W9-APY-618

Publications

OF THE

STATE DEPARTMENT OF ARCHIVES AND HISTORY

THE PAPERS OF
THOMAS JORDAN JARVIS

Thomas Jordan Jarvis (1836-1915)

(Photograph copied from Kemp P. Battle, *History of the University of North Carolina from Its Beginning to the Death of President Swain, 1789-1886.*)

The Papers of
Thomas Jordan Jarvis

———

Edited by

W. BUCK YEARNS

VOLUME I

1869-1882

———

Limited Edition of 750 Copies

Raleigh
State Department of Archives and History
1969

100645

FOREWORD

The years between the end of the Civil War and the beginning of the twentieth century were years of great change in North Carolina. Thomas Jordan Jarvis witnessed and participated in this period of rapid development of the state. His papers reflect events of the times; his correspondence with leading state and national figures reveals thought and action which affected the lives of citizens of the Tar Heel State.

The editor of *The Papers of Thomas Jordan Jarvis* is Dr. W. Buck Yearns. Dr. Yearns, professor of history at Wake Forest University, is the author of *The Confederate Congress* and of a number of articles and book reviews.

The State Department of Archives and History wishes to express appreciation to Dr. Yearns for assuming the editorship of the Jarvis material. Mrs. Barbara R. Hall and Mrs. Nancy S. Bartlett, formerly on the staff of the Division of Publications of the department, prepared copy for the printer. The preparation of front matter, proofreading, and other technical details were handled by Miss Brenda M. Smith and Miss Beth G. Crabtree, editorial assistants. Thanks is hereby conveyed to each of these people for her part in making this book possible.

Memory F. Mitchell, *Editor*

February 1, 1969

CONTENTS

LIST OF ILLUSTRATIONS

LIST OF SYMBOLS

A&H-GLB   Governors' Letter Books, State Department of Archives and History, Raleigh

A&H-GO   Governors' Office Papers, State Department of Archives and History, Raleigh

A&H-GP   Governors' Papers, State Department of Archives and History, Raleigh

A&H-JDW   John D. Whitford Papers, State Department of Archives and History, Raleigh

A&H-SAA   Samuel A. Ashe Papers, State Department of Archives and History, Raleigh

A&H-SPI   Papers of the Superintendent of Public Instruction, State Department of Archives and History, Raleigh

A&H-ZBV   Zebulon B. Vance Papers, State Department of Archives and History, Raleigh

DUKE-TC   Trinity College Papers, Manuscript Collection, Duke University Library, Durham

DUKE-TJJ   Thomas J. Jarvis Papers, Manuscript Collection, Duke University Library, Durham

UNC-ABA   Alexander B. Andrews Papers, Southern Historical Collection, University of North Carolina at Chapel Hill

UNC-DFC   David F. Caldwell Papers, Southern Historical Collection, University of North Carolina at Chapel Hill

UNC-DMC   David M. Carter Papers, Southern Historical Collection, University of North Carolina at Chapel Hill

UNC-KPB   Kemp P. Battle Papers, Southern Historical Collection, University of North Carolina at Chapel Hill

UNC-MG   Moore-Gatling Papers, Southern Historical Collection, University of North Carolina at Chapel Hill

UNC-MWR   Matt W. Ransom Papers, Southern Historical Collection, University of North Carolina at Chapel Hill

UNC-RPB   Ralph P. Buxton Papers, Southern Historical Collection, University of North Carolina at Chapel Hill

UNC-SMT   Samuel M. Tate Papers, Southern Historical Collection, University of North Carolina at Chapel Hill

UNC-UP   University Papers, Southern Historical Collection, University of North Carolina at Chapel Hill

UNC-WJH   William J. Hawkins Papers, Southern Historical Collection, University of North Carolina at Chapel Hill

BIOGRAPHY OF THOMAS JORDAN JARVIS

THOMAS JORDAN JARVIS

For some years before North Carolina became a colony, people had been drifting down from present day Virginia into the Albemarle Sound area and acquiring land there from the Indians. In 1662 Governor William Berkeley of Virginia announced that he would no longer recognize land titles obtained from Indians and that the Albemarle settlers must take out patents for their land under the Virginia law. Among those hastening to comply was one Thomas Jarvis, who was then occupying land in the area now known as Harvey's Neck.[1] The early records do not make clear the direct lines of his progeny, but by the middle of the eighteenth century the records of deeds for the Albemarle counties show large numbers of landowners bearing his surname. And occasionally a Jarvis slipped into the record of events. The original Thomas Jarvis became deputy governor of North Carolina in 1691; a Thomas Jarvis was a leading member of the Assembly; and during the Revolution a Samuel Jarvis was commanding general of the Albemarle militia. The census of 1790 lists three Thomas Jarvises living in Currituck County. One of these men sired Bannister Hardy Jarvis, who became a Methodist minister and a farmer. He married Elizabeth Daley, and in their home at Jarvisburg, on January 18, 1836, their first child, Thomas Jordan Jarvis, was born.[2]

Tom Jarvis, as he was always known to his friends, spent his boyhood on his father's farm. Bannister Jarvis was one of the many Currituck farmers of moderate circumstances, able to provide his family the necessities of life but few cultural amenities. He owned about three hundred acres of farmland,[3] and his home was a plain, rather large frame house situated near a narrow through road. With a father who had varied outside interests, and with only five slaves to help with the farm work,[4] Tom, his brother George, and his sisters Ann, Margaret, and Elizabeth spent their youth in arduous, wholesome farm labor.

---

[1] "Information on Thomas Jarvis," typescript, Manuscript Department, Duke University Library, Durham.

[2] For the fullest account of Jarvis' heritage, see Samuel A. Ashe and Others (eds.), *Biographical History of North Carolina: From Colonial Times to the Present* (Greensboro: Charles L. Van Noppen, 8 volumes, 1905-1917), I, 332-333, hereinafter cited as Ashe, *Biographical History.*

[3] Records of Deeds, Currituck County, Book 43, p. 23.

[4] *Eighth Census of the United States, 1860,* XI, Agriculture Schedule, 705, Archives, State Department of Archives and History, Raleigh, hereinafter cited as *Eighth Census, 1860.*

The highlights of the boys' simple existence were probably the occasions when they and their father drove their market cart to Norfolk to sell their farm produce and to purchase supplies for the family.[5]

After attending the nearby common school, Tom Jarvis worked for his father for several years. But as he matured farm life palled on him, and at the age of nineteen he decided to attend college and prepare himself for a more attractive livelihood.[6] Bannister Jarvis should have been able to help him, for his farm was worth about $8,000.[7] But the records of Currituck and Tyrrell counties show that he speculated in land constantly and unprofitably, and he probably seldom had much for long-term cash investment. So young Jarvis had to pay his own college expenses. Between 1855 and 1860, with several interruptions, he put himself through Randolph-Macon College, at that time located at Boyton, Virginia. More than once he borrowed money from John Sanderson of Tyrrell County. During the summers of 1857 and 1858 he earned $175 by teaching school near his home.[8] In 1860 he graduated with honors, and in 1861 he received the Master of Arts degree. He immediately opened a school in Pasquotank County and was engaged in teaching when North Carolina entered the Confederacy.[9]

Jarvis then enlisted in the 17th North Carolina Regiment.[10] On May 16, 1861, he was commissioned first lieutenant of Company B, 8th North Carolina Regiment, of which Henry M. Shaw was colonel. On April 22, 1863, he was promoted to the rank of captain. After a brief sojourn at a camp of instruction near Warrenton, in 1861, the regiment was assigned to Roanoke Island on September 18. For the next several weeks the men devoted most of their energies to building fortifications and to making occasional forays against the enemy scattered around Pamlico Sound. In October the regiment went into winter camp

---

[5] *News and Observer* (Raleigh), June 19, 1885, published as *News-Observer-Chronicle* July 2, 1893-August 11, 1894, but for purposes of this sketch hereinafter cited as *News and Observer.*

[6] Ashe, *Biographical History,* I, 333.

[7] *Eighth Census, 1860,* XI, Agriculture Schedule, 705.

[8] Ashe, *Biographical History,* I, 333; Reports of Benjamin T. Simmons, Chairman of the Board of Superintendents of Common Schools in Currituck County, October 12, 1857, and September 4, 1858, in Common School Reports, Cumberland and Currituck counties, Papers of the Superintendent of Public Instruction, State Archives.

[9] Ashe, *Biographical History,* I, 333.

[10] The account of Jarvis' military service taken from Ashe, *Biographical History,* I, 333-334; Walter Clark (ed.), *Histories of the Several Regiments and Battalions in the Great War, 1861-'65* (Raleigh: State of North Carolina, 5 volumes, 1901), I, 387-403.

on the island near Fort Bartow. On February 8, 1862, a Federal army of about 15,000 overwhelmed the island's defenders and made prisoners of Jarvis and his 1,400 comrades in arms. They were held prisoners for about two weeks before being sent to Elizabeth City, where they were paroled and sent home. As a result of an exchange of prisoners negotiated in September, 1862, the regiment was able to reassemble.

The 8th Regiment, now a part of Clingman's Brigade, spent October and November, 1862, in relative inactivity, first near Kinston and then Wilmington. In mid-December it helped repel an enemy attempt to seize Goldsboro. In February, 1863, it journeyed to James Island near Charleston, South Carolina, then to Savannah, Georgia. By March 1 it was back at Wilmington. In July the regiment returned to James Island, this time to help defend Battery Wagner on nearby Morris Island. After a fifty-eight day seige, during which the 8th North Carolina saw almost constant service, the Confederates were forced to evacuate the Island. After brief tours of duty in eastern North Carolina, the regiment was ordered to Petersburg, Virginia, arriving there on December 14, 1863, and bivouacking in the streets. In January, 1864, it moved once again into North Carolina. In early February it successfully defended Kinston, and in April it participated in the capture of Plymouth, losing 154 men in the latter effort. In May it was engaged in an attempt to recapture New Bern when orders came to proceed to Petersburg. At the battle of Drewry's Bluff on May 14-16, 1864, Jarvis received a wound in his right arm that necessitated a resection of a part of the bone. Permanently crippled, he never rejoined his regiment and when the Confederacy ended he was on sick leave in Norfolk, "penniless and unknown." [11] He remained in Norfolk until he was paroled in May, 1865, and then returned to Jarvisburg.

To comply with President Andrew Johnson's requirements for the restoration of North Carolina's government, Governor William W. Holden on August 8, 1865, called an election for September 21 for delegates to a constitutional convention. The voters of Currituck gave their wounded hero all but fourteen of the votes cast,[12] and Jarvis' political career was launched. When

[11] *News and Observer*, June 19, 1885.
[12] Election returns of Currituck County from Thomas C. Humphries, sheriff, to Governor W. W. Holden and to the President of the Convention, September 23, 1865, Election Returns, Delegates to Convention, Papers of the Secretary of State, State Archives, hereinafter cited as Papers of the Secretary of State.

the convention assembled, Jarvis and most of the delegates faced their task realistically. Old issues were dead, and they worked toward the one goal of restoring the state government as speedily as possible. On one matter, however, Jarvis won for himself a reputation which served him well in future years. The main work of the adjourned session of 1866 was the writing of a new constitution. Jarvis and approximately one-third of the delegates believed that the convention had not been called for this purpose and had no such authority. They repeatedly, though unsuccessfully, tried to block the proposed constitution, and were vindicated when the electorate subsequently rejected it.[13]

In late 1865 Jarvis formed a business partnership with William H. Happer of Tyrrell County. The two young men bought a stock of goods on credit and borrowed the money to pay the freight on it from Norfolk, Virginia, to Columbia. They then opened a small general store in the Gum Neck community several miles from Columbia. Business was poor, and in March, 1867, Jarvis bought out Happer for $5.00.[14] But apparently Jarvis had been looking beyond the Tyrrell County swamp. During his spare moments from storekeeping he read law, and in the spring of 1867 he spent considerable time in Norfolk intensifying his studies. In June, 1867, Jarvis obtained a license to practice, gave up his store, moved to Columbia, and opened a law office.[15]

It was in 1868 that Jarvis permanently contracted the fever of politics. In the spring of that year the state adopted a new constitution in compliance with the Reconstruction acts of Congress, and in the following elections Jarvis won a seat in the House in an uncontested Tyrrell County election.[16] In the fall of the same year the Democratic party nominated him as an elector on the

[13] R. D. W. Connor, *North Carolina: Rebuilding An Ancient Commonwealth, 1584-1925* (Chicago: American Historical Society, Inc., 4 volumes, 1929), II, 268-271, 280, hereinafter cited as Connor, *Rebuilding An Ancient Commonwealth.* For the efforts by Jarvis and his colleagues to block the adoption of a new constitution, see *Journal of the Convention of the State of North Carolina, at the Adjourned Session of 1866*, 12, 13, 16, 17, 30, 85, 185, 186.

[14] For Jarvis' mercantile transactions, see Record of Deeds, Tyrrell County, 1860-1873, sale of chattel, March 26, 1867, 287-288 (microfilm copy), State Archives.

[15] Ashe, *Biographical History*, I, 334; Henry Groves Connor, "Thomas Jordan Jarvis and the Rebuilding of North Carolina," *Proceedings of the Sixteenth Annual Session of the State Literary and Historical Association of North Carolina* (November 8-9, 1915), 84, hereinafter cited as Connor, "Thomas Jordan Jarvis"; *News and Observer*, April 24, 1894.

[16] Election returns from Tyrrell County, April 21-23, 1868, Election Returns, Congressional, State, and County, Papers of the Secretary of State.

Seymour-Blair ticket. Jarvis then made the first of his many statewide canvasses, though the state went for Grant.

When Governor Holden called a special session of the legislature to meet in July, 1868, Jarvis was one of the small group of young Conservatives who united in stubborn dissent to the program of the Republican majority. They used a variety of parliamentary devices to prevent the passage of a bill issuing special tax bonds for railroad construction, but to no avail. Jarvis himself was particularly active in opposing suffrage changes and the organization of special militia forces to police certain counties.[17] At the last of the session he sought to impose a two-thirds of one per cent limit on all taxes upon real and personal property, but he had no more success here than with his other efforts.[18]

When the legislature met again during the winter of 1869-1870 the Conservatives succeeded in establishing the Bragg-Phillips Committee to investigate corruption in the passage of the special tax bond laws. Its report was damaging, and the Conservatives sprang to the initiative. Jarvis introduced, and after a long struggle the legislature passed, a bill repealing recent acts authorizing bond issues, ordering railroads to return all state bonds still in their possession, and stopping interest payments on the special tax bonds.[19]

With the defeat of the Republicans in 1870, the Conservatives commanded a majority in both houses, and they elected Jarvis as speaker of the House. In this capacity he exercised a controlling role in impeaching Governor Holden, reducing the costs of state government, investigating other railroad frauds, and outlawing secret societies.[20]

In 1872 he was Democratic candidate on the Greeley ticket as elector-at-large. Though he distinguished himself a second time in state-wide speaking engagements, he went down to defeat

---

[17] *Journal of the House of Representatives of the General Assembly at its Session of 1868*, 12-16, 133-136, 142, 149, 154, hereinafter cited as *House Journal; House Journal, 1868-'69*, 17, 20, 43-49.

[18] *House Journal, 1868-'69*, 266-267; *Daily News* (Raleigh), May 25, 1880, hereinafter cited as *Daily News.*

[19] B. U. Ratchford, "The North Carolina Public Debt, 1870-1878," *North Carolina Historical Review*, X (January, 1933), 2, hereinafter cited as Ratchford, "The North Carolina Public Debt."

[20] Ashe, *Biographical History*, I, 334; Hugh Talmage Lefler and Albert Ray Newsome, *North Carolina: The History of A Southern State* (Chapel Hill: University of North Carolina Press, c. 1963), 469, hereinafter cited as Lefler and Newsome, *North Carolina.*

again with Grant's victory.[21] It was during this campaign that Jarvis made the decision to move to Greenville, which became his home for the remainder of his life. In Greenville he formed a partnership with David M. Carter[22] and devoted the next three years to reestablishing himself. In 1874 he married Mary Woodson of Goochland County, Virginia, daughter of Judge John Woodson. His bride had won for herself some literary reputation for several articles which she had contributed to northern periodicals and from her little novel *The Way It All Ended.*[23] The Jarvises had no children.

But even these readjustments in his existence had not dimmed his enthusiasm for politics. Not long after he arrived in Greenville the leading Democrats there asked him to help rebuild their county organization. He accepted the chairmanship of the party's Central Committee and was given the right to choose the other members. He then set up committees for each township, which in turn divided their township into districts and subdistricts with a committee over each. Jarvis' secretary prepared a list of all registered voters in the county, and the party was thus organized to get out the vote and to prevent nonregistered Republicans from voting. The results were that the Democrats won an amazing victory in the county elections of 1874 and Jarvis' reputation was established.[24]

In 1875 the legislature called for a convention to revise once again the state constitution. By this time the partnership of Carter and Jarvis was prospering and the latter decided to seek public office once again. During the summer he campaigned vigorously for constitutional reform and obtained his party's nomination to one of the county's two seats.[25] Then using the party organization which he had recently fashioned, he launched a "brilliant" and "magnificent" campaign against the Republican adversaries.[26] It was largely due to his efforts that Pitt County elected two Democratic delegates to the convention.[27]

In the convention there were 58 Democrats, 58 Republicans, and 3 Independents. Nevertheless, according to the recollections

---

[21] Unidentified newspaper clipping in the Jarvis Scrapbook, Thomas Jordan Jarvis Papers, 1790-1915, State Archives, hereinafter cited as Jarvis Scrapbook.
[22] Ashe, *Biographical History,* I, 335.
[23] *Morning Star* (Wilmington), June 28, 1876, hereinafter cited as *Morning Star.*
[24] *Morning Star,* July 9, 1880.
[25] *Morning Star,* July 4, 1875.
[26] *Morning Star,* July 28, 1875.
[27] *Morning Star,* August 10, 1875.

of his friends, it was Jarvis' maneuverings on and off the convention floor that welded the Democrats into an effective majority.[28] Though unable to repudiate the entire 1868 Constitution, they added to it thirty significant amendments. Samuel A. Ashe credited Jarvis with the most important amendment adopted, one which placed in the hands of the legislature the appointment of justices of the peace and county commissioners. This amendment insured white control of any county government regardless of the racial distribution there.[29] In addition he introduced, but failed to secure the passage of, an amendment to Article I, Section 6, which would have repudiated the special tax bonds of 1868.[30]

The next year Jarvis set his political sights higher. The Democratic party[31] had controlled the legislature since 1870, and in 1876 it was determined to win the executive branch of government. During the spring candidates for each executive position abounded, but by June the need for party harmony had compelled the weaker contenders to withdraw. When the State Democratic Convention met on June 14 the ticket seemed set. The delegates then nominated by acclamation Zebulon B. Vance for governor, James Engelhard for secretary of state, and John M. Worth for secretary of the treasury. Jarvis had sought the nomination for lieutenant governor, but by June General William R. Cox seemed assured that honor. On the first ballot Cox received about two-thirds of the Convention vote, but for some unexplained reason the result was not immediately announced. During a long and tiresome speech that followed there was noticeable activity on the floor, allegedly caused by Jarvis forces persuading several county delegations to change their votes. At the end of the speech these delegations announced their changes and Jarvis emerged the winner by the margin of 482 to 469.[32]

The campaign of 1876 was one of the most dramatic in the state's history. All candidates competed vigorously, and the Republicans further intensified the pitch of battle by seeking

---

[28] Lefler and Newsome, *North Carolina*, 471; Connor, "Thomas Jordan Jarvis," 87.
[29] Lefler and Newsome, *North Carolina*, 471, 507; Ashe, *Biographical History*, I, 336.
[30] *Journal of the Constitutional Convention of the State of North Carolina, Held in 1875*, 82, 129, 196-197.
[31] The state Conservative organization adopted this name for purposes of cooperation with the national Democratic party.
[32] *Morning Star*, June 15, 1876; *Observer* (Raleigh), May 19, 1878, hereinafter cited as *Observer;* unidentified newspaper clipping in the Jarvis Scrapbook.

joint debates with Democrats in order to obtain exposure to partisan white audiences. Vance and Jarvis complemented each other admirably, the one providing eloquence and showmanship, the other furnishing an endless supply of facts and arguments. Together they demanded white supremacy and an honest and frugal government. Vance and the Republican's vulnerable Reconstruction record carried the Democrats to a small but decisive victory.[33] Vance defeated Thomas Settle by a margin of 123,265 to 110,256, while Jarvis won over William R. Smith by 123,863 to 109,580.[34] In addition, the Democrats won control of the legislature, the congressional delegation, and the presidential electors.

After two years as lieutenant governor, with little official responsibility except to preside over the Senate, Jarvis unexpectedly fell heir to the governorship. The six year term of United States Senator Augustus S. Merrimon was to expire in 1878, and in the spring of that year Vance announced his own candidacy for the position. With his friendship for Vance as well as his own career in mind, Jarvis "donned his old war clothes" [35] and campaigned vigorously for Vance. The newspapers supporting Merrimon accused Jarvis of unethical political manipulations, particularly of packing the county conventions with Vance's adherents. Vance naturally defended Jarvis, saying that the "great and only danger to our party arises from so-called independents. If we cannot maintain discipline the party will go to pieces. . . ." [36] Vance won the party's nomination and the legislature duly sent him to Washington.

When Jarvis assumed the governorship on February 5, 1879, he already possessed those characteristics with which the public always identified him. Physically he was heavy-set, with broad shoulders, a strong neck, and a large head. He spoke in clear and convincing language, with little imagery or embellishment. His colleagues considered him an efficient organizer and a practical politician, talents greatly needed during the revival of Democracy. The accurate capsule evaluation of the Wilmington *Morning Star* was that he had "administrative talents, and without being a great man, or a finished orator, or a fluent and force-

---

[33] For a brief description of this "Battle of the Giants," see Lefler and Newsome, *North Carolina*, 471-472.

[34] Election Returns for Governor and Other State Officers, November, 1876, Election Returns, 61-64, Papers of the Secretary of State.

[35] *New York Times* (New York), April 6, 1878, quoted in *Observer*, April 9, 1878.

[36] *Observer*, July 27, 1878.

ful writer, or a man of erudition, he is a man of fair natural parts, is cautious and conservative and well-balanced, and has a good stock of common sense." [37]

In 1879 North Carolina was preeminently agricultural. Except for wheat, farm production had recovered from the distresses of the previous generation, and North Carolina was the only state that was a large producer of both cotton and tobacco. Along with rising production came lower prices, accentuated by the mounting costs of tools, machinery, credit, and transportation. By 1879 the farmers of the state, comprising over 90 per cent of the total population,[38] had already begun to seek relief through the legislature. Conceivably the "plough-boy of Currituck" owed his first loyalty to them.

But at the same time North Carolina had an industrial revolution under way. The state had many advantages for the development of light industries, particularly those based on cotton, tobacco, and forest products. By 1879 local capitalists had made considerable progress in developing these industries; so much, in fact, that northern investors as well were becoming interested.[39] With industrial development came pressure for legislation inherently inimicable to agriculture. Even in so agrarian a state as North Carolina political leadership could not ignore, and might even see cause to favor, this industrialism.

The Democrats had also to decide how to live up to their political promises. For years they had freely denounced the "Black Republican" era of 1868-1870 as one of ineptness, extravagance, and corruption. As antidotes they had promised a government of "retrenchment and reform" once back in power. In 1876 the Democrats gained clear command of the state machinery, and thereafter the Negro vote and the Republican party gradually declined. The Vance administration began cautiously to instigate certain changes but had achieved little by 1879. This left upon the Jarvis administration the burden of deciding which Republican policies to repudiate, which to modify, and which to accept.[40]

---

[37] *Morning Star*, February 6, 1879.

[38] Lefler and Newsome, *North Carolina*, 483.

[39] For the status of North Carolina industry at the beginning of Jarvis' governorship, see Lefler and Newsome, *North Carolina*, 476-477; and Connor, *Rebuilding An Ancient Comonwealth*, II, 361-375. For an example of northern interest in the North Carolina lumber industry, see Paul W. Gates, "Federal Land Policy in the South, 1866-1888," *Journal of Southern History*, VI (August, 1940), 303-330.

[40] For a general discussion of this situation, see Lefler and Newsome, *North Carolina*, 472-473.

In his inaugural address, Jarvis explicitly and implicitly revealed a set of attitudes that determined the tenor of his administration as governor. As a self-made man and as a true conservative, he felt that the government should play a negative role in the state's economic development. To be sure, the government had to accept some responsibility for certain dependent elements, like the wicked, the incompetent, and the very young. But agriculture and industry must chart their own destiny. The government should not show partiality toward any interest group, and it should not aid one of them except indirectly. The primary function of government should be to provide an honest and efficient environment in which all such groups could flourish. This, Jarvis believed, had been the pledge of the Democratic party and this was what he intended to accomplish.

The Governor maintained that close attention to "the little things" of government would save the state thousands of dollars a year and that a careful watching of pennies would save thousands more. Additional amounts could be saved by simplifying the administration of the criminal and civil law, by a greater use of convict labor, by a careful supervision of expenditures for county administration, and by numerous other such methods. For the best use of convict labor he suggested a board of internal improvements with full power to lease convicts where they were most needed and to assure their proper treatment. He advised the legislature, however, not to reduce appropriations to the public schools or to the Department of Agriculture. His chief constructive promise was to promote railroad construction throughout the state, and he felt that the wisest use of convicts would be on this kind of work.[41]

The legislature which met from January 8 to March 14 achieved a solid record along the lines suggested by Jarvis. To pare the costs of government by attention to "the little things," it reduced the compensation for public printing, abolished a number of superior court terms, made several small improvements in the handling of criminal procedure cases, required justices of the peace to keep active and permanent records, redefined the duties of the county treasurers so as to place them under better supervision, reduced somewhat the state salary scale, and made other small changes designed to save from a few

---

[41] Inaugural Address, February 5, 1879, Thomas J. Jarvis Letter Book, 1879-1883, 1-11, Governors' Letter Books, State Archives, hereinafter cited as Jarvis Letter Book.

hundred to several thousand dollars.[42] A questionable economy was made by abolishing the position of state geologist and making the Geological Department a branch of the Department of Agriculture with a reduced expense account.[43]

Following this same talk, the legislature revised the state's role in the care of the insane. Due to inadequate facilities, the state for several years had been contributing money to the counties for the local care of these unfortunates. An investigating committee found this system wasteful and dishonestly administered, and the legislature decided to end the practice. As compensation, it voted $50,000 and $20,000 to hasten the completion of the Western Asylum at Morganton and the Colored Asylum near Goldsboro.[44]

The greatest opportunity for economy lay in the handling of the state debt. On October 1, 1878, the total gross debt was $44,730,698, of which $28,360,045 was principal and $16,404,653 accrued interest. The treasurers' reports commonly divided this debt into the "recognized" and the "special tax bond" debts. The first was $27,120,228, of which $16,960,045 was principal and $10,160,183 was interest. There were $11,366,000 of the special tax bonds outstanding, on which the interest was $6,244,470. The recognized debt had been incurred over the past several decades, chiefly for railroad construction, and its validity was unquestioned. But the money raised by the special tax bonds issued during the legislature of 1868-1869 had largely been wasted and the indebtedness itself was considered fraudulent. All efforts by the state and the bondholders to compromise the indebtedness failed, and for several years Democratic leaders had debated how much of the recognized debt the impoverished state should pay, and whether it should totally repudiate the special tax bonds. Governor Vance had openly advocated partial repudiation of the one and complete repudiation of the other;[45] Jarvis, while of the same opinion, left the initiative to the

---

[42] *Laws and Resolutions of the State of North Carolina Passed by the General Assembly at Its Session of 1879*, cc. 1, 3, 5, 6, 33, 45, 49, 80, 96, 240, 264, hereinafter cited as *Laws of North Carolina*.

[43] For a full explanation of this legislation, see Stuart Noblin, *Leonidas LaFayette Polk, Agrarian Crusader* (Chapel Hill: University of North Carolina Press, 1949), 95-100.

[44] "Report of Joint Committee on Retrenchment and Reform," *Executive and Legislative Documents of the State of North Carolina, Session 1879*, Document No. 24, hereinafter cited as *Public Documents; Laws of North Carolina, 1879*, cc. 174, 331.

[45] Ratchford, "The North Carolina Public Debt," 13, 19, 20.

legislature. In 1879 it attacked the problem with ruthlessness and finality. All told, it settled a debt of over $44 million by issues of new bonds amounting to $6,534,511.

The law of March 4 to "Compromise, Commute and Settle the State Debt" repudiated all the accrued interest on the recognized debt. It then classified the principal into three groups. Bonds issued before May 20, 1861, were made fundable into new 4 per cent, thirty-year bonds to the amount of 40 per cent of the principal of the old bonds. Class two were those bonds issued for internal improvements during and immediately after the Civil War, and they were made fundable at 25 per cent of par. Class three were the funding bonds of 1866 and 1868, to be funded at 15 per cent of par. On March 14 the legislature proposed a constitutional amendment,[46] subsequently ratified by popular vote, prohibiting forever the payment of the special tax bonds.

The bonds issued to buy stock in the North Carolina Railroad were treated differently. They were secured by a lien on the railroad's stock and were known as "construction bonds." There were outstanding $2,795,000 of these bonds. Since they would mature during 1883-1885 some provision had to be made for them; otherwise, the bondholders would be able to sell the stock pledged as security and the state would lose control of the railroad. Because of the strong legal position of the bondholders, none of these bonds could be repudiated. On March 14 the legislature authorized Governor Jarvis to appoint a commission to negotiate with these bondholders and contract with them for a renewal of the debt by a process of funding the construction bonds into a new issue of state bonds. Any terms reached by the governor and the secretary of the treasury.[47] In October Jarvis appointed George Davis, Montford McGehee, and Donald W. Bain as commissioners to negotiate with the bondholders.[48]

Since its return to power in 1870, the Democratic party had sought to disengage the state government as much as possible from internal improvement projects. And the determination to economize of this and succeeding Jarvis legislatures compelled them to follow this conservative policy. The result was that any such improvements must be at the initiative of county govern-

---

[46] *Laws of North Carolina, 1879,* cc. 98, 268.

[47] *Laws of North Carolina, 1879,* c. 138.

[48] For a thorough study of this issue and its settlement, see B. U. Ratchford, "The Adjustment of the North Carolina Public Debt, 1879-1883," *North Carolina Historical Review,* X (July, 1933), 157-167.

ment or private enterprise. The Jarvis legislatures authorized numerous boards of county commissioners to have their local swamps drained and to pass on most of the cost to the landowners affected. They empowered many boards of commissioners to have public roads constructed. They chartered several new canal companies, none of which became operative, and they granted numerous railroad charters authorizing either the construction of a new railroad or of a spur line to an existing one. The legislatures shared none of the costs of any of these projects, though they frequently promised certain numbers of convict laborers if they were available. The only innovations in this area by the legislature of 1879 were laws which placed the justices of the peace and the county commissioners in charge of township and county roads, respectively, and which required every man to work on these roads seven days a year or to buy his exemption for seven dollars.[49]

The problem of the Western North Carolina Railroad, however, endangered the entire retrenchment program of the Democratic party. Since 1870 the state had not only ceased to subsidize railroad construction, it had leased the state-owned North Carolina Railroad to a syndicate of northern and Virginia capitalists. But the Western North Carolina constituted a unique problem. On its completion depended the development of the western part of the state as well as the connection of the state's railroads with those in the Mississippi Valley. For years private management sought to push construction across the rugged Appalachians but made little progress. In 1875 the state bought the railroad and the Democrats pledged to complete it. Nevertheless, when Jarvis became governor the railroad had not yet reached Asheville, was heavily in debt, needed constant subsidies for its operation, and existed as two corporations—the Eastern Division and the Western Division.[50]

With the West's development and the party's integrity seemingly at stake, the legislature of 1879 had no choice but to continue bearing this cross. In March it appropriated $20,000 to the railroad for operating expenses and ordered the state to keep at least five hundred convicts at work on it.[51] A number of

---

[49] *Laws of North Carolina, 1879*, cc. 82, 83. In 1883 these requirements were reduced to three days or $2.50. *Laws of North Carolina, 1883*, c. 228.
[50] Cecil Kenneth Brown, *A State Movement in Railroad Development* (Chapel Hill: University of North Carolina Press, 1928), 155-173, 188-226, hereinafter cited as Brown, *A State Movement in Railroad Development.*
[51] *Laws of North Carolina, 1879*, cc. 169, 278.

legal difficulties had developed because of the division of the railroad into two corporations, and on March 13 the legislature reunited the two divisions in the hope of speeding up construction.[52]

The legislature contributed to two other areas of public service. In 1877 it had authorized a normal school for each race. Soon there were established normal schools at Fayetteville and at Chapel Hill for Negro and white teachers respectively. In 1879 the legislature authorized additional ones at Davidson, Trinity, and Wake Forest colleges, and opened all its normal schools to both men and women. It also organized the North Carolina Board of Health on a state and county basis and defined its duties and jurisdiction.[53]

Believing that it had reduced appreciably the costs of government, the legislature lowered the poll tax from 89 cents to 72 cents, and reduced the ad valorem tax on real estate, personal property, and corporate stock and bonds from $29\frac{2}{3}$ cents to 24 cents on each $100 valuation. It also ordered a reassessment of all property to make its book value more nearly approximate its real value.[54] The results of these tax changes, however, were unexpected. The reassessment of property increased its book value by about $16 million. But the tax reduction had overbalanced this gain, and the receipts for 1879 were $54,000 less than those for 1878.[55]

But the fact of a limited treasury never seemed to worry Governor Jarvis. He considered himself the responsible head of his party as well as the chief executive of his state. The Democratic party stood for conservatism, for "retrenchment and reform." To fulfill its pledges would require executive leadership rather than a bountiful treasury.

Much of his work as governor, of course, was quite routine. During the summer of 1879 he began communicating with the governor of Georgia for a resurvey of the line between Raburn County in Georgia and Macon County in North Carolina.[56] In August he held the first of many conferences with foreign and

---

[52] *Laws of North Carolina, 1879,* c. 230; *Observer,* May 25, 1879.

[53] *Laws of North Carolina, 1876-'77,* c. 234; *Laws of North Carolina, 1879,* cc. 54, 117, 226.

[54] *Laws of North Carolina, 1876-'77,* c. 156; *Laws of North Carolina, 1879,* cc. 70, 71.

[55] "Treasurer's Report," *Public Documents, 1881,* Document No. 5.

[56] Thomas J. Jarvis to Alfred H. Colquitt, August 28, 1879, Thomas J. Jarvis, Governors' Papers, State Archives, hereinafter cited as Governors' Papers.

northern groups interested in settling in the eastern counties where land was almost free.[57] In November he addressed the first Industrial Exhibition by the Colored People and advised them to work hard.[58] At the instigation of President Kemp P. Battle he circularized throughout the state an appeal for contributions to the University.[59] And from time to time he presided at the dedication of monuments and spoke at Revolutionary centennials. These duties were often time consuming, but they appealed to his rather gregarious nature.

Jarvis soon found that the costliest part of state government was the program for the care of the physically, mentally, and morally deficient. By the end of 1879 construction on the Western Asylum had come to a halt for lack of money, and its directors pleaded for an additional $10,000. Jarvis requested this sum in March, 1880, from the special session of the legislature, but it was not until the following March that the legislature appropriated the money to complete the central building of the Western Asylum.[60] In April, 1880, the directors of the Colored Asylum at Goldsboro indicated that they could finish the first stage of their building program with a like amount. This time the Governor arranged for the state treasurer to advance as much as $10,000 to the Colored Asylum, and that institution opened in August, 1880.[61] This largess continued, for Jarvis and the legislature consistently gave these and other institutions essentially whatever they requested. The treasurer's reports indicate that money for the three asylums; the Institution for the Deaf, the Dumb, and the Blind; the Penitentiary; the Oxford Orphanage; and the support of leased convicts comprised over half the operating expenses of the state.

In November, 1880, the commissioners appointed to negotiate with the holders of the construction bonds received a proposal from the bondholders. The latter agreed to surrender all bonds with coupons due after October, 1877; coupons due before that date were to be paid out of the dividends received from the stock

---

[57] *Observer*, August 19, 1879.
[58] *Observer*, November 19, 1879.
[59] A copy of this circular, which is undated, may be found in the University Papers, Southern Historical Collection, University of North Carolina at Chapel Hill.
[60] "Thomas J. Jarvis to the Senate and House of Representatives," *Public Documents, 1880*, Document No. 8; *Laws of North Carolina, 1881*, c. 182.
[61] Thomas J. Jarvis to J. A. Bonitz, April 28, 1880, Jarvis Letter Book, 1879-1883, 198; "Report of the Chairman of the Board of Directors of the Asylum for the Colored Insane," *Public Documents, 1881*, Document No. 12.

in the North Carolina Railroad owned by the state. In exchange they should get, to an amount equal to the principal of the old bonds, new 6 per cent forty-year bonds. Any surplus of the dividends on the state-owned stock was to constitute a sinking fund to retire the bond issue.[62] Jarvis and the commissioners had the legal authority to accept this settlement, but chose to leave the decision to the legislature scheduled to meet in just two months. When the latter took no action, Jarvis and the commissioners eventually worked out by 1882 a settlement much like that described above.[63]

A recurring problem was the best disposition of the state's convicts. Jarvis was always a hearty protagonist of the convict lease system, believing that such labor would reduce the expense of keeping the prisoners and would help rehabilitate them by teaching them good work habits. Since there were always many internal improvement projects in need of cheap labor, these were the natural places for the assignment of convicts. Consequently, each session of the legislature enacted several laws promising certain numbers of convicts to the more worthy projects. But the demand for convicts always far exceeded their supply, and Jarvis had the responsibility of advising the Penitentiary authorities which undertakings deserved labor priority. Generally he gave preference to railroads, and the demand here was so great that county commissioners wishing to cut a road or drain a swamp seldom received the convicts promised them. They never abated their demands, however, and frequently reinforced them with political warnings. Regardless of where leased convicts worked, Jarvis always required specific guarantees for their care, and he periodically sent commissions to investigate their living and working conditions.

Another set of problems stemmed from the Democrats' determination to relinquish railroad development and management as much as possible to private business. The legislature of 1879 had written laws forbidding pooling and rebates and had ordered all freight agents to post their rates in conspicuous places and to change these rates only after a fifteen-day notice of intention. But the laws provided no special agencies for their enforcement and only slight penalties for noncompliance.[64] At this same

[62] "Report of Commissioners to Adjust a Portion of the State Debt," *Public Documents, 1881*, Document No. 15.
[63] "Governor's Message," *Public Documents, 1883*, Document No. 1.
[64] *Laws of North Carolina, 1879*, cc. 182, 237.

session the legislature even refused to establish a state railroad commission.[65] It was small wonder that Jarvis received so many reports of railroad abuse and discrimination.

Jarvis' hands-off attitude toward railroads embroiled him in several other controversies. The legislature of 1879 authorized the Western Railroad to consolidate with the Mt. Airy and Central, to change its name to the Cape Fear and Yadkin Valley, and to build a line from Mt. Airy to some place on the North Carolina Railroad.[66] Local interest groups immediately started beseeching Jarvis to steer the proposed line through their town, something over which he had no authority and chose to exert no influence. In another instance, citizens of Wilmington claimed that Jarvis' policy made it more profitable for North Carolinians to ship their produce to Norfolk than to a North Carolina port.[67] They were further incensed when the Atlantic and North Carolina Railroad, whose stock was two-thirds state owned, hired as its superintendent A. B. Andrews, an official of the Richmond and Danville. Andrews' task was to increase the traffic of the Atlantic and North Carolina by making contracts with other railroads and with steamship lines.[68] But Wilmingtonians blamed Jarvis for allowing a Virginia corporation enough influence in a North Carolina railroad to destroy its autonomy.

The greatest vexations arose from the state's efforts to complete the Western North Carolina Railroad to Ducktown and Paint Rock on the Tennessee boundary line. Eastern North Carolinians complained that the state was wasting money in building a railroad through the almost valueless mountain counties. Landslides began to cover roadbeds as soon as they were cut around mountainsides, and costs became alarming.[69] Meanwhile the directors of the East Tennessee, Virginia and Georgia Railroad clamored for the road to be completed and link their line to the Atlantic Ocean.

Toward the end of 1879 the Democratic leaders apparently decided that to complete the Western North Carolina quickly

---

[65] *Observer*, June 17, 1879.

[66] *Laws of North Carolina, 1879*, c. 67.

[67] *Morning Star*, January 1, February 6, August 13, 1879.

[68] Brown, *A State Movement in Railroad Development*, 240.

[69] For the difficulties being encountered in completing the railroad, see "Report of the Committee of Investigation on the Western North Carolina Railroad and the Western Insane Asylum," *Public Documents, 1879, Document No. 27.*

would bankrupt the state. They spread word through the northern financial centers that the railroad was for sale, and in mid-December William J. Best, James D. Fish, J. Nelson Tappan, and William R. Grace, four wealthy New Yorkers, made a tentative offer to buy the railroad and complete it.[70] Their plan was to buy this line and the Atlantic and North Carolina, link them together, and thus form a through line from Beaufort to Tennessee. After receiving the blessings of the North Carolina congressmen, Jarvis asked Best and his associates to submit a formal offer. On January 10, 1880,[71] they complied and Jarvis then began a lively correspondence with Best designed to protect the state's interests at every point of the contract.

A flood of letters on the advisability of the Best contract deluged the Governor's office. Those who favored the sale maintained that only a syndicate of outside capitalists could command enough resources to complete the railroad in the near future, that careful attention to the details of the contract would safeguard the state's interests, and that the sale would remove the railroad from politics. Those who opposed the sale argued that the state would be selling a valuable asset for a pittance, that the new owners would direct their traffic toward Virginia rather than North Carolina ports, that the long-term value of the road would warrant any sacrifice by the state to complete it, and that the Best contract contained insufficient guarantees that it would be built or managed properly. The railroad's own board of directors advised against the sale; the Council of State advised an immediate special session of the legislature.[72] Without any clear mandate, Jarvis had to make the lonely decision. On February 21 he called an extra session for March 15 to consider the sale.

When the legislature convened, the Governor explained that completing the Western North Carolina would take $6 million and thirty years if undertaken solely by the state. And the people of the state were neither willing nor able to be saddled with new bond issues or taxes. He advised the legislators to

[70] For the earliest indication of this negotiation, see Zebulon B. Vance, Robert B. Vance, and Robert F. Armfield to Thomas J. Jarvis, December 19, 1879, Governors' Papers.
[71] William J. Best to Thomas J. Jarvis, January 10, 1880, Governors' Papers.
[72] George P. Erwin to Thomas J. Jarvis, February 11, 1880, Governors' Papers; George L. Dudley to Thomas J. Jarvis, February 21, 1880, Governors' Papers.

examine the contract in detail, see that it protected all the interests of the state, and then ratify it. On March 29 both houses passed the bill selling the railroad by comfortable majorities.[73]

The act authorized the purchasers to organize a new Western North Carolina Railroad Company. The company could issue $4 million of preferred stock, $212,500 of which must be assigned to the private stockholders. It had to assume an existing mortgage of $850,000, and it had to pay the state $550,000 of new mortgage bonds for its interest in the road.[74] The line must be completed to Paint Rock by July 1, 1881, and to Murphy by January 1, 1885. A commission[75] of three men was to see that the purchasers lived up to the terms of the contract. For its part the state had to promise to keep at least 500 convicts on the road until work was completed.[76]

Subsequent events, however, soon began to cast new doubts on the wisdom of the sale. In May, 1880, Best's associates deserted him and assigned all their interests to another group of Virginia and northern financiers. These men intended to lease a number of railroads and organize them into a system operating between Richmond and Atlanta. They had first acquired the Richmond and Danville Railroad, and in 1871 they had leased the state-owned North Carolina Railroad, which stretched from Greensboro to Charlotte.[77] Now that this "Richmond and Danville syndicate," as Best's new associates were generally called, controlled the Western North Carolina Railroad, they were in a position to channel much of the state's traffic into Virginia rather than to North Carolina ports. When they ousted Best from the presidency of the Western North Carolina,[78] the state's dream of a central line extending from the mountains to the coast seemed shattered.

But Best was not yet out of the picture. During the fall of 1880 he had acquired another group of associates, known through the state as the "Boston syndicate." They immediately bought control of the Midland North Carolina Railway Com-

---

[73] "Governor's Message," *Public Documents, 1880,* Document No. 1; *Laws of North Carolina, 1880,* c. 26.

[74] This was the approximate amount which the state had spent on the railroad since 1875.

[75] The commissioners appointed were Jarvis, Vance, and John M. Worth.

[76] *Laws of North Carolina, 1880,* c. 26.

[77] Brown, *A State Movement in Railroad Development,* 163, 228; *News and Observer,* October 2, September 1, 1881.

[78] *News and Observer,* April 13, 1881.

pany, essentially a paper corporation which had been trying since 1873 to form a line from Beaufort to Tennessee. In November they offered to lease the Atlantic and North Carolina Railroad, which was two-thirds state owned, for thirty years. At the same time Best began to insist that he still controlled the Western North Carolina.[79] The groundwork thus laid, they publicized their plan to combine the Western North Carolina, the Midland, and the Atlantic and North Carolina into an east-west trunk line. On such weighty matters Jarvis preferred the advice of the legislature, which was scheduled to meet the following January. Consequently, he refused to commit himself on the ownership of the Western North Carolina, and he ordered the state's proxy on the Atlantic and North Carolina's board of directors to prevent its sale or lease until after the Legislature met.[80]

Jarvis had an early opportunity to test the popularity of his railroad policies when he sought reelection as governor. During April, 1880, several leading Democrats announced their candidacy for the party's nomination, but by May the field had narrowed to Jarvis and Daniel G. Fowle. For the sake of party harmony the two men chose not to debate the wisdom of having sold the Western North Carolina, and the contest between them was largely personal. The Jarvis forces derided the unheroic nature of Fowle's Civil War record and accused him of opposing the call for a constitutional convention in 1875. The Fowle supporters could do no better than disparage in general terms Jarvis' intellect, leadership, and personality.[81] On May 21 the Raleigh *Observer* stimulated the only excitement when it published an anonymous letter accusing Jarvis of having voted for the special tax bonds during the legislature of 1868-1869.[82] Jarvis retaliated by an open letter of his own in which he demonstrated how his votes and proposals had been parliamentary tricks designed to obstruct rather than support the bond issues.[83] On June 17 the Democratic convention met in Raleigh and on the first ballot gave Jarvis nearly a one hundred-vote majority.[84]

[79] Brown, *A State Movement in Railroad Development*, 241, 247; *News and Observer*, February 16, 1881.

[80] Thomas J. Jarvis to F. M. Simmons, November 20, 1880, Jarvis Letter Book, 1879-1883, 168; Thomas J. Jarvis to F. M. Simmons, November 23, 1880, Governors' Papers.

[81] *Morning Star*, June 15, 30, 1880; *Daily News*, May 5, 20, June 5, 6, 12, July 20, 1880.

[82] *Observer*, May 21, 1880.

[83] *Daily News*, May 30, 1880.

[84] *Daily News*, June 18, 1880.

Jarvis waged his campaign against Ralph Buxton, who had resigned his position as district judge in order to run for governor on the Republican ticket, on time-tested Democratic issues. Republican government in North Carolina had been extravagant and corrupt; the Democrats had reduced both taxes and expenses. The Republicans had accomplished essentially nothing for railroad development; the Democrats had sold the Western North Carolina with guarantees that it would be completed quickly and at no further expense to the state. Buxton himself had avoided military action during the Civil War, had used his judicial garb to favor Negroes and Republicans, and had always opposed using convict labor on state internal improvements. In turn, the Republicans portrayed the Democratic party as one of reaction and hate, disunion and secession. They chastised the Democrats for neglecting internal improvements; they accused them of enormous corruption and of quashing any attempted investigation of their own conduct; and they insisted that true democracy had existed in the state only under the Republican administration. They accused Jarvis himself of delivering the Western North Carolina Railroad into hands indifferent to the best interest of the state. Both candidates spoke frequently, and sometimes in joint debate. Jarvis himself spoke in nearly every county.[85]

Jarvis won reelection as governor by the narrow margin of 121,827 to 115,590.[86] He scored best in the Piedmont and Mountain sections, while Buxton's strength was in the East. The general distribution of votes was much the same as that of the Vance-Settle election. But ten counties, five in the East and five in the West, shifted from Democratic to Republican in the two elections; only one county changed from Republican to Democrat.[87] Vance's immense personal magnetism certainly had been partially responsible for the larger margin of his victory, but the voting trend during these years was toward democracy. Apparently the sale of the Western North Carolina Railroad, the issue of the day, operated to Jarvis' disadvantage despite its

---

[85] *Morning Star*, June 1, July 24, August 4, 1880; *Daily News*, July 18, 20, 25, 27, 30, August 4, 5, 15, 1880; *News and Observer*, September 18, 19, 23, 24, 29, October 1, 21, 24, 1880.
[86] Abstract of votes, November 27, 1880, Election Returns, Governor and State Officers, 1880, Papers of the Secretary of State.
[87] R. D. W. Connor (comp. and ed.), *A Manual of North Carolina . . . 1913* (Raleigh: North Carolina Historical Commission [State Department of Archives and History], 1913), 1001-1004.

general popularity. He probably would have at least held his own without this issue.

In his address of January 5, 1881, Jarvis spoke optimistically of conditions in the state. Trade and business were increasing, evidences of "thrift and prosperity were seen in the country and in town," and whites and Negroes were "working together in peace and harmony." The Department of Agriculture had made a good start in bringing immigrants into North Carolina, and it saved the farmers thousands of dollars by keeping inferior fertilizer out of the state. Work on the Western North Carolina Railroad was progressing slowly but should accelerate by spring-time. Since the last legislature, over $7 million of old bonds had been funded into only about $2.2 million of new bonds. It was true that the state's income was small, but its expenses were being kept to a minimum.

The legislation that the Governor proposed was conservative and generally based on the assumption that the state needed no further major reforms. He recommended a new Supreme Court building, which should also serve as a repository of the state's valuable records. He requested a Supreme Court librarian to do research for the over-worked justices. The state's law had not been codified since *Battle's Revisal* of 1873 and needed to be recodified. The pardoning power was too much responsibility for one man, and a pardoning board was needed. The state also needed stronger laws to regulate the traffic in and sale of alcoholic beverages. The Atlantic and North Carolina Railroad was "fairly prosperous," but several groups of businessmen wanted to lease it. If the legislature did not act, the Governor would leave the decision to the railroad's directors.

Some of Jarvis's recommendations, however, indicated less than commitment to retrenchment. He complimented the managers of the charitable and penal institutions and urged the legislature to grant them whatever they needed. He requested more money for the normal schools and even suggested trebling the tax rate to provide an adequate school system. He proposed that the swamp lands belonging to the Board of Education be sold and the money assigned to the education fund. And to the consternation of the denominational colleges, he requested a small annual appropriation of $7,500 to the University and an increase in the number of tuition scholarships from one to two for each county.[88]

---

[88] "Governor's Message," *Public Documents, 1881*, Document No. 1.

The Democratic legislature found these recommendations generally acceptable. As yet, the ultraconservative Bourbons had not taken over the party, and the legislators still reflected the moderate conservatism implied by the Democrat's slogan of "Retrenchment and Reform." They rejected totally only the requests for a new Supreme Court building, a new mansion, and a state pardoning board.

They acted most vigorously on educational matters. The act "to revise and consolidate the public school law" included the following reforms: county superintendents were to be elected by a joint meeting of the county board of education and board of magistrates; the superintendent of public instruction for the first time received an expense account of $500 a year and was empowered to employ a clerk; grades of teachers' certificates were defined; a system of county teachers' institutes was established; a standard of examinations for public school teachers was fixed; and a list of recommended textbooks was to be drawn up.[89] The state treasurer was ordered to restore to the school fund, from the general fund, the money hitherto spent for the support of normal schools. This official was also authorized to distribute to the counties according to the number of school children entitled to the benefits of the common schools the $214,000 then possessed by the education fund.[90] The Board of Education was permitted to sell its swamp lands and use the proceeds as needed.[91] The legislature began a policy of allowing certain towns to vote special taxes for setting up graded schools for each race.[92] Higher education was encouraged by beginning annual appropriations to the university, by establishing eight normal schools and giving $2,000 to those of each race, and by donating one acre of land to Shaw University for a medical school.[93]

Legislation for the state's charitable institutions was also constructive. Their boards of directors had pleaded for extra funds for expansion and improvement, and the legislature

---

[89] *Laws of North Carolina, 1881*, c. 200.

[90] *Laws of North Carolina, 1881*, cc. 82, 91.

[91] *Laws of North Carolina, 1881*, c. 150.

[92] *Laws of North Carolina, 1881*, cc. 189, 231. The schools for each race were to be supported by taxes paid by citizens of the same race. The North Carolina Supreme Court eventually ruled such laws unconstitutional on the grounds of racial discrimination. Frenise A. Logan, "The Legal Status of Public School Education for Negroes in North Carolina, 1877-1894," *North Carolina Historical Review*, XXXII (July, 1955), 354, 355.

[93] *Laws of North Carolina, 1881*, cc. 141, 149.

granted the amounts that each of these boards requested.[94] The asylums at Goldsboro and Morganton were incorporated in order to give their directors more freedom of action.[95] The one at Raleigh was authorized to acquire additional property as needed.[96]

Taxation had to be increased slightly to bear the added costs of these latter programs. The poll tax was raised from 72 cents to 84 cents, and the ad valorem tax from 24 cents to 28 cents per $100.[97]

Governor Jarvis had only recommended better controls over the sale and use of alcoholic beverages, but the state's temperance forces were clamoring for total prohibition. A compromise law forbade the manufacture of liquor and beer, but not wine and cider, and permitted the sale of liquor only by druggists and doctors. A referendum was to be held in August to determine whether the law should go into effect.[98]

Largely due to the persuasive powers of Secretary of State William L. Saunders, the legislature contracted with John W. Moore to prepare a roster of North Carolina troops who had served in the Civil War. It also authorized the trustees of the Public Library to publish the state's Colonial and Revolutionary records.[99]

Other laws of significance ordered a resurvey of all the state's boundaries, incorporated the North Carolina Pharmaceutical Association and defined its duties, permitted the lease of convicts to county and town authorities, and ordered the laws of the state to be recodified.[100] Rather than decide whether to sell the state's interest in the Cape Fear and Yadkin Valley Railroad, the legislature established a commission with full power to act.[101]

In the campaign preceding the prohibition referendum, Jarvis stated that he "should be false to the 1,400,000 people of North Carolina" if he remained silent.[102] At the prohibition convention in Raleigh he urged ratification of the law, and later he re-

---

[94] *Laws of North Carolina, 1881,* cc. 96, 182.
[95] *Laws of North Carolina, 1881,* cc. 206, 297.
[96] *Laws of North Carolina, 1881,* c. 133.
[97] *Laws of North Carolina, 1879,* c. 70; *Laws of North Carolina, 1881,* c. 116.
[98] *Laws of North Carolina, 1881,* c. 319.
[99] *Laws of North Carolina, 1881,* cc. 50, 88.
[100] *Laws of North Carolina, 1881,* cc. 127, 145, 347, 355.
[101] *Laws of North Carolina, 1881,* c. 374.
[102] *News and Observer,* April 29, 1881.

quested all county commissioners to refuse to license any more liquor dealers until after the election. Nevertheless, on August 4 the voters rejected statewide prohibition by a vote of 166,325 to 48,370.[103]

To assist the Board of Education to prepare a list of recommended textbooks, Jarvis sent a circular letter to all principals in the state asking their preferences.[104] The scores of responses had so much agreement that the superintendent was able to submit this list in his next report. On the other hand, the Governor chose to have no part in selecting the locations of the new normal schools. Despite much pressure, he left these decisions to the Board of Education and the superintendent of public education.[105]

With adequate financing provided by the legislature, the state's asylums developed rapidly. In April, 1881, the directors of the Goldsboro asylum decided to add another wing to their building and construction was soon under way. In December, 1882, the directors of the Morganton asylum reported that the first stage of their building program was completed.[106]

The law permitting the lease of convicts to local authorities increased the competition for the limited number of convict laborers. Jarvis became so harried by requests for them that he asked Attorney General Thomas S. Kenan for a solution. Kenan decided that the state was legally bound by specific commitments only to the Western North Carolina and the Cape Fear and Yadkin Valley railroads; the Governor could allocate the remainder where he wished.[107] Since the state could not even meet its primary commitments, Jarvis could only reply to eager supplicants that they must wait until the state had more convicts or fewer commitments.

---

[103] For the full story of this referendum, see Daniel J. Whitener, "North Carolina Prohibition Election of 1881 and Its Aftermath," *North Carolina Historical Review*, XI (April, 1934), 71-93.

[104] One of these circulars, dated March 21, 1881, is in the Governors' Papers.

[105] *News and Observer*, May 1, 1881. Soon after the General Assembly authorized the new normal schools, graded school principals and county teachers' associations began writing Governor Jarvis and suggesting their community or county as a desirable location for such a school. Jarvis turned these letters over to the superintendent of public instruction.

[106] *News and Observer*, April 20, 1881; "Report of the Board of Directors of the Western North Carolina Insane Asylum," *Public Documents, 1883*, Document No. 13.

[107] Thomas J. Jarvis to Thomas S. Kenan, October 7, 1881, Jarvis Letter Book, 1879-1883, 367; Thomas S. Kenan to Thomas J. Jarvis, October 10, 1881, Governors' Papers.

The decision to sell the swamp lands belonging to the Board of Education stimulated some interest in North Carolina among outsiders. Several northern lumbermen made inquiries about timber tracts, though sales went slowly. John T. Patrick, the state's immigration agent, reported that he had begun to receive from two to ten letters daily asking about free farm land,[108] and the newspapers seemed to believe that the number of immigrants was increasing.

The law establishing a commission to sell the state's stock in the Cape Fear and Yadkin Valley Railroad afforded Jarvis another opportunity to enlist outside capital in North Carolina's development. In August Doctor A. H. Canedo, representing a group of New York investors, informed Jarvis that they were interested in the railroad as a link of a projected trunk line connecting Wilmington and Cincinnati.[109] After the usual negotiations, Canedo submitted a formal offer in January, 1882.[110] His company would pay the state $55,000 for its stock, would pay the private stockholders $100,000 for their floating debt, and would complete the road within three years "from Wilmington to some convenient point in the extreme west." [111] The Governor and his Council and the private stockholders then successively approved the contract and presumably the railroad was sold.

When Canedo and his associates began the customary hedging, Julius A. Gray, president of the railroad, and some of his friends decided to buy the line themselves. Jarvis and the commissioners were delighted at the prospect of North Carolinians owning the railroad and turned a deaf ear to Canedo's entreaties. The New Yorkers eventually forfeited their contract and Jarvis recommended the new contractors to the next session of the legislature. The latter consented to the sale, and it was Gray and his North State Improvement Company that eventually completed the construction.[112]

Jarvis followed no set pattern in pursuing ideas of his which the legislature of 1881 had rejected. During his first years as governor he acquired some notoriety for his sparing use of the

    [108] John T. Patrick to Thomas J. Jarvis, May 23, 1882, Governors' Papers.
    [109] A. H. Canedo to Thomas J. Jarvis, August 17, 1881, Governors' Papers.
    [110] *News and Observer*, December 20, 23, 1881; January 12, 1882.
    [111] *Laws of North Carolina, 1881*, c. 374.
    [112] For the complete story of this last transaction, see Roland B. Eustler, "The Cape Fear and Yadkin Valley Railroad," *North Carolina Historical Review*, II (October, 1925), 427-441.

pardoning power, and this reputation had undoubtedly motivated his request for a pardoning board. But when denied this assistance, he remained as implacable on pardoning as ever. Detractors called him "Bloody Tommy" and claimed that he was trying to build up the convict labor force. But Jarvis himself believed that idleness caused crime, that "swift and certain punishment" were its best preventative,[113] and that the governor should seldom overrule criminal sentences. The legislature had also refused to authorize a new governor's mansion, and he felt that he could only renew his request at the next session.

But he was unable to resist two bargains that presented themselves. In April, 1881, the National Hotel property, adjacent to the Capitol building, went up for sale. Jarvis without legislative authority, quickly had the Board of Agriculture buy it for $13,000.[114] The legislature had also refused to finance an exhibition of the state's resources at the Atlanta Exposition of October, 1881. But Jarvis considered this false economy, and with his blessings the Department of Agriculture undertook to see that the state was well represented. State Geologist Washington C. Kerr gathered thirty-five boxes of wood, minerals, and field products, and the Richmond and Danville Railroad gave them free transportation to Atlanta. Both Jarvis and Vance attended the Exposition and reported it a great success.[115]

On April 30 President A. B. Andrews of the Western North Carolina Railroad requested a four-month extension of the date for completing his contract. He maintained that construction had been unnecessarily hampered by the state's failure to keep enough convicts on the road and by the severe winter of 1880-1881. The contract of sale had allowed such an extension at the discretion of a majority of the commissioners appointed to supervise the contract. Commissioners Jarvis, Worth, and Vance met and unanimously agreed to the extension.[116]

William A. Best and his Boston associates chose this as an opportune moment to reassert themselves. By its inaction, the

<hr>

[113] Thomas J. Jarvis to Joseph S. Amis, November 23, 1881, Jarvis Letter Book, 1879-1883, 387-388.

[114] *News and Observer*, April 17, 20, 1881; "Governor's Message," *Public Documents, 1881*, Document No. 1.

[115] *News and Observer*, July 20, October 16, 27, 1881.

[116] *News and Observer*, September 1, 1881; Proceedings of the Commissioners on the Western North Carolina Railroad Company, 1881-1884, April 30, 1881, 2, Governors' Office Papers, State Archives, hereinafter cited as Proceedings, Governors' Office Papers.

of the Western North Carolina and the lease of the Atlantic and North Carolina. By June, Best had convinced the commissioners that only the Midland Company could build the much desired east-west trunk line. Best then deposited $250,000 with the commissioners to reimburse the Richmond and Danville for its expenditures on the Western North Carolina; in return Jarvis assured Best that he would do everything possible to make the Richmond and Danville accept the money and forfeit the railroad.[117] Best was so convinced that the railroad was his that he leased the Atlantic and North Carolina and deposited $85,000 as surety.[118]

On August 1 the commissioners peremptorily informed the management of the Richmond and Danville of the new agreement with Best.[119] They then attempted to browbeat the railroad's officials into surrendering their contract. The commissioners accused the Richmond and Danville management of charging discriminatory rates; they accused Andrews of lagging behind schedule and using deceit to obtain the extension of his contract. Jarvis challenged the Richmond and Danville groups to disprove these charges or suffer the legal consequences.[120] To the chagrin of the commissioners, the management repudiated each allegation and politely dared Jarvis to bring suit.[121] Over Vance's objections, Jarvis and Worth chose an ignominious retreat rather than involve the state in a protracted lawsuit.[122] In November the Boston syndicate asked Jarvis to resort to the courts as he had promised. Jarvis replied legislature had left to the Executive Department the ownership

---

[117] News and Observer, June 15, 1881; Thomas J. Jarvis to W. W. Carruth and D. J. Sprague, November 14, 1881, Jarvis Letter Book, 1879-1883, 377-382; Proceedings, August 1, 1881, 13, Governors' Office Papers.

[118] News and Observer, July 6, 1881; Proceedings, August 1, 1881, 13, Governors' Office Papers.

[119] Thomas J. Jarvis et al. to W. P. Clyde et al., August 1, 1881, in the News and Observer, September 13, 1881.

[120] Zebulon B. Vance and John M. Worth to Thomas J. Jarvis, August 25, 1881, Governors' Papers; Thomas J. Jarvis to A. S. Buford, August 26, 1881, Jarvis Letter Book, 1879-1883, 348; News and Observer, August 28, 1881. Andrews' reliability seemed questionable in another instance. The previous winter had been so severe that his convict labor had suffered hardship and disease, and during the summer an epidemic of scurvy had broken out in the camps. News and Observer, September 1, 2, 1881.

[121] A. S. Buford et al. to Thomas J. Jarvis et al., August 25, 1881; A. S. Buford to Thomas J. Jarvis, September 1, 1881, Governors' Papers.

[122] Thomas J. Jarvis to A. S. Buford, September 2, 1881, printed in the News and Observer, September 13, 1881; A. S. Buford et al. to Thomas J. Jarvis et al., September 27, 1881, Governors' Papers; Proceedings, Novembers 17, 1881, 35-39, Governors' Office Papers.

that the work was now going well along the Western North Carolina and he could do nothing.[123]

This defeat wrecked all hopes by Best and his associates for a trunk line, and they showed little interest thereafter in developing the Midland system. Charges of violation of contract proliferated, and in November the disgusted stockholders declared the lease forfeited.[124] The directors of the Midland declined to surrender the railroad, and the case was before the courts during the 1883 session of the legislature.[125]

When Jarvis once again addressed the legislature, he devoted most of his attention to continuing or completing existing programs. The Code had been revised and needed the legislature's approval. The old National Hotel adequately housed the Department of Agriculture and the Geological Museum. But Jarvis wanted the building remodeled and expanded so as to include quarters for the state library, the Supreme Court, and the Secretary of State. He renewed his request for a new governor's mansion. The Atlanta Exposition had been a great success, and Jarvis thought that North Carolina should also be represented at the one scheduled at Boston. Basic construction on penal and charitable institutions was about completed, though the Morganton asylum needed an additional wing. The Constitution required a board of public charities for the general supervision of these institutions, and the Board of Health could serve in this capacity. The Governor's Office still needed a board of pardons.

The Governor felt that the state's railroad system was developing satisfactorily. Construction on the Western North Carolina was on schedule. The leasers of the Cape Fear and Yadkin Valley had forfeited their contract, but new prospects existed; the commissioners should have more latitude in making subsequent leases. The Midland Company had begun the Atlantic and North Carolina railroad from Goldsboro to Salisbury, but had stopped at Smithfield; the Governor or a commission should have the authority to give the state's stock in the Atlantic and North Carolina to anyone who would finish the line to Salisbury. Soon the state would have a surplus of convicts, and a law was

[123] W. W. Carruth and D. J. Sprague to Thomas J. Jarvis, November 7, 1881, Governors' Papers; Thomas J. Jarvis to W. W. Carruth and D. J. Sprague, November 14, 1881. Jarvis Letter Book, 1879-1883, 377-382.

[124] "Proceedings of the Twenty-Ninth Annual Meeting of the Stockholders of the Atlantic and N. C. Railroad Co.," *A.&N.C.R.R.*, 1882-'89, 12, John D. Whitford Papers, 1770-1896, State Archives, hereinafter cited as "Proceedings," Whitford Papers.

[125] *News and Observer*, December 15, 1882; February 10, 22, 27, 1883.

badly needed letting the penitentiary directors assign them to any railroad that needed them.

The state's school system was improving, but it was still underfinanced. The Constitution limited the total tax burden that could be imposed on the people to $2.00 on the poll and 66⅔ cents on each $100 of property. Because of the low valuation of property throughout the state, routine government expenses required most of the proceeds from these taxes, and an amendment was needed to permit extra taxes for the support of the common schools. The legislature should also urge congressmen to support the Blair Bill then before Congress, which proposed to distribute the federal surplus among the states for education according to each state's illiteracy rate. Jarvis complimented the eight towns which were levying special taxes to support graded schools, and he felt that the state needed a general law letting any town do this.

Finally, Jarvis commented that the tax valuation on land and personal property was much too low. If they were reassessed and the valuation doubled, the state could halve its tax rate without losing any income. The consequent high property values and low tax rates would undoubtedly induce many more outsiders to invest in North Carolina.[126]

The work of the legislature of January-March, 1883, indicated that this body had become appreciably more conservative than its immediate predecessors. As yet it had not turned to the unashamed favoritism to business that later typified Bourbonism. Nevertheless, its determination to economize was becoming inflexible, and its reluctance to innovate hinted at future indifference to public ills. Favoritism to business was merely the next development. By comparison, the always consistent Governor seemed almost liberal.

The legislature gave Jarvis permission to sell some state property in Raleigh and to use the proceeds, plus convict labor, to build a new governor's mansion.[172] It denied him any funds to develop the National Hotel property.

Its actions on educational matters indicated a growing indifference in the Democratic leadership toward providing a better public school program. On March 8 it enacted a general law whereby any unit of local government could hold a referendum on the question of special taxes for a segregated graded school

---

[126] "Governor's Message," *Public Documents, 1883,* Document No. 1.
[127] *Laws of North Carolina, 1883,* c. 134.

system.[128] Presumably this law would gradually reduce the enrollment in the common schools and thereby save the state part of the cost of educating its children. Another law reduced the pay of county superintendents and restricted their duties so much that they were unable to provide good leadership.[129] The legislature's only action favorable to public education was a resolution urging the congressmen to support the Blair Bill,[130] and even this proved futile when Congress eventually decided against any such distribution of the federal surplus.

Internal improvement policies were more standard. The legislature authorized the Governor and the Council of State to give to the Newbern and Beaufort Canal Company the state's 2,500 shares of capital stock in the Albemarle and Chesapeake Canal Company, provided the former completed its work by January 1, 1885.[131] It wrote a new contract with the Richmond and Danville Company which made several concessions to the latter regarding the construction of the Ducktown branch of the Western North Carolina. In return the Richmond and Danville agreed to buy for $600,000 the $520,000 of bonds that the first contract required be delivered to the state treasurer.[132] The legislature authorized the Governor and a special commission to sell the state's stock in the Cape Fear and Yadkin Valley Railroad to Julius Gray and his associates, subject to the approval of the stockholders. It then offered to give the proceeds of this sale to any company that would build a railroad from a point on the Western North Carolina near Salisbury to either the Tennessee or the Virginia boundary.[133] It rejected, however, Jarvis' plan to secure a railroad from Smithfield to Salisbury by a similar offer of the state's stock in the Atlantic and North Carolina. Finally, it permitted the use of county prisoners for general road work.[134]

When William L. Saunders began to prepare for publication the early records of North Carolina, he found so many gaps in them that publishing only those records possessed by the state would be useless. At his request, Jarvis asked the legislature to

---

[128] *Laws of North Carolina, 1883,* c. 148.
[129] *Laws of North Carolina, 1883,* c. 121.
[130] *Laws of North Carolina, 1883,* resolution on 607.
[131] *Laws of North Carolina, 1883,* c. 105. In January, 1881, this stock had been valued at $8.00 a share. "State's Interest in the Albemarle and Chesapeake Canal Company," *Public Documents, 1881,* Document No. 24.
[132] *Laws of North Carolina, 1883,* c. 241.
[133] *Laws of North Carolina, 1883,* cc. 190, 371.
[134] *Laws of North Carolina, 1883,* c. 234, ss. 23, 24.

enable Saunders to search other archives for material relating to Colonial North Carolina and to copy it for inclusion in his publications. The legislature responded generously, and Saunders brought out his first volume in 1886.[135]

The legislature passed other laws of importance as follows: It approved the revised North Carolina Code; it consolidated and clarified the state's insurance laws; it ruled against a board of public charities, and instead drew up a detailed set of rules for the management of the asylums; and it voted $70,000 for another wing of the Morganton asylum.[136]

This conservative program permitted the legislators to write new tax laws quite at variance with Jarvis' recommendations. They ignored his request for a constitutional amendment permitting higher school taxes. Instead, on the basis of their new school laws, they lowered the poll tax from 84 cents to 75 cents. Jarvis' request for a more accurate tax assessment seemed directed against large property owners, and the legislators received it coolly. Their only concession was a general requirement that the county boards of commissioners assess all land and other real property every four years.[137] Worst of all, the legislature ordered all taxes to be suspended for the year in which the treasury received the $600,000 for its Western North Carolina Railroad bonds. This money was paid in May, 1884, and the Democratic party thus reneged on its promise to devote the proceeds of the sale to public education.[138]

When the legislature again declined to finance any participation in the various expositions being held around the country, Jarvis and the Board of Agriculture once more acted on their own. At the Boston Exposition of September, 1883, North Carolina had "the most conspicuous" exhibit of resources of any of the states.[139] The Governor and many other prominent North Carolinians attended. Jarvis himself delivered such an exciting "New South" type of address that the Boston *Post* later suggested him for the vice-presidency.[140] After leaving Boston, the party took the state's exhibit on a tour as far west as Chicago. The exhibit was later shown at the New Orleans Exhibition of

---

[135] "Message from the Governor," *Public Documents, 1883*, Document No. 21; *Laws of North Carolina, 1883*, resolution on 619-620.

[136] *Laws of North Carolina, 1883*, cc. 57, 156, 191, 419.

[137] *Laws of North Carolina, 1881*, c. 116; *Laws of North Carolina, 1883*, cc. 136, 363.

[138] *Laws of North Carolina, 1883*, c. 136.

[139] *News and Observer*, September 9, 1883.

[140] *News and Observer*, March 4, 1884.

1884 and at the North Carolina State Fair of the same year.[141]

In April, 1883, the Council of State instructed Jarvis to begin the new governor's mansion. He employed Samuel Sloan of Philadelphia as the architect and contracted with the Penitentiary authorities to build the mansion for $25,000.[142] The construction required six years and was done almost entirely by convict labor and with convict-made material.

The best disposition of the Atlantic and North Carolina Railroad remained an aggravating dilemma. In March, Judge Samuel F. Phillips appointed John Gatling, a Raleigh lawyer, as receiver of the railroad and ordered the Midland Company to pay it $28,493 in back rent.[143] In May Gatling turned the railroad over to its directors, and soon new offers of lease began to come in from other parties. Generally thereafter the affairs of the road were handled contrary to Jarvis' preferences. He had favored giving away the state's stock to encourage further construction, and his correspondence showed that he still favored leasing the railroad under favorable terms. Nevertheless, the legislature had chosen not to honor the one; and in regard to the other, Jarvis wrote the directors of the railroad that he would leave the decision to them.[144] At the December meeting the stockholders voted to lease the railroad to the Eastern North Carolina Railroad Company.[145] But in January the directors wrote the Governor that they had decided against another lease; they preferred to improve the road themselves and make it an effective servant of eastern North Carolina.[146] Jarvis then began lending them all possible assistance. In the next few months he thoroughly familiarized himself with the needs of the railroad, helped the directors borrow money for repairs and improvements, and even urged them to buy several small adjacent lines.[147]

---

[141] *News and Observer*, October 11, 16, 20, December 7, 1883.

[142] Journal of the Council of State, 1885-1889, April 3, May 15, 1883, 264-270, Governors' Office Papers.

[143] *News and Observer*, March 11, 1883; Brown, *A State Movement in Railroad Development*, 249.

[144] Thomas J. Jarvis to the Directors of the Atlantic Railroad Company, December 19, 1883, Jarvis Letter Book, 1883-1885, 22-25.

[145] "Proceedings," 45ff., Whitford Papers.

[146] John D. Whitford *et al.* to Thomas J. Jarvis, January 3, 1884, Governors' Papers.

[147] *News and Observer*, March 7, 28, 1884; Brown, *A State Movement in Railroad Development*, 250; John D. Whitford *et al.* to Thomas J. Jarvis, January 3, 1884; John D. Whitford to Thomas J. Jarvis, January 24, 1884, Governors' Papers; Thomas J. Jarvis to C. C. Clark *et al.*, January 23, 1884, Jarvis Letter Book, 1883-1885, 42-43.

Meanwhile, President Andrews pushed construction rapidly on the Western North Carolina. He occasionally reminded Jarvis that the state seldom honored its guarantee of five hundred convicts, but the Governor could only reply that they were not available.[148] Indeed, he sometimes received veiled political warnings from easterners when he insisted that the Western North Carolina had a legal first lien on such labor. About the only way by which he could alleviate this labor problem, and he did so consistently, was to check frequently on the health and care of the convicts at work. By September, 1884, Andrews had completed the railroad as contracted, and on September 17 Jarvis conveyed to the assignees all the state's interest in the railroad.[149]

Some of the optimism which Jarvis had expressed in his message of January, 1883, was not borne out by events of the next two years. Though every legislature of his administration had generously supported the state's charitable institutions, the latter seemed as needy as ever. Late in 1884 their directors reported that their new quarters were already overcrowded and that they neded more space and better equipment.[150] During 1883 and 1884 out-of-state farmers and lumbermen still continued to show interest in the swamp lands in the eastern part of the state. But the treasurer's report of January, 1885, reveals that for these two years the Board of Education received only $16,310 for its land and timber rights.[151] The Superintendent of Public Instruction stated that the law of 1883 reducing the pay of county superintendents and restricting their duties had made these men ineffective school leaders. This in turn had caused a sharp reduction in the number of teacher institutes held each summer. He pleaded for a new law to revitalize the county superintendencies.[152] After several years' delay, Jarvis finally

[148] A. B. Andrews to Thomas J. Jarvis, May 24, 1884, Governors' Papers; Thomas J. Jarvis to S. M. Dugger, May 26, 1884, Jarvis Letter Book, 1883-1885, 70.
[149] Thomas J. Jarvis to United States Trust Company, September 17, 1884, Jarvis Letter Book, 1883-1885, 81-82.
[150] The most pressing need of the asylums was more space. "Governor's Message," *Public Documents, 1885,* Document No. 1. The reports which the directors of other institutions submitted to the 1885 session of the General Assembly indicated general satisfaction with their building program, but a dire need for furniture, heating equipment, tools, and other accouterments.
[151] "Biennial Report of the Treasurer of North Carolina," *Public Documents, 1885,* Document No. 4.
[152] "Biennial Report of the Superintendent of Public Instruction," *Public Documents, 1885,* Document No. 8.

decided that the resurvey of the state's boundaries authorized by the law of 1881 would be too expensive. He preferred to leave its eventual survey to the United States Coast and Geodedic Survey Office.[153]

In his message to the legislature of 1885, given two weeks before the inauguration of Alfred M. Scales as his successor, Jarvis reported that the "affairs of the State are in a most Satisfactory condition." The Department of Agriculture had attracted "thousands of settlers," and the publicity gained at the various expositions had lured hundreds of thousands of investment dollars into North Carolina. Construction was completed on the Western North Carolina Railroad, was almost completed on the Cape Fear and Yadkin Valley, and was prospering on the Atlantic and North Carolina so much that the state should stop trying to lease it. The treasury showed a balance of $947,069. There were no great expenditures in sight, so taxes could be kept low, and the counties could use the opportunity to get out of debt. In fact, the state was so flush that its salary scale should be raised to attract the ablest talent.

Any deficiencies that still remained could easily be remedied. The state had excellent school laws, so that all the public school system needed was better financial support. Jarvis emphasized the value to the state of higher education and urged the legislature to increase its appropriations to the University at Chapel Hill. The state's asylums were adequate, but they needed expanding and modernizing to anticipate future needs. Finally, he reiterated his requests for more Superior Court judges, for an enlargement of the Department of Agriculture's facilities, and for a new Supreme Court building.[154]

Jarvis' long governorship had been an administrative as well as a Democratic success, and he fully expected an appointment to some important federal position. The legislature unanimously endorsed him for a place in President Cleveland's Cabinet,[155] and Senators Vance and Matt W. Ransom pleaded his case eloquently. But Cleveland had better political use of these select appointments and could only offer Jarvis the post of United States minister to Brazil. The Jarvises were nonplused at the thought of living abroad, but the generous minister's salary of $12,000[156] would partially compensate for years in low-salaried

[153] C. V. Boutelle to Thomas J. Jarvis, May 12, 1884, Governors' Papers.
[154] "Governor's Message," *Public Documents, 1885*, Document No. 1.
[155] *Laws of North Carolina, 1885*, resolution on 678-679.
[156] *News and Observer*, March 28, 1888.

state offices, and Jarvis eventually accepted the appointment. He and Mrs. Jarvis left Newport News on June 13, 1885, and arrived at Rio de Janeiro on July 7.

Minister Jarvis found his quarters at Rio cramped and in great disorder. The "Legation" consisted of two rented rooms in the Candidois Hotel. They were sparsely furnished, but they did contain several hundred public documents which Jarvis often consulted.[157] The records of the Legation for the past half century were stored in the hotel attic, and one of Jarvis' first undertakings was to classify those of value and discard the remainder.[158] His staff consisted of one secretary, a young American of whom Jarvis grew quite fond and whose duties consisted mainly of translating and copying.

Life in Brazil for the Jarvises was pleasant but dull. They lived in the Hotel dos Estrangaros, about a half mile away from the Legation. During the summer Rio was hot and unhealthy, so they spent about half of each year at Petropolis, a mountain city about thirty miles in the interior. Mrs. Jarvis never quite adjusted to the climate or the food, nor Jarvis to the idleness. He wrote home that he had so little work to do that he was studying French, Spanish, and Portuguese, and had become proficient in the latter.[159] Half way through his appointment Jarvis obtained a leave of absence, and the lonely couple visited in North Carolina from November, 1886, to April, 1887.[160]

It was small wonder, then, that Jarvis worked so industriously on the few cases that merited his services. Some United States citizens had organized the Central and South American Telegraph Company and wanted to extend a line from Texas to Argentina. They needed permission to run it through the waters near Rio, but to their perplexity the Brazilian government denied them this right. Jarvis eventually discovered that the government already owned a line between Rio and New York and did

---

[157] Thomas J. Jarvis to Thomas F. Bayard, August 7, 1885, and Thomas J. Jarvis to Thomas F. Bayard, October 23, 1885, Despatches from United States Ministers to Brazil, National Archives, Washington, D.C., hereinafter cited as Despatches from Ministers to Brazil.

[158] Thomas J. Jarvis to Thomas F. Bayard, August 21, 1885, Despatches from Ministers to Brazil.

[159] Thomas J. Jarvis to John D. Whitford, February 2, 1886, Whitford Papers.

[160] Thomas J. Jarvis to Thomas F. Bayard, December 22, 1886, and Thomas J. Jarvis to Thomas F. Bayard, May 19, 1887, Despatches from Ministers to Brazil.

not want any competition.[161] In 1888 the State Department queried him on the advisability of a commercial treaty with Brazil. Jarvis submitted a thoughtful report, arguing that Brazil would never become a rival manufacturing nation and that such a treaty would benefit both nations.[162]

His most interesting encounter was with Hinton R. Helper, who arrived in Rio in December, 1885, and began "an unnecessary" and "unpleasant" correspondence with Jarvis.[163] At this time Helper was trying to settle a long-standing claim of the Fiedler Steamship Company against Brazil. According to Helper, Brazil had leased a Fiedler ship and would not pay the lease price of $450,000. The Brazilian government insisted that the lease had been made by an unauthorized private citizen, and it denied any responsibility. Helper became bitter and sarcastic when Jarvis insisted that he could do nothing except present the Fiedler case formally and await instructions from his government.[164]

As early as mid-1886 Jarvis began to think about reentering public service at home. He asked his correspondents about his popularity in different sections of the state, whether he could successfully contest Ransom's seat in the United States Senate, and whether there was any way to get the Democratic party to draft him for governor.[165] To place himself once again in the public eye he wrote letters expressing his views on issues of the day and had his friends insert them in North Carolina newspapers. He damaged his candidacy for the governorship, however, when he wrote home that he could not return to North Carolina until after the election.[166] Possibly he expected the party to draft him and thus afford him an excuse for an earlier return. But the party could hardly risk nominating an absentee candidate and his friends took him at his word. At the State

---

[161] Thomas J. Jarvis to Baron de Cotigipe, September 25, 1885; Thomas J. Jarvis to Thomas F. Bayard, April 26, 1886, Despatches from Ministers to Brazil.

[162] Thomas J. Jarvis to Thomas F. Bayard, August 27, 1888, Despatches from Ministers to Brazil.

[163] Thomas J. Jarvis to Thomas F. Bayard, February 17, 1886, Despatches from Minister to Brazil.

[164] Jarvis copied his entire correspondence with Helper and sent it to the Secretary of State, enclosed in Thomas J. Jarvis to Thomas F. Bayard, February 17, 1886, Despatches from Ministers to Brazil.

[165] Thomas J. Jarvis to A. B. Andrews, May 10, 1886, Alexander B. Andrews Papers, Southern Historical Collection; Thomas J. Jarvis to T. F. Davidson, November 4, 1887, Allen T. and Theodore F. Davidson Papers, Correspondence, State Archives.

[166] *News and Observer*, April 14, 1888.

Democratic Convention in May, 1888, Jarvis was never nominated and the convention selected Daniel G. Fowle on the twenty-third ballot.[167] After Cleveland's defeat in November, Jarvis resigned his diplomatic post and returned home. Shortly after his resignation some of his friends predicted that he would contest Ransom's senatorial position, but Jarvis scotched the movement before it could develop.[168] He had political fences to mend and this would take some time.

Once back in Greenville the Jarvises settled into the routine of community life. Mrs. Jarvis was a Presbyterian and Jarvis was a Methodist, and both took an active role in church work. In 1891 Jarvis represented the North Carolina Conference in the Ecumenical Conference in Washington, D.C.[169] Mrs. Jarvis joined several book clubs and appeared often on their programs. She helped organized the Singletary Chapter of the Daughters of the Confederacy and became its first president.[170]

Jarvis reopened his law office, this time in partnership with Alexander L. Blow. Jarvis' long years of public service now rewarded him with a thriving practice, while his political knowledge of the law and his untiring industry won him a statewide reputation as a successful attorney. His most sensational case occurred in 1889, when he headed a team of prominent lawyers who successfully defended Eugene Grissom, Superintendent of the North Carolina Insane Asylum, against charges of immorality, corruption, mismanagement, and cruelty.[171] In 1889 the Board of Trustees of North Carolina State College offered him the first presidency of that institution, but he declined.[172] In 1891 he bought at public auction most of the property of William Whitehead, who had recently gone into bankruptcy. The Pitt County records of deeds show that for the rest of his life Jarvis received a modest income from selling tracts of this land and from leasing timber rights upon it.

But he could not stay away from politics. He never lost his affection for or his loyalty to the Democratic party, and he was distressed at what was happening to it. By the early 1890's it

[167] News and Observer, May 31, June 1, 1888.
[168] News and Observer, December 20, 1888.
[169] News and Observer, January 25, 1891.
[170] Daily Reflector (Greenville), May 27, 1899, hereinafter cited as Daily Reflector.
[171] News and Observer, June 27, July 21, 1889.
[172] David A. Lockmiller, History of the North Carolina State College of Agriculture and Engineering of the University of North Carolina, 1889-1939 (Raleigh: Edwards & Broughton Co., 1939), 41.

had become so much the guardian of the "special interests" of the business world that the Farmers' Alliance, originally a non-political organization, was contemplating bolting the party and fusing with the Republicans.[173] Staunch organization man that he was, Jarvis exerted every effort to prevent such a rupture. Though he had sometimes been accused of toadying to business interests, he had never lost his concern for agriculture's plight. He always maintained that the Democratic party was equally concerned with both interest groups.

In 1892 he was permanent chairman of the State Democratic Convention and worked for party unity. In his address to the Convention he announced himself "a candidate for the office of peace maker in the Democratic party." He asked the Convention to avoid controversial issues and concentrate on victory. "Lay aside your professions, lay aside the third party, lay aside the St. Louis platform, and as Democrats and as North Carolinians, let us go forward shoulder to shoulder and whip this common enemy, the Republican party." [174] He could hardly have been more gratified when the Convention wrote a meaningless platform but angled for the farmer vote by nominating for governor Elias Carr, conservative ex-president of the Alliance.[175]

From August until November, Jarvis campaigned almost continuously for Carr and the other Democratic candidates. Sometimes speaking on the same platform with Carr and at other times speaking alone, he generally delivered a lengthy middle-of-the-road stump speech devoted largely to scoring the opposition. He attacked the Republicans for their pension frauds, their high tariff policy, the proposed Force Bill, and for their callousness toward agriculture's distress. And, lest he alienate North Carolina businessmen, he condemned the Populists for "monstrous and impracticable" financial ideas and the "naked deformity" of their prejudice toward railroads.[176] In private, Jarvis visited numerous bankers, railroad officials, and manufacturers and secured large campaign pledges from them.[177] All told, Jarvis contributed at least as much as any individual to

---

[173] For a survey of North Carolina political conditions at this time, see Lefler and Newsome, *North Carolina*, 512-514.
[174] *News and Observer*, May 19, 1892.
[175] Lefler and Newsome, *North Carolina*, 515.
[176] *News and Observer*, September 20, 1892.
[177] J. Fred Rippy, *F. M. Simmons, Statesman of the New South, Memoirs and Addresses* (Durham: Duke University Press, 1936), 23.

the Democratic victory. In April, 1894, Senator Vance died and Governor Carr appointed Jarvis to fill the vacancy.[178]

During his brief senatorship Jarvis took special interest in financial matters before Congress. He worked diligently to fulfill the party's pledge to lower the tariff, but party factionalism made the resultant Wilson-Gorman tariff little better than its predecessor. Nevertheless, as a true party man, Jarvis publicly defended the new law as "infinitely superior" to the McKinley Tariff and one which would cause "a general decrease in the cost of family supplies." [179] During debate on an income tax law, he advocated the principle of a graduated tax. When a fellow Democrat retorted that such a law would wreck the party, Jarvis indignantly replied, "If the Democratic party has no higher mission than to bow at the foot stool and worship at the shrine of the accumulated wealth of the country, the sooner it does the better." [180] For the most part, however, he worked quietly at a job which he did not consider particularly exciting.

In the spring of 1894 Jarvis decided against being a candidate for the two remaining years of Vance's term. Instead he would seek a full term by attempting to unseat Senator Ransom.[181] The legislature would almost surely prefer a western man as Vance's successor, while Ransom was an easterner and therefore fair game. By this time, however, the Republicans and the Populists had joined forces, and the Democrats could ill afford intraparty rivalries. The result was that both Jarvis and Ransom directed most of their shafts at the Fusionists, while engaging in quiet infighting against each other. The Ransom forces confined their attacks to gentle barbs at Jarvis' conciliatory attitude toward the Populists, particularly their demand for the free coinage of silver.[182] In turn, Jarvis sought to overcome Ransom's advantage as the incumbent by proposing that the State Convention call for a senatorial primary rather than decide the nomination at the Convention itself.[183] On August 8 the Convention voted overwhelmingly against a primary[184] and Jarvis was virtually out of the race.

For the next three months he campaigned just as vigorously

[178] Ashe, *Biographical History*, I, 337.
[179] *News and Observer*, August 24, 1894.
[180] *News and Observer*, June 23, 1894.
[181] *News and Observer*, April 20, 22, 1894.
[182] *News and Observer*, June 6, August 2, September 7, 27, 1894.
[183] *News and Observer*, June 24, 1894.
[184] *News and Observer*, August 11, 1894.

for Ransom and the other Democratic candidates. In contrast to most party speakers, however, he cast his appeal largely to the yeoman class, concentrating mainly on the party's demands for tariff reduction and the free coinage of silver.[185] But it was to no avail. The Republicans and Populists avoided their mistake of 1892, when they refused to join forces against the Democrats, and in 1894 they united behind a single platform and a single ticket. They swept the November elections, and the following January the legislature elected Populist Marion Butler and Republican Jeter Pritchard to the Senate.[186]

For the next several months Jarvis devoted his political efforts toward using the issue of free silver to rebuild the Democratic party. While he seems to have abandoned hope of obtaining public office for himself, he urged his younger friends to take more active roles in politics. And he attempted to convince conservative Democrats that the gold standard was playing havoc with the nation's economy. In August, 1895, he attended a conference in Washington, D.C., the chief object of which was to discuss the best way to insure a silver platform and a silver candidate in the next national convention.[187]

In September an interparty silver convention was held in Raleigh. At the outset Jarvis sought to establish a bipartisan aura in the convention by arguing "that the question of silver rose above party." [188] But once the delegates began work, he and others felt that the Populists were trying to turn the convention to their own advantage. Most Democrats then boycotted the convention after its first day. In a subsequent interview, Jarvis explained, "I intend to keep myself free to act, when the time comes, as I may think best for the good of the cause of silver and the good of the country." [189]

In 1896 Jarvis attended the Chicago National Democratic Convention as delegate-at-large. He hoped to be elected national committeeman and favored the nomination of Richard "Silver Dick" Bland for president. But a majority of the delegation supported William Jennings Bryan and selected Josephus Daniels as committeeman over Jarvis by a vote of thirteen to eight.[190]

---

[185] *News and Observer*, September 13, 25, November 6, 1894.
[186] Lefler and Newsome, *North Carolina*, 515-517.
[187] *News and Observer*, August 9, 17, 1895.
[188] *News and Observer*, September 25, 1895.
[189] *News and Observer*, September 26, 1895.
[190] *News and Observer*, July 7, 8, 1896; Josephus Daniels, *Editor in Politics* (Chapel Hill: University of North Carolina Press, 1941), 159-160, hereinafter cited as Daniels, *Editor in Politics*.

According to Daniels, Jarvis became a confirmed Bryan man on hearing the latter's "Cross of Gold" speech and "shouted with the boys." [191]

For the next decade Jarvis acted as an elder statesman of the Democratic party. He campaigned in each general election and could always be depended on to deliver "one of Jarvis' old-time speeches—full of sense and wisdom." [192] He steadfastly advocated free silver, legalized primaries, a lower tariff, the regulation of trusts and corporate wealth, and a general reorientation of his party toward the common man—ideas liberal enough to make conservative Democrats suspect him of Populist tendencies. He wrote several articles in the Democratic handbooks which were models of clear statement.[193] He served several times on the Democratic Executive Committee, and in other years he faithfully attended each party convention. In 1900 the Democrats ordered their first senatorial primary, and Jarvis was one of several who announced their candidacy. He hoped that his years of experience, particularly his brief senatorship, would be in his favor. But he soon realized that local leaders and organizations wanted new blood, so he withdrew from the race.[194]

In 1898 Jarvis helped "redeem" North Carolina for a second time. The Fusionist legislature of 1895 had redistricted Greenville so that it had two Negro wards electing four councilmen and two white wards electing two councilmen. Since the councilmen chose the town officials, by 1898 Greenville had a Republican mayor and chief of police, two Negro policemen, and a Negro clerk.[195] At his party's request, Jarvis provided the Democratic managers with details of "Negro rule" in Greenville.[196] He and a team of speakers then conducted a statewide white supremacy campaign, urging all white voters to unite within the Democratic party and elect a legislature which "will undo this infamous wrong." [197] Between speaking engagements, Jarvis visited businessmen friends of his and assured them

---

[191] Daniels, *Editor in Politics*, 164.
[192] *News and Observer*, September 8, 1896.
[193] Ashe, *Biographical History*, I, 339.
[194] *Daily Reflector*, September 21, October 15, 1900.
[195] *Daily Reflector*, April 6, 1898; Helen G. Edmonds, *The Negro and Fusion Politics in North Carolina, 1894-1901* (Chapel Hill: University of North Carolina Press, 1951), 130, hereinafter cited as Edmonds, *The Negro and Fusion Politics*.
[196] Edmonds, *The Negro and Fusion Politics*, 130.
[197] *Daily Reflector*, April 6, 1898.

that in the event of a Democratic victory their taxes would not be increased.[198] As a result of a sweeping Democratic victory, the legislature of 1899 eliminated the Negro from North Carolina politics, and the government of Greenville soon returned to normal.

By the early 1900's the temperance forces had triumphed in hundreds of local option elections, and the Democratic managers sensed the popularity of this issue. The town of Greenville had thirteen barrooms, and Jarvis joined wholeheartedly the crusade to prohibit them. For the next several years he spoke and wrote advocating statewide prohibition. He had the insight to reconcile politics and morality, arguing that since a majority of the counties had already outlawed intoxicants by local option, the legislature should respect the majority wish and enact a blanket law. In 1909 the Turlington Act provided statewide prohibition.[199]

In 1904 President John C. Kilgo offered Jarvis the deanship of the new Trinity College law department, but Jarvis felt too old and settled to begin a new career.[200] He and his wife had simple habits, and after the turn of the century he chose law cases more for their interest than their emolument. In 1901 the House of Representatives brought impeachment charges against two Republican members of the State Supreme Court, Justices David M. Furches and Robert M. Douglas. Jarvis and four of his old friends handled the defense and secured acquitals on all charges from the less partisan Senate.[201] He was the leading counsel of Josephus Daniels when a federal judge held that newspaperman in contempt of court because of several pungent editorials. Jarvis hastened to Washington and consulted with Chief Justice Melville Weston Fuller of the United States Supreme Court and Justice Jeter C. Pritchard of the Circuit Court. When Justice Pritchard eventually tried the case he promptly discharged Daniels from arrest.[202]

As a citizen of Greenville, Jarvis involved himself in one civic movement after another. He was chairman of the building committee entrusted with erecting a new Methodist church build-

[198] Lefler and Newsome, *North Carolina*, 525.

[199] *Daily Reflector*, August 4, 1902; Lefler and Newsome, *North Carolina*, 537, 538; Daniels, *Editor in Politics*, 521.

[200] Thomas J. Jarvis to John C. Kilgo, August 9, 1904, John C. Kilgo Papers, Duke Manuscript Department.

[201] *Daily Reflector*, February 25, March 4, 6, 1901; Lefler and Newsome, *North Carolina*, 533.

[202] Ashe, *Biographical History*, I, 338.

ing.[203] This handsome structure was completed in 1907 and became Jarvis Memorial Methodist Episcopal Church South. He took an active part in establishing a system of graded schools for Greenville and for some years was chairman of the board of trustees of this system. In 1907 he and his friend William Ragsdale secured the passage of a law establishing a teachers' training school in Greenville. Jarvis became chairman of the building committee and persuaded the town and county governments to appropriate $100,000 for the construction.[204] It was largely through his personal supervision that East Carolina Teachers' Training School, now East Carolina University, was able to open in 1909.

Soon after his seventy-ninth birthday his health began to break. He was in ill health for much of the summer of 1913, and for the last ten days of his life was critically ill. He died at nine o'clock at night on June 17. He left his entire estate, consisting of about $2,000, to his wife, who outlived him for only a short while.

---

[203] Thomas J. Jarvis to Benjamin N. Duke, February 7, 1906, Trinity College Papers, Duke Manuscript Department.

[204] Thomas J. Jarvis Memorial Issue, *East Carolina Training School Quarterly* (July-September, 1915), 20, 21.

Remarks of Mr. Jarvis, of Tyrrell, on Revenue and Taxation, delivered in the House of Representatives, February 17, 1869.

Interview, July 18, 1878, with Thomas J. Jarvis by P. H. Wilson, City Editor of the Raleigh *Observer*.

Address to the Senate of North Carolina, January 2, 1877.

Inaugural Address, February 5, 1879.

Notice of Public Auction. Sale of real estate of Roanoke Navigation Company in Halifax County, June 28, 1879.

Thanksgiving Proclamation, November 11, 1879.

Speech of November 18, 1879, delivered at the formal opening of the Colored Industrial Fair at Raleigh, North Carolina.

Pamphlet to the Friends of Higher Education, February 2, 1880.

Printed circular of a proclamation by the governor, February 21, 1880, convening the General Assembly in extra session, March 15, 1880.

The Western North Carolina Railroad, statement of the case given by Governor Jarvis, March 4, 1880.

Report of William Johnston to Jarvis, March 15, 1880, on condition of convicts employed on Cape Fear and Yadkin Valley Railroad.

Notice from W. H. C. Price to Jarvis, relative to World's Fair Committee, April 24, 1880.

The Governor to the People, May 28, 1880. Jarvis' statement defending his administration.

Printed circular, to the Friends of Higher Education, June 10, 1880.

Thanksgiving Proclamation, November 13, 1880.

Proclamation, November 20, 1880, giving list of electors of President and Vice President.

Proclamation relative to proposed amendments to Constitution, December 11, 1880.

Governor's Message to the General Assembly, January 5, 1881.

Inaugural Address, January 18, 1881.

Resolution by Governor Jarvis before the Board of Public Buildings, relative to repairs to the Capitol, January 23, 1881.

Proclamation to relinquishment of lands for sites for lighthouses, beacons, and other navigational aids to the United States, March 1, 1881.

Circular on textbooks for use in public schools sent by Jarvis to educational institutions in the state, March 21, 1881.

Address by Jarvis before The Society of Alumni of Randolph Macon College, June 15, 1881.

Proclamation giving result of election on prohibition, held, August 4, 1881.

Proclamation, inviting the people of North Carolina to unite with other states in prayer for the recovery of the President, [September 4, 1881].

Proclamation urging people of the state to cease work during hours of funeral ceremonies of James A. Garfield, September 23, 1881.

Jarvis' speech before the Atlanta Exposition, October 27, 1881.

Thanksgiving Proclamation, November 16, 1881.

Proclamation requesting meeting of Commissioners appointed to receive propositions for purchase of state stock in Cape Fear and Yadkin Railway Company, November 23, 1881.

Report on Jarvis' speech before the State Democratic Convention in Raleigh, July 5, 1882.

Thanksgiving Proclamation, November 17, 1882.

An open letter to Jarvis, P. M. Hale, and John Spelman, from CATO. The undated broadside concerns Jarvis' vote on special tax bonds.

Jarvis to George Franklin Drew, May 22, 1879.
G. F. Drew to Jarvis, May 27, 1879; [May 31, 1879].
J. W. Lee to Jarvis, May 29, [1879]; [May 29, 1879]; May 30, 1879; May 31, 1879.
Thomas P. Devereux to Jarvis, July 11, 1879.
E. W. Thompson to Jarvis, July 11, 1879.
Thomas P. Devereux to Jarvis, July 12, 1879; July 15, 1879; July 18, 1879.
Thompson to Thomas J. Jarvis, July 19, 1879.
James H. Pool to Jarvis, August 21, 1879.
Thomas Michael Holt to Jarvis, January 28, 1880.
W. J. Best to Jarvis, [February] 17, 1880.
J. M. Worth to Jarvis, [February] 17, 1880.
R. A. Lancaster to J. M. Worth, [March] 23, 1880.
Jarvis to A. B. Andrews, May 22, 1880.
W. R. Grace to Jarvis, May 27, 1880.
Jarvis to W. R. Grace, May 27, 1880.
Jarvis to J. W. Wilson, May 28, 1880.
J. B. Manning to Jarvis, November 4, 1880.
Jarvis to F. M. Simmons, November 23, 1880.
F. M. Simmons to Jarvis, November 23, 1880.
E. K. Hyndman to Jarvis, [January] 24, 1881.
Jarvis to E. K. Hyndman, January 24, 1881.
W. J. Best to Jarvis, September 13, 1881; November 6, 1881.
Jarvis to David N. Bogart, December 29, 1881.
Jarvis to John Whitaker Cotten, December 29, 1881.
D. M. Bogart to Jarvis, December 29, 1881.
Jarvis to Cyrus Wiley Grandy, December 29, 1881.
Jarvis to G. L. Dudley, [December], 30, 1881; January 2, 1882.
Jarvis to Harry Skinner, December 30, 1881.
Jarvis to A. H. Canedo, July 27, 1882.
John Gatling to Jarvis, August 5, [1882].
Jarvis to John Gatling, August 11, 1882.
Jarvis to M. W. Ransom, August 29, 1882.

THE JARVIS PAPERS

LETTERS FOR 1869-1877

REMARKS OF MR. JARVIS, OF TYRRELL,

On Revenue and Taxation, delivered in the House of Representatives, February 17, 1869[1]

The bill to raise Revenue being under consideration, on the 15th of February, Mr. Jarvis introduced the following proviso to section 1, class [*sic*] 1: [Section 1, class 1, reads, subject to the exemptions allowed by law, there shall be an *ad valorem* tax of two fifths of one per cent, in addition to the special taxes, which have been or may be levied to pay interest on bonds issued to or for Railroad or other corporations, levied for the purpose of paying the expenses of the State government; the interest on the public debt; and such other liabilities of the State as General Assembly may direct, upon the moneys, credits, investments in bonds, stocks, joint stock Companies or otherwise; on the real and personal property.]

The proviso of Mr. Jarvis to come in at the end of the above quoted section reads: "Provided, that all the taxes imposed upon the real and personal property of the State for State and county purposes shall, in no case, exceed two-thirds of one per cent."

The proviso was adopted by a vote of 48 to 29.

A motion was immediately made to reconsider the vote by which the proviso was adopted.

Pending the motion to reconsider, on the 17th of February, Mr. Jarvis said: Mr. Speaker[2]—Having introduced this proviso to the Revenue bill on Monday, I feel it my duty to give some of the reasons which induced me to do so, and to state why I think the motion to reconsider should not prevail. I am influenced by motives worthy of the thoughtful consideration of this House.

---

[1] Taken from the *Daily Sentinel* (Raleigh), February 27, 1869, hereinafter cited as *Daily Sentinel*.

[2] Joseph William Holden, son of William W. Holden; newspaperman and novelist of Raleigh; served in the General Assembly, 1868-1870. Samuel A. Ashe and Others (eds.), *Biographical History of North Carolina: From Colonial Times to the Present* (Greensboro: Charles L. Van Noppen, 8 volumes, 1905-1917), VI, 320-328, hereinafter cited as Ashe, *Biographical History*.

First—The proviso is the plain provisions [*sic*] of the Constitution according to my understanding of that instrument. Sec. 1 of Art. V of the Constitution reads:

"The General Assembly shall levy a capitation tax on every male inhabitant of the State over twenty-one and under fifty years of age, which shall be equal on each, to the tax on property valued at three hundred dollars in cash. The Commissioners of the several counties may exempt from capitation tax, in special cases, on account of poverty and infirmity, and the State and county capitation tax combined shall never exceed two dollars on the head."

For our purposes of investigation, this section may be made much shorter and much plainer by letting John Smith represent the class of persons subject to capitation tax in the first sentence of the section. In the second sentence of the section, we can leave out all in regard to exemptions including the word "infirmity," without, in the least, changing the sense so far as it effects the subject under consideration. Then the section, thus simplified, will read:

"The General Assembly shall levy a capitation tax on 'John Smith,' which shall be equal to the tax on property valued at three hundred dollars in cash. And the State and County capitation tax, combined, shall never exceed two dollars on the head."

This section, as it now stands, as well as in the original, is composed of two sentences. The first, I will call the first division of the section, and the second, the second division. The meaning of the word "equal," in the first division, is not variable and uncertain, but is fixed and determined. The word "equal," in the first division, thus defined and used, established an absolute equality in value between the tax on John Smith (the capitation tax) and the tax on three hundred dollars worth of property. —The capitation tax and the property tax must go hand in hand. If one is increased the other must, in order to keep up the EQUALITY. If the tax on John Smith is one dollar, the tax on my three hundred dollars worth of property *must* be one dollar also. I suppose all agree, that if the section contained only the "first division," the General Assembly would be compelled to keep good this equality, and that this would be the only restriction upon its action. If the section stopped with the first division, the General Assembly would not be limited as to the extent of the tax, but only as to the manner of levying it. It would be *compelled* to preserve the equality, and nothing more. It might tax John Smith five dollars, but it would be required to tax my three hundred dollars worth of property also. Whenever the tax on John Smith and on my three hundred dollars worth of property is not the same in value, the equality is destroyed, and the provisions of the first division of the section violated. Hence, we see that the whole scope and meaning of the first division of the section is to establish an absolute and unalterable equality between the tax on property and the tax on persons. The object of the framers of the Constitution is very apparent and praiseworthy. They did not intend that persons should oppress property, or property oppress persons, but that all should feel the weight and responsibilities of the Government alike. Now, it is a principle in mathematics, that things equal to the same thing are equal to each other. The converse of the proposition is also true, to wit: that things equal to each other are equal to the same thing. Suppose I say that Tom's house is equal in length to Bill's house, and that John's house is also equal to Bill's house. Then, if I tell you that John's house is twenty feet long, do you not at once know the length of Tom's house! Hence, I lay this down as an established principle in physics and in ethics, that when two things are declared to be equal, any limitation upon the one will operate as a limitation upon the other; and that to limit the one, it is only necessary to limit the other.

Then, the question arises is either the tax on the head or on property limited; for according to the principles just laid down, if the one is, the other must be. In the second division of the section we find the following language: "And the State and county capitation tax combined, shall never exceed two dollars." Here is a clear and distinct maximum limitation upon the tax on the head. It may be anything less than two dollars, but can never be greater. So long as the poll tax is less than two dollars, we are only required to look to the equality established in the first division, but when it reaches two dollars the second division commands us to stop, for the limit is reached. On the other hand so long as the tax on three hundred dollars worth of property is less than two dollars, we are only required to preserve the *equality* of the first division, but when we make it more than two dollars and the capitation tax being compelled by the several divisions, to stop at two dollars, is it not clear that we violate the provisions of the first division—to wit: the equality! From this I conclude that when you undertake to tax John Smith FIVE dollars on his head, and to tax me TWO dollars on my three hundred dollars worth of property, you violate the section under consideration. It is also true, that when you undertake to tax John Smith TWO dollars on his head, and to tax me FIVE dollars on my two hundred dollars worth of property, you destroy the equality, and therefore violate the same section. The true meaning of the section is, that we must tax both alike, till we reach two dollars, and then stop. Any other mode is a violation of the section. It is worthy of notice, that the two divisions of the section are connected by the conjunction *and*. After declaring the equality in the first division it does not say, but the capitation tax shall not exceed two dollars, thereby intimating that the property tax might, but the equality of the first division is connected with the limitation of the second division by the conjunction AND, thereby showing that the equality and the limitation are the great leading ideas of the section, and that both must be preserved. Hence, I conclude, that property can only be taxed, under this section, two thirds of one per cent, which is the principle contained in my proviso.

I know, sir, that the law of construction requires the instrument to be taken together as a whole. I propose now to go briefly through the whole Article to see if there is anything in conflict with the construction I have put upon the first section.

The 2nd section provides how the capitation tax shall be applied—nothing in conflict there.

The 3rd section provides how all other things, except real and personal property, shall be taxed, and it requires the laws taxing them to be *uniform*. It also requires the laws by which the money value of the real and personal property is ascertained to be *uniform*. Here again we see this great idea of equality in levying the tax. No conflict in this section.

The 4th section provides that a part of the money raised under the 1st and 4th sections shall be applied to the payment of the interest on the public debt. No conflict in this section.

The 1st sentence of section 5 directs how new debts may be contracted on the part of the State. It provides that no new debt shall be contracted in behalf of the State unless there is a special tax levied to pay the interest on the same, except it be to supply a casual deficit, to suppress insurrection or invasion. Here I think we have a strong proof that it was the intention of the framers of the Constitution to limit the powers of the Legislature to levy taxes. They excepted from this restricted power of the Legislature, the three great emergencies when the very existence of the State government might depend upon the prompt action of the General Assembly in obtaining money. It was not deemed expedient to put any check upon the action of the General Assembly if any one of these great emergencies should arise. In all other cases the Legislature is required to levy the tax. Now if the levying [of] the tax is the only restriction, why make an exception in the three cases above referred to. It is clear to my mind, that the makers of the Constitution required the tax to be levied so that the legislators should be compelled to keep before their minds the limitation in the first section. The other part of the section directs how the Legislature may aid railroads and other corporations, but this aid must be in conformity with the limits of the 1st section. I think this section is in harmony with the first section.

The 6th section provides for exemptions from taxation.

The 7th section provides how Counties may raise Revenue. Here some suggests [sic] a difficulty, but to me there is none. It says they "shall be levied in like manner with the State taxes, and should never exceed the double of the State tax, except for a special purpose, and with the special approval of the General Assembly." When the Constitution was made, the authors of it had before their mind the fact that, heretofore, the State tax was but ten cents on the hundred dollars worth of property. Taking this as the State tax they intended to allow the counties to tax twenty cents on a like amount of property, but not to go beyond that, except by special permission of the Legislature. So, if the State only taxed five cents, the counties would be limited to ten, unless, by special permission of the Assembly. The Legislature may give this special permission to the counties, to exceed the double of the State tax, until it reaches the limit established in the first section, and then it must stop. I think this section harmonizes with the others. I have thus briefly taken up the whole Article on taxation, and I no where find any thing in conflict with the construction placed upon the first section. There is no jarring or discord between the two different sections of the Article; but all are in perfect harmony, and, taken as a whole, form a more complete canoply [sic] to the people against oppressive taxation than any Constitution of North Carolina has ever furnished.

The first section establishes the orbit of taxation in which the Legislature is to move. The other sections prescribe the manner in which it is to move. While the planets move in their regular orbits, harmony prevails among the heavenly bodies; but when one shoots madly out of its orbit, it produces confusion among the others. So, as long as this Legislature moves in its regular and well-defined orbit, the people will be at rest, but when it goes outside of the orbit, the people will rise up in their might, and drive those from power who produced this confusion.

But it is argued, that if we place this construction upon the Constitution we cannot raise money enough, by taxation, to carry on the government and to pay the interest on the old bonds. I assert that we can. The Chairman of the Finance Committee,[3] himself, admits that two fifths of one per cent, on the real and personal property of the State, together with the tax on incomes, professions, trades, &c., will raise *one and a half million dollars*. Ought not *this* to be enough? Under the new order of things it may not be sufficient to meet the wants and to supply the demands of those who administer the affairs of State. But who will say that, in the good old honest days of North Carolina economy, it would not have been enough, and to spare! If, however, it does not yield money enough, shall we, on this account, trample the Constitution under our feet! If it serves as a check upon the wild extravagances of this Legislature and the Republican party, shall we, on this account, violate it! If we find that, under a policy of strict economy, the necessary funds cannot be raised, let the Constitution be changed. If not enough to encourage extravagances, let our expenses be curtailed; but, under no circumstances, let the Constitution be violated.

Now, Sir, for the policy of this proviso. It is said, by gentlemen on this floor, that if we adopt this proviso, as a permanent feature of the tax bill, it is death to the system of Railroads contemplated by this Legislature. A direct appeal is made to those who voted for these appropriations to be active to defeat this proviso, by striking it from the bill. Even if it be true that the proviso would be injurious to the Railroad interest, which seems to be so dear to some gentlemen, *shall* we be more awake to the interest of these projected lines of Railroads, which are not yet begun, and may never be completed, than we are to preserve the Constitution of the State? —Shall we be less mindful

---

[3]Llewellen G. Estes of New Hanover County, member of the General Assembly, 1868. R. D. W. Connor (comp. and ed.), *A Manual of North Carolina . . . 1913* (Raleigh: North Carolina Historical Commission [State Department of Archives and History], 1913), 724, hereinafter cited as Connor, *Manual, 1913.*

of the interest of an impoverished and over-taxed people than we are of soulless corporations! The warmest opponents of this proviso admit it is not clear that the Constitution does not limit taxation. If this doubt exists, is it not better to give the Constitution and the people the benefit of the doubt!

But sir, if the Constitution does not limit taxation, the ability of the people to pay does. It is an easy matter for us to pass tax bills and direct the Sheriffs to collect them. It is but the work of a day and a few strokes of the pen to prepare these bills. But in levying these taxes we should not lose sight of the people's ability to pay them, for it is useless to levy the taxes, if they are to remain unpaid. I contend that two dollars on the three hundred dollars worth of property, is all the people in their present impoverished condition can pay. —It will be remembered that last year the State tax was only ten cents on the hundred dollars worth of property, and that but little of the personal property of the State was taxed, while under this bill everything is to bear its part. It will be remembered that last year the entire revenue of the State for State purposes was less than three hundred thousand dollars. Will you look back over the Journal of the Legislature at the large number of Sheriffs we have been called upon to relieve from fines, because they could not collect this small amount? As before stated, this bill will raise *fifteen hundred thousand dollars* for State purposes alone, besides the tax for County purposes, to carry on the County governments. Here you have increased the amount of taxes which the people are to pay for State purposes, five times. Have you increased their ability to pay? Not at all. From all sections of the State there comes up a cry of want, of poverty, of scarcity and "hard times." If the people found it difficult to pay the small tax last year, will they not find it almost impossible to pay five times that amount this year? —But that is not all. In the section to which I propose to add this proviso, you read that this tax of two-fifths of one per cent, shall be in addition to the *"special taxes"* levied for Railroad purposes. The aggregate of the "special tax" is six tenths of one percent, levied for Railroad purposes. This bill, as it now stands, authorizes the collection of that tax. Now, putting the estimated value of the property of the State at two hundred millions of dollars, and we have under this "special tax" twelve hundred thousand dollars as a "special tax" to pay interest on bonds issued or authorized by this Legislature. Now add the "special tax" and the general tax together, and we have a tax of *twenty seven hundred thousand dollars*, to be paid by the people during this year. Only nine times the amount we paid into the State Treasury last year. Can the people pay it? The answer comes up from every hamlet in the State, *No!* Is this the cheap and economical government the Republican orators promised the people under the new Constitution? Is this what Republican orators meant when they held up that Constitution to the people and told them that under it their taxes could never be high? Will the people call this a cheap government, think you?

Mr. Speaker, it is known that when this Constitution was before the people for ratification, the Republican speakers, from the seaboard to the mountains, told the people that it limited taxation to sixty six and two-thirds cents on the hundred dollars worth of property. The people ratified it with that belief, and this is the construction they put upon it. They were educated to this opinion by you gentlemen of the Republican party. You know you urged this upon them as one great reason why they should ratify the Constitution. You told them it would throw a wall of protection around them, over which the Legislature could not go. Will you, to-day, assist in tearing away that wall of protection? —Many of you hold seats upon this floor, to-day, that would be at home digging in some corn-field, had you told the people you would not respect their expressed and known will on this great question of taxation. This proviso proposes that you shall do, officially, what you told the people you would do. My proviso proposes to put that limit upon the Legislature which you told the people the Constitution did. It proposes to give the people that protection which you said the Constitution gave them.

Republicans, I call upon you to day, to redeem your promises! To act out here, in practice, what you preached last Spring and Fall. If you do not, the people shall know who have deceived them!

Mr. Speaker, you will remember that the Railroad bills, which passed this House, did so by a combination known as the "Omnibus," and those who voted for these appropriations are said, by gentlemen on this floor, to be riding in the "Omnibus," —each passenger being pledged to each other on the principle, "you tickle me and I will tickle you." Not a single one of these bills could have passed this House on its own merits; but by putting them all into the "Omnibus" together, they have been driven through. This proviso has created quite a stir among the passengers, and I see them begin to gather around the old "Omnibus" again, which is hastily being put in motion to gather up all the Railroad men to defeat this proviso. Already, the "*whipper in,*" with his burly form, is in his seat, and with powerful and strong muscular arm, is cracking the whip over those who are halting by the way because they love the Constitution and do not wish to violate it. The bugle of the "Manager" has sounded for it to move forward! In the name of the people of North Carolina, I cry, stop! Republicans, let not that Omnibus move an inch! The Constitution of your State lies in its way! I have thrown it there by this proviso. It is your Constitution! It is the work of your own hands. Will you preserve it, or will you drive rough shod over it, as you go thundering along the high road, to the ruin of the people and the bankruptcy of the State. Railroad men, I appeal to you to stop and think what you are doing before you go farther. Your combined bills of "special taxes" levying a tax of 60 cents on the one hundred dollars worth of property; the Revenue bill in addition to the "'special tax" levies a tax of forty cents on the same hundred dollars worth of property, and then, finally, the counties must tax thirty or forty cents more. All of these taxes together amount to at least one dollar and thirty cents on the one hundred dollars worth of property, which is just twice the amount your Constitution permits you to tax. I know, in your eagerness to have a railroad to run by your door you are apt to forget the ruin you are about to bring upon the people. I must think you all mean to do right; but you have allowed railroads to run away with your better judgment. In your heated imagination, you hear nothing but the whistle of the steam engine as the iron horse, with his hoofs of iron and ribs of steel, goes dashing by your door. Let me tell you, before you hear that shrill sound, you will hear other sounds that will be more piercing, and that will carry sorrow instead of joy to your heart. If you strike out this proviso and persist in collecting this large amount of tax, you will hear, instead of the rattling of the cars, the murmur of the populace for relief—instead of the sweet notes of the maiden, the wailing of the mother as she surrenders some cherished household good to the taxgatherer—instead of the merry songs of the son, the curses and imprecations of the father against those who have brought this trouble and ruin upon him, as he gathers around him his wife and children to bid farewell to the home of his

childhood which he has been compelled to vacate to give place to
its new occupant from a foreign land who has just purchased it
at the Sheriff's sale, "for taxes."

But, Mr. Speaker, what do we hear said in reply to these unpleasant truths. It is said let me levy the tax and then if any
one thinks it is unconstitutional, let him test it before the Supreme Court of the State. —Now, sir, I have confidence in the
Judges of the Supreme Court, but I do not wish to leave this
an open question. It will cost more to take a case up to the Supreme Court than to pay the tax, and there are but few men
able to incur the expense. I know, sir, the Judges occupy a high
position in the confidence of the people of North Carolina, because they are men incorruptible, and learned in the law. So far
the waves of party faction have broken harmless at the base of
the throne upon which they quietly sit. But after the innovations
and attacks that have been made upon the Judiciary of our land,
who can say that this bulwark of the peoples rights, may not
soon be swept away and all be left to the pitiless mercy of the
cormorants that hover around the capitol of the dear old State,
feeding upon the life blood of the people, and whose constant
cry is a few more millions of bonds. It is to avoid the costs of
bills of injunction, to check mate these men who are too selfish
to be just, to save the credit of the State and to prevent the utter
ruin of the people, that I have offered this proviso.

I demand of the Republicans to stand by it. You are already
committed to its doctrines, and, if you reject it, you shall not
escape the responsibility. It was placed in this tax bill, in part,
by your votes. Keep it there, and the people are safe. Strike it
out, and the ruin of the people is as certain as your political
death. Everywhere, the people of all parties are uneasy on account of the alleged extravagance of this Legislature, and the
Republican party. I confess there is a just cause of alarm. The
papers have gone out to them containing the glad news that
this proviso has been adopted. A new life springs up within
them. —A new energy quickens their every motion. Their countenance, so lately shaded, again beams forth with joy and glad-
ness. They see that they are not to be stripped of their homes
and their all to pay the interest of the millions of bonds authorized by this Legislature. The same paper contains the names
of those who voted for my proviso. They read this list with
eagerness to see if the name of their Representative is there!
Just below that list, of which they approved, they see a motion

has been made to reconsider the vote by which the proviso was adopted. They are again anxious, thoughtful and uneasy! Their eyes are beseechingly turned towards the Capital of their State. Me think I hear neighbor ask neighbor, will our Representatives stand firm? Will they redeem the pledges they made us when we sent them there, or will they desert us now in the hour of our peril? When the Democratic and Conservative speakers told us last spring, that our taxes, under Republican rule, would be eight or ten times as great as ever before, these men, whom we have trusted with our interests, told us that it was a "Rebel lie." The Republicans told us the Constitution limited taxation, and, if we would ratify it, we would be safe. The Democrats told us, in reply, that the Republicans would find some way to dodge the limitation. The Republicans retorted that it was a lie, that the provisions of the Constitution in this respect were plain, that it limited the tax to two-thirds of one per cent, on property, that they would stand by the limitation, and that all the talk about high taxes, by the Democrats, was simply to frighten us. We believed the Republicans, we ratified the Constitution, and we selected the Republicans to guard our interests, expecting them to be faithful servants. The hour has now come when their integrity, their fidelity to principle, and their devotion to truth, is to be tested.

Mr. Speaker, to those who in good faith redeem their pledges, their constituents will say, "well done, thou good and faithful servant," enter thou into the full confidence o' thy people. To those who do not, they will say, depart from me ye recreant servants, ye have deceived me once, you shall not deceive me again.

UNC-DMC

Thomas J. Jarvis to David Miller Carter[4]

Raleigh, March 15th '69

Yours of the 10th is to hand and in my opinion merits an immediate reply

Enclosed I send you a copy of the bill I introduced in regard

---

[4]Prominent lawyer and planter of Washington; member of the General Assembly, 1862, 1864. Moved to Raleigh, 1875. Samuel A. Ashe and Edward McCrady (eds.), *Cyclopedia of Eminent and Representative Men of the Carolinas of the Nineteenth Century* (Madison, Wisconsin: Brant and Fuller, 2 volumes, 1892), II, 68–70, hereinafter cited as *Cyclopedia of the Carolinas.*

to the practice of the courts and which has been called a Stay
Law, Relief Bill &c. Some law of the kind was determined upon
by the Legislature. I thought this was just to debtor and creditor
for it restored the same remedies that obtained when the debts
were contributed[.] I do not think the bill unconstitutional but
manifestly just. The House put in two other sections to the bill
to which I objected and which I fear makes the bill a bad one.
The bill as it passed the House is substantially the same as this
ref to the obtaining of the judgmt. The two sections to which I
objected delays the execution till 30 'days before the Spring
Term 1870—

Capt Farrow[5] is still on pay or at least he will be paid when
Jenkins[6] gets the money to pay with. The State Treasury is now
empty. It is a great pity that Hyde is no better represented. Miss
G.[7] is still in Raleigh—I saw her yesterday. She is a lovable
woman. I think I am on good terms with her. I cannot yet tell
what her answer would be were I to propose.

I do not think the Legislature will adjourn before the 15th of
April notwithstanding the House has just determined by a resolution to adjourn on the 29th of March.

It is generally believed that Clingman[8] will take charge of the
Standard in a few days. Jo Turner[9] still continues to play the
fool in the Sentinel.

He will not be control[l]ed. He has at least stirred the
rad[ical]s up—they are threatening to assassinate him.

I wanted you with me so much to help me "cuss' the conservative members of the Legislature in to voting for the 15th Act. I
did my best but could not get them all up to "sticking point"

I hope to meet you in Edenton soon and to be introduced to
Mrs Carter.

---

[5]Probably Tillman Farrow, gristmill proprietor of Okracoke and member
of the General Assembly, 1868. Connor, *Manual, 1913*, 659; Rev. L. Branson
(ed.), *The North Carolina Business Directory, 1877 and 1878* (Raleigh: L.
Branson, 1878), 159, hereinafter cited as Branson, *Directory, 1878*.
[6]David A. Jenkins of Gastonia; member of the General Assembly, 1865,
1866; state treasurer, 1869-1876. *Cyclopedia of the Carolinas*, II, 379–380.
[7]Unable to identify.
[8]Thomas Lanier Clingman, lawyer of Asheville; member of the General
Assembly, 1840; Democratic representative in Congress, 1843–1845, 1847–
1861; delegate to the Democratic National Convention, 1868. Allen Johnson,
Dumas Malone, and Others (eds.), *Dictionary of American Biography*
(New York: Charles Scribner's Sons, 22 volumes and index, 1928—), IV,
220–221, hereinafter cited as *Dictionary of American Biography*.
[9]Josiah Turner, previously a lawyer and newspaper editor in Hillsboro,
now editor of the *Daily Sentinel*, a newspaper established in 1865 to oppose
Reconstruction. Member of the General Assembly, 1852, 1854, 1858, 1860,
1879; of the conventions of 1861 and 1875; and of the Confederate Congress, 1863–1865. *Dictionary of American Biography*, XIX, 68–69.

16th of March

The relief Bill as it is called has just passed the Senate as it was passed by the House.

Sects. one, two, three, four, five, six, eight, nine and ten of the bill that passed both Houses are the same as the bill enclosed— Sect. 7th has a proviso to it that provides that all the pleadings heretofore had under the "stay laws" are void; so that all cases in which issues have been joined and which does not refer to old debts stand for trial at this Spring Term—

The two features of the bill that passed and to which I objected are that the property sold under the executive must bring ¾ of its value, and no sale of property to be made till 30 days before the Spring Term of 1870.

The other was that no sales of property under any deed of trust or mortgage should be made till the debt secured by such trust or mortgage was reduced to a judgmt.

In all other respects the bill that is now a law is substantially the same as the one enclosed—

UNC—WJH

Thomas J. Jarvis to William Joseph Hawkins[10]

Raleigh N.C.
January 13th 1872

A friend of yours is in great need of fifteen hundred to meet his present wants. It occurs to me that you can help him without any inconvenience to yourself. If you can do so you will *greatly* oblige one who will not soon forget the kindness. Your risk will be it is *possible* you may loose the money—it is *probable* you will not. I hope for the sake of a friend you will be willing to take the risk. It is now about time I had told you the man. Well I am the man and I am really in earnest and if you can do me the favor you will greatly oblige me. Please let me hear from you at once.

---

[10]Originally a physician in Raleigh, Hawkins abandoned medicine and in 1870 founded the Citizens National Bank and became its president. Subsequently he became president of the Raleigh and Gaston Railroad Company and owner of Florida orange groves. Ashe, *Biographical History*, V, 169–173.

William Joseph Hawkins (1817-1894) was a Raleigh physician who became more interested in business than in medicine. He was president of the Raleigh and Gaston Railroad and one of the founders and president of the Citizens National Bank, Raleigh. (Photographs of individuals, unless otherwise indicated, copied from Samuel A. Ashe and Others (eds.), *Biographical History of North Carolina: From Colonial Times to the Present.*)

UNC—DMC

Thomas J. Jarvis to D. M. Carter

Raleigh N.C.

Aug 23rd 1872

I am now only able to go about—have been sick all the time since I was in Pitt but now confined to the house only at intervals. As soon as the election was over I deemed it best to come up the country to recruit. I am now much better and will start for home via Wilson on Monday so as to reach home by the 1st Monday of Sept. which is our Court. I have decided positively to go to Pitt and will do so at once, or at least just as soon as I can move after our Court. I shall pack up at once and get over as soon as I can after court. I am bound to leave Tyrrell.

Now a word about the elections. I hope you are not as you say shelved for life. You have run about as well as the rest of the defeated candidates and I have no doubt as well as any one else could have run.[11]

I shall live and die in the belief that if Leach[12] had been nominated at Greensboro he would have beatten Caldwell.[13] Any how I wish he had been nominated. Caldwell'[s] majority as reported is about 1900—the feeling in favor of contesting the election is pretty strong—I do not think Merrimon[14] will do it—he wants to run again for the Senate of U.S. I doubt the propriety of a contest unless we are prepared with such proof as will make out a

---

[11]Carter had been a candidate for Congress in 1872.

[12]James Madison Leach, lawyer of Lexington; member of the General Assembly, 1848–1856, 1865, 1866; Democratic representative in Congress, 1859–1861; member of the Confederate Congress, 1863–1865. *Biographical Directory of the American Congress, 1774–1927: The Continental Congress, September 5, 1774, to October 21, 1788, and the Congress of the United States from the First to the Sixty–Ninth Congress, March 4, 1789, to March 3, 1927, Inclusive* (Washington, D.C.: United States Government Printing Office, Sixty–Ninth Congress, Second Session, *House Document No. 783*, 1928), 1, 212, hereinafter cited as *Biographical Directory of Congress.*

[13]Tod R. Caldwell of Morganton, member of the Convention of 1865, lieutenant governor under William W. Holden, and Republican governor in 1871 upon Holden's impeachment. Re-elected governor in 1872 over Augustus S. Merrimon, but died in 1874 before the expiration of his term of office. *The National Cyclopedia of American Biography* (New York: James T. White & Co., 52 volumes and index, 1898–1960), IV, 428, hereinafter cited as *National Cyclopedia.*

[14]Augustus Summerfield Merrimon of Raleigh; member of the General Assembly, 1860, 1861; Superior Court judge, 1867–1868; Democratic Senator in Congress, 1873–1879; state Supreme Court justice, 1883–1892; chairman of the Democratic State Central Committee in 1868. *Dictionary of American Biography*, XII, 569-570.

clear case. So far but little of such proof has come to hand and I doubt if it can be found. I have no doubt large frauds was committed but getting at it will be troublesome—
The Greely[15] canvas begins to look up a little in this State—

UNC—DMC

Thomas J. Jarvis to Edward Jenner Warren[16] and D. M. Carter

Charlotte, Oct. 21st, 1872

I got here yesterday and am booked for a great speech to–morrow night. I have been pressed to go to Stokes, Surry, Yadkin & Forsythe and I have partially consented—There is more interest in the election in this than in our section. I saw Clingman Saturday and he told me that he spent yesterday and to–day week ago with Greeley and that Greely has well calculated the chances of his election and that he (Greely) says it will turn upon N.C. I do not believe any such stuff myself yet if by any sort of turn it should turn out to be so and we should loose the State on account of our inactivity we would not soon forgive ourselves—it will therefore be well for us to do what we can in the short time now left us to get out a full vote if possible.[17]

I have just had a long talk with Vance[18] and seen his roll and he figures up for himself on the 1st ballot 60 votes for the U.S. Senate. He says he knows he will get a majority of the transmountain members. Tom C. Fuller[19] and Gen Scales[20] are on the look out but from the best opinion I can form Vance will

---

[15]Horace Greeley, candidate for the presidency in 1872 on the Liberal Republican and the Democratic tickets.
[16]Lawyer of Washington; member of the conventions of 1861 and 1865; member of the General Assembly, 1862–1865, 1870; Superior Court judge, 1865–1868. John H. Wheeler, *Reminiscences and Memoirs of North Carolina and Eminent North Carolinians* (Columbus, Ohio: Columbus Printing Works, 1884), 19, hereinafter cited as Wheeler, *Reminiscences*.
[17]In the presidential election of 1872, Greeley lost North Carolina to Ulysses S. Grant by approximately 22,000 votes. Connor, *Manual, 1913*, 252.
[18]Zebulon Baird Vance, originally from Asheville, was practicing law in Charlotte at this time. For his varied and stormy career before 1872, see *Dictionary of American Biography*, XIX, 158–160. Vance was the Democratic candidate for the United States Senate in 1872 but was defeated by a combination of Republicans and bolting Democrats.
[19]Thomas Charles Fuller, lawyer of Fayetteville; served in the Confederate Congress, 1863–1865; unsuccessful candidate for elector on the Greeley ticket in 1872. *Dictionary of American Biography*, VII, 66.
[20]Alfred Moore Scales, lawyer of Greensboro; member of the General Assembly, 1852–1856, 1866–1869; Democratic representative in Congress, 1857–1859, 1875–1884. *Biographical Directory of Congress*, 1,497.

certainly be elected.

They are making great preparations here for the fair and are expecting it to be a great success. I shall remain here to see something of it for a day or two and will then leave for the field to discharge a public duty and in that spirit alone I do it.

If Coke[21] cannot go to Greenville to meet Ransom[22] on the 2nd of Nov Carter must go and give him the devil for his impudence last Summer—

UNC—DMC

Thomas J. Jarvis to D. M. Carter

Greenville, Nov. 12th 1872

A grief like yours is too sacred to be intruded upon even by a friend and generally silence, in such cases, is the best evidence of genuine sympathy. But in your case it must be different. I loved dear little Hattie so well that I must ask to be permitted to share with you and Mrs. Carter the great grief over her death. And yet we ought not to grieve. It is true she was bright and joyous, the pet and the pride of the household. But in that spirit land where we must soon join her she will be so much brighter. A little angel here she will be a big angel in heaven. Had she lived on earth to an old age her life might or might not have been happy. She lives in heaven now and it is certain she is safe from the troubles and ills that attend this life. How I shall miss the dear little creature when I visit you. I was so much attached to her. Yet it is our duty, without a murmur, to bow to the will of Him, Who doeth all things well. My regards & kindest sympathy to Mrs. Carter[.]

---

[21]Octavius Coke, lawyer of Chowan County; member of the General Assembly, 1876, 1880; secretary of state, 1891–1895. Wheeler, *Reminiscences*, 449; Connor, *Manual, 1913*, 441.

[22]Matt Whitaker Ransom, lawyer and planter of Weldon; member of the General Assembly, 1858, 1860; Democratic senator in Congress, 1872–1895; United States minister to Mexico, 1895–1897. *Dictionary of American Biography*, XV, 379.

Thomas J. Jarvis to D. M. Carter

26th of June 1873

. . . .

Crop prospect at this time good and farmers hopeful.

Reade's[23] recent "crust of bread" decision[24] stops the Bankrupt business of which I was about to have considerable to do. I advise all who consult me to make a safe harbor now while the storm is, for the time, held in check. It will eventually burst upon them. Some one will take a case to the Supreme Court of the U.S. Then farewell homestead. It will be shaken from "turret to foundation stone," will topple and fall. Beneath its ruins will lie in poverty and want the hundreds who have trusted in Reade's sophistry. The number will be so great that he will not be able to give them a "crust of bread."

But I must be a little more cautious how I talk about the legal opinion of Miss Lizzie's uncle. There is sometimes virtue in silence. This may be one of the times.

Thomas J. Jarvis to D. M. Carter

Greenville N.C.
Aug. 7th 1874

When about two years ago you suggested to me to move to Pitt you also suggested to me to take charge of the politics of the County. When I moved here I thought I would have but little to do with politics and seemingly I did have but little to do with such things for a long time.

The first political meeting held in the County this year was held in May. At that meeting I was made chairman of the County Ex: Committee and in this I was rather forced into active service. I there determined to do as you had directed me to do—"take charge of the politics of the County" I immediately

---

[23]Edwin Godwin Reade of Roxboro; representative of the American party in Congress, 1855–1857; Confederate senator, 1864; member of the Convention of 1865; state Supreme Court justice, 1865–1879. *Dictionary of American Biography*, XV, 432.

[24]A reference to *Garrett v. Cheshire*, 69 N.C. 396 (1872), which held that the North Carolina homestead law was not an increase, but a restriction, upon former bankruptcy exemptions; that the law was not made to defeat debts, but to secure "necessaries and comfort" to citizens.

set to work to organize the Party and after weeks of hard work I succeeded in getting a very thorough organization. On the 13th of July I took the field myself and gave the County a complete canvass. In all things connected with the campaign I have had my own way without opposition. I have had every body to obey without asking any questions. Dr. [Illegible] stood aside and called the canvass in derision a "sugar candy canvass," and would have nothing to do with it. I paid no attention to him but pushed the Canvass on to suit myself. The result is all that heart could wish for. Our candidates to the legislature are elected by an average of *175* each. Our county candidates are elected by an average of *125* each. We have made a clean sweep—not a radical elected in the County. Modesty forbids me to tell you what the people say of the cause of this great victory. The women folks always impulsive and enthusiastic say I have saved them and their children from the horrors of the Civil Rights Bill. My room to–day is orderous with the scent of a thousand flowers sent by them. Hundreds of staid old men have been to my room and almost with tears in their eyes thanked me for the redemption of the County. But enough of that. I only mention it because I think it will be gratifying to you to hear it.

My present impression is that this ends my political life. I am too poor to have anything more to do with politics. I like the excitement of the thing and so far I have been wonderfully successful but just here I must stop. I think now that I have got a hold upon the people of Pitt that will give me a good yield so that I hope in a few years by attention to business and by economy to be independent. Our lives are checkered—luck to day and disappointments to morrow. Mine is not an exception. . . .

A&H—JDW

Thomas J. Jarvis to John Dalton Whitford[25]

Richmond, Va. Nov. 28th 1874

It has been a long time since I heard from you or saw you yet I have not forgotten you. At last I am about to sign away my

---

[25]Whitford, a New Bern businessman whose main interests were in shipping and railroad management; president of the Atlantic and North Carolina Railroad Company; served in the Constitutional Conventions of 1861 and 1865. John Gilchrist McCormick, *Personnel of the Convention of 1861* (Chapel Hill: University of North Carolina Press [Volume 1 of *James Sprunt Studies in History and Political Science*], 1900), 87-88, hereinafter cited as McCormick, *Personnel of the Convention of 1861.*

liberties. I am to be married in this City at 12. hr on the 23rd of Dec, 1874. I write this to beg you to come to Richmond with me. The woman I am to marry[26] is in deep mo[u]rning and she may not have any brides maid. But she will be married at the 1st Presbyterian Church by the Rev Dr Hayes and I am anxious to have you come with me to take charge of me. If you come you will leave home on the 21st—Monday—and join me at Rocky Mount. We will leave here at once after the ceremony is over for Norfolk. From Norfolk I shall take my *wife* out to Currituck to my fathers[27] where I will spend a week or so. I will turn you loose at Petersburg or Norfolk as you may like best. Write me at Greenville at once if you can come with me and I beg you to come. SILENCE!

UNC—MWR

Thomas J. Jarvis to M. W. Ransom

Greenville N.C.
Jan. 4th 1876.

I write to day to beg your influence in behalf of Miss S. C. Moon[28] who desires a place in one of the departments. I owe her a debt of gratitude for kindness when I was wounded in Richmond. She wrote to me a few days ago from Washington asking me to give her my influence in securing her a place. I most gladly beg you to champion her cause and I know success will be assured. She is a woman of fine character and one that you can endorse without hesitation. My dear General she sat by my bedside weeks and weeks when all thought I was gone. She did much to save me. She was then rich and independent. I naturally feel a great interest in her and beg as a personal favor to myself that you will interest yourself in her behalf.

Hope you may do much this winter to secure our success in 1876. Send me some documents—those that are political.

---

[26]Mary Woodson, daughter of Judge John Woodson of Goochland County, Virginia; author of a novel, *The Way It All Ended*, and contributor of several articles to northern periodicals. *Morning Star* (Wilmington), June 28, 1876, hereinafter cited as *Morning Star.*
[27]Bannister Hardy Jarvis, Methodist minister of Currituck County. Ashe, *Biographical History*, I, 332.
[28]Unable to identify.

A&H—ZBV

Thomas J. Jarvis to Z. B. Vance

Greenville, N.C., Nov. 16th 1876

Let me join you in the joy you must feel over your splendid triumph.[29] The infernal Radicals lied on you so that such a great vindication by the white people of the State, I know, must be gratifying to you. I undertake to say that no man in the history of our good old State ever had as bitter a personal campaign waged against him. It was unjust, and malignant devilish. Your vindication is perfect and complete. It is grand as it is great. Thank God Truth has triumphed over falsehood—Right over wrong.

If Holden[30] and Settle[31] and their aiders and abetters did not defeat you, it was not because their stock of lies was ever *exhausted;* but because the people knew them too well to believe them.

I feel the canvass has identified me with you. The attack was upon you and it was for you that I fought; and believe me when I say that I feel as proud over your great victory as your dearest friends can feel. Holding the second place on the ticket, I tried to do my full duty towards you; and I hope now the battle is over you can say I did it well.

Address to the Senate of North Carolina,

January 2, 1877[32]

Senators:—Having been called by the people of North Carolina to preside over your deliberations, I am here at the time appointed by the Constitution, and having taken the oath of office, am prepared to enter upon the discharge of my duties.

---

[29] In 1876 Vance was elected governor of North Carolina, defeating Thomas Settle by a majority of 118,000 to 104,000. Connor, *Manual, 1913,* 1,001–1,002. In the same election Jarvis was elected lieutenant governor.

[30] William Woods Holden, named postmaster of Raleigh, 1873; from 1843 to 1865, edited the Raleigh *Standard,* the state's leading Democratic paper; served as Republican governor, 1868–1870. *Dictionary of American Biography,* IX, 138–140.

[31] Thomas Settle, of Rockingham County; member of the General Assembly, 1854–1858, 1865; member of the Convention of 1865; state Supreme Court justice, 1868–1876; United States district judge for Florida, 1877–1888. *Dictionary of American Biography,* XVI, 598–599.

[32] Taken from the *Journal of the Senate of the General Assembly of North Carolina at Its Session of 1876-'77,* 123–126, hereinafter cited as *Senate Journal,* with proper date.

When I look around me and see the many distinguished gentlemen who are to take part in the proceedings of the Senate over whom I am to preside, I am deeply impressed with the dignity and responsibility of the position I am about to assume. Every emotion of my heart goes out in gratitude to the people for this great manifestation of their confidence. I shall at all times labor with singleness of purpose to prove myself worthy of their esteem by faithfully and fearlessly, but kindly and impartially, discharging every duty imposed upon me. In doing this, gentlemen, I earnestly invoke your assistance and friendship, and beg that you will aid me by your wisdom, and strengthen me by your kind encouragement.

Pardon me, Senators, if I pause to indulge in a few reflections suggested by our present surroundings. We stand to-day upon the threshold of a new year. Its solemn and mysterious import is breaking upon the world. We must take our share of its labors and responsibilities. The old year with its history lies burried in the graves of the past. With a tear for its sorrows and a smile for its joys, let us turn from it to the living present and hopeful future. With the year that has died certain features of the government of North Carolina passed quietly away. In bidding them farewell, let no bitter words be uttered. Our business is with the propitious present, and to it let us turn.

Yesterday we inaugurated Zebulon B. Vance Governor of North Carolina. It was the magic power of his name that worked this mighty revolution in the State, and that brought such a concourse of our countrymen to the Capital yesterday. To him the people have committed the execution of the laws with an assurance of their confidence never before given to any man. We know that that confidence has not been misplaced. We well know that he will execute every law with kindness to all, with partiality to none—the whole people will be the objects of his solicitude and care. His mighty powers will be used to bring back to his and our old State her former grandeur and greatness; to her people unexampled prosperity and happiness.

But, Senators, what law is he to execute? The answer is with us. Whether it be good or bad, wise or unwise, depends upon how well we keep our pledges to the people. We promised them laws that should know no man in the protection they give, or the burdens they impose. We promised the people reform and relief. If we fail to give it to them, we cannot plead, as other Legislators have done, that we did not have the power. Yesterday the amendments to the Constitution, so recently ratified by the people, became a portion of our organic law. They give us enlarged powers. Many of our people opposed this grant of power. Not a few of our colored fellow–citizens even to–day fear it will be used to their detriment. Let our acts teach them there was no cause for such fears, and that all their rights will be held sacred by us. If you fail to use the power given you by these amendments, the people will not hold you guiltless. If you abuse it, they will condemn you. Varied and manifold are the questions that are to come before you. An appeal for relief will come up from one section. Another will ask for aid to help them open up their land of hidden wealth and sublime grandeur and beauty. All sections will demand the most rigid economy.

Wise statesmanship calls for the education of the rising generation. The means to do this, so far as it is done by the State, must be provided by you. Many other grave questions will demand your attention.

You then have a great work before you. In this work I am to be a co-laborer with you. I am to administer the rules which you yourselves have made for your own government. I am not unmindful of the fact that, upon a proper enforcement of these rules depends, to a great degree, the speedy conclusion of your labors and the good order and decorum of your body. It shall be my purpose to perform well my part. With your kind assistance I hope to be able to do so. I earnestly hope nothing will occur to disturb the harmony and good feeling that should at all times mark your deliberations.

I enter upon my duties with the kindest feeling to all. Some of you I meet to–day for the first time. Many are friends of years, and a few of you the friends of my childhood. It will be my pleasure to cultivate these friendly relations. May each day of our intercourse add strength to the ties of friendship that now bind us, so that we may hold each other in high esteem, and carry with us to our homes only pleasant recollections.

I am sure I shall have the co-operation of the officers of the Senate. They shall certainly have mine. With these remarks, gentlemen, and invoking the friendship and support of you all, I am ready to proceed with the business of the Senate.

A&H—ZBV

Thomas J. Jarvis to Z. B. Vance

Greenville, N.C., April 16th 1877

. . . .

I found myself unable to attend the meeting of the Board. But I see that you did quite as well as if I had been there.

The Methodist ladies at this place have been after me for several weeks to write to you for them to *beg* you to deliver your address on "the Scattered Nation"[33] at this place (May 15th—Court week) the proceeds to go to aid them in building a new Methodist [church] here. I have declined to write because I did not know whether it would embarrass you or not. I will say this much in confidence. If you could consent to come I myself would be glad on many accounts. I would be glad to see you here and you would be helping the poor Methodists. If you can possibly come give me a confidential word and I will say to the ladies I think you may be induced to come. If you say positively you cannot I think I can put them off. Some of them are after me every day to write to you. This is only as an inquiry for my own guide and not for them. I shall be governed in the matter by your inclinations.

LETTERS FOR 1878

A&H—ZBV

Thomas J. Jarvis to Z. B. Vance

Greenville, Pitt Co., N.C., May 20th 1878

You know I want to see you and to hear your address but at the same time I feel that I can speak to you frankly and plainly.

The Methodist and Baptist are at war here and I am of the opinion that it will be the safe side of the question to avoid the least appearance of participating in the conflict.

I hope Peace will be proclaimed by the Fall and then we will have you with us if it is then convenient with you to come. At

---

[33]Speech on the history of the Hebrew people which Vance frequently delivered, among other occasions, at fund-raising activities. The speech may be found in Clement Dowd, *Life of Zebulon B. Vance* (Charlotte: Observer Printing and Publishing House, 1897), 369-399, hereinafter cited as Dowd, *Vance.*

this time I suggest that you give an excuse for not coming. Edwards[34] and the Supreme Court of the U.S. has done us much harm in this Section. The debtor class is about to stampede and as Edwards is a Democrat our party is blamed for the decision. But it will have its good results—it will, I think, keep off independent candidates as success is more doubtful. I know of no trouble in any eastern county—Merrimon men are few and can do nothing.[35]

Interview, July 18, 1878, with Thomas J. Jarvis by P. H. Wilson,
City Editor of the Raleigh OBSERVER[36]

Q. Governor, what do you think of this new National party, or National Greenbackers as they call themselves in our State?

A. I don't think that the Democratic party in the State has much to fear from the organization,[37] for the reason that the chief principle advocated by them is warfare against the bondholders of the country, and the Democratic party has been so much more closely allied to the greenback feeling and interest than the Republican party has, that I don't think that any very considerable number of its members will desert its ranks. The movement is fostered in this State at least by the Republicans, who are without organization, and only look for local successes by defeating the regular Democratic nominees with independents of any complexion of principles. In any National contest the Democratic and the Greenback principles are too closely allied to admit of a serious distinction. We have got too little money to make a financial plank the plank of a platform for any party in North Carolina.

Q. What are the general political prospects in the State?

A. Well, it's a[n] off year you know. We have no organized opposition to fight, and I think that our prospects are good under

---

[34]Unable to identify.

[35]Merrimon was seeking re-election to the United States Senate, but Vance was hoping to secure the Democratic party's nomination for the position. *Dictionary of American Biography*, XII, 570.

[36]Taken from the *Observer* (Raleigh), July 19, 1878, hereinafter cited as Raleigh *Observer*.

[37]Jarvis was correct here. In the next presidential election, the Greenback candidate polled only 1,126 votes in North Carolina. Thomas H. McKee, *The National Conventions and Platforms of All Political Parties, 1789 to 1904* (Baltimore, Maryland: Friedenwalk, 1904), 198, hereinafter cited as McKee, *National Conventions and Platforms*.

the circumstances. Our majority in the Legislature will be large, quite as large as it was in 1876.[38]

Q. Were you in Raleigh during the election for a Senator in December, 1872?

A. I was not in Raleigh at any time during that winter, and all my information about that election comes from the papers and the conversations of men who were present.

Q. Will the people stand to the party rather than to its leaders?

A. I think that a very large majority of the Democratic members, who will be elected to the next Legislature, will come here determined to uphold the organization of the Democratic party. I doubt very much if a single regular nominee elected will bolt the party; and I want to say this: I think there is a general disposition in the State to uphold the organization of our party at all hazards, and the man who puts himself in conflict with this organization must take the consequences. The Democratic party, in my opinion—and I believe that opinion is shared by the great mass of the people of the State—is the only party that can carry the country safely through the dangers of Imperialism on the one hand and communism on the other. While the Democratic party offers an asylum to the laboring man, seeks to better his condition and is pledged to protect every right to which he is entitled under the laws of the land, it will not aid him in an improper warfare on capital; nor will it permit the capitalist and moneyed interest of the country, if it is so disposed, to trample upon the rights of the laborer. The Republican party is in the hands and is the servant of the moneyed interest of the country, and cares very little for the toiling masses. The people of this State are going to stand by the Democratic party and maintain its organization. If any man, whatever may have been his status or his services in the party, undertakes to set the party at defiance the people will set him aside. Particularly is this so in view of the great conflict in which we are to engage only two years hence, when nothing but a thorough and rigid organization can crush the party and men that committed the great fraud of stealing the Presidency from the people.

---

[38] A reference to the fact that in 1872 the Democratic caucus had nominated Vance for United States senator but that a few Democratic legislators had rejected the party mandate and had been able to secure the election of A. S. Merrimon by the joint session of the General Assembly. For details, see Samual A. Ashe, *History of North Carolina* (Greensboro: Charles L. Van Noppen, 2 volumes, 1925), II, 1,158-1,160, hereinafter cited as Ashe, *History of North Carolina*.

Q. Well, Governor, everybody is talking about the next Senatorial election; do you think that any danger is imminent to the party from the contest ahead of us?

A. I do not. The people intend to uphold the means or machinery of organization as well as the organization itself. County, District and State Conventions and Legislative caucuses express the will of the party and by them alone it can be ascertained and declared. The man who prates against party machinery is, whether designedly or not, undertaking to prejudice the people against the only method for making the organization effective, and will find but little favor with the great mass of democratic voters.

Q. Suppose a candidate for election before the Legislature declines to submit his name and claims to the action of a caucus, do you consider him a good democrat?

A. I think that when a County, District or State Convention or Legislative caucus, has named the candidate for the party that every good democrat is bound to support that nominee. It is no excuse for a man to say that he is not bound by the action of his party because he did not submit his claims to the party in caucus or convention.

Q. Then you don't think him a very good Democrat?

A. I do not. My opinions may be very decided, but I have grown up with them. I was acting in the ranks of the Democratic party in this State after the war, when it was a weak minority. I was in the Legislature in 1868, when there were less than half a hundred of us in both houses. I then helped in the work of organization, and have worked with the party and for the party continuously, till now I see it in its prosperity; and if I hold these strong opinions against any man who in any manner seeks to destroy the organization or impair its usefulness, I do so because he is pulling down the only protection that the people have against present dangers.

Q. Do you think that the nominees of conventions ought to be instructed?

A. The propriety of giving instructions, as a general rule, I doubt; but I think that the people assembled in convention have a right to indicate their preferences, and the nominee acting in good faith ought to carry them out. The people must be the judge of the necessity for instructions, and there may be special occasions that make the necessity apparent, as when a great wrong has been done the organization, as was the case in 1872,[39] and the people fear its repetition.

A&H—ZBV

Thomas J. Jarvis to Z. B. Vance

Greenville N.C.

July 24th 1878

I have been to Martin [County] and seen Henry D. Robinson[40] who is the support of the Independent candidate for the House.[41] I could not induce him to withdraw the Independent—He said the thing had gone so far that he must run through. But he gave me the most positive assurances that the Independent is a good Democrat, will, if elected, vote with the party and will vote for *you*. I am assured and I rely upon it that we have nothing to fear from that quarter.

The canvass in the East is progressing well. I think we will elect in all the counties where we have elected and all of them are for Vance.

I hope Mrs V. is doing well. Remember Mrs. J and myself to her[.]

Thomas J. Jarvis to Joseph Jonathan Davis[42]

Greenville, N.C., Oct. 4th, 1878.

You will remember that in travelling with you on the North Carolina Railroad on your way to your appointment at Selma, in Johnston county, on September, the 11th, you told me that Mr. Turner charged in his speeches with you that my offer to

---

[39] In the election of 1876, the Democrats had from 80 per cent and 70 per cent of the seats in the Senate and House respectively. In the election of 1878 their majorities fell to 68 and 66 per cent. Volume III of *History of North Carolina*, by R. D. W. Boyd, J. G. de Roulhac Hamilton, and Others (Chicago and New York: Lewis Publishing Company, 6 volumes, 1919), 192, 199, hereinafter cited as Hamilton, *North Carolina Since 1860*.

[40] Henry Daniel Roberson, businessman and farmer of Robersonville; member of the General Assembly, 1879. John W. Tomlinson, *Tar Heel Sketch-book* (Raleigh: Raleigh News, 1879), 95–96, hereinafter cited as Tomlinson, *Sketch-book*.

[41] A reference to N. B. Fagan, farmer of Jonesville. Fagan won this race, but died before he could take his seat, and was succeeded by Henry D. Roberson, Tomlinson, *Sketch-book*, 95–96.

[42] Prominent lawyer of Louisburg; member of the General Assembly, 1866; Democratic representative in Congress, 1875–1881; state Supreme Court justice, 1887–1892. *Biographical Directory of Congress*, 887. Letter taken from the Raleigh *Observer* of March 5, 1880.

buy the *Sentinel* for the Ring, as he called it, was made through Thomas Sparrow,[43] Esq., of Beaufort county.

I was then on my way to Currituck Co., *via* Norfolk, Va., and on reaching that city that night I addressed Maj. Sparrow the following letter, which was mailed to him at Norfolk:

> Purcell House,
> J. R. Davis, Proprietor,
> Norfolk, Va., Sept. 11th, 1878.

Thomas Sparrow, Esq:

My Dear Sir:—The Hon. Josiah Turner time and again charged in the *Sentinel* that I offered him $15,000 for that paper for "the Ring." I cared nothing for it so long as it affected myself alone.

He has recently renewed his charge but this time on the stump in his canvass with Mr. Davis, and as it may affect that gentleman, I felt called upon to notice it. I authorized Mr. Davis to say that I never had a word of conversation with Mr. Turner relative to the purchase of the *Sentinel* in my life. When confronted with my denial, he, now for the first time that I have ever heard of, says that the offer was made through you. It is impossible that you could ever have made him any such offer. I certainly never authorized you to do so.

I do not pretend to say that I never talked with you about the purchase of the *Sentinel* of Mr. Turner by the Democratic party. I think likely I did. You know that it was the general talk among the members of the Legislature in 1871–'72. I think it possible you and I talked often about it.

We were much together, and both held prominent positions. There was, as you well know, a general feeling among the Democratic members of the Legislature that the *Sentinel* failed, under the management of Mr. Turner, to meet the wants of a party organ. The leading members of the party outside of the Legislature, so far as I know, generally held the same view. There was much talk, in and out of the Legislature, about establishing a new paper to be the organ of the party.

A caucus of the party was called to take the matter into consideration. It was largely attended by the Democratic members

[43]Lawyer of Aurora; member of the General Assembly, 1858, 1870, 1881. Branson, *Directory, 1878*, 31; Connor, *Manual, 1913*, 498–499.

of the Legislature, the State Executive Committee of the party, and other prominent members of the party then in the city of Raleigh. I have no doubt you were in the caucus. I certainly was. I favored not the establishing of a new paper, because that would be unfair to Mr. Turner, but to buy the *Sentinel* and put it under the control of the party. This I think was the general view. Anyhow, a committee was appointed by the caucus to see Mr. Turner and ascertain what he would take for the paper. I rather think the committee was appointed upon my motion, but of this I am not certain. I do not now remember all of the members of the committee, but I do remember the Hon. D. M. Barringer,[44] then chairman of the State Executive Committee, the Hon. A. S. Merrimon, then a member of the committee, and Col. H. C. Jones,[45] State Senator from Mecklenburg county, were three of the members of said committee. I do not think there was a dissenting voice to the action of the caucus. The result of this action you no doubt remember—Mr. Turner refused to sell.

This was going on for weeks, and I think it quite likely that I gave you my views in full about the matter. I had decided opinions and I did not hesitate to express them. I heard from those who profess to know (I did not) that the *Sentinel* office and all its fixtures was not worth to exceed $5,000. I was in favor of paying Mr. Turner $15,000 as an inducement for him to sell and as a reward for his services. I heard it said that one difficulty in the way of his selling was that he had in different companies $30,000 of insurance upon his life which he was paying for in advertising, and that if he sold that his insurance would have to go down, as he was not financially able to keep it up. I was in favor of putting it into the contract of purchase that the party should keep up and carry out his contracts with the companies, free of charge to him, as a further compensation for his services. All of these things I may have mentioned to you, I do not now remember. But of one thing I am positively certain. I never spoke to you about the purchase of the *Sentinel* except by the party and for the party. I do not believe you ever represented to Mr. Turner anything I ever said in reference to the

---

[44]Daniel Moreau Barringer of Cabarrus County; member of the General Assembly, 1829–1835, 1840, 1842, 1854; Whig representative in Congress, 1843–1849. *Biographical Directory of Congress,* 674.

[45]Hamilton Chamberlain Jones, lawyer of Charlotte; member of the General Assembly, 1870; for many years, chairman of the Mecklenburg County Democratic Executive Committee. Ashe, *Biographical History,* VII, 268-273.

matter in any other light, if you ever spoke to him at all. Please say whether you did or not.

I thought it would be to the interest of the party to buy the *Sentinel*, and that we could afford to pay $15,000 for it rather than to fail. How far I was mistaken subsequent events have shown.

I saw Mr. Davis to–day and travelled with him from Wilson's Mill, on the N.C.R.R. to Selma, and from him first heard of Mr. Turner's new charge. Please write me at Greenville, where I will be in a few days, what you have to say about it.

Very truly yours,
Thos. J. Jarvis.

On my arrival at home I found the following reply from Maj. Sparrow:

Washington, N.C., Sept. 20, 1878.

Hon. T. J. Jarvis:

My Dear Sir:—I have been in receipt of yours of the 13th for several days, in which you desire to know whether you ever authorized me, in the interest of a Ring, to offer Josiah Turner, Jr., $15,000 for the purchase of the *Sentinel* office.

As often as I read in that paper the charge that "the Ring" had offered to buy him out at that or any other price, the suspicion never entered my mind that I was associated with such offer in the remotest degree. I do not remember that in any conversation had with Mr. Turner in Raleigh while a member of the Legislature of 1871–72 in reference to a sale of his paper, I ever used your name. I had a motive for not doing so, as I supposed there was no very good feeling existing between you. I do not remember to have named the sum of $15,000 in any conversation had with him about the sale of his paper, nor of any other specific amount. I am very sure I never represented any Ring and that I never mentioned Ring to him at any time.

Your recital of the anxiety of the Democratic members of the Legislature to purchase his paper, with a view of establishing a party organ, which would better subserve the party purposes, and the caucuses which were held with a view to this end, and the committee which was appointed to wait upon him and failure of all these efforts, is in exact accord with my own recollection.

There is, however, one circumstance which occurred between you and myself in reference to Mr. Turner and his paper, which you seem to have forgotten. The recollection of it is very distinct in my mind. It is this: Mr. Turner and I had been friends from our boyhood and my sympathies were with him in his troubles. He knew this no doubt. On one occasion he talked to me about his embarrassments and his need of assistance in such a way as to lead me to suppose that he would be glad to sell out. I suggested this belief to you in your room at the National the same afternoon. This was before any caucus had been held, and before I had any idea of a purpose on the part of any one to buy Mr. Turner out. The suggestion was made by me to you with the one thought of aiding Mr. Turner. Your reply to my remark that I thought Mr. Turner would sell out was this: "If he will I will give him _____ thousand dollars for his paper, and raise the money for him in twenty–four hours." I do not remember the amount named, but I think it was much less than fifteen thousand dollars. Nor am I certain as to the *twenty–four hours,* but it was some short time. Your prompt offer surprised and gratified me, and I told you that I would see Mr. Turner at once. You made no reference whatever as to who was to furnish the money, nor had I any idea as to the source from which it was to be derived. I went to see Mr. Turner at his room at the Yarborough, and had a long talk with him. Without the use of your name, and without the mention of any amount, (as I now believe) I sounded him as to his disposition to sell the *Sentinel,* and informed him that a reliable party would purchase if he wished to sell. He spoke of the mortgages held by his father and others, and interest owned by his wife. He expressed his anxiety to relieve his father and his willingness to this end to sell all his (Jo T.'s) interest except that owned by his wife. He spoke of his great sacrifices, his consequent embarrassments, and insisted at all hazards in retaining his wife's interest. "It was all the living he would have," and he would under no circumstances surrender the control of the entire establishment. He was willing to sell an interest, but must retain a controlling influence in the management and conduct of the paper. This ended the interview, and I reported the result to you. You were emphatic in your refusal to purchase a partial interest in the paper. I do not remember to have talked with Turner or yourself on the subject after this, except the general conversation to which you refer, as of every day occurrences, and common to all the

Democratic members of the Legislature. I am very curious to know how Mr. Turner ever came to associate your name with this transaction, and how he ever came to associate my name with an offer of a Ring to buy out his paper. If his oft repeated declarations to the effect rest on no better foundation than this interview they are slanderous indeed. Very Sincerely yours,

T. Sparrow.

Professional business in the midst of a Court prevented me from forwarding Maj. Sparrow's letter to you immediately after its reception. It and mine are with you to make such use of as you may deem necessary to let the people know the truth of the attempted purchase of the *Sentinel*, so far as I had anything to do with it, or know anything about it.

UNC—MWR

Thomas J. Jarvis to M. W. Ransom

Greenville, Pitt Co., N.C.
Oct. 22nd 1878

Yeates[46] and his three op[p]onnents—Martin,[47] Respass[48] and Chamberlain[49]—have been with us the 19th & 21st. Yeates seems to be in a bad temper generally. What the cause is I do not know. His prospect of election I consider fine.

I leave here to–morrow, at his request, to make a canvass of Beaufort, Washington, Tyrrell and Hyde and will not get back till the Sunday night before the election. This will take me away from my own County entirely. I do not think I would have con-

---

[46]Jesse Johnson Yeates, lawyer of Murfreesboro; member of the General Assembly, 1860; Democratic representative in Congress, 1875–1879, January–March, 1881. *Biographical Directory of Congress*, 1,735.

[47]Joseph John Martin, Republican lawyer of Williamston; defeated Yeates by 54 votes in the congressional elections of 1878. Yeates contested the results; replaced Martin in January, 1881. *Biographical Directory of Congress*, 1,293.

[48]James Thomas Respass, farmer of Yeatesville; member of the General Assembly, 1879, 1881; ran for Congress against Yeates as an Independent Republican in 1878; defeated and accepted earlier—won seat in the General Assembly. Tomlinson, *Sketch–book*, 7.

[49]John L. Chamberlain, lawyer of Camden County; member of the General Assembly, 1870, 1872; member of the Convention of 1875. Branson, *Directory, 1878*, 54; Connor, *Manual, 1913*, 534, 871. In 1878 he was an Independent Republican candidate for Congress.

Matt Whitaker Ransom (1826-1904) of Northampton County, graduate of the University of North Carolina and lawyer, was state attorney general (1852-1855) and a member of the legislature (1858-1860). He was a brigadier general in the Civil War, succeeding to command of the 24th North Carolina Regiment (1863) upon promotion of his brother Robert to major general. His contemporaries wrote glowing accounts of his capacity for leadership and ability to command the confidence and affection of his fellow officers and volunteer soldiers. Ransom was a member of Congress (1872-1895) and minister to Mexico (1896-1897) during President Grover Cleveland's administration. (Photograph copied from Walter Clark (ed.), *Histories of the Several Regiments and Battalions from North Carolina in the Great War, 1861-'65.*)

sented to be away so much but for your promise to speak here on Monday the 4th of Nov. I am anxious for this County to increase its majority and I am sure it will do it if you will only come. Monday the 4th is the 1st day of our Court and you will have a tremendous crowd. You can leave Weldon Sunday and reach Tarboro at 3pm where he will have a comfortable carriage to take you direct to Greenville. You can speak Monday and we will send you to Tarboro in time to take the train at 12m on Tuesday. You can thus get home in time to vote.

Please write to A. L. Blow[50] that [you] will certainly come so that he can post you and have a carriage at Tarboro to meet you. I shall not be here myself to attend to it. I shall certainly expect you. Do not fail to come. Write Blow at once—

UNC—MG

Thomas J. Jarvis to Henry Augustus Gilliam[51]

Dec 13th 1878

Yours of the 10th to hand yesterday. I am deeply concerned about Carter.[52] I hope he may yet be spared to us. Louis[53] and I were talking about trying to get up to see him. If he goes to Balt. we will not be able to do so, but we both trust he will find help and relief by going.

I have looked after the Hyde representative.[54] I was down there the second week in November attending Court. I did not see him but had a friend to do so. Having been elected an *Independent* he will not say he is for Vance, He say he is for Carter first and the choice of the party next. But I was assured

[50]Alexander Lillington Blow, lawyer of Greenville and at one time Jarvis' law partner; clerk of the Pitt County Superior Court, 1881–1882; member of the General Assembly, 1903, 1909. Henry T. King, *Sketches of Pitt County, a Brief History of the County, 1704–1910* (Raleigh: Edwards and Broughton Printing Company, 1911), 254, hereinafter cited as King, *Sketches of Pitt County.*

[51]A practicing lawyer in Plymouth for several years; later law partner of John Gatling in Raleigh; member of the General Assembly, 1854 and 1856, and Superior Court judge in 1882 and 1883. *News and Observer* (Raleigh), March 1, 1882, hereinafter cited as *News and Observer.*

[52]Carter had recently suffered a severe heart attack. He died in Baltimore, Maryland, in January, 1879. *Cyclopedia of the Carolinas,* II, 70.

[53]Probably Louis Charles Lathan, lawyer of Plymouth; member of the General Assembly, 1864, 1870; Democratic representative in Congress, 1881–1883, 1887–1889. *Biographical Directory of Congress,* 1,206.

[54]Theodore Pickett Bonner, Democratic member of the General Assembly, 1879. He practiced law from 1873 to 1879 and then became a Methodist minister. Tomlinson, *Sketch-book,* 87.

by Henry Wahab,[55] the man who elected the whole independent
Ticket in Hyde, that I need give myself no concern about Bonner;
It is true if Carter lives he will absolutly own Bonner, and
can control *all* his votes. But in any event he will be all right on
the Senator[i]al question.

It is thought that old Jim Joyner[56] is the writer of the Quarters letter in the Observ– of the 11th from Pitt. Old man Jim has
quit strong drink and he now has a mania on Temperance. He
has heard that Merrimon never took a drink and therefore he is
a great Merrimon man.

In his Township that gives 250 Democratic votes[,] himself
and three others are the only Merrimon men although he says
all are for him. *I know this to be so*[.]

A&H—GP

Thomas J. Jarvis to Z. B. Vance

Greenville N.C.
Dec. 17th 1878

After writing you yesterday I received a letter from Jim
Moore[57] giving information about Martin. I think our friends
have acted wisely in not nominating a candidate. The radicals
will and a great many Democrats will vote for Henry Roberson.
Some out and out Democrats will probably run against him and
while I am quite certain Roberson will be elected it makes no
difference so far as our interests are concerned which is elected.
If our friends had made a nomination I fear the candidate would
have been beaten by a Radical. As it is now we can safely rely
upon the member from Martin.

Now as to the Merrimon letter.[58] I think the public is tired of

---

[55] A merchant of Sladesville, active in Hyde County politics. Branson,
Directory, 1878, 159.

[56] Possibly James Joyner, Greenville grocer. Levi Branson, *Branson's
North Carolina Business Directory for 1884* (Raleigh: Levi Branson, Office
Publisher, 1884), 537, hereinafter cited as Branson, *Directory for 1884*.

[57] James Edwin Moore, lawyer of Williamston; member of the General
Assembly, 1865–1868. Branson, *Directory, 1878*, 186; Connor, *Manual, 1913*,
692, 842.

[58] The Democratic members of the General Assembly had agreed in caucus
to support Vance instead of A. H. Merrimon for the United States Senate.
Merrimon had published a letter claiming his "right" to re-election by
virtue of his six-year record as senator. He also stated that in 1876 Vance
had denied any interest in a senatorship. Vance had been publicly denying
both of Merrimon's allegations. *Morning Star*, October-December, 1878,
passim.

this controversy and the only effect it can [have] upon the members elect by continuing it is to encourage the idea to give up both M. & V. and take some one else. I have thought I would have some friends of ours to write a strong paper to be published in the [Raleigh] Observer demanding that the controversy shall end but I was afraid it might interfere with your plans. I think the members elect all have their minds made up and nothing that can be said or written will change a single one as between you and M. What I fear is that some of them may conclude that the harmony will best be promoted by giving up both and going for a third man. If any thing can bring about such a result as this I think this continued controversy will. I think the best thing you could do, if you can do it, is to have a stop put to it so far as you are responsible and leave the whole matter with the members where it belongs. If the public come to understand this to be your position I think it would give you strength. While this is my opinion I will defer to your better judgment.

As I wrote you yesterday hurriedly the letter was actually sent Robinson.[59] He told me himself that he kept a copy which he intended to publish. This he told me before the "Maimed Confederate Soldiers" met at his office and before he agreed to withdraw it. I think if I were to see the copy I would know if [it] was a true copy. Jim Robinson knows more about the matter and whoat [sic] became of the copy he had than any one else and if necessary I will write to him. My very distant recollection is that it was destroyed. I remember that John Gilmer,[60] Benton Withers,[61] Jim Robinson and myself were among those at the meeting in M's office. There were many others—some sixteen or eighteen but it has been so long I do not remember who they were. The main points in the letter were his withdrawal from the Ex: Com: because the Party was a war party and that union men stood no chance of promotion in its ranks. It was the point he made against the Party about its hostility to union men that made me so anxious to suppress the letter. That was the very issue the Radicals were trying to make with us and it being just

---

[59]James Lowrie Robinson, farmer and merchant of Franklin; member of the General Assembly, 1868–1879; lieutenant governor, 1879–1885. Branson, *Directory for 1884*, 430; Connor, *Manual, 1913*, 476–477, 688.

[60]John Adams Gilmer, Jr., lawyer and financier of Greensboro; adjutant general, 1866–1867; delegate to the Democratic National Convention of 1868; member of the General Assembly, 1870; Superior Court judge, 1881–1889. *Cyclopedia of the Carolinas*, II, 149–151.

[61]Probably Elijah Benton Withers, lawyer of Caswell County. Branson, *Directory for 1884*, 191.

before the campaign of 72 I feared the publication of such a letter would greatly injure us. Who will say the *effect* of such a
letter was not to practically withdraw from the Party? But if
they have a copy why not demand of them to publish it.
What I say ending the controversy
applies to the whole matter

LETTERS FOR 1879

DUKE—TJJ

Thomas J. Jarvis to Appleton Oaksmith[1]

Raleigh, N.C., Jan. 22nd 1879
It will be my purpose in administering the high office of
Governor to induce our people, so far as I can, both by example
and precept to build up the Cities, Towns and highways of their
own state. If that be a North Carolina policy then it will be mine.
I shall be glad to hear any suggestion you may have to make
on that or any other subject. In fact it will be my pleasure to
listen patiently to the suggestions of all persons touching what
they deem to be the interest of the State.

A&H—GLB

Inaugural Address

February 5, 1879[2]

Fellow Citizens:

A time honored custom requires that I should, on assuming
the duties of Chief Executive of the State, give some expression
of my views on public affairs. In yielding to this custom to–day,
I shall be as brief as the subjects upon which I shall touch will

---

[1]Businessman of Carteret County, at one time quite wealthy but now of
moderate circumstances. For a full biographical sketch, see the Appleton
Oaksmith Papers, Duke University.

[2]On Governor Vance's election to the United States Senate, Lieutenant
Governor Jarvis succeeded him to the governorship for the completion of
the term. The North Carolina House of Representatives refused to appropriate money for the printing of Jarvis' Inaugural Address, apparently
assuming that the printing of Vance's address in 1877 had sufficed for one
administration. *Journal of the House of Representatives of the General
Assembly of the State of North Carolina at Its Session of 1879*, 755, hereinafter cited as *House Journal* with proper date.

permit. As I am simply filling out the Term of an Administration which was begun and continued so well, it will not be my purpose to address a General Assembly formally which is in possession of so exhaustive a message from my predecessor.

Yet as I speak today at their request and by their courtesy, as well as in accord with my own inclinations I will make some suggestions intended for their special consideration,

Government has its blessings and its burdens. Good laws properly administered constitute its blessings, the taxation necessary to its support its burdens. How to make its burdens so small & its blessings as great as possible should be the constant study of all to whom the people have committed their interests either as makers or ministers of the law. This study should embrace the substance as well as the shadow and if it is as searching as it should be it will not disdain to look carefully after the little matters. In fact the little things should receive the special care & attention of the public official. It is here in my opinion that those who wish to practice economy & lighten the burdens of the people can be most successful. And yet because of their seeming [un]importance these little amounts are so often overlooked or indifferently examined. It is too often said what is a hundred dollars to a great Government like the United States or two dollars to a great State like North Carolina or a dollar to a great county like _____ and yet it is the aggregate of these very items that swells the disbursements accounts of these governments to their millions their hundred of thousands & thousands.

The time was when in making contracts for the government, the agents exercised the same care & economy as if he were spending his own money. Then we had true economy & the burdens of the people were light. Now, with some, it has become unfashionable to stand on a few dollars & undignified to look after these little things and the man who attempts it, is by some called penurious and laughed at as an old fogy.

The people are as much interested in how their agents perform their duties as they are in what they pay them[.] And the retrencher whose purpose is to serve the people and not to make a little cheap notoriety for himself will devote himself earnestly; and impartially to the work of publishing to the people how the public official does his work as well as what he is paid. If he is proved to be faithful in the performance of all his duties, cautious & prudent in his contracts & always on the lookout to save every dollar for the people he possibly can, the people ought to know it. On the other hand if he is found wasteful or extravagant or indulgent or corrupt or in any way unfit or unfaithful it ought to be known & published. For after all this question of practical retrenchment & economy rests with the people. They choose the officials. Upon their choice turns the whole question. If they choose proper men they secure practical economy. Therefore it is that the people are entitled to know the whole truth; what a man does as well as what he gets—So that when they come to make their choice of public servants they may act knowingly. The public mind, has recently become greatly excited upon this question of retrenchment. It is no new question with me. I have been laboring for it for ten years. I have studied it, talked for it & practiced it. Under its banners I have called the people to rally. I have worshipped at its shrine & I believe it is for my devotion to its cause, that I am today so richly rewarded. It will always be one of the cardinal principles of my political creed & must be of my political party with which I act. But I want the substance & not the shadow, the genuine & not the false. I can not & will not yield to this cry of false economy that stops the wheels of progress, undo what has been done to help the farmers & cripple the efforts of the State to educate the rising generation. These are great interests upon which depend the future greatness & glory of the State. A wise statesmanship in my opinion demands that there shall be no decrease in the appropreation [sic] for the normal & common schools. It would be unwise to strike down the Department of Agriculture or to paralize its energies

This Department was created but two years ago. It was the first organized effort by the State to foster & aid the great agricultural interest. That its workings should as yet be imperfect & its benefits but dimly seen is not surprising. But when the plan of its operations are better matured & the farmers have taken hold of it more cordially, I hope to see great benefits flow from it to the farming interest of the State upon which rests every other interest. I speak of these matters because they have been attached to this cry of false economy[3]

The property of the State is taxed for the support of the State Government & for the support of the County governments The whole amount of tax collected from property for State purposes including tax for the support of the Asylums for the Insane, for

[3]For an explanation of these references to the Department of Agriculture, see Jarvis to Battle, February 21, 1879, n. 31.

the Deaf the Dumb & the Blind & the Penitentiary was, as shown by the last Auditor's report $434,232,45. The aggregate amount of tax collected from the same property is shown by the same report to support the several County governments proper was $1,024 459,89 Add to this the County tax for school purpose, $327,143,04 & we have $1,351, 603, 42 tax collected for County purposes. There was $917,569.98 more collected for County purposes than for State purposes. The people pay annually nearly a million of dollars more to the Counties than to the State. Where the burden is heaviest is the place where the burden most needs help, But the relief given here can not be so easily shown to the relieved & hence this broad field for retrenchment is I fear, too much neglected. And yet a dollar saved here is worth just as much to the people as if it could be demonstrated to them by palpable facts.

One of the chief items of expense in these County governments is the administration of the criminal law. The witness tickets & officers cost paid by the counties embrace small amounts but the aggregate is great I will here make these suggestions by which I think money may be saved to the tax payers without any detriment to the public good. First by simplyfing the forms of all bills of Indictment. How often is it the case that a Solicitor in the hurry & pressure of the court fails to put in his bill a "not," a "said" or a[n] "aforesaid" with which our bills of Indictments bristle so frightfully. Witnesses are subpoenaed & attend from Court to Court—officers fees & costs accumulate—and when the trial is had the bill is quashed or judgement arrested. The result is a guilty man escapes & the County has a big bill of costs to pay.

We need a statute which enacts, "That every bill of indictment which charges in words sufficiently clear without regard to form the offence for which the defendant is to be tried so that he can know the charge he is to meet shall be held by the Courts to be good." Second By giving justices of the peace power to try & determine certain petty cases upon proper complaint so as to largely reduce our crowded State docket, But it ought to be expressly forbidden for the County to pay any costs incurred in any trial before any justice of the peace who he takes final jurisdiction. Third By making it mandatory by statute, that in a certain class of cases the the Solicitor shall not send a bill of Indictment before the grand jury without endorsing thereon a prosecutor & that the judges shall have the power in all cases & at any time before judgement to direct the Solicitor so to do.

The tendency of legislation in this State since the war has been to create a large number of mere statutory offences to protect private rights which were formerly redressed by civil suits. Injury to real estate, injury to personal property, injury to live stock entering upon lands after being forbidden to do so, removing or destroying mortgaged property, removing crop by tenant before rents & charges are paid & the like are some of them. The public is not interested in this class of cases & the Counties ought not to have the costs to pay. Then too where a man resorts to the criminal law, as is often the case to harrass & annoy his neighbor & it so appears to the court, the tax payer ought to be protected against the costs in such cases.

I think these modifications in our system of administering the criminal law coupled with a rigid scrutiny of every bill of costs to be paid by the County before it is allowed will save to the tax payer an average of one thousand dollars to the County per annum In some counties it will be more [,]in many less. If I am correct this gives a net saving to the people of $94,000 every year. But if I am too high in my estimate & it shall be reduced one half then it will amount to $47,000.

This question of costs paid by the Counties in proceedings in criminal cases is of much more importance than one who has never investigated the subject is likely to suppose. But add to this the $115,000 paid annually for the maintenance & custody of the convicts & one may well say "the crime of the country is eating up the property of the country." The subject is well worthy of the thoughtful consideration of the tax payer & the retrencher. It is the part of wisdom & sound economy to make this crime contribute as much as possible to develope & increase the value of that property which it so heavily taxes. And for one I desire the declaration to go forth now to all men that they will find it to their interest as well as their comfort to live by honest toil & labor. The man who commits crime expecting to live in idleness while in the custody of the law will so far as I am concerned find he has made a great mistake. If he never knew what work work [sic] was the State will teach him. I have no patience with crime or idleness & a provision of law to hire out persons by County authorities who commit crime & will not voluntarily work to pay for it will in my opinion tend to lessen crime & relieve the burdens that rests upon honest men.

We have already accomplished enough with this convict labor to teach us that if properly used we can make it an important

factor in developing the wealth & resources of the State With it
we have slowly but steadily climbed the mountain side filling
here an immense gorge & there making a huge excavation till a
splendid passway has been made for the locomotive where but a
few years ago the way was impassable for man or beast. With it
we have removed barriers that rose up in our way mountain high
& when they were too high to be scaled we bored through them.
With it the engineer passing under the very backbone of the
mighty Blue Ridge will in a few days appear on the Western
slope to make glad the hearts of those whose hopes have so long
been deferred.[4]

In addition to this great work which I hope to see pushed
forward as rapidly as possible there are other enterprises for
the development of the wealth of the State in which this labor
may be beneficially employed. The Railroad from Fayetteville to
Egypt[5] in which the State has a large interest claims our attention The States interest in this road should be secured & then
the Road with the convict labor extended up the fertile valley of
the Yadkin into the rich mineral deposits of the Northwest.
Where this is completed the force may be withdrawn & with it
extend the road from Fayetteville to Wilmington thus giving
railroad facilities to a large portion of our people & greatly increasing the wealth & prosperity of the sections through which
it passes. There are several lines of projected railway on which
this may be profitably employed. Thousands of acres of lands in
the Eastern Counties through which the moor fowl now wings
its weary flight, but need the canals which can be cheaply constructed by this labor to make them contribute rich harvists
[sic] to their owners and much to the aggregate wealth of the
State.

But in the employment of this labor there are certain principles of business & State policy that ought to be observed. It
ought to be farmed out where it will be kept actually at work
& never allowed to be idle. The great work upon which it is
most likely to be employed will not be completed in [sic] years to
come

In our impoverished condition the process of construction &
development will necessarily be slow. What we do now ought to
be so done that those who are to direct & control years hence

---

[4]A reference to efforts being made to extend the Western North Carolina
Railroad to the Tennessee line.
[5]The Western Railroad of North Carolina.

may wisely build upon the foundations laid by us. But above all it ought to be used to enrich North Carolina, to build up her cities & towns & make more valuable her lands by constructing lines of travel & ways of transportation which tend in that direction and which conserve a North Carolina policy & a North Carolina system.

I very much doubt if these ends can best be obtained by farming out the convicts by legislative enactments. When it is done in this way there is not power that can change it till the Legislature meets again, although there may be manifest reasons why there should be a change. A better plan it seems to me is to organize a Board of Internal Improvements which may be composed of certain State officers & certain members of the now existing Boards which may be done without any extra cost to the State. Give this Board sole power to farm out convicts for the local interest of the State under such rules & regulations as may be prescribed by law. Such a Board will be free from local influences & I have no doubt can make better contracts for the State than is secured by the present system

This Board can also hear & determine all complaints as to treatment of convicts or alleged failure in compliance with the terms of the contract.

A common interest & a common patriotism require every citizen of the State to contribute all he can to the development of the resources & the increase of her wealth. Did I say a common interest. Yes. It can be demonstrated upon the simplest principles of political economy that the farmer in Currituck is pecuniarily interested in an increase in the value of the lands of Cherokee. The poorest tax payer in Buncombe is interested in seeing Raleigh grow to be a great and wealthy city. Raleigh in seeing Beaufort & Wilmington put on a new era of prosperity & all in seeing Charlotte maintain her steady step to wealth & what is true of these sections is true of every other section & its people. The taxable property of the State as shown by the last report of the Auditor is $146,170,493. To raise enough money from this property for State purposes requires a tax of twenty nine cents & two thirds cents on each hundred dollars worth of property. Now suppose by constructing highways that leads to our own cities & towns by encouraging our own people in their efforts to develope [sic] the manufacturing interests of the State by fostering our own trade & commerce & by a just and equal system of valuation we could in a few years double the taxable value of the property of the State and it may be done Is it not perfectly clear that any one individual no matter in what section he resides would only would only [*sic*] have to pay half as much tax on the same property then as now for as you increase the value of the property to be taxed the amount of money to be raised remaining the same, you decrease in like proportion the amount each hundred dollars worth of that property has to pay.

But this common interest & common patriotism not only requires the construction of our lines of communication so that they lead to our own cities & towns but they require that our people shall patronize them.

While I am free to admit that the trade & commerce of the State can not be controled by legislation without injury to many of our citizens I at the same time insist that if the shipper in Raleigh or Charlotte can get an outlet on our own coast on as good terms as he can by a route that tends to build up the cities & towns of other States he is in duty bound to give North Carolina the preference. So when our people can buy at home as cheaply as they can abroad they ought to encourage their home merchants, their home mechanics, their home manufacturers and every enterprise of their own State.

All petty jealousies & rivalries between individuals & sections which tend to keep one down because it may outstrip another ought to cease and as the devoted children of one grand old Mother we ought to labor together to help each other & make her prosperous & great.

I hope I will be pardoned for an allusion to myself on this occasion. In my childhood I read about the Governors of North Carolina and invested him with the highest honors that beface mankind. As I toiled & labored on the little farm by the side of the sea in noble old Currituck, I wondered if it were possible for me ever to reach that high & exalted position. The prospect then seemed gloomy but I said I will try. Guided in all things by the lessons of integrity & honesty taught me by a pious mother & a holy father, aided by devoted & generous friends & favoured by a noble & chivalrous people I have today reached the goal of my youthful ambition and am about to enter upon the discharge of the duties of that office which there seemed so far away out of my reach. Now it is mine by the free gift of the people; but I still think it is an honor of which the greatest & best of men may be proud. Although it comes by indirection & by what some may call accident I think it none the less great.

I am aware of the fact that while this position confers upon me such great distinction, it at the same time places upon me great responsibilities. Now my ambition is to so meet these responsibilities as to merit the approval of the people. To this end all that I have & am shall [be] unreservedly dedicated. All that I do shall be done with an eye single to the public good and with entire impartiality. The humble & the weak shall have a protection in all their rights of the strong arm of the law. The strong & the mighty must obey its mandates.

And in all things so far as in me lies I will try to so discharge my duties, that the people will feel as little as possible their loss of a great man who today surrenders into my hands the important trust they commit to him.

UNC-UP

Thomas J. Jarvis to Kemp Plummer Battle[6]

Executive Department
Raleigh, Feby 10th 1879

If you have not already done so, will you allow me to suggest that you had best attend to the matter, which the Board of Agriculture imposed upon you as chairman of the committee to propose amendments to the Ag. law, at your earliest convenience.

A&H—GLB

Thomas J. Jarvis to the General Assembly

Executive Department
Raleigh, N. C. Feby 14th 1879

I have the honor to herewith transmit the excellent report of the Adjutant General[7] of the State for the year 1878.

---

[6]Battle, a lawyer, banker and planter of Raleigh before the Civil War, served as state treasurer, 1866–1867; president of the University of North Carolina, 1876–1891; and professor of history, 1891–1907. *Dictionary of American Biography*, II, 57–58.

[7]Johnstone Jones, lawyer of Mecklenburg County; clerk of the House of Representatives, 1874–1875; adjutant general, 1877–1891; member of the General Assembly, 1885. Connor, *Manual, 1913*, 476, 518. For the report mentioned, see "Annual Report of the Adjutant-General of the State of North Carolina for the year 1878," *Public Documents of the General Assembly of North Carolina, Session 1879*, hereinafter cited as *Public Documents*, with proper date and number.

The State Guard is composed of the best young men of the State. They have uniformed themselves at a large personal expense. The organization itself has been a benefit to its present efficient condition at a very small expense to the State.

While there is little apprehension of riot or insurrection within our borders, still it is important that the State should have a force like this ready at all times to be called upon to assist the civil power in the enforcement of the laws in case a serious emergency should arise.

The State Guard is thoroughly organized & armed and well disciplined. It may be concentrated rapidly, upon short notice, at any point as occasion demands. It answers every purpose of a trained militia, and I respectfully recommend that no legislation tending in the least to impair its efficiency or to cripple the Adjutant Generals Department be adopted. The Department of the Adjutant General is being conducted at a very small cost to the State, & with the closest economy. It is essential to the proper management of the military affairs of the State that this department be kept up; and I would earnestly repeat the recommendation of my predecessor that the salary of the Adjutant be increased to six hundred dollars a year.[8]

A&H—GP

Committee from Greene County to Thomas J. Jarvis

Snow Hill, Greene Co.
N.C. Feby. 15th 1879.

The undersigned, a portion of the people of the County of Green, trust that you will not consider us presumptious in presenting to you the claims of a gentleman well known to us and to you, for the presidency of the A.&N.C.R.R. This county, though it does not touch that road, is in a large measure dependent upon it for supplies and for facilities for shipment, and has a very considerable interest in its proper management and well being. We feel fully assured that in the hands of A. J.

---

[8]The adjutant general's salary was $300 a year without any expense account. *Laws and Resolutions of the State of North Carolina Passed by the General Assembly at Its Session of 1879*, c. 240, hereinafter cited as *Laws of North Carolina*, with proper date. In 1883 it was raised to $600. *Laws of North Carolina, 1883*, c. 283.

Galloway,[9] Esq. of Goldsboro, the best interests of the road and of the people would be subserved with great ability—both from his well known views as to the policy of the conduct of the former, and his long experience and high standing as a railroad man—and we respectfully recommend him to the favorable consideration of your excellency in connection with the presidency of said railroad.

Theo Edwards[10]

A. L. Darden[11]

John Patrick [12]

Jno. H. Freeman[13]

R. C. C. Beaman[14]

Owen W. Jones[15]

S. Wooten[16]

Aned Sugg[17]

John G. Britt[18]

Ed. T. Albritton[19]

Jno. Murphy[20]

Wm. W. Carraway[21]

Wm. A. Darden[22]

Wm. J. Jones[23]

A&H—GP

John Hughes[24] to Thomas J. Jarvis [*with enclosure*]

Newbern, N.C., Feb 17 1879.

I take the liberty of inclosing to you a copy of a letter that I have just written to Col Buford[25] Prest of the Richmond &

---

[9]Soliciting agent for Atlantic and North Carolina Railroad. The identification of all names relating to this petition is taken from the following sources: Branson, *Directory, 1878*, 134–136; Branson, *Directory for 1884*, 337–341.

[10]Theophilus Edwards, lawyer of Snow Hill.

[11]Farmer of Snow Hill.

[12]Merchant and farmer of Hookertown.

[13]Gristmill owner of Snow Hill.

[14]Gristmill owner of Speight's Bridge.

[15]Farmer of Snow Hill.

[16]Shade Wooten, farmer of Snow Hill.

[17]Farmer of Snow Hill.

[18]Farmer of Snow Hill.

[19]Lawyer of Snow Hill and superintendent of the Greene County public schools.

[20]Merchant of Snow Hill.

[21]Farmer of Carr's township.

[22]Farmer of Speight's Bridge.

[23]Physician of Snow Hill.

[24]Lawyer and banker of New Bern, and president of the Atlantic and North Carolina Railroad. Branson, *Directory for 1884*, 239–242.

[25]Algernon Sidney Buford of Richmond, Virginia. A lawyer before the Civil War, he became president of the Richmond and Danville Railroad in 1864 and served for twenty-two years. Lyon G. Tyler (ed.), *Encyclopedia of Virginia Biography* (New York: Lewis Historical Publishing Company, 5 volumes, 1915), V, 701–703, hereinafter cited as Tyler, *Virginia Biography*.

Danville R R Co— It will explain itself and, I hope, meet with your approval—

I presume that it is hardly necessary to say to you that Gov Vance and myself (I in making and he in ratifying) were actuated by no feeling of hostility to the great North Carolina system,[26] when the present "combination" was formed—[27] It was done from a stern sense of duty— We saw that a valuable property in which the State as well as private citizens were largely interested as stock-holders was going to ruin— Its physical condition was such that it was with extreme danger that trains could be run over it— The bridges were decayed and unsafe, the road-way rotten and almost falling to pieces, its debts piled up mountain high and its Treasury almost empty— The hands had not been paid for months, material men were in a worse fix— More than $10,000 of interest on its bonds was due and unpaid— Suits and judgments on every hand and a total loss of credit everywhere— Under this state of affairs it became necessary either to take the impossibility of a total temporary change in the policy of the Road or to let it go to sale— The change was made— I knew that it would not be popular but I thought that it would be effective— I therefore concluded to breast the storm and leave the result to justify the propriety of my action— That result has more than met my most sanguine expectation— For in a period of great depression in all R.R. business we have brought the Road from the verge of ruin and placed it in a condition of prosperity— We have expended vast sums of money in bettering the permanent way of the Road and in repairing the rolling stock— the bridges are sound and good— and I believe that there is not in the state a road more entirely equal to the demands of trade than this one is at the present time, nor one having better credit or owing less floating debt—

I yield to no man in my devotion to what is known as the

---

[26] A term implying a system of railroads in North Carolina that would tap the resources of the entire state and direct the traffic to the North Carolina ports.

[27] On October 16, 1877, the directors of the Atlantic and North Carolina Railroad had entered a combination with the Raleigh and Gaston and the Wilmington and Weldon railroad companies to maintain rates on through traffic to the North. This agreement was designed to carry the traffic of eastern North Carolina to Norfolk, Virginia. Many in eastern Carolina felt that this agreement broke faith with the steamship companies operating out of New Bern and Morehead City. Cecil K. Brown, *A State Movement in Railroad Development* (Chapel Hill: University of North Carolina Press, 1928), 239, hereinafter cited as Brown, *State Movement*.

"North Carolina system"— I have always been its firm and enthusiastic supporter and have worked as hard and spoken as much for it as any man in this section of North Carolina, and will hail with delight the day when it can be *established*, for it has not heretofore at any time existed—

John Hughes to A. S. Buford
(*enclosure*)

New Bern, N.C., Feby 17th 1879

In the editorial columns of the "Observer" of Saturday the 15th inst, I find under the caption "Our commercial possibilities," a paragraph which reads as follows, "In respect to this Danville connection and the Richmond & Danville lease of the North Carolina Railroad",[28]— the *management* of that great interest assured us yesterday, as they have frequently stated in the past, that if the Governor and the people of the State were in earnest about the establishment, development & pursuit of a North Carolina policy and desired to have operated the Atlantic, the North Carolina and the Western North Carolina Rail Roads as an entirety, and a unified east & west line terminating at Beaufort Harber [*sic*], the management of the Richmond & Danville Railroad would clasp hands with the State over the compact of a North Carolina system"

This is indeed good news over which many true North Carolinians will greatly rejoice, if it is true— Will you please inform me by return mail, if possible, whether or not you sanction the statement and are prepared to carry it out

P S. I presume of course that the whole length of the North Carolina Rail Road from Charlotte would be included and that we would have an equal showing, at least, with the R&DRR for all through freights

A&H—GLB

Thomas J. Jarvis to John Hughes

Executive Department
Raleigh, N.C. Feby 20th 1879

Yours of the 17th inst was rec'd some days ago & the answer

---

[28] In 1871 the North Carolina Railroad was leased for thirty years to the Richmond and Danville for a rental of $260,000 a year. Brown, *State Movement*, 173.

has been delayed by the untimely death of the late Secty of State.[29] I have carefully read your letter & the copy of the one to Col. Buford. I trust Col Buford's reply will be all you desire. I have no ref[l]ection to make on your management of the Road. Whether the combination made by you & approved by Gov Vance was a wise policy or not I am sure you both did what you thought best,

UNC—UP

Thomas J. Jarvis to K. P. Battle

Executive Department
Raleigh, Feb. 21st 1879

I agree with you that Prof. Kerr[30] is the best qualified man in the State for State Geologist. But the action of the Legislature was prompted mainly, I think, out of hostility to him.[31] After that can I afford to force him upon the Senate. I think not, and yet if I do not take him who can I get. There are so few persons who devote themselves to Geology that his place will be hard to fill and especially in this State.

You are much more familiar with the muse of science than I am. I want you to help me. How will Dr. Ledoux[32] or Prof.

---

[29]Josephus Adolphus Engelhard, a lawyer after the Civil War in Tarboro and then in Wilmington; also editor of the Wilmington *Journal*, 1866–1876; appointed secretary of state in 1877. Daniel Lindsey Grant (ed.), *Alumni History of the University of North Carolina* (Chapel Hill: General Alumni Association, Second Edition, 1924), 185, hereinafter cited as Grant, *Alumni History of the University*.

[30]Washington Caruthers Kerr, state geologist from 1866 to 1882; in 1882 he entered the employment of the United States Geological Survey. *Dictionary of American Biography*, X, 258–259.

[31]For several years Kerr had been making a geological survey of North Carolina. There was considerable hostility to this survey on the grounds that it was too expensive a project. The Department of Agriculture was also under attack for much the same reason. In line with its "retrenchment" program, the General Assembly in 1879 abolished the position of state geologist. It then divided the Department of Agriculture into three equal subdepartments, one of which was filled by Kerr as state geologist. Kerr was able to continue his survey, but with reduced funds and without clerical help. Stuart Noblin, *Leonidas LaFayette Polk, Agrarian Crusader* (Chapel Hill: The University of North Carolina Press, 1949), 119–126, hereinafter cited as Noblin, *Polk*.

[32]Albert Reice Ledoux, Ph.D., of Geottingen University, state chemist from 1876 until 1880, when he moved to New York City and became a consulting mining engineer and chemist. *National Cyclopedia*, XII, 449.

Simons[33] do? Suggest some good men to me, and if possible come to Raleigh.

A&H—GLB

Thomas J. Jarvis to the General Assembly

Executive Department
Raleigh, N.C. Feby 22dn 1879

It is known to your Honorable body that under the Administration of Gov. Caldwell G W Swepson[34] & M S Littlefield[35] were indicted in Wake Superior Court at Oct Term 1874 for obtaining the Bonds of the State by false representations.

Counsel learned in the law were employed by Gov Caldwell to conduct the prosecution on the part of the State. The case went to the Supreme Court where it was held until the last days of the Court at June Term 1878 where Justice Rodman[36] delivered the opinion which will be found on page 632 vol. 79 of the N.C. Reports. The effect of this opinion was to reinstate the case for trial on the Superior Court Docket. Both of the Counsel employed by Gov Caldwell having been made Judges, Gov Vance felt called upon to employ other Counsel who now have the case in charge in Franklin Superior Court to which County it has been removed.[37] It is represented to me that most of the witnesses for the State & whose testimony is absolutely necessary live in Buncombe & counties beyond and that some of them

---

[33]William Gaston Simmons, professor of chemistry and natural history at Wake Forest College, 1855–1888. George W. Paschal, *History of Wake Forest College* (Raleigh: Edwards & Broughton Company, 3 volumes, 1935–1943), III, 498–501, hereinafter cited as Paschal, *History of Wake Forest*.

[34]George W. Swepson, prominent Raleigh banker, who had been involved in railroad frauds in North Carolina during Reconstruction. During the 1870's the governors of the state devoted much of their time and energy attempting to punish Swepson and to recover the state's funds. C. K. Brown, "The Florida Investments of George W. Swepson," *North Carolina Historical Review*, V (July, 1928), 275–288, hereinafter cited as Brown, "Florida Investments of Swepson."

[35]Milton Smith Littlefield, Civil War general who came to North Carolina in 1868 to speculate in depreciated railroad bonds. He and Swepson cooperated closely in defrauding the state. For the full story of Littlefield's activities relating to North Carolina, see Jonathan Daniels, *Prince of Carpetbaggers* (Philadelphia: J. B. Lippincott Company, 1958), *passim*, hereinafter cited as Daniels, *Prince of Carpetbaggers*.

[36]William Blount Rodman, state Supreme Court justice, 1868–1879. *National Cyclopedia*, VII, 385.

[37]A copy of this bill of indictment is in the Governors' Papers. For additional information on the prosecution of this suit, see Stewart to Jarvis, April 7, 1879, in this volume.

are not able to travel so great a distance at their own expenses

If it is the purpose of your Honorable body that this prosecution shall be continued I ask you to authorize the Treasurer to advance to such indigent Witnesses their actual expenses so that their attendances may be had

DUKE—TC

Thomas J. Jarvis to Braxton Craven [38]

Raleigh, Feb. 22nd 1879

Yours of the 20th has been received. I am glad to have your assurance of your interest in public affairs. It was only what I supposed. I cannot now say what will be the result of the proposed Legislation in regard to the Asylum for the Insane. I hardly think from what I hear that the Bill to reorganize the Institution will pass. In fact I think it will hardly be pressed.

As to the suggested resignation of some of the Directors[39] I see no reason now why that course should be persued [*sic*]. At least it is a matter they must determine for themselves. I shall not make any suggestion of the kind.

I will however make this suggestion to you personally. The Methodist Church is very dear to me. The least whisper whether true or not that one of its leading Ministers does any thing wrong gives me pain. While I would dislike to lose your valuable services on the Board I will take the liberty to suggest for your consideration whether the cause of religion and the interest of the Church do not require your non acceptance of any place where jealousy or malice may whisper their foul suspicions. There has been for the last two years and I fear will be for years to come more or less criticism about the management of the Asylum. It is and will be first one charge and then another. Whether any of them be true or not it is to be regreted that one

[38]President of Trinity College, Durham, North Carolina. *Dictionary of American Biography*, IV, 516–517.

[39]The state's care of the insane was under heavy criticism. Newspapers and legislators claimed that the Insane Asylum was being mismanaged, and that the state's practice of contributing money to counties for local care for the insane was wasteful. *Morning Star*, February 7, 14, 1879. An investigating committee of the General Assembly, however, gave the Asylum a clean bill. *Public Documents, 1879*, No. 27. In the same session, the General Assembly ended the practice of contributing funds for local care of the insane. *Laws of North Carolina, 1879*, c. 331.

[40]Craven refused to resign his directorship. Nora C. Chaffin, *Trinity College, 1839–1892: The Beginnings of Duke University* (Durham: Duke University Press, 1950), 262, hereinafter cited as Chaffin, *Trinity College*.

so high in the Church as yourself should be in the remotest degree associated with them.[40]

I throw out these suggestions in all love and kindness for your consideration. I am sure you will receive them in the proper spirit and that you will be guided by a high sense of duty to your God and your Country.

A&H—GP

G. W. C. Clarke to Thomas J. Jarvis

United States Board of Trade
New York, March 3rd 1879

The President, Vicepresidents and Executive Committee of this Board invite you to appoint four Delegates to attend the National Convention convened by the Board, to be held here on the 12th instant, as mentioned in the enclosed Notice.

I shall esteem it a great favor if you send me the names of the Delegates this week.[41]

A&H—GP

Carlton Brandaga Curtis[42] to Thomas J. Jarvis

New Bern   March 3 1879

The daily journals here informed me of the passage of the bill for funding North Carolina Bonds.[43] The terms are hard, very hard, and I do not believe the creditors will be willing to accept them, hoping that a sense of justice will prompt your State to offer terms something near the equity. It does seem unreasonable that after calling on the creditors to surrender nearly two thirds of the principal they should be asked to give up one third of the

---

[41]There is no record of Jarvis having made these appointments.

[42]New York businessman with varied interests in banks, oil wells and railroads; served in the United States House of Representatives 1851–1855, 1873–1875. *Biographical Directory of Congress*, 871.

[43]In February, 1879, the General Assembly adjusted the state debt by funding its "old bonds," worth almost $27,000,000 in principle and interest, into new bonds worth $3,644,511. This act included all bonds outstanding except the construction bonds authorized by the Convention and the General Assembly of 1868, and one issue authorized and sold during the Civil War. For a full account of this phase of North Carolina financial history, see B. U. Ratchford, "The North Carolina Public Debt, 1870–1878," *North Carolina Historical Review*, X (January, 1933), 1–20, hereinafter cited as Ratchford, "The North Carolina Public Debt;" and B. U. Ratchford, "The Adjustment of the North Carolina Public Debt, 1879–1883," *North Carolina Historical Review*, X (July, 1933), 157–167, hereinafter cited as Ratchford. "The Adjustment of the North Carolina Public Debt."

interest on the small remainder, — and in addition to all that they are told they must wait nearly two years longer before they will receive the first payment of interest on their claims. This seems to be clipping the corners all round, and so near to the centre that there is but little substance left.

I have one bond received by me for past due coupons on ante-war bonds then and now held by me. I find I would have been better off if the state had paid me one single years interest and then cancelled the bond.

I think the creditors are disposed to be reasonable, and I believe that if the law recently passed should be amended so as to pay the customary rate of interest, they might accept the reduction of the principal. I think its even probable that they might accept 4 per cent for five years, 5 per cent for five years and afterwards 6 per cent.

I hope the law will be amended in some such way and that the interest will be made to commence Jan 1 1879 & I hope you will use your influence to pressure such a modification.

A&H—GP

Cornelius Tate Murphy[44] *to Thomas J. Jarvis*

Ashland Va
March 6th 1879

It has been my purpose to have visited the State Capitol during the Sessions of the State Legislature to meet with the "Board of Public Charities" of the State and to consult with you upon the general purposes and intents of the Board and as to the propriety of making further efforts before the Legislature for rehabilitating the Board with some Legislative assistance or some appropriation that would enable the Board to inaugurate a system of visitation to the various counties for the purpose of introducing much needed reforms in the management of the Jails and Poor Houses of the State[45] but having attended faith-

---

[44]"Physician of Clinton; member of the General Assembly, 1870, 1872; chairman of the State Board of Public Charities, 1879–1886. *Sampson County M.D.'s* (Clinton: Commercial Printing Company, 1957), 46–47, hereinafter cited as *Sampson County M.D.'s*.

[45]The only expenses allowed the Board of Public Charities was compensation for its members' traveling expenses. William H. Battle (reviser), *Battle's Revisal of the Public Statutes of North Carolina, Adopted by the General Assembly at the Session of 1872-'3* (Raleigh: Edwards, Broughton & Company, 1873), c. 93, s. 2, hereinafter cited as *Battle's Revisal.*

fully and assiduously upon the Session of the General Assembly of 1876 & 7 & used every effort for the passage of a bill in accordance with the views and desires of the Board and having failed entirely to receive the cooperation of that branch of the State Government I have felt that any effort before the present Legislature with its tendencies and expressions of economy & retrenchment would more than likely prove useless and abortive and feeling myself this neglect of the Legislative Session of 1876 & 7 which would not even appoint successors to members of the Board whose terms had expired I declined to call together the only remaining members of the board in Annual Meeting during the past winter or during the present sittings of the State Legislature.

Upon reflection however I have concluded to indite this brief communication to your Excellency suggesting the propriety of asking the Legislature to fill up the vacancies upon the Board with such names as your Excellency in his wisdom may think best fitted to fill the position and whose influence upon the Board might in this as in many of the other States of the Union aid the other branches of the State and county governments to solve the difficult problem of Systemitizing and cheapening the expenses of caring for and properly providing for the paupers— prisoners and indigent persons accumulating so rapidly in every county in the state

It has been the custom of this Board to hold one of its annual meetings during the sittings of the State Legislature for the reasons partly set forth previously in my letter viz the Strict *pecuniary construction* so very prominent in the working of the present Legislature   I deemed it almost useless to tax the State treasurer with the expense of a meeting of the members of the Board whose terms have not expired

These unexpired terms of the board exist as you will see by reference to the enclosed "Ninth Annual Report of the Board" [46] only with D[r] G. W. Blacknall [47] J. T. Morehead [48] & myself— So you will percieve it will be necessary for the Legislature to appoint four persons as members of the Board whose terms should

---

[46]Located in the Governors' Papers.

[47]George W. Blacknall of Raleigh; planter, owner of the Yarborough House, and pioneer in developing the North Carolina tourist trade. Josephus Daniels, *Tar Heel Editor* (Chapel Hill: University of North Carolina Press, 1939), 309–311, hereinafter cited as Daniels, *Tar Heel Editor*.

[48]James Turner Morehead, businessman of Rockingham County, with large interests in textiles, mining, and railroads. Ashe, *Biographical History*, II, 259–264.

begin at the Expiration of those expiring as will be seen by reference to the Enclosed Report. It has been customary for the Board at their annual meeting to nominate successors to those whose terms were expiring but as no meeting has transpired during the present Legislative Session I thought I would as President of the Board ask you to nominate them to the Legislature & by concurrent Resolution have them appointed each one for five years—terms to begin as necessary to fill out those expired & expiring This I think would perhaps be the better plan I intended calling at the capitol & saying verbally to you what I have written or to have a canvass of the subject with you but the extreme illness of a son of a friend and townsman of mine who is a student at the college "Randolph & Macon" here has prevented me from going & I fear if the matter is postponed it will be too late to have it attended to the present Session. Therefore I shall submit the entire case to you as a ruler of the people and a lover of the prosperity and wellbeing of our state I have thought that something good for our Poor House & Prison System ought to be made out of this constitutional mandate but thus far the Legislature has failed to appreciate by Legislative assistance any good or profitable results from this Board and I have felt disinclined to be continually harrassing them upon what appeared to be an uninteresting subject Perhaps we have had the wrong men at the helm of the Board if so I earnestly hope that if your Excellency will take some interest in the matter & select four men in the state of intellect & influence they may have the proper influence over the Legislature to grant such aid as to make the Board a *living acting reality* & not a dead letter as it has been hitherto Gov Vance was very anxious to have the Legislature do something for the Board in 1876 & 7 but all failed[.] if we could get an appropriation of even one thousand dollars per annum that would serve as some compensation for a secretary & travelling agent great good could be accomplished it has done much good in other states & surely would in ours if properly managed.

I leave the matter Governor with you with the hope that you will be able to suggest such names as will give new strength & life to the Board or if your Excellency in your wisdom should think that the whole matter is unworthy your attention or that the constitutional requirement can be subserved without any filling up of the Board then I am & shall be satisfied. There is no personal interest to be justified with me. I love my good old mother state and love whatever will promote her best interest. I was first appointed upon this Board without any personal solicitation I have thought a good deal and corresponded right largely with the members of similar Boards in other states and they all seemed anxious that our State would clothe our Board with some pecuniary Strength & try its effects in reforming the old and in many cases worthless & corrupt management of the Poor Houses and Prisons of our State.

I will forbear I have to beg you to pardon style—arrangement haste & everything about this communication as I did not think at the outset I would fill a single sheet but as I wrote on I felt warmed up a little & have written thus much in case the Legislature will have adjourned or will not have time to ratify the appointments the unexpired terms can be filled by your Excellency which might be better anyway. I leave the matter with you. Wishing you every sort of good wish happiness health and enjoyment of every happy faculty I remain

A&H—GLB

Thomas J. Jarvis to the General Assembly

Executive Department
Raleigh N.C. Mar 7th 1879

I herewith transmit to your Honorable body the enclosed letter of Eugene Grissom,[49] Supt of the Asylum for the Insane.

I beg to call your attention to the suggestions therein made.

While I join with you in your purpose to reduce the expenditure as low as possible consistent with the public service, I ask that you will not have the unfortunate persons confined in the Asylum unprovided for in a manner creditable the State & beneficial to them.

---

[49]Physician and psychiatrist of Granville County; member of the General Assembly, 1862–1865; member of the Convention of 1865; became superintendent of the North Carolina Insane Asylum in 1868, and as such he was a member of the Board of Public Charities. In 1890 he moved to Colorado. *National Cyclopedia*, XXII, 98. Grissom's letter has not been found.

A&H—GLB

Thomas J. Jarvis to C. B. Curtis

Executive Department
Raleigh—N.C. Mar 7ᵗʰ 1879

In reply to yours of the 3rd inst in reference to the action of the General Assembly on passing the bill to compromise & settle the State Debt, I think I can say their action is final   It may seem hard to the Creditors & I cant blame them for thinking so, it is but natural I sincerely [wish] we were able to pay more. We are not in my opinion, this is the last offer. It is better to pay what we promise than to promise a larger amount & then a few years hence have to propose another compromise. We have been slow to make an offer not from a want of disposition to pay, but the want of ability. Now we have made this & we propose to stand by it. Those who accept it may rely upon its being complied with on our part in perfect good faith. Such as do not accept, will wait in my opinion, for something better

A&H—GP

John Hughes to Thomas J. Jarvis

Newbern, N.C. March 10 1879

At a meeting of the Board of Directors of this Company [A. & N.C.R.R.] held on the 7ᵗʰ day of March inst. a resolution was adopted in the following words "Ordered by the Board that the President of this Co confer with the Governor of the State in regard to claim of this Company against the N.C.R.R. Co. and request him to recommend to the latter that the Statute of limitations shall not be pleaded by them against said claim, and that then a proposition of reference under the Statute shall be made to the N.C.R.R. Co. for the purpose of settling and adjusting the mutual accounts between the two companies"—

I had hoped to be able to go to Raleigh to–day or to–morrow to see you personally in regard to the matter, but I have other pressing engagements which conflict with my doing so. I have, therefore, concluded to write, with the understanding that if a personal interview prove necessary, I will go to Raleigh later—

In 1865 the military power of the U.S. (then in possession of this and the N.C.R.Ro) took a quantity of R.R. iron from the line of this R.R and placed it in the track of the N.C.R.R. The claims for this iron with interest on its *true* price amounts to about $10,000— No claim was made for it until after the Statute of limitations had run against it— Under these circumstances as it was known that the N.C.R.R. Co would plead the Statute, Gov Brogden,[50] (as I am informed by Col Humphrey[51]) wrote a letter to the Directors on the part of the State, in which he instructed them not to plead the Statute, upon the ground that as they were both State Roads the matter should be settled according to right and justice without regard to the Statute— Gov Vance subsequently took the same view of the subject—I am now informed that they still propose to plead the Statute— Of course if they do, the claim will be lost, but as they do not allege that the iron has ever been paid for our Board thought that you would be willing to give similar instructions to them of Gov Brogden especially as it is reality a sort of family matter—

In July 1876, Col Humphrey, then Prest of this Co, borrowed from the N.C.R.R. Co $4.500 to pay his semi-annual interest bonds— This sum has been paid by his administration except about $800 which was left for us to settle— I decline to pay it unless they could come to a mutual settlement of all matters in controversy between the two companies— Now they threaten to sue and I suppose will do so unless you intervene—

Our idea as expressed in the resolution, is that the whole thing should be reformed under the statute and a full settlement made. Please let me know your views on the subject. If you concur with us oblige me by writing a letter of instructions to the State Directors of the N.C.R.R.

---

[50]Curtis Hooks Brogden; member of the General Assembly for sixteen years between 1840 and 1868; collector of internal revenue, 1869; lieutenant governor from 1872 to 1874 and, upon Governor Caldwell's death, governor from 1874 to 1876; Republican representative in Congress, 1877–1879. *National Cyclopedia*, IV, 428.

[51]Lott William Humphrey, lawyer and businessman of Goldsboro; member of the General Assembly, 1872. He had once been prominent in local Democratic politics, but in 1876 he turned Republican. Daniels, *Tar Heel Editor*, 176; Frank A. Daniels, *History of Wayne County* (Goldsboro: 1914), 41–42, hereinafter cited as Daniels, *Wayne County*.

A&H—GP

W. G. Curtis to Thomas J. Jarvis

Office of Quarantine Physician
Smithville March 11th 1879

Since my last report to the Executive, there has nothing occurred of importance at this Quarantine Station—Great vigilance has, and continues to be exercised with regard to the probability of vessels from South American ports, where yellow fever and small pox both prevail extensively—An occasional vessel arrives with sickness on board, but so far none of a contagious nature

.   .   .   .

A&H—GLB

Thomas J. Jarvis to John Hughes

Executive Department
Raleigh N.C. Mch. 11th 1879

Your letter of the 10th has been recd. It is the first information I have had directing my attention to the matter therein referred to. I will look into the matter at once & have no doubt will pursue the course suggested. I can see no reason why the N.C.R.R.Co. should plead the Statute of Limitations—Has there been a suit instituted by your Company against the NCRR Co. & if so when & where?

A&H—GLB

Thomas J. Jarvis to the Senate of North Carolina

Executive Department
Raleigh N.C. Mch. 11th 1879

By an Act of the General Assembly ratified Feb'y 20th 1879, I am required to appoint by & with the consent of the Senate a suitable person to conduct under the supervision of the Agriculture Department, a Geological Survey of the State.[52] Since the passage of the Act I have used all the means available to arrive at the best way in which to discharge this important and difficult duty. The number of men, who have devoted themselves

[52]See Jarvis to Battle, February 21, 1879, *n.* 31, in this volume.

to the study of Geology in the State, are very few & my information as to the qualifications of that few is very limited, although I have sought all the information I possibly could. I have also inquired into the present condition of the work & I find as a fact, that the labors of the last five years of the Geologist, have been devoted to gathering the subject matter for the 2nd Vol.[53] of his Report. This matter is now in the form of mere notes & memoranda of which were collected at a cost to the State of at least $25,000. It is worthless as I understand in the hands of any one except the man who made it; because it can not be understood by any one else. It seems to me it would be unwise to throw away this material as it has been [acquired] at such a cost. I learn from direct information from Prof Kerr, that it will take from six to twelve months to write up this material into manuscript form for publication. For these reasons I have concluded if it meets the approval of the Senate not to make a nomination at this time for the Office of the Geologist, but to direct Prof Kerr to continue the work & to apply himself to putting the material now in hand in such shape, that it may be used.[54] After this is done I shall then be better prepared to make a change in the management of the Department if one is desired & the work could then be suspended without such loss, if such a cause be deemed advisable

A&H—GP

John Hughes to Thomas J. Jarvis

Newbern, N.C., March 13, 1879

I have just rec'd your letter of 11th in reply to mine of the 10th inst: I am glad to know that I was not in error in supposing that you would give the instructions asked for—

No suit has ever been brought by this Co against the N.CRR Co on account of the iron— Our hope has always been that this matter could be adjusted amicably, and I still think so, if they will not set up the Statute—

---

[53]Volume I of W. C. Kerr's *Report of the Geological Survey of North Carolina* was published in 1875.

[54]The Senate approved Kerr's continuation as state geologist, but declining health prevented him from completing his *Geological Survey*. He retired in 1883 and died in 1885. Volume II was completed by George B. Hanna and published in 1888.

A&H—GP

William Joe Boney[55] *to Thomas J. Jarvis* [*with enclosure*]

Enclosed find formal organization of commissioners for canalling Angola Bay as pr recent act of the Legislature &c.[56]

1st   I am directed to inquire of you as to the appointment of a civil engineer and general overseer for said work.

There has been a survey made by civil engineer James[57] of Wilmington from Crooms' Bridge into said Bay 2¾ miles and He reported a rise of 27 feet in that distance which survey was on exhibition during the discussion and passage of said Bill before the Legislature and is probably on file. This survey is of recent date and can be traced easily. And we the Commissioners do not think it necessary to make such an appointment at a large Salary there by creating a heavy expence as there seems to be no obstacles in the way   But it will be necessary to appoint some man to oversee and push the work on unless the Guards are required to do that part of the work. Neither of the Commissioners can oversee it from day to day as will be necessary for the early completion of the same   It is about Six miles from the said N.E. River to the east side of the Public lands and 3¼ miles from Angola to Cypress Creek across the Piney woods

2nd   How shall we proceed in case of any party owning lands on the proposed Route between the said River and Public lands should they object [to] the said Canal (or claim damage)   There is only one party that owns land on said proposed Route and he is the owner of the canal we propose to use. his canal is about of sufficient size already cut about 500. yards from said N.E. River and in the exact direction of the Route of the canal we are directed to cut   And he says we may cut through and use his canal If we will have the damage paid and our body does not think it will damage him at al[l] as it will drain a large tract of his land beyond his canal

3rd   There are some outbuildings that can be used for Quarters until stockades can be built. And Logs & building material is convenient and can be had free of Rent for those Buildings

A weekly line of Steamers from Wilmington to Crooms Bridge

---

[55]Farmer of Wallace, Duplin County, and secretary of the Duplin County Democratic Executive Committee. Branson, *Directory for 1884*, 284; *Raleigh Observer*, July 20, 1878.

[56]The General Assembly intended to have Angola Bay, in Duplin and Pender counties, drained in order to convert a great area of swamp land into farm land. *Laws of North Carolina, 1879*, c. 143.

[57]William H. James.

South Washington Station W.&.W. Rail Road Six miles from said Bridge

It will probably be necessary to employ a practical surveyor at intervals to stake off the work but we do not think it necessary to make a permanent appointment by order of the board.

Crooms Bridge Pender County, N.C.

Pursuant to a recent act of the Legislature of North Carolina to canal Angola Bay

We Daniel Shaw[58] & Asa B. Croom[59] of Pender County and William J. Boney & Edward T. Pigford[60] of Duplin County Commissioners appointed by said act met and organized by electing Daniel Shaw Ashton Post Office Pender County as chairman and William J. Boney of Wallace P.O. Duplin County as secretary and

On Motion the said commissioners proceeded to examine the sites for said canal and unanimously agree that Lot[t] Crooms[61] Canal just above Crooms' Bridge on the east side of North East River in Pender County is the best point for locating said canal

Resolved that the secretary be requested to write to his Excellency Gov. T. J. Jarvis

1st   In regard to the appointment of a civil engineer for the proposed work

2nd   In regard to other matters of interest in the putting said work into execution

3rd   That all communications be addressed by mail to the secretary

On Motion we adjourned to meet at the Call of the Chairman

March 20th 1879
To his Excellency
Gov. T. J. Jarvis
Raleigh N.C.

---

[58]Farmer and chairman of the Pender County Board of Commissioners. Branson, *Directory for 1884,* 521, 524.

[59]Farmer of South Washington. Branson, *Directory for 1884,* 524.

[60]Merchant of Wallace. Branson, *Directory for 1884,* 282.

[61]Farmer of Point Caswell. Branson, *Directory, 1878,* 241.

William Simpson Pearson[62] to Thomas J. Jarvis

Morganton, N.C.,
March 22ᵈ 1879

The Bᵈ Comssrs of the W[estern] I[nsane Asylum] find the
season for work now upon them & have made arrangements to
begin operations at once.[63] Mr [Samuel] Sloan of Phil. the architect is of opinion that the finished wing should be floored & furnished, temporary accomodations provided for officers & employees & all effort directed to care for 200 patients by 1880. The
present Board are, I feel sure, disposed to build the centre or
main building & leave to the next Legislature the provision for
officers & patients.

Inasmuch as the one or the other of these policies must be
speedily adopted and all work of detail made to fit in & go along
with the chosen plan, I submit that we should know the pleasure
of your Excellency in reference to the continuance in office of
the present Board before we in any way undertake to bind or
trammel our successors. Under the act of assembly we hold for
two years, which is now out or until our successors are appointed—

Suggesting to Your Excellency the necessity of taking such
steps in the matter of appointing a new Board or continuing the
present one, as to you may seem proper at as early day as is
possible & for the above given reasons, I have the honor to be

Thomas J. Jarvis to K. P. Battle

Executive Department
Raleigh, March 31ˢᵗ 1879

I have seen Mr. S.[64] and had a long talk with him. He will
write you by this mail and give his consent to the employment

⁶²Editor of Asheville *Pioneer*, 1874 and 1875; he then moved to Morganton and entered railroad management. He held several appointive state
positions, one being a commissioner to supervise the construction of the
Western Asylum for the Insane at Morganton. In 1880 he entered the legal
profession. Ashe, *Biographical History*, VII, 375–379.
⁶³In 1877 the General Assembly authorized the completion of the construction on the Western Insane Asylum building. For progress to date, see
Public Documents, 1879, No. 12.
⁶⁴Barnas Sears, for many years president of Brown University, and later
general agent for the Peabody Fund. *Dictionary of American Biography*,
XVI, 537–538.

of Ladd.[65] He was very generous about it and said he was willing to do whatever I advised. I hope his letter will be all that you desire. If it is not write me and I will see him again. He will not be in the way but on the contrary he will do all he can to make the Normal School a grand success.

I return you Dr Sears letter suppose you may desire to keep it.

A&H—GLB

Thomas J. Jarvis to W. S. Pearson

Executive Department
Raleigh N.C. Mch 31ˢᵗ 1879

Yours of the 22ⁿᵈ has been rec'd & for a reply thereto I will say, that as I understand the law the present Board continues for two years and *until their successors are appointed.* It is my wish that the present Board continues the work as I know of no reason why any change should be made. Their management was fully endorsed by the Committee of the Legislature which made the examination. I will leave the manner of carrying on the work with the Board and therefore can not give you a definite answer to your inquiry about the details of the work. I can only say, that I think it wise to have a portion of the Building ready for the reception of patients as soon as it can be done with due care to the final completion of the building. I beg that your Board will enforce the most rigid economy & require the most faithful performance of duty of all contractors & employees in the further progress of the work.

I send you enclosed a certified copy of the last Act

A&H—GP

Joseph B. Stewart[66] to Thomas J. Jarvis

New York, April 7ᵗʰ 1879

For reasons which will appear in what I shall proceed to state I address you this communication.

---

[65] John J. Ladd of Vermont, for several years teacher in the Vermont public schools, and since 1877 superintendent of the Normal School at Chapel Hill. Kemp P. Battle, *History of the University of North Carolina* (Raleigh: Edwards & Broughton Printing Company, 2 volumes, 1907–1912), II, 143, hereinafter cited as Battle, *History of the University.*

[66] Attorney of New York City. Daniels, *Prince of Carpetbaggers,* 285–286.

In the latter part of the year 1870, or 1871, suits were instituted in the Supreme Court of the state of New York by the Western Division[67] of the Western North Carolina Railroad Company against various parties to recover its assetts [sic] or the proceeds thereof which it was alleged had been misappropriated to a very large amount. In this litigation I was not concerned except so far as I was occasionally consulted by the counsel employed by the Company in the prosecution. But from such consultations I learned something of the character of the suits and that they terminated adversely to the interests of the Company in or about the year 1873.[68]

Soon after this time litigation involving the same interests took a new shape in the States of Georgia and Florida, wherein the Western Division Company was sued,[69] and, failing to appear and properly to defend, was placed at great disadvantage in asserting its rights, whatever they were.

In December, 1874, I was employed specially to go to Ga. & Fla. and look after these suits, and see what, if anything, could be done to establish the interests of said Company therein.

In accepting this employment it was made known to me that the W.D. Co. had nothing whatever with which to pay expenses or costs—much less to fee counsel, and that I would have to look wholly to results for compensation. I did visit Ga. & Fla. and carefully investigate the condition of the suits, and adopt such measures as I thought would prevent further injury until I could prepare myself fully for taking the aggressive by the institution of proper judicial proceedings. This was attended by a great deal of labor and expense—it soon becoming apparent to me that the Company was as ignorant of the real facts, and its rights in the premises, as it was destitute of money or means to assist the same.

In addition to this litigation in which the W.D. Co. was involved, a new element of attack appeared in a scheme and com-

[67]In 1868 the General Assembly divided the Western North Carolina Railroad into two separate corporations, the Western Division and the Eastern Division. George W. Swepson became president of the Western Division. Brown, *State Movement*, 191, 202–203.

[68]During his presidency, Swepson defrauded the Western Division of over $1,000,000, most of which he invested in the Florida Central Railroad. In 1870 the state of North Carolina began trying to recover its losses but by 1873 had had little success. For the full story, see Brown, *State Movement*, 196–203; and Brown, "Florida Investments of Swepson," 279–283.

[69]Because of Swepson's malfeasance, North Carolina repudiated the state bonds issued to the Western Division, and the bondholders brought suit against the state for their redemption. Brown, *State Movement*, 202.

bination by one Charles D. Willard, Frank R. Sherwin, W^m. H. Gleason, Henry R. Jackson, Charles R. Simonton, Calvin H. Allen, and others ranging to New York, England, and Holland, for the purpose of absorbing both the Jacksonville, Pensacola, & Mobile, & the Florida Central railroad, in which the interests of the W.D. Co. had become involved. The plan was to have them seized and speedily sold by the Gov. of Fla.[70] under the provisions of a statute of that state providing for the exchange of bonds between said companies and the state.[71] The bonds had been bartered off in Europe at nominal prices because of their alleged fraudulent issue, and were subsequently declared unconstitutional and void by the Supreme Court of the State of Fla.[72]

Nevertheless the roads were seized and advertised for sale; which, if permitted to take place, would at once terminate all interest of the W.D. Co. in them,[73] though it had been the subject of litigation for years. To encounter this new and threatening element of attack at once required new and extraordinary labor and exertion, and the immediate and continued expenditure of large sums of money, not a dollar of which was or could be contributed by the W.D. Co. as I have stated.

To meet this condition of things the W.D. Co. executed to me a power of attorney, and entered into an agreement with me under its corporate seal, giving me full and plenary power to prosecute and defend its interests in such manner as I might deem best, with full power to settle or compromise according

---

[70]Harrison Reed, governor of Florida, 1868–1872. *National Cyclopedia,* XI, 380.

[71]In 1870 the Florida General Assembly authorized the issuance of state bonds to seven Florida railroad companies for the purpose of improving and expanding their facilities. The governor then executed and delivered to Littlefield, in exchange for a like amount of railroad bonds, $4,000,000 of state bonds issued to the Florida Central and the Jacksonville, Pensacola, and Mobile railroads. If the railroads defaulted on their interest payments, the state was authorized by law to take possession of the roads. Reginald C. McGrane, *Foreign Bondholders and American State Debts* (New York: Macmillan Company, 1935), 300–301, hereinafter cited as McGrane, *Foreign Bondholders.*

[72]*Holland v. Florida,* 15 Fla. 455 (1876).

[73]Early in the 1870's the Florida Central and the Jacksonville, Pensacola, and Mobile defaulted on their interest payments and the state took possession of these railroads. Florida wished to sell the roads immediately, but for some time was blocked by the Western Division of North Carolina which, through Littlefield's investments, had acquired a first mortgage lien on the Florida Central. McGrane, *Foreign Bondholders,* 303. Essentially the question was whether the Western Division had first claim on the Florida Central because the latter had been financed by money stolen from the Western Division, or whether the first claim was held by the state of Florida.

to my best judgment—the W.D. Co., however, not to be subjected to any debts or liabilities, or provide any means for conducting said litigation—all of which was to be borne by myself and associates if we elected to accept the terms—otherwise the field was to be abandoned.

Having then already devoted so much time & labor, and incurred such heavy expenditures I had no alternative but to go on or suffer considerable loss. I therefore summoned to my aid such means and assistance as I deemed necessary, & did commence a most vigorous attack upon the Willard & Co. conspiracy —and after employing means and incurring expense in possessing myself of the facts and proof of their transactions and schemes in Washington, New York, London, Amsterdam, Savannah, Tallahassee, and at Jacksonville the objective point, I brought my pleadings and proofs to a hearing before the Hon. U.S. Circuit Court, at its May Term, 1877, wherein I was successful in breaking down the conspirators so far as to get the Gov. of the state enjoined from selling either of the roads, and soon after, by further Judicial Proceedings, succeeded in getting possession of the Florida Central road in the interest of the W.D. Co.,[74]—which I believe was regarded by the Courts and the bar, as well as the community at large, as a very creditable achievement.

During all this time in '74, '75, '76, & '77, I never saw or heard of a man in N.C. or out of it who claimed sufficient interest in the W.D. Co. to manifest a willingness to contribute $1.—towards defending its rights except its president, Major Rollins,[75] who did, and seemed willing to do, all in his power. But no sooner had I made a success and brought to light something in the shape of value than I was assailed in a most extraordinary manner by another scheme and conspiracy, gotten up by one Thomas D. Carter, and one Mike L. Wood,[76] claiming to represent the W.D. Co., united with Willard and his co-conspirators, whom I had just defeated in Fla. by which they sought to drive me out of control of the suits which I had instituted and was conducting successfully in the name of the W.D. Co. At the same time, and by another proceeding in the name of the fraudulent Bondholders, which was aided by said Carter and others in N.C.

---

[74]Actually, all the Western Division received at this point in its series of suits was $94,000 in first mortgage bonds of the Florida Central Railroad. *Public Documents, 1879*, No. 15.

[75]Wallace W. Rollins, lawyer of Marshall. Branson, *Directory, 1878*, 184.

[76]Neither Carter nor Wood has been identified.

it was sought to wrench the Florida Central road out of my control, and place it in the hands of a Receiver for their own benefit. They did not succeed.[77]

I shall attempt no description of this performance except to say that it was malicious and personal to a damnable degree. Nothing was left undone—nothing left unsaid—nothing refrained from that the conspirators supposed would enable them to succeed in their purpose. At one time they claimed to own and represent the stock of the W.D. Co.—at another time they asserted it had no stock to be represented—at another time they claimed to act in the corporate name of the W.D. Co.—and then again would deny that it had any corporate existence to use because of some alleged fraud in its organization. While assailing me in one breath for abusing its rights, in the next they would allege that it had no rights to abuse.

The material for these attacks was either manufactured or furnished by said Carter and others co–operating with him in N.C. so far as they affected the W.D. Co. But I again defeated them. These attacks were renewed a third, a fourth, and a fifth time with increased malignance and virulance [sic] devolving upon me heavy additional labor and expense—but with no better success for the conspirators.

In the meantime, on my part, I was so fortunate as to be able to rid the Florida Central road of the troubles surrounding it, & to hand over to the officers of the W.D. Co. $94,000. of good, well secured 7% Bonds upon which the interest has been promptly paid to the present date, the efforts of Carter Wood & Co & Willard & Co—including the Florida confederates to the contrary notwithstanding. And I will be able to ′add $150,000 more to that amount if I am not defeated by the acts of these conspirators through the aid of recent legislation in your state.

The latest of these attacks was made on the 22d of January last, and ended about the 1st of March,—being another attempt to get a Receiver for the Florida Central road, in which the conspirators suffered another disastrous defeat.

Having stated thus much for your general advice, and which, if my many communications to your predecessor have been preserved, you will find was made known to him substantially as the events occurred down to the last and recent one. This brings me

---

[77]No information has been found on this "conspiracy." The fact that North Carolina newspapers for 1879 make no mention of it seems to indicate that it did not exist.

to the immediate matter I desire now to impress upon your official consideration.

I have stated that the last raid by Willard and his co–conspirators on the Fla. Cen. road terminated about the 1ˢᵗ of March last. He and those engaged with him soon thereafter left Jacksonville. About the time they left I was told in the office of the U.S. Circuit Clerk that Willard had declared that if they could not break my hold any other way they would legislate me out of existence by repealing the charter of the W.D. Co.; and that such would be done before the 1ˢᵗ of April, or language to that effect.

On going to Tallahassee a few days later to take testimony, and being in the office of the Attorney General the same story, substantially, was repeated to me by a party there present, to which I replied that such a thing was impossible. Leaving Fla. for Raleigh to take further testimony I stopped at Greensboro and met there two gentlemen, who, I was told, were members of your state legislature. I availed myself of the opportunity to inquire of them if any such legislation had occurred or been proposed. They replied that they had heard of nothing of the kind and were sure that no such law had been passed. Arriving next at Raleigh I went to the office of your Secretary of State[78] to get some certified laws for use in the trials in Florida. I repeated my inquiry to him and was informed that on the very last day of the Session such a law had passed, and was shown the law.[79]

I read the act with no little astonishment, as must be the case with all others who do read it, and I took a copy of it. I showed it to C. M. McLoud,[80] Esq., one of the directors of the W.D. Co. from Asheville, who told me that the Co. knew nothing about it, and were not consulted about it or apprized of it by its promotors, who prepared it and hastened it through the legislature at the last moments of the Session. He expressed great sur-

---

[78]William Laurence Saunders, secretary of state from 1879 until his death in 1891. He began practicing law in 1858 but later turned to newspaper work. He was editor of the *Wilmington Journal* from 1872 to 1876; in 1876 he and Peter M. Hale established the Raleigh *Observer*. Ill health forced him to abandon newspaper work and accept public position. *Dictionary of American Biography*, XVI, 384.

[79]On March 13, 1879, the General Assembly reunited the Western and Eastern Divisions of the Western North Carolina Railroad. This was done because of the legal difficulties existing in the way of constructing the road beyond Asheville should the Western Division be allowed to remain in existence. Raleigh *Observer*, May 25, 1879.

[80]Calvin H. McLoud, lawyer of Asheville and member of the General Assembly, 1883. Branson, *Directory, 1878*, 41; Connor, *Manual, 1913*, 518.

prise that it was done—said the Company were not all responsible for it, and would seek to protect themselves in the courts against its enforcement. He at once sent a copy of the law to the Company at Ashville[sic], where he said it would take every body greatly by surprise, unless it should be the immediate promotors of it whose names be used.[81]

Upon a careful reading of the law, it seemed to me not to repeal the Charter of the Company, coupled with provisions for liquidating and winding up its affairs, paying its debts, and fulfilling its obligations in the manner known to the law; but simply and positively obliterated the W.D. Co. (or sought to do so) and transferred all its estate to the Eastern Division without any regard to stock, stockholders, debts or obligations, or private vested rights, and without notice or hearing, in court or otherwise. And in order to impart a more vigorous effect to its extraordinary provisions, there is added, in lieu of a civil trial, a penal clause punishing with fine and imprisonment all who refuse to surrender what they suppose to be their property and rights, when commanded to do so by the Governor, by declaring them to be guilty of a misdemeanor!

All this, and more too, is apparent on the face of this act, which certainly must have passed your Legislature without due consideration. Indeed I was informed by several members whom I met at your Capitol that the matter was not considered at all, and that they did not believe any one besides those who introduced the Bill really knew what it contained, or the monstrous character of its provisions.

But, nevertheless, there is such an act, and I cannot fail to see that it is well designed to impose upon me increased trouble in the trial of my suits for the W.D. in Fla., which are set for the 19th of May. Not, indeed, that it is in the power of the act to in any manner impair the obligation of my contract and agreement made and executed under the seal of the W.D. Co., not to impair

---

[81]No irregularities in the passage of the consolidation bill have been found. Two factors, however, may support Stewart's charges. (1) Now that the Western Division no longer existed, a final compromise of all its claims on Florida railroads was made in September, 1879, whereby the parent company, the Western North Carolina Railroad, received only $25,000. Brown, "Florida Investments of Swepson," 287. (2) The President of the Western Division refused to turn over the assets of his railroad to the Western North Carolina Railroad on the grounds that the private stockholders of the Western Division had not been consulted about the consolidation. He complied only after the consolidation law and been declared constitutional by the state Supreme Court. *Morning Star*, August 12, 1879; Raleigh *Observer*, August 30, 1879.

or deprive me of my vested rights thereunder, even if such were the intention, which, from its allusion to suits pending in the state or Federal Courts, seems highly probable, and that Willard and his co–conspirators, whom I have so far defeated in the courts were justified in their threat I should be legislated out of the causes by the repeal of the Charter of the W.D. Co. before the 1st of April.

But what I do fear is that it will be availed of to attack my suits by a motion in abatement with a view of forcing me to change my position before the court, and to otherwise demoralize my suits in which your state and people are so largely interested, and for whom, as I have stated, I will be able to secure full $250,000. in good interest–paying securities within the next sixty days if I am not defeated or postponed by the extraordinary legislation to which I have referred.

In order to show how completely this scheme was concocted by a secret conclave outside of the legislature, and for what purposes, I will remark that besides being told in Jacksonville and Tallahassee that such legislation would be had, even before the Bill was introduced into your Assembly, on my arrival at Washington, D.C., I was told that such had occurred, as coming from Thomas D Carter & Mike L. Wood, and with a statement of the reasons and object for which it was done; and on my arrival in N.Y. to take testimony before U.S. Commissioner Stilwell [sic].[82] he informed me that he had been told by Ex Judge Birdseye,[83] the counsel for Willard and Carter opposed to me in this city—that "the W.D. Co. had fizzled out, and that it suits in Florida never would be tried;" thus showing that Willard, Carter, and their associates were able to proclaim the passage of this act in Fla., Washington, and N.Y. city even before a Bill for it was introduced into your Legislature. Of course there is no misinterpreting these revelations however discreditable to those engaged in the transaction.

Now, it is not my purpose to advise or attempt to settle questions of law or right between the state of N.C. and its citizens,

---

[82]Probably United States Commissioner Richard E. Stilwell of New York. *Register of Officers and Agents, Civil, Military, and Naval, in the Service of the United States on the Thirtieth of September, 1877* (Washington: Government Printing Office, 1878), 330, hereinafter cited as *Register of Officers of the United States, 1878.*

[83]Probably United States Commissioner John T. Birdseye of Ohio. *Register of Officers of the United States,* 326.

or the corporations created under its laws; but I do beg leave to call your attention to the large interest affected by this law *outside* of your state, wherein the rights of myself and others, created under sealed covenants with the W.D. Co., which have been in good faith carried out on our part are seriously involved. These rights I do not believe you will permit to be disturbed.

I have been engaged in these suits for the W.D. over 5 years, and over $40,000.—in money have been advanced and expended in their prosecution by myself and associates, besides our time and labor, compensation for which is only arranged in the sealed contracts with the W.D. Co. which it is proposed to destroy by the attempted enforcement of the act to which I have referred.

We are now in the trial term of the court, and, as I have stated, the cases are set for the 19th of May, when I shall be ready for trial, and feel confident of success. After the cases are tried, and I settle my transactions with the Co., in the event of success (and without such success I am not aware of any estate of the Co. to administer upon) I shall, of course feel it my duty to deliver and pay over anything I may collect, in addition to what I have done, to whomsoever Your Excellency may direct or order, as I shall by no means attempt to settle or adjust the local questions or policy of your state; but I do ask, without the slightest doubt about my right to do so, that, as the act seems to be left in your hands especially for execution, you will defer any enforcement of it in a manner that will disturb or delay the efficient and successful prosecution of the suits on the part of the W.D. Co. in Fla.

Indeed the facts that the state bonds issued to the W.D. Co. have been ignored by the state, and indictments found against Swepson and Littlefield for fraud in the organization of the Company have been and are being used against me with unpleasant effect by the counsel employed by Willard, Carter, and their associates, and I do not think it fair or just that I should have this repealing act, be it good or bad, loaded upon me just on the eve of the trial. In hopes to contribute to the prevention of this useless injury, if not destruction of the rights of all parties I have taken pains to address you this communication in your official capacity, believing you will not fail to see therein sufficient to justify me in assuming to address you.

I regret not having found you at home when I was taking testimony in Raleigh for it would have afforded me great pleasure to have explained these matters more fully to you personally.

I will only add that it will relieve my mind of some anxiety if you will be so good as to let me have your views on this subject at your earliest convenience.

A&H—GLB

Thomas J. Jarvis to W. J. Boney

Executive Department
Raleigh April 8th 1879

I have held back my answer to your letter concerning the use of convicts on the Angola Bay Canal[84] to see if the details of operation could be agreed upon by letter. I am of the opinion that it will be absolutely necessary for the Chairman or some member of your Board to come up here and have an interview with the Board of Education & the Board of Directors of the Penitentiary with a view to arranging the plan of operations. Bringing with him the map of the Survey so that the Board of Education may fully understand all the questions involved. I will further suggest that the member of your Board who comes be prepared to submit some plan for our consideration and that he have at his command all the needed information. Instead of paying landowners through whose canals we drain, damages, I think they ought to help us to cut the Canal. At least they ought to be glad to give us the right way.

UNC—MWR

Thomas J. Jarvis to Blount C. Pease[85]

Executive Department
Raleigh, April 15th 1879

.   .   .   .

And you have had another shooting in Pitt. It is getting so common to use deadly weapons for the destruction of human life that unless it is stopped no man's life will in a little while be safe. If the Courts and juries can ever be induced to do their

---

[84]See **Boney** to Jarvis, March 20, 1879, in this volume.
[85]Resident of Greenville and personal friend of Jarvis. See Jarvis to Ransom and Vance, April 14, 1879, Ransom Papers, not included.

duty it can be put an end to. After conviction and judgment I will take care of the balance and will undertake to see the r[e]igns of the law rigidly enforced.

No man in Pitt need commit crime expecting any mercy from me.

With kind regards to all. I am most truly and Sincerely Yours,

A&H—GP

Braxton Craven to Thomas J. Jarvis

President's Office, April 18 1879

Some two weeks ago, I sent a communication to the State Board of Education, through Supt. Scarborough,[86] in reference to the Normal School at Trinity.[87] I have received no reply.

If the matter has not been considered, Trinity will be greatly obliged, if you will promptly have a meeting for that purpose. I assume that the State Board will be prompt and disposed to do in this case whatever the Law either enjoins or permits. As soon as action is had in this case, I will submit an Announcement for the signature of yourself and the Supt of Pub. Instruction

A&H—GP

Braxton Craven to Thomas J. Jarvis

President's Office, April 18 1879

In accord with a sentiment you lately wrote me upon another matter,[88] I suppose Your Excellency will not only "adhere strictly to the spirit and letter of the law," but will require others to do the same.

to the spirit and letter of the law," but will require others to do

---

[86] John Catre Scarborough of Johnston County; superintendent of public instruction for North Carolina, 1877–1884; commissioner of labor statistics, 1889–1897; president of Chowan College, 1897–1909. Norman Wade Cox and Others (eds.), *Encyclopedia of Southern Baptists* (Nashville: Broadman Press, 2 volumes, 1958), II, 1,186, hereinafter cited as Cox, *Encyclopedia of Southern Baptists.*

[87] In 1879 the General Assembly authorized normal schools at Davidson, Trinity, and Wake Forest colleges. *Laws of North Carolina, 1879,* c. 226. These, plus the one at Chapel Hill, were held only during the summer months. Chaffin, *Trinity College,* 306–308.

[88] See Jarvis to Craven, February 22, 1879, in this volume.

sembly, establishing a Normal School at the University. Laws 1876–77. Page 437; and to the report of the said school in Mr Scarborough's Report, and also to the late Announcement.

The points raised are—

1. Is the teaching done and proposed to be done, according either to the "letter," or spirit of the Act?
2. Is the application of the money, according to the last part of Sec 1.
3. Are all who enter "required and expected to teach at least three years," or is Sec 3. exacted in any reasonable sense?

I do not intend any captious inquiry; but only a reasonably fair interpretation of the law.

A&H—GLB

Thomas J. Jarvis to J. B. Stewart

Executive Department
Raleigh April 19th 1879

Your letter giving a history of the litigation in Florida of the West Dv. of the Western. N.C.R.R. so far as you have been connected with the same has been received. After your account of the events & trials you have had in the conducting of the said litigation, you make these points in your letter which I will now notice.

1st you charge that the Act of the Legislature of which you complain was inspired by the Florida Conspirators as you call them. In this I know you are mistaken. Whether the legislation serves their purpose or not, it was not inspired by them. It was however expected that if you failed in your suits in Florida and nothing came of them, that you would try and cover your retreat with the Acts of the North Carolina Legislature and for this reason I am not at all surprised to hear you begin to denounce it. I can however assure you the Act will not be in the way of your success nor will it hide your failures. It was for this very reason put in the Act that it shall not go into effect until such time as I shall order I will give full time to fight it out on the line you have marked out and upon which you expect to succeed.

2nd You charge that the Act was clandestinely stolen through the Legislature. This I also know to be a mistake. It was talked of and discussed for weeks by the friends of the great work before it was passed and I think concurred in by all   Those engaged in its passages are gentlemen whatever you may say or think of them

3rd You say, you and your associates have spent out of your own money $40,000 advanced for your clients. This is so unheard of in a lawyer and so incredulous that you must excuse me when I say in this you must likewise be mistaken. So much am I impressed with the belief that you are so mistaken, that I will thank you to furnish me with an itemized statement of the amount you and your associates have paid out to whom paid & for what paid. This statement which I beg you will furnish at once I desire to lay before you, the Board of Directors of the West Dv. of the Western NC. RailRoad. It will be of great service to them in dealing with the affairs of the company and its organics & will no doubt be thankfully received.

A&H—GLB

Jarvis to George Franklin Drew[89]

[Telegram]

Raleigh May 22. 1879

I hear Littlefield is in Florida[90] probably at Jacksonville. Inquire. And if so arrest him & hold him until I can send messenger. Requisition on file in your office. Answer.

---

[89]Prominent lumberman of Jacksonville, and governor of Florida, 1876–1880. *National Cyclopedia,* XI, 381.

[90]Littlefield had spent much of the past eight years in Florida where he invested heavily and disastrously in Florida railroads. By 1879 he could hardly pay his hotel bills. Daniels, *Prince of Carpetbaggers,* 267–288, *passim.* In the fall of 1878 Governor Vance had requested Littlefield's extradition for trial on the grounds of conspiracy and embezzlement. On being informed that Littlefield had recently moved to New Jersey, Vance sought his extradition from that state, but it was denied on a technicality. Meanwhile Littlefield had moved back to Florida. Jarvis was now taking up the chase. Raleigh *Observer,* May 29, 1879.

A&H—GP

John Morehead Brower[91] *to Thomas J. Jarvis*

Mt. Airy, Surry County, N.C. May 22 1879

I learn this evening that on last night Mr R L Patterson[92] of Salem addressed a meeting in Winston in which he stated he had an interview with you in regard to the Mt Airy & Ore Knob R R & the Cape Fear and Yadkin Valley R Rs[93] coming by Winston & said he had told you it was all predjudice of our people against Winston & Salem for not coming by there and that you had said that this difficulty must & should be settled before you would consent to give our portion of the road any hands; I will say most emphatically that it is not prejudice of our people that we dont want to come by Winston, but for the following reasons 1st our people are not able nor willing to build a road for the benefit of another section when they have all to loose and nothing to gain. We are about as near Kernersville as we are Winston the distance to Winston being 42 miles and to Kernersville 45 miles[.] then when we get to Kernersville we are only 17 miles from Greensboro & very light work to do if we cant make terms with the Northwestern road[94] from Kernersville to Greensboro. and when we are at Winston we are 29 miles from Greensboro with no earthly hope of making any terms with the N.WNC road to Greensboro and 6 or 7 miles of the road between Winston & Kernersville very rough and cost as much or more than the Balance of the road from Winston to Kernersville so I am informed by men who had the road in charge while building And further Winston & Salem have made no proposition to do any-

---

[91]Planter and businessman of Mt. Airy; member of the General Assembly, 1876, 1892–1898; Republican representative in Congress, 1887–1891. *Biographical Directory of Congress,* 743. In 1879 Brown was president of the Mt. Airy Railroad Company.

[92]Rufus Lenoir Patterson, merchant and manufacturer of Salem; member of the conventions of 1861 and 1865. In 1879 he was mayor of Salem. Ashe, *Biographical History,* II, 334–344.

[93]In 1879 the General Assembly authorized the consolidation of the Western Railroad with the Mt. Airy Railroad and incorporated them as the Cape Fear and Yadkin Valley Railroad Company. The goal of this consolidation was to connect Mt. Airy with Wilmington, but by 1879 the Western had been constructed only from Fayetteville to Gulf, and the Mt. Airy Railroad Company had laid no rails. Brower was concerned about the location of the route from Gulf to the town of Mt. Airy. For the full story, see Roland B. Eutsler, "The Cape Fear and Yadkin Valley Railway," *North Carolina Historical Review,* II (October, 1925), 427–441, hereinafter cited as Eutsler, "The Cape Fear and Yadkin Valley Railway."

[94]A railroad from Greensboro to Salem, at this time being operated by the Richmond and Danville. Henry V. Poor (comp. and ed.), *Manual of the Railroads of the United States for 1876–77* (New York: H. V. & H. W. Poor, 1876), 313, hereinafter cited as Poor, *Railroad Manual.*

thing toward building the road Well I beleive [*sic*] now that in
the same talk I understand Mr Patterson asked that they vote
$15000⁰⁰ & when we get to Winston then we have a very Rough
country this side of Winston for several miles. now is there any
justice, in Winston saying that we should spend our money to
accomodate them when they are able to pay $100⁰⁰ to where
we are able to pay one & refuse to do anything. I think you will
say there is none I tell you Winston has all they want & they
dont [want] a road built to this country [.] they have fought this
section for years, to keep us out of a road but if one is to be
built they want it but dont want to help do it. from Kernersville
within 20 miles of Mt Airy we run on the ridge that divides
the waters of Dan River & the Yadkin & cross but one branch
in the whole 25 miles & it will not cost $500 dollars a mile to
Grade it with hired labor & we have only limited means & we
want to build our road the most practable & most direct route to
Fayeteville Winston wants our back country here to keep them
up[.] we have built them & are keeping them up still & all they
want is to keep us out of the road. Now I will give you a short
history of their proceedings & manouverings towards our section[.] in the first place the Northwestern N C Road was chartered to this place with $20000 per mile of State bonds which
could have been sold at one time for 76¢ in the dollar[.] the
Winston Salem people made up the subscription required and
organized the company and went [to] work[.] we went to the
President with a subscription from here begged him to survey
the road & agreed to pay for the survey & begged him to sell the
bonds & go to work all along the line but it was never done and
by holding back to keep us out of the road they didnt realize anything on the bonds & had to as you are aware turn them all back
into the Treasury & give their road to a foreign company to
compleet it[.] we the[n] procured a charter for a narrow guage
road from here to some point on the N C road[.] we asked them
to help us[.] they never would subscribe a cent & said the road
would not be built &c. & done evrything to obstruct us as they
are doing now, in 1877 we asked Surry County to subscribe fifty
thousand dollars to the capital stock of our road. here we had
Winston & Salem to fight Some of the citizens of Winston came
here & took the stump against the subscription & defeated it,
again last May I went to Raleigh & had 50 hand assigned to our
road[,] had money sufficient to work them together with an
additional 50 the board had promised us[.] we were going to

commence at Kernersville for the reason we could get help there
& could build the road much cheaper on that line[.] Winston
were on hand again[.] they sent a delegation here immediately
& made a proposition to our people that if we would hold off for
a few weeks or untill after the 17th of June they would call a
meeting & invite our people down there & they were authorized
to say Winston would give at least $20 000 to our road & we
must start from that point. Some of our people thought as the
committee sent felt so sanguine of the earnestness of Winston &
Salem, that we had best wait but have never had the invitation
yet & never heard from them any more only of their making
their brags they had stopped the work on the road. Then again
wehen [sic] we went to Fayetville on the 4 of April for the
purpose of consolidation [,]a portion of our delegation went by
Winston & Salem to see what they would do[.]they would not
talk to us about it at all[.]said there would be no consolidation
&c but now since they have learned that there is a certainty of
the road being built they are using evry effort against it they
can to stop the work[.]our people are in earnest about this
road[.]we went to Fayetville for the purpose of making proposition of consolidation we agreed on terms came home and asked
our township to take $20 000⁰⁰ which she did last thursday by
the folowing vote 401 votes for taking the stock and only 57
against it[.]so you see how unanimous our people are. We have
now sent twenty thousand dollars to the President to compleet
the terms of consolidation which reached him today or ought
to have done so[.]and now Governor we ask that you turn over
the hands to us & give us all the aid you can & not to throw any
obstacle in the way of the progress of the only State enterprize
in the State. I was the first President of the Mt Airy road &
have been evry year except one since the company was organized
& I know what the Winston people are driving at & I have just
submited the facts of the case to you. Col Alspaugh[95] & Maj
Brown[96] were the gentlemen sent to us last may who afterwards
said they had stopped the work on our road Governor I will
submit the whol thing to you & hope you will consider it & I
ask you is it right or just that all of northwestern N C should

[95]John Wesley Alspaugh of Winston. First a lawyer, then editor of the
Western Sentinel, Alspaugh in 1876 organized the First National Bank of
Winston and became its cashier and then its president. Ashe, *Biographical
History*, VIII, 1–6.
[96]John Lewis Brown, merchant of Charlotte; member of the General
Assembly, 1879. In 1879 he was a director of the Western North Carolina
Railroad. *Cyclopedia of the Carolinas*, II, 533–536.

be kept from having Railroad facilities because one town wishes it should be otherwise for the only reason of their own Self interest I hope you will give me your views fully in regard to this matter

Thomas J. Jarvis to K. P. Battle

Executive Department
Raleigh, May 23rd 1879

I wish you to write to the R.R. Coms.[97] and make terms for the Normal. I will help you all I can, and will see Andrews[98] in person. If there is anything special you wish me to do let me know and I will back you all I can.

.   .   .   .

Thomas J. Jarvis to K. P. Battle

Executive Department
Raleigh, May 27th 1879

A mass of letters accumulated in my absence on the Western R R. and at the Charlotte celebration caused me to overlook yours of the 22d.[99]

The best I can say to you about drawing the funds for the Normal is to do as you desire—draw it as you need it or in bulk.

I thank you for the assurance that my action in the case of the Chapel Hill Burg:was approved by the *good* people.[100]

I knew nothing of their denial till I saw it published, But the

---

[97]This is one of many instances in which Jarvis sought to obtain special passenger rates for worthy causes.

[98] Alexander Boyd Andrews, prominent railroad builder and operator. At this time he was superintendent and vice–president of the Richmond and Danville Railroad. His main accomplishment in North Carolina railroad development was his role in extending the Western North Carolina Railroad to the western border of the state. *Dictionary of American Biography,* I, 282.

[99]Not found.

[100]During 1878 and 1879, Chapel Hill had been terrorized by a series of daring burglaries. Finally the guilty parties were captured and three of them were sentenced to hang. Jarvis had refused to pardon them or to commute their sentences. For a full account, see Battle, *History of the University,* II, 150–151.

fact that they denied on the verge of the grave gave me no concern. It is the history of four fifths of those who die upon the gallows.

G. F. Drew to Thomas J. Jarvis

[Telegram—not dated]

Your man has been arrested in Jacksonville, and awaits your wishes.[101]

A&H—GP

G. F. Drew to Thomas J. Jarvis

[Telegram]

Tallahassee Fla 8[50] p May 27 1879

I will have him there[102]

A&H—GP

J. W. Lee[103] to Thomas J. Jarvis

[Telegram]

Jacksonville, May 29 [1879]

Arrived here, arrested Littlefield, have him in jail. Is trying to get a writ of habeas corpus. Must I employ counsel?[104]

---

[101]Littlefield had been arrested in Florida in compliance with a requisition for extradition by Governor Jarvis. See Jarvis to Drew, May 22, 1879, *n.* 90 in this volume. An official copy of this telegram has not been found. The version included was taken from the *Raleigh News* and printed in the *Morning Star* of May 31, 1879.

[102]Jarvis had apparently asked Governor Drew to have Littlefield at the latter's trial, which was scheduled for May 30.

[103]Chief of police of Raleigh, who had been armed, equipped with the necessary papers, and sent to Florida to bring Littlefield back. *Morning Star*, May 31, 1879.

[104]In response to this telegram, Jarvis telegraphed Drew to arrange counsel for Lee. Raleigh *Observer*, May 30, 1879.

J. W. Lee to Thomas J. Jarvis

[*Telegram*]

Jacksonville [May 29, 1879]

Is the bill of indictment published in The Observer a true copy? Criminal Court, November Term, 1878. Answer immediately.[105]

J. W. Lee to Thomas J. Jarvis

[*Telegram*]

[May 29, 1879]

He has sued out a writ of *habeas corpus.* Will try it at 5 o'clock.[106]

A&H—GP

J. W. Lee to Thomas J. Jarvis

[*Telegram*]

Jacksonville Fla, 9 40 am, May 30 1879

If the Case goes against us this morning we will take an appeal to the supreme Court which Convenes Tuesday week if not directed to the Contrary.

A&H—GLB

Thomas J. Jarvis to J. W. Lee

[*Telegram*]

Raleigh May. 30 1879

If the Judge decides against us appeal   Have Judge Baker[107] or some other good lawyer to take charge of the case

---

[105]This telegram has been found only in the Raleigh *Observer,* May 30, 1879. Jarvis answered Lee's question in the affirmative. Raleigh *Observer,* May 30, 1879.

[106]This telegram has been found only in the Raleigh *Observer,* May 30, 1879.

[107]Probably James McNair Baker, lawyer of Jacksonville; member of the Confederate Congress, 1862–1865; Florida Supreme Court justice, 1866–1868. *National Cyclopedia,* V, 88.

A&H—GP

J. W. Lee to Thomas J. Jarvis

[Telegram]

Jacksonville Fla, 405, May 31 1879

Think State authorities is all right.

A&H—GLB

Thomas J. Jarvis to J. W. Lee

[Telegram]

May 31, 1879. Raleigh NC.

Push the case to extremities. Say to the Attorneys to leave nothing undone. Keep me informed.

A&H—GP

J. W. Lee to Thomas J. Jarvis

[Telegram]

Jacksonville Fla, 406 PM, May 31 1879

Archibald[108] Judge Thompson & Hartridge[109] atty s point raised flaw in indictment. Statute limitations argument pending on our demurrer to Littlefields traverse of sheriffs return appeal in any event I leave for home this evening.

A&H—GP

J. W. Lee to Thomas J. Jarvis

[Telegram]

Jacksonville Fla [May] 31 1879
Received at Ral N C 5 45

Our case is postponed until monday Judge is very sick

---

[108]Robert Burns Archibald of Jacksonville, Florida. In 1868 his parents immigrated from Scotland to Illinois. In 1868 he received his law degree from the University of Michigan, and a year later he opened a law office in Jacksonville. He was a prominent and active citizen there, and from 1873 to 1875 was judge of the Fourth Judicial Court of Florida. Pleasant D. Gold, *History of Duval County, Florida* (St. Augustine, Florida: The Record Company, 1928), 359, hereinafter cited as Gold, *History of Duval County.*

[109]E. W. Thompson and John E. Hartridge were Jacksonville lawyers employed by J. W. Lee to secure Littlefield's extradition.

A&H—GP

J. B. Stewart to Thomas J. Jarvis

Jacksonville, Fla., May 31ˢᵗ, 1879.

This will be handed you by your messengers sent for the body of M. S. Littlefield. These gentlemen arrived here just at heel of the abatement of the Suits of W.D. Co. because of the Repealing act of the 13ᵗʰ of March, forcing me to review under many disadvantages.[110] And added to this the assertion made current about the Commencement of the trial two of my most material witnesses were to be tried upon an indictment charging fraud in the creation of the W.D. Co., and that the latter was under requisition from your state for the offense charged.

Being forced to trial under these circumstances I fully realized the disadvantage, and the arrival of your messenger for the body of Littlefield pending the hearing of the case fully confirmed all that had been said, and has evidently had its worst effects on the result.

The decision of the Court has just been rendered adverse to the N.C. Co's interests. The decision fully concedes that we had shown by the proofs that the N.C. Co's money purchased the roads, and its right legal and equitable therein was fully declared; but that in consequence of the acts of the Legislature of N.C. creating the Woodfin Com.[111] in March, 1870, & in consequence of the agreement of said Com. of the 16 April 1 1870, in their settlement with Swepson & Littlefield in the city of Washington, and their agreement to participate in the proceeds of the Fla. State Bonds, and also in consequence of the acts of Mr. Woodfin as chairman of said Com. in London, in 1870, coupled with the former repeal of the Charter of the W.D. giving said Com exclusive power to act, the Company had become estopped from denying the prior equity of the Holders of the Fla. State bonds, though admitted and adjudged to be unconstitutional and void.

Or in other words, the court has decided that the admitted and well defined equities of the N.C. Co. had been destroyed or lost in consideration of a void bond issued under a statute declared

---

[110] See Stewart to Jarvis, April 7, 1879, *n.* 79, in this volume.

[111] Nicholas W. Woodfin was chairman of a commission appointed by the General Assembly to regain the funds fraudulently obtained by Swepson and Littlefield during their venture in North Carolina railroad construction. For the activities of the Woodfin Commission, see Brown, "Florida Investments of Swepson," 279–289. The five reports of the Commission are in the North Carolina *Public Documents, 1870–1873.*

unconstitutional. This is, in substance the decree agai.
the ground of the decree, wherein we have been defeate
send you a copy of the opinion upon which the decree is f\
as soon as I can obtain one.

I do not believe this decree will stand the test of review
reasons too numerous to mention, and I have therefore pray
and appeal on the part of the N.C. Co, & both the F.C.&J.P.&
M.Cos have done the like. To make this appeal effective a large
Bond has to be given, which will require prompt and efficient
action, and a resort to responsibility beyond what can be availed
of either in Fla. or N.C. so far as I am at present advised. But
guarding against such a possibility, before I left N.Y. such arrangements were made as will require my early presence there,
and will also require the presence of M. S. Littlefield, as Pres.
of the J.P.&M.Co. to sign and execute the proper papers, as it is
not possible for me to get along without it, because, being President, and in existence no one can substitute him in the executing of said papers. Besides this the arrangements I made in
N.Y. included his personal participation and arrangement which
I cannot alter, or substitute, in the short time which I have to
give an appeal bond.

I therefore send you this advise [*sic*] of the situation of the
interests of N.C. as involved in these suits, and to inform you of
what is necessary to be done to protect an appeal, which I feel
well assured will result in a reversal of the decree rendered
against us, and cause the ordering of one to be entered in favor
of the N.C.Co., & to suggest to you as counsel, the importance
and absolute necessity of withdrawing the proceedings against
Littlefield so that I can immediately avail myself of his assistance in N.Y. in the very important matters above stated, &
hope you will be so good as to advise me of your conclusion in
this matter by telegraph upon the receipt of this letter.

A&H—GP

E. W. Thompson to Thomas J. Jarvis

Jacksonville Fla
2 June 1879

I sent to MrJW. Lee on yesterday, for your information, a
statement of all that had transpired in the matter of Littlefields
extradition—This morning the argument on our Demurrer to

their Traverse of the Sheriff's Return was contravened— Mr Jno. T. Walker for Littlefield— The points he undertook to make were that the Court must inquire beyond Gov Drews Warrant, and determine the questions as to whether the indictment charges an offense, whether it is barred by the No. Ca statute of limitations, and whether there is sufficient evidence that Littlefield is a fugitive from your State—. There was nothing in his positions, his arguments or his authorities and only one case was cited which even partially sustained the view that the Court must look beyond the Warrant—that was a case reported in the Albany Law Journal of a decision by Judge Wythe of the US. Dist. Ct. Southern Dist Michigan— The overwhelming array of authority is undoubtedly with us and in my reply to Mr Walker I undertook to emphasize the authorities I had before produced and which decided the questions of law raised by the Demurrer in direct and emphatic language, as precise and positive as possible— I also directed the Judges attention to the principles, which control the exercise of the Constitutional power to demand the extradition of fugitives, laid down in the case of Dennison 24 Howard— That was an application to the Supreme Court (US) to Mandamus the Governor of Ohio to remand a fugitive on the requisition of the Governor of Kentucky. The Court denied the application, on the ground that it had no power to enforce the Writ of Mandamus against the Chief Executive of a State, but the opinion discusses the whole subject in its Constitutional and legal aspects and if this Judge decides in conformity to the principles announced, he must remand the prisoner— The matter has been taken under advisement and we will have a decision on tomorrow morning. If it is unfavorable we shall give issue, go to trial on the issue of fact and if judgment is rendered against us, take the Writ of Error—

During Mr Walker['s] argument he took occasion to refer to the Revised Statutes of No. Ca. published in 1855 to show that the offense of Littlefield was a misdemeanor and barred by the Statute. He referred to Mr Badgers[112] statement that the Statute read was still in force, quoting him as authority & stating that he was a high toned, honorable lawyer who would not mislead the Court by a false statement. While he was speaking I received your telegram of today, whereupon I exhibited it to the Judge

---

[112]Probably Richard Cogsdell Badger, lawyer of Raleigh. Grant, *Alumni History of the University*, 26.

and upon its authority denied the truth of Mr Badgers statement. I very much regret that the books you refer to are not to be had here—

In respect to the future conduct of this matter, I recommend that if Archibald overrules the Demurrer, and judgment is rendered against us that we go to the Supreme Court If they hold that any defects exist in the pending Requisition or in Gov. Drews Warrant, they can be readily reminded by a new Requisition— If they decide for us and I can not believe that they will do otherwise the matter will be at an end and Littlefield can be forwarded at once I do not think there is any danger of his escaping from the State in case he is released by Judge Archibald— He has little or no money and no prospects of any thing from the Railroad litigation—for some time— He can manage to live here and he can not elsewhere— It would be well in case a new Requisition becomes necessary, to have the Warrant send in amnesty lawsuit say at Live Oak, the junction of the J.P.M& Savannah Railroads— Had that course been followed in this instance there would have been no difficulty— L frequently passes Live Oak, and it is a matter of no difficulty for the Sheriff of that County (Suwannee) to arrest him, turn him over to your agent and have him conveyed into Georgia within a few hours— Besides the Judge of that Circuit is an upright and able man and would make no difficulties about his rendition— My only apprehensions about the decision of Archibald are attributable to the fact that he is a Republican & a bitter party man— Do not understand however that he has said or done any thing to indicate what his decision will be— He has listened patiently and attentively to the whole argument and appears inclined to do justice. Will keep you advised of all that occurs—

A&H—GP

John Hughes to Thomas J. Jarvis

Newbern, N.C., June 2nd 1879.

Since seeing you, I am in receipt of information that someone has said to you that it was impossible to ascertain the *true* condition of this Company because the report of the Finance Committee for last year has not been published. It is true that none has been published, the reason being that we had no meeting of the stockholders and consequently no order for publication was made. but the report[113] has been constantly on file subject to the inspection of any stockholder— I send a manuscript copy for your inspection and I know that it cannot fail to be satisfactory

P.S. There is a long list of enclosures acompanying this report which I do not send as I presume they would not prove interesting to you, but I will send them if you desire to see them

A&H—GLB

Thomas J. Jarvis to J. M. Brower

Executive Department
Raleigh N.C. June 5 1879

Your communication of the 22nd was received yesterday and least I may be misunderstood I hasten to reply.

Col Patterson, Mr Mathes[114] & Mr Buxton[115] came to see me in the interest of the line the disent adopted. They represented to me that it was a fight between Greensboro & Winston—that Greensboro had been injured by the Road to Winston and that the Greensboro people now desired to injure Winston in turn by cutting it off My reply to them was that I did not propose to take any part in the fight between sections. If Greensboro or Winston wanted to build a road with their own money, that they could build it whenever they desired & which town was benefited or which hurt was a matter that did not concern me. But since the State was building it, that I desired to see the Road located where the greatest benefit would be given to the greatest number, and where the Road would be most likely to pay. This I said then and I now repeat it to you. I have no prejudice for or against any line or route or any town or community. I am a friend to the great enterprize and intend to help it all I can upon the principles I have laid down. I do not intend to take any part in any local quarrels, nor do I intend for the labor & money of the State to be used for any such purpose, if I can

---

[113]The report referred to is the June 26, 1878, report of the finance committee of the stockholders of the Atlantic and North Carolina Railroad. Governors' Papers, not included.

[114]Probably George M. Mathes of Winston, editor of the *Western Sentinel*, a weekly Democratic newspaper. Adelaide Fries and Others, *Forsyth, A County on the March* (Chapel Hill: University of North Carolina Press, 1949), 88, hereinafter cited as Fries, *Forsyth County*.

[115]Probably John Cameron Buxton, lawyer of Winston and later its mayor. Fries, *Forsyth County*, 76, 82.

help it. What line will give the North Western section the greatest good & at the same time give the State the best paying road is a matter about which I am not now fully informed. When I became satisfied where that route is, that will be the line I shall favor for the C.F.&Y.V.R.R. regardless of what particular locality is benefitted or not. As to the convicts, it is not a question whether *I* will or will not furnish them. The *law* has directed their distribution & that will be the guide.[116] I assure you, that all the authority conferred upon me will be used to push forward work on the C.F.&YV RailRoad.

A&H—GP

G. F. Drew to Thomas J. Jarvis

Executive Office,
Tallahassee, Fla., June 6th 1879

In accordance with your request by Telegraph of the 3d Inst,[117] I have caused a careful search to be made for the requisitions made upon my predecessors for Littlefield and can find no such documents the only paper I can find that relates in any way to the extradition of Littlefield is a Long Lecture from Gov Caldwell to Gov Hart[118] as to his duty about giving up Littlefield to the authorities of North Carolina. If you will issue another requisition for Littlefield and cause certified copies of those indictments upon which the original Requisitions were based, to be attached to Your requisition I will submit the papers to Attorney General Raney[119] and if there is no prospect of Judge Archibald being able to find some flaw in them I will issue my warrant at once and hope it will result in more good to our respective states than the former papers did—

---

[116]The allocation of convicts for work on internal improvements was to become a major problem for Jarvis' administration. Usually whenever the General Assembly granted a charter to an internal improvement corporation, the charter included a promise of a certain number of convicts for use in the heavy construction work. Generally, however, the number of able-bodied convicts was insufficient for the demand, and Jarvis was forced to decide which projects deserved the available convicts.

[117]Not found.

[118]Ossian Bingley Hart, governor of Florida, 1873–1874. *National Cyclopedia*, II, 380–381.

[119]George Pettus Raney. A native of Apalachicola, Raney studied law at the University of Virginia and returned home to practice. He served as attorney general of Florida for eight years. Rowland H. Rerick, *Memoirs of Florida* (Atlanta, Georgia: Southern Historical Association, 2 volumes, 1902), II, 103, hereinafter cited as Rerick, *Memoirs of Florida*.

A&H—GLB

Thomas J. Jarvis to Roger P. Atkinson[120]

Executive Department
Raleigh. N.C. June 9th 1879

In reply to yours of the 6th [121] I will say it is my desire & the order of the Board of Internal Improvements, that you proceed at once or as soon as the nature of the case will admit, to consolidate the convict force on the W.N.C.R.R. so as to save all you can consistent with a proper prosecution of the work. Retain the best men as Stewards & Overseers & Guards without any regard as to who they are or from what section they come. As soon as the consolidation is made report to us what persons have been discharged & what ones retained. Keep no man in the public service who is not absolutely needed, and who fails to do his full duty. We hold you responsible for those under you and you may therefore rely upon our support

A&H—GLB

Thomas J. Jarvis to G. F. Drew

Executive Department
Raleigh—N.C. June 10th 1879

I am having prepared certified copies of a half dozzen Indictments against Littlefield ranging as to time from 1870 to 1878 upon which to base my Requisition. I will send also proof of at least a dozzen Requisitions made for Littlefield also ranging from 1870 to 1879. I will also furnish ample proof that he *is* a refugee from justice.[122] In fact I will make the case so plain that I believe even Judge Archibald will be obliged to yield. I am anxious to get Littlefield and have him tried. His plunder in the State the two years he cursed it with his presence is without a parallel except it may be the doings of some of his fellow thieves in South Carolina. His protestations of injured innocence is all a

---

[120]Civil engineer of Greensboro and supervisor of convicts assigned to work on the Western North Carolina Railroad. *Public Documents, 1879,* No. 27, *passim.* In 1881 he resigned after being accused of allowing scurvy to break out among his convicts. He then became chief engineer of the Cape Fear and Yadkin Valley Railroad. *News and Observer,* September 2, 1881.

[121]Not found.

[122]See Jarvis to Drew, May 22, 1879, *n.* 90, and Drew to Jarvis, June 6, 1879, in this volume.

sham and his statement that he has the permission of the Gov
of N.C. to pass through this State a false hood.[123]

I beg to thank you, my Dear Gov, for your prompt response
to my Requisition and to assure you of my appreciation of any
further assistance you may render me in bringing this man to
trial With high regard and the hope of knowing you personally.

A&H—GP

Hartridge and Calhoon to Thomas J. Jarvis

Jacksonville, Fla. 11th June 1879

Our firm was associated with Mr. E. W. Thompson of this city
in the representation of the state of North Carolina in the matter
of the Littlefield habeus corpus case. We arranged with the agent
of North Carolina for a fee of $100—for Mr. Thompson and our
firm. This amount has not been remitted as yet. We would be
obliged if your Excellency would give the matter your early
attention.

A&H—GP

George Washington McCrary[124] to Thomas J. Jarvis

War Department
Washington City
June 25th 1879

Your letter of the 16th instant,[125] requesting the use of the
Barracks at Fort Macon, Georgia, for the 1st North Carolina
State Guard during their encampment in August next, has been
received, and, in reply, I beg to inform you that in consequence
of the bad condition in which the buildings were left by the
State Militia who occupied it in 1877, the Department feels compelled to decline the request.

---

[123]For an explanation of why Littlefield wished to go to New York, see
Stewart to Jarvis, June 28, 1879, in this volume.
[124]Jurist, congressman, and secretary of war from 1877 to 1879. *Dictionary
of American Biography*, XII, 2–3.
[125]Jarvis to McCrary, June 16, 1879, Governors' Papers, not included.

A&H—GP

[*Endorsement*]

Z. B. Vance to Thomas J. Jarvis

Washington, July 1st

I have seen the Sec: of War relative to the enclosed matter, and he has consented to reconsider his decision. If you will become personally responsible for the property I think there will be no doubt of acquiescence in your request.

A&H—GP

[*Notice of Public Auction*]

Notice!   Notice!

By virtue of certain Ven Ex's in my hand for collection against the Roanoke Navigation Company I shall on the 4th day of August 1879 it being the first Monday in said month expose to the highest bidder for cash at the Court House door in the town of Halifax the following real estate belonging to said Roanoke Navigation company, to wit, the real property of said Company lying in the town of Weldon along its canal bed, in and along and on both sides of its said canal from Rock Landing on the south side of Roanoke River to the terminus of said canal near and below the town of Weldon; also the short canal on which J. W. Whites mill is located including and embracing the real estate in and along and on both sides said last mentioned canal, All of the above real estate situate in Halifax County, to satisfy said Ven Ex., This 28th June 1879

J. T. Dawson, Shff.
T. H. Dickens D S

[*Endorsement*]

Raleigh N.C.
July. 3ʳ 1879

Referred to Col Thoˢ S. Kenan[126] Atty General with a request that he investigate the case at an early day and report what can be done, if anything, to protect the interest of the State[127]

Thoˢ. J. Jarvis
Gov

A&H—GP

J. B. Stewart to Thomas J. Jarvis

Jacksonville Fla June 28ᵗʰ 1879

Mr Wᵐ T. Dorch[128] who was appointed by yourself or the Directors of the Western NC.RRCo to visit Florida and examine the situation of the suits against the Florida Railroads and others and the records of the court as to my proceedings therein as solicitor[129] has performed that duty and has recommended the signing of the appeal Bond[130] by the Western N.C.Co the new complainants in the suits. While it is by no means pleasant to an attorney who feels concious of having done his full duty to be subjected to such supervision, it at the same time affords me pleasure to be able to thank yourself and the directors for having sent both a gentleman and a jurist so thoroughly capable to discharge the duties imposed upon him as Mr Dorch, with whom I found it pleasant and instructive to communicate. But the signing of the Bond by the Western Co only goes so far as to

---

[126]Thomas Stephen Kenan, lawyer of Wilson; member of the General Assembly, 1865–1867; attorney general, 1876–1885; clerk of the Supreme Court, 1876–1912. Ashe, *Biographical History*, III, 248–252.

[127]For an explanation of the state's interest in this sale, see Kenan to Jarvis, July 16, 1879, in this volume.

[128]William Theophilus Dortch, lawyer of Goldsboro; member of the General Assembly, 1852–1861, 1879–1883; member of the Confederate Congress, 1862–1865. Jerome Dowd, *Sketches of Prominent Living North Carolinians* (Raleigh: Edwards & Broughton, 1888), 120–121, hereinafter cited as Dowd, *Sketches of North Carolinians*.

[129]See Stewart to Jarvis, April 7, 1879.

[130]The United States Circuit Court in Florida held that the Western Division of the Western North Carolina Railroad had not held a first lien on the bonds of the Jacksonville, Pensacola and Mobile Railroad. The Western North Carolina Railroad then decided to appeal the case to the Supreme Court. Brown, "Florida Investments of Swepson," 286–287. See also Stewart to Jarvis, April 7, 1879, in this volume.

put the bond in a legal form to be signed by the sureties and then be supported by the auxiliary bond of the two Companies, that is the Florida Central of which E M L'Engle[131] is President and the Jacksonville Pensacola & Mobile Co of which M S. Littlefield is President.

Now as my sureties all reside in New York being persons connected with Railroads and transportation business, the further Execution of the appeal Bond or other bonds must of course take place in New York when the Bondsmen must be qualified as it is impossible to have them come to Florida. This of course will require the presence of both Mr L'Engle and Mr Littlefield in New York. Mr. L'Engle has now gone but Mr Littlefield declines to go unless I can assure him that he will be exempt from Molestation while doing so on the part of the authorities of North Carolina. I therefore ask you to be so good as to favor me with this assurance for such time at least as I shall require the presence and assistance of Mr Littlefield in New York in completing the appeal Bond and signing such papers as the law requires and which he alone can sign as President of such Company. This I beg to say is a very important business matter involving a very large interest to your State and people which [I] feel assured can be secured if the appeal is promptly prosecuted. But you must observe that waiting to get the signature of the Western Co has consumed half my time and I have now got to be very vigilant in order to do all that is necessary to be done so as to perfect our appeal within the time prescribed by law.

I hope therefore you will see the importance of my request and will advise me that pending the time I require the services and assistance of Mr Littlefield in New York that I can assure him he will not be molested by further proceedings 'til after such time as I advise him he is no longer there at my request which I will do as soon as that time arrives.

Your prompt attention to this matter will not only serve an important interest to your state and people but greatly oblige

---

[131]Edward McCrady L'Engle, wealthy lawyer of Jacksonville, Florida. Daniels, *Prince of Carpetbaggers*, 216.

A&H—GP

W. G. Curtis to Thomas J. Jarvis

Office of Quarantine Physician
Smithville June 30th 1879

I have the honor to report, that the health of the Port of Wilmington continues excellent so far as it is affected by commercial intercourse with foreign nations

Contrary to my expectation, a good many vessels have come to the port, which required inspection, and it has been necessary to detain several, on compliance with the ordinance of the city of Wilmington—I am able to state that no vessel has yet arrived in which there was any danger, but the city ordinance being arbitrary, there was no discretion allowed, and these vessels, although from healthy ports, and in remarkably good sanitary condition, had to be excluded— I beg to be allowed to state to your Excellency that my position is one of extreme difficulty— While I desire as a matter of first importance to preserve the health of the city, and recognize the fact that no private interest should be allowed to imperil the health of our people, still I am inclined to deal out justice to all concerned, and to inflict as little injury as possible to the commercial growth of Wilmington— Hence it is nearly if not quite impossible to satisfy the varied interests involved in the enforcement of quarantine, under the present regulations—

Your Excellency, having a deep interest in the welfare of North Carolina and in common with a large number of our most intelligent citizens desiring that the Port of Wilmington should attain a position of first rate importance among the cities of the Atlantic coast, must naturally desire that while the risks of disease should be reduced to a minimum, the obstructions should also not be greater than is absolutely necessary, and this is the position I endeavor to maintain—

Having had a good deal of experience during the last thirty years in quarantine matters I feel prepared to say that with a judicious system, there need be no danger to the city of Wilmington— With the present system I can also say there is little danger, although it is rather hard upon commerce

I hope that my efforts to maintain an efficient quarantine will meet your Excellency s approval, and I beg leave to subscribe myself

A&H—GP

James W. Wilson[132] *to Thomas J. Jarvis* [*with enclosure*]

Morganton Ju[ly] 2nd 1879

I enclose a letter from Stewart which explains itself. T. B. Long[133] whom you no doubt know was also to see me with messages from Littlefield to the effect that Stewart cld. accomplish nothing in the suit without his (Littlefields) assistance and that he was tired being hunted down and if prosecutions w[d] be stopped he could get a compromise giving us 75 or $100 000.[134] I mention these facts Gov[r] with no wish to urge you to any such course, but to give you all the facts in my possession. How far Littlefield could be of service to us we will never be able to find out until he is put upon the stand as he openly proclaims that he expects to be paid.

He & Stewart are I am satisfied in full accord. Mr Dortch advised signing the bond which I have done, I hope it is right but I have my misgivings in regard to it.

[*enclosure*]

J. B. Stewart to J. W. Wilson

Jacksonville, Florida June 28, 1879

Your director, Hon. W. T. Dorch has been here and examined what I have done in the prosecution of the suits for your company and recommends the appeal which ought to have been perfected before now.

I enclose you herewith a copy of a letter which I have just addressed to Gov. Jarvis[135] and in the requirements of which I hope you will render me all the assistance in your power. The time being now half expired, it is absolutely indispensable that I should have the presence of Mr Littlefield in N. York and he

---

[132]Businessman of Morganton, who had worked for the Western North Carolina Railroad since his youth and who was now its president. At this time he was chairman of the Burke County Democratic Executive Committee. A. Davis Smith & Company (Pub.), *Western North Carolina, Historical and Biographical* (Raleigh: Edwards & Broughton, 1890), 262–266, hereinafter cited as Smith, *Western North Carolina.*

[133]Thomas B. Long of Rowan County, special agent for the Post Office Department. In 1880 Long became postal inspector for the Atlantic and Gulf Coast states. James S. Brawley, *The Rowan Story, 1753–1953* (Salisbury: Rowan Printing Company, 1953), 212–213, hereinafter cited as Brawley, *The Rowan Story.*

[134]See Stewart to Jarvis, April 7, 1879, *n.* 81, in this volume.

[135]See Stewart to Jarvis, June 28, 1879, in this volume.

positively refuses to go unless I get the assurance from the Governor asked in my letter and pay his personal expenses there and back.

The latter I will do but the former depends upon the action of the Governor, & I hope you will be good as to unite with me in procuring the assurance from the Governor I have asked.

I feel sure I will reverse this decree and decision of the Court which was evidently the result of prejudice engendered by surrounding circumstances & that I will receive on appeal the relief prayed for in our bill. But the appeal must be taken, & to do which there is no time to be lost, as you are well aware, it requires time & details to perfect appeal bonds for such large amounts and I hope therefore, you will aid me in this matter all in your power

The truth is, I, and the lawyers here all believe that the matter as to Littlefield's extradition is in fact *res adjudicata* & than [*sic*] no court in any state would refuse to discharge him upon habeas corpus while the late decision of a court of competent jurisdiction remains in full force & unreversed. But Mr Littlefield feels that he might be annoyed, & hence I am burdened with the necessity of seeking to remove his objections which I don't think at all unreasonable under the circumstances. Please give me all the assistance you can in this matter & oblige.

A&H—GP

E. W. Thompson to Thomas J. Jarvis

Jacksonville Fla
4 July 1879

Your favor of 30 ult reached me on yesterday and I at once called on Mr Bowden Sheriff of this County and engaged his services to execute the plan you suggest:

L. [ittlefield] lives at the Grand National Hotel which is located about 75 yards from the RR Depot. He usually dines at 3 to 4 P.M. and is at the Depot almost always when the train Departs— It would be a very easy matter at all events to secure his attendance there on the train leaving time, which is 5^{10} P.M. I proposed to Bowden that he should bring with him a capable assistant, arrest and secure Mr L. take the train and depart. There could be no danger of Habeas Corpus after the train left here as it makes no delay beyond a few minutes at any place in Florida— Anticipating however that his friends at this place, hearing of his arrest might telegraph to Savannah to some attorney there to have Habeas Corpus proceedings in readiness when the train should arrive there next morning, at 9 oclock, I suggested that Bowden should leave the train, with his prisoner at Live Oak, the junction of the A&G. & Florida Railroads, go down to Albany, thence to Macon & Atlanta and thence by the Air Line route to North Carolina— This would throw his friends off the scent, and he would probably be in your State, before they ascertained the route Bowden had taken— This plan I am fully satisfied will succeed—as L. is apparently unapprehensive of danger. I know his habits and associations and am posted respecting his daily movements.

Mr. Bowden may be fully relied on. I have known him for many years and he is a man of the highest character— He only requires that I shall assure him *professionally*, that the Extradation [*sic*] Papers and our Governors Warranty are made out in due form of law. He is brave, resolute and energetic. L. knows him and neither he nor his friends would undertake to resist Bowden— In short the plan can be executed as easily as netting a partridge—

If you wish this done, write to me at once. I can meet your agent in Tallahassee, and see that Gov— Drews Warrant is properly executed— I can then bring the papers here deliver Gov. Drews Warrant to Bowden and have the plan executed at once under my personal supervision— Of course it would be necessary for you to designate Bowden as your agent and for this purpose I give you his name in full—Uriah Bowden—

In case there should be any miscarriage (which is scarcely possible) and a Habeas Corpus should be taken before Archibald I think then there would be no difficulty, in case the papers are drawn in conformity to the act of Congress —

Bowden's expenses would probably be say $150 or $200— which sum you can remit to him, by express or New York Exchange— In case he succeeds in carrying L. to Raleigh you & he can settle the matter of his compensation there, and he can account to you for his expenditures—

I confess that I feel great interest in this matter and shall at all times be ready to respond to your orders. I trust you will fall in with this plan, as I assure you it is easy of execution in the hands of a resolute man like Bowden[136]

---

[136]This plan to arrest Littlefield and hurry him out of Florida before he could obtain a writ of habeas corpus was foiled when one of Littlefield's

UNC—UP

Thomas J. Jarvis to K. P. Battle

Executive Department
Raleigh, July 9th 1879

While I know of no important business to come before the Bd. of Agriculture yet I think it important that a meeting be held. While these attacks upon the Department are going on[137] I think unwise for the Bd to seem to be flagging in interest as will be the case if we do not meet. It may furnish Clark[138] & Tourgee[139] subject matter for an article on "Military Agriculture."[140]

I therefore hope you will be here on Tuesday if it is only to come in the morning and go back in the afternoon

I will try to be with you at the close of the Normal.

A&H—GP

Thomas P. Devereux[141] to Thomas J. Jarvis

[Telegram]

Savannah Ga, 11 40 am, July 11 1879

Have heard from T[hompson] Will arrive in morning

---

friends in North Carolina telegraphed him word of the plot. Consequently, when Jarvis' agent, Thomas P. Devereux, arrived in Florida with the necessary papers for Littlefield's arrest, the latter had prepared his plans for resisting this new attempt to return him to North Carolina. *Morning Star*, July 17, 1879, quoting the *Raleigh News* of July 13.

[137]At this time the Department of Agriculture was being criticized as not worth the cost of maintaining it, and of being of little practical benefit to the mass of poor farmers. Noblin, *Polk*, 122–124.

[138]Walter Clark, lawyer of Raleigh and editorial director and part owner of the *Raleigh News*. He served as Superior Court judge from 1885 to 1889, and as Supreme Court justice from 1889 to 1924. For a rather thin account of Clark's early career, see Aubrey L. Brooks, *Walter Clark, Fighting Judge* (Chapel Hill: University of North Carolina Press, 1944), *passim*, hereinafter cited as Brooks, *Walter Clark*.

[139]Albion Winegar Tourgée. At this time Tourgée was ending his long and varied career in North Carolina—in August he and his family left Raleigh and returned to New York. His most recent undertaking had been his "C" letters for the Greensboro *North State*, consisting of attacks upon the Ku Klux Klan and the Democratic party for their mistreatment of the Negro. Roy F. Dibble, *Albion W. Tourgée* (New York: Lemcke & Buechner, 1921), 57–58, hereinafter cited as Dibble, *Tourgée*.

[140]Because of Secretary of Agriculture Polk's driving executive ability, his critics called his approach to his job "Military Agriculture." Noblin, *Polk*, 124–125.

[141]Raleigh lawyer. Branson, *Directory, 1878*, 293. For the explanation of this telegram, see Thompson to Jarvis, July 4, 1879, *n.* 136, in this volume.

E. W. Thompson to Thomas J. Jarvis

[Telegram]

Jacksonville Fla, 4 PM, July 11 1879

Money received I leave for Savannah at five & will do all in my power to effect your purpose Saw Littlefield this morning money less and poverty stricken We will capture him—

T. P. Devereux to Thomas J. Jarvis

[Telegram]

Savannah Ga, 2 09 PM, July 12 1879

T[hompson] is here We will write you after consultation

J. E. Hartridge to Thomas J. Jarvis

Jacksonville, Fla. 14th July 1879.

Mr. Devereux called this morning and handed me for our firm Fifty Dollars. Our firm had drawn on you for this Fifty Dollars. We regret having done so, since the amount had been forwarded and it would needlessly subject you to the annoyance of its prevention Any costs that may have been occasioned thereby our firm will sustain, though we *instructed* that there should *be no protest.*

It is rumored here that Gen— Littlefield will leave for New York on the steamer City of Dallas on Thursday next. I will go to New York on the same steamer. She will, *en route,* stop at Brunswick Georgia and Beaufort S.C. If Littlefield should take passage I will keep you posted as to his movements by telegraph from both Brunswick and Beaufort. My New York address will be care of Drew Lowell & Drew 35 Broadway. In the meanwhile Mr. Calhoun will remain in Florida and will give Mr. Thompson any aid that he can, & that you wish

T. P. Devereux to Thomas J. Jarvis

[*Telegram*]

Tallahassee Fla, 5 55 PM, July 15 1879

The following was received by Gov Drew since dinner "Have arranged for Littlefield to go to New York without molestation He must start immediately" Answer tonight & explain at request of Attorney General

Wilkinson Call[142] to Thomas J. Jarvis

Washington, July 15 1879.

I have great solicitude for the protection of the people of Florida against the great wrongs which are now about to be perpetrated against them in the sale of their Railroads, & in the control of them by persons who in the judgment of our people are unfriendly to all the real and best interest of the State and to the continued control of the political power of the state by the intelligent—property holding and white portion of her people—

In the hope of accomplishing the prevention of this great wrong I have had frequent opportunities of conversation with Govr Vance. and have addressed a communication to you enclosing an opinion of the Hon B H Hill[143] a Lawyer and a man certainly not surpassed in soundness of judgment and legal acumen by any member of the Profession in the United States

There is no expense and labor which I would not be willing to encounter to prevent this great wrong to my people.

I know of but one way in which it can now be accomplished and that is by an original suit in the S C of the US— *immediately* brought— If there is any *hope* of accomplishing this result by any explanation or argument which I might submit to you I will be glad to stop on my way South *within* the next ten days and confer with you on the subject. Will you do me the kindness to write me on the subject at this place on the receipt of this letter

---

[142]Democratic United States senator from Florida, 1879–1897. *Biographical Directory of Congress*, 778.

[143]Benjamin Harvey Hill, prominent Georgia statesman and at this time United States senator. *Dictionary of American Biography*, IX, 25–27. Hill's opinion was not found.

I think a combination may be made by which the State of N C may be relieved of expense in the prosecution of the suit— if you think it right that it should be so.

A&H—GP

T. S. Kenan to Thomas J. Jarvis[144]

Attorney Genl's office
July 16. 1879.

I made a report concerning the affairs of the Roanoke Nav. Co. to Gov. Vance,[145] and he sent it with a special message to the last legislature (1879) as will appear from the letter book in the office of the Private Secretary. I called his attention to the act authorizing the action to vacate the charter, Acts 1874 '75. Ch. 198. And he asked that the legislature take some action in regard to an execution against the company then in the hands of the sheriff of Halifax. But no legislative action was had.

Since then, there has been a sale under said execution, and a case is now before the Supreme Court involving the question, as to whether the property was subject to sale at the instance of one creditor, during the pendency of the action under the above act of 1874 '75, to dissolve the corporation. Since your Excellency referred the within to me, I went to Halifax, and found that there were several judgments against this company. I know of no law which would authorize you to pay them out of the public fund. While the stock was once valuable, yet I am informed by reliable persons, that it is now worthless, and if you had the right to pay these judgments, it might be a useless expenditure of money, in view of the fact that the legislature has authorized the said action for dissolution. Until the determination of the case now pending in Supreme Court, I would suggest that your Excellency request the sheriff, or plaintiff in this execution, to postpone the contemplated sale.[146]

---

[144]This letter is in response to Jarvis' endorsement on the Notice of Sale, dated June 28, 1879, in this volume.

[145]See *Public Documents, 1879*, No. 23.

[146]For the final disposition of this matter, see Worth to Jarvis, February 21, 1880, in this volume.

A&H—GP

T. P. Devereux to Thomas J. Jarvis

[*Telegram*]

Tallahassee Fla, 3 25 PM, July 18 1879

Govr D[rew] advised by atty Genl not to issue warrant Res Judicata[147] Shall I take writ of error to supreme Court from archibalds former decision Go to Jacksonville tonight to see thompson answer there tomorrow Start home in afternoon

A&H—GP

E. W. Thompson to Thomas J. Jarvis

[*Telegram*]

Jacksonville July 19 1879

No train from here to Savannah until tomorrow afternoon five oclock will go there if you decide it—will have to go to Savannah thence to Tallahassee to procure Governor Drews warrant thence return if you wish me to go send telegraphic money order one hundred Dollars for expenses—Littlefield is here & can be easily taken with present arrangements

UNC—UP

Thomas J. Jarvis to K. P. Battle

Executive Department
Raleigh, July 22[d] 1879

I shall be obliged to forego the pleasure of being with [you] at the close of the Normal. I feel such a deep interest in the School and believe so much in the good work it is doing that I really regret that I cannot visit it.

I have ten important engagements for to–morrow of State interest. A man has been here from Richmond a week waiting for Stamps[148] to come to make a contract concerning the Peniten-

---

[147]The Raleigh *Observer*, July 22, 1879, reported that Drew thought that he would be guilty of disrespect to the Florida judiciary if he had Littlefield arrested after the latter had already been discharged under the writ of habeas corpus.

[148]Edward R. Stamps, Raleigh lawyer who at this time was president of the board of directors of the penitentiary. Branson, *Directory, 1878*, 293; *Public Documents, 1881*, No. 8, 4. In 1884 he became president of the State National Bank of Raleigh. Branson, *Directory for 1884*, 657.

Kemp Plummer Battle (1831-1919) was born in Franklin County but moved to the state capital with his family. He attended the Raleigh Male Academy, entered the University of North Carolina at thirteen, graduated at seventeen, and stayed on as a tutor of Latin and mathematics. Battle had wide interests and held various executive positions—with the Chatham Railroad Company, State Agricultural Society, and the North Carolina State Life Insurance Company. He also wrote treatises on ecclesiastical and state history. In 1875 Battle led in the movement to reorganize the University of North Carolina, following its decline in the post-war era; he was named president in 1876 and served fifteen years. Perhaps his greatest contribution was his two-volume history of the University.

tiary. He will return to morrow and I feel obliged to attend to it as soon as he returns.

Besides I am really unwell and want to go to Beaufort as soon I can leave the city—certainly by Friday.

With best wishes for you and the School,

A&H—GP

Joseph Hyrum Parry[149] *to Thomas J. Jarvis*

Brasstown, Cherokee Co., N.Carolina

29 July, 1879

Permit me to call your attention to the very dangerous and most deplorable state of affairs now existing in the township of Brasstown, Clay county, of this State.

A few months since, a number of Latter–day Saint, or "Mormon," Elders came into this part of the State as ministers and preachers of the Gospel. Religious prejudices ran high, and about the first of April last, a mob arose, threatening to forcibly eject the Elders from the State. But believing that they would be protected by the laws and authorities of the State in the free exercise of their religious principles, and being assured of such religious liberty by the Constitution of the United States, the Elders took no notice of these lawless threats, but continued their peaceful avocation of propagating the principles of the Gospel, violating no law nor interfering with anyone.

The members of this unlawful assemblage were never brought to account for their threats of molestation, although well known to the three Justices of the township.

A Latter–day Saint Church was established, with some seventeen baptized members, and many more adherents. Seeing the growth and prosperity of this so–called "new doctrine," the mob spirit revived, and made itself manifest in a very violent manner. A raid was made upon the members of the Church, and also upon non–members. Men and women, old and young, were dragged out of their beds and whipped and clubbed in a most cruel manner, some being nearly killed. Property was also interfered with; one man had his mill partially destroyed. All this occurred between 12 o'clock and daylight on Sunday morning,

---

[149]Unable to identify.

July 20th. After whipping them, the marauders threatened to kill every member and friend of the cause if they do not leave the State within four weeks. Some have since been told to leave at once on pain of death. Those of our members and friends who were not whipped at the first are threatened every moment. Homes are now being broken up, and the people are disposing of their chattels and effects at ruinous prices; and also of their lands and standing crops, for almost a mere nothing, when they can find a buyer. The people are leaving the country, several have already left, and the rest will go so soon as they can raise sufficient means to leave, whether they dispose of their property or not. And all this because they are afraid to remain here, and they have just cause for fear. The people are even forbidden to assemble together in a Sacramental meeting.

Myself and companions, the Elders, are in imminent danger, being threatened with death *at sight,* being in danger of being waylaid at any time; and this, too, for simply preaching the Gospel. We have violated no law, for if we had, you may be sure we should have been put through long since. The same of our members and friends also.

At a place called Shoal Creek, in Cherokee County, mobs have organized, and are threatening and trying to waylay our friends and Elders there also.

Can such things take place, and there be no redress, in one of the first States of this great Confederacy of free America? What, "the home of the brave, and the land of the free," where the downtrodden and the oppressed of all lands, and all creeds, are invited to a home and a refuge, come to this—that a man cannot believe and practice the religion of Jesus Christ without grevious molestation and threats of life? That he cannot entertain a stranger of a particular faith without a challenge from a mob?

It has come to a terrible straight, too, when officers of the peace are afraid of their own safety when called on to deal in such matters.

If there is any virtue in the Constitutional guaranty of religious liberty and protection to all creeds, or any power in the good government of North Carolina to protect us in our rights in trying to do good to our fellow creatures,— and we have every hope and assurance that there is,—we appeal to your Excellency for redress of our grievances, and protection in our common rights as American citizens to "worship God according to the dictates of our own consciences."

By your early attention to this matter, you may save much suffering and inconvenience, and perhaps some lives.[150]

P.S.—I patiently await an answer. J. H. P.

A&H—GLB

Thomas J. Jarvis to Theodore Fulton Davidson[151]

Executive Department
Raleigh N.C. Aug. 18th 1879

Enclosed I send you the proposition of Mr Fain[152] to which I beg to call your attention. You will remember I spoke to you about the matter while at Beaufort, and asked you to call the attention of the Board of Directors to it. Some provision must be made to take care of these convicts when they are turned over to your Board. I send this to you as Maj Wilson, the Prest. of the Road is absent on important business for the Company. Please call his attention to it as soon as he returns. I refer you to Ch 146. pages 143–4 Laws of 1876–7. I desire to do my duty as imposed by this as well as any other Law.

James H. Pool[153] *to Thomas J. Jarvis*[154]

[Telegram]

Beaufort, N.C., Aug. 21st, 1879.

Our people are in great distress and in danger of pestilence from the great amount of rubbish in front of the town. Can't

---

[150]Jarvis' correspondence contains no further mention of Mormons and their problems, but the *Morning Star* of August 13, 1879, stated that Jarvis "promptly notified the Solicitor of the District to 'look after the Saints.'"

[151]Lawyer of Asheville; member of the General Assembly, 1879–1883; attorney general, 1885–1893. *Cyclopedia of the Carolinas*, II, 64–67.

[152]Mercer Fain, mine operator in Cherokee County and president of the Georgia and North Carolina Railroad Company. This railroad was projected to run from Murphy, North Carolina, to Marietta, Georgia, but it was never built. Branson, *Directory, 1878*, 72; *Laws of North Carolina, 1870–1871*, c. 167.

[153]Possibly intended to be L. A. Potts, mayor of Beaufort. Branson, *Directory for 1884*, 184.

[154]This telegram was taken from the Raleigh *Observer* of August 22, 1879.

you let us have two or three hundred dollars from the State funds?[155]

A&H—GP

Alfred Holt Colquitt[156] to Thomas J. Jarvis

Executive Department
Atlanta, Ga., Aug 28th 1879

I have the honor to transmit to your Excellency a copy of an Act just passed by the General Assembly of Georgia to establish the State line between Georgia and North Carolina so far as the same is the line between Rabun County in Georgia and Macon County in North Carolina, and to provide for the survey of the same.[157]

You will see by Section 2nd of said Act that I am authorized to appoint a Commissioner on the part of Georgia to cooperate with a Commissioner on the part of North Carolina to be appointed by you as the Governor of your State, the said Commissioners being authorized to have said survey made.

Your consideration is respectfully invited to the matter.

UNC—DFC

Thomas J. Jarvis to David Franklin Caldwell[158]

Executive Department
Raleigh, Sept. 16th 1879

In reply to yours of some days ago[159] I beg to say that I shall always give a willing ear to your advice and suggestions, on any

---

[155]On August 19 a great storm had struck the entire North Carolina coast, with Beaufort suffering the greatest damage. Jarvis had no authority to extend relief from the public treasury, but he turned this telegram over to a Raleigh citizens' committee, which raised $288.45. Raleigh *Observer*, August 22, 24, 1879.

[156]Governor of Georgia, 1876–1882. *National Cyclopedia*, I, 291.

[157]In 1821 a North Carolina commission had surveyed this line, and in 1861 the Georgia General Assembly had accepted the findings of the survey. By 1879 some confusion had arisen as to the precise location of the line between Macon and Rabun counties. Marvin L. Skaggs, *North Carolina Boundary Disputes Involving Her Southern Line* (Chapel Hill: University of North Carolina Press, 1941), 205, hereinafter cited as Skaggs, *North Carolina Boundary Disputes*.

[158]Businessman of Greensboro, Caldwell helped to organize the Cape Fear and Yadkin Valley Railroad and owned stock in this and other lines. In addition he had large interests in land and cotton factories. He served in the General Assembly, 1848–1858 and 1879; and he was a member of the Convention of 1865. *Cyclopedia of the Carolinas*, II, 336-338.

[159]Not found.

subject and especially on one with which you are so familiar as you are with the Rail Road interest of this State.

I think the proposition of the Board of Directors of the C.F.&Y.V.R.R. to commence work at Mt Airy[160] has so little merit in it that the Board itself will not attempt to begin it. It would be such a waste of the means of the company that I think so prudent a man as Mr. Gray[161] is would not permit it. I can hardly think I should be called upon to take any action about it.[162]

A&H—GP

Alfred Augustus McKethan[163] *to Thomas J. Jarvis*

Fayetteville, N.C., Sept 26th 1879

I learn through Col L. C. Jones[164] that there is some talk of appointing "state Proxy"[165] for the Cape Fear and Yadkin Valley R R" I therefore write to inform you I have this morning seen the mortgage bonds of the "Old Western R Road"[166] that has given us so much trouble burned with the exception of $5000. now held in New York. So we are now beginning to see our way clear to build the Road, if we can only be let alone, and can work in harmony with the state of N.C. We therefore earnestly wish in filling this place you will give us the best man possible and one that will work in harmony with our county and Town which hold $200.000 in the Road and those men who have saved the Road to the stockholders—

[160]See Brower to Jarvis, May 22, 1879, *n*. 93, in this volume.

[161]Julius Alexander Gray of Greensboro, banker, railroad entrepreneur, and at this time president of the Cape Fear and Yadkin Valley Railroad. Ashe, *Biographical History*, V, 110–116.

[162]The state owned $1,000,000 of stock in the Western Railroad. Since this road was now part of the Cape Fear and Yadkin Valley Railroad, the state had the same interest in the later company. *Public Documents, 1879,* No. 3, 8.

[163]Businessman of Fayetteville, with interests in mills, stores, manufactories, and land. He had been a director of the Western Railroad at the time that it was merged into the Cape Fear and Yadkin Valley Railroad. John A. Oates, *The Story of Fayetteville and the Upper Cape Fear* (Fayetteville: John A. Oates, 1950), 846–847, hereinafter cited as Oates, *Story of Fayetteville*.

[164]Resident of Fayetteville. He had been president and general superintendent of the Western Railroad at the time of its merger. Poor, *Railroad Manual*, 558.

[165]Usually whenever the state held stock in a particular railroad, the governor appointed a "proxy" to attend the meetings of the stockholders and vote for the state's interests.

[166]See Brower to Jarvis, May 22, 1879, *n*. 93, in this volume.

I feel a great interest in this road being one of its first Directors and continuing as such untill was forced to get out the way for A. J. Jones[167] and party—and as soon as we by *Elections gained control of the county and Town was again put back,* so may say have been a Director continuously from the beginning, and for past 8 years have held the county proxy and desire that I may witness the completion of this undertaking on which I have spent so much time, labour, Thought & money— The county and Town own $200.000 which gives us the balance of power although we agreed to give the state one more Director expecting to get the appropriation made by the last Legislature[168] and which I think we are still entitled to.

I am for building the *road as straight and as cheap from the Gulf to Greensboro as possible* and as fast as we can. This I know does not suit the views of some men in N.C, but they have not put large amounts of money in the Road as we have done and only pay their proportion of taxes as we do. I have no ax to grind or friend for the place and only write to let you know the views of our people on the subject and with the hope may be of some advantage to you in making a selection of a suitable man for the place. We are well pleased with our selection J A Gray Esq as President and dont believe we could have done better in the entire state as he has gone to work in earnest to build the Road—

A&H—GP

W. G. *Curtis to Thomas J. Jarvis*

Smithville Sept 30th 1879

I am pleased to report that no infectious disease has thus far been imported into the State by way of this Port, and the season being now well advanced, the danger of yellow fever may be considered nearly over—

I am also pleased to see that the citizens and authorities of the City of Wilmington are becoming aware that the policy of

---

[167]Andrew Jackson Jones of Brunswick County, who had been a partner with G. W. Swepson in defrauding North Carolina during Reconstruction. During that period he had been president of the Western Railroad. Daniels, *Prince of Carpetbaggers,* 214.

[168]This is a reference to a promise by the state to buy $50,000 of first mortgage bonds of the company after the grading of the road had been completed. *Laws of North Carolina, 1879,* c. 67.

non intercourse is injuring their city, and that such extreme stringency is both unwise and unscientific—[169] The authorities of the city are now interposing no obstacle to vessels entering the city from healthy ports in South America and the West Indies after they have undergone such quarantine as is considered proper at this station—

A&H—GLB

Thomas J. Jarvis to J. W. Wilson

Executive Department
Raleigh N.C. Oct 3rd 1879

I am glad to hear that Lt. Gov. Robinson and Mr Fain will visit you soon to confer with you in regard to the employment of the convicts now in Cherokee. And in this connection I beg to suggest one of the greatest difficulties that I fear in going forward to carry out in good faith the Acts of 1876–7 for the completion of the Western N.C.RR.[170] will be getting the right of way & in getting rid of the claims and hinderances of the creditors of the West Dv. of the W.N.C.R.R., I beg that you will press this view upon Robinson & Fain & if possible enlist their support & help in getting clear of this trouble. Would the funds you received from the Florida suits be sufficient do you think to procure a perfect right of way? If so for the sake of getting so desirable a thing would it not be well to consider the propriety of using that fund to pay off & satisfy the *bona fide* claimants. Think of it. I am glad you wrote the letter to Col Myers[171] about the Charlotte & Wilmington freight. I approve of it fully. It is just what I call a North Carolina policy—if there is to be any descriminations let it be in favor of North Carolina cities & Towns. If you have not done so I wish you would send Johnston[172] of the C.C. Road a copy of the letter. I

---

[169]For Curtis' criticism of Wilmington's port regulations, see Curtis to Jarvis, June 30, 1879, in this volume.

[170]Since before the Civil War the ultimate destination of the Western North Carolina Railroad had been Paint Rock and Ducktown on the Tennessee line. For the story of the slow progress made to these points, see Brown, *State Movement, passim.*

[171]Possibly Charles D. Myers, Wilmington merchant. Branson, *Directory for 1884,* 489.

[172]Probably V. Q. Johnson of Lincolnton, assistant superintendent of the Carolina Central Railroad. Poor, *Railroad Manual,* 636.

trust if complaints are now made by the people of Wilmington & Charlotte it will not be against the W.N.C.R.R or its management

Thomas J. Jarvis to Frederick William Mackay Holliday[173]

Executive Department
Raleigh. N.C. Oct. 6th 1879

Yours[174] inviting myself with the other Governors of the Colonial States to meet you in Philadelphia on the 18th inst to make the proper arrangements for the celebration at Yorktown Va. Oct 18th. 1881 of the surrender of Lord Cornwallis has been received   It [is] my purpose unless prevented by some unforseen contingency to attend in person on that occasion; and I hope to meet all the other invited Governors. While the Surrender of Cornwallis belongs to the whole nation, and its celebration is an event in the history of our common country in which every citizen may earnestly join yet I trust I will not be chargable with sectional feelings when I say that Virginia & North Carolina are entitled to claim in it a special property. As the surrender at Yorktown was the end of hostilities between the people of this and their mother Country, so I pray God, this proposed great National celebration may be, in *fact* & in *truth* the end of all bitterness & estrangement among the people of the different sections of our Country

Thomas J. Jarvis to the Council of State

Executive Department
Raleigh Oct 7th 1879

The Act of March the 14th 1879 entitled "An Act to adjust and Renew a portion of the State Debt" makes it the duty of the Governor to appoint three Commissioners to negotiate with the

---

[173]Governor of Virginia, 1878–1882. *National Cyclopedia*, V, 454.
[174]The invitation was extended on October 2. Governors' Papers, not included in this volume.

holders of that part of the Debt "incurred to aid in the construction of the North Carolina Rail Road."[175]

I have delayed action in the matter till now for the reason among others that I wanted to see what action our creditors would take in regard to other portions of our debt under the general Act. Up to this time about four and a third million of the old Bonds have been exchanged for about one million three hundred thousand Dollars of the new Bonds and the old Bonds burnt

At least one third of the whole amount of the recognized Debt of the State exclusive of the Debt known as the construction Bonds of the N.C.R.R.—having been taken up we may safely conclude the rest will come in.

The powers given to the Governor and the commissioners under this Act to fix a new debt upon the people of the State are very large. In the exercise of this power I desire that all that I do shall be a matter of record open at all times to inspection; and that the commissioners shall be men of such high and irreproachable character, that whatever is done shall command the unqualified confidence of the entire people. The Constitution Art III 14 makes you my advisors in the execution of my office.

The matter upon which I desire your advice at this time is,

1st Has the time come for the appointment of the commissioners contemplated by the Act?

2nd Who shall the commissioners be if you advise their appointment?

I will thank you for your advice upon these two subjects

---

[175]The state bonds issued to pay for stock in the North Carolina Railroad were secured by a lien on that stock, and were known as "construction bonds." There were outstanding $2,795,000 of these bonds, and by 1879 almost $700,000 in interest had accrued. Because of the strong legal posi-in the same way as the remainder. (See Curtis to Jarvis, March 3, 1879, n. 43, in this volume.) The bonds would mature in 1883–1885, and so some provision had to be made for them; if not, the holders would be able to sell in the same way as the remainder. (See Curtis to Jarvis, March 3, 1879, the stock pledged as security. This condition prompted the General Assembly to pass the law of March 14 mentioned above. This law authorized the governor to appoint a commission to negotiate with the holders of the construction bonds and contract with them for a renewal of the debt by a process of funding the construction bonds into a new issue of state bonds. Any terms reached by the commission and the bondholders must be satisfactory to the governor and the secretary of the treasury. *Laws of North Carolina, 1879*, c. 138.

A&H—GLB

Thomas J. Jarvis to George Davis[176]

Executive Department
Raleigh N.C. Oct 7th 1879

At a meeting of the State Council held in the Executive office this day in reference to the adjustment of that part of the State debt incurred in aid of the construction of the North Carolina Rail Road, the Hon George Davis Montford McGehee[177] and Donald W. Bain[178] were recommended to the Governor as Commissioners to carry out the provision of said Act.

It is with peculiar pleasure to myself personally that I tender you the appointment and ask your acceptance of the same. I send you inclosed a copy of the Act that you may see by easy reference what are the duties imposed by said Act.

Will you be kind enough to reply as soon as you may be conveniently able to do so[179]

UNC—UP

Thomas J. Jarvis to K. P. Battle

Executive Department
Raleigh, Oct 30th 1879

I thank you truly for the interest you have taken in setting me right in reference to my Wake Forest talk. I have just looked over the Reports in the Observer and [the Raleigh][180] News of Sept. 4th and there is nothing in either that in the very slightest degree warranted Mrs S. to assign to me any such position.[181]

---

[176]Lawyer of Wilmington with a special interest in legal matters pertaining to railroads. He had served as congressman and then as attorney general of the Confederacy. *Dictionary of American Biography*, V, 114–115.

[177]Lawyer and planter of Person County; member of the Convention of 1865; member of the General Assembly, 1862–1879; commissioner of agriculture, 1880–1887. Grant, *Alumni History of the University*, 390.

[178]Donald W. Bain of Raleigh; chief clerk of the Treasury Department, 1865–1885; state treasurer, 1885–1893. *Cyclopedia of the Carolinas*, II, 311–313.

[179]All three appointees accepted.

[180]These two newspapers were combined in 1880 into the *News and Observer*.

[181]At Wake Forest Jarvis had said that the church was "the greatest educator." He urged that the "four leading denominations should through their pulpits demand of the legislative power of the State appropriations for their various colleges." In an editorial in the Chapel Hill *Weekly Ledger*, Miss Cornelia Phillips Spencer, who advocated complete separation of

But the report did me no [harm] and so let it go.

I had a fine time in Phil[182] and I have reason to know that I made a good impression. It is very gratifying to me to feel that the State did not suffer in my hands on that occasion.

I hope the University is doing well and that the boys are giving you no trouble.

A&H—GLB

Thomas J. Jarvis to the President and the Board of Directors of the Western North Carolina Rail Road Company

Executive Department
Raleigh N.C. Nov 8th 1879

I have received a letter from the Managers of the Tenn. & Kentucky Roads a copy of which I herewith enclose.[183] You know the means at your command and can answer the inquiry more intelligently than I can Will you be kind enough to give me your best opinions that I may forward the same to these gentlemen. The prospect of having direct connection with the Ohio River and the great West through North Carolina with our own Sea Ports should induce us to push forward to the Tenn. Line as rapidly as possibly [*sic*]. Having as we will the shortest line from the Ohio to the Atlantic we may reasonably hope that the W.N.C.R.R. will become a self sustaining and a paying institution

A&H—GLB

Thomas J. Jarvis to Elisha David Standiford[184]

Executive Department
Raleigh N.C. Nov 8th/79

Your letter of the 29th ult[185] was rec'd at this office in my absence. I have forwarded a copy of the letter to the President &

---

church and state, replied that the church "has no commission from her Head to teach reading, writing and upbeing, it is not her business." Louis R. Wilson (ed.), *Selected Papers of Cornelia Phillips Spencer* (Chapel Hill: University of North Carolina Press, 1953), 338–339, hereinafter cited as Wilson, *Spencer*.

[182]See Jarvis to Holliday, October 6, 1879, in this volume.

[183]This copy has not been found. For partial clarification of this letter, see Jarvis to Standiford, November 8, 1879, and McGhee to Jarvis, December 8, 1879, in this volume.

[184]Farmer and businessman of Louisville, Kentucky, and president of the Louisville and Nashville Railroad from 1875 to 1879. A Democrat, he served in the House of Representatives from 1873 to 1875. *Biographical Directory of Congress*, 1,559.

[185]Not found.

Board of Directors of the W.N.C.R.R. asking for their opinion and if theirs differ materially from mine I will forward theirs also.

With the limited means at our command it is, as you can readily see, difficult to say exactly when a work of that magnitude can be completed. The completion of the Road to the Tenn. line is now an assured fact; and the work will be pushed forward as rapidly as possible. I think we will be at Asheville by the 1st of Feb'y or March unless delayed by the heavy rain of winter

We will be there by the 1st of April anyhow. From Asheville to the Tenn. line the grade is comparatively easy and a part of the work has been done. We ought and I think can complete that part of the work in a year and a half, some well informed persons say in a year. This will bring us to the Tenn. line say from the 1st of July to 1st of October 1881 & upon this I think you may safely rely. We will do better if we can

If the Directors of the Morristown Road[186] would go to work & complete that Road to the North Carolina line I think it would help us in our efforts to hurry up our work. I beg to suggest that a force be put to work there as soon as the Board may find it practicable to do so.

I trust that the completion of these links in this great line of Rail will be the begin[n]ing of closer relations socially and commerc[i]ally between the people of your great section and the people of North Carolina.

A&H—GLB

Thanksgiving Proclamation, November 11, 1879

Executive Department

By authority of law I Thos J. Jarvis, Governor of North Carolina, do set apart Thursday Nov. 27, 1879. as a day of prayer and thanksgiving to Almighty God for the manifold mercies and blessings He has vauched safe to us during the year now passing away.

And in order for its proper observance I request the people on that day to close up their places of business and abandoning all secular pursuits to attend their respective places of worship to return thanks to the Great Ruler of individuals and nations

---

[186]Local name for the Cincinnati, Cumberland Gap and Charleston Railroad. Poor, *Railroad Manual*, 22–23.

for the peace and tranquility which we have enjoyed; for the exemption from pestilence and disease which He has given us; for the kind and friendly relations that have existed among all classes of our citizens; for the general and growing prosperity that has pervaded the whole State and for all His varied blessings bestowed upon us; and to invoke a convenience of His watchful care and protection over us during the coming year.

And while it will be becoming on that day to remember the widow and the orphan and the poor and needy every where among us; and to minister to their wants I especially commend to the prayers and gifts of the people the orphans in the Asylum at Oxford who are now dependent for a support solely upon the charity of the people, the State appropriation for that purpose being entirely exhausted.

Speech of November 18, 1879, Delivered at the Formal Opening of the Colored Industrial Fair at Raleigh, N.C.[187]

My Colored Friends: —When requested some week or more ago to open this, the first Industrial Exhibition of the products of the colored race, I consented with pleasure. I did not expect to be so much gratified as I am at the display made here to–day, for it far exceeds what was expected. In the few remarks I shall make I shall point out as plainly as I can the great work before you and your race. I do not know better how to begin than by quoting a motto I saw in one of your halls to day. It was: "God helps those who help themselves." He helps in this way, that whenever in this life a man is found trying to live up to his duty, and is true to himself, honor and truth, that man, rich or poor, black or white, educated or ignorant, will have friends to advise and friends to help him.

In the providence of God your condition from that in years agone is changed. You are freemen in the sight of God, of men and of the law. Your destiny is therefore in your own keeping; it belongs to yourselves. You may be told that in some place you can find a land where you can live without labor. Believe it not, for it is indeed a true saying, that he only succeeds who works. By this alone can any one succeed. No man of his means is going to support you in idleness. You will find in North Carolina as genial a home, as promising a future as anywhere on God's earth. It affords me particular pleasure as the Executive of your

---

[187]Taken from the Raleigh *Observer*, November 19, 1879.

State, to say that at this time, in all sections of our State, from the mountains to the sea, in every county, the most amicable relations exist between the two races. There is no reason why things should be otherwise. So far as I am concerned I feel a deep and abiding sympathy for the colored race. So long as I am Governor the poorest colored citizen shall have equal justice with the richest white one.

Right here, where your forefathers were born, lived, died and sleep their last sleep, you will find the place to stay and work out your destiny. (Loud cheers.) But your destiny is with yourselves. Your best interests will be promoted by getting homes of your own, to dwell in. I wish every colored man had his own home, and his own piece of ground. I wish to tell you that there are many grades of character in the white, as in the colored race. There are mean white men, who will cheat and swindle you; but let me advise you, that there are plenty of white men who will not. Be honest yourselves and deal with honest men. When you need advice, as you surely will, go to some one you know to ask for it. You will need the advice, and for a time yet.

Another practical thing is this. I take it that I now speak to the better class of your race. I hope there are classes among you. Every people has such distinctions and so must you. The lesson must be impressed that if you wish to lift your race up as near the plane the white race occupies as possible you must make such distinctions as to character. This is not the place to talk politics, nor will I do so, but I will give you an illustration in point. A colored man in an eastern county voted for a ticket his people did not like. He was, as the result, ostracised. I make no comments, but tell you a simple truth. If you apply the same social ostracism to one of your race who goes wrong, it will be the best preventive to wrong–doing. The best means therefore of preventing wrong–doing is by drawing lines in your own race. I ask you to practice this principle. I give another incident to urge this matter. In Hyde county, a colored man returned from the penitentiary. He was made a preacher. After a few months occupancy of the pulpit he went back to the penitentiary. This brought a reproach upon the congregation and the neighborhood. It was rather an encouragement to crime. If they had closed the doors against him, it would have deterred others from doing wrong. He that doeth right shall be blessed of his race, and he that doeth wrong shall be accursed. I repeat that I am gratified at this exhibition in all its departments. The stock display of hogs and poultry is better than that made at the State fair. I am truly glad to see it. Every farmer should try to raise his own meat and bread. When you make your money don't throw it away. Buy a home, adorn it, educate your children. Then you will feel that you have something to live and to work for. I assure you that whatever I can do, as an individual and official, to make the next exhibition a greater success than this one, shall be done. I feel an interest in the good work the colored people of North Carolina are doing.

UNC—DFC

Thomas J. Jarvis to D. F. Caldwell
Executive Department
Raleigh, Nov. 29 1879

I have read with interest your letter on the Mud cut Boom and its effect upon the Democratic party.[188]

I do not apprehend much trouble from it. The statements in the circular are so false in fact that when the truth is told I do not apprehend that many votes will be effected by it. I have great confidence in the good judgment of our people and they are not [to] be moved about by every wind of doctrine The W.N.C.R.R. must be built through to Paint Rock so as to make connections with the great west at as early a day as possible. The C.F.&Y.V.RR must be pushed up the Yadkin Valley as speedily as possible. The Mud Cut Boom would would [*sic*] stop work on both of these great works by hireing out the convicts and taking off the public works. It can't be done.

---

[188]The managers of the Western North Carolina Railroad were having difficulty building their road through the four miles of rugged terrain from Henry to the tunnel at Swanannoa Mountain. The worst obstacles had been a series of land slides in this area. Mud Cut was a six hundred feet long cut along the side of Round Knob Mountain, and since April, 1878, several slides had occurred here. At one time all but 8,000 of 77,000 cubic yards of material had been removed, when further slides deposited 110,000 more cubic yards. *Public Documents, 1879*, No. 27, 10–11; *Morning Star*, December 19, 1879; Raleigh *Observer*, May 12 and July 22, 1879. "Mud Cut Boom" refers to a series of letters by Walter Clark which were published in several newspapers. In these letters Clark advocated discontinuing construction of the Western North Carolina Railroad on the ground that the cost of the railroad would exceed in value all the property west of Asheville. Daniels, *Tar Heel Editor*, 187. Caldwell's letter referred to has not been found.

A&H—GP

Charles McClung McGhee[189] *to Thomas J. Jarvis*

[with enclosure]

Knoxville, Tenn., Dec 8th 1879

In view of the deep interest which our Company feel in the early completion of the connection between Wolf Creek and Asheville N.C. our Board of Directors at its session, yesterday, appointed a Committee of the Board, whose duty it was made to visit Raleigh and confer with your Excellency, and with the President and Board of Directors of the Western North Carolina Railroad, with a view of obtaining detailed information as to the views, purposes and ability of that Company to construct their Road to a connection at the line

It was unanimously agreed in the Board that it was the duty of our Company to facilitate, aid and encourage the people of your State to a more vigorous prosecution of the work. That the link to connect the North Carolina line should be at once built:— provided the work could be taken up and immediately extended forward in the direction of Asheville

Having heard, unofficially, that a meeting of the President and Board of Directors of the Western North Carolina Railroad was to be had in Raleigh on the 10th of next month, I write to know whether such is the fact; and, if so, whether it would be agreeable that our Committee should present themselves before that meeting— An early reply will very much oblige

C. M. McGhee to Rufus Yancey McAden[190]
[enclosure]

Knoxville, Tenn., Dec 8th 1879

Yours of 17th November was received

In my absence Maj O'Brien sent you the information asked for[191]

Our Board of Directors at its recent Session appointed a com-

---

[189]Banker of Knoxville, Tennessee, and vice–president of the East Tennessee, Virginia, and Georgia Railroad. *Dictionary of American Biography,* XII, 48.

[190]Banker and textile manufacturer of Charlotte. At this time he was president of the Atlantic, Tennessee, and Ohio Railroad from Charlotte to Statesville. Ashe, *Biographical History,* V, 198–202.

[191]Not found. Major O'Brien has not been identified.

mittee to visit Raleigh for the purpose of conferring with the Governor and with the President and Board of Directors of the Western North Carolina RRd, in view of the fact that the Governor has expressed a desire that we should build the few miles yet remaining in Tennessee to reach the North Carolina line. We will build the four miles at once, provided by doing so, we can get the Western North Carolina Road to take up the work and build from that End

I understand there is to be a meeting of the Directors of the Western N.CRR at Raleigh on the 10th of next month, and have written to Governor Jarvis and President Wilson of the W.N.C. RR this morning asking if such is the case, and also asking if it will be agreeable that our Committee should meet them at that time. Would it not be well for you to be in Raleigh upon that occasion You could give me much valuable information as you understand the people there better than myself

A&H—GLB

Thomas J. Jarvis to A. H. Colquitt
Ex. Dept: Raleigh Dec. 10th 1879

I beg to inform your Excellency that I have this day appointed L. T. Howard[192] Commissioner on the part of the State of North Carolina with a commissioner to be appointed by your Excellency on the part of Georgia, to establish the State line between the County of Macon of the former and Rabun of the latter State; and would request, that as soon as you have made the said appointment you will cause information of it to be made to me

A&H—GP

James H. Rumbaugh[193] to Thomas J. Jarvis

Warm Springs, N.C.
Dec 16. 1879

I attended the convention & meeting of the Stockholders of the E.T.Va.&Ga.R.R. last week, and am glad to report, with considerable success, as the Board of Directors appointed a committee to meet with the Board of the Directors of the W.N.C.R.R.

---

[192]Possibly Lewis Howard, farmer and civil engineer of New Hanover County. Grant, *Alumni History of the University*, 300.
[193]Merchant and farmer. Branson, *Directory for 1884*, 433–434.

at their next meeting, to consult in regard to the completion of their Road to the State line.

I urged upon them the necessity & importance of *leaving* that portion of the Road that lays between the State line & this place, a distance of six miles, and showed them the Law, (which I refer you to, Laws of N.C. '71 & '72. Chap. 150. Sec. 10. Page 236) which gives the Board of the W.N.C.R.R. full power to do;[194] & I think they were favorably impressed with the idea. And if our Board was fully apprised of the importance of the Tenn: Road coming to this place, I think, they will make every effort to accomplish it; as it will save the State considerable money & time, as well as increasing the income of the State in the way of taxes & population, & giving to the Road a suitable place for connecting the Roads, which it is *impossible* to do at the State Line, thereby insuring the *completion* of the Road, & *connection* with the *Great N. West.*— So I hope you will do all in your power to have *a large force* put on this end of the Road, & give every encouragement to the speedy completion of *Our* Road. There are many reasons why the force should be put *on this end* of the line, but, I will confine myself to a few; from Asheville to Marshall then on 17 miles of grading finished, so if the force is put on this end, we could grade the 20 miles easily before the Legislature meets, & with cars running to this Place, & the whole Road graded, we would have plenty of credit without any assistance from the State, to *iron* & equipt the Road, as we can bond the same from this place to Salisbury, for not less than $10,000 per mile, which amounts to neary *$2,000,000.*, leaving, after paying the indebtedness of the Road, of *$850,000.* a large surplus, to expend, going west.

In fact there are so many reasons, that I will not attempt to take your valuable time, in explaining them.

So I hope, you will have Col. C. H. McGee's Committee notified, when the Board of the W.N.C.R.R. meets, & do all that your good judgement may dictate in the interest of *our* great enterprise.

N.B.

You will greatly oblidge me also, to give me full & timely notice when the Board of the W.N.C.R.R. meets, *so* I can have

---

[194]The section referred to stated that the directors of the Western North Carolina Railroad could "lease or sell or otherwise dispose of the whole or any part of said road to any person or corporation upon such terms as may be agreed upon. . . ."

Col: McGee's committee to pass over the entire Road with me, by so doing you will greatly oblige & confer a great favor, on your obedient Servant.

A&H—GP

A. H. Colquitt to Thomas J. Jarvis

Executive Department
Atlanta, Ga., December 18. 1879

In accordance with the request made in your Excellency^s communication of the 10th inst. I have the honor to inform you that I have appointed H. W. Cannon, of the County of Rabun to co–operate with the commissioner appointed by your Excellency in establishing the State line between the counties of Macon N.C. and Rabun Ga. The address of Mr Cannon is "Tiger" Rabun County. Ga.

A&H—GP

Z. B. Vance, Robert Brank Vance[195], and Robert Franklin Armfield[196] to Thomas J. Jarvis

United States Senate Chamber
Washington, Dec. 19th 1879

We have carefully read the proposition of Mr. W. J. Best[197] concerning the W.N.CR.Road.[198] The prefatory statement we believe to be fair and accurate and the estimates for completing

---

[195]Originally a farmer and merchant in Buncombe County, R. B. Vance, a Democrat, served in the House of Representatives from 1873 to 1885. After being defeated for re-election in 1884, he served from 1885 to 1889 as assistant commissioner of patents. He was a nephew of Z. B. Vance. *Biographical Directory of Congress*, 1,642.

[196]Lawyer of Statesville; member of the General Assembly, 1874; Democratic representative in Congress, 1879–1883; Superior Court judge, 1889–1895. *Biographical Directory of Congress*, 648.

[197]William J. Best, an immigrant from Ireland to New York City some years before the Civil War, he became a successful accountant and by the 1870's was connected with several prominent financial concerns. *Biographical and Genealogical History of the City of Newark* (New York: Lewis Publishing Company, 2 volumes, 1898), II, 316, hereinafter cited as *Biographical History of Newark*.

[198]See the following document for the proposition of Best and his associates to buy the state's interest in the Western North Carolina Railroad and to finish the road to Paint Rock and Ducktown. For the role of the state in the previous history of this railroad, see *Jarvis' Message to the General Assembly, March 15th, 1880*, in this volume; and Brown, *State Movement*, chs. 8, 11, and 12.

the Road quite reasonable. In our opinion the proposition is so beneficial and the matter so important to the interests of the State as to justify the Governor in submitting it to the Legislature at as early a day as possible.

A&H—GP

[*n.d.*]

The Western North Carolina Railroad Company—its condition, the cost to finish and equip it and the time required to do so, under existing laws; together with a plan whereby it may speedily be completed to Paint Rock and Ducktown without farther expense to the State.[199]

Existing laws forbid the contracting of any debt upon the franchises and property of the W.N.C.RR. Company to complete and equip its road. Moreover, the expenditure of public moneys for these purposes is restricted to $70,000 annually. This does not include the interest upon the bonds heretofore issued by the Railroad Company, amounting to about $60,000 per annum, for which the State is obligated. In addition to these sums, the State is required to furnish at least 500 convicts during the progress of the work and until it shall have been completed. The approximate annual cost of the support of these convicts is $41,000. The State's expenditure on account of this corporation is, therefore, at least $170,000 per annum.

To complete the Paint Rock branch, repair and ballast the roadway from Salisbury to Ash[e]ville, relay it with new iron, wherever necessary, and provide rolling stock, will involve an outlay of at least $700,000, including the convict labor. Were the whole appropriation devoted to these objects, Paint Rock would, probably, be reached in about seven years. As the law stands, however, after reaching Ash[e]ville the appropriation must be divided equally between the Paint Rock branch and the main line to Ducktown. Without new legislation, therefore, it is impossible to finish even this portion of the road in less than ten years; and it is certain the people to be benefitted by the Ducktown line will never consent to the diversion from their section of any part of the State aid to which they are entitled.

---

[199] This was the tentative proposal by Best and his associates to purchase the state's interest in the Western North Carolina Railroad and to finish the road to the Tennessee line. The proposal was considerably revised before Jarvis submitted it to the Council of State and the General Assembly.

As matters stand, the State is in duty bound ultimately to finish this division of the road, the cost of which will exceed $1,750,000. With the present appropriation this generation will hardly live to see the work completed.

To finish and equip the whole road, including interest upon the Company's outstanding bonds during the period of construction, $4,000,000 will yet have to be expended to place the road in a position to earn dividends upon its cost.

What security will the State hold for this large outlay? Merely a *second* lien upon the franchises of the Company, its rolling stock and roadway; for it must be borne in mind that the $850,000 mortgage heretofore executed by the Company covers its franchises and all its property. Should that mortgage be foreclosed, a contingency by no means remote and for which the State must be prepared, the holders of the bonds to secure which it was given would take the corpus and property of the Company, unless the State became the purchaser, in which event it would have to raise $850,000 either by taxation, or by the issue of new bonds.

The Ducktown line, though the most expensive to build, is the least valuable portion of the road. In the opinion of railroad experts, it will scarcely pay operating expenses for several years after completion. On the other hand, the road from Salisbury to Paint Rock is likely to prove remunerative as soon as finished.

In view of these facts is the present policy of the State a wise one? On the contrary, would it not be better to assign to responsible parties all its interest in the property of the Company upon conditions that would ensure the finishing of the road without farther State aid? The following is presented as the basis of an agreement, which would accomplish the object suggested

1   The State to assign to the United States Trust Co., of New York in trust for John Doe all its stock in and claims against the W.N.C.RR. Company, subject to the conditions which follow:

A. John Doe to enter into a contract with the State of North Carolina to finish the railroad of the W.N.C.RR. Company to Paint Rock on or before July 1, 1881, and to Ducktown on or before January 1, 1885, and provide the equipment therfor—

B. Upon the execution of said contract, John Doe to succeed to all the rights of the State, so far as relates to the control of the Board of Directors of said Company.

C. From and after the execution of said contract, John Doe to hold the State harmless in the matter of the payment of interest upon $850,000 of mortgage bonds heretofore issued by the Company.

D. John Doe to begin said work within two months from the date of the execution of said contract, and prosecute the construction of the main line to Ducktown and the Paint Rock branch simultaneously and with equal diligence and energy.

E. During the construction of said road the State to furnish John Doe not less than 500 convicts upon such terms as may be agreed upon.

F. John Doe may reorganize said Company upon the basis of a capital stock of $4,000,000. Of this stock, $500,000 to be set aside and reserved to said state in lieu of the convict labor given to the construction of said road and the interest paid upon the bonds of said Company since its reorganization in 1875; said $500,000 of stock to entitle said State to two representatives in the Board of Directors as reorganized by John Doe.

G. John Doe may cause to be executed by said Company a mortgage upon its franchises and property to secure the payment of such bonds as it may issue to aid in the construction and equipment of its road; provided, that until the whole of said road shall have been completed and equipped no bonds shall be issued to exceed $12,500 per mile, nor shall any bonds be issued in smaller amounts than $250,000 for every 20 miles of road finished and in actual operation.

H. Should John Doe fail to carry out his said contract, the grants made to him thereunder to become null and void, and upon due proof of such failure said Trust Company shall deliver to said State the stock of and claims against said Railroad Company assigned to said Trust Company in trust for John Doe.

I. In the contingency last provided for, the State may, with–or without notice to John Doe, repossess itself of the control of the Board of Directors of said Company, together with all the property of said Company as the same shall exist at the time of such default.

2   Three experienced railroad men, two of whom shall be residents of North Carolina, to be appointed a commission to super-

vise the building and equipment of said railroad:— one of said commissioners to be named by the State and one by John Doe:— the two thus chosen to select the third, and the decision of a majority to be alike binding upon the State and John Doe. Said Commissioners shall examine said road not less than once in ninety days, and whenever said John Doe shall notify them that 20 miles of roadway has been graded, and again when the same shall be ready to open for traffic. The expenses of said Commission to be borne by said Company, and the pay of the Commissioners to be fixed at $10 per day, each, exclusive of actual traveling expenses.

A&H—GP

M. W. Ransom, A. M. Scales, and J. J. Davis to Thomas J. Jarvis
United States Senate Chamber,
Washington, Dec 19th, 1879

The proposition submitted by Mr. Best of N.Y. impresses us on first sight with such force that we feel it our duty to say, that the subject deserves the most serious consideration of the Governor of N.C. And if he should be satisfied that the State can have proper security for all its rights & interests in the premises, and sufficient safeguards against any disappointment in the accomplishment of the great object of the completion of the Road to Paint Rock & to Ducktown in a reasonable time, and that this consumation depends upon prompt action, then that the matter should be submitted as soon as necessary to the Legislature of the State.

A&H—GP

John Bernard Manning[200] to Thomas J. Jarvis

New York Dec 23^d 1879

I again beg to address you on the subject of exchanging the North Carolina bonds issued to aid construction of the North Carolina RR.[201] Why is not the exchange effected according to the provisions of the Act passed by the last Legislature. It is true one part of the Act has been complied with in appointing

---

[200]New York stock broker and owner of varied shipping interests. *National Cyclopedia*, XXX, 336–337.
[201]See Jarvis to the Council of State, October 7, 1879, n.175, in this volume.

the Commissioners to negotiate the exchange, but for all they have done they might as well not have been selected for the purpose. There seems no disposition on their part to effect a compromise. I have been in correspondence with Messrs Bain and Davis on this subject but can get nothing definite from them as to what terms they will treat with the bondholders on. Some of the largest holders of the construction bonds have been in consultation lately at this office and all profess to meet the Commissioners liberally but there [sic] willingness to compromise is brought to a standstill by the non-committal policy of Commissioners. This is much to be regretted, the time is slipping past and nothing is being done. The bondholders are now ready and willing to trade but if their patience is taxed much longer I think it will revert to the detriment of the State.

We did intend holding out for an exchange at par of our bonds for a new 6% State bond; secured *in the same way as the present construction bonds,* but the temper of the bondholders now is to take the new bonds at say 98½ to 99^c on dollar thus allowing the State a little leeway for expenses &c, and to surrender the coupons on our present bonds—that is the coupons due January or April 1877. The unpaid portion of coupons due 1876, must be provided for in cash; as also those coupons due prior to 1876 which have not yet been presented to the Receiver for payment. These terms are a concession to those we had intended asking, but are willing to accept them sooner than have the matter remain longer in abeyance.

We were informed that the Commissioners wanted a decree from the Court to enable them to go on with the exchange and when I wrote Mr Davis asking for an abstract of the decree required, in order to submit it to the bondholders, it appeared they did not exactly know what was wanting.

If the Commissioners will only talk business and let us know what they require the exchange of bonds I feel assured, can be easily effected, we will throw no obstacles in the way but on the contrary do our utmost to bring about the desired result. This hesitating policy adopted by the Commissioners will do no good.

Since writing the foregoing I have seen some large holders and they with myself are willing to take 97½^c in new 6% bonds sooner than have the compromise go uneffected. This is the lowest. Awaiting a reply

A&H—GLB

Thomas J. Jarvis to J. B. Manning

Executive Department
Raleigh N.C. Dec 26ᵗʰ/79

Yours of the 23ʳᵈ has been recd and referred to the Commission for their consideration

The effort to compromise that part of the State Debt incurred in aid of the N.C.R.R. is in the hands of the Commissioners While I would not interfere with their duties yet I do not wish that you shall have any complaint to make. Hence I frankly reply to your letter.

1ˢᵗ I do not see that there is any *Compromise* on the part of the holders of the Bonds in asking the State to pay 98½ or 99 (C) for a Bond that is worth in the market less than 70 (C)

2ⁿᵈ I fear the great difficulty in the way of a compromise is that the holders put too great a value upon their security, the North Carolina. R.R.—

3ʳᵈ The Road now has the "care and protection of the State and while it is thus protected is good property."

4ᵗʰ It will be different if the State ceases to have an interest in it—as she will if the stock is sold and the projected hostile lines are constructed.

5ᵗʰ The State recognizes her obligations and in her poverty will meet them as fully as she is able.

6ᵗʰ She desires to treat all her credits as nearly a like as possible.

7ᵗʰ The Construction Bonds are no more binding upon her than her other anti-war Bonds

8ᵗʰ We are taking up other Bonds just as binding upon her as these at 40 cents with a new 4 per cent Bond.

9ᵗʰ The holders of these Bonds *happen* to have an advantage in that they have a Rail Road pledged for their redemption

10ᵗʰ The holders propose to take advantage of this fact to demand par less one cent.

11th This they have a right to do if they choose—but I beg they will not call it a *Compromise*.

12th I have generally found Northern creditors liberal in compromising with their Southern debtors—I regret to see their dispositions in this particular case are exceptions. I hope they will think better of the matter and will meet the Commission in a more liberal spirit

LETTERS FOR 1880

Thomas J. Jarvis to Z. B. Vance

[*Telegram*]

A&H—ZBV

Raleigh NC Jany 4 1880

Business engagements makes it impossible next week.[1] will write

A&H—GP

J. M. Brower to Thomas J. Jarvis

Mt. Airy N.C., Jan 9 1880

I rec'd a letter from you sometime since[2] in which you stated you had not interfered in the working of convicts on the CF&YVRR although President Gray states to the contrary, he was in our place this week & he says you told him it would not do to put hands to work here nor neither would you allow it to be done and also that he had seen some of the members of the board of Internal Improvements & they also refused & said it would not do to put hands to work on this end of the road. And he further says you told him you would call the board together & take action on it if he wished it & he told you he thought it was useless as you all had expressed yourselves in the matter. Governor as Mr Gray says the reason for not putting the hands

---

[1]Jarvis was probably trying to find a convenient time to visit Washington, D.C., in order to consult with the North Carolina congressmen about the sale of the Western North Carolina Railroad. See Jarvis to Wilson, February 3, 1880, *n.* 24, in this volume.

[2]See Jarvis to Brower, June 5, 1879, in this volume.

to work here I ask you in behalf of our people who are badly treated to call your board together & direct that the President of the CF&YVRR to place one hundred of the hands to work here the 100 the law gives us. by so doing you will do a favor which will never be forgotten by the people of north western NC, the people of this section of the state are very much displeased with you in regard to this matter, they are putting all the blame on you & the board of Internal Improvements for the work not being commenced on this end of the road. Gray refuses to do anything here untill the work is done below Greensboro when the law is plain & Imperative on him to put 100 of the hands to work west of Greensboro as soon as the two companies are consolidated.[3] Governor I appeal to you & ask that you interfere in this matter & see that we have justice done us in this matter. I have com[m]enced a suit against the company to compell them to commence the work to be heard before Judge Graves[4] on the 20 but I do hope it will be adjusted before for I know it damages the whole road to keep this suit up which I intend to do if we cant get what is due us otherwise & this is the reason I appeal to you to see that we have our hands put to work & I am satisfied Gray will do as you say and if your Board will order him to put the 100 hands west of Greensboro as is provided for in the act to change the name of the western road & consolidate the same with the Mountairy RR Co he cant nor wont refuse to do so. Please let [us] hear from you soon in regard to this whole matter

---

[3]The law incorporating the Cape Fear and Yadkin Valley Railroad specifically instructed its president and board of directors to place one hundred convicts on the road west of Greensboro. *Laws of North Carolina, 1879,* c. 67. s. 4. Jarvis, however, preferred to concentrate on building the eastern section of the road (see Jarvis to Caldwell, September 16, 1879, in this volume.), therefore, choosing virtually to ignore the mandate of the law. See Jarvis to Brower, January 17, 1880, in this volume.

[4]Jesse Franklin Graves of Mt. Airy; member of the General Assembly, 1876–1879; Superior Court judge, 1879–1894. *North Carolina Biography,* Volumes IV, V, and VI of *History of North Carolina,* by R. D. W. Connor, William K. Boyd, J. G. de Roulhac Hamilton, and Others (Chicago and New York: Lewis Publishing Company, 6 volumes, 1919), V, 128–129, hereinafter cited as *North Carolina Biography.*

A&H—GP

W. J. Best to Thomas J. Jarvis

Raleigh, N. Carolina
Jany. 10th. 1880

I have the honor herewith to enclose a draft of a bill[5] covering the proposition which I submit for the consideration of the honorable Council of State with the view to the sale of the State's interest in the Western North Carolina Railroad. The early decision of this question by the Council is important, both to the State, and myself. Please send me the decision of the Council to 120 Broadway, New York. On my return home, I shall submit a proposition to purchase the State's interest in the "Atlantic and North Carolina Railroad" [6] My reason for not doing so now is that I wish to consult certain friends in reference to the matter.

Hoping soon to hear from you

A&H—GLB

Thomas J. Jarvis to W. J. Best

Executive Department
Raleigh Jany 13th 1880

Your letter, with the draft of a Bill proposing the purchase of the interest of the State of North Carolina in the Western North Carolina Railroad Company, is on file in this office, and in due time will be laid before the Council of State.

The Western North Carolina Railroad, as I am fully aware, in the hands of Capitalists, and judicialy managed, will be, when its connections are made, very valuable property. By the Paint Rock Route, Louisville, St Louis, Cincinnati, and the vast North West will find its shortest way to the Seaboard, either at Wilmington, Beaufort, Norfolk or Richmond, by the Carolina Central, the North Carolina, the Raleigh and Augusta or the Richmond and Danville Railroad.

---

[5] Jarvis returned the proposed bill to Best (see Best to Jarvis, February 2, 1880, in this volume), and no copy has been found.

[6] The capital stock of the Atlantic and North Carolina Railroad was $1,800,000, of which the state owned $1,266,600. *Daily News* (Raleigh), August 4, 1880, hereinafter cited as *Daily News.*

The Baltimore and Ohio Road has its Southern terminal at Danville Virg^a and is anxiously seeking to extend its connections still further South Westwardly, and one of its proposed routes is to push on to Statesville, a point on the Western North Carolina Railroad. By a reference to the map you will see that Statesville, Asheville, Danville and Chatanooga are almost on an Air–line—thus giving the shortest possible route to the Great South West. In addition to this the route will penetrate one of the finest sections on this Continent. The scenery climate and fertility of the soil from Asheville to Ducktown cannot be excelled. The mineral wealth, consisting of Gold, Silver, Copper, Iron, Mica and a great variety of Marbles, is incalculable. In fact this Section of our State but needs Capital and opportunity to make it all that could be desired.

The many evidences, recently developed, of the interest which Capital from widely distant parts of the Union, is taking in this Road and its connections, are surely well founded, and show that its great value is known and duly appreciated.

I mention these facts to show you our appreciation of the value and magnitude of the purchase you propose, and the foundation of whatever opposition there may be (and it is likely to be not inconsiderable) on the part of the people of North Carolina to part with their interest in it on any terms.

If the General Assembly convenes to consider your proposition, I desire that it shall be in such shape as to insure its favorable action, and for this reason I beg to suggest a few amendments to the Bill which you have submitted to me.

In Section 11. after the words, "as it may then exist" insert: free and discharged from all claims or demands of whatever kind which said Best and his Associates may have acquired therein, and free and discharged from all claims, demand, debt, lien or obligation they may have asserted, permitted, or suffered thereagainst in favor of any person, or persons except the State of North Carolina.

This is in furtherance of what I understand to be your original idea.

In same section the words "and upon due proof of such failure" seem to me vague, and may lead to trouble. I would suggest that they be stricken out and in lieu thereof insert: Upon the certificate of the Commissioners provided for in Section 12 of this Act.

The $500.000 in First Mortgage Bonds which you propose to

deliver to the State in compensation for money expended since the Mortgage to secure of the $850.000 Bonds now outstanding, will not cover the amount actually expended, to say nothing of interests, and as this fact when known to the Legislature would likely lead to discussion and objection, I suggest that you make the amount sufficient to cover actual expenditures. An additional $54.000 will do it. This will make the amount of Bonds to be paid to the State $554.000.

To call the Legislature together is assuming a very grave responsibility, and to justify myself in so doing, I must have a substantial, tangible guarranty, which can be reached in this State; and for this purpose, I shall require that you deposit in the Citizens National Bank in this City $30.000 to be held by the Bank for the following purposes and subject to the following conditions, Viz 1. If the Legislature declines to adopt your proposition the deposit to be subject immediately to your order. 2. If the Legislature does adopt your proposition and you fail to close the contract or purchase as agreed upon, the Treasurer of the State shall apply the deposit to the payment of the expenses of the Session of Legislature. 3. If the proposition is adopted and closed according to agreement, the deposit to remain as a further security for the payment of the interest on the $850.000 First Mortgage Bonds now outstanding (and which you agree to pay) until the said Bonds are paid and cancelled.

While those who knew you are satisfied that your proposition is made in good faith, and they believe that you will honestly execute it if it is accepted, you will readily understand why it is that I in a matter–of such great importance, insist that nothing shall be left to accident whereby the Public interest might be prejudiced.

A&H—GLB

Thomas J. Jarvis to J. W. Wilson

Executive Department
Raleigh Janey 14th 1880

I send you enclosed two letters forwarded to me by Lt Gov Robinson—one from Mr Fain and one from Mr Herbert—[7]

As before suggested I think it best for you to make your contract with one responsible man to include everything—pay

---

[7]Unable to identify.

of guard, feed, clothing, Dr Bills and everything—Then you will know exactly what you are doing—The contractor can be clothed with authority to control the convicts and he may employ as many men at his own expense to assist him as he chooses.

Please attend to this in due time

A&H—GLB

Thomas J. Jarvis to Alexander Ramsey[8]

Executive Department
Raleigh Jany 14th 1880

I have the honor herewith to transmit to you, through Senator Vance, certified copy of Resolution[9] passed by the General Assembly of North Carolina, and to ask your compliance with the expressed of wish of the same—

These Letter Books of the Executive of this State are of great value to us; and I trust the time has come when they will not longer be withheld from us—Their return to the Archives of this State will be taken by this State Administration as an evidence on the part of the Government of the United States to remove, as far as it can, every hindering cause to a full and complete reconciliation in any section of the Country.

I beg that you will order those Books to be delivered to Senator Vance to the end that he may return them to his State

A&H—GLB

Thomas J. Jarvis to J. M. Brower

Executive Department
Raleigh Jany 17th 1880

In reply to yours of the 9th I beg to say that I have no power or inclination to direct Mr Gray and his Board of Directors as to what part of their road they put their force to work on— They ought to know better than I do what is best for the Com-

---

[8] Governor of Minnesota, United States senator, and, from 1879 to 1881, secretary of war. *Dictionary of American Biography*, XV, 341–342.

[9] This resolution, enacted February 19, 1877, asked for the return of these North Carolina Civil War letter books. It further ordered the governor of the state to have copies made of the letter books if they were not returned. *Laws of North Carolina, 1876–1877*, 593–594. The original letter books were not returned until, November, 1962.

pany and if they do not then I would advise the stockholders in April when they meet to select better men—For one I have confidence in them and if I had the power to interfere with them I would not—I shall furnish the Board of Directors with all the means and support that I can under the laws to help them push forward the C.F.&Y.V.RR which I consider one of the most important enterprises in the State—How they shall use this means the law leaves with them, and you are in part responsible for this law.

You refused to even allow the Gov to appoint the Directors on the part of the State and hence it is wrong for you to allow me to be blamed as to how the work is done or where the force is worked—

A&H—GP

Robert McKnight Furman[10] *to Thomas J. Jarvis*

Strictly Confidential

Washington, Jany 18th, 1880

The very great interest I feel in the completion of the W.N.C.R.R. to its termini is my apology for troubling you with this letter. I have heard nothing of the action of your council upon the proposition submitted to it, through you, by Mr Best. I have heard some things in Washington, that I did not hear of in Raleigh, relative to the opinions of certain gentlemen concerning the matter of sale, which opinions it is also asserted have much weight with our State authorities. I feel very sure, however, that their opinions will receive the consideration their respective personal interests would suggest they deserve. Sincerely believing that no mere individual considerations will be considered or prevail, I will proceed to discuss the subject direct. The laws now contemplate the *completion* by the State, of the road to Murphy and Paint Rock. It involves an annual outlay of $170,000,00. To give the entire appropriation of labor and money to the Paint Rock branch, the latter could not be finished within two years—I have been assured by contractors three

---

[10]Furman had been editor of the *Asheville Citizen* since 1872. From 1876 to 1893 he was clerk of the state Senate, and from 1893 to 1897 he served as state auditor. For many years he was chairman of the Buncombe County Democratic Executive Committee. W. F. Tomlinson, *Biography of the State Officers and Members of the General Assembly of North Carolina, 1893* (Raleigh: Edwards & Broughton, 1893), 12, hereinafter cited as Tomlinson, *Biography of North Carolina.*

would be required. Then to complete the Western Division, after the P. Rock branch is completed, will require, under present laws which no one can hope to have amended so as to allow larger sums of money—twenty years; thus 22 years will have been spent before that country can be opened up with Railroad facilities, and an outlay by the State of over three and a–half millions, independent of equipment &c. Do you believe the State will go on with this taxation year after year in this manner? Dont you believe the State will repeal, at its next session, the appropriation for the Western Division? It has been suggested to me by an influential member of the board of Directors for the Road, Col Scales, that the State will cut off the W.D., build at once to P. Rock, and then use the proceeds of that line to build the W.D. whenever there are any proceeds on that road, would the State not require as much of said proceeds as might be necessary, to go towards paying the $60,000 interest, and *if* (?) these should be more, use it to liquidate the principal of that debt? How much would be left, under your most sanguine expectations, to carry on the work west of Asheville. Suppose it might be suggested that the State should put a mortgage on the road to complete it west. There being already a mortgage on the *entire* property, from Salisbury to P. Rock *and Ducktown*, for $850,000, do you believe you could possibly dispose of a second mortgage, calling for enough to finish the road? And granting bonds might be disposed of, aside from their selling at a great sacrifice, would they not ultimately take the road & property for their payment? Dont you believe, Governor, to rely upon such contingencies to build that road, will result *only* in cutting off that western division entirely? I know, and every man acquainted with the matter will tell you, that the road already built *must be used as the basis* for the completion of the Ducktown branch. It must be worked together by the State, or in selling, the contract of sale must be based upon the completion of the W.D. Any other course will destroy that W.D. for this generation at least.

Have you discovered that our State has ever made anything by managing railroads? Has one under State (political) management ever paid expenses, much less made money? If this road should remain under such control can you hope for any better results?

It is not worth the while to disguise the matter, the eastern *taxpayers*, not thinking, aspiring politicians, are tired of the tax for the western road. The next legislature will as certainly repeal the law applying to the W.D. as you are to-day the Governor of the State, your inclinations and recommendations, and the pledges of *politicians* in State convention to the contrary notwithstanding. I hazzard nothing in asserting, that if the proposition could be submitted to the people of the State, to keep up taxation as it now exists, for this road, or sell the property and thus secure the early completion of both lines, the latter would carry by an overwhelming vote. I found no man who did not say unhesitatingly, if the State can be made anything like whole for her late expenditures on behalf of this road, and secure satisfactory guarantees of the completion of the 170 miles yet remaining, let it go by all means. Suppose some prominent man should come out advocating this sale under the circumstances proposed, do you think for one moment he, if he has any strength at all, would not receive the strong endorsement of our convention and party? I do not hesitate to believe he would, *knowing as much as I do of the feelings of leading men in all sections.* Should you refuse to call the legislature and let it take the responsibility of choosing between the completion by the State as now provided, or selling to responsible parties, will you not subject yourself to the charge, in the east, of refusing to do what was or might be in your power to relieve them of what they think to be a burden, and in the west, jeopardizing the dearest interests of those people, possibly losing them this road, for fear *you* might suffer because of calling an extra session of the legislature? On the other hand, if you should call the body together, the road sold and its entire completion secured, and the people of the entire State relieved of taxation to the amount now appropriated, would it not result in the grand triumph of the party *and of yourself at its head*? Certain Railroad gentlemen may oppose it. Can their personal interests outway [*sic*] the great interests of the people of the State—the taxpayers generally and the material interests of 20 000 square miles of our territory?

I know several parties have expressed a desire to buy and build the road, to *Paint Rock*—but will say nothing of the W.D. Upon hearing of the proposition to build both, Mr McGee of the E—Tenn. Road endeavored to buy a majority of the *private stock,* so as to control it against any action of the State looking to a completion of the W.D., because the latter could, when completed through, compete with his road. Some others are fearful, lest when completed other roads which connect with it may also be beneficiaries of the trade and traffic over the line, and could doubtless defeat any action of yours, or possibly prevent any, which looks to the selling of the road. Can all the interests involved in this matter, the interests of the taxpayers, of our party, and our section, be made subservient to such influences?

I have put every phase of this matter to you as plainly and frankly as I can. My regard for you personally and deep interest in this matter would not allow me to do otherwise. I hope to hear something within a few days, of good to our every interest. I sincerely trust all may turn out for the best.

I have heard of criticisms in the State upon members of congress for endorsing the proposed plan. They have not had the effect to weaken one of them in their opinions as to the necessity [of] taking early steps to settle this R.R. matter, nor to remove from their minds the great advantage to our party and people of the sale of the road and the securing of its early completion. Would be glad to hear from you.

A&H—GP

W. J. Best to Thomas J. Jarvis

New York 19 Jany 1880

Your favors of 12th and 13th inst. were duly received and have been acknowledge. I shall now proceed to answer them.

Respecting the Atlantic and North Carolina Railroad I am not yet prepared to submit any proposition. This road, as you are aware, is of little value by itself. It may, however, be made very valuable as a part of a through line from the Tennessee system of railways to the Seaboard. To make it available in connection with the Western North Carolina Railroad, it would be necessary to use the N.C. Division of the Piedmont Air Line, from Salisbury to Goldsboro: I have, therefore, written to Col A. B. Andrews to ascertain what terms, or running arrangements, can be made with that Company. As soon as I hear from him, I shall probably send you an offer for the State's interest in A.&N.C.R.R.

I accept the second amendment you suggest to Section. 11. of the draft of an Act embodying my offer for the interest of the State in the W.N.C.R.R. As to the additional $50,000 of the mortgage bonds which you ask, I feel sure I can arrange in accordance with your views. Further, I deem eminently just and proper, your suggestion in reference to the deposit of $30,000, for the purposes and subject to the conditions named by you, should the Legislature be convened in special session and ratify the Act which I have submitted. Regarding the depository, I do not doubt we shall be able to agree. I prefer, however, to keep the question open until I shall have been able to confer with yourself and my friends. In fact, you have raised only one point to which I cannot assent, viz, to amend Section. II. by inserting the following: "free and discharged from all claims or demands of whatever kind, which said Best and his associates may have acquired therein, and free and discharged from all claims, demand, debt, lien or obligation they may have created, permitted or suffered there against in favor of any person or persons except the State of North Carolina."

Upon this basis it would be merely a waste of time to attempt to raise the money to complete and equip the road. It would place the investor absolutely at the mercy of the Commissioners provided for in Section 12; for they, or a majority of them, when the work had been progressed almost to completion, might find it to their interest to declare the deed of trust forfeited. You may regard this view of the matter rather extreme. To my mind, however, it is not impossible, and, were I to lose sight of it, I would not be exercising ordinary business caution. With such a contingency before you, could you, in my place, advise the public to risk from $3,000,000 to $4,000,000. in the construction & equipment of this road? My proposition has been made in good faith and will be faithfully carried out. That such is the fact is evidenced by the following provision, which you will find in section 7: "and said bonds shall have printed thereon that they are issued for the purpose of completing the railroad of said Company and that the mortgage deed of said Company executed for the purpose of completing the railroad of said Company executed to secure the payment of said bonds cannot be foreclosed until said railroad shall have been completed to Paint Rock and Murphy aforesaid, and that no interest shall become due and payable upon said bonds until the interest period, six months, next ensuring the completion of said railroad to Paint Rock."

Beside the notice printed upon the bonds, I propose that each bond shall carry a considerable amount of stock, thus giving the bondholder a voice in the management of the Company, and the means of seeing his funds properly applied. I am not aware of such precautions ever having been taken in any similar enterprise. Indeed, I believe I have made the most ample provision for the protection of the State's interest, as well as that of myself and friends.

A&H—GLB

Thomas J. Jarvis to William T. R. Bell[11]

Executive Department
Raleigh Jany 19th 1880

I hardly think it would be possible for me to be present on the 21st of Feb at the unfurling of the Centennial Flag on Kings Mountain.

I am very much engaged with public matters, and am likely to be for some time.

I trust all the preparation will be made to make the celebration in Oct a grand success. It will be my pleasure to contribute whatever I may be able to do then or before to this most patriotic undertaking.

A&H—GLB

*Thomas J. Jarvis to the Board of Directors of
the Penitentiary*

Executive Department
Raleigh Jany 20th 1880

I look to the judicious use of the convict labor as an important factor in the future development of the resources of the State.

There is, as I am informed, a fair probability of a Rail Road being speedily built to Chapel Hill, and its projectors desire to have the benefit of some of this labor.

It seems to me that the State has some indirect interest in this work. It will increase the prosperity of the State University —It will develop a valuable mica mine whose ore is now of no practical value and the opening this mine will give work to the North Carolina and Atlantic Rail Road in the way of freights, both of which belong chiefly to the State.

---

[11]Principal of King's Mountain Military Academy; member of the General Assembly, 1874. *Cyclopedia of the Carolinas*, II, 442-443.

Any arrangement you may make with the authorities of the Chapel Hill Road for a hundred convicts by which the State looses nothing, will have my approval, if at any time it should be deem necessary for my approval to be given.

A&H—GP

Albert Smith Marks[12] *to Thomas J. Jarvis*
[*with enclosure*]

Executive Office
Nashville, Tenn. 21st Jany 1880

In compliance with the direction of the General Assembly of Tennessee I have the honor to transmit to your Excellency a copy of a joint resolution of that body suggesting a Centennial Celebration of Kings Mountain. As Kings Mountain was the key to Yorktown, and Yorktown, the key to American Independence the General Assembly of Tennessee deemed it appropriate to suggest to her sister States, whose troops participated with hers in that interesting event, the propriety of its Centennial Celebration. You will observe that the proposed celebration is dependent upon the concurrence and cooperation of your Excellency. If approved by your Excellency it is important that your approval be signified as soon as it may be done with convenience in order that the preliminary steps for the celebration may be taken without delay.

[*enclosure*]

Senate Joint Resolution No 3

Whereas the One hundredth anniversary of the battle of "Kings Mountain" will occur on the 7th day of October next, in which the gallant Soldiers from Tennessee (then a portion of North Carolina) Virginia North and South Carolina participated, winning Victory, and
Whereas it is proper that we should commemorate their gallant deeds, and show to the world that we appreciate and cherish the great blessings of civil and religious liberty for which our forefathers so nobly struggled, Therefore

---

[12]Governor of Tennessee from 1879 to 1881. *National Cyclopedia*, VII, 212–213.

Be it resolved by the General Assembly of the State of Tennessee, That the Governor is hereby requested to communicate with the Governors of North and South Carolina and Virginia, for the purpose of inaugurating a movement to celebrate on the grounds the anniversary aforesaid

Resolved; That should said Celebration meet with the approval of the Governors of the aforesaid States, the Governor of Tennessee shall appoint a committee of ten, three from each grand division of the State and one for the State at large who shall meet similar committees at Charlotte North Carolina on the 22nd of June 1880, for the purpose of making all arrangements necessary for the celebration of the Centennial of "Kings Mountain"

Resolved that the Historical Society of Tennessee, and the Historical Societies of the three other States if such there be, be, and are, hereby invited to co-operate in said Celebration.

Adopted Dec 24th 1879

A&H—GP

Thomas J. Jarvis to W. J. Best

Executive Department
Raleigh N.C. Jany. 24, 1880

If the state parts with the Western N.C. Railroad, the consideration will be not so much, what she gets from the work done, as to get the railroad completed without further expenditure by the State.

The only guarantee you offer in your proposition to go on with the work, is the right of the state to enter, if you fail to carry out your contract.

This right, as you can well see, would be a barren right, if the state is to take the road back, subject to all the encumbrances you choose to put upon it—It would be so easy for you and your associates to put such a mortgage upon it, that the right of the state to enter, would be practically worth nothing, and the state in this may lose the work already done and the Road thus remain uncompleted. But you will say, this cannot happen, for you are acting in good faith and intend to complete the work. I have no doubt you are acting in good faith, but how do I know that you will live to act at all, or who your associates are, or what they will do in the event of your death. I think the failure of yourself and associates is quite as likely as the positive act of bad faith on the part of the state suggested in your letter of the 19th. I would not have the State take any advantage of you, and you must excuse me for seeing to it, that nothing is left open, whereby, you and your associates could take any advantage of her. The tribunal which is to pass upon this question is one of your own creation, in part, and I think you can well afford to trust it. Certainly I think there is no cause to apprehend the extreme view suggested by you. We can agree upon men of such high character, that they will not be liable to any suspicion. Then, if they were to permit the fraud, suggested in your objection, the Courts would protect you against its consumation.

But if this kind of guarantee does not suit you, suppose you change your proposition to let the State pass out entirely, based on these two ideas. Pay the State in her own bonds for the money, she has put into the work, then put up some of her bonds; the amount to be agreed upon; as a guarantee for the faithful completion of the work.

A&H—GLB

Thomas J. Jarvis to R. M. Furman

Executive Department
Raleigh N.C. Jany 26th 1880

My time was so much taken up with the different Boards that met in my office last week that I really did not have the time to make an earlier reply to your letter.

Many years ago it was said by a man of some wisdom "Save me from my friends" and all along through life we see instances of the kind illustrating this fact. Well might the W.N.R.R. say this if it had a tongue to speak. The last number of the [Asheville] Citizen on the proposed purchase of the Road is the worst blow the work has received. It is more damaging to the continuance of the work than all that its enemies can write or say or do in a year. When the Citizens [sic] declares the Road to Paint Rock cannot be completed in three years and Ducktown in ten it makes itself a living witness to all that is said in the "Mud Cut Boom." As a fact it is not true. If it be true that thirteen years more of work is before us, let the people of the State so understand it and good–bye Road.

I am in favor of a sale of the road, if it can be done on proper terms. I am more particular about the terms that looks to the completion of the road than I am about the amount we are to receive for the Road. I shall stickle more about the guarantees for the completion of the Road than I do about the security for the money—

The proposition of Mr Best as made by him does not give this guarantee. I do not intend to leave anything to chance, but to provide if possible for every contingency. I have a hope that Mr Best will satisfy me on this point. When he does, the difficulties in the way of a sale will be, so far as I know, removed, I am determined, if I have brains enough to do it, to see to it that if the State gives up the Road that the man that takes *it shall build* it.

Mr Best may be and for all I know is in every way reliable; but I cannot trust alone to that. The contract before I can give it my approval must be such that neither the State nor its Western Section, which has the deepest interest in this matter, shall be left without the means to *force* a compliance with the terms of the contract, if a voluntary compliance is refused.

I know this course is obliged to secure your approval as well as the rest of the friends of the road and the State.

A&H—GLB

J. W. Wilson to Thomas J. Jarvis

Washington D.C.
Jany 26th 1880

Can you meet Mr B[est] and myself in Greensboro Wednesday night. Reply at Willards [Hotel]

A&H—GLB

Thomas J. Jarvis to J. W. Wilson

Executive Department
Raleigh Janey 27th 1880

Cant leave you and B. come here

A&H—GP

T. S. Kenan to Thomas J. Jarvis

Attorney General Department.
Raleigh, 27 Jany 1880

In reply to your inquiry as to whether under existing law you have the authority to pay the Beaufort Light Infantry for services rendered during and immediately after the terrible storm of August 1879,[13] I have the honor to state, that under the facts as contained in the papers, the authority is given by the Act of 1876–77 chapter 272 section 2. They were ordered on duty by competent authority, and a refusal to obey would have subjected them to penalties. And it must be presumed that the emergency of the occasion and the overruling necessity for efficient protection to life and property were sufficient to induce the General commanding, to interpose his commands for the purpose of arresting any anticipated riot or disturbance. The circumstances disclosed by the facts warranted a reasonable apprehension of trouble, and it seems to me, that to require the services of an organized body of men on such an occasion to protect property, and possibly life, was a precautionary measure well taken, and not the subject of just criticism. At all events, duty was performed by the company in obedience to orders, and for which they are entitled to pay.

A&H—GP

Thomas Michael Holt[14] to Thomas J. Jarvis

[*Telegram*]

Jany 28 1880

Will you meet Best at my house friday evening. He prefers not to go to Raleigh. if you will come to Haw River answer

---

[13]See Jarvis to Kenan, January 26, 1880, Governors' Papers (not included in this volume). For the storm referred to, see Pool to Jarvis, August 21, 1879, n. 154, in this volume.
[14] Textile manufacturer of Haw River; member of the General Assembly, 1876–1879, 1883–1887; governor of North Carolina, 1891–1893. For twelve years Holt was president of the North Carolina Agricultural Society. *National Cyclopedia*, IV, 430.

Thomas J. Jarvis to T. M. Holt

Executive Department
Jany 28th 1880

Care Senator Z B Vance
Senate Chamber
Washington D.C.

I shall be glad to visit you at some other time. Cant go Friday,
say to Mr B. to come to Raleigh, if he desires to see me

Thomas J. Jarvis to A. S. Marks

Executive Department
Raleigh Jany 28th 1880

Your communication of the 21st enclosing a copy of certain
resolutions recently adopted by the General Assembly of Tennessee and approved by yourself in relation to the celebration
of the coming centennial anniversary of the battle of Kings
Mountain has been received.

It gives me great pleasure I beg leave to assure your Excellency to see the interest manifested by yourself and the General
Assembly of Tennessee in the proposed celebration. One hundred
years ago the territory whose people now so justly take pride
in the name of Tennessee was fully as much apart of North
Carolina as that which still bears the name. We were all North
Carolinians then, and it is gratifying to know that though no
longer one in name, and no longer one in territory we are still
one in affection and one in admiration for the great achievements
of our common ancestors, and in our determination on suitable
occasions to make that admiration known to the world.

The success that befell the American Arms on Kings Mountain[,] a success achieved by Southern Troops under Southern
leaders upon Southern soil[,] was the turning point in the war
of the Revolution. But for Kings Mountain there would have
been no Guilford Court House, and without Guilford Court
House there could have been no Yorktown. It was the meaning
of the day that was to bring forth assured success, success that
meant the indication and establishment of the right of self

government, after a long night of despotism despair and defeat.
And that our forefathers bore so conspicuous a part in our
achievement so conspicuous for the brillant genius of its con-
ception and the grand daring of its execution no less than for its
magnificent and momentous consequences, we may well be
proud whether we call ourselves Tennesseans or North Carolinians. It gives me pleasure therefore to inform you that measures have already been taken by the people of North and South
Carolina also looking to a proper observance of the centennial
anniversary of the battle of Kings Mountain on the very field
upon which the battle was fought. On the 22ᵈ of next month a
magnificent flag of mammoth size will be raised upon the highest
point of the battle field there to remain; when and where various preliminary arrangements for the celebration will also be
perfected—In all our arrangements honored the presence and
participation of our brethren of Tennessee and Virginia have
been affectionately contemplated and anxiously anticipated.

I beg leave therefore to assure your Excellency that I take
great pleasure in signifying to you my approval of the proposed
celebration, and that I will at once proceed to designate suitable
gentlemen to meet in Charlotte on 22ᵈ June next, then and there
to confer with the gentlemen of the committee appointed by
yourself and with the gentlemen of similar committees from
South Carolina and Virginia; and further that from time to time
as opportunity may offer, I will do every thing in my power
that may tend to make the celebration of the coming centennial
commensurate with the importance of the magnificent achievements it is intended to commemorate.

A&H—GLB

Thomas J. Jarvis to W. T. R. Bell

Executive Department
Raleigh Jany 29ᵗʰ 1880

Since writing you on the 19ᵗʰ inst I have had a correspondence
with Gov Marks of Tennessee; copies of which I herein enclose.

I beg to suggest that at the first meeting of the Citizen's Committee which now has in charge the Kings Mountain celebration
you lay before the Committee this correspondence; and suggest
to them the propriety of taking such steps as in their wisdom
may seem best looking to a participation of Tennessee; and Va

in the proposed celebration, and a cooperation with the Committee suggested by Gov Marks.

I would further suggest that the Governors of South and North Carolina be requested to invite the Governor and people of Virginia to participate in the preliminary arrangements and in the final grand celebration.

With renewed assurances of my readiness to cooperate in this patriotic work

A&H—GLB

Thomas J. Jarvis to William Dunlap Simpson[15]

Executive Department
Raleigh Jany 29th 1880

I send you enclosed copies of a correspondence recently held with Gov Marks of Tennessee.

I presume you have had similar letter from him yourself. If not the papers accompanying this will explain themselves.

King's Mountain is upon the line that divides our State, being partly in one and partly in the other. The Battle Field lies, I believe, wholly in your State—as we say—by a mistake of the Commissioners who established the line. So you see we are not without some claim to the actual soil made so dear to every American heart. While time has bared our right to an assertion of that claim it can never obliterate the memory we cherish for our heroes whose deeds helped to immortalize the spot.

The Mountain with its hallowed association standing as it does between us will always serve, I trust, to bind us closer together in bonds of mutual regard and interests. Upon its historic heights I hope to see the people of both States gather next October, in multitudes, to commemorate, in the Centennial celebration, *the* great *victory* of 1780.

As a part of the patriots who fought for Liberty that day were from our Sister State Virginia I beg to suggest that, in addition to the adoption of the suggestions of Governor Marks, we write the Governor of Virginia and the people to participate in the preliminary arrangements; and in the grand celebration.

I would that the people of North and South Carolina of Ten-

---

[15]Governor of South Carolina from 1878 to 1880. In 1880 he became chief justice of the state Supreme Court. *Dictionary of American Biography*, XVII, 184.

nessee and Virginia attest to the world, by their commemoration of the Battle of King's Mountain, that they will maintain, at all hazards, the principals [*sic*] of civil liberty for which their revered ancestors died.

A&H—GP

J. W. Garrett [16] *et al. to Thomas J. Jarvis*

Kings Mountain N.C.
Jan'y 29th 1880

In obedience to instructions from the Executive Committee of the Kings Mountain Centennial Association we have the honor to invite you to attend a public meeting to be held on the pinnacle of Kings Mountain Feby 21st 1880

The meeting is intended to awaken an interest in the proposed Centennial Celebration of the Battle of Kings Mountain, to be held Octo 7th 1880. As it is intended to make that a national affair your attendance on the 21st Febry will be gratifying to the Committee. Distinguished speakers from this state, South Ca and Georgia will be present.

A&H—GLB

W. D. Simpson to Thomas J. Jarvis

Executive Chamber
Columbia S.C. Feby 2[d] 1880

Your letter of the 29th inst has been received with the copies of the correspondence with his Excellency Governor Marks

I had received some days before a similar letter from Governor Marks, and had responded assuring him of every cordial approval and cooperation. I neglected however to state to him that an association of citizens of North and South Carolina had been organized with Col A. Coward of Yorkville, S.C. as Chairman, looking to the centennial celebration of the battle of King's Mountain in October 1880. I am glad to find that you brought the fact to the attention of Governor Marks.

I agree with you—that the battle of King's Mountain was a most important event in the Revolution of 1775. It was in fact

---

[16]Merchant of King's Mountain. Branson, *Directory, 1878,* 79.

the pivotal point in the Southern Campaign of that day. And in those centennial celebrations, this grand natural momument—King's Mountain—to the gallantry and devotion of our forefathers in the great cause of self government should not be overlooked. I do not know so well about the Commissioners having made a mistake in the line between us as referred by you so as to throw this glorious battle field on our side. We will not however raise that issue at this time—it is so near the line that we can regard it in sentiment at least as common property, and in view of the common sacrifices and gallantry of our ancestors made and illustrated thereon for a common good we may look upon it as a bond that would bind us their descendants together forever. And we should join heart[i]ly in the commemoration of the noble deeds of those who were conspicuous on that devoted field on the 8th of October 1780, nearly a century ago.

You suggest that we should invite the Governor of Va to participate in the preliminary arrangements in Feby as well as the grand celebration in October.

I have just received from Col Coward chairman of the Association referred to an invitation to attend, and I have no doubt that you will also receive a similar invitation, and that the Governor of Va will also be invited. And inasmuch as the Association seems to have taken charge of this matter, would it not be better for them to go on, and let us write a letter to the Gov of Va urging his cooperation.

UNC—UP

[*Pamphlet*]

Executive Office
Raleigh, N.C., Feb'y 2, 1880

To the Friends of Higher Education:

The Board of Trustees of the University, at their late meeting, instructed President Battle to appeal to the friends of higher education in this State and elsewhere in his discretion, for pecuniary aid to relieve the Institution from present embarrassment and to enable it more effectually to carry out its great objects.

The University was re–organized in 1875 in the midst of a financial depression, of a severity almost unparalleled, which has continued to a recent date. The sums contributed by its friends during that year have been mostly spent in repairs absolutely necessary, and for purchase of apparatus essential for instruction.

It was hoped that the income of the University would, within four or five years, suffice to pay its annual expenses. The stringency of the times has prevented this happy result. The attendance of students is as large as during any year prior to 1850. But a considerable number of these students pay no tuition—some by reason of their appointment by the counties as allowed by law, others by the free gift of the University. The University is proud of its beneficiary work. It desires and expects that this work shall not be diminished—that in the future, as in the past, no worthy young man shall be turned from its doors for want of means.

But from these causes the University is in need of further help, to discharge its floating liabilities incurred since its re-organization and to effect such improvements as will place its educational facilities abreast with the demands of the age.

Being entirely satisfied that all contributions to the University will be economically and wisely used, I cordially commend this application as eminently worthy of a liberal response.

THOS. J. JARVIS,
Governor and ex-officio Ch'm'n B'd of Trustees,
of the University of North Carolina.

A&H—GP

W. J. Best to Thomas J. Jarvis

Raleigh N.C. Febry 2ᵈ 1880

Referring to my letter of 10ᵗʰ inst., I beg to acknowledge the return of the draft of an act, then submitted, embodying my offer to purchase the interest of the State in the Western North Carolina Railroad. As a substitute, I herewith enclose a draft[17] which substantially embodies the amendments suggested in your letter of the 13ᵗʰ ult. In accordance with our recent conversation, I have added a proviso to section 3, in reference to discriminations against the towns and cities of North Carolina in the matter of freight and passenger rates, which, I believe, will fully meet your views.

---

[17]Not found.

After careful consideration, I have concluded not to submit any proposition for the Atlantic and North Carolina Railroad.[18]

A&H—GP

Armand John De Rossett,[19] David Reid Murchison,[20] and

Donald McRae[21] to Thomas J. Jarvis

Wilmington N.C. Feby 2. 1880

A report having been circulated in the papers, that a proposition has recently been made in behalf of Northern Capitalists for the purchase of the State's interest in the Western North Carolina Rail Road—a private meeting of some of our leading Citizens has been held to consider the Subject in connection with the interests of our State & particularly of this City—

The undersigned was appointed a Committee to communicate with Your Excellency, & ask for such information as you may be authorized & deem proper to give in regard to the terms of such proposition (if any has been made) and to request earnestly & respectfully that no steps shall be taken for consummating any disposition of the property refer'd to until the people of Wilmington & such other Citizens as may unite with them, shall have had an opportunity of submitting a proposition for the purchase, or that they shall have the first offer of such terms as may be decided upon by the proper Authorities, if it shall be deemed best for the interest of the State to dispose of its property in the said Road—

We do not doubt that an arrangement can be made for raising a Company to purchase the property & to provide for the management & control of its operations by the people of our own State, rather than to see it placed in the hands of Strangers who might make it instrumental in working the most ruinous damage to the best interests of North Carolina—

---

[18]For the nature of this proposition, see Best to Jarvis, January 10, 1880.

[19]Wealthy businessman of Wilmington. A physician and a shipping and commission merchant, for many years he served as director of the Wilmington and Weldon Railroad. *Cyclopedia of the Carolinas,* II, 249-251.

[20]Banker, merchant, and businessman of Wilmington, and at this time a large stockholder in the Carolina Central Railroad. Ashe, *Biographical History,* I, 392-397.

[21]Businessman of Wilmington, with interests in railroads, securities, textile mills, and the Navassa Guano Company. Hugh Lefler, *History of North Carolina* (New York: Lewis Historical Publishing Company, 4 volumes, 1956), IV, 576, hereinafter cited as Lefler, *History of North Carolina.*

We are also instructed to protest against any present change in the gauge of the Western N.C. Road, which we understand has been proposed, to make it conform to that of the line owned & controlled by the Richmond & Danville Rail Road Company[22]— any such change being in our opinion calculated to have a most disastrous affect upon the best interests of the State generally & especially upon this & other Commercial Cities within its borders—

Hoping that this communication will receive your serious & careful attention, we are

A&H—GLB

Thomas J. Jarvis to J. W. Wilson

Executive Department
Raleigh Feby 3[d] 1880

The weather is too bad for Mr B. to make inspection of Road.[23] Ask him to meet me at Washington.[24] Our delegation may want to make some amendments to which he will agree. I think of one.

A&H—GLB

Thomas J. Jarvis to A. J. de Rossett, D. R. Murchison, and Donald McRae

Executive Department
Raleigh Feby 3[d] 1880

Your communication bearing date February 2[d] 1880 came to me this morning and has I assure you received the careful and serious attention that it merits and that you bespeak for it.

A proposition was made to the Board of Directors of the Western North Carolina Rail Road at their meeting in this city to make some amendments to which he will agree. I think of one

---

[22]In 1871 the North Carolina Railroad had been leased to the Richmond and Danville line. In 1875 the Richmond and Danville Railroad changed the gauge of the North Carolina Railroad from 4' 8½" to conform to its own gauge of 5'. Brown, *State Movement*, 174, 181. The two roads leading into Wilmington, however, had a guage of 4' 8½". For this and other reasons, businessmen of Wilmington feared that railroad traffic was being directed away from that city to those of Beaufort, North Carolina, Charleston, South Carolina, and Norfolk, Virginia. *Morning Star*, 1875–1880, *passim*; Poor, *Railroad Manual*, 360, 635.
[23]Nevertheless, Best spent several days on a tour of inspection of the Western North Carolina Railroad. *Morning Star*, February 10, 1880.
[24]At this time Jarvis was preparing to visit Washington, D.C., to consult with the North Carolina congressmen about selling the Western North Carolina Railroad. *Morning Star*, February 12, 1880.

on the 9th of January last by Mr W. J. Best of the city of New York acting for himself and his associates, for the purchase of the State interest in said Road. That proposition was promptly declined by the said Board of Directors.

Since then a proposition has been submitted to me by the same parties, which, as I understand it, is much more advantageous to the State and much more certain to secure the completion of the Road to Paint Rock and to Ducktown.

There has been between Mr Best and myself considerable correspondence about this proposition, looking to perfecting it and arranging a more complete protection of the interests of the State. This correspondence is recorded in my letter book in this office and belongs to the public.

On last Thursday night Mr Best returned to Raleigh and on Friday in the presence of Col W. L. Saunders, Secty of State, Dr J M Worth[25] Public Treasurer, Col Junius Scales[26] and R H Battle[27] Esq of the Board of Directors of the Western North Carolina Rail Road and Charles M. Cooke[28] of the Board of Internal Improvements presented to me the draft of a bill which embraced the general features of the proposition previously submitted to the Board of Directors of the Western North Carolina Rail Road and, substantially, the suggestions made by me. The said draft is now in the possession of Mr Best, but I am informed and believe will be sent to me to day or tomorrow by mail for my final action. If it does come to me I propose to submit it to the Board of Directors of the Western North Carolina Rail Road for their consideration, and if approved by the Board of Directors, then to the Board of Internal Improvements, and if approved by the Board of Internal Improvements then to the Council of State—These meetings will be held in this City and due notice thereof will be given, when and where your Committee or those interested or any other persons desiring to purchase the States interests in said Rail Road can make their

[25] John Milton Worth, physician and merchant of Randolph County; member of the General Assembly, 1870, 1872; state treasurer, 1877–1885. Ashe, *Biographical History*, III, 454–460.

[26] Junius Irving Scales, lawyer of Guilford County; member of the General Assembly, 1876–1879. Grant, *Alumni History of the University*, 548.

[27] Richard Henry Battle, planter and businessman of Raleigh; state auditor, 1864–1865; member of the Convention of 1875; member of the General Assembly, 1880, 1911; chairman of the State Democratic Executive Committee, 1884–1885. *National Cyclopedia*, XXXVIII, 406.

[28] Charles Mather Cooke, lawyer of Louisburg; member of the General Assembly, 1874, 1879, 1881, 1889; secretary of state, 1895–1896; Superior Court judge, 1903–1915. Ashe, *Biographical History*, VI, 151–161.

offers so to: But I will remind you that there is no power that can dispose of the States interest in said road except the Legislature, and the Legislature cannot assemble until January 1881, unless [by] my proclamation which can only be made by and with the advice and consent of the Council of State, which proclamation must state the purpose for which the Legislature is convened in extra–session; So that our friends in Wilmington will have the amplest opportunity either to oppose the proposition of Mr Best or to make one of their own. If they shall find themselves prepared to make an offer to purchase the States interest in said road there is no man in the State that will be more rejoiced than myself. It will be to me the double assurance that we have those among us who are willing to devote their means to maintain a proper North Carolina pride and enterprise, and that the value and importance of the Western North Carolina Rail Road and its connections are deemed sufficient to awaken this home interest. If the States interest in the road is to be sold I trust that neither your committee nor those whom you represent will hesitate for a moment to believe that as between our own people and all other peoples my sympathies will be with those amongst whom I was born and in whose midst I expect to die.

The details of Mr Best's proposition I cannot now unfold, because they are not in my possession, but when they shall have been submitted to the Board of Directors and approved by them they shall at once have the greatest and speediest publicity.

In general I will say that the proposition binds Mr Best and his associates to provide for the Eight hundred and fifty thousand dollar mortgage now resting on the property; to relieve the State from any further payment of interest on said mortgage; to complete the road to Paint Rock by July 1st 1881, and to Ducktown by January 1st 1885; to deliver to the State $550.000. of the first mortgage bonds of the Company in payment of the expenditures made by the State since it purchased the road in 1875; in the management of the affairs of said company to make no discrimination in freight or passenger traf[f]ic against any city or town in North Carolina nor in favor of any city or town in North Carolina against another. In the event of the failure to comply with the terms of this proposition on the part of Mr Best and his associates the grant made by the State to them is to be void.

The State for its part is to furnish 500 convicts to work upon said road until it shall be completed, the said Mr Best and his associates paying—dollars—per annum for the same, which amount is to be sufficient to cover all expenses of guarding, feeding, clothing, &c the same, and is to be paid quarterly.

As to the change of guage [*sic*] referred to in your communication I know nothing, and beg to remind you that any protest on that subject ought to be made to the Board of Directors of the Western North Carolina Rail Road, who alone have the authority to make such a change.

P.S.

Since writing the above I am informed by telegram that the Board of Directors of the W.N.C.R.R. will meet in this City the 10th I will gladly submit to them any communication you may desire.

A&H—GLB

Thomas J. Jarvis to J. W. Garrett & others

Executive Department
Raleigh Feby 4th 1880

I am in receipt of yours of the 29th ult inviting me to be present Feby 21st at the unfurling of the Centennial flag in King's Mountain battle field.

I can not speak with certainty, that I will be able to attend. It will however give me pleasure to do so, if my official engagements will permit. I shall therefore be compelled for the present, to leave the acceptance of your kind invitation an open question. But whether I attend or not, I beg to assure you of my readiness to cooperate heartily in the great Centennial of the battle of King's Mountain; and the preliminary arrangements necessary to its success. I enclose you a paper containing a correspondence between myself and the Governors of South Carolina and Tennessee on the subject, and beg that your Committee will initiate the proper steps to secure the practical cooperation of Virginia and Tennessee in the celebration.

I will thank you to inform me of your action in this particular, so that I may conform thereto—

A&H—GP'

Henry Conor Bost[29] to Thomas J. Jarvis

South River N.C.
Feby. 5th 1880

I see per The Raleigh Observer that there is a probability of the early assembling of the Legislature in extra session. While such a thing could only be a misfortune to that class of the Genl— Assembly to which I belong still, I think, all would cheerfully bear it if anything so desirable as the sale of the W.N.C.R.R. could be effected.

The great desideratum in this matter is the early completion of the Road. This if I am correctly informed is promised at least ten years sooner by the proposed purchasers than can be done by the State. It is very desirable to get the matter out of State politics.

I trust that no expedient will be left untried that might promise good results in the perfection of a sale on advantageous terms to our State. I saw what a profound sensasion [sic] Mr. Rawley's bill created last winter and hope no occasion of the kind will arise again in our legislature.[30]

P.S. Let the assembling be as early as the importance of matter will allow, as there are many farmers in the Genl. Assembly

A&H—GLB

Z. B. Vance to Thomas J. Jarvis

Febry 6th 1880

I have carefully examined the proposition of Mr W J Best and associates for the purchase and completion of the Western NCRR and am of the opinion that the interest of the State would be promoted by an acceptance of the same. I advise you to call the Legislature togather [sic] that they may take it into consideration

---

[29]Farmer of Rowan County; member of the General Assembly, 1879. Tomlinson, *Sketch–book*, 114.

[30]Probably a reference to a bill giving the Raleigh and Augusta Air Line a charter to build a spur line from Hamlet to Charlotte. Many prominent North Carolinians felt that such a line would injure the state's seaports by draining off much of the state's produce to Norfolk and Baltimore. The *Morning Star* and the Raleigh *Observer*, February and March, 1879, *passim*. This bill, however, failed to pass. *House Journal, 1879*, 321. The threat of such a railroad accentuated the need for completing a through route across North Carolina.

A&H—GP

M. W. Ransom to Thomas J. Jarvis

Washington City, Feby 6th 1880

In response to your request, my opinion is, that you should call the legislature together as soon as necessary to consider the proposition of Mr. W. J. Best, now submitted. In a matter of so much importance I know that you will require the best evidence of the capacity of Mr Best to perform his promises, and that you will and can do nothing that will not give to persons in North Carolina the amplest opportunity also of securing the Road.

A&H—GP

Walter Leak Steele[31] and Others to Thomas J. Jarvis

Washington D.C. Febry 6th 1880

Having been consulted by you in regard to the propriety of calling the General Assembly of the State in special session to consider a proposition relating to the transfer of the States interest in the Western North Carolina Railroad to parties who have the means and willingness to complete it, and having examined the proposition submitted by Mr W J Best of New York and approving the general provisions of the same; and believing that it presents a prospect for the speedy completion of said road, without further taxing the people and that it is best for the State and the people most directly interested that the public should no longer be burdened with the expense of constructing said road we do not hesitate to advise that the General Assembly be convened at as early a day as practicable with the view of voting upon the proposition submitted

We have the honor to be.

Your Excellencys obt servts.

W H Kitchin[32]
R. F Armfield
Robt. B. Vance
Jos. J. Davis
Walter Steele

---

[31]Banker, manufacturer, and lawyer of Rockingham; member of the General Assembly, 1846-1854, 1858; Democratic representative in Congress, 1877–1881. *Biographical Directory of Congress*, 1,563.

[32]William Hodges Kitchin, lawyer of Halifax County; Democratic representative in Congress, 1879–1881. *Biographical Directory of Congress*, 1,189.

A&H—GP

R. M. Furman to Thomas J. Jarvis

Washington, Feb'y 8th, 1880

I desire to mention your reasons for caution and prudence— Knowledge on your part that the W.R.R. was becoming a burden to the people and party, and anxiety, and determination so far as you are concerned that the *W.D.* should not be sacrificed. Recognizing not only certainty of sale, but necessity, you were determined to see that no disposition should be made of the property unless its earliest completion to Ducktown should be assured beyond per–adventure. Having satisfied yourself of the personal and financial character of party proposing to buy, you then devoted yourself to arranging the terms of interest to be submitted as would protect the State, build the road, and secure good fruits. This accomplished, you propose to submit to the proper person to grant you authority to carry out this contract. Any other ideas you may think of.

Mr Best desires me to say to you that he left the words "first of such mortgage deeds," in, because, while it could not possibly affect the State's interest or protection it would act as a 'sop' to his friends; and besides, it might be found necessary to put a second mortgage, which, while it would not affect the first only in which the State would have an interest, it could or might be of great advantage to the holders of the 1st to have the second also, and therefore not hesitate to advance the money needed.

After the whole road could be completed of course all interest of the State would cease only so far as the $550,000 first mortgage, which of course would be good. I write hurriedly. Hope you reached home safely.

A&H—GLB

Thomas J. Jarvis to the Board of Directors of the Western North Carolina Railroad

Executive Department
Raleigh N.C. Feb' 10th 1880

Immediately after your adjournment on the 10th of January Mr W. J. Best of the City of New York submitted to me a proposition to purchase the State's interest in the Western North

Carolina Rail Road which differed I am informed, from the proposition rejected by you on the said 10th of January in that the proposition made to me proposed to give the State Five Hundred Thousand Dollars of the First Mortgage Bonds of the proposed new company in place of the Eight Hundred and Fifty Thousand Dollars of stock offered in the proposition made to you.

Considerable correspondence between Mr Best and myself ensued on this subject and has finally resulted in his formulating the changes made into the draft of a Bill which I submit to you for your consideration

You are the special custodians and guardians of of [*sic*] the state's interest in the property and at my request you are assembled by the President of your Board to consider the proposition and I beg that you will do so with all diligence care and patience.

I will thank you to return to me the proposition which I this day lay before you with your conclusions as to the propriety of making the sale upon the terms and in the manner therein set forth together with such suggestions as to the propriety of calling an extra-session of the General Assembly to consider the same as you may deem proper

The correspondence between Mr W. J. Best and myself as well as all other information in my possession is at your disposal

A&H—GP

George Phifer Erwin[33] *to Thomas J. Jarvis* [*with enclosures*]

Raleigh, NC
Feb 11—1880

By direction of the Board of Directors of the W.NCRRC., I have the honor to transmit herewith copies of two resolutions which have this day been passed upon by said Board—and return the proposition submitted by Mr Best.

---

[33] Lawyer of Morganton, and secretary and treasurer of the Western North Carolina Railroad from 1871 to 1886. W. A. Withers and Others (eds.), *The Semi-Centennial Catalogue of Davidson College, Davidson, N. C., 1837–1887* (Raleigh: E. M. Uzzell, 1891), 47, hereinafter cited as Withers, *Davidson College.*

[enclosure—extract]

The following resolution was offered by Mr Henderson:[34]—

Resolved—That we recommend to His Excellency the Governor to convene the Legislature to consider the proposition of Mr W. J. Best & his associates, for the purchase of the Western North Carolina Railroad but we suggest that the draft of the bill which has been submitted to us by the Governor, shall be amended in some material particulars, so as to more perfectly protect the interests of the State.

which resolution was rejected—

.   .   .   .

The above resolution of the Board was rejected by a vote of five in favor of and six against the resolution. The President stating that Mr Shober[35] who was absent, would have voted in favor of Mr Bests proposition

[enclosure—extract]

Mr [Junius I.] Scales offered the following

Resolved:—That this Board does not deem it necessary to the true interests of the State of North Carolina or its Western portion, that the question of the sale of the W.N.C.R.R. should be considered in special session of the General Assembly, but on the contrary, believe that those interests will be best subserved by referring such question and all propositions to purchase, to the next regular session in January 1881—when the wishes of the people will be better known and the chances of competition much increased— which resolution was adopted by a vote of six in favor of and five against the resolution:—

.   .   .   .

---

[34]John Steele Henderson, lawyer of Salisbury and private stockholder in the Western North Carolina Railroad; member of the Convention of 1875; member of the General Assembly, 1876, 1878, 1900, 1902; Democratic representative to Congress, 1885–1895. *National Cyclopedia*, IX, 438–439.

[35]Francis Edwin Shober, lawyer of Salisbury; member of the General Assembly, 1862–1865; Democratic representative to Congress, 1869–1873; member of the Convention of 1875; chief clerk of the United States Senate, 45th Congress. *Biographical Directory of Congress*, 1,521.

A&H—GLB

Thomas J. Jarvis to William Johnston[36] and C. M. Cooke

Executive Department
Raleigh Feby 11th 1880

Will you please be kind enough to examine a Draft of a Bill which I herewith hand you looking to the purchase of the States interest in the W.N.C.R.R. and return it with such suggestions, as you may desire, either as to amendments or submitting the same to a called session of the Legislature

A&H—GP

W. J. Best to Thomas J. Jarvis

Raleigh, Feby 12, 1880

In compliance with the request made at our conference last evening, I now beg to hand you the names of gentlemen who will be associated with me in the purchase of the State's interest in the Western North Carolina Railroad, and in the completion of the same. These, or other gentlemen equally acceptable to the Commissioners provided for to make the conveyance of the State's interest, will sign the contract with me, and I agree that the deposit of Thirty thousand dollars shall have the additional condition attached, that it shall be forfeited to the State if they do not sign. You will oblige me by making the most searching inquiry as to the financial and social standing of these parties. As a favor, however, I would ask that you do not permit their names to be made public until the passage of the act, which I have submitted. Permit me, also, to suggest that, in the inquiries you shall make, no allusion be made to the Western North Carolina Railroad. The reason for this is, that, possibly, some of

---

[36]Promient lawyer, banker and railroad executive of Charlotte. Ashe, *Biographical History*, I, 341–348. Johnston and Cooke were members of the Board of Internal Improvements.

the parties to whom you may apply are interested in other railroads, whose interests might seem to be jeopardized by our control of the W.N.C.R.R.

William J. Best
James D. Fish[37]
William R. Grace
J. Nelson Tappan
Arthur Leary

A&H—GLB

Thomas J. Jarvis to J. M. Worth

Executive Department
Raleigh February 12th 1880

Mr W. J. Best, of the city of New York, who has for a month past, as you know, been engaged in perfecting a proposition for himself and his associates for the purchase of the State's interest in the Western North Carolina Rail Road handed me to day the names and places of residence of those whom he calls his associates and are expected by him to join in the purchase and completion of said Road Their names and addresses are:
James D. Fish, President, Marine National Bank, Wall St New York.
William R. Grace of the firm W[m]. R. Grace & Co, William St Near Pearl, New York. J. Nelson Tappan, City Chamberlain of the City of New York, New County Court House, New York.
Arthur Leary, Shipping Merchant William St. New York
I also hand you a copy of the letter of Mr Best in which he furnishes these names   I will thank you to make at once a rigid and searching investigation into their moral and financial standing and report to me by letter at as early a day as practicable. In making this investigation I will suggest that you make known as little as you think proper the purpose for which it is made. At your request made in a conversation with you to day, I telegraphed the Hon Joseph J. Davis at Washington to aid you in this matter and he has answered me that he will gladly do so

---

[37]For identification of Best's associates, see Best to Worth, February 12, 1880, and Anderson to Jarvis, February 21, 1880, in this volume.

A. D. Brooks[38] to Thomas J. Jarvis

Statesville, N.C.,
Feb. 12th, 1880

I hope you will pardon me for the liberty I may seem to take in writing you this hasty letter— I do it as a Jarvis man.

Ever since Mr. Best made his first proposition to you with reference to the sale of the Western N.C.R.R., I have been travelling in Western N.C., and have had opportunity of hearing a vast deal said on the subject. I have heard no one express himself that was not strongly in favor of the sale of the R'd. The universal sentiment of the people of Western Carolina seems to be for the sale, but at the same time they want the interests of the people well secured. They want every safeguard thrown around the State's interest. The people beyond the Blue Ridge want a R'd. The Democratic Party has been promising them one, but they now have no hope of that promise ever being fulfilled. They say if the R'd is built at all it must be built by some foreign corporation. They will never vote with that party that prevents that corporation from doing it.

I was induced to write this letter by a remark I heard a gentleman make in this town to–day. He said he wrote Judge Fowle[39] that the universal sentiment of the Western people was for the sale, and that he must by all means take that side of the question.

Samuel James Ervin[40] to Thomas J. Jarvis

Morganton NC
Feby 12—80

Permit me although a stranger to you but as one interested in the success of the Democratic party and in the material prosperity of the state which I think is closely connected with it to that of the sentiment of the West in regard to the sale of the

---

[38]Principal of the Classical School in Statesville, and enrolling clerk of the House of Representatives, 1879–1880. Tomlinson, *Sketch–book*, 138.

[39]Daniel Gould Fowle, lawyer of Raleigh; member of the General Assembly, 1862–1865; Superior Court judge, 1867; governor of North Carolina, 1889–1891. *National Cyclopedia*, IV, 429–430. Fowle was Jarvis' main rival for the Democratic gubernatorial nomination in 1880.

[40]Lawyer of Morganton. *North Carolina Biography*, IV, 563.

WNCRR according to the terms of the proposition submitted by Mr Best. I have heard many people speak of it prominent men and any number of voters and taxpayers who are not so prominent and the people of Burke are almost as one man in favor of selling—in favor of calling a special meeting of the General Assembly in order that they may pass upon the proposition They think that with guarantees providing against any discrimination against any of our NC towns and cities the honor of the state is protected that by a sale the road will sooner be completed taxes will be lower the convicts can be used in building other roads and finally that the Democratic party will be much more comfortable in the next campaign For these reasons and for many other they desire the sale of the road Hoping that you will trust and believe that my attachment to my state and party is alone the occasion of my writing

A&H—GLB

Thomas J. Jarvis to Robert Rufus Bridgers[41]

Executive Department
Raleigh, N.C., Feb 13th 1880

Mr W. J. Best of the city of New York, who, as you have no doubt heard has been for some time proposing and perfecting a proposition to purchase the State's interest in the Western N.C. Rail Road, goes to your city this P.M and will take with him the proposition as now perfected.

I will thank you to examine the said proposition in detail and especially that section of it which looks to a protection against discrimination against North Carolina cities and towns.

I have great confidence both in your patriotism and judgment and if the section referred to does not give protection to North Carolina interests in the way of freight and passenger traffic I will thank you to make such suggestions to Mr Best, and to myself if he does not adopt your suggestions as will secure these interests in the amplest manner without imperiling the success of the road

---

[41]Lawyer and businessman of Wilmington, with large investments in banks, mines, land, manufacturing, and processing; member of the General Assembly, 1844, 1856–1861; member of the Confederate Congress, 1862–1865. At this time Bridgers was general manager of the Wilmington and Weldon Railroad. *Dictionary of American Biography*, III, 33–34.

Col Pope[42] is familiar with the details of such matters and if desired by you it will be entirely agreeable to me for you to consult him

A&H—GP

Samuel McDowell Tate[43] to Thomas J. Jarvis

Morganton N.C
Febry 13. 1880

You no doubt find many ready to advise you. Some from interested motives, others perhaps, because they have little else to do. But I believe I have not been forward enough to volunteer my opinions to your Excellency upon any subject, altho' in the matter of the Western N.C. Railroad I have a large interest and ought to have as much knowledge as any private citizen.

Therefore, after first assuring you that I have no interest in Mr Best or his proposal other than as a stockholder in the Western road, I venture to "post" you on public sentiment here about. It is, of course, to be looked for that the people beyond the line of completed way would favor almost any proposition that promised them an earlier realization of its benefits; but I confess surprise at the unanimity of sentiment among those who already enjoy its uses, whether stockholder or mere tax payer, as developed by the publication and discussion of the "Best" proposal. There is but one opinion up this way, and that is to *accept*.

The modern Reformer has aroused such ultra feeling in behalf of retrenchment that I see little hope of continuing much longer even the present progress in construction and, therefore, it seems to me little less than Provedential [*sic*] that a means of accomplishing this great work of improvement is open to us, while yielding to the popular clamor for a reduction in public expenditure.

---

[42]A. Pope, general freight and passenger agent of the Wilmington and Weldon Railroad. He was also general passenger agent for the Associated Railways of Virginia and the Carolinas Railway Company. *Public Documents, 1881*, No. 9, 21.

[43]Businessman of Morganton; member of the General Assembly, 1875, 1881, 1883; state treasurer, 1893–1895. He is credited with initiating the convict lease system in North Carolina during his presidency of the Western North Carolina Railroad, 1865–1868. *National Cyclopedia*, XXXVI, 86–87.

As a citizen, loyal to North Carolina interests, I can see no better arrangement practicable and, as a democrat, would gladly see the thing removed from the domain of politics. There can be no doubt as to what position the democracy should take upon this question, but I have too much respect for the Governor of North Carolina to suggest the influence that heroic action would have upon a state Convention. Your Excellency is familiar with the history and an admirer of the character of Andrew Jackson. Such men succeed and deserve success. If I were Governor and believed it was to the public interest, "by the Eternal" I'd call the Legislature.

A&H—GP

Alphonso Calhoun Avery[44] *to Thomas J. Jarvis*

Morganton
Feb 13th 1880

In a conversation with Major Wilson this afternoon I learned, that you were seriously considering the propriety of acting on your own matured judgement in reference to calling the Legislature together and without the approval of the Directors. As you know, I fully concur with you in opinion as to the course, that would be wisest and best for the State of North Carolina and especially for the mountain people, who have so much at stake.

It is your duty as well to consider what is the interest of the democratic party in the decision of the question. A week since I visited Charlotte and made it my business, while in transit, to enquire particularly as to public sentiment. Throughout the piedmont region the people will almost unanimously approve of selling the road, and calling the Legislature together in order to effect it, and they will not only approve of a sale and sustain you in prompt action, but they will condemn you, if you fail to act. Every paper published west of Greensboro except the Charlotte Observer will sustain you, and there is no show of opposition except on the part of a few leading men in Catawba County,

---

[44] Lawyer of Morganton; member of the General Assembly, 1866; member of the Constitutional Convention of 1875; Superior Court judge, 1879–1888; state Supreme Court justice, 1889–1897. In 1880 Avery was on the board of directors of the Western North Carolina Railroad. *National Cyclopedia*, III, 424–425.

who have heard nothing but Dr Powell's[45] explanation. A majority of his own neighbors could be influenced against him by a fair statement of Best's proposal.

I have heard several leading men of our county say within a week past, that after the matter had been made public and freely discussed, it would be difficult to carry Burke County for the democratic ticket this year, if the sale should not be effected. You know, that along the line of all roads, owned or controlled by the state, a war between the *ins* and the *outs* will sooner or later arise, and this strife, which is raging from Rowan to Buncombe, can be allayed effectually only by turning the road over to private individuals. I would not willingly urge you to take any step, that would injure you or endanger the success of the democratic party; but I am satisfied, that you would be sustained overwhelmingly by the people, and would save the democratic party to say the least from very great jeopardy by exhibiting the boldness and nerve, that you have shown on many occasions heretofore.

I believe, that it will be worth 1500 to 2000 votes to the democratic ticket along the line of the road from Salisbury to Buncombe to say nothing of the Northern counties, where they have such a holy horror of taxation or the extreme Western counties. I have never talked to or rather explained to any intelligent man (out side of the Directors) the exact terms of the proposal, who did not endorse it readily.

Fortify yourself by inviting expressions of opinions for a few days and I think, you will concur with me as to public sentiment

I understand, that Best is willing to give $400 000 in money, $550,000 in mortgage bonds on $830 000 in stock. Let him shape his proposition so as to offer to the Legislature a chance to take either. If he could afford to prefer the $550 000 in mortgage bonds it would remove the only argument, against his scheme that attracts any attention.

I thought tonight of telegraphing you as to public sentiment and may do so tomorrow.

With kindest regards to Mrs Jarvis

---

[45]Probably Dr. A. M. Powell, physician and planter of Catawba County. Branson, *Directory for 1884*, 200–201.

A&H—GP

Burgess Sidney Gaither[46] to Thomas J. Jarvis

Morganton February 13ᵗʰ 1880

I hope you and your Council, will have the wisdom and the nerve to convene the Legislature, in extra session, to consider the proposition of Mr Best to purchase the Western North Carolina Rail Road. The question is one of such magnitude and of such vital importance to the whole state, as to justify an extra session of the legislative department to consider and determine— I regret the action of the majority of the Board of Directors of that Company, upon that proposition and hope their opinion may not be sustained by the intelligent, public sentiment of the state— I have no doubt that you are in possession of the opinions of many of the leading gentlemen of the different parts of the state including the opinions of our representatives in Congress of the several districts of the state and our senators— and of the well informed rail road men of the state, in the premises, and can form a more correct opinion of the public feeling of the entire state on this subject, than any other gentleman in the state. I am fully satisfied that a large majority of our western people without distinction of party are decidedly in favour of a sale of the road, with the necessary and proper guarantees, to secure the early completion of both branchs to the Tennessee line and to guard against and prevent the new company from ever making improper discriminations against our other railroads, and important cities and towns of our state— Our people desire the road to be completed in the early future and do not see any hope of such consummation by the state under the present plan of opperations [*sic*]. If the state should determine to act with more energy in the future, than in the past and make larger appropriations to facilitate the work the result would be a large state debt created or probably another Mortgage upon the road and a foreclosure by sale and the road pass into the hands of capitalists under much more unfavourable circumstances than those now proposed

This question is now before the state and it has to be met and decided, whether we will sell or whether [we] will continue the appropriations and go on under the present plan, or whether

---

[46]Lawyer of Morganton; member of the Convention of 1835; member of the General Assembly, 1841, 1845; state solicitor, 1844–1852; member of the Confederate Congress, 1862–1865. *National Cyclopedia*, VII, 185.

we will stop the road at Asheville and give up all hope of a connection with the roads of the west and the commerce of that vast country

In a political point of view, it is a matter of vast importance to our party that this question shall be settled in such manner as may harmonize all sections of the state— If we fail to do so we all know that the radical party will take issue with us in what ever course the party may determine to take in the matter and I do assure you that my candid opinion is that if we reject this proposition to sell and refuse to make liberal appropriations to carry on the work beyond Asheville we will be defeated in our state and national elections this year and be and remain in a minority for many years. I am not informed of the state of public opinion in other parts of the state, but I am informed and think I know that this section of the state will sustain any party which will advocate & sustain the early completion of this great state work and the opinion is very generally entertained that our legislature should effect a sale either to Mr Best & his associates or some other company who have the capital & make the road at once and relieve the state from the present debt incurred in the purchase & the extension of this road. I have written you more than I intended when I commenced and for yourself & your Council & not for the public print. This is a pleasure I do not indulge in

A&H—GP

Alfred Martin Erwin[47] to Thomas J. Jarvis

(Private)   Marion, N.C., Feby 13 1880

I have just seen & heard the decision of Board of Directors on our Road— Really I am surprised— & more so because of the vote of my friend J S. Brown—[48] I know whereof I speak when I know there is not ten men in McDowell Co opposed to the sale— Those men who have taken the trouble to inform themselves upon the subject do not hesitate to advocate the sale & the necessity of sale can easily be satisfied— The reasons of the sale you know better than myself— & more convincing so I'll say no more about that— Another view, how will it affect the .

---

[47]Lawyer of Marion; member of the General Assembly, 1874, 1879. Tomlinson, *Sketch-book*, 43.
[48]Farmer and gristmill owner of Marion. Branson, *Directory for 1884*, 442–443.

party— I am free to confess if the Road [is] not sold I fear the result in the West— this will draw the line between East & West I am satisfied But as a matter of economy & for benefit of the State the people of the State, I cannot conceive of a valid reason for a refusal to sell— The Road must stop at Asheville under present appearances & then the West cut off from all communication & the Road as built now will pay a dividend— My only object or reason in writing you, to let you know how public sentiment is— I was in Asheville this week & met with one man alone who was opposed to sale— I have heard & know from Yancy & Mitchell Countys—

Tho a member of Legislature I hope you will not misconstrue my motive in writing, I hope far higher motives control me— If the sale could be effected without the Legislature I would prefer—

A&H—GP

William Johnston to Thomas J. Jarvis

Charlotte N C
Feby 14th 1880

In reply to your request[49] that I give you any suggestions & amendments in regard to Mr Best bill offering to purchase the WNCRR; also my opinion of the propriety of calling the Legislature in extra session to consider it, I beg to submit the following views

In the first place the bill gives no sufficient responsible parties to guarantee the fulfilment of the conditions of sale — involving the expenditure of millions of dollars, or of the performance of the contract for building the entire road

Second   In a private conversation with Mr Best (sought by himself) as to his associates— who were to sign the contract with him— their responsibility &c he failed to satisfy me that any responsible party would sign the contract with him

3rd The contract (which is in the form of a bill) provides no sufficient indemnity or security for specific performances for the State of North Carolina in case of failure to build the road as specified

4th The provision prohibiting discrimination against North Carolina interests, is general, indefinite & unmeaning

---

[49]See Jarvis to Johnston, February 11, 1880, in this volume.

5th The provision that the mortgage bonds of $15,000 are not to create any lien upon the property & franchises until the road is completed, appears unbusinesslike, distroys the value, or credit of the bonds in open market for five years, or until the road is finished, as well as impairs the credit of the company in the very means of building the Road. If the company (new purchasers) can build the road without the use or sale of the bonds why make a mortgage until it is finished or hesitate to give ample guarantees for the fulfilment of the contract.

6th The road is destined to become of immense value to North Carolina as soon as it is completed Under proper state management it will add millions in values to the wealth of the people of our state, create an identity of interest and unity in state policies, which has never heretofore existed and these were the great and patriotic objects of the venerable authors of the North Carolina system — so much derided by some of the present day. This great road cutting through the Appalachian chain of mountains connects directly by the shortest line every section of North Carolina — including her mountains & seaports with the inexhaustable productions of the northwest and will thus by an exchange of comodities add greatly to the wealth & power of both under a proper state policy. In the interests of others it may generate increased sectional feelings and prejudices, repress the energies & resources of our citizens and make North Carolina truly "a strip of land between two states"
The pecuniary profits of the road which will be great when completed, are but a small portion of the benefits & blessings to be derived from it by the people of North Carolina if operated in their interests, instead of that of other states.

7th After a long period of depression & financial embarrasment throughout our entire country it is now rapidly emerging, a new impulse has been imparted to all values & thus appears likely to continue for some time. The property of this road is partaking of these influences, and as it approaches completion, is rapidly growing in public importance We have passed the cricis. North Carolinians have spent over four millions of dollars in credit & cash on this state work. The great chain of mountains has been penetrated, the battle has been fought & won by the people, the prize is within our grasp and let us not barter it away for a mess of potage. Not less than five or six corporations besides private capitalists are anxiously watching the progress of the WNCRR. Its control is not only desirable but important to each one of them. Two are now not in a condition to become bidders, but probably will be, by the time of the meeting of the next regular session of the Legislature. If the State should then desire to sell her interest in the road and it is known to these corporations with the number of competitors, the opinion is entertained that she can secure better terms and a more certain and speedy completion of the entire road to Duck town & Paint Rock than by the only proposition now offered. By next winter the intelligent public mind of the state will be better prepared to act with unanimity than in the present divided expression of public sentiment. For these and other reasons I would respectfully suggest that all action be suspended and the entire subject of sale be referred to the next regular session of the General Assembly

I have thus briefly but frankly given you some of the reasons which govern my judgment unbias by any consideration except the good of my state, and knowing that your every impulse is patriotic & your sole purpose is the greatest good to North Carolina

A&H—GP

Charles Wetmore Broadfoot[50] *to Thomas J. Jarvis*

Fayetteville N– C–
Feby 14 1880

I have closely read the proceedings of Bd of Directors of W.NCRR. and was forced to the conclusion that they are a set of pigmies — not one of them seemed to realize the importance of the matter. Their action has sent joy to the hearts of the radicals of this section. Unless this matter of sale or appropriations to W.RR is settled before the next campaign I greatly fear it may rend our party in pieces. Wilmington folks since they succeeded in bulldozing the last Leg—[51] are puffed up like the frog in the fable. I think they will do you all the harm they can. We of the upper Cape Fear have suffered for a long time from their vanity and conceit and paid for it in last Cong. election.

---

[50]Teacher, then lawyer, of Fayetteville; member of the General Assembly, 1870. Grant, *Alumni History of the University*, 73.
[51]See Bost to Jarvis, February 5, 1880, n. 30, in this volume.

They now propose to try the same game with us in approaching nominating Conv.

Can't you secure another proposition from capitalists which the Board will dare not decline & recommend— I should think you had made strong friends with the West or "Over the Ridge" men as they delight to be called. You ought to have had the strong support of the whole East, but as I have said the Board did not rise to the occasion— I have written this out of high personal regard to yourself and to show that your action is heartily endorsed here—

William Henry Malone[52] *to Thomas J. Jarvis*

Marion N.C.
Feby 15.th 1880

I find great indignation and mortification expressed at the refusal of the Directors to favor the "Best" proposition. The people including most of the private stockholders are an almost unit for a sale of the Road.

I greatly fear that the "democratic ship" will "strand on this rock" if left for discussion next summer. It appears to me that the Legislature should be called, for 2 reasons

1. To consider the "Best" proposition
2. If not proper to sell — then to provide a remedy for the difficulties.

For it is a fixed fact that the work must suspend in a few months if something is not done.

I think Dor[t]ch's position[53] full of fallacy — his policy would ultimately pass the road into a corporation or bondholders. I cannot see why the Cape Fear region should object to calling the Legislature for a comparison of views

It is utterly impossible to build this road by the State in the manner now proposed. The people will not submit to the tax. Why not sell? — that facilities may be early presented for a rapid development of the "old North State"? Tis the only hope of the West.

---

[52]Lawyer of Asheville; member of the General Assembly, 1868. *Cyclopedia of the Carolinas*, II, 172–174.
[53]At the meeting of the board of directors on February 10, Dortch wanted the state to remortgage the Western North Carolina Railroad and finish the work itself. *Morning Star*, February 13, 1880.

I fully appreciate the delicacy and responsibility of your Excellency's position, but I believe a bold move and a call of the Legislature in extra session is the proper course.

The issue is presented — it cannot be ignored — the breach will widen. But when the Legislature has given expression public opinion will be better settled.

Excuse this perhaps improper offer of advice, but knowing the great desire of your Excellency to right in the premises and to serve the interest of the entire people I venture to write

A&H—GP

Mrs. Cicero W. Harris[54] *to Thomas J. Jarvis*

Wilmington Feb 16th 1880

I fear a short note written you sometime last week failed to reach you. Recent developments[55] in this city cause me to write another.

For reasons strengthened by those "recent developments" I would like very much to get $5000. for the revival of the "Sun." The "Review" has no weight and the "Star" no politics. I have secured a good business man. Mr Harris is amply able to edit it, and managed on an economical basis the paper will pay handsomely. I am already ahead of everybody else as regards campaign funds, with Senators Barnum,[56] Ransom & Vance, Speaker Randall,[57] Hon Clarkson Potter[58] and W. W. Corcoran.[59] See enclosed letter which you will please return.

Can you, and will you, help me get the necessary $5000 to

---

[54]Mrs. Harris at this time was editor and proprietor of the *South Atlantic*, a monthly literary magazine published in Wilmington. Her husband had served as editor of the Wilmington *Morning Star* and then of the Wilmington *Sun*, but in 1877 he went to work on the Goldsboro *Messenger*. Mrs. Harris remained in Wilmington and commenced publishing the *South Atlantic*, See *Morning Star*, 1875–1880, *passim*.

[55]Probably a reference to the fact that the Jarvis administration was being vigorously criticized in Wilmington for contemplating the sale of the state's interest in the Western North Carolina Railroad. See de Rossett and others to Jarvis, February 2, 1880, *n.* 22, in this volume.

[56]William Henry Barnum, Democratic United States senator from Connecticut, and at this time chairman of the Democratic National Committee. *National Cyclopedia*, XII, 389.

[57]Samuel Jackson Randall, Democratic congressman from Pennsylvania and Speaker of the House during the 45th and 46th Congresses. *Dictionary of American Biography*, XV, 350–351.

[58]Lawyer of New York and Democratic representative in Congress, 1877–1879. *National Cyclopedia*, III, 60.

[59]William Wilson Corcoran, banker and broker of Washington, D.C. *Dictionary of American Biography*, IV, 440.

begin with from Geo. W. Swepson (he know me) and the R.R.
man Mr Best. If you will, get it quietly, and I will meet your
private Secretary in Goldsboro and take the money from him —
or from any other safe, reliable party — so that *no one* will ever
dream of where the money came from — or how it came.

This is confidential. I hope you will destroy it, and return
enclosed at once.

Finally, I know how to return a favor, and my friends never
found me wanting.

A&H—GLB

Thomas J. Jarvis to W. J. Best

Executive Department
Raleigh Feb 16th 1880

Return with your associates all right,[60] and I am ready to act.
They need have no apprehension. I can pledge the honor of the
State to act fair and liberal, as long as they act in good faith

A&H—GLB

J. M. Worth to Thomas J. Jarvis

New York, Feb 16th 1880
4 PM

I have had the fullest satisfaction that the men named by Mr
Best are all Right as to character and money and by the merest
accident found out that they had not fully agreed amongst
themselves about the matter.[61] I felt that after knowing the fact
that it was my duty — (altho not instructed to enquire as to
that) to look into that matter — and in the last 30 minutes
have learned that Mr Best is here— and a message from him
requesting me to stay over tomorrow which I will do and longer
if necessary to be able — to give you the information you wish
so there can be no doubt. I hesitated about saying anything to
the men that I was enquireing about but [J.J.] Davis insisted
that it was my duty after learning that they had not fully agreed

---

[60]Jarvis had been to Washington to check the credit and reputation of
Best's associates. See Jarvis to Wilson, February 3, 1880, *n.* 24, in this
volume.

[61]See Best to Jarvis, May 21, 1880, *n.* 150, in this volume.

upon the matter   I have not seen any of them but negotiated through Mr Lancaster   Best and party are now holding a meeting   I feel sure that it will all come out right— now that Mr Best is on the ground   If I get satisfied fully I shall notify by wire — I propose to be able to give you a square answer before I leave

A&H—GP

W. J. Best to Thomas J. Jarvis

[Telegram]

New York 17 1880

Associates all right
will start tonight or tomorrow—

A&H—GP

J. M. Worth to Thomas J. Jarvis

[Telegram]

New York 17 1880

Everything satisfactory
Will be home Thursday noon   Best same time —

A&H—GP

W. R. Grace, J. D. Fish, and J. N. Tappan to Thomas J. Jarvis

New York February 17th. 1880.

We propose to take an interest with William J. Best in the purchase of the State's interest in the Western North Carolina Rail Road and in the completion of the same.

In case the General Assembly of North Carolina is convened in extra session and pass the bill submitted to you by Mr Best authorizing the sale of said road, or with such amendments to said bill, as may be assented to by Mr Best, We will sign the contract provided for in said bill, to be signed by said Best and associates.

A&H—GLB

Thomas J. Jarvis to Henry F. Grainger[62]

Executive Department
Raleigh N.C. Feby 18th 1880

Enclosed you will find a "Bill" to provide for the settlement of accounts with certain Railway Companies now pending in the U. S. Senate together with the Report thereon,[63] and the letter of Senator Vance to me.

You will please examine the Bill and Report carefully and if necessary go to Newbern to see and consult with C. C. Clark[64] Esq and Col J D Whitford Prest &c. Senator Vance's letter explains the necessity of immediate attention to this matter.[65]

A&H—GP

J. J. Davis to Thomas J. Jarvis

Washington, D.C., Feb. 18th. 1880

My Dear Sir:— in compliance with your request, I went to New–York with Dr. Worth and ascertained, from sources that I deem entirely reliable, the character & standing, financial and personal, of Jas. D. Fish, Wm. R. Grace, J. Nelson Tappan and Arthur Leary. The first two are gentlemen of large means and all of them gentlemen of high character, commanding the confidence of business men—

A&H—GP

Mrs. C. W. Harris to Thomas J. Jarvis

Feb 18 [1880]

Your reply to my letter was rec'd after I had mailed a second letter to you. I fear you misunderstand me some what. I would

---

[62]Lawyer of Goldsboro; member of the General Assembly, 1881. At this time he was director of the Atlantic and North Carolina Railroad on the part of the State. Daniels, *Wayne County,* 40.

[63]See Worth to Jarvis, March 19, 1880, in this volume.

[64]Charles C. Clark, lawyer of New Bern; member of the General Assembly, 1860; member of the Convention of 1865. At this time he was the lawyer for the Atlantic and North Carolina Railroad. Branson, *Directory for 1884,* 239; Connor, *Manual, 1913,* 572, 875.

[65]Representative A. M. Scales introduced this bill, but the House refused to discuss it. *Congressional Record,* 46th Congress, Second Session, 1,143.

not accept money from Mr Best, or any one, either for *"Sun"* or "South Atlantic" unless I thought I could offer a quid pro quo.

I am anxious to revive the *"Sun,"* I confess, and would resort to any honorable expedient to raise from $5000 to $10.000 for that purpose. The papers here are provincial and contracted and a good paper is needed. Governor Vance was once of great service to me. Ex Officio, I thought you might favor me by your advice and assistance with regard to Mr Best. You acted very promptly and placed me under obligations to you for it.

I think something may come of it yet. If you see any opportunity, let me hear from you, and I will never forget to show my grateful appreciation.

I am sorry the "Star" and "Review" wont allow you to leave the State without their written permission! High–handed, isn't it?

Wilmington is no more able to buy the Western R.R. than I am to purchase the State House — and what is more, she has no idea of trying to do so. They the business men are *very* uneasy about the Carolina Central[66] which is of vital importance to them. This is sub rosa.

If you are in Washington City 22, 23, or 24th of this month, *you* can get at least $5000 for "Sun" from Nat. Ex. Com. They are thoroughly informed by all *parties,* Senators, Congressmen, N.Y. Capitalists &c. *Speaker Randall is interested too.* Verbum sap.

A&H—GP

Terrell Wilkie Taylor[67] *to Thomas J. Jarvis*

Hendersonville N° Cᵃ —
Feby 18th. 1880 —

I write to give you as far as I am able the Sentiment of this Section in regard to the Sale of W.N.C.R.R and the call of the Extra Session according to my opinion and observation There is but One feeling among my people They are urgent for the Sale

---

[66]As part of their railroad plans, Best and his associates contemplated a system extending from Beaufort to Ducktown and including the Western North Carolina Railroad, the North Carolina Railroad, and the Atlantic and North Carolina Railroad. The Carolina Central, running from Wilmington to Shelby, would have difficulty competing with the proposed Best system. See map opposite page 138 in Brown, *State Movement.*

[67]Farmer and merchant of Hendersonville; member of the General Assembly, 1874, 1879. Tomlinson, *Sketch–book,* 48–49.

of the Road — and they also think that you Should convene the General Assembly at once that there may be no further delay in the matter that the Sale may be consimated [*sic*] and the work proceed to completion Supposing that you would like to be advised as to public Sentiment in my Dist— I take the liberty of addressing you this communication—

A&H—GP

J. M. Worth to Thomas J. Jarvis

Treasury Department
Raleigh, Feby 20ᵗʰ 1880

Immediately upon the reception of your letter of the 12ᵗʰ inst. requesting that I should make rigid and thorough enquiry into the personal and financial standing of several persons whose names were mentioned therein as the associates of Mr William J. Best in the purchase of the Western North Carolina Rail Road; I repaired at once to the City of New York in compliance with said request. Upon arriving at Washington City I was there joined by the Hon J. J. Davis, and through his, and the assistance of Genls. Ransom, Scales, Gov. Vance, and all of our members of Congress on whom I was able to call, procured letters of introduction to gentlemen of the highest standing residing in the City of New York. Upon arriving in New York Mr Davis and myself began the enquiry as you directed, and continued the same until we were perfectly satisfied of the unexceptionable character, business capacity and strong financial standing of Mr Best and his associates.

Through the courtesy and interest of Senator Ransom I was greatly aided by letters of introduction from Senator Randolph[68] from New Jersey.

I am glad to report to you that I am perfectly satisfied in every respect that Mr Best and his associates possess the financial ability to fulfill the contract submitted to you by them, and that their personal character and standing is such as to give positive assurance that they honestly intend to carry out any contract they may enter into.

---

[68]Theodore Fitz Randolph, Democratic senator from New Jersey, 1875–1881, *Biographical Directory of Congress*, 1,443.

A&H—GLB

Thomas J. Jarvis to the Council of State

Executive Department
Raleigh N.C. Feby 21ˢᵗ 1880

A proposition was submitted to me about the 10ᵗʰ of January by W. J. Best, for himself and his associates to purchase the States interest in the Western North Carolina Rail Road, which proposition in its perfected form I herewith submit to you. The names of Mr Best's associates are W. R. Grace, J. Nelson Tappan and James D. Fish whose letter agreeing to enter into the contract are also herewith submitted. The financial ability and personal integrity of Mr Best and his said associates have been investigated by the State Treasurer the Hon J. J. Davis and Col Wᵐ E. Anderson[69] at my request and their report made thereon. This I also submit to you. My letter book containing all the correspondence between Mr Best and myself on this subject is likewise placed in your possession for your inspection. I ask you to consider the proposition and the other matters herein referred to and, if you shall deem it proper to give me your advice as to to [*sic*] the necessity and propriety of convening the General Assembly in Extra–session at an early day to consider the same.

I have required Mr Best to make a deposit of Thirty thousand dollars on the conditions in my letter of January 13ᵗʰ, which you will find upon my letter–book all the details of this deposit, and the supervision of the same I shall leave with the State Treasurer, and shall reply upon his written authority that it has been properly made.

A&H—GP

Guilford Lafayette Dudley[70] to Thomas J. Jarvis
[*with enclosure*]

Executive Department
Raleigh, Feby 21 1880

In compliance with the instructions of the Council of State, I

---

[69] Businessman of Raleigh, president of the Citizens National Bank and a director of the Western North Carolina Railroad. Grant, *Alumni History of the University*, 13.

[70] Private secretary to Governor Jarvis since November, 1879. Before this he had been chief clerk of the State Department. *Public Documents, 1881,* No. 4, pp. 61 and 73.

have the honor to transmit herewith a copy of a resolution unanimously adopted by the Council at its meeting to day in response to the communication of your Excellency enclosing the proposition of Mr Best and associates for the purchase and completion of the W.N.C.R.R., and asking advice, as to the necessity of convening the General Assembly in extra session at an early day to consider the same.

[*enclosure*]

Executive Department
Raleigh Feby 21ˢᵗ 1880

[*copy*]

Resolved: That it is the sense of the Council of State that the General Assembly should be convened under article three, Section 9 of the constitution, at an early a day as practicable for the purpose of considering the proposition of William J. Best and associates, and such other propositions as may be submitted for the purchase and completion of the Western North Carolina Railroad to Paint Rock and Ducktown.

A&H—GP

[*enclosure*]
J. M. Worth to Thomas J. Jarvis

Treasury Department.
Raleigh, Feb. 21, 1880

I have this day received a certificate of deposit for thirty thousand dollars, given by the United States Trust Company of New York, to William J. Best, and transferred to me as State Treasurer by him, said amount being held by me for the protection of the interests of the State in the matter of the sale of the Western North Carolina Railroad, the conditions upon which said deposit is made being known to you. I herewith enclose copy of the conditions of the deposit.

[*enclosure*]
W. J. Best to John H. Stewart

Copy of the Conditions

Raleigh. N.C.
Feby 21ˢᵗ 1880

Please take notice that I have this day assigned to J M, Worth,

Esq Treasurer of the State of North Carolina, a certificate of deposit for Thirty thousand dollars, issued by the United States Trust Company, January 21st. 1880, and made payable to the order of myself and James D. Fish, jointly. I have signed the name of Mr Fish by authority of a power of attorn[e]y heretofore filed with your Company. Following are the conditions upon which said certificate is assigned:

1st   If the Legislature of North Carolina shall be convened in special, or extra session, and shall decline to ratify the draft of an act heretofore submitted by me, embodying my offer to purchase the interest of said state in the Western North Carolina Railroad, the assignment of said certificate to be null and void, and the amount thereof, together with the interest thereon, to be subject immediately to the order of myself and said James D. Fish, jointly.

2nd   If the Legislature of said state shall be convened in special, or extra session, and shall ratify the aforesaid act, I and my associates are to close a contract to purchase the interest of said state in said railroad, in accordance with the provisions of said act, or, failing so to do, the amount of said certificate of deposit, with the interest thereon, shall be withdrawn by the Treasurer of said state and applied to the payment of the expense of said special, or extra session, of the Legislature.

3rd   If the Legislature of said state shall be convened in special, or extra session, as aforesaid, and shall ratify the act submitted by me, I and my associates closing a contract to purchase said railroad as provided by said act, said certificate of deposit is to remain in the name and to the credit of the Treasurer of said state as security for the payment of the interest on $850,000 first mortgage bonds now outstanding as a lien upon the property of said company, until said mortgage bonds shall be paid.

4th   If the Legislature of said state shall ratify said act, as it now is, or with such amendments as I shall approve, the contract to be made according to said act is to be signed by me, W. R. Grace, James D. Fish, and J. Nelson Tappan, or other gentlemen equally satisfactory to the commissioners provided for in section one (1) of said act, and should failure be made in this regard said certificate of deposit shall be forfeited to said state

I herewith enclose a copy of the act spoken of above.

A&H—GP

W. E. Anderson to Thomas J. Jarvis

Raleigh, N.C., Feb 21 1880

I am in receipt of yr letter of this date asking me to give you any information I may have in regard to the financial and personal standing of certain parties, residents of New York City, and hasten to reply.

Mr Wᵐ R Grace is one of the Directors of the Marine Natnl Bk of New York, is a man of the highest character as regards ability & integrity, and is worth between $800,000. & $1,000,000.

Mr James D Fish is President of the Marine National Bank of New York, has been receiver for several prominent institutions and is President of a Rail Road running out of St. Louis, is reputed and believed to be worth from $300,000. to $400,000., and occupies a leading position in the business community as well as in society.

Mr J Nelson Tappan, who is Chamberlain of the City of New York, is said to be worth from $250,000. to $300,000., and stands high in business and social circles, having occupied many prominent & responsible positions in the City.

You are entirely at liberty to show this letter to whom you please, or use it in any manner you see fit, as the sources from which I have drawn my information are varied, and of the highest respectability in New York City, and they all agree that these are men "who would not intentionally enter upon any undertaking which would involve their good names, or which they might not be able to carry out."

A&H—GP

Printed Circular

A Proclamation by the Governor.

By and with the advice of the Council of State, I, Thomas J. Jarvis, Governor of North Carolina, in the exercise of the power conferred upon me by the Constitution, do issue this my Proclamation, convening the General Assembly in extra session, on Monday, the Fifteenth day of March, in the year of our Lord one thousand eight hundred and eighty, on which day at twelve o'clock, meridian, the Senators and Members of the House of

Representatives of the General Assembly of North Carolina, are hereby notified and requested to meet in their respective Halls in the Capitol, in the city of Raleigh, for the purpose of considering a proposition for the purchase of the State's interest in and the completion of the Western North Carolina Rail Road to Ducktown and Paint Rock, made by W. J. Best, W. R. Grace, J. N. Tappan and James D. Fish, of the city of New York, of whose financial responsibility and personal integrity I have satisfactory assurances; and for considering such other propositions as may be made for the same purpose. In Witness Whereof, I, Thomas J. Jarvis, Governor and Commander–in–Chief have hereunto set my hand and caused to be affixed the Great Seal of State.

Done at our city of Raleigh, this the twenty–first day of February, in the year of our Lord one thousand eight hundred and eighty, and in the one hundred and fourth year of American Independence.

A&H—GP

J. M. Worth to Thomas J. Jarvis

Treasury Department
Raleigh, Feb. 21st 1880

I favor and advise the convening of the General Assembly in extra session, for the purpose of considering a proposition for the purchase of the State's interest in the Western North Carolina Rail Road, and for the completion of the road, made by William J. Best and others, and such other propositions as may be made for the same purpose, and submit briefly some reasons therefor.

The State has engaged in Rail Road, Navigation, and other enterprises, almost from their beginning, either by becoming a stockholder, or otherwise lending its aid. Such a policy has been diastrous, and the failure to receive returns from the State's investments is just such as other States have experienced in like enterprises.

The following exhibit is sufficient, without extended comment, to show the results of our investments.

Wilmington and Weldon Rail Road Company.

Amount of stock in this company, held by the State Board of Education, and for many years a part of the School fund of the

State, was $400,000. It was sold by the Board in 1869 for $148.000, and invested in special tax bonds which are worthless— Lost.

Wilmington and Manchester Rail Road Company.

Amount of stock held by Board of Education $200.000. Sold by the Board in 1869, for $10.000 and invested in special tax bonds.— Lost.

Roanoke Navigation Company.

Since 1832 the State has been a stockholder in this Company to the amount of $50,000,[00] (increased from a previous investment) and for many years the stock has been almost entirely unremunerative. An act was passed March 18, 1875, directing the dissolution of the company. The interest of the State was sold under execution and brought less than fifty dollars.

Cape Fear Navigation Company.

Stock, $32.500; sold by Board of Education in 1869, for $3.250. Money paid into the Treasury.

Fayetteville and Western Plank Road Co.

The State subscribed to the stock of this Company in the year 1849, to the amount of $120.000, and issued bonds for its payment. Dividends were received by the State for a few years, but were much less than the interest paid by the State on its bonds. The road had gone down and the State's interest is absolutely worthless.

This remark applies to the Fayetteville and Centre Plank Road and Fayetteville and Warsaw Plank Road, which the State aided by the issue of bonds in payment of stock, authorized by acts of 1854–'55, the former $50.000, the latter $10.000.

Under act of January 27th, 1849, $65.000 of bonds were appropriated for improving the navigation of these rivers, and a similar appropriation of $15.000 under act of Feb. 14th 1855, was made for Tar river, all of which is absolutely worthless.

Atlantic and North Carolina Rail Road Co.

The State contracted a liability on account of this company, by issuing bonds in payment of stock and loan, to the amount of $1.466.500. Nothing has ever been received from this investment. The private stock in the company is now selling, as I am informed, for less than five cents in the dollar.

Albemarle and Chesapeake Canal Company.

Under the act of 1856 the State became a stockholder in this company to the extent of $350.000, paid in bonds. This liability has been reduced by the return to the State of $100.000 of old

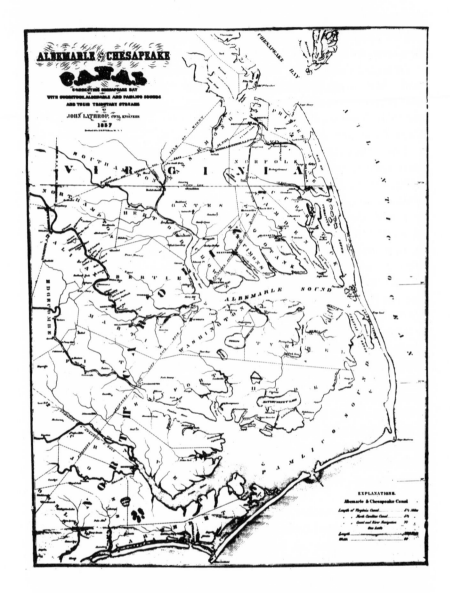

The Albemarle and Chesapeake Canal was a successor to the Great Bridge and Lumber Canal Company chartered by the Virginia legislature, March, 1854, to connect the Elizabeth and North rivers with Currituck Sound, establishing communication between the Albemarle, Currituck, and Pamlico sounds and the ocean. Construction was begun by 1857 and bonds guaranteed by the state were issued in the amount of $500,000. The board of internal improvements was authorized to subscribe $250,000 and the governor was empowered to appoint three directors. In 1871, with the idea of increasing business, the president of the company was authorized to subscribe capital stock to any other canal in North Carolina connected by navigable water with the Albemarle and Chesapeake canal. The 1874-1875 General Assembly authorized a committee to investigate the company and, in 1881, the treasurer was instructed to exchange stock of the state in the company for bonds of the state of North Carolina; upon exchange, the state's interest in the corporation ceased to exist. (Photographs, unless otherwise indicated, copied from files of the Museum of Natural History, State Department of Agriculture, Raleigh, N. C.)

bonds, in exchange for a like amount of stock surrendered under act of 1879. No money derived from the investment.

Western Rail Road Company; (from Fayetteville.)

Original liability on account of this company, incurred in 1858 and 1860, was $600.000. Nothing has been received from this investment. Nearly two hundred shares of this stock have recently been sold for two dollars and fifty cents per share.

Cape Fear and Deep River Navigation Co.

The State assumed the bonds of the company and issued its own bonds, under acts of 1854 and 1858, to the amount of $400.000, in aid of this company. Entirely lost to the State.

Wilmington, Charlotte and Rutherford Rail Road Co.[71]

The State exchanged bonds with this company to the amount of $2.000.000, under act of 1858, but has received no income from it, and lost all claim to the stock or property of the road.

New River Navigation Company.

By act of February 14th, 1855, the State subscribed $20.000 to the capital stock of this company, which is a total loss.

North Carolina Rail Road Company.

The outstanding liability on account of this Company is principal, $2.795.000 (originally $3.000.000) and past due interest over $500.000 What the fate of this stock will be is an open question. Amount of stock $3.000.000. But few dividends have been paid into the Treasury.

Western North Carolina Rail Road Co.,

Original appropriation of bonds under act of 1854-'55, $4.000.-000. Of this amount $957.000 have been retired in exchanges with other companies for stocks or bonds since the war, under authority of law, leaving amount of bonds outstanding $3.043.-000. All lost.

It is not necessary to state in detail the recent liabilities and expenses incurred by the State on account of this road, amounting to $1.300.000, as full information concerning them has already been given.

Raleigh and Gaston Rail Road Co.,

The stock of the State in this company was $682.500, and sold in the year 1866, under ordinance of Convention of 1865, for a like amount of State bonds, at their then depreciated value.

No mention is made of Turnpikes and other roads aided by the

---

[71]In 1875 this railroad became the Carolina Central Railway. Poor, *Railroad Manual*, 635.

State in cash appropriations, amounting in the aggregate to at least $50.000, and which have become worthless.

The aggregate of the liabilities and investments as stated, is $13.496.500, to which it is proper to add the interest on the bonds endorsed or issued by the State, paid in cash to the first year of the war, $2.200.000, making the total cost in connection with these investments $15.696.500. I make no mention of bonds issued or stock acquired under ordinances of Convention of 1868, or acts of 1868 and 1869, as they are not recognized in the compromise of the State debt.

The dividends received by the State from its investments have been far less than the interest paid by the State on its bonds.

The above exhibit ought, I think, to satisfy every citizen of the State that it is best for the State to make no further investment in any internal improvements, and I strengthen my advice to you, by urging that the General Assembly be convened for the purpose of selling the Western North Carolina Rail Road, and, as soon as possible, sell all the interest the State has in all other corporations.

I am surprised to hear, as a serious objection to selling this road, that it is to pass into the hands of *foreigners,* when it is well known that a large part of our roads now belongs to foreigners, and that nearly all of the three million of bonds outstanding against the North Carolina Rail Road are held by non residents of the State with a lien that virtually makes them the owners of the road. I have yet to learn that it makes any difference who builds a Rail Road to make it useful to the country, whether citizens of the State or non residents. The State can enforce any law against *foreigners* as well as our own citizens.

It is due to Mr. D. W. Bain, Chief Clerk, to say that the above statistics and data were furnished by him at my request, and are the result of his examination of the records here; and his long service in this department and familiarity with its details are sufficient evidence of their correctness.

A&H—GP

Mrs. C. W. Harris to Thomas J. Jarvis

Wilmington, Feb. 27th [1880]

Do not destroy my letters, please, recently forwarded you by me. I mean those signed by Hon. Messrs. Davis, Ransom, and

Vance. Will you add a fourth letter to them signed by yourself and send them all to me—for I expect to go to New York soon.

Be kind enough to tell me whether the "School Bill" will be allowed to come up before the extra session of the Legislature.[72] Answer this question, for if the Appletons of N.Y. can get that bill altered and their books adopted, it will be worth $20.000. to me. If you will help me do this, I will pledge you the most effective assistance a man ever had—and I will spend $5000 of it in a way that you will endorse—a way designated in those letters, just referred to.

Verbum sapientis.

Answer me fully with regard to School Bill.

Maj [W.P.] Hix of Columbia a prominent lawyer of this city, a shrewd agent, of this State and Mr C. W. Brown, Manager of Appletons Educational Department will be on hand as my agents and representatives in Raleigh if anything can be done. I will be there too, but very few must know it. I have trusted you with a secret. You must keep it. I have a written contract of the Appletons to pay me if I succeed. The smallest amt. is $20.000.

A&H—GP

Thomas J. Jarvis to Mrs. C. W. Harris

Executive Department
Raleigh, Feb 28ᵗʰ 1880

In reply to your letter I can only say again I regret that I cannot assist you. I have no money of my own to lend and if I had my official position would forbid my investing it in so powerful an engine of public and political opinion as a daily newspaper In regard to your request that I could see Mr. Swep-

---

[72]In March, 1879, the General Assembly passed a law making it the special duty of the commissioners of each county to levy a special tax for whatever was needed beyond the annual state grant to conduct their county schools for four months each year. Raleigh *Observer*, March 8, 1879. In the busy moments preceding adjournment, the speaker of the House and the president of the Senate neglected to sign the bill. Raleigh *Observer*, March 18, 1880. The superintendent of public instruction sought a mandamus compelling the secretary of state to receive the bill as duly in effect. Raleigh *Observer*, May 30, 1880. The Supreme Court, however, decided that the bill was not law because affixing these signatures to a bill was the finishing act of legislation and was not under the control of the judiciary. Neither could the bill be signed after the adjournment of the General Assembly. Raleigh *Observer*, August 27, 1880.

son in your behalf I must tell you that I never had any communication with him in my life and I feel sure that upon reflection you will see what a false light it would place me in to enter into negotiations with him even for you at this time.

My relations with Mr Best are simply what business relations justify and I can form no opinion of what his views about aiding you might be.

An answer as complete as this is renders in [*sic*] unnecessary to go into detailed replies to the other matters mentioned in your letter. In all proper ways I will be glad to aid you because I like to see intelligent industry succeed

I am very far from supposing that you had an idea of compromising me in your requests because I believe that they were preferred in honest endeavor or to establish again your newspaper. I enclose the letter sent me

A&H—GP

Thomas J. Jarvis to Mrs. C. W. Harris [*with enclosure*]
[*copy*]

Executive Department
Raleigh Mar 1st 1880

I returned a few days ago the letters referred to me in yours of the 27th.

I herewith send you the letter to supplement those of Messrs R. D. and V. as requested.

I hardly think the School Bill will be taken up at the **Extra** Session.

The Legislature can take it up and pass it, if they so desire. When the General Assembly meets, whether in general or extra session it can do anything within the limits of the Constitution.

This is quite as definite as I can speak

[*enclosure—copy*]

Executive Department
Raleigh Mar 1st 1880

The "Sun" a daily paper published some time since at Wilmington N.C. by C. W. Harris was a sprightly, prudent useful Democratic Paper.

Its revival under the same management would in the coming great campaign of 1880 be a blessing to the Democratic Party.

Tho⁸ J. Jarvis

The Western N. C. Railroad[73]

Statement of the Case Given by Governor Jarvis.

The proposition of Mr. Best and his associates, as perfected, briefly stated, is this: The State, through its proper commissioners, is to make a deed, without any warranty of title, to Mr. Best and his associates for the State's interest in the Western North Carolina Railroad. This deed is not to be delivered to the purchasers until the railroad is completed both to Ducktown and to Paint Rock, nor until all the other stipulations of their contract are performed; but until then it is to be held in trust by the United States Trust Company, of New York, upon the following conditions:

If the road is completed as agreed upon in the contract, and all the other conditions therein stipulated are faithfully performed, the deed is to be delivered to the purchasers; but if they fail in any one, the grant becomes void, the property reverts to the State, the United States Trust Company is to re-deliver to the State the deed and all papers pertaining thereto, and the State re-enters at once into the possession, control and ownership of the entire property.

Before the delivery of this deed to the United States Trust Company, the purchasers are to enter into a contract, binding themselves, their executors, administrators and assigns, to build the branch railroad to Paint Rock by July 1st, 1881, the Ducktown line by January 1st, 1885. From the day the act authorizing the sale is ratified, the purchasers are to pay all the interest on the $850,000 mortgage bonds which the State is now paying, and are in due time to take up and cancel the said bonds.

The purchasers are to have the right to mortgage any mile of the said Western North Carolina Railroad that has been completed and is in operation, to the extent of $15,000 per mile, but the aggregate amount of their mortgage bonds shall include the $850,000 heretofore issued, until these latter bonds shall be canceled. Of these bonds issued by the purchasers they are to deliver

---

[73]Taken from the *Union Republican* (Winston–Salem), March 4, 1880, hereinafter cited as *Union Republican.*

to the State Treasury $550,000 to re–imburse the State for its expenditures made since the purchase of the road in 1875. The mortgage to be made by the purchasers is to contain a condition that it cannot be foreclosed until the railroad is completed both to Paint Rock and to Murphy, in Cherokee County, and this condition is to be explicitly stated in the body of all the mortgage bonds, so that no defalcation in the payment of interest or anything else can work a sale of the railroad until it is completed. If the parties shall fail in their contract, the remedy is two–fold. First, the State has the legal right and the ability to enforce its performance. But if from any cause it shall become impracticable or inexpedient to enforce its performance, the railroad again becomes the property of the State, which takes that part from Salisbury to Paint Rock with all the rolling stock and equipment, free and discharged of all mortgage, lien or incumbrances of any and every kind, in favor of the purchasers or any other person or corporation, except the $850,000 now on it, and the actual expenditures made by the purchasers in the construction, repair and equipment of the said road, not to exceed in the aggregate $850,000. But this lien or indebtedness shall not be due or in any manner collectable until the completion of the Ducktown line to Murphy.

So that whatever money the purchasers shall have expended upon the work will be absolutely forfeited unless the road shall be completed both to Murphy and to Paint Rock. If, therefore, the purchasers build the Paint Rock branch and stop there, the State will take possession of the road, which is reasonably estimated to be worth $3,000,000. The only incumbrance upon it will be the $850,000 which is now a lien upon it, and which will be due in 1890, and the amount expended, not to exceed $850,000, which latter amount will not be due until the Ducktown line is completed to Murphy; and if the road shall never be completed to Murphy this amount will never be due. It will be seen, therefore, that unless the purchasers build the road to Ducktown, the State will get a completed road, said to be worth $3,000,000 cash for $850,000.

The proposition also contains a provision that the said purchasers, in the matter of transportation, shall not discriminate against any North Carolina city or town, or against any one North Carolina city or town over another. The State is to *hire* to the purchasers—not *give* them—five hundred convicts, for which they are to pay to the State $125 each per year, amounting in the aggregate to $62,500 annually for five years, or $312,500 in all.

The reasons that have influenced me to convene the General Assembly in extra session are:

1. The Western North Carolina Railroad belongs to the people of North Carolina. It has been built up to its present condition by your money, it is slowly progressing towards completion by the aid you give it, and surely you have the right to say whether you will sell it to those who will complete it, or will continue to be taxed for its construction.

2. Under existing laws, the appropriations for the building of the road, to be paid in cash out of the State Treasury, annually, are: For interest on the first mortgage bonds, $59,500; for the purchase of iron and material, $70,000, and for the support of convicts about $45,000—making in all $174,500. To collect this money and place it in the treasury the sheriffs get 5 per cent. commission, amounting to $8,725, which, added to $174,500, amount collected, makes $180,000 in money collected out of your property every year.

3. The taxable property of the State is $157,967,481. To raise $180,000, therefore, out of this property requires a tax of 12 cents on every $100 worth of property. It is a simple matter of calculation for each taxpayer to know the exact sum he pays annually and will continue to pay if you decline to sell the road, and decide to go on with the work yourselves.

4. The price to be paid for the convicts, that is to say, $62,500 a year, or $125 a head, payable quarterly in cash, will entirely relieve you of the burden of the maintenance of 500 convicts.

5. I think you have a right to the opportunity of saying, through the Legislature, whether you will relieve yourselves entirely of this burden, or whether you will use the money to hasten the completion of the Western Insane Asylum at Morganton, so that those of our fellow–beings whom God has bereft of reason may be provided for with decent comfort, instead of languishing in our common jails.

6. You have a right to say whether you will continue in force the existing laws, or use the money now appropriated to this purpose for fostering public schools and the education of your children, in which so much has been left undone by North Carolina.

7. You have a right to say whether or not this property shall pass from your hands into those of private capitalists, who will

speedily complete both lines of this important railway without further burden to you.

8. You have a right to say whether you are willing that these capitalists shall invest $4,000,000 of their own money in developing in the near future one of the grandest and most important sections of your State, a section that bids fair to be the great mining camp of the Union, and whether this investment shall be followed by other almost equally important.

9. It is for you to say whether capitalists, who have been urged by appeals, constantly and earnestly made, to come and invest their money among you, shall be permitted to do so.

10. It is for you to say whether your fellow-citizens of the West are again to be disappointed. For nearly half a century they have appealed to you for help. For a quarter of a century you have responded to their appeals with all the means in your possession. During that time, after expending millions, you have been able, of the three hundred and forty miles of railway which you projected nearly thirty years ago, to complete only one hundred and forty, and the track upon the part completed is almost worn out. You have in your political conventions often pledged yourselves to complete the other two hundred miles, and appropriate legislation has been participated in by both parties to redeem this pledge. Private capitalists now offer to relieve you of this obligation. Whatever may be the speculation on that subject, who can say when another offer will be made? You are entitled to have an opportunity to accept this offer or to decide to run the risk of another.

11. You have a right to say that you will keep your faith. Every plan yet suggested for the State to go on with the work without further taxation looks to the abandonment of the main or Ducktown line, and the completion of the branch to Paint Rock alone. Before your plighted faith is broken, you are entitled to the opportunity of accepting, if you desire, a proposition that will enable you to keep that faith and to strengthen rather than loosen the bonds that bind the mountains to the plains.

12. This is the first offer you have had for the purchase of the road and for its completion by private means. It may or may not be the last. But if I knew absolutely that one equally advantageous would be made to the General Assembly as its regular session next year, I would still deem it my duty to place it in your power to act now. The extra session, I find upon investigation, will cost you about $13,000, detailed as follows:

One hundred and seventy members, $4 per diem $680
Two presiding officers, $2 per diem additional 4
Seven clerks at $5 per diem 35
Four door–keepers at $4 per diem 16
Four servants at $1.50 per diem 6
Five pages at $1 per diem 5
Printing, fuel, lights and stationery, estimated at $29
    per diem (ample) 29
                                       ———

    Total per diem $775

It is thought that ten days will be amply sufficient for the Legislature to pass upon this question. Then, ten days at $775 per diem, will aggregate, without mileage, $7,750. To which add mileage, taken from the Auditor's book, $5,637.75. Total cost, $13,337.75.

This is less than one cent on each $100 worth of property. To wait until next January means that the sheriffs shall collect of you for the railroad this year $175,000; that is to say, twelve cents on the $100 worth of property, the appropriations for the road being that amount. To act now, rather than a year from now, will cost $13,000, and save $175,000. In other words one cent on the $100 worth of property, and save twelve cents. Now, I think you have a right to say whether you desire to have that eleven cents collected this year or not, or what you will have done with it if collected.

Of the million and a quarter of people in your State, I am the only one, on account of the position in which you have placed me, who can give you the power to answer these questions and exercise these rights for yourselves, through your representatives, and to say what you will have done with this property and the money you are annually contributing to build it. After mature deliberation, I have determined, whether wisely or unwisely the future will demonstrate, to give you this opportunity. The way is now open to you, and it is for you to say what shall be done.

                           Respectfully, Thos. J. Jarvis.

A&H—GP

William Johnston to Thomas J. Jarvis
Report

Charlotte N C March 15th 1880

In obedience to your directions to examine the condition of the Cape Fear & Yadkin Valley Railroad and the convicts employed thereon, I went to Greensboro on the eving of the 8th, expecting to meet Cap[t] C M Cooke co–member of the Board of Internal Imprment & M[r] J A Gray Prest of the Road The former did not arrive

In company with the President I proceeded along the line of the graded track to Cable stockade 12 miles South East of Greensboro   Here I found 125 convicts and 19 guards, the former at active work and in good health and condition. The examination of their work, quarters, habits, sanitary regulations were thorough and proved to be very satisfactory. The necessity of frequent washing the persons, clothes & sunning the bedding of the convicts, was enjoined upon those in charge. Under the supervision of Major Jones[74] these regulations seem to have been well executed. There was not a single invalid in the hospital. The work of the hands on the track was as active & vigorous as that of the best laborers

Thence we proceeded along the line about 12 miles in the direction of the Gulf to the Staley stockade under the control of M[r] Cha[s] E Houston.[75] The condition and management here were not so satisfactory The filth in the stockade was too great, the washing of persons, bedding & clothing, had not received proper attention, and as a consequence there were six patients in the hospital. Proper instructions were given to the Supervisor in all these matters in regard to his duties & responsibilities. He had only been in charge for two months, without experience & instruction and only required to know his duties, and I doubt not will in future faithfully carry them out. He is a worthy & ingenious young man of good judgment and active habits. The force here numbering with 19 guards in all 114 was doing efficent work, notwithstanding the inclement weather. The graduation is done almost entirely with shovels & wheelbarrows, mules and cars being more expensive than the cheaper labor of

---

[74]Unable to identify.
[75]Merchant of Mt. Vernon Springs, Chatham County. Branson, *Directory for 1884*, 207.

convicts. Thence we proceeded along the line & track of the road to the Gulf—the terminus of the Fayetteville & W R Rs on the night of the 11th inst. The general management of the convicts has been good on the work especially in the Greensboro division and a large amount of labor has been accomplished by a force amounting in all to from 240 to 260 convicts. As the term of imprisonment expires the convict is discharged, hence the changing number on the work. Several have escaped & one was shot in the attempt to escape

The food & cooking appear to be good and nutricious. The President informs me that the cost of care & maintenance of convicts amounts to 31cts per day—each   The line of the road appears to have been well located, although it runs through a rolling country, with some physical obstacles in fills, cuts & rock to encounter   The wagon road from Greensboro to the Gulf is numbered 55 miles   The survey makes the rail line 51½ less by 3½ miles. Of this 31 miles are graded and ready for the rails except Buffalo Creek bridge and a few inexpensive trestles— leaving about 20 miles to be graded, commencing about 12 miles from Greensboro and extending towards the Gulf. Ten miles of this is light work and the estimate is that the entire graduation can be finished before the 1st day of October, with the present force maintained on it. I was much gratified to find the lands of Chatham & Randolph counties penetrated by the road, so rich & fertile—covered with a heavy growth of hickory, white oak, & other valuable timbers. Besides the beds of coal and iron ore, the number of cotton factories, saw & grist mills within ten miles of the road far exceeded expectation   This railroad when constructed will do much to develop the middle portion of the state and add greatly to their taxable resources by giving increased value to the lands, timbers, water power, coal & iron mines on its line.

My inspection of the convicts—their management & discipline has been critical, as it is the policy of the state, and according to the enlightened progress of the age to endeavour to improve their moral status, cultivate a higher taste, and elevate them in the scale of humanity, as much as possible during imprisonment; while at the same time efficient work should be required of them

To Mr J A Gray President I am indebted for every courtesy & attention—giving me all information desired and showing me every portion of the railroad work & stockades I have the honor to submit the foregoing report for your consideration, while I remain

MESSAGE TO THE GENERAL ASSEMBLY, MARCH 15TH, 1880[76]

Gentlemen of the Senate and House of Representatives:

I have convened you in Extra Session to–day to consider a proposition made by W. J. Best, J. N. Tappan, W. R. Grace and J. D. Fish, of the city of New York, for the purchase of the State's interest in the Western North Carolina Railroad, and for its completion, and to consider any other proposition having the same end in view, and I have done so because you are the representatives of the real owners of the property proposed to be purchased.

To have refused to submit such an important proposition to you would, in my opinion, have been in effect, a gross usurpation of a power nowhere in the Constitution confided to me by the people of North Carolina. Reading that Constitution, by the light of true Democracy, the authority given to the Governor "on extraordinary occasions, by and with the advice of the Council of State, to convene the General Assembly in extra session" seems in no sense a restriction upon the right of the people to consider and determine their own affairs, but, on the contrary, a solemn enactment in furtherance of that right. Provision was first made in the Constitution for the people to be heard at regular stated periods through their representatives in General Assembly, and then in view of the possibility that emergencies at other periods might arise, in which it would be equally important for the voice of the people to be heard, machinery for that purpose also was provided. In a word, it was to enable the people to make known their will, and not to clothe the Governor with a veto power on that will, that authority was given to him to convene the General Assembly in extra session; to give the people voice and not to silence them in matters of their own concern. The people of North Carolina have steadily refused, from the organization of the State government in December, 1776, to the present time to confer upon their Governor a veto power, or any power in the nature of a veto power. Not

---

[76]This is Document Number 1 of *Public Documents, 1880.*

proposing, therefore, to usurp a prerogative that rightfully belongs to you as the representatives of the people, I have deemed it my plain duty to call you together and submit the proposition to you.

In view of the importance of the subject matter which you are to consider, it is my duty to put you in possession of all the information I have concerning both the proposition and the property to which it relates.

On the 10th day of January, of this year, Mr. William J. Best, of New York city, submitted to me, for himself and others, a proposition to purchase the State's interest in the Western North Carolina Railroad, and for the speedy completion of the entire line of road, both to Paint Rock and to Duck Town. After considerable correspondence, and several interviews with Mr. Best, and after assurances of the financial and personal character of himself and his associates, and of their connection with him, the proposition was so shaped as in my opinion to possess sufficient merit to require its submission to you. This proposition was first submitted to the Board of Directors of the Company and then to the Board of Internal Improvements, with requests for their advice, suggestions and action. These Boards were, in point of fact, as I was informed, divided in their opinions.

On February 3rd, I received a letter, dated February 2d, from Messrs. A. J. DeRosset, Donald McRae and D. R. Murchison, in behalf of themselves and other leading citizens of Wilmington, enquiring if a proposition had been submitted for the purchase of the State's interest in the Western North Carolina Railroad, and what the terms of the proposition were, and stating that there was an arrangement being perfected in Wilmington to raise a company to purchase the property. I replied to these gentlemen on the 3rd, the same day I received their letters, stating that a proposition had been made, giving them as accurately as I could (it then not being in my possession) its terms, and stating that I would submit it to the Board of Directors on the 10th, then to the Board of Internal Improvements, and finally to the Council of State. I assured them "that our friends in Wilmington would have the amplest opportunity to oppose the proposition of Mr. Best, or to make one of their own," and expressed the hope that they would "find themselves prepared to make an offer for such purchase," with the assurance that "as between our own people and all other people, my sympathies were with our own." I then laid the proposition, together with my correspondence, letter book, and all the information I had, before the Council of State, made by the Constitution my advisers, and asked their advice as to the propriety of convening the General Assembly in Extra Session, to consider the same. I was officially informed that the Council was unanimous, and earnest in opinion that I ought to call together the General Assembly in Extra Session at as early a day as practicable to consider the proposition. In accordance with that advice, I issued my Proclamation on the 21st day of February calling you together in Extra Session to-day.

Immediately after issuing my proclamation I caused the proposition of Mr. Best and his associates to be printed and circulated throughout the State, so that the people might know what it was and you might learn their will concerning it before you were required to act.

There has been much discussion on the merits of the proposition, the language in which it was written and the propriety of a sale of the property on any terms, which I take it will aid you in coming to your conclusions. When I published the proposition, though I thought its main features sufficiently set forth to be submitted to the General Assembly, it was not claimed by myself or by the Council of State so far as I am informed, that it was absolutely perfect either in form or in substance, and such amendments as mature deliberation might show to be necessary I confidently relied upon your wisdom to make and to this end, as I said in my recent address to the people of the State, I desired that "the speediest, greatest and most detailed publicity" be given to the proposition. And to aid you in this work of perfecting the proposition in its details as far as I could, (the Attorney General being constantly engaged in official duties connected with the Supreme Court) I availed myself of the services of Hon. George Davis, of Wilmington, and Hon. Thomas Ruffin,[77] of Hillsboro, whose rare legal attainments and whose unsullied personal integrity you know full well. At my request these gentlemen, after a careful study of the proposition, and after full conference with Mr. Best and the Attorney of his associates, and with their full concurrence, made a redraft of the entire proposition, which, together with the draft as first printed, I transmit herewith. I am sure, if you desire the property to be sold on the terms proposed, you will have but little trouble

[77]Lawyer of Greensboro; member of the General Assembly, 1850; Superior Court judge, 1861–1862, 1881–1883. *National Cyclopedia*, VII, 366.

in framing a bill that will protect the interest of the State and be acceptable to the parties who desire to become the purchasers.

The history of this road naturally divides itself into three periods. *First*. Its management from the date of its charter to the date of its sale under execution in 1875. *Second*. Its management from its purchase by the State at the sale in 1875, to its reorganization in April 1877. *Third*. Its management from its reorganization to the present time. The charter for this road from Salisbury to Duck Town and to Paint Rock was granted by the General Assembly at its session in 1854–'55 and work under it was begun soon thereafter. From that day to this there has seldom been in the State a political campaign in which this road has not in some way or other been a topic of discussion. Pledges for its speedy and early completion have been freely made by all parties that have had an existence in the State. Hopes have been excited, deferred, destroyed and renewed until the people have well–nigh despaired of its completion.

The State issued her bonds for four millions of dollars for this work prior to 1868. During the same period one million and three hundred thousand dollars were paid in money or labor by counties and individuals along the line of the road. The Company also issued its mortgage bonds to the extent of near a million and a half dollars to aid in the work. I think that I can safely say that not less than seven millions of dollars in actual cash, from time to time, including that derived from the sale of the six millions, six hundred and forty thousand dollars of so–called Special Tax Bonds,[78] went into the hands of the officers of the two divisions of the Company, during the first period, with which to build and equip this great work, and yet not a rail was laid beyond Old Fort, in McDowell County. From causes not now necessary to discuss, the whole property was, in 1875, put up and sold at public auction to the highest bidder, and bought by the State.

The amount bid for this property, by the State, was eight

---

[78]For developing the state's railroad facilities, the General Assembly of 1868–1869 had issued over $12,000,000 of special tax bonds, on which about $7,000,000 in interest had accumulated by 1879. The money had been spent so corruptly that little railroad improvement had resulted. The people of North Carolina hated these bonds so bitterly that in 1880 an amendment to the constitution was ratified forbidding the payment of any of the principal or the interest of these bonds. Ratchford, "The Adjustment of the North Carolina Public Debt," 165–166.

hundred and fifty thousand dollars, which she paid by executing a mortgage for that amount upon the property itself, and issuing, through the Commissioners appointed to make the purchase, mortgage bonds for that amount to be due in 1890, and bearing seven per cent. interest. The interest on these bonds the State guaranteed by making the coupons receivable for taxes due the State; but she did not bind herself to pay the principal.

Three Commissioners were then appointed by the State, who took possession of the property, and managed it until the organization of the present Company, in April, 1877. Of this management it is sufficient to say, generally, that it had a small convict force, and completed the road to Henry, and did considerable grading on the mountain section.

In the great campaign of 1876 pledges for the completion of the road were again given by both parties, and in the General Assembly of 1876–'77 both parties participated in the legislation under which the present Company was organized, and under which the present appropriations have been made and expended. Under the management of the present Company the State has furnished a convict force, averaging about five hundred, which has been fed, clothed and quartered at her expense. She has supplied the rails and material necessary to lay the track, and has paid for the same, and the iron laid by the Commissioners, with money drawn from the treasury and raised by taxation. In the same way she has paid all the interest on the eight hundred and fifty thousand dollars First Mortgage Bonds up to the present time. The amounts thus paid out, up to March 1st, 1880, are:

For Iron, &c	$150,173 43
" Interest	266,175 00
" Support of convicts	140,031 00
Total	$556,379 43

Under this management twenty–six miles of track have been laid, a part of the grading for which had been done by prior managements, and to–day the terminus of the road is at Gudger's Ford, six miles East of Asheville.

It gives me pleasure to say that I believe the affairs of the Company have been well conducted by the present management, and that a great deal of work of a difficult character has been done under it with but small means.

Any proposition to sell the State's interest in the road must to a very great extent be a business matter, and should be considered upon business principles. If an offer were made to one of you for the purchase of your own property, you would, after hearing the terms of the offer, be influenced in its acceptance or rejection by the condition and value of the property, and your supposed advantage in keeping or selling it. Presuming you would act in this way with the people's property, in the exercise of your responsible duties, I requested the President of the Company of the Western North Carolina Railroad to prepare a report, to be submitted to you, showing the condition and value of the property. This report I herewith transmit,[79] and commend to your careful attention. From it you will see the completed part of the road is by no means in good condition. The road–bed and an important and costly bridge need repairs; the iron is worn, and much of it needs replacing with new; the rolling–stock is insufficient, and much of it old and needing repairs. He estimated, as you will see from his report, that the sum of $220,000 will be needed in the next two years to put the road from Salisbury to Asheville in fair condition. From Asheville to Paint Rock is forty–five miles, and the sum of $650,000, according to his estimate, will be needed to build and equip this part of the road. From Asheville to Ducktown, he reports, is one hundred and thirty–five miles, and to build and equip this line the sum of $5,330,000 will be required. The time required to build and equip these two lines, under existing laws, he estimated to be thirty years; and this estimate supposes that every dollar of the annual appropriation be paid by the State and used for that purpose. The gross earnings of the company were last year $82,422.37, and the net earnings $22,157.60, which were used to aid in the construction and more speedy completion of the road to Asheville. Had the net earnings been used for the purpose of keeping up the old part of the road, they would have been wholly insufficient for that purpose. In fact, they would have been insufficient to have paid off the floating debt of the Company, which has been permitted to remain unpaid in the anxiety of the directors, officers and employees of the Company to reach Asheville as early as possible. The gross earnings for the next two years, if applied wholly to that purpose, would not be sufficient to repair and equip that part of

[79] "Western North Carolina Railroad—Special Report of President Wilson," *Public Documents, 1880*, No. 2.

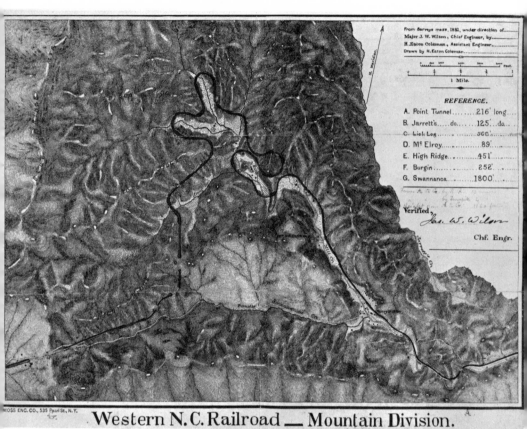

Western N. C. Railroad — Mountain Division.

This map gives some idea of the difficult route followed in the construction of the Western North Carolina Railroad to the Tennessee line. See also pictures, page 600.

the road already built, unless they should be greatly increased. So the managers of the property, if the State continues to own it, will have to look elsewhere for the means actually necessary to keep the road in proper running order.

The place to which they naturally would look is the State treasury, for the funds there are the property of the State equally with the road. With this view, I have called upon the State Treasurer for a report, which I herewith transmit,[80] and likewise commend to your careful consideration. From this report you will see there is not a dollar in the Treasury that can be used for any such purpose, and will not be next year, unless you increase the rate of taxation. In fact, you will see that not a dollar of the annual appropriation for iron can be paid. So that unless other means are devised or taxation shall be increased the further construction of the road must practically be stopped. It is a rule with the Treasurer, in the administration of the affairs of his office, to first pay the expenses of the State government proper, including the support of the charitable and penal institutions, and then the appropriations of money for specific purposes according to their priority. Acting upon this rule, he has not yet been able to pay off the liens on the Cape Fear and Yadkin Valley Railroad, and still acting upon this rule, he will be unable this year to pay anything to the Western North Carolina Railroad.

What to do, then, with this property becomes a very grave question for you to determine. Ought the State to keep the road or ought the State to sell the road? If you decide to keep it, how do you propose to complete it? There are, so far as I can see, but three ways in which this may be attempted: To issue more State bonds, which to me seems perfectly inadmissible; I do not desire ever to see another State bond issued to build this or any other road: To still further mortgage the property, which in my opinion will inevitably lead to another foreclosure and sale and to its purchase by parties who will build and use the road when and how as to them may seem best, or who, it may be, will never build it all all: Lastly by moneys derived from increased taxation. To increase the taxes already laid upon the people, without an absolute necessity therefor, I am persuaded you will not do. Governments are necessary, and their machinery is necessarily costly, but the moment a govern-

[80]"Treasurer's Special Report," *Public Documents, 1880*, No. 3.

ment exacts a dollar from the people more than the requirements of its existence may demand, that moment it becomes an oppressor. As I said to you in my inaugural address: "Government has its blessings and its burdens. Good laws properly administered constitute its blessings; the taxation necessary to its support, its burdens. How to make its blessings as great and its burdens as small as possible, should be the earnest, constant study of all to whom the people have committed their interests, either as makers or ministers of the law." What I said then I repeat now. Nor am I to be deterred from pointing out to my fellow citizens how they may lighten their burden of taxation by the fear of having it said that such a course is an appeal to the sordid passions of the people, and having it characterized as the act of a demagogue. Such an opportunity now presents itself and I do not for a moment hesitate to pursue the course that patriotism and duty so plainly mark out for me. In my opinion, further taxation for the completion of the Western North Carolina Railroad is entirely unnecessary, even at existing rates, for the simple reason that by a sale of the road upon the terms offered, it can be completed as originally designed without one dollar of additional cost to the State, and not another dollar ought to be so spent. The State in its expenditures for works of internal improvement has never sought dividends, or any profit indeed, other than that inseparable from the greater conveniences of the people and the necessary increase in values sure to be caused by such works. But whether she sought such dividends from such expenditures or not, her sad experience in investments in other public works forbids the hope of any return to the State Treasury of any money expended on the Western N.C. Road so long as she may own and operate it.

But there is still higher consideration involved in the acceptance or rejection of the proposition now before you. North Carolina should do equal and exact justice to each and every portion of her people and territory, and only by so doing can she do the greatest good to the whole State, and only by so doing can she make her citizens everywhere proud to be called North Carolinians. Daily and hourly may be witnessed in various sections the increased means of travel, trade and intercourse which have so greatly added to the general wealth of the State. There are, however, a few sections of the State still unprovided for, and of these notably, is that whole section of the State west of the Blue Ridge. The only means of transportation for person or produce in all that section is to–day as it was a century ago, while during the whole period from that day to this, these people have responded with their lives and their scant means to every call of the State. In the proposition now before you I believe the State has an opportunity, without laying further burdens upon the other sections, of speedily giving to those people what they have so long hoped for and so patiently waited for. I do not hesitate to avow my confidence in the honesty, integrity and ability of the gentlemen proposing this purchase, and my firm belief that if they make the purchase they will carry out in good faith and in good time any contract they may enter into with you.

The sale of the road is the only security of the people against taxation. Simply to repeal the legislation of 1876–'77 will not give relief. The only additional taxation placed upon the people by that legislation was for the purchase of iron which in 1877 amounted to $34,000, in 1878 to $48,000 and in 1879 to $69,000, and can in no one year exceed $70,000. The reason the amount paid for iron in 1879 so greatly exceeded that paid for it in either of the preceding years was because I bought in the fall of that year, anticipating a rise in the price of iron, 650 tons at $42 per ton, nearly enough to iron the road to Asheville, and which could not be bought now for $80 per ton. This appropriation for iron is the only part of the burden which can be lopped off. You cannot if you would and you would not if you could repeal the act which binds the State to pay the interest on the $850,000 first mortgage bonds of the Road. The State has pledged her faith to this by making the coupons of these bonds receivable for taxes and her faith must be kept inviolate. The amount of interest thus to be paid is $59,500 per annum, and must so continue for ten years, when these bonds mature. It costs the State $50,000 per annum to take care of 500 convicts. She cannot and will not refuse to provide for these. It is true she may work them elsewhere, but that will not get clear of or lessen the cost of maintenance. There is no place to put these convicts at work at the cost of private parties. The Oxford and Henderson and the Chapel Hill roads are the only enterprises that have made offers to the Penitentiary authorities to hire convicts and both of these roads have been supplied. So that there is $110,000 of the burden that must still remain in any event if you refuse to sell this property. And just here I beg to call your attention to another fact in the report of Treasurer

Worth, to which I have not yet alluded. He states that there will be a deficiency in the Treasury under existing laws at the meeting of the next General Assembly of $216,675.28. If the appropriation of $70,000.00 for iron be omitted—and that as I have shown is the only item than can be repealed—then there will be a deficiency of $146,675.28, if you refuse to sell the road and the State meets her obligations. There is but one way to supply this deficiency and that is by increase of taxation, and the increase necessary for that purpose will be ten cents on each hundred dollars worth of property.

The State should never, as I have said, issue another bond to aid in any public work in any section. She can, though, do much in the way of aid for all sections that choose to avail themselves of it with her convict labor. Our experience has shown it to be the best labor ever employed in this State on works of improvement. A force of one hundred and twenty–five convicts has nearly graded, since last October, the most of the line from Oxford to Henderson, for which the State receives compensation in cash sufficient to cover all expenses. Another force of now nearly one hundred is at work on the road running to the State University, and it is expected will complete the grading by the first of the Fall. This force is likewise paid for in cash. The force on the Cape Fear and Yadkin Valley Road will complete the grading of that road to Greensboro by the last of the summer, and then can be placed west of Greensboro, and well organized as it is, will, if kept at work push quite rapidly up the Northwestern section of the State through and into a section rich in mineral and agricultural resources, and much in need of railroad facilities. This force is paid for in the first mortgage bonds of the company, which is the same sort of security that those who pay for the iron and superstructure are to take for their money. This much the State can do, and should do for other sections, and it can better be done by leaving it with the penitentiary authorities than by legislative enactments. In this way, I think many projects which have been much talked of and discussed in our more eastern counties, may be greatly aided without any additional burdens to the people. In fact, I think at the same time the State is giving this aid she may, by proper legislation, lessen the burdens in the counties, for I am prepared to advise that the criminals who are now an expense to the counties, be taken out of jail and put to work on these roads. If men will commit crime, I believe in making them work for the public to pay for it. If the State continues this work on the Western N.C. Railroad for twenty or thirty years longer, it will cut her off for long years to come from doing anything with this labor for other sections.

The introduction into the State of the amount of money and energy necessary to the completion of this great work by foreign capitalists, is, in my opinion, worthy to be considered, and if you believe in the good faith of the parties proposing such completion, should have its influence on your action. The speedy development of the large section of the State beyond Asheville, consequent upon the completion of this road, and the investments there by other capitalists from abroad, will become a reality and no longer be a prophecy.

And now, gentlemen, having given you all the information in my possession, and for fuller details placing my letter book containing all my correspondence on the subject at your disposal, I leave the matter in your hands, confidently believing that your action in this crisis, so fraught with good or evil to the people of the West, and of the whole State, will be taken with an eye single to the good of those whom you represent.

In conclusion, gentlemen, I beg leave to say that I know of no other subject for your consideration which may not be postponed till the regular Session of the General Assembly next winter, and I trust that I am not infringing upon your prerogatives, in earnestly advising you not to enter upon general legislation.

A&H—GP

A. R. Ledoux to K. P. Battle

Chapel Hill, N.C., March 17th, 1880

In response to your request for information concerning the attitude past and present of Col. L. L. Polk[81] to the Experiment Station, I beg to state the following particulars: It is my firm conviction that the Station is popular today in *spite* of rather than because of the Commissioner. In my opinion he has sys-

---

[81]Leonidas LaFayette Polk; member of the General Assembly, 1860, 1864; member of the Convention of 1865; first North Carolina commissioner of agriculture, 1877–1880; editor of the *News and Observer*, 1880–1881; publisher of the *Progressive Farmer*, 1886–1892. Polk was always interested in politics, and was a prominent Alliance and Populist leader in the South. For an excellent biography, see Noblin, *Polk*.

tematically and constantly belittled this branch of the work, whenever he could not make it appear as if some of the credit arising from the work of the Station was due to himself. When I first came into the State from my first conversation with him I saw that he considered *himself* the "Department of Agriculture." He paid me my salary in the first instance by putting his hand into his pocket and pulling out the money, ignoring the Treasurer entirely and informed me that I must apply to him when I wanted funds. He so arranged it that all my reports and even news–paper articles relating to the Station had to be examined and approved by himself before printing. He wrote and spoke of me as "my Chemist" and ordered me about as if *he* had hired me. I was constantly in receipt of letters from him saying "I wish you to do this at once", "I wish you to do that", "I wish you to devote yourself to my work [Fertilizers] to the exclusion of everything else," &c. &c. In his speeches throughout the State, as I am informed and as I have seen reported in the news–papers, he spoke of me and "my Chemist" and of the Department as his Department. Before the Committee of the Legislature, as he has elsewhere done, to my personal knowledge he arrogated to himself all the praise that could be claimed for the Board of Ag. and laid upon them all the blame that he himself deserved. Until April 1879 he invariably published my reports, my formulae and analyses at the back of his crop reports as "an appendix" with no name but his own upon the title–page and nothing to indicate that anything in regard to the Exp. Station was contained in the publication. Thus my directions for making vinegar, my report upon the Ville formulae, my report upon the Savannah lands, my directions for composting, my second quarterly report for 1877, my fourth quarterly report for 1878, my report to the Assembly for 1879, &c, &c. everyone appeared as an appendix to or at the end of some pamphlet of the Commissioner's, without anything on the title–page to indicate their presence. My sugar–beet report—a pamphlet of fifty pages—only escaped the same fate after an appeal to the Executive Committee and a direct order from them that it should appear alone. In publishing the expenses of the Dept. of Agriculture for the Legislature of 1879, he ingeniously mixed up the items so that it was impossible to tell how much had been spent at the Station and how much had been expended by him. It was only with great difficulty that I obtained from Capt. Robinson[82] the true figures. In a recent publication of expenses the Commissioner attempts to make it appear that the Station is the most expensive branch of the work of the Dept. by separating ingeniously the fish–hatching work from his work in Raleigh, although Mr. Worth[83] reports through him and requests through him and he is not responsible for the appropriations and expenditures of that branch. In a recent report published by him, in the face of emphatic and formal protests made in the past, he publishes, without my knowledge, portions of my report to the Board of Agriculture. He knew that I considered my reports confidential. On page 4 of said report he makes a false statement as to the publications requested and ordered for the Station. On page 5 he omits portions of my report, thus causing it to appear that I had been unjust and partial in bestowing praise upon my assistants. On page 6 he maliciously publishes a portion of a recommendation of mine which he well knew I did not desire made public.

From a number of letters, received this year and last from manufacturers of fertilizers I learn that in reporting to them my analyses he omits my name entirely, not stating in some cases who made them, in others stating that they were made by "my chemist", in others by "our chemist." In 1877 they appeared as made "for the Commissioner" and recently in the Raleigh Observer as made "*by* the Commissioner." As you know, I am soon to leave the State and have little more to gain or lose by the continuance or discontinuance of the Dept. of Agriculture, nevertheless I affirm it as my solemn conviction based on Col. Polk's statements to the Committee of the Legislature in 1879, upon his statements to myself, and upon his general conduct that he is not only a secret enemy to, and jealous of the success of the Exp. Station, but also that he is completely ruining the whole Dept. of Agriculture. The present system of collecting fertilizer samples would work admirably, with the proper man to supervise it, but with his jealousy of the Station not only is there no provision made for carrying out portions of the law, (e.g. compelling fertilizer bags to bear a proper analysis,) but I honestly believe the Commissioner has attempted to, or

[82]T. J. Robinson of Cumberland County, secretary of the Board of Agriculture until his death in November, 1879. "Report of the Board of Agriculture," *Public Documents, 1881.* No. 9, 1.

[83]Stephen G. Worth of Fayetteville, superintendent of the fish hatcheries at Morganton. "Report of L. L. Polk, Commissioner of Agriculture for 1877 and 1888," *Public Documents, 1879,* No. 8, 8.

through gross forgetfulness and carelessness has involved me in several disputes past and present with the manufacturers.

You are aware that after three years of compliance with that portion of the plan suggested by me for fertilizer control which provided for our being informed whether the samples contained Potash or Ammonia, or both, that he refused to continue the same and denied that it ever had been the custom, *only yielding after I threatened to bring the matter before the Board* and forwarded to him positive proofs that the system *had been* followed by him in every case in the past. This act of the Commissioner's caused considerable delay in the publication of analyses, as well as an increased expenditure of time and a waste of costly reagents.

It has been only by assuring Legislators and others that my sub–department and that of the Commissioner were at present almost entirely disconnected that I have been able to render the Station as popular as it is. A month rarely passes in which I am not compelled to take decided ground in opposition to some new encroachment of the Commissioner's.

You have perfect liberty to use my opinion in any way that you deem to be for the good of the Station.

A&H—GP

William A. Courtenay[84] to Thomas J. Jarvis

Mayor's Office,   Charleston, S. C.   Mch 17   1880

As chairman of the Committee of arrangements for the Cowpens Centennial, I have the honor to transmit an official communication which will present to your attention, and, I trust, to your favor, our plans for the observance of the coming anniversary.

The large outlay for this proposed Centennial Commemoration will be provided by the citizens of South Carolina, but it is particularly desired that the old thirteen States of the Union, through their Executives, should make a contribution specifically to the cost of this Memorial column, and thus identify their people with this permanent memorial, on South Carolina soil, to the victors in this important and decisive battle for American Independence. For the sole purpose of the identification of your

---

[84]Prominent businessman and mayor of Charleston, South Carolina. *Cyclopedia of the Carolinas*, I, 367–372.

State with the erection of this granite column, I am asked to suggest to you that the small sum of Two hundred and fifty dollars ($250) be subscribed for this National work; the thought being to name an amount so small that there would be no disability in making the contribution and thus unite the original States in the old bonds of fraternity and union. The purpose of the Committee is to make a record of this unity of the States in the erection of this memorial, on the column itself, and the assent of each at an early day will further our monumental plans.

I beg, also, most Respectfully, to add, that your Excellency will honor the coming occasion with your presence.

In the programme of the day, there will be expected a Speaker from the Southern States, one from the Middle States and one from the New England States. This selection from the Southern States, the Governors of North Carolina, Virginia, Maryland, So. Carolina and Georgia will be requested to make.

At this early day it is only necessary to add that you will be warmly welcomed to South Carolina, and that His Excellency, the Governor of South Carolina is deeply interested in having a successful and happy Re–union on the 17th January 1881, at Spartanburg. S. C., and will, in person, welcome you to our Commonwealth

A&H—GP

Thomas Wallace[85] *to Thomas J. Jarvis*

New York March 18, 1880

The New York parties represented by G. A. Fitch[86] in the purchase of the North Carolina Rail Roads, are amply able and ready to take this property if that the Legislature decides disposing of them, and passes the necessary legislation to carry it into Effect.

---

[85]Manufacturer of Ansonia, Connecticut, and then of New York, New York. Beginning his career with the production of wire products and sheet metal, in 1872 he added the manufacture of dynamos and electrical supplies to his metal interests. *National Cyclopedia* XL, 49.

[86]Unable to identify.

A&H—GP

J. M. Worth to Thomas J. Jarvis

[March 19, 1880]

[Copy of Contract &c]

I am informed by Col John N Staples[87] that the Atlantic and North Carolina Rail Road, and the North Carolina Rail Road Companies have commenced proceedings to realize from the Government of the United States by congressional action or otherwise taxes collected some ten years ago from the said Rail Road Companies by the Government as income tax upon the stock.[88] Col Staples is interested in behalf of said Roads as Attorney, and is familiar with the matter.

I would respectfully suggest and recommend that you employ Col Staples in behalf of the State to collect from the Government or such other source as he may be able, whatever claim or interest the State may have in the said recovery, and he be allowed compensation for his services out of the recovery only, and that said compensation be the same as that be allowed and agreed to be paid to the attorneys by the said Rail Road Company or Companies and no more, and upon the further agreement on the part of Col Staples that if he fails to recover, he is to receive nothing for his services, and that the state shall be at no expense whatever in the matter, and that his said compensation shall become due and payable when a recovery is had, and payable solely out of the amount recovered.

By this arrangement the State will lose nothing, in the event of a failure to prosecute successfully; but will be that much the gainer by whatever amount is realized.

[Copy of Governor's Endorsement]

Executive Dept
Raleigh Mch 19. 1880

I hereby approve the suggestions and recommendations in the foregoing letter of Treasurer Worth and this is to certify that I

---

[87]Lawyer of Greensboro; member of the General Assembly, 1874–1881. James W. Albright, *Greensboro, 1808–1904, Facts, Figures, Traditions and Reminiscences* (Greensboro: Jos. J. Stone & Company, 1904), 45–46, hereinafter cited as Albright, *Greensboro*.
[88]This effort to recover such taxes had already failed once in Congress. See Jarvis to Grainger, February 18, 1880, *n*. 64, in this volume.

have this day employed Col John N. Staples to represent the State of North Carolina in the collection of the claim of the State for taxes collected by the Government as referred to in said letter, upon the terms and according to the stipulations referred to in Mr Worths letter, and I have this day given him a power of Attorney with full and ample authority to represent the State of North Carolina for the purposes mentioned in said letter. In testimony whereof I hereto set my hand and cause the Great Seal of the State to be hereto affixed.

A&H—GLB

Thomas J. Jarvis to the General Assembly

Executive Office
Raleigh, N. C.   March 20th 1880

I have had some official correspondence with the Governors of South Carolina and Tennessee in regard to the proper celebration of the centennial anniversary of the Battle of King's Mountain on the eighth day of October next, and I have received from others assurances of their intentions to make the day worthy of the event.

Both these states have made appropriations for this purpose and their Legislatures have shown their appreciation of its importance by patriotic resolves.

I desire to bring the matter to your attention in order that you may express the sense of the people of the State in such form as you may deem best suited to the magnitude of a victory won by the blood and bravery of our ancestors, and to the end that you may enact such laws as will enable me to spend a sum not exceeding two thousand dollars to give North Carolina her proper rank and dignity on that day.[89] King's Mountain was the decisive Battle of the campaign of 1780. The brilliant victory there won reanimated the flagging hopes of our people and made Yorktown possible. It is one of North Carolina's priceless honors, and I confidently entrust to your pride and patriotism its proper recognition.

---

[89]The General Assembly authorized the governor to spend $1,500 for this celebration. *Laws of North Carolina, 1880,* 110–111.

A&H—GP

Committee to Thomas J. Jarvis

Greensboro N. C. March 22/80

Sir:

At a mass meeting of the residents of Guilford county held at Greensboro N.C. on the 2nd day of March 1880, it was resolved to celebrate with becoming ceremony the one hundreth anniversary of the battle of Guilford Court House which will occur on the 15th day of March 1881.

With a view of perfecting arrangements for such celebration the meeting was adjourned to Tuesday April 6th 1880 at Greensboro N. C.; when it is expected that many of the eminent men of the nation will be present and assist by their eloquence and influence in so shaping matters as to ensure a grand and enthusiastic centennial celebration of one of the most remarkable struggles in the revolutionary war.

In behalf of the citizens of Guilford county we extend to you a cordial invitation to be present and join us on the 6th day of April next.

Very respectfully
Cyrus P Mendenhall[90]   Committee
Thomas B Keogh[91]   on
R. G. Fulghum[92]   Invitations

A&H—GP

G. Fitch to Thomas J. Jarvis

Raleigh, N. C. March 22[d] 1880

I have the honor of submitting to your Excellency, for and in behalf of Thomas Wallace and others, of the City of New

---

[90]Lawyer and mayor of Greensboro; member of the General Assembly, 1860. Ethel S. Arnett, *Greensboro, North Carolina, The County Seat of Guilford* (Chapel Hill: The University of North Carolina Press, 1955), 35, 222, hereinafter cited as Arnett, *Greensboro.*

[91]Lawyer of Greensboro and editor of the Greensboro *North State.* Branson, *Directory for 1884,* 351, 354. The newspapers of the day show that for several years Keogh had been chairman of the Republican State Committee.

[92]Richard G. Fulghum, owner of the Greensboro *Patriot.* Sallie W. Stockard, *The History of Guilford County, North Carolina* (Knoxville: Gaut–Ogden, 1902), 68, hereinafter cited as Stockard, *Guilford County.*

York and elsewhere, the following proposition for the purchase of the interest of the State of North Carolina in and to the "Atlantic and North Carolina," the "North Carolina," and the "Western North Carolina" Railroads, as follows:

The said Thomas Wallace and his associates will pay the State for its interest in the Atlantic and North Carolina Railroad, the sum of Two Hundred Thousand Dollars in cash;

And for its interest in the North Carolina Railroad they will liquidate at maturity the bonds issued by the State in aid of the construction of that road, amounting to Two Millions Seven Hundred and Ninety–four Thousand Dollars, or thereabouts;

And for its interest in the Western North Carolina Railroad they will pay the sum of Five Hundred and Fifty Thousand Dollars in cash.

This purchase, if so made, is understood to be subject to all the liens on said corporations, and the existing lease of the North Carolina Railroad. I am informed that there is a judgment in the United States Circuit Court of Two Hundred and Thirty–four Thousand Dollars on the Atlantic and North Carolina Railroad,[93] and a mortgage of Eight Hundred and Fifty Thousand Dollars on the Western North Carolina Railroad, on the latter of which the State is paying the interest. The said Wallace and his associates will indemnify the State against the payment of said mortgage lien of Eight Hundred and Fifty Thousand Dollars, and the interest on the same.

The payment of said sums of Two Hundred Thousand Dollars, and of Five Hundred and Fifty Thousand Dollars, shall be made to the Treasurer of the State, upon the transfer of the interest of the State in said incorporations to said Wallace and his associates.

Ample security, guaranteeing the State of North Carolina against the payment of the principal or further interest on the said Eight Hundred and Fifty Thousand Dollars of mortgage bonds of the Western North Carolina Railroad, shall be deposited with the said Treasurer, and shall so remain until said bonds are paid, or until the State is discharged from all further liability thereon.

The said Wallace and his associates will agree to complete the Western North Carolina Railroad from its present terminus to

---

[93] For the judgment in the "Hawkins suit," see Brown, *State Movement*, 245–246.

Paint Rock on or before the thirty–first day of December, 1881, for which satisfactory guarrantees will be given.

The State of North Carolina shall grant a charter to said Thomas Wallace and his associates, containing the conditions and provisions usual in such acts of incorporation in the State of North Carolina, that shall enable them to consolidate, under one organization, the three railroads in question, from Morehead City to Charlotte, and *via* Salisbury to Paint Rock.

If these proposals are accepted by the State, the said Thomas Wallace and his associates will meet the duly authorized agents of the State of North Carolina without unnecessary delay, and reduce these propositions, with other necessary details, to the formal conditions and provisions of a contract, and will enter at once thereafter upon the obligations so undertaken.

In addition to the above, but with the express understanding that it shall be considered as a separate and distinct proposition, and in no manner connected with the foregoing, the said Thomas Wallace and his associates will agree and guarantee to iron, equip and operate a line of railroad from Asheville to Ducktown, if the State, or the citizens interested therein, will "grade, bridge and tie" the road so projected.

Contracts for work remaining to be done shall be open to competition for the employment of the convict labor of the State, when it can properly be so employed, and upon the same terms offered to other contractors, the said Wallace and his associates assuming no responsibility for the care or custody of the convicts while so employed.

I beg to assure your Excellency that in submitting these propositions we are actuated and governed solely by business considerations, and by the openly avowed purpose of completing a through line of railroad from the sea–port of North Carolina, to Louisville, Cincinnati, St. Louis, Chicago, and other commercial centres of the West and North–west, and to connect as well with the Southern and South–western railway system of our country.

A&H—GP

W. A. Courtenay to Thomas J. Jarvis

Mayor's Office, Charleston, S.C. Mch 22ᵈ 1880

I have the honor to invite your attention to the joint action taken by the citizens of Spartanburg, S.C., and the Washington

Light Infantry, at their meetings held on 17 January, 1880, and embodied in the following Resolution. We will feel very much honored if you assist us in the successful achievement of our work by accepting this position.

"Be it further Resolved, That the Governors of the Old Thirteen States, and of the State of Tennessee be cordially invited to co-operate in this undertaking by acting as an honorary advisory Committee, lending their counsel and influence to this patriotic work of erecting, with fitting ceremonies, an enduring memorial, on South Carolina soil to the brave men, who, one hundred years previously, devoted their lives and services to the establishment of American Independence; and, by so doing, bring together the people of the 'Union' in the bonds of country and of Washington."

A joint Resolution was, some weeks ago, offered in the U. S. Senate and House of Representatives, providing for a bronze statue of Gen[l]. Daniel Morgan, of New Jersey, to be delivered, through the Governor of South Carolina, to the Cowpens Centennial Committee, with which to crown the memorial column and thus identify the whole country with the celebration in January next.

It is of primary importance to secure early action in Congress, as, with such a work of art, the time remaining is growing short for its preparation and delivery in season for the Commemoration.

Would your Excellency lend your personal influence to expediting this result, by communicating, at your earliest convenience, with your Senators and Representatives in Congress on the subject.?[94]

The success of our undertaking will be complete and potent for good, if concurrent with the action of the old thirteen States, in the erection of the column; the United States Congress, speaking for the whole people of the Union, will give to South Carolina and the country the form of the chief actor in this important victory of the American Revolution.

---

[94]By May 26, 1880, such a resolution had passed Congress and had been approved by the president. *Congressional Record,* Forty-sixth Congress, Second Session, 3,857.

Thomas J. Jarvis to G. A. Fitch

Executive Office
Raleigh N.C. Mar 23, 1880

Your communication looking to the purchase of the States' interest in the Atlantic and North Carolina Rail Road, the North Carolina Rail Road, and the Western North Carolina Rail Road. has been received. In this communication you represent Thomas Wallace and others of the city of New York and elsewhere, as the proposed purchasers.

Will you be kind enough to furnish me at once. with the residence and business of Thomas Wallace:

The residence and business of each of his associates: and also to file with me your power of Attorney to represent the said Thomas Wallace and such of his associates whose names you furnish me with.

I will further thank you to furnish me with proper references as to yourself, your business, profession, occupation and financial standing.

Please put me in possession of the information asked for at once.

Thomas J. Jarvis to J. M. Worth

Executive Department
Raleigh March 23ᵈ 1880

Will you please be kind enough to inquire at once as to who and what Thomas Wallace of 61 Broadway New York is, and what is his standing.

J. M. Worth to Thomas J. Jarvis
[with enclosure]

Raleigh, Mar 24 1880

In reply to yours of the 23 inst. requesting me to ascertain "who and what Thomas Wallace of 61 Broadway is, and what is his standing," I herewith hand you telegram received in reply to inquiries made as requested.

[*enclosure*]

R. A. Lancaster to J. M. Worth

[*Telegram*]

New York [March] 23 1880

Wallace returned Californian not well known here Can not find out anything reliable about him

G. A. Fitch to Thomas J. Jarvis

Raleigh N.C. March 24 1880

I have the honor to acknowledge the receipt of your note of yesterday, and to say in reply that Thomas Wallace Esq. late of San Francisco Cal, and now of the city of New York, is well known to George D. Roberts Esq. James R. Keene Esq, Charles L. Wright Esq Eugene Kelly Barker. and the Banking House of Lazard Freres, all of the city of New York., also to Ramon Pacheco, N.C. and to Senators J. P. Jones, James Farley and Newton Booth, now in Washington D.C. any of whom I have no doubt can give your Excellency any information you desire as to the financial ability of Mr Wallace whose place of business is I understand. No. 61 Broadway New York. City.

Thomas J. Jarvis to G. A. Fitch

Executive Office Raleigh N.C.
March 24 1880

Your communication of even date with this has been received The only information asked for by me which you furnish me is that you understand the place of business of Thomas Wallace is No 61, Broadway New York.

I again ask you, will you be kind enough to furnish me at once with the residence and business of each of his associates and also to file with me your power of attorney to represent the said Thomas Wallace and such of his associates whose names you furnish me with. I will further thank you to furnish me with proper references as to yourself your business, profession occupation and financial standing. Please put me in possession of the information asked for at once

A&H—GP

George Davis to Thomas J. Jarvis

Wilmington, N. C.
29 Mar, 1880

I have been laid up ever since my return, and though in my office today, am not fit to be here.

Col. Ruffin and myself, after deliberate consideration, are immovably resolved that it is impossible for us to accept any compensation for anything connected with the Best proposition.[95] Our friend Col Saunders agrees with us that this is the right position; and I beg you to believe that we cannot be, and ought not to be, shaken in it. I am therefore compelled to renew my request that you will not look to me for any further services in relation to drawing papers &c. It is too great a burden for me. My business at home now requires all my time, and I cannot afford to neglect it any more. I can only regret that my ability is not equal to my wish; and appeal to you as my friend to take this only reasonable view of the subject

A&H—GLB

Thomas J. Jarvis to J. D. Whitford

Executive Department
Raleigh March 31st 1880

It may not be improper for me to say in writing substantially what I said to you verbally before leaving Raleigh.

I propose to leave with the Board the acceptance or rejection of the proposed offer of Mr Best to lease of you the A&N.C.R.R.[96]

I will only add that if the proposition — I do not know what it will be — shall in the opinion of the Board give protection to that section of the state East of Goldsboro; for which the road was chiefly built; and shall amply protect the interest of the State and the property of the Company I would not disapprove its acceptance by the Board.

---

[95] For the work of Davis and Ruffin in regard to the Best proposition, see "Governor's Message," *Public Documents, 1880*, No. 1, 4.

[96] Best proposed to lease the Atlantic and North Carolina Railroad, of which Whitford was the president, for ninety-nine years. He would pay $25,000 a year for the first thirty years, $30,000 a year for the next forty-nine years, and $35,000 for the remaining years. *Daily News*, April 7 1880.

I shall however leave the Board and so desire them to act as they think best.

A&H—GP

William Edwards Clarke[97] to Thomas J. Jarvis

New Berne N.C.
March 31st. 1880

The chairman of our Road Commissioners has this day made formal application to Col W. J. Hicks[98] for the 25 convicts to be fed clothed and guarded at the expense of the State for the purpose of building a road through the State's land for ten miles: We desire to know exactly how to proceed to get these few convicts as speedily as possible for Jones, Craven and Onslow Counties.

Please give us all the help you can for this little scheme for the East that our Western brethren reluctantly allowed us to pass.

We filed our application addressed to the Penitentiary Board with Col W. J. Hicks.

Any help on this scheme so that we can get the stockades erected and the work begun at once will be very much appreciated by your eastern friends.

P.S. Mr Jacob F. Scott,[99] who is now in Raleigh is one of the Commissioners, and can give you all the particulars.

A&H—GP

C. B. Curtis to Thomas J. Jarvis

New York April 2 1880

About six months ago I had the honor of receiving a letter[100] in which you informed me that Commissioners had been ap-

---

[97]Lawyer of New Bern; member of the General Assembly, 1876–1883. *Cyclopedia of the Carolinas*, II, 126–127.

[98]William Jackson Hicks of Raleigh. Originally a building contractor, he became architect and warden of the state penitentiary in 1872 and served until 1898. He was superintendent of the Oxford Orphanage from 1898 until his death in 1911. Ashe, *Biographical History*, II, 167–173.

[99]Farmer and merchant of Trenton; member of the General Assembly, 1866, 1872–1876; member of the Convention of 1875. Branson, *Directory, 1878*, 172; Connor, *Manual, 1913*, 677, 886.

[100]Not found.

pointed under the Act to provide for funding the Bonds of your State issued to the North Carolina Rail Road Co, and that they would shortly visit New York.[101] I have not heard of their being in this City, nor have I heard that any steps have been taken to accomplish the purpose named in the law. I have however heard a rumor that the proposition they had it in their minds to offer was to give new bonds at about par for the old ones including all the interest. As your Legislature is now in session I have thought it might not be inopportune to offer some suggestions which may be useful in case any further measures are proposed.

To begin with, I suppose it may be taken for granted that the creditors will be governed by their views of self interest, and that they will not sacrifice a considerable part of their claim unless it is shown to be for their advantage. They have now bonds which with interest represent about $12.50. each. The payment of the interest may be considered secure, and although the proving of outstanding bonds will probably make the payments somewhat irregular and deficient for two or three years to come, yet in the end the whole amount is pretty certain to be paid. The question is, whether the great certainty of prompt and full payment of interest will be an inducement sufficient to secure the surrender of the 25 per cent back interest which the bonds now bear. I have talked with some of the creditors and it does not seem to me that they will consent. They feel that the state is able to pay something *herself* besides what may be realised on the securities, and do not feel that she ought to hold aloof entirely, and to tell them that not only will she pay nothing but that she will not assist her creditors in receiving the sums collectable on the collatterals, unless they will pay her three quarters of a million dollars for doing so.

I think however they would do something. The present bonds are ragged and shapeless, and an eyesore to the owners. I think they would pay something to have clean and wholesome looking papers. And they would be glad to have their interest payable in this City. For these advantages, which are rather sentimental than practical I think they would pay say 5 per cent.

Such a bond as the Act provides for would be a desirable security. When issued some of the old bonds might be exchanged for them and I believe they would command a good price. But

---

[101]See Jarvis to the Council of State, October 7, 1879, *n.* 175, in this volume.

it must be borne in mind that every advance in their value would also increase the value of the bonds which can be exchanged into them. The old bonds could by no possibility fall below the price of the new ones, and if there is a chance that they might some day be worth 25 per cent more they would probably always sell higher.

If I am correctly informed the state owns about $300.000 of these bonds on which she receives no interest and can receive none so long as any interest remains unpaid on any of the $2.700.000 outstanding. The creditors will hardly feel that they ought to discount nearly three quarters of a million from their just claims in order that the State may make a profit of $300.000 by depreciating her own debts. On the contrary it would seem as if the State ought to pay something herself, if the securities are insufficient.

Suppose she was to offer new bonds for the principal and interest of the old ones in full. How would the case then stand? I have heard it estimated that from 200000 to $300.000 of these bonds have been lost. This is probably an exagerated estimate, but some have certainly disappeared. If however all should be presented, say $2.700.000 with past due coupons amounting to 25% there would be an aggregate of $3.375.000. The Rail Road rental will pay the interest on all this sum except $375.000, and this sum will be diminished by bonds and coupons lost, so that I think $200.000 is all it would cost the state to pay in full. At any rate I think the creditors would settle at that sum.

In these days of paying large debts with small sums of money it may seem hard that the State should pay nearly 95 per cent of its obligations but private debtors sometimes do even more than this and is the honor of a state of less value than that of an individual

North Carolina is improving her financial condition so much that in a short time her indebtedness will be adjusted except as to this small remnant. A very small suming is required to settle and I hope your Legislature will be wise enough to authorise a settlement which the creditors may think just and equitable, and advantageous for them to accept.

I will be glad to hear if anything is proposed to be done at this session of the Legislature and also to know the names and addresses of the Commissioners

A&H—GP

A. R. Ledoux to Thomas J. Jarvis

Chapel Hill N. C., April 2d– 1880

I regret very much to be obliged to inform you that Dr. Goessmann[102] has decided to remain where he is. The Legislature has made arrangements by which the permanency of the fund at the disposition of the Mass. Agricultural College is insured. With his fees as Inspector of Fertilizers his income will be more than our Board of Agriculture would feel warranted in offering him.[103]

There is no other thoroughly satisfactory candidate in the field at present. I shall propose to the Board to direct the work from New York during the Summer.

Trusting that by Sept. a suitable Director can be secured,

A&H—GLB

Thomas J. Jarvis to J. D. Whitford

Executive Department
Raleigh April 12th 1880

The failure to call the meeting of the stockholders for the 29th I beg to assure you, gives me no trouble. If the whole matter goes over till the Regular meeting in June I have nothing to say against it. In fact I propose as I have said and done heretofore to leave the management of the Road with the Board. I shall not depart from this rule in this proposed lease.[104] After the Board has expressed its opinion I will frankly give mine if it is desired. I pursue this course because the Board is presumed to know what is best for the Road, better than I do. If I were to undertake to suggest to the Board my views some of the members might act according to my suggestions and not according to their own judgment, and harm result to the property. As long as it is my duty to appoint a Board of Directors I shall

---

[102]Charles Anthony Goessmann, German–born chemist who had been at Amherst College since 1868. By 1880 he had achieved considerable prominence as a practical chemist. *National Cyclopedia*, XI, 350.

[103]At this time Ledoux was preparing to resign as state chemist and was helping Jarvis and Kemp Battle to find his successor. The salary offered Goessmann was $2,500 a year. Goessmann to Battle, April 3, 1880, Governors' Papers. Letter not included in this volume.

[104]See Jarvis to Whitford, March 31, 1880, *n.* 96, in this volume.

try to appoint good ones and after that the work is with them.

Acting upon this rule I have left the whole matter of the lease with the Board; and shall continue to do so unless I see some interest of the State about to be sacrificed and then I shall feel bound to interfere but in doing so I shall go direct to the Board with my wishes

With kind regards for yourself and best wishes for the Company

A&H—GP

A. R. Ledoux to Thomas J. Jarvis

Chapel Hill N.C., April 12ᵗʰ 1880

It becomes my duty to write to you concerning a matter of great importance to the welfare of the Experiment Station. I write in the fullest confidence and trust that you will understand my motives.

In view of the uncertainty as to who shall succeed me and especially since Dr. Goessmann's refusal there is an effort being made to have one of my assistants, Mr. Phillips,[105] appointed temporarily or permanently Director of the Station. I shall not be at your meeting and, if I were there, it would be exceedingly unpleasant for me to be obliged to state anything against the young man. Nor am I willing to send a communication to the Board concerning him, in view of the fact that it is not certain that he will be before them as a candidate. I write to you to say that, while he is a hard worker and conscientious, he has certain faults, scientific as well as of disposition, which would render him *totally unfit* to do the work required by *this* position.

My object in writing this is to request you that, *in case* Mr. Phillips *becomes* a candidate and there *seems to be a likelihood of his election,* to state to the Board that, in a communication, I had expressed to you the opinion that Mr. Phillips was not at all fitted for the place.

I hope sincerely that it will not be necessary for my opinion to be made public before the Board, since it is very painful to be obliged to state what I have.

At his request I have given him two or three letters recom-

---

[105]William Battle Phillips, who served as assistant chemist of the Experimental Station at Chapel Hill from 1877 to 1882. In 1885 he became professor of chemistry at the University of North Carolina. Grant, *Alumni History of the University,* 492–493.

mending him for the position of teacher or professor in different Institutions. For such a position he has many qualifications, the requirements being *very different* from those necessary to successfully conduct the practical work and correspondence of an Experiment Station. Should any of these letters be placed before the Board as my opinion of Mr. Phillips, I respectfully request that you state that they were given for a special purpose and are not my opinion as to his fitness to direct the Station.

Prof. Kerr who is a warm friend of Mr. Phillips and of his family is well acquainted with the reasons which unfit Mr. P. for the position in question and can tell you, if desired, what they are.

I hope, as I said, it will *not* be necessary to lay this communication before the Board, but feel it my duty, unpleasant though it be, to inform your Excellency in the premises.

A&H—GP

Joseph Pearson Caldwell[106] to Thomas J. Jarvis

Statesville, N.C., April 16, 1880

It is proper, I suppose, that I should make some report to you of the proceedings of the meeting of the private stockholders in the Western North Carolina Railroad, held yesterday (15th) at Hickory. The proceedings were, generally speaking, harmonious. Shortly after the organization, with Col. T. Geo. Walton,[107] of Burke, as chairman, and discussion of the three alternatives presented to the private stockholders — to–wit: to accept $212,500 of the reduced, non–assessable stock; to remain in the company with Mr. Best and his associates on the basis of one–fourth interest; or to sell to the owners of the State's late interest for $50,000 in cash and pass out — a motion was made by D. C. Pearson,[108] of Burke, that final action be postponed until another meeting.

Messrs. D. C. Pearson, of Burke, M. L. McCorkle,[109] of

[106]Owner and editor of the Statesville *Landmark*, 1880–1892; editor of the Charlotte *Observer*, 1892–1909. Ashe, *Biographical History*, I, 213–217.

[107]Thomas George Walton, farmer of Morganton; member of the General Assembly, 1850. Branson, *Directory, 1878*, 46; Connor, *Manual, 1913*, 523.

[108]Clerk of the Superior Court of Burke County. Branson, *Directory, 1878*, 44.

[109]Matthew Locke McCorkle, lawyer of Newton; member of the General Assembly, 1864–1866; member of the Convention of 1875. *Cyclopedia of the Carolinas*, II, 156–158.

Catawba, and R. M. Allison,[110] of Iredell, argued in favor of this motion, and Maj. J. W. Wilson, J. G. Bynum[111] and myself insisted on immediate action. The motion to postpone was put and failed.

It was then submitted to a vote of the stockholders to get their sense as to which of the three alternatives should be accepted. Two stockholders, representing 186 shares, voted in favor of accepting the reduced stock; 91 stockholders, representing 8,470 shares voted to sell.

The disaffected stockholders generally refrained from voting but the majority sentiment, very decidedly, was that the Stockholders did very well — much better than they had for many years expected — to get even $3\frac{1}{2}\cancel{c}$ in the dollar on their shares.

A&H—GP

W. A. Courtenay to Thomas J. Jarvis

Charleston S C April 17 1880

Your esteemed favour of 16th inst[112] at hand to–day and I hasten, to Reply to your Several inquiries — 1st The memorial column will be in the Doric Style 22 feet high, including the base — 2d The equality of the States is *fixed* by the Request to each, to unite in a *limited Sub*n for the erection of the column say $250 each — This has been done to avoid the point you inquire about — 3d The inscriptions have not been concluded upon, for all the States have not yet been heard from — These and other details, the comee— will be too glad to have suggestions from the Governors about & I feel sure that you will aid us personally by your counsel & officially by your active co-operation — The granate [sic] column is partly finished, the main block, on which the inscriptions are to go, is octagonal in form, as presenting a more symetrical appearance & the eight panels may be utilized for inscriptions of any kind, that the States may agree upon — This will be the last work done & only, with the concurrence of all concerned. Of course the com-

---

[110]Richard Monroe Allison, lawyer of Statesville. Grant, *Alumni History of the University*, 10.

[111]John Gray Bynum, lawyer of Morganton; member of the General Assembly, 1879; Superior Court judge, 1888–1895. Tomlinson, *Sketch–book*, 42–43; Connor, *Manual, 1913*, 450.

[112]Not found. For the significance of this letter, see Courtenay to Jarvis, March 17, 1880.

memoration expenses fall upon the host,* the column will be the united & Equal contribution of the States named — The Resolution, in congress, is still neglected — There can be no opposition and yet it does not come up — If you would ask the members in both houses from your State to aid this movement for a Bronze Statue of Gen Morgan, it would be greatly appreciated — Charleston will be strongly Represented at Kings Mountain in oct & also at Spartanburg in Jany—We will show you a fine Brigade of troops in all arms & the Wᵐ Washington Flag in a good State of preservation —

Hoping to have at an Early day, the official assurance of your co operation —

* South Carolina

A&H—GLB

Thomas J. Jarvis to E. R. Stamps

Executive Department
Raleigh April 21ˢᵗ 1880

Mr. Simmons[113] of Jones County has had an interview with me about an Act recently passed to place twenty five convicts to work on the road on the State lands in Jones and Onslow Counties.

I tell him I appreciate the difficulty you have on account of a want of funds; and have suggested to him that possibly as you have to feed and *clothe* the convicts any how, that you can do that much for him if he will agree to raise the means to bare all the other expenses such as resting quarters, guarding washing & c I hope you will be able to do this much for them as it will be the beginning of opening up the State lands—an enterprise in which I feel a very great interest as I believe great good will come to the State from its success.

---

[113]Probably Furnifold McLendel Simmons, Democratic representative in Congress, 1887–1889, and senator, 1901–1931. In 1880 he was practicing law in Jones County, and, though quite young, was already taking an active role in Democratic politics. *National Cyclopedia*, XXXV, 39.

A&H—GLB

Thomas J. Jarvis to E. R. Stamps

Executive Department
Raleigh April 21st 1880

As the force on the Western North Carolina R.R. will now be under the undivided and unrestricted control of your Board I beg to suggest that you or some other member of the Board proceed at as early a day as convenient to the Western Road and make a rigid and th[o]rougher investigation into the treatment of the convicts by the present officers. It seems to me you will need this information to determine your course as to whether you will retain the present officers or any of them. Then in view of charges already made by one of the City papers as well as my earnest desire that the convicts shall be humanely treated I trust you make the investigation. I am sure each member of the Board shares with me in my desire to have these convicts properly cared for and properly worked.

I believe this has been done of the Western Road but if it has not it is my wish that it shall be known and the men who have been negligent in their duty discharged.

A&H—GP

D. F. Caldwell to Thomas J. Jarvis

Greensboro NC April 23d 1880

I wish to say to you a few words in *confidence* Fulgum left to night for Raleigh on recevng a telegram from someone in your place He is doing all he can to defeat your geting the nomination He is for Fowl[e], but is trying to bull up [A.M.] Scales to try to prevent this county from casting her votes for you That is my opinion He hasnt paid me a cent for this where he seems to have paid me before this $12.00 the fourth payment

I had some sharp words with him a night or two since—he said some bitter and unjust things against you & Worth[114] and I replied as I thought his remarks deserved I have not spoke to him since He is making a good paper but I have no confidence in his stability There is no danger of this county if the Scales

---

[114]In the spring and summer of 1880, Jarvis and J. M. Worth, who were running for re-election as governor and secretary of the treasury respectively, did most of their campaigning together.

movement does not lead over delegates in this county & others of his district to throw off on the first ballot, which I hope will not be done I shall not be able to attend this convention and as I am assured that you should receive this nomination I have thought it might be well to inform you of the Fulgum Scales — *pro* Fowl[e] movement I[t] might be well for some of your friends to write to Gilman Grady[115] J H Lindsay[116] etc I will do what little I can to squelch this movement, as I am sure it a flank movement on behalf of Fowl[e] I have nothing in the world against Judge Fowl[e] but as you are in harness I am willing you should remain for another term But I fear that my friend Hall[117] will not, if nominated for L G, give the ticket much strength It will be a hard fought campaign and we ought to have good speakers and will have to have much and good speaking and that by men who are well posted in the politics of the country I hope that you will not think I have taking too great liberty in intruding this hasty note upon you for your consideration

A&H—GP

J. B. Stewart to Thomas J. Jarvis [copy]

Raleigh. N.C. April 23rd 1880

The decision of the Supreme Court of your state recently made in the suit of the Western North Carolina Rail Road Company v^s W. W. Rollins[118] imposes the position of *trustee* upon the said Western NC.R.R. Company as to all and several the estate and assets of the Western Division Company: or is at least designed to do so eventually. Upon the rendition of the decision I could not fail to see that unforseen, as well as undesirable complications must at once attach to the corporation thus created a trustee, (not by the letter of the law but by the decision) unless the situation of *trustee* and *cestui qui trust* between the Western N.C.R.Co– and the Western Division Company were at once dissolved by closing the trust and the more especially in view of the recent legislation terminating

---

[115]Editor unable to identify Gilman and Grady.

[116] Editor of the Kernersville *News*, a weekly Democratic newspaper. Branson, *Directory for 1884*, 710.

[117]E. D. Hall, mayor of Wilmington; unsuccessful Democratic candidate for Lieutenant Governor in 1868. *News and Observer*, June 12, 1896.

[118]See Stewart to Jarvis, April 7, 1879, *n.* 81, in this volume.

the present and transferring over the corporate existence of the Western N.C.R. Co— under operation of the legislative contract with Best and associates who are authorized and empowered by law to hold and direct the *trustee* company as by said legislative contract provided.

While attending U.S. Circuit Court at Greensboro last week my attention was called to the decision referred to and in conversation with Col. Thos. Ruffin it was suggested that a settlement of the matter should be made immediately in order to avoid embarrassment and injury to all parties. Concurring in the views of Col— Ruffin and actuated by my personal desire to terminate an unnecessary controversy— I prepared a *proget* of settlement that seemed to me would be sufficient to close up and end the alleged *trust* at once with the same effect and producing the same result as if it were litigated to the utmost extent that the law will allow.

This paper I submitted to Col. Ruffin who expresses approval of the same and said he would submit it to your Excellency with his favorable recommendation which he informed me on Wednesday last he had done and I was in hopes I should have heard something on the subject and for that reason have deferred any steps that would tend to create further complications.

In a conversation I had with M. McCloud on Thursday evening after an interview he had had with you he informed me that you were favorable to the settlement as indicated in the *proget* handed you by Col— Ruffin and was willing it should be consummated.

I therefore address you this communication as a proposal and request that you may be pleased to advise such action as will bring the proposed settlement into practical operation. To facilitate this object I have telegraphed Mr— Rollins to come here immediately and I believe he is now on his way.

I believe I can at once consummate the settlement upon the basis stated in the paper handed you by Col— Ruffin if such a settlement is desirable without resort to further litigation and it shall not be my fault if the effort fails.

As to the terms of the proposition it will be observed that treating the Western NC.R. Co as a *trustee* (though in direct contradiction of the letter of the Statute) it must sooner or later settle up the trust imposed upon it.

This settlement is at once effected by transferring the Road bed and the appurtenances thereto to the Western N.C. Co– or its assigns Messrs. Best and Associates while its assets and cause of action are ceded over to its creditors & stockholders which is just what must result from the pending litigation if continued: And this too without the peril of loss or depreciation by unnecessary litigation. In truth the proposition substantially executes itself by mere adoption. I hope it may meet your views as a base of settlement.

I beg also to make this further statement. I have been informed (and among others by M^r McLoud) that you were under the impression that I am seeking to oppose and embarrass the consummation of your legislative contract with Messrs. Best and associates. This is not so and any such representations are erroneous and unfounded. On the contrary while not allowing myself to intermeddle with matters not subject to my control I have nevertheless done and said all in my power to promote your transactions with Mr. Best and to say such things when interrogated as would tend to influence his friends at home to support him in the fulfillment of his agreement: and this I have done several times both verbally and in writing.

A&H—GP

Hector McAllister McKethan[119] to Thomas J. Jarvis

Fayetteville Apl 23 1880

We see in some paper that a meeting of stockholders of the Atlantic & N C Road is called for 29 Apl to consider proposition of Best & Co to lease the road for 33 years for $30.000 anualy &c   if this be so we are glad of it and will send our proxy to vote for lease — the last we heard before this was the matter was indefinately pos[t]poned &c If we include Julius A Gray Pres of our road who holds 9 shares we have in all 60 shares A & N C in this Town and 47 shares by Carolina Citty Co chiefly owned here by John D Williams[120] — E L Pemberton[121] & A A M^c-Kethan Sen[ior] of this Town Some of the stockholders are

---

[119]Son of A. A. McKethan, and junior partner in the many business enterprises of McKethan & Sons of Fayetteville. Branson, *Directory for 1884*, 249–253.

[120]Merchant, manufacturer, and banker of Fayetteville. Branson, *Directory for 1884*, 249–253.

[121]Edmund Lilly Pemberton, flour and corn merchant of Fayetteville. Branson, *Directory for 1884*, 251.

dead & left Bankrupt estates — others went into Bankrupsy &c &c and D G McRae[122] *Radical* Deputy U States Marshall in Banrupsy has often demanded & tried to vote on all Bankrupsy stock &c — a question so plainly unjust we cant submit to unless compelled by the high courts & should be decided soon for all Roads   A A McK my father has 8 shares in the Road and owns lots in Morehead C and is the principle own[er] of lots & lands of Carolina Citty Co. & since we invested our money in road say about 24 years ago not one cent in divadin have we recd or expected and the stock had no market value— We know Col Whitford and regard him a safe worthy man — we dont care for our R Road stock but hope to enhance our lands &c about Carolina Citty   R K Bryan[123] senator frm Pender & N Han ishued the Examiner here yesterday and will make a *No 1 paper* — he like Geo Davis *sustains* you & the *sale* and Bryan *voted for it* and was much blamed by some— Please get a copy of Examiner frm Ashe[124] or Hale[125] & see what Pres Gray says of you & Worth in his anual report — The splendid speach of Geo Davis is again printed— Let us know if the stockholders of A & N C Road meet on 29 Apl at Newbern we suppose but dont know for certain as to time or place

Dont fail to see Fay Examiner of 22 Apl   I gave my coppy away or would send it

---

[122]Duncan Granger McRae of Cumberland County; member of the Convention of 1865. Connor, *Manual, 1913,* 875.

[123]Robert Kedar Bryan, lawyer, planter, and newspaperman of Scot's Hill; member of the General Assembly, 1858, 1879. Bryan had wide newspaper experience, and from 1880 to 1883 he published the Fayetteville *Observer. North Carolina Biography,* IV, 229–230.

[124]Samuel A'Court Ashe of Raleigh. He practiced law from 1867 to 1879, when he bought the Raleigh *Observer* and became its editor. In his last years he returned to the law, and for a while he was clerk of the United States District Court for the Eastern District of North Carolina. He was chairman of the Democratic Executive Committee from 1876 to 1879, and he was a member of the General Assembly from 1870 to 1873. He wrote several volumes of North Carolina history. *National Cyclopedia,* XXVIII, 9.

[125]Peter Mallett Hale. From 1850 to 1876 he was in the publishing business in Fayetteville and New York with his father, E. J. Hale. In 1876 he and W. L. Saunders bought and began publishing the Raleigh *Observer.* After selling the *Observer* in 1880, he published *Hale's Weekly* for a short while and then became a member of P. M. Hale, Edwards, Broughton Printing Company. Ashe, *Biographical History,* VII, 185–190.

A&H—GP

Thomas J. Jarvis to J. B. Stewart

Executive Department
Raleigh, Apl 24ᵗʰ 1880

Your letter of the 23ᵈ inst was handed me at 4 oclock P.M. today and I herewith hand you my reply.

Col. Ruffin handed me the paper referred to in your communication which I read and handed in his presence to Mr. Best. I made no reply to the proposition as it was not addressed to me.

I have never since I came in office as Governor taken any part in the litigation pending in the State of Florida to recover for the Western division of the W.N.C.R.R the proceeds of the sale of special tax bonds invested by Swepson & Littlefield in certain Florida Rail Roads.

I have never recognized the validity of these bonds and have persistently refused to commit the state to any act that created any moral obligation upon the people to pay any part of them

You will no doubt remember that I have refused to authorize anybody to represent the state in this Florida litigation and the above were my reasons therefor

So far as the board of directors of the W.N.C.RR. have participated in said litigation they have done so without any direction or suggestions from me. I mention these facts that you may appreciate the only part that I can take to bring about an adjustment and final determination of that litigation.

The state has sold and will in a few days transfer all of her interest in the W.N.C.R.R. to W. J. Best and associates, so that it occurs to me that the only parties now to be consulted about the proposed settlement are the directors of the W.N.C.R.R. (whom you say are made trustees) and Best and associates who may be parties in interest, on the one hand and those whom you represent on the other. After the conveyance referred to is made the state will have no direct interest in the matter

I desire the work of constructing and completing the W.N.C.R.R both to Paint Rock and Ducktown [to] go on without any interruption or delay. I would also be glad to see the creditors of the late Western division of the WN.C.RR. provided for. To aid in the first I shall use all my personal & official influence and will be glad to aid in the second as far as I can consistent with my views herein expressed.

I expressed these sentiments to Mr. McLeod without saying that I fully concurred in the plan contained in the statement given to Col. Ruffin or not, and while there is no official action that I can take in the matter I will advise the adoption by those, who value my suggestions, of any plan that looks to me fair equitable.

I will suggest that the practicable way of getting at it will be to have a conference of Rollins & McLoud on the one side and those of the directors that you can conveniently get together & Best on the other side. I believe that in this way it is possible to come to an under standing and bring about a settlement.

Finally and in conclusion I am glad to hear that you have taken no part in the effort to embarrass the consumation of the sale of the W.N.C.R.R to Best

A&H—GP

W. H. C. Price to Thomas J. Jarvis

WORLD'S FAIR COMMITTEE

New York, April 24th. 1880

I am instructed by the Executive Committee of the World's Fair Committee to inform you of the passage of the bill by both Houses of Congress authorizing the holding of a World's [Fair] in this City during the year 1883, and that the bill has received the signature of the President and is therefore a law.

The Honorable Secretary of State[126] informs us that he will give the necessary official notice to the Governors of the different States and Territories with a request to nominate to the President the names of the Commissioners.[127] Under the provisions of the law two Commissioners and two alternate Commissioners are to be nominated from each State.[128] One Commissioner and one alternate from the Territories and the District of Columbia.

This Committee will cooperate with the Commissioners named in the bill and to be nominated by the Governors, until such

---

[126]William Maxwell Evarts, lawyer and statesman of New York. He held many high public offices, among which was the position of secretary of state from 1877 to 1881. *Dictionary of American Biography*, VI, 215–218.

[127]See Evarts to Jarvis, May 7, 1880, Governors' Papers. Letter not included in this volume.

[128]Jarvis nominated as commissioners R. Y. McAden of Charlotte and Donald McRae of Wilmington. As alternates he nominated Julian S. Carr of Durham and Thomas M. Holt of Haw River. Jarvis to Evarts, June 22, 1880, Governor's Letter Books. Letter not included in this volume.

time as they may legally organize, and will continue to aid the movement actively in every way, in order to make it a grand success. It has been de[e]med proper to thus acquaint you from our Committee of the action already taken, and of requesting you at the same time, that you send your nominations to the President, and that you would inform the Secretary of this Committee of the names proposed, in order that we may have a complete record of them as fast as made.

Permit me also to state that the Head–Quarters of this Committee is at Room #16, St. Nicholas Hotel, and that it will be the pleasure of the Secretary to furnish you, or the Commissioners named by you, such information with reference to the origin and progress of this movement as may be desired, and to extend through you to them a most cordial invitation to call at the office of the Committee when they are in this City.

A&H—GP

Thomas Branch and Company to Thomas J. Jarvis

Richmond, Va. Apl 24. 1880

When the law was passed for the exchange of North Carolina R R Construction Bonds for new 6% state–bonds,[129] the former could be purchased at $60 or less, and had the Commission acted promptly a very favorable exchange could have been made[.] now on account of the increased value of the construction Bonds and as they continue to improve we expect soon· to see them @ 100$.

We understand a motion will be made at the next session of the Court to sell Stock enough to pay the past due interest which amounts to over $600th which will take at least $1200th of the Stock will be sold in a short time to pay for the interest so large amount is thrown on the market[.] in this way all of the Stock will be sold in a short time to pay for the Company leaving $2.794.000 Bonds out and not paid and whilst you may say they will not be paid with the present feelings of the people, they will have to be liquidated by the next generation: but if your Commission will act *promptly*, they can all be exchanged now on very favorable terms: and whilst we have no authority to act for all of the bond holders, We believe they would ex-

---

[129]See Jarvis to the Council of State, October 7, 1879, *n.* 175, in this volume.

change $1000 bond with $210 past due interest for $1000 new
6% Bond. We would be willing to Exchange all One Million of
the bonds on these terms and have no doubt the balance would do
likewise—

You are no doubt aware One Million of the bonds become due
in 1883 & the balance very shortly afterwards and the longer
the delay more will be required by the bondholders and unless
your State has made up its mine to loose this property which is
worth far more than the bonded debt and must in a few years
increase in value over 100% — it has no time to loose

The South was the most prosperous part of this country for
the decade before the War and will be for the next decade. Our
fathers made money in making cotton @ 6¢ and hence the
profits now are very large when we get 10¢. The South is much
less in debt (we mean the merchants and farmers) The negroes
are much more extravigant than their masters were, as they
spend all they make which makes trade for the merchants and
tonage for the Rail Roads and the time will come when a double
track will be needed to carry the freight of the NCRR: and if
you in your wisdom save this property to your state [you] will
deserve more praise than Calvin Graves[130] who as Speaker cast
the vote that created the act to build said road. but should the
property be sold to foreigners to pay the construction bonds the
state cannot blame the creditors:

We think your State did wisely in selling the Western NCRR
Co: but they should hold the NC RR Co & A & NC RR Co for
they hold the key of the situation and so long as they are
owned by the state they can control the policy of all the North
Carolina Roads.

Permit us to say in all candor and at the same time with that
respect due you both personally and in your official position —
that we think you made a mistake in your appointment of the
Commissioners, for whilst they are all gentlemen of high
character and wish to promote the interest of your State, they
evidently think it to its interest to sell its Rail Road property.[131]

---

[130]In 1849, Graves, president of the Senate from Caswell County cast
the deciding vote in the Senate for the passage of the bill chartering the
North Carolina Railroad Company. Rufus Barringer, "History of the North
Carolina Railroad," *Papers of the North Carolina Historical Society at
the University of North Carolina* (1894), 18–19, hereinafter cited as Barringer, "History of the North Carolina Railroad."
[131]The strategy of the commissioners appointed under the law of March
14, 1879, to negotiate with the holders of the construction bonds seems to
have been to bluff the bondholders into accepting terms favorable to the

This is certainly not carrying out the wish of your people, for the Legislature would never have passed the act to appoint the Commission, had it not been their wish to save its interest in the NC RR — If the Commission are not willing to carry out the will of the Legislature (and we believe the law was passed nearly unanimously certainly by a very large majority) others should be appointed in their place:— We cannot close this long letter (which is much more than we intended to say) without predicting that the time will come when the NC R R Co will pay twice 6% dividends p anum and why not? is the South never to be any richer than it is now? & where is there another road in the *United States* that shows so small a debt which is now only about $125th (after deducting good assets on hand) and one six months lease will pay this road *entirely* out of debt—: There is no property that pays so well as Rail Roads when well managed: We remember when the New York Central RR had a small debt and a capital of stock of less than $10 millions now it has a debt of over $40 millions and $89. millions of capital and they now talk of increasing the capital to $100 millions making a total of 140 millions on 740 miles of road by watering it: and all this increase has been made by good management— The road now pays 8% dividend on the Stock— which is selling @ $135: and there are many other roads that would show nearly as well. and with this showing who will not say there is a brighter future for Rail Roads in North Carolina

A&H—GLB

Thomas J. Jarvis to Julius A. Bonitz[132]

Executive Department
Raleigh April 28th 1880

I have just had an interview with the Treasurer and he authorize[d] me to say that he will be able to pay out from

state. The commissioners had met in October and addressed a circular to the bondholders. It stated that, while the North Carolina Railroad was a valuable asset to the state, rather than pay off the construction bonds on unfavorable terms, the state would allow the road to be sold. Raleigh *Observer*, November 1, 1879; *Morning Star*, November 4, 1879; see also Jarvis to Thomas Branch & Co., May 6, 188, in this volume.

[132]For a decade after the Civil War Bonitz was a merchant and manufacturer in Goldsboro. In 1876 he began publishing the Goldsboro *Messenger*, which soon became a prominent journal. Dowd, *Sketches of North Carolinians*, 178–182. This letter from Jarvis concerns Bonitz's position as secretary of the Board of Directors of the Colored Insane Asylum at Goldsboro.

time to time during the balance of the year as much as $10.000 for the support of the Asylum if so much shall be needed.

With this assurance I think the Board can safely open the Institution[133] by the 1st of June. I know it is the purpose of the Board to run the Institution as cheaply as possible; and with this purpose I believe you can do the work the balance of the year on this amount.

The $2.500 you can draw for at anytime you need it, and the $10.000 will be monthly as your expenses require.

The Board shall have my hearty co–operation in its efforts to make the Institution a credit to the State and useful in its purpose.

A&H——GP

J. D. Williams to Thomas J. Jarvis

Fayetteville April 30/80

As a believer in the importance of the Cape Fear and Yadkin Vally Railway, when finished, not only to this place but the other section through which it runs, as well as incidentally to the whole State, I desire to thank you for the uniform encouragement you have given the enterprise, and especially for your influence with my good friend the Treasurer, in supplying Mr Gray with the $24.000 which enabled the Co. to free itself from all Lines [sic][134] (which had heretofore greatly hindered the progress of the work) Although the Treasurer has been a little slow to see his duty in the past, we will be disposed down here, to continue him in possession of the key to the shares if such shall be his wish. As to you we cannot allow any personal choice, you must continue at the Head, at least another Term

---

[133]For a brief history of the construction of the Colored Insane Asylum, see "Report of the Chairman of the Board of Directors of the Asylum for the Colored Insane," *Public Documents, 1881*, No. 12, *passim*.
[134]When the General Assembly chartered the Cape Fear and Yadkin Valley Railroad Company in February, 1879, it authorized the state treasurer to buy $50,000 of the first mortgage bonds of the company in order to help it discharge the existing liens against it. *Laws of North Carolina, 1879*, c. 67. Williams is referring to the fact that State Treasurer J. M. Worth had recently appropriated part of the allotted sum. "Treasurer's Report," *Public Documents, 1881*, No, 5, 7.

A&H—GLB

Thomas J. Jarvis to W. A. Courtenay

Executive Department
Raleigh May 4th 1880

In reply to your enquiries on that subject it gives me pleasure to say that North Carolina will contribute her share to the erection of the Granite Column upon the Battle field of the Cowpens. Its erection can awaken no memories but those that speak of a united people and a heroic past while the Column itself will be a sign that the children love the land and the law which the valor of their forefathers gave them.

I have written as requested to the North Carolina Congressmen to aid in the passage of the resolution by Congress providing a bronze statue of Gen¹ Morgan with which to crown this column and have received from them favorable replies.[135]

I will gladly cooperate with the friends of the celebration and will willingly render any service I can in making it worthy of the Deed which it is to commemorate.

A&H—GLB

Thomas J. Jarvis to Thos. Branch & Co

Executive Department
Raleigh N.C. May 6th 1880

Yours of the 24th ult came to hand in due time. I have given the subject of which it treats much though[t] and consideration before and since I received the letter.

While the Western North Carolina Railroad belonged to the state I was anxious to preserve for the state the North Carolina Rail Road, but since the sale of the Western Road the same reasons for desiring to continue to own the North Carolina Road, in my opinion do not exist.

At any rate I am not willing to sanction the creation of a new debt of $3.000.000 upon the state in order for the state to own it.

The holders of the construction Bonds are now among our favored creditors. They have had their interest now for years.

---

[135]See Courtenay to Jarvis, March 22, 1880, *n.* 94, in this volume.

No other creditors have, although holding bonds just as binding upon the state.

The present Board of Directors have done all they could to make the property pledged for these construction Bonds as valuable as possible, and in this way have taken care of the interest of the creditors.

The stock is now worth about as much as the Bonds so that if the creditors get the stock of the state they will get something—no matter what they bid it off at—of equal value to these bonds.

If they choose to sell now for their interest they will have nothing to sell when their principle falls due. So the sale now is a matter for them to consider, and in determining their line of action they had better act upon the settled fact that the road is all they will get if a sale is had, I am sure the state will never pay one penny of what remains unpaid by the sale.

I beg to assure you I have not written thus plainly out of any spirit of unkindness to any of the holders of these Bonds; but because I think it proper for them to understand our position.

I shall be glad to join in any adjustment of the matter that is fair to the state and satisfactory to the creditors, if such a basis of settlement can be agreed upon.

A&H—GLB

Thomas J. Jarvis to Noah Porter[136]

Executive Department
Raleigh May 6th 1880

I was informed that Yale College became the purchaser recently of a pamphlet entitled "Political Tyranny in North Carolina" and printed in 1705.[137] A misapprehension of instructions prevented its purchase for this state. It seems to me that the state Library of North Carolina is the proper place for such a pamphlet, and as one of its Trustees I wish to express the hope that you concur with me in this view of the case.

The title of this pamphlet is all we know about it, but it is

---

[136]Congregational clergyman, educator, and, from 1871 to 1886, president of Yale University. *Dictionary of American Biography*, XV, 97–99.
[137]Daniel Defoe, "Party–tyranny: or, An occasional bill in minature," (London, 1705). No reply has been found to Jarvis' enquiry about this pamphlet.

fully hoped that it will throw light on a period to which attention is just now being directed in this state.

If you concur with me in the view I take of this matter any expense you may have incurred in the premises will be promptly paid.

A&H—GP

W. A. Courtenay to Thomas J. Jarvis

COWPENS * CENTENNIAL * COMMITTEE.

Charleston May 8th 1880

Your letter was considered so admirable, and so pertinent to the occasion, the Com^ee Sent it to the News & Courier for publication and the editors used the extract from it in their editorial, and a copy of the paper was mailed to you

I enclose a supplimental paper from the Com^ee [138] which is not at all necessary, as your State is already enrolled, but you may as well file it with other papers connected with the Centennial. In regard to the Sub^m of $250—that can be provided by 1st July as we begin chiseling the 60 tons of granate about then, & expect to lay the foundation, during the warm weather to ensure it against the cold weather—and shall need ready mony later on.

In behalf of the Com^ee I thank you for your interest in the Statue of Morgan & for your enclosure from Mr Scales.

A&H—GP

G. P. Erwin to Thomas J. Jarvis

Salisbury N.C.
May 14, 1880

At a meeting of the Board of Directors of the Western North Carolina Rail-road Company, this day held at Salisbury N.C.: the following resolution was passed & I was directed to inform you —

On motion it was resolved that the Secretary inform the Governor, at once, that the Board is ready to turn over the property of the W.N.C. R R Co. to the grantees, as soon as they shall be notified by him that said grantees have complied with Section 2

---

[138]Governors' Papers, letter not included in this volume.

of their contract with the State:[139] and Section 24 of the Act providing for the payment of the floating debt of the Company shall also be complied with

AN OPEN LETTER.[140]

[n.d.]

Hon. T. J. Jarvis, Messrs. P. M. Hale and John Spelman:[141]

Gentlemen:

Upon the House Journal of the session of the General Assembly of 1868 and 1869, I charge as follows:

1st. Gov. T. J. Jarvis voted for the first special tax bonds[142] ever authorized to be issued in North Carolina.

2nd. That the bonds he so voted to have issued amounted to ten million and three hundred thousand.

3rd. That the special tax bonds he so voted to have issued were *"Littlefield's pets."*

4th. That he voted to issue these bonds to Swepson's Road, Hawkin's Road, and the Williamston and Tarboro Road,[143] in which two last Jno. Pickrell,[144] the lobyist, was largely interested.

5th. That he voted for these special tax bonds not only *once* but *twice.*

6th. That he never moved to reconsider these votes or either of them, and never manifested an intention or disposition to do so, though ample opportunity was afforded him therefor.

7th. That Gov. Jarvis and James L. Robinson voted for these special tax bonds after they knew that the majority of the

---

[139]For the final terms of the contract selling the state's interest in the Western North Carolina Railroad to Best and his associates, see *Public Documents, 1880,* No. 12.

[140]This open letter was circulated about the state in broadside form and was published in several newspapers. The copy quoted herein was taken from a printed broadside in the Randolph A. Shotwell Papers, Southern Historical Collection, University of North Carolina, Chapel Hill, hereinafter cited as Shotwell Papers.

[141]Spelman had been in newspaper work all during the 1870's. Since November, 1879, he had been publisher of the *State Journal* (Raleigh). *Daily News,* April 15, 1880.

[142]See Message to the General Assembly, March 15, 1880, *n.* 78, in this volume.

[143]For the railroads, persons and legislation referred to, see Brown, *State Movement,* 170–171.

[144]See The Governor to the People, May 30, 1880, in this volume.

Legislators by whose votes they were authorized were plunderers and thieves.

6th. That Governor Jarvis failed to vote on over one hundred important bills at that session of the Legislature, though he was present in Raleigh and not sick.

Gentlemen, I charge these things to be the truth. If they are not the truth. If the record does not show them to be the truth deny them by citing the pages or evidence upon which you rely to controvert the printed record I have referred to. If you will deny these eight charges or any of them in the Raleigh News of the 28th, your denial shall be printed verbatum to accompany this letter. If you do not deny these charges, or any of them, I shall assume fairly, I think, that you cannot.

On the 29th instant I shall publish this letter anyhow. If you deny any of these charges I will publish with it such denial.

I am, gentlemen, your servant,

CATO

A&H—GP

Thomas J. Jarvis to Edward William Pou[145]

Raleigh N.C.
May 21st 1880

I send you to–day a marked copy of the Raleigh Observer containing a communication signed "Cato" charging me with voting for and being in sympathy with the Special Tax Bond.

I am sure you never will entirely forget the days and doings of the Legislature of 1868–9.

In those days we consulted much together and associated much together; and I know of no one now living who knows more of my views and *acts* in that Legislature than you.

You know whether or not I ever had any sympathy with the Special Tax Bonds. I think you will remember that I held that the proper construction of the constitution was that the Taxes for all purposes both State and County never could exceed sixty six & two thirds cent on the hundred Dollars; and that it was upon this question that we hoped to defeat the whole issue of Special Tax Bonds. That when the Revenue Bill came up in

---

[145]Lawyer of Smithfield; member of the General Assembly, 1868. *Cyclopedia of the Carolinas*, II, 129–130. This letter to Pou is a rough draft, signed by Jarvis. Pou replied the next day.

Feb. 69. I did offer and try to have incorporated in the Bill such a feature and that after being defeated we then had long and repeated interviews about taking a case to the Supreme Court on that question and that when such a case was instituted I wrote you from Tyrrell urging you to argue the case before the Court for the people of North Carolina.

So strongly have I contended for this construction of the constitution that I never voted, as I am sure you will remember, to lay any tax upon the people to exceed sixty six and two thirds cents on each hundred worth of their property; not even to vote for a special Tax Bill for a County. I have always believed that sixty six & two third cents on each hundred Dollars worth of property was sufficient to run the State and County governments if properly and economically administered; and if it was not I do not believe that taxation can exceed that under the constitution

By reference to the Journal of 68–9 you will see that I voted against every one of the Bills to issue Bonds — and I have no doubt this is your recollection — except the Bill "to reenact and confirm certain acts of the General Assembly authorizing the issue of State Bonds to and for certain Rail Road Companies." This Bill referred alone to appropriations made to the Chatham Road, the Williamston and Tarboro Road and the Western North Carolina Road at the summer session and was a Senate Bill, for which I am recorded as voting aye.

Your seat in the Hall was immediately under the Clock on the left of the Speaker and mine just to your left and front. When this Bill was called up I was standing at your seat talking to you then about the best way to fight the villians upon which the Democrat party was about to vote. I remarked to you at the time that the President of the Chatham Road[146] and the Williamston and Tarboro Road[147] had made some bona fide Contracts with the Bonds issued under that acts that this Bill proposed to Ratify which I thought involved the honor and credit of the State. That I thought that all Bonds not used ought to be returned and their actual bona fide purchases for which the State was to be benefitted paid for. That the Bill was imperfect and went too far, that I would vote for it and then move to reconsider. If this motion prevailed I would then move to strike out any authority to issue other Bonds and then we would begin the fight. I did vote in the affirmative and having a Speaker in

---

[146]W. J. Hawkins. *Public Documents, 1869–'70,* No. 5, 9.
[147]J. R. Stubbs of Williamston. *Public Documents, 1869–'70,* No. 5, 9.

the Chair[148] hostile to us he recognized some one else and the ordinary motion to reconsider and lay on the table was made and carried.

I am thus left in the Journal as voting in the affirmative and the fact that I am thus recorded has been distorted and misrepresented by one who knows better into a charge that I voted for all the Special Tax Bonds. While the fact is as you know and as the journals will show that after that Bills were passed making appropriations to the Western North Carolina Rail Road, to the North Western North Carolina Rail Road, to the Western Rail Road to Atlantic Tennessee & Ohio Rail Road to the Wilmington Charlotte and Rutherford Rail Road, to the University Rail, to the Wilmington Charlotte and Rutherford Rail Road, to the Plymouth and Wilmington Rail Road and possibly others amounting in the aggregate to $20.000.000 or more and not one of these did I vote for; and it was by authority of *these* acts that the Special Tax Bonds were issued. The fact that I stood recorded in the Journal as voting for the Bill referred to above has never given me any concern nor does it do so now except that it shall not be perverted. I had always supposed that my hostility to the Rail Road Legislation of 1868–9 was too well known of all men to be questions. I have no doubt you will remember the fact that I introduced into the House the Bill at the Session of 1869–70 to repeal all this Legislation and what I [sic] struggle we had to get it through, and I here wish to say that it could never have passed but for the efficient aid you gave me in that long struggle.

I know you will remember whether I had any sympathies with the villians of the Legislature of 1868–69 and whether I did anything to defeat it and protect the people of the State or not.[149]

Will you be kind enough to write me at your earliest convenience and give me your statement of my acts and doings in that Legislature with permission to make such use of it as I may desire.

---

[148]Joseph W. Holden.
[149]A careful check of the *House Journal* supports all of Jarvis' allegations. See also Remarks of Mr. Jarvis . . . February 17, 1869.

A&H—GP

Thomas J. Jarvis to S. A. Ashe[150]

Raleigh N.C.
May 21st. 1880

Will you be kind enough to inform me as to the authorship of the communication in your paper of to–day signed "Cato."

It is proper for me to state that I propose to make such use, as I may choose of the information I get in reply to this.

A&H—GP

S. A. Ashe to Thomas J. Jarvis

Raleigh, N.C., May 21, 1880

In reply to your note making enquiry as to the authorship of the communication in this mornings Observer, signed *Cato,* I desire to say that I will furnish the name if you propose to take any action legal or otherwise with reference to the contents of the communication. Otherwise I do not understand that you can ask to be informed of the name of a correspondent who has chosen to withhold his name from the public.

A&H—GP

Thomas J. Jarvis to S. A. Ashe [copy]

Raleigh N.C.
May 21st 1880

In reply to yours of this date I will say that I do propose to take action "otherwise," unless I shall see the public pay no attention to the misrepresentations of one "who chooses to withhold his name from the public."

I therefore hope you will favor me with the name as a matter of courtesy, if not as a matter of right.

---

[150]This is a signed copy of a letter from Jarvis to Ashe.

A&H—GP

W. J. Best to Thomas J. Jarvis

New York May 21st 1880.

During the past two weeks, I have left no effort untried to get my co–grantees together to reorganize the W.N.C.RR. Co. in accordance with the provisions of the act ratified by the general assembly on the 29th day of March, 1880. I regret to inform you that Mess Grace, Fish & Tappan, who appear to be represented by Mr Flint, a partner of Mr Grace, decline to advance any portion of the money necessary to carry out the contract entered into with the State.[150] These gentlemen have also refused to meet and organize and assign their rights to the Company, which would enable me to find others who would join in completing this road. Mr Flint, acting I presume in the interest of my co–grantees has demanded of me the right absolutely to control the grants made to us, with the view of negotiating their sale to one of the Railroad companies immediately interested. Strange as it may seem to you, I would have made this great sacrifice had not Mess Grace & Co refused to give any gu[a]ranties for the performance of their contract with the State. Their action has surprised and disappointed me. I fear they mean no good either to the State or myself. I have concluded, therefore, to separate from them without delay. They will not, however, assign their interest without the assent of the commissioners named in the act. Will you, therefore, telegraph Mr Grace that it is agreeable to you and your co–commissioners that he assigns to me all the rights which he acquired under the act of Mar 29th. If you will do this, I believe I can find several gentlemen, in all respects more desirable than Grace & Co., who will take their place. Free to act, I am satisfied a few days will suffice to put me in position to pay the State its disbursements and vigorously to begin the work. Without such freedom, I fear much mischief to the State and the Democratic party. So impressed am I with the gravity of the situation, I send this com-

---

[150]Best and his associates were to meet with the representatives of the state on May 15 and take over the Western North Carolina Railroad according to the terms of the contract. Samuel M. Tate reached New York shortly before that date, and he soon reported that the members of the syndicate disagreed as to the management of the railroad and that they planned another meeting for May 24 at which they hoped to settle their differences. *Morning Star*, May 27, 1880.

munication by Mr Caddagan[151] and hope to receive an answer by wire tomorrow night. Mr C can explain to you the position of affairs with more particularity than I would be justified in useing in a letter.

North Carolinians, in whose judgement and patriotism you rely, who are now in New York, will, at the proper time, inform you that I have done all that I could do to induce my co–grantees to perfect their organization and faithfully carry out their contract. Having failed to do so, I earnestly urge upon you at once to agree to their withdraw[a]l. That done I shall find good and strong men to join me. I shall make sure of the success of the enterprise and that nothing reaches the public as to any change in the parties until the work of construction shall be well under way.

A&H—GP

Thomas J. Jarvis et al. to W. J. Best.

Executive Department,
Raleigh, May 22d, 1880

In reply to yours just received, we will state that the Act of 29th of March, 1880, gave the Commissioners therein named the power to assign and transfer the interest of the State in and to the property and franchises of the Western North Carolina Railroad Company to W. J. Best, W. R. Grace, J. D. Fish and J. Nelson Tappan. This we did, and they executed to the State their obligation in the form of a contract to complete the road. The Act gives the Commissioners no power to release them or any of them from that obligation. If we were to assume such authority, it would be of no force and effect. If they or any of them desire to sell their interest in the property, they could do so without our consent, and even against it. All we can ask is, that the work shall begin by the grantees, or some one for them, on or before the 29th, the day fixed in the Act and in the contract, and be continued in conformity therewith. We greatly regret that there should be any delay in the organization and work.

---

[151]John P. Caddagan, Best's private secretary and later treasurer of the Midland North Carolina Railroad. *News and Observer*, February 23, 1882.

If it were possible for us to remove the obstacles, we would do so at once; but anxious as we are to aid in the matter, we do not see at this time anything we can do.

We are yours respectfully,

Thos. J. Jarvis,
J. M. Worth,
W. L. Saunders,
Thos. S. Kenan,
Commissioners

A&H—GP

George A. Dichte[152] to Thomas J. Jarvis

Raleigh N.C. May 22ᵈ 1880

I have the honor to state that about one year ago Mr. J. White-law of this City, reopened part of the States rockquarry at the terminus of east Davie street, and in front of this Cemetery.

I presume Mr. Whitelaw had permission from the proper authorities.

An excavation about 20 feet wide, 50 feet long, and from 8 to 10 feet deep was thus made at the bottom of the former quarry, and the vein of water which supplied the well in this Cemetery was tapped, which drained the well into this excavation, where the water now stands about six or eight feet deep.

This standing water is fast becoming foul and extremely unhealthy to those living in the neighborhood. It is also a place for people to cast the carcasses of death [*sic*] animals by s[t]ealth.

My family and self have to live within a few rods of this nuisance and much of our sickness has been caused by it. As the hot season approaches the danger from this pest hole increases, and I would respectfully request that steps be taken at an early date to have the water drained off or the excavation filled up.

Please inform me whether or not the above request will be granted.

---

[152]Superintendent of the National Military Cemetery in Raleigh. Branson, *Directory, 1878*, 304.

A&H—GP

E. W. Pou to Thomas J. Jarvis

May 22nd 1880

If your nearest comrade who saw you struck down, by a Federal shot at Drewry's Bluff, should hear the charge made that you are not a proper man to be nominated by your party for Governor, because you fought in the late war under the Federal colors, his surprise could not be greater than mine was, yesterday, to see it gravely asserted, in a public journal, that you were a promoter of the Special Tax Bond Legislation of 1868 & 1869

I left the State House in the Spring of 1870, with such a deep disgust for the public service, that I have allowed much of the details of what I had just then seen & heard, to escape my recollection. I have even lost or mislaid my Copies of the Journals. But I never can forget that I looked on you then as being as faithful to the State & to the *right,* as I knew myself to be.

I do not remember that under any circumstances you voted *aye,* on the passage of any of the bills we were then opposing. I am sure, if the journals of the House record such a vote, & the record is true, that I was then satisfied your vote was, nevertheless, that of an opponent & not a friend of the bill.

I did not get your letter until late yesterday afternoon; & have not been able, since, to get a Copy of the House Journal—

I will refresh my memory as best I can by Monday & will forward you on that day my recollections of your services in opposing the Special Tax Bond & other vallainies [*sic*] in the Legislatures of 1868, '69 & '70; & you will be at liberty to use what I may write as you see proper—

UNC—ABA

Thomas J. Jarvis to A. B. Andrews
[Telegram]

Raleigh, N.C., May 22 1880

I have telegraphed Vance to go over to New York   he can control B[est] the thing must be fixed   much talk here

A&H—GP

W. R. Grace to Thomas J. Jarvis
[Telegram]

27 May 1880

Grantees met for organization and adjourned till you approve
by wire and letter of the following gentlemen as directors of the
Western North Carolina Rail Road. W. J. Best President W. T.
Dortch A. C. Avery F. F. *Milne*[153] R. B. Vance W. E. Anderson
A. B. Andrews Vice Presdt T. M. Logan[154] John Hoey.[155] Answer
by wire & letter.

A&H—GP

Thomas J. Jarvis to W. R. Grace [copy]
[Telegram]

May 27 1880

The persons named as directors of W.N.C.R.R. are satisfactory

A&H—GP

W. J. Best to Thomas J. Jarvis
[Telegram]

Raleigh, N.C., May 28th, 1880

Organization completed will be in Raleigh Sunday noon Have
advised Andrews Vice President to take possession of road immediately

THE GOVERNOR TO THE PEOPLE[156]

Raleigh, N.C., May 28th, 1880

To the People of North Carolina:
During the unusually bitter canvass that has been going on
for the nomination for Governor I have tried to act in a becom-

---

[153]Unable to identify.
[154]Thomas Muldrup Logan of Richmond, Virginia. Beginning in 1878
with the Richmond and Danville, Logan and various associates bought the
controlling interest in several railroads, and in 1894 they organized the
Southern Railway System. *Dictionary of American Biography*, XI, 367–
368.
[155]Unable to identify.
[156]Taken from *Daily News*, May 30, 1880.

ing manner. I have remained constantly at the Capital; have been nowhere during the year and have not attempted to control the action of any man or community. I have been silent under the most unprovoked and malignant misrepresentations of my political record and the most unfeeling sneers at the crippled condition of my helpless right arm.[157]

Taking courage from that silence, my enemies have proceeded to attack my personal integrity, finding a convenient vehicle for both sneers and slanders in a newspaper at the head of whose columns stands the name of the Chairman of the Democratic State Executive Committee.[158] In face of such charges so gravely affecting my personal integrity, and so circulated, I am unwilling to remain silent.

SPECIAL TAX BONDS.

It is charged and insisted that in the Legislature of 1868–9 I favored the issue of Special Tax Bonds, and that I was a friend to the Legislation that fixed that debt upon the people. The facts are these: At the summer session of 1868 appropriations were made to various railroads, and among them to the Williamston and Tarboro Road, to the Chatham Road and to the Western North Carolina, for none of which did I vote except for $300,000 to the Williamston and Tarboro Road. In October, 1868, these Bonds were issued and went into the hands of the Presidents of the several companies. When the Legislature met in regular session in November, 1868, it was concluded that these bonds were unconstitutional and void. Some of them had been used by the President of the W.&T. Rail Road, and by the President of the Chatham Road, in making *bona fide* purchases for those roads. A bill passed the Senate to allow the Presidents of these three roads to return to the treasury these void bonds and get others in their place of like amount to those returned, which were thought to be valid. My decided views on this bill, were, 1st: The void bonds ought to be returned. 2d: That the actual *bona fide* obligation incurred with these bonds for which the

[157]At the Battle of Drewry's Bluff, Jarvis received a wound in his right arm, necessitating a resection of a part of the bone, from which he never fully recovered. Ashe, *Biographical History*, I, 333. Jarvis' political opponents often charged that he made a great show in public of nursing this arm.

[158]This was Samuel A. Ashe. Ashe was removed as chairman of the Democratic State Executive Committee soon after Jarvis received the Democratic nomination for governor in 1880. *Daily News*, June 18, 1880; *Morning Star*, July 1, 1880.

State was to be benefitted, ought to be redeemed, when those who had taken them did not have notice. This amount, however, was but small. In this I thought the honor and credit of the State were involved. 3d: That the feature of the bill which authorized the issuing of other bonds over and above what was necessary to redeem those *bona fide* obligations, ought to be stricken out. The bill was passed under the call of the previous question, and my only chance to move to amend was to vote with the majority, which I did. I was cut off the first day by a motion to adjourn and the second day by the motion to reconsider being made by another member and a friend of the bill. After that *nine* other separate and distinct bills were before the House, (eight of which passed), to appropriate Special Tax Bonds to the Railroads, not one of which did I vote for but opposed as best I could.

I believed then and believe now that the Legislature was limited in its power to tax the property of the State to sixty–six and two–thirds cents on the $100 worth of property, and that this must include all taxes. In February 1869, I tried to have that feature made a part of the Revenue Bill for the express purpose of defeating the Special Tax Bonds as I then so declared. At the session of 1869–70 I was the mover in the House of their repeal and repudiation. And in the Convention of 1875 I sought to have it put in the Constitution that the people should never be taxed to pay them. I have always been an enemy of the Special Tax Bonds and always expect to be.

My hostility to all the Special Tax legislation was so well known at the time, and not apprehending that a day would ever come when I would be charged with favoring such legislation, the fact that the record was left as it now stands gave me no concern.

THAT I MISSED ROLL CALL

How many times I did miss I do not know; probably quite as many times as charged. There were many special tax bills for local purposes in different counties. I could not vote for any of them and very frequently failed to vote on them at all. In addition to this I often refused to vote on either side of a question before the House as the only means of fighting the villainies of that Legislature, thus in many notable instances defeating them. It is now only after the lapse of more than ten years, during which time I have been almost continuously before the people, that a whisper even has been heard impeaching my fidelity to my constituency. Until now I have been universally commended for my course then.

BRIBERY AND CORRUPTION.

So long as the charges against me affected only my political record, grave though they were, and so long as my helpless physical condition was sneered at, I was content to remain silent; but now that I am charged with positive bribery and corruption I am forced to the only redress my position as the Chief Magistrate of your State leaves open to me, that is to say, a plain statement of the facts to you. I am charged with having corruptly received from John F. Pickerel $1,500.

The circumstances under which I received the money were these: In 1865 I went into a mercantile partnership with a gentleman who afterwards became my brother–in–law.[159] The business was fairly prosperous, and in 1868 I sold to him my interest, taking his obligation for the purchase for about $5,000. In the summer of 1868 I was in Raleigh. In the fall of that year I was on duty as an elector for my district in the SEYMOUR and BLAIR campaign. From November, 1868, till April, 1869, I was in Raleigh. In November, 1869, I again returned to Raleigh, where I remained until about April 1, 1870, when I returned home to find my brother–in–law in failing health and business, and myself not only a loser of $5,000 but involved for him in the city of Norfolk for some $4,000. I was not able to pay in full. Not wanting this indebtedness to hang over me, I asked for and obtained a compromise for cash, to meet which I wrote to Col. JOHN D. WHITFORD, who was then living in New York, to go to see Mr. BALTZER, of the firm of BALTZER & TAAK, Bankers of that city, and try to get for me $1,500 on long time, explaining to him my condition and the cause of my needs. The reason I applied to Mr. BALTZER was that in the winter of 1869–70 he was in Raleigh and stopped at the Yarborough House, where I was also boarding. I was introduced to him and frequently saw him. He mentioned to me that he thought Special Tax Bonds, which were then very low, a good investment, and that he intended to put his money into them largely, and asked me what I thought of it. I replied to him he had better see the Treasurer

---

[159]From 1865 to 1867, Jarvis and William H. Harper were partners in two Tyrrell County general stores. Record of Deeds, Tyrrell County, Volume 22, pp. 242-243, 287.

and Governor.[160] He said he did not think they represented the tax–payers, while I did, and he preferred my opinion. I told him I did not think the white people of the State would ever pay one dollar of them; that for one, I would not vote to pay a dollar of them nor would I vote for any man that would. This conversation was several times repeated, and the result was that he declined to purchase the bonds, and when he was leaving he said to me he was satisfied from what he had seen that I was correct, that he felt under great obligations to me for having by my advice saved him much money, and was warm and earnest in his expressions as to the service I had done him, assuring me that if ever he could serve me in any way, I had only to let him know how it could be done. It was the warmth and the earnestness of these assurances so recently given me that led me to apply to Mr. BALTZER, when I had need of money. When Col. WHITFORD received my letter he was, as he afterwards told me, in Mr. PICKEREL'S office, and mentioned the fact of having received the letter and its contents, and of his purpose to call on Mr. BALTZER in my behalf. Mr. PICKEREL, as Col. WHITFORD wrote me and has often told me since, said there was no need to take that trouble as he would gladly let me have the money, and drew his check at once for $1,500 and handed it to Col. WHITFORD. This check Colonel WHITFORD sent me. I received it and did not hesitate to use it. I deposited the check with Messrs. C. W. GRANDY & SONS, in Norfolk, and drew upon it for different amounts in favor of my creditors there with whom I had made the compromise. I have since repaid to Mr. PICKEREL near $1,400. The balance due is in judgment in Halifax county in the name of NINA PICKEREL, which I hope to be able to pay at no distant day.

INSOLVENCY.

I am charged with being at that time and the present insolvent. That unfortunately for myself and my creditors is too true. In 1860 I left college with a debt of over $2,000 hanging over me for money that I had borrowed to pay for my education, which was secured by a policy on my life. In May, 1861, I enlisted in the State Guard, under Capt. W. F. MARTIN. I was dangerously wounded in the arm and shoulder on the 14th of May, 1864. When the war ended, with my shattered arm in a sling, and with no possessions in the world but one suit of Con-

---

[160]D. A. Jenkins and W. W. Holden, respectively.

federate gray, and with this debt of $2,000 with accumulated interest hanging over me, I went to work as best I could to make an honest living, and have struggled on ever since. Unfortunately for me, I was quickly forced to the front in politics, in consequence of the disfranchisement of so many of the older men in 1868. I never like to do anything in a half-hearted way and the campaigns through which I have gone have cost me no little. As a result of all of this, I am still in debt, a fact that I regret more than any one else can.

Painful as it is to me to go into all this, I have felt that after the bitter assults on my character there was no other course left open to me. I have a clear conscience before my GOD, that I never knowingly wronged my State, or any fellow being, out of one penny in all my life, and if, to–day, I am still a poor man and in debt, it is because I devoted so much of my time and so much of the proceeds of my labor to the service of my party and State.

All the facts stated above are within the knowledge of witnesses now living, and I have no fear for the result of any scrutiny, no matter how searching, or how rigid, and no matter even how harsh.

A&H—GLB

Thomas J. Jarvis to J. W. Wilson

[*Telegram*]

Executive Department
Raleigh May 28ᵗʰ 1880

The grantees have paid to State Treasurer $15.000 to cover expenditures,[161] and are ready to take possession. Get ready to turn over. Communicate at once with A B Andrews who will take possession at once for grantees. Can you come to Raleigh Sunday.

---

[161]This sum for $5,000 in interest on the first mortgage bonds due the state, and for $10,000, which was the amount of money spent by the state on the Western North Carolina Railroad between the signing of the contract of sale and the time the purchasers took formal possession of the railroad. *Morning Star,* June 1, 1880.

A&H——GP

S. A. Ashe to Thomas J. Jarvis

Raleigh May 31 1880

You say in your address to the People of North Carolina that your enemies have found "a convenient vehicle for both sneers and slanders" against you in the Observer of which I am Editor and Proprietor.

I respectfully ask you to designate specifically the sneers and slanders to which you refer and to enumerate them.

You also state that you have been charged in the Observer with positive bribery and corruption. This statement I deny and I respectfully request you to designate by quotation the language covering such a charge and on which you rely to sustain your allegation.

The same with regard to your allegation that you have been charged in the Observer with missing roll–call.

I shall publish this note and your reply if you shall choose to make one during the day; and I shall repel the imputation that the Observer has contained any slander upon yourself.

A&H——GP

Thomas J. Jarvis to S. A. Ashe[162]

Executive Department
Raleigh, May 31, 1880

In reply to yours of this date I have to say, that the only reference I make to you or your paper in my letter to the people is to be found in the following extract.

"Taking courage from strict silence my enemies have proceeded to attack my personal integrity finding a convenient vehicle for both sneers and slanders in a news paper at the head of whose columns stands the name of the Chairman of the Democratic State Executive Committee. In face of such charges so gravely affecting my personal integrity and so circulated I am unwilling to remain silent."

It is therefore clear that the only thing of which I complained

---

[162]This is a rough draft of a letter in Jarvis' handwriting. An edition of the Raleigh *Observer* for this period has not been found.

of you is the circulation of that which affected my personal integrity and character.

The "Sneers" and "attacks upon my personal integrity" of which I complain are the following. First—Sneers—

In your paper of the 20th of May is this language. "Mr. Jarvis' friends claim much for him on account of his war record and point with pride to the indelicate way he nurses his wounded right arm." and in the same column speaking of another gentleman it is said "He has no wounded arm to publicly caress." Now it seems to me that this is a "sneer" at me Whether it is so or not I leave you and the public to say.

Second. As to the attack on my personal integrity.

In your paper of the 28th May will be found what purports to be a letter dated Raleigh April 15th 1871. addressed to John F. Pickerell with such parts quoted and such parts and the name of the writer left out as suits the purposes for which it was intended together with the following skillfully put language.

"Governor Jarvis voted for the special tax bonds. He borrowed $1.500 from Pickerell, the lobbyist in manner above, and has not returned it. Can the Democratic Party afford to carry him at the head of its ticket? How will the candidates for sheriff, register of deeds and members of the Legislature answer when upon every stump the questions will be asked—are you in favor of the adoption of the constitutional amendments repudiating the infamous special tax bonds? Do you endorse the action of Gov Jarvis in voting for the special tax bonds? Did he borrow of Pickerell the lobbyist, $1.500 in the manner stated by Mr Cooke? Has he returned the amount to Pickerell? Was not Governor Jarvis then insolvent? What motive actuated Pickerell in lending $1.500 to an insolvent without security?"

Will you say that this does not "charge me with corruptly receiving from John F. Pickerell $1.500. The adroit way in which it is put by an astute lawyer by questions and inuendo does not relieve it of the character of a "charge." If this does not constitute such a charge and if it was not intended to insinuate such a charge it is utterly pointless

No where in my letter do I complain of the Observer for circulating my political record. That is public property and had the Observer contained nothing else I should have continued my silence but as I felt bound to go to the public with an explanation of the attack, as I conceived it, on my personal integrity I chose to set myself right in the matter of the record also from the tenor of your note it is evident that you do not realize that the Observer has contained any slander upon me. I am glad to know this. In the years of intimate personal acquaintance with you I had learned to greatly esteem you and I was much pained when I saw these things in your paper which to me seemed so plainly slanderous.

A&H—GP

Printed Circular

Executive Office,[163]
Raleigh, N.C., June 10, 1880

To the Friends of Higher Education:

The Board of Trustees of the University, at their late meeting, instructed Prof. G. T. Winston[164] to appeal to the friends of higher education in this State and elsewhere in his discretion, for pecuniary aid to relieve the Institution from present embarrassment and to enable it more effectually to carry out its great objects.

The University was re-organized in 1875 in the midst of a financial depression, of a severity almost unparalleled, which has continued to a recent date. The sums contributed by its friends during that year have been mostly spent in repairs absolutely necessary, and for purchase of apparatus essential for instruction.

It was hoped that the income of the University would, within four or five years, suffice to pay its annual expenses. The stringency of the times has prevented this happy result. The attendance of students is as large as during any year prior to 1850. But a considerable number of these students pay no tuition—some by reason of their appointment by the counties as allowed by law, others by the free gift of the University. The University is proud of its beneficiary work. It desires and expects that this work shall not be diminished—that in the future, as in the past, no worthy man shall be turned from its doors for want of means.

---

[163]This appeared as a printed circular.

[164]George Tayloe Winston. After a distinguished academic education, Winston taught mathematics at Cornell, then became professor of Latin and German literature at the University of North Carolina. He was president of the University from 1891 to 1896. He later served as president of the University of Tennessee and then of North Carolina State College. Ashe, *Biographical History*, II, 460–466.

But from these causes the University is in need of further help, to discharge its floating liabilities incurred since its re-organization and to effect such improvements as will place its educational facilities abreast with the demands of the age.

Being entirely satisfied that all contributions to the University will be economically and wisely used, I cordially commend this application as eminently worthy of a liberal response.

Thos. J. Jarvis.

Governor and ex officio Ch'm'n B'd of Trustees,

of the University of North Carolina.

A&H—GLB

Thomas J. Jarvis to F. M. Simmons

Executive Department

Raleigh June 21st 1880

I herewith hand you the Proxy of the state in the A&N.C.R.R. Company.[165] I desire you to attend the meeting of the stockholders and to guard as best you can the interest of the state and all other interest which may depend upon it.

The administration that control[l]ed this road prior to the present one I am sure did all that could be done to preserve this property and yet when I became in some way responsible for its safety I could but have grave apprehension for it on account of the large debt that so greatly imperrelled it.

I believed then and I believe now that the future of the Road was very precarious if left to its own resources. Its natural ally is the North Carolina Road and impressed with this belief I favored a project to operate the A&N.C. Road in connection with the N.C. Road. But because of the lease of the N.C. Road to the R&D. this project has not only not met with favor but has been violently assailed as a matter of sentiment more than in substance. But even with the weak support that has been given this project it has, as I am informed, succeeded to the extent of meeting all the current liabilities of the company. Had it been more warmly supported I have no doubt it would have succeeded bet-

---

[165]The state owned about two-thirds of the capital stock of the Atlantic and North Carolina Railroad, but had only about one-seventh of the voting power among the stockholders. *Daily News*, August 4, 1880.

ter. When it was inaugerated it never occurred to me that any one interested in the development of Neuse River section would object to the Lessees of the N.C.R.R. doing a part of their business over the A&N.C.C. but it seems in this I have been mistaken.

A new project is now proposed: to wit: to lease the Road to the W&W.R.R. Company.[166] Upon this question my views have been asked and to President Whitford and President Bridgers I have replied, that the proposition to lease to any one must protect the property, the interest of the state therein and the interest of that section of the state east of Goldsboro for which the Road was chiefly built, before it could get my approval. I repeat the same thing to you now.

I am not one of those that hope for dividen[d]s from this or any other road while under the control of the state; and in making any arrangement for the future of this road I will be guided chiefly by what I believe is the interest of the section of the state this Road was intended to benefit.

The state contributed largely to the W&W. Road, the W&M Road and the W.C&R Road. All she put into those roads she lost so far as the Dollars are to be counted, but she did a great work in developing the Cape Fear section and building up Wilmington, the value of which cannot be told. The same may be said of other sections and other Roads. These roads have been, so far as I know, operated and managed in the interest of the sections for which they were constructed, and if in doing that they were lost to the state they were saved to the sections.

What I most desire is that the A&N.C.R.R. shall be so operated as to secure its safety and be of the greatest service to that section of the state East of Goldsboro. If in the opinion of the stockholders and people along its line a lease of the Road is the best means of doing this the state will permit that to be done which the interest of that section demands.

Hence I desire you to ascertain, if possible, what is the interest of that section and the wish of the people interested in its development and improvement and then cast the influence of the state to secure that end.

I trust that nothing will be done in this matter hastily, but that both private stockholders and the state will deliberate to-

---

[166]On June 9, 1880, R. R. Bridgers, president of and on behalf of the Wilmington and Weldon, offered to lease the Atlantic and North Carolina Railroad for thirty years at a rent of $33,000 a year. Brown, *State Movement*, 247.

gether and work together for the best interest of the Road and the section through which it runs.

A&H—GP

Levi T. Oglesby[167] to Thomas J. Jarvis

Newport June[th] 30th 1880

You will please allow me to make a statement of a few facts in connection with myself. At the last convention the vote of *Carteret* would have been divided but for my earnest effort to cast it solid for you. At an unexpected time and without a moments warning I was stabed in the back in the house of my friends for having done my whole duty. The Doctors in my section say the wound is a fearful one and have prescribed some remedies but I have steadily declined to take any thing or apply any of the proposed remedies until you shall have been consulted. Please let me hear from you. For 42 years I have never failed to vote the democratic ticket without a scratch. For 8 years I carried the democratic banner from 52 to 60 though in a hopeless minority of 200. In the second canvass I carried it to victory by 60 majority being the first Democrat ever elected in this county from the time party lines were drawn by Jackson and Adams.— A word if you please as to my record as a Rail Road man. In 1854 the canvass was made between C. R. Thomas and myself upon its location in case we could get the charter through the Legislature. I defeated Thomas went to Raleigh voted its charter and after the Legislature returned home and backed up what I had said and done by taking my self and family more stock than was taken by all others in the county.

I served for 2 years as director while the Road was being built. I then declined the appointment in favor of C. R. Thomas who had come to the Democratic party. I then held the state Proxy for 2 years this brings us up to the war. Since that time until last year I have had no connection with the Road except to pay taxes fare freight bills &c.

But enough, my character & reputation is worth more to me than the Road with all its offices combined.

---

[167]Large land owner of Carteret County; member of the General Assembly, 1884. Branson, *Directory for 1884*, 188; Connor, *Manual, 1913*, 539. For the cause of Oglesby's grievance, see Jarvis to Oglesby, July 3, 1880, in this volume.

A&H—GP

Thomas J. Jarvis to L. P. Oglesby

Executive Department
Raleigh, July 3ᵈ 1880

The Democratic record you show in yours of the 30ᵗʰ ult. is one of which any good Democrat may be proud, as I have no doubt you are, and justly so too. That in all this you acted from a high and noble sense of duty to your State and section I have no doubt.

For your services rendered me at the late State Convention I here beg to thank you although you acted in that matter from the same high sense of duty.

But I presume your real purpose in writing was to enquire of me why I did not reappoint you a Director on the A&N.C.R.R. Whether bound to give you my reasons or not I do so frankly and they are these. I too felt that I had been stabbed in the house of my friends. Before calling the Legislature together last winter I saw proper to require the proposed purchasers to deposit in one of the Banks of this City $30.000, as a guarantee for the faithful performance of their proposed contract in the purchase and completion of the Western North Carolina Rail Road. In a public meeting held in Newport, in which you are reported as participating, a resolution was passed the object of which was to charge that I had consented to the Legislature being paid by those who were seeking its favors and in an insinuating way denouncing the act.

That the people of Carteret or any other County had the right to meet and criticize anything I do, or was about to do I will be the last to deny, and will be last to complain of them for exercising this undoubted right. In fact I think it is the duty of the people to fully express their opinions on all important questions and it is likewise the duty of all officers and servants to pay due regard thereto. But I do not think the people have the right to pervert the act of an officer which is right in itself into a crime and then proceed to denounce him for it.

I do not complain of you that [you] expressed your opinion in the most decided manner in that meeting as to anything I did do, but what I do complain of is that you assumed I had done an act disgraceful to the State, which had not been done, and then proceed to censure it.

I have thus frankly and as briefly as I could given you my reasons for my action. If I have in anything done you injustice I regret.

A&H—GP

Walter Calton Murphy[168] *to Thomas J. Jarvis*

So. Washington Pender Co. N.C.
July 7th 1880

At the request of friends I write to urge the compliance by the Penitentiary Board with the law in regard to canaling Angola Bay.[169] The Board have repeatedly provided that as soon as proper arrangements could be made for their care they would be sent forward.

A&H—GP

Levi T. Oglesby to Thomas J. Jarvis

Newport N.C.
July 10th 1880

Your favor of the 3rd Inst. is received by me and duly considered; Permit me to thank your Excellency for the frankness and candor which characterizes its statements

The object of the meeting refered to was solely to instruct our representatives and was intended in no way to reflect upon you or your administration. it is true, we believe our interest in this section particularly, and the whole state generally, requires adherence to what you have been pleased to call "the North Carolina system of Railroads"

The particular resolution which appears to have given offense, we think does not fairly admit of the construction placed upon it, and certainly we know it was very far from the thoughts of any person in that meeting to charge the deposit made by Mr. Best was intended as a corruption fund upon the contrary the Governor was commended for his precaution in protecting the

---

[168]Physician, and secretary of the state medical society during 1884 and 1885. Mattie Bloodworth, *History of Pender County, North Carolina* (Richmond, Virginia: Dietz Printing Company, 1947), 170–172, hereinafter cited as Bloodworth, *Pender County.*

[169]See Boney to Jarvis, March 20, 1879, and Jarvis to Boney, April 8, 1879, in this volume.

interests of the state Notwithstanding this, we believed then and believe now that inasmuch as the deposit was made upon the condition that the Legislature should accept the proposition of Mr. Best, they should not be paid out of this fund if we were ever jealous of the fair honor of our party and our representatives, this is the head and front of our offending.

A&H—GP

Joel Henry Davis[170] *and Julius F. Jones*[171] *to Thomas J. Jarvis*

Beaufort   Carteret Co. N.C.
July 12th 1880

At a meeting of the citizens of Carteret County irrespective of party held at Beaufort on Saturday the 10th inst the following Resolutions were unanimously adopted, and the undersigned instructed as per the 4th Resolution to send a copy to your Excellency.

Resolutions

Whereas the citizens of Carteret County are burdened with a debt of over $100.000 arising out of her subscription to the Stock of "The Atlantic & North Carolina Railroad Company" and for this reason, and the fact that she possesses the best harbor in the State, her interests and her opinions ought to be treated with respect, in any disposition which may be made of said Railroad,

—And whereas "The Wilmington & Weldon Railroad Company" has lately made propositions to lease said "Atlantic & N. C Railroad,"[172] which propositions it is said have been favorably considered by certain stockholders having more regard for their personal advantage than the interests of Carteret County and the public;

And whereas through some proceeding of which the citizens of this County are not informed and do not approve, 500 Shares of

---

[170]Farmer of Beaufort; member of the General Assembly, 1868. Branson, *Directory, 1878*, 58; Connor, *Manual, 1913*, 540.

[171]Sheriff of Carteret County and a cotton gin owner. Branson, *Directory for 1884*, 183–184.

[172]On June 24, 1880, the stockholders of the Atlantic and North Carolina Railroad passed a resolution in favor of leasing the road if good terms could be secured. Brown, *State Movement*, 247. See also Jarvis to Simmons, June 21, 1880, *n.* 166, in this volume.

Stock in the "Atlantic & North Carolina Railroad Company" belonging to the County of Carteret have illegally passed from the control of said County, and it is claimed will be voted in favor of said Lease, and against the interests of this County:—

Therefor the citizens of Carteret County have

Resolved—

—1st That the proposed Lease of "The Atlantic & North Carolina Railroad" to the "Wilmington & Weldon Railroad Company" would be fatal to the future prosperity of said County, detrimental to the best interests of every County from Carteret to Wayne, and a death-blow to all the hopes which have centered for half a century, throughout the State, upon Beaufort Harbor,

—2nd That we concur in the opinions heretofore expressed by the Governor of the State that the people speaking through their chosen Representatives should alone decide as to the disposal of all State works of Internal Improvements, and we earnestly request that the disposal of "The Atlantic & North Carolina Railroad should be left to the next General Assembly, and that he will use his prerogatives to see that this end and object are attained,

—3rd That the Commissioners of this County be requested and instructed to appoint a Proxy to vote 500 Shares of Stock in the next Stockholders meeting of "The Atlantic & North Carolina Railroad" Company, and that said Proxy claim his right to vote under Sections 36 and 37 of the Charter of said Company, and that he be instructed to vote against any Lease of said Railroad, until the General Assembly shall convene;—and that said commissioners also appoint on Agent to take steps for the recovery of said Stock, and employ counsel if necessary for its recovery, and to prevent its being voted against the interests of this County.

4th That copies of these Resolutions signed by the chairman and secretary, be sent to His Excellency Governor Jarvis and published in the "Raleigh Observer" The [Raleigh] "News" the "Goldsboro Messenger" and "The Newbernian."

Trusting that the Resolutions may meet your favorable consideration, the undersigned avail themselves of this opportunity to renew the assurances of their high consideration

A&H—GP

Thomas J. Jarvis to L. T. Oglesby [*copy*]

Raleigh July 13th/80

In reply to yours of the 10th I will say. It never was in the range of human possibilities that the Legislature or any member of it could be out of the $30.000 deposit. And this is just what I complained of that when it was impossible that a dollar of the Deposit could be used to pay any member of the Legislature that a public meeting should be held and a resolution passed which, if it meant anything, said I was a party to the Legislature being paid in a way that reflected upon the honor of the State. I trust I am as mindful of the honor of the State as any man, and I think I would guard it as jealously. I really felt hurt when I read this resolution in the Newport meeting. It was all right for the people to meet and oppose or favor the sale. I invited such meetings. I wanted to know the will of the people. But it was not right for them to indirectly censure me (I was the only man that had anything to do with requiring the deposit) for something that I had never thought of and that could not be done.

I wish however I had had your disclaimer sooner. I really felt that you had wronged me and it gives me pleasure to know that you did not so intend it.

A&H—GP

A. R. Ledoux to Thomas J. Jarvis

New York, July 15, 1880

I have seldom been placed in a position as embarrassing as that which causes me to write the present letter. After thinking it all over, I have deemed it my duty to write directly to you, relying implicitly upon your discretion, and believing my letter will be considered confidential. My friend, Prof. Kerr, writes to me requesting that I recommend *him* for the position of Director of the Experiment Station, to be elected at the meeting of the Board next Tuesday. He says he is willing to direct the work at Chapel Hill for $1000 in addition to his present salary, as State Geologist, that he would require a first class chemical assistant at a salary of $1200 or $1500.

As a scientific man, I consider Prof Kerr perfectly competent to act as Director of the Station, and think that, with his knowledge of the people and needs of the state, he *could* do the work with satisfaction. I cannot disguise the fact, however, that he is very unpopular, and, am forced to say, deservedly so, in some instances at least. I fear that having him for Director, even temporarily, might cause adverse criticism, and result in some trouble for the Board. However, you understand the situation, and I shall be obliged to write Prof. Kerr that I have written to you "speaking of" him as a candidate for the position. My great reluctance to say a word against him is materially increased by the fact that I am drawing a salary from the Board and uncharitable persons, or those who did not know me, might think that I was selfishly acting the dog in the manger. No one has regretted more than myself that a suitable candidate has not appeared, and Pres. Battle will bear me witness that I have done my best to secure the right man to succeed me. I shall write to Capt. Thigpen[173] about Prof. Kerr, but shall say nothing whatsoever against the Prof. I have known the latter longer than anyone else in the state, and obtained my late position through him, and nothing but a sense of duty would tempt me to say a word excepting in praise. A line from Pres. Battle to day informs me that he is thinking of advocating the election of Mr. Phillips. Here again is an embarrassing position. You know my feelings in regard to him, as contained in my letter to you of April. I then requested you to make known the contents of that letter, should there seem *imminent* danger of Mr. P.'s election. I now request that you use it only in the event of his being a candidate for *permanent* Director.

Thanking you for many past kindnesses, and believing that you will understand and appreciate my position,

UNC—RPB

Thomas J. Jarvis to Ralph Potts Buxton[174]

Raleigh N.C.
July 22nd 1880

I hereby inform you that it is my purpose to canvass the State as the Democratic Candidate for Governor.

---

[173]James R. Thigpen, important farmer of Edgecombe County, and member of the Board of Agriculture. In 1875 he had been an editor of the *Reconstructed Farmer* of Tarboro. Noblin, *Polk*, 103, 108, 127.

[174]Prominent lawyer of Fayetteville; member of the constitutional conventions of 1865 and 1875; Superior Court judge, 1865–1881. He was the Republican nominee for governor in 1880. Ashe, *Biographical History*, V, 41–46.

Presuming it is your purpose to canvass as its Republican Candidate and that you like myself prefer to keep up the time honored custom of a joint discussion, I beg you to name an hour to–day or as soon as possible when I can have a conference with you to arrange a list of joint appointments.

I will thank you for an early reply.

A&H—GP

John O'Brien[175] to Thomas J. Jarvis

Baltimore. Aug. 4th 1880

The State of N.C. has a lot in the Stonewall Cemetery at Winchester, Va. in which are interred the remains of the soldiers from your State who fell in the war in that section.

I thought that commemorative of your dead in said cemetery, through you a movement could be started to erect a monument over their remains by an association, general contributions or such other plan as your judgement might suggest. I was the sculptor and associate contractor of the work erected over Marylands Confederate dead dedicated on the 5th of June last. I herewith send you a photograph of it,[176] and a copy of the "Baltimorean" conveying to you some details of the matter, and as an artist "what manner of man" I am.

Should I be intrusted to execute similar work for your State lot, I would keep in view the pleasure I would have of rendering it in every way worthy of my commission.

If further corespondence should follow this, I shall be glad to furnish original design and estimates conformable to what you may propose.

A&H—GP

H. Pinckney Walker to Thomas J. Jarvis

British Consulate
Charleston S. Carolina
August 9. 1880

I have the honor to ask Your Excellency's attention to a subject now under the consideration of Her Britannic Majestys

---

[175]Sculptor of Maryland, who moved to Texas in 1882. George C. Groce and David W. Wallace, *The New–York Historical Society's Dictionary of Artists in America, 1564–1860* (New Haven: Yale University Press, 1957), 475, hereinafter cited as Groce and Wallace, *Dictionary of Artists.*
[176]Found in Governors' Papers.

government and to beg for certain statistical information which I presume, from the Public Records of the State, Your Excellency may be able to furnish.

The subject I refer to is Criminal Homicide and I am directed to ascertain the number of Committals for Murder in North Carolina during the ten years ended on the 31. December last, the number of Convictions—the sentences passed in each case and if extreme penalty whether it was executed or not, and if not, why not?

I have prepared and inclose a specimen of a tabulated form[177] to embody the desired information which may perhaps lessen the labour of the officers to whom Your Excellency may be pleased to refer this Communication; and humbly begging Your Excellencys aid in the performance of this task, I have the honor to be,

C. W. McLean to Thomas J. Jarvis[178]

An Open Letter to His Excellency, Gov. Jarvis:

Newbern, August 10. 1880

Hon. Thomas J. Jarvis:

Dear Sir:—As I understand that the offer[179] of Mr. Lazarus Silverman,[180] of Chicago, made through me in July last, to lease the Atlantic & North Carolina Railroad for the sum of $35,000 for the term of thirty years, was not considered by some members of the committee as a *bona fide* bid, I take this way of informing the people of North Carolina, through you, that it was

---

[177]Governors' Papers, form not included in this volume.

[178]Taken from the *Daily News*, August 12, 1880. C. W. McLean has not been identified.

[179]This offer was considered by the stockholders at their meeting on September 16, 1880. The meeting was adjourned until November 23, however, because of the inability of Silverman and one other bidder to be present. *Proceedings of the Occasional Meeting of the Stockholders of the Atlantic and North Carolina Rail Road Company, 1880.* By the time of the November meeting, Silverman's bid had been withdrawn. *Report of the Atlantic and North Carolina Rail Road Company, 1881.*

[180]In 1849 Silverman immigrated from Bavaria, Germany to Alabama. After five years of peddling goods, he accumulated some capital. In 1863 he moved to Chicago and entered the real estate and then the banking business. During his successful business career, which ended with his retirement in 1893, he was a director of several important mining and manufacturing corporations. In 1873 he submitted to United States Senator John Sherman a plan for the resumption of specie payment by the government. The plan was adopted and became known as the "Sherman Bill." John W. Leonard (ed.), *The Book of Chicagoans* (Chicago: A. N. Marquis & Co., 1905), 529, hereinafter cited as Leonard, *The Book of Chicagoans.*

made in good faith; and that Mr. Silverman proposes, should his bid be taken, to deposit in the hands of the Treasurer of the State, ample securities for the annual payment of the lease money.

There is, among the influential and wealthy Hebrews of Europe and the United States, a movement for the relief of the Hebrew peasantry of Romania, who are not allowed to hold land in that country, but only to till it for the Russian owners. Baron Rothschild[181] is at the head of this movement, and a million of dollars has already been deposited for the purpose of removing these men and their families, and settling them in the United States. The plan is to buy lands for them in different localities, purchase stock and farming implements, and give them ten years to pay for the same; they pledging themselves not to engage in trade, beyond the sale of their own produce and manufactures; the object being to elevate the race from mere hewers of wood and drawers of water into producers. Mr. Silverman's attention having been drawn by me to this section of the country, and one of our mutual friends, a gentleman of wealth and standing in Chicago, having visited North Carolina and reported favorably of the advantages of this particular location, he had almost determined to purchase land in Wayne, Lenoir, Craven, Carteret and Jones counties and begin at once to bring out settlers. But hearing of the proposed lease of the Atlantic & North Carolina Railroad, he felt it would not be well to locate on its line, should it pass into the hands of the Wilmington & Weldon Railroad Company, whose interest it will be to close our port of Morehead, at which point he proposed to land his colonists from steamers direct from Europe.

The interest of my colony at Havelock[182] being identical with his I induced him to make this bid for the Railroad, believing that if the people of North Carolina could fully realize the extent of this movement they would not allow so magnificent an opportunity for the developing of the resources of the State to slip from them. The fact that Baron Rothschild and his associates are willing to expend a million of dollars in this State would of itself be an advertisement of its merits to the whole civilized world, which would end in the settlement of every

[181]Lionel Nathan Rothschild, banker and philanthropist of England. Leslie Stephen, Sidney Lee, and Others (eds.), *The Dictionary of National Biography* (London: Oxford University Press, 28 volumes, 1922–1959), XVII, 304–306, hereinafter cited as *Dictionary of National Biography*.
[182]Community in Craven County.

acre of the State land. So that although Mr. Silverman is willing to give more for the Road than the Wilmington & Weldon Railroad Company offers, the State could in reality well afford to give her interest in it to him and his associates. My friends will be at the meeting on the 16th of September prepared, not only to renew their bid, but to deposit their securities. It is thought by some that the Wilmington & Weldon Railroad Company will be able to lease the road at *less* than Mr. Silverman offers; but I ask you, sir, if the property–owners at Morehead, Beaufort and along the line of the Road will quietly submit to see the Atlantic & North Carolina Railroad put into the hands of a monopoly? Or if they are so blind to their own interest, will the people of the State at large be? The battle–cry of those who favor leasing to the Wilmington & Weldon Railroad Company has been that the Atlantic & North Carolina Railroad will be sold out at the end of eight years to the Bondholders. My friends will, if it is desired, extend these bonds to the end of their lease, which ought to remove all fear of such a sale from the minds of the people.

A&H—GP

John D. Davis[183] *to Thomas J. Jarvis*

Beaufort N.C. Aug. 10. 1880

I learn that a protest[184] has been sent from Newport against Oglesby's removal and Perry's[185] appointment as Director of the A & N C R R Co. and among other things, I further learn it is charged that Mr Perry published a Republican newspaper in this town in 1876. If it is so charged, I will state, that I was a subscriber to that paper & very likely read every copy, and can bear testimony to the fact, that it endorsed & supported the National, State & County Democratic measures, although it was silent as to our Congressional ticket and he did oppose Col Askew.[186] These are the facts in the case, and Mr Perry was up to that time & has been since a good Democrat.

---

[183]Merchant and farmer of Beaufort. Branson, *Directory for 1884*, 185, 187. At this time he was chairman of the Board of Directors of the Atlantic and North Carolina Railroad.

[184]See Oaksmith to Jarvis, August 12, 1880, enclosure, in this volume.

[185]Benjamin Leecraft Perry, businessman and hotel owner in Wilmington. *Cyclopedia of the Carolinas*, II, 553–554.

[186]Benjamin Askew, coach manufacturer of Trenton; member of the General Assembly, 1876. Branson, *Directory, 1878*, 181; Connor, *Manual, 1913*, 677.

A&H—GP

J. F. Jones to Thomas J. Jarvis

Beaufort, N.C. Aug. 10, 1880

I am informed that a petition,[187] remonstrating against the appointment of Mr. B. L. Perry as a Director on the A & N.C.R.R. in the place of Mr. L. T. Oglesby has been sent to you, in which I appear as one of the petitioners. If this be true, I then desire to explain my position: at the time when this petition was being gotten up I happened to be in Newport & was approached for my signature to it, which I refused to do stating, that Mr. Perry & myself were intimately connected in the same family & our relation to each other had always been very friendly, though I censured you, for removing Mr. Oglesby because he had expressed himself in a public meeting on the sale of the Western Road, & for appointing a Beaufort man & thus ignoring the west end of our county, the portion that was entitled to the most consideration. Upon being pressed on all sides, however, to sign it & with the private assurance of the holder of the petition that my name should be erased before it was sent off, I very reluctuntly consented to do so. Since he has been recreant to his promise I here desire to state that I do not wish to be considered one of the petitioners & take no stock in the petition. By request, I have made inquiry concerning the charge against Mr. Perry as the Editor of the Beaufort Eagle & learn from good authority that it is false. Our delegation to the State convention should be able to vouch for Mr. Perry's true democracy as he was their chairman.

In conclusion allow me to say that though we in the western portion of the county think you treated us badly, yet we intend to support you. With my best wishes for your election & for the success of the Democratic Party

A&H—GP

Appleton Oaksmith to Thomas J. Jarvis [*with enclosures*]
Confidential

Hollywood—
Carteret Co N.C. August 12th 1880

In sending you the accompanying papers *officially*, I desire that you should understand how thoroughly I appreciate the

---

[187]See Oaksmith to Jarvis, August 12, 1880, enclosure, in this volume.

embarassments of this question. Several of our *strongest* men have consulted me privately upon the subject, and looking at it impartially, *solely in the* interests of party, and without any personal bias, we are *at a loss to see what you can do at present.*

In a recent local contest, where the *Arendells*[188] *opposed my motion to join your name with Hancocks*[189] in the title of a Campaign Club, Oglesby supported me; which certainly looked as though *he* had no ill feeling. Many of your warmest friends here think it will be wisest to *let all Railroad questions* rest until after the election.

I think it would be well to write me such a letter as your judgement approves to submit to this Committee, *as the result of my action.*

Pray notify me a few days in advance *when you are coming to Morehead* that I may see you *personally* about these matters.

[*enclosure*]

Appleton Oaksmith to Thomas J. Jarvis

Hollywood Carteret Co N.C.
August 12th 1880

I have received the accompanying Petition from Messrs D. McCain,[190] S. H. Newberry[191] and Jno H. Mann,[192] sub Committee with a letter as to its disposition of which I inclose copy. In regard to the suggestion that the matter should be referred to the State Committee, I presume it arose from the prevailing impression that any citizen who accepts a party nomination places himself, as it were, in the hands of that party, as expressed by its highest authority, during the Canvass—and should, in a measure act under its counsel's. Under *all* the circumstances it seems to me that this is *not* one of those cases requiring such action. Agreeable therefor to the alternative, as expressed in the Com-

---

[188]A prominent Carteret County family.

[189]Jarvis had favored Winfield S. Hancock as the Democratic nominee for president. He had been asked by the Democratic organization of the city and county of New York to address a meeting in New York held for the purpose of ratifying Hancock's nomination. Democratic Committee to Jarvis, July 15, 1880, Governors' Papers. (Not included in this volume.) Jarvis, however, had been unable to accept the invitation.

[190]David McCain, hotel owner of Newport. Branson, *Directory for 1884*, 184.

[191]Carriage manufacturer of Newport. Branson, *Directory for 1884*, 184.

[192]Merchant of Newport. Branson, *Directory for 1884*, 186.

mittees letter, I send the Petition to you—not doubting that you will give the subject proper consideration.

I shall take the liberty of sending the Committee a copy of this communication and your reply; and trust you will command my services whenever they can be employed in the interests of *harmony* and Party success.

[*enclosure*]

Petition[193]

To His Excellency Thos. J. Jarvis

We, the undersigned citizens and voters of Carteret County, in view of your failure to appoint our patriotic fellow citizen and tried and true democrat and foremost Rail Road man, Capt. L. T. Oglesby, as one of the Directors of the A.&N.C.R.R., therefore do most earnestly request that you revoke the appointment of B. L. Perry, a man whose political distinction consists in his sneaking but unavailing attempt to disorganize the democracy in the memorable struggle of 1876. In the begining of that campaign he commenced the publication of a paper in Beaufort called the "Beaufort Eagle" to which he procured a large Democratic patronage. who were soon disappointed by their paper's turning from the Democratic Eagle to a Republican "Buzzard," and to see its Editor, this same B. L. Perry, take the field as an Independant against Col. Benjamin Askew the regular Democratic nominee in this Senatorial District, and against Col. A. M. Waddell,[194] the Democratic nominee in the 3rd Congressional District. We, therefore further most earnestly ask in the name of true Democrats of Carteret Co., in the name of Democrats of this Senatorial District, in the name of the Democrats of the 3rd Congressional District, that B. L. Perry be removed from the Directory of the A.&N.C.R.R. and your petitioners will ever pray

---

[193]This petition was signed by 107 individuals.

[194]Alfred Moore Waddell, lawyer of Wilmington; Democratic representative in Congress, 1871–1879; editor of the Charlotte *Journal–Observer*, 1881–1882. *National Cyclopedia*, VIII, 124–125.

[*copy*]

Newport Carteret Co N.C.
July 31–1880

Appleton Oaksmith Esq
Member from Carteret of the Dem
Executive Committee of the State

Dear Sir, The undersigned sub–committee to whom was referred the subject of the inclosed Petition, after due consideration have thought it best to send the same to you for such action as you may deem proper for the welfare & harmony of the party It was the intention to send the Petitions directly to Gov Jarvis, but prominent Democrats have advised that they should be sent to the State Executive Committee, It has therefore been decided to place them in your hands requesting that you would lay the matter before the State Executive Committee if you should approve of that course, Should you not do so, we request that you forward them to Gov Jarvis with such endorsement as you think right and proper—Yours Respectfully.

sgnd—

D Mᶜ Cain
S. H. Newberry
Jno. H. Mann—

A&H—GP

Hyde Clarke to Thomas J. Jarvis

London E.C. 12ᵗʰ August 1880

I am directed on behalf of the Council of the Corporation of Foreign Bondholders, again to request Your Excellency to lend your aid to the Library of this Institution, by adding to the publications it contains, relative to the resources and finances of the State of North Carolina

The Council have formed a collection of works on fiscal subjects, unique of it's kind, for which they have been in a great measure dependent upon the liberality of the Governments of many countries, who have generously responded to their requests for contributions, and they take this opportunity of offering their grateful thanks for them.

All persons of every nationality can avail themselves of the information which the Council possesses, and they hope that the appeal they now make to Your Excellency will induce you to contribute to the Library, any works of financial or general interest connected with North Carolina.

Allen Jordan[195] *to Thomas J. Jarvis*

Troy, August 17, 1880

I have just understood that Judge Buxton will not meet you to-morrow. If you will divide time with me I will represent him. Please let me hear from you as soon as convenient and oblige,[196]

Thomas J. Jarvis to Allen Jordan

Troy, August 18, 1880

Sir:—Referring to your note of the 17th inst., I beg to say that immediately after Judge Buxton, the Republican candidate for Governor, tendered his resignation as Judge, I addressed him a note asking him to name a time and place where I could have a conference with him for the purpose of arranging appointments for the joint canvass of the State.

This he declined to do, giving as his reason that his plans for canvassing were not matured. I then published a list of appointments and invited the Judge to go with me. He accepted this invitation and has been canvassing with me up to this appointment, and I did not know until Saturday that he would not be here to-day.

Under these circumstances I do not recognize the right of any one to represent him; he ought to be here to represent himself. He has, after a consultation with his Executive Committee, voluntarily abandoned the joint canvass and gone off to himself in a distant part of the State.

Notwithstanding all this, if you will state that you are authorized to speak for Judge Buxton, and that you will pledge for him that when he visits this county, the man I may send here or

---

[195]Lawyer of Troy. Branson, *Directory, 1878,* 202.

[196]On several occasions when Buxton was unable to keep an appointment for a joint debate with Jarvis, an ambitious local Republican volunteered to substitute for Buxton. This was such an occasion. This and the following letter were taken from the *Daily News,* August 22, 1880.

my friends may select to reply to him shall have ample opportunity to do so, and that no other persons shall participate in
the discussion that day, I will divide time with you to–day.

A&H—GP

James Rumley[197] *to Thomas J. Jarvis*

Beaufort, Carteret County, N.C.
Augt. 1880

I have just learned that some parties at Newport are getting
up a petition to you, asking for a change in the appointment
lately made by you of Mr. B. L. Perry of this place to a Directorship in the Atlantic & N. C. Rail Road Company.[198] I regret very
much to hear that you are likely to be annoyed in this way. But
I most sincerely hope you may not be induced to make any change
in the appointment of Mr. Perry

About the time you made this appointment a feeling of deep
concern as to the future destiny of our little town pervaded the
minds of our citizens, having its origin, I support, in the dread-
ful storm which occurred here on the 18th of August last. After
the commencement of the new hotel at Morehead City, daily reports reached our Beaufort people that leading men interested
in that place intended to make an effort to make that place the
capitol of the County, & of course have the Court House, Jail,
and even the Custom House located there—in short that Morehead City was *going up* & Beaufort was *going down.* These reports increased the solicitude of our people—at least of all who
were attached to the old town, as their native place. While this
feeling existed, we heard that you had determined to make a
vacancy in the Directory of the A.&N.C. Rail Road Co. It seemed
to me that if you appointed any person at Morehead City to fill
this vacancy, under the circumstances, your action would cause
great dissatisfaction in Beaufort, that therefore the appointee
ought to be selected on the East side of Newport River. Mr.
Perry was then engaged in a correspondence with Robert Graham[199] about the scheme of a new hotel at this place, and also

---

[197]Clerk of the Superior Court of Carteret County; member of the constitutional conventions of 1865 and 1875. Branson, *Directory, 1878,* 55;
Connor, *Manual, 1913,* 871.
[198]See Oaksmith to Jarvis, August 12, 1880, enclosure, in this volume.
[199]In 1880 Graham was a lawyer and a hotel owner in Wilmington, but
in 1884 he entered government service in Washington, D.C. Grant, *Alumni
History of the University,* 228.

had charge of the Front Street House. It seemed to me he ought to have a place in that Directory, where he could guard & promote his own interests, which are identical with the interests of *Beaufort*. I wrote to you & urged his appointment. I think his appointment under the circumstances was eminently proper. Of course I know that other influences, besides those alluded to by me, operated with you to cause his appointment.

As to the charge some of our friends have brought against Mr. Perry, they are certainly mistaken in making such a charge. As editor of the "Eagle," in this place, in 1876, Mr. Perry did refuse to advocate the cause of Mr. Waddell, & Mr. Askew—the former a candidate for Congress, & the latter, a candidate for the state senate. He said not a word about the candidates for these offices of either party. But with these exceptions, he supported the entire state & national tickets. At that time there was a good deal of *disaffection* in regard to Mr. Waddell, in this County. So I think the charge on this score amounts to—*nothing*. Our friends speak of the votes you will lose, &c. I think they are in error. I think the voters on the West side of Newport River have better sense than such fears concede to them. But our friends forget that the voters on the East side of that River might have been greatly dissatisfied by the appointment of some person on the West side. If voters are to be governed by such things you might have lost five times as many on the East side as you will lose on the West side. I sincerely hope however, you may be fully able at the next election to lose all you can lose in this County.

.   .   .   .

A&H—GP

William Henry Hurlbert[200] *to Thomas J. Jarvis*

New York, Sept 28 1880

I take the liberty of asking your cooperation in a measure which cannot fail, I think, at this stage of the campaign to be of great and immediate benefit to the Constitutional cause. The letter of General Hancock which I enclose has had a most beneficial effect throughout the North and West—so beneficial in-

---

[200]Originally a Unitarian minister, Hurlbert entered newspaper work in 1855. He was editor of the New York *World* from 1876 to 1883. *Dictionary of American Biography*, IX, 424.

deed that the Radicals are trying everywhere now to counteract it by asserting that he will not be supported by the Southern people in the position which he has taken. Absurd as we know this assertion [to] be, it has its effect not only upon the ignorant and prejudiced members of the Radical party but even, I am sorry to say upon men who ought to know better. This being the case it occurred to me that brief peremptory endorsement of General Hancock's position in regard to these alleged "Rebel Claims" by the leading men of the South would have a most important effect on public feeling just now.[201] May I ask you therefore, on receiving this letter to telegraph me here at once (at my expense) authority to sign your name to this brief statement:

The undersigned, Governors of the States of (here I shall insert the names of the several States) cordially agree with the Democratic candidate for the Presidency that no legislation providing for the consideration or payment of claims of any kind for losses or damages by persons who were in rebellion, whether pardoned or not, ought to be approved by him if elected to the Presidency.

As it is important that this demonstration should be made at the earliest possible moment, and effectually and once for all, I hope you will allow me to ask that you will oblige me with your reply be [sic] telegraph at the earliest possible moment. It will be sufficient if you will simply telegraph me the words "Your suggestion approved, act upon it," as it is desirable to avoid any premature publicity on the subject[.]

---

[201]In 1871 Congress set up the Southern Claims Commission, which received petitions from professed southern unionists during the Civil War for payment for quartermaster and commissary supplies furnished to the federal armies. During the decade of its activity it received 22,298 petitions claiming $60,258,150.44. During his campaign for the presidency in 1880, Hancock announced that he would veto all measures concerning "rebel claims." Frank W. Klingberg, *The Southern Claims Commission* (Berkeley and Los Angeles: University of California Press [Volume 50 of University of California Publications in History], 1955), VII, 184, hereinafter cited as Klingberg, *Southern Claims Commission*. Hancock's letter to which Hurlbert refers has not been found. There is no indication that Jarvis signed the endorsement as requested by Hurlbert.

A&H—GP

W. G. De Saussure²⁰² to Thomas J. Jarvis [with enclosure]

State Society of the Cincinnati of South Carolina
Charleston S°C.ª 29 September 1880

I enclose herewith a circular from the Cowpens Centennial
Committee: Also a circular from myself to the Presidents of
some of the other State Societies of the Cincinnati:²⁰³ And also
a proposed inscription, for the panel, on the monument, reserved
for the Southern States.

The purpose is to get the inscriptions prepared by 15 October, if practicable, if not, as early thereafter as possible. Inasmuch as in the Southern States there are but two State Societies
of the Cincinnati now in existence, I have undertaken, at the
desire of the Committee, to address the Governors of the Southern States directly, asking that they will suggest such inscriptions as they desire, or signify whether the enclosed inscription meets their approval.

The Committee also desire that an orator be named by the
Governors of the Southern States, to speak for the Southern
States, upon the unveiling of the monument on 17 January 1881.
I take the liberty of suggesting to the Governors of the Southern
States, as their representative orator, the Honble Wade Hamp-
ton,²⁰⁴ whose ancestors bore gallant part in the War of the
Revo[lu]tion, of which the battle of Cowpens was a turning
point. But asking that each Governor will name such person as
he prefers, as the representative orator of the Southern States.

Upon receiving replies from the Governors, I will report to
the Committee, such inscription, and such orator, as a majority
of the Governors approve, and recommend.

May I ask for an early answer

---

²⁰²Wilmot Gibbes De Saussure, lawyer and prominent citizen of Charleston. In the field of public service, he had served as member of the South
Carolina General Assembly, as adjutant general and as inspector general.
He took an active part in organizing the Huguenot Society of South Carolina and was a member of the Charleston Harbor Commission. At the time
of his death in 1886 he was president of the Cincinnati Society and of
several other Charleston societies. Information taken from the Charleston
News and Courier of July 23, 1947, and furnished the editor by Mrs.
Roberta Bonnoit of the Charleston County Library.

²⁰³Governors' Papers. Circular not included in this volume.

²⁰⁴Governor of South Carolina, 1877–1879; Democratic senator to Congress, 1879–1891; United States railroad commissioner, 1893–1897.
Dictionary of American Biography, VII, 213–215.

[*enclosure*]

Proposed inscription for Southern States panel
in the Cowpens Memorial Column.
One hundred years ago
The men of the North and the South fought together,
and, by their blood, secured
The Independence, and cemented the Union
of the American States.
The Bond that then bound them together is the
Bond of their fellow–countrymen to–day
The common country they created is the
Heritage of all their sons.
The perpetuation of the Republic of our
Fathers is the Safety and honor of
North and South
Alike the sentiment and duty of all the States.
"Esto Perpetua."

A&H—GP

Claude Baker Denson[205] *to Thomas J. Jarvis*

Raleigh, N.C., Oct. 6th 1880

I have the honor to forward to you complimentary tickets for
the 20th State Fair of North Carolina.

Allow me, in behalf of the Executive Committee, to tender you
their sincere thanks for the kindly interest you have manifested
in behalf of the Society, and its efforts to preserve the State
Fair, as a permanent institution, in our midst.

They ask of you the favor to open the Fair formally on Tuesday 19th at 12 M. and tender the proper escort for the occasion.

A&H—GLB

Thomas J. Jarvis to W. G. De Saussure [*with enclosure*]

Executive Department
Raleigh N.C. Oct 8th 1880

In reply to the request contained in your letter of 29th Sept,
which reached here during my absence, I herewith enclose the

---

[205]Farmer and nurseryman of Pittsboro; secretary of the North Carolina
Agricultural Society. Branson, *Directory, 1878*, 68, 304.

inscription that seems to me to be suitable for the panel on the Cowpens Monument reserved for the southern states.

In further reply to your letter I herewith suggest, and with great confidence in his fitness for the position; Hon George Davis of Wilmington, N.C. late Attorney General of the Confederate States as a suitable person to speak for the Southern States as their representative orator.

I have as you desired notified the Governors of the other Southern States of my recommendation in the premises.

[enclosure]

Copy of the inscription enclosed

One hundred years ago
Our fathers on this spot staked their lives in desperate battle
To secure to Americans the right of self government
    To day
In admiring recognition of their glorious cause
And of their no less glorious heroism in its behalf
And in grateful remembrance of the manifest blessing
Of the Constitution and Government
They devised to perpetuate, for our benefit,
The fruits of their valor and patriotism
    We, their children
Have erected this monument

A&H—GP

W. G. De Saussure to Thomas J. Jarvis

State Society of the Cincinnati of South Carolina
Charleston 15 October 1880

I have the honor to acknowledge the receipt of your letter of 8 Inst. with the inscription proposed by you for the panel reserved, on the Cowpens Monument, for the Southern States. Gov Colquitt of Georgia prefers your inscription—Gov[r]. Hamilton[206] of Maryland, Holliday of Virginia, Jeter[207] of South Carolina, and Marks of Tennessee, have approved the inscription a

---

[206]William Thomas Hamilton, governor of Maryland, 1879–1883. *Dictionary of American Biography*, VIII, 191–192.
[207]Thomas Bothwell Jeter, ex–officio governor of South Carolina, 1880. *National Cyclopedia*, XII, 178.

copy of which was sent you. In accordance with my previous letter to you, I have reported to the Committee by furnishing them with copies of all the letters received by me, and with a copy of the inscription furnished by you, so that they may act understand[ab]ly. All of the Governors of the other Southern States who have been corresponded with, have expressed a preference for Honble Wade Hampton as the orator. Will you permit me to suggest that if you can concur in such selection, it would enable the Committee in their invitation to Genl Hampton to say that he met the unanimous approval of all the Governors.

A&H—GP

J. B. Manning to Thomas J. Jarvis

New York Nov 3ᵈ 1880

I understand there will be a meeting between the Directors of the North Carolina R R Company and the Commissioners appointed to adjust the bonds issued by the State for the construction of the road, at Raleigh on Friday next.[208] As a holder of the bonds I sincerely trust a settlement of this question will be reached at that time. I am willing to accept a new 6% State bond for the face of the construction bonds, but the unpaid coupons on them must be provided for in some way; and I would suggest, the issuing of certificates for these coupons—such certificates to be paid out of the surplus earnings of the road during the next Fifteen years. This can be very easily accomplished I believe. The road is doing well now with a very fair prospect ahead. Of course the stock of the company should be retained as it is now for the security of the bondholders, we don't want the stock but wish to be protected as we are now.

---

[208]For explanation, see Jarvis to the council of state, October 7, 1879, *n.* 175; and Thomas Branch and Company to Jarvis, April 24, 1880, *n.* 131, in this volume.

A&H—GP

J. B. Manning to Thomas J. Jarvis
[*Telegram*]

New York Nov 4 1880

I will forego and surrender unpaid coupons mentioned my letter am satisfied all holders of Construction Bonds will accept forty year six per cent state Bonds at face surrend[er]ing unpaid Coupons but nothing Less

A&H—GP

Richard T. Merrick[209] to Thomas J. Jarvis

Washington, D.C., Nov. 11th 1880

I regret to inform you that Mr. Justice Wylie[210] has granted the motion to discharge Perry[211] on the writ of *habeas corpus.*

This decision is, in my judgment, plainly contrary to well established principles of law, and entirely unsupported by either sound reason or logic, as you will see from the opinion of the Judge, taken down by a stenographic reporter, and a copy of which I will send to you.

I regret to say that I do not believe the Judge would have reached the conclusion indicated, but for the influence of the political prejudices appealed to in the case.

I have taken great trouble with this case, and argued it fully, both before the Chief Justice of our Court, when called upon to perform the executive function of extradition, as well as before Judge Wylie when exercising judicial authority on the Petition for the writ of *habeas corpus.*[212] I was stimulated to

---

[209]Prominent lawyer of Washington, D.C. *National Cyclopedia,* VII, 323.

[210]Andrew Wylie, justice of the Supreme Court of the District of Columbia. *Register of Officers of the United States, 1877,* 314.

[211]Some years earlier, Samuel L. Perry, an ex–slave, had been engaged in persuading Negroes to leave North Carolina for other states, mainly Kansas and Illinois. Upon his return to North Carolina in 1880, Perry was indicted for assisting in forging papers, but before his case came up he had forfeited his bond and fled. Joseph H. Taylor, "The Great Migration from North Carolina in 1879," *North Carolina Historical Review,* XXXI (January, 1954), 22, 26, hereinafter cited as Taylor, "The Great Migration from North Carolina." Merrick represented North Carolina in its effort to obtain a bill of extradition against Perry from Judge Wylie.

[212]Upon reading North Carolina's requisition for Perry, Judge John V. Carter ordered Perry arrested. But Perry sued out a writ of habeas corpus on the grounds that, if he returned to North Carolina, he would not get a fair trial and his life would be in danger from the Ku Klux Klan. The

more than ordinary effort, by having superadded to the duty of serving my client, an earnest desire to protect our Judges from the discredit of yielding to a fanatical clamor which is not, at all times, without force, even in judicial proceedings. North Carolina may well indulge a reasonable pride in contrasting her methods of the administration of justice, as shown by the evidence, (taken upon the hearing of the motion) with those of this District, in so far as the latter are illustrated by the case under consideration.

The substance of the Judges opinion was, that the indictment against Perry was defective and did not *charge a crime.* He held that the omission to aver in the indictment, that the "school committee" was empowered by law to draw on the Treasurer of the County, or to aver that the draft set out, would have been available, if genuine, were omissions of *essential elements* of the crime of forgery, and that, therefore, the indictment did not charge a *crime.*

I had shown him that by your public statutes the "school committee" was expressly authorized to make drafts on the Treasurer of the County precisely similar to that set out in the indictment, and for the precise purpose for which that draft purported to have been made; and reasoned to the manifest and inevitable conclusion, that the authority being conferred by the public general law known to all people, and of which Courts were, compelled to take judicial cognizance, it was not necessary that it should be either averred in the indictment, or proved as a substantive fact at the trial. Admitting that it was necessary, under the Constitution and laws of the United States that the indictment should charge a *crime* in all such cases, nevertheless, the particular act constituting the *crime* need not be a *crime* under the law of the State demanding the surrender.

This argument, the Judge in his opinion, failed to notice.

I also submitted the equally plain proposition, that even if the averments contended for as essential, were necessary to constitute a valid indictment for forgery *under the provisions of your criminal code,* nevertheless, they were not essential to a valid indictment at common law for that offense, and that the indictment fully and completely described the common law crime of forgery, without any such averments. This had been ex-

---

District of Columbia court looked into the situation and decided that there was no evidence that Perry would be denied a fair trial. It still refused to extradite Perry, however, on the grounds explained herein by Merrick. *News and Observer,* November 13, 1880.

pressly decided in the State of North Carolina, by whose adjudications and laws, he was to be controlled in the premises. I referred him to the cases of *State vs. Lamb* 55 N.C., and the *State vs. Seak*, 80 N.C. Both of these cases, as you will see, are directly in point. The Judge *may* have failed to appreciate their force and application, but it would be a harsh criticism to suppose that he did.

The Chief Justice,[213] who, though a party man of strongest prejudice, has a wonderfully broad mind, and an iron-like intellectual grip, stood up noble to his duty, and much as it would, resisted all outside fanatical appeals, and yielded submissive obedience to the logical conclusions of his great big mind.

By our law Mr. Justice Wylie, who made the order discharging the fugitive on the writ of *habeas corpus*, cannot participate in hearing the case on appeal.

Our court, as a whole, is a good one, and reliable, and though there may be some possible question of the right of appeal, in such a case, I think the right exists, and am satisfied that, if the appeal is entertained, Judge Wylie's decision will, certainly, be reversed.

Your telegram, leaving it somewhat discretionary with me, as to whether the appeal should be taken or not, was received last night; and regarding it due to the dignity of the State of North Carolina, that the appeal should be prosecuted, and inferring that such was your own view, I have taken the necessary steps to have it perfected.

At the same time, I would suggest that, unless your statute of limitations bars the right to find an indictment at this time, another indictment should be found against Perry, containing every possible averment consistent with the facts, that could be supposed or imagined of any use in any possible view. I have not looked at your statute of limitations, but I presume that, even if the prosecution is barred by any general provision, there will be found a saving in the law, for the State and justice, against those who have spent the period of the limitation beyond the borders of the State, as fugitives from justice; but your prosecuting attorney must look at the law, if there be any such, *very carefully,* for Perry *returned to the State after having left it, subsequent to the commission of the crime.*

For any further information in reference to what took place

---

[213]John V. Carter. *News and Observer*, November 13, 1880.

here, you can see Mr. Bagby,[214] the States agent, who is a gentleman of most remarkable coolness, sagacity and intelligence.

You will oblige me by remitting $500 for my professional services. I employed a stenographer to take down the testimony, and will send you his bill when I receive it.

I do not know what arrangement Mr. Bagby had with Mr. Davis, and the fee indicated above has no relation to him.

A&H—GP

Thanksgiving Proclamation, November 13, 1880

Custom, Law and Gratitude alike require us, before the close of each year, to devote one day to giving thanks to Almighty God for the mercies and blessings which he has bestowed upon us. In obedience to these just and proper requirements, I, Thomas J. Jarvis, Governor of North Carolina, do issue this my proclamation, setting apart

Thursday, November 25th Inst.,
As a Day of Thanksgiving and Prayer,

and do earnestly request all the people of North Carolina properly to observe the same. Let the churches and other places of public worship be opened, and the places of business closed. Let the people, resting from their labors, spend the day devoutly, as becomes a Christian people who have been peculiarly blessed during the year with abundant harvest, tranquility and prosperity.

On that day forget not the poor, the widow and the orphan, but remember that to give to these is to lend to Him from whom all these blessings come. I especially commend to the generous consideration of the people the Oxford Orphan Asylum, and beg that they will show their gratitude for this year of unexampled plenty by suitable gifts to that noble charity.

A&H—GP

Proclamation, November 20, 1880

Whereas, The Secretary of State has, under his hand and the seal of his office, in the manner prescribed by law, certified to

---

[214]Dr. George K. Bagby, dentist and hotel proprietor of Kinston, who had been sent to Washington to claim Perry. News and Observer, November 13, 1880.

me that the following named persons received the highest number of votes for electors of President and Vice–President of the United States at the election held therefor in this State on November 2d, 1880, to–wit:

Fabius H. Busbee,[215]
>Of the Fourth Congressional District.
James M. Leach,
>Of the Fifth Congressional District.
Thomas R. Jernigan,[216]
>Of the First Congressional District.
Henry R. Bryan,[217]
>Of the Second Congressional District.
Daniel H. McLean,[218]
>Of the Third Congressional District.
William F. Green,[219]
>Of the Fourth Congressional District.
Frank C. Robbins, [220]
>Of the Fifth Congressional District.
David A. Covington,[221]
>Of the Sixth Congressional District.
Theodore F. Kluttz,[222]
>Of the Seventh Congressional District.
James M. Gudger,[223]
>Of the Eighth Congressional District.

Now, therefore, I, Thomas J. Jarvis, Governor of North Carolina, do as directed by law, issue this my Proclamation declaring

---

[215]Raleigh lawyer; United States district attorney, 1885–1889. Grant, *Alumni History of the University*, 89.

[216]Lawyer of Hertford County; member of the General Assembly, 1874; consul to Japan, 1885–1889. In 1889 he moved to Raleigh and entered the newspaper business. *Cyclopedia of the Carolinas*, II, 456–457.

[217]Lawyer and planter of New Bern; Superior Court judge, 1890–1897. Grant, *Alumni History of the University*, 81.

[218]Lawyer of Lillington; member of the General Assembly, 1876, 1898. *North Carolina Biography*, VI, 72.

[219]Lawyer and planter of Franklinton; member of the Convention of 1875; member of the General Assembly, 1883. Branson, *Directory, 1878*, 119, 122; Connor, *Manual, 1913*, 611, 879.

[220]Lawyer of Lexington. Grant, *Alumni History of the University*, 526.

[221]Lawyer of Monroe; member of the General Assembly, 1865, 1866, 1879. Dowd, *Sketches of North Carolinians*, 59–60.

[222]At first a druggist in Salisbury, Kluttz became a lawyer in 1881 and practiced the profession the remainder of his life. He was Democratic representative in Congress from 1899 to 1905. *Congressional Directory*, 1,191.

[223]Lawyer of Marshall; member of the General Assembly, 1864. Branson, *Directory for 1884*, 432; Connor, *Manual, 1913*, 517.

that the said Fabius H. Busbee, James M. Leach, Thomas R. Jernigan, Henry R. Bryan, Daniel H. McLean, William F. Green, Frank C. Robbins, David A. Covington, Theodore F. Kluttz, and James M. Gudger, have been duly elected as Electors for President and Vice-President of the United States, and I do hereby warn each of them to attend at the Capitol, in the city of Raleigh, at noon, on the Tuesday preceding the first Wednesday of December, 1880, to discharge the duties imposed upon them by law.

A&H—GLB

Thomas J. Jarvis to F. M. Simmons

Executive Department
Raleigh Nov 20th 1880

I believe there have been for some months and are now several propositions pending before the stockholders of the A&N.C. R.R. Company for the lease of said Road.[224]

I understand that a meeting will be held on the 23d inst, for the consideration of those propositions. I will thank you to ask the private stockholders, if they are prepared to do so, to take some definite action, at this meeting.

If they accept either of the propositions pending, have the proposition put in a definite shape, and forward the same to me, with a copy of the proceedings of the stockholders thereon. I hope the record of the proceedings will be so made up as to show distinctly how the vote of the private stockholders stood on the proposition accepted.

I desire you to give the private stockholders the amplest opportunity to express their wishes in any manner they may desire, but I do not wish you to cast the vote of the state so as to make the action of the stockholders final and conclusive.

To lease the Road, for twenty or thirty years is almost equivalent to selling it, so far as the present generation is concerned. I do not think it would be a proper thing to do, to make such a change in the status of the property, within forty (40) days of the meeting of the Legislature. Two thirds of this property belongs to the people of the state, and as the people will so soon assemble, through their representatives, I prefer not to make any change in the status of this property without consulting its owners.

---

[224]For the propositions still pending, see Brown, *State Movement,* 247.

Were it a long time to the meeting of the Legislature, or were there a pressing necessity for immediate action, then in that case we might be required to exercise such delegated powers as have been given us. I think you will concur with me in the propriety of submitting this matter to the Legislature, so soon to assemble; particularly as it is likely the Legislature will feel called upon to consider some matters touching the state's interests in the North Carolina Railroad.

I will submit to the Legislature, as soon as it assembles, any proposition, accepted and approved by the private stockholders, together with the action and proceedings of the Stockholder's meeting. I will thank you for any suggestions or recommendations you may desire to make touching the matter, and will also transmit the same, with the other papers, to the Legislature.

A&H—GLB

Thomas J. Jarvis to F. M. Simmons
[Telegram]

Executive Department
Raleigh Nov 23ᵈ 1880

I take it you understand my instructions to mean that no vote is to be taken that will be final. My letter is not private if you wish to use it

A&H—GP

F. M. Simmons to Thomas J. Jarvis
[Telegram]

New Bern Nov 23 1880

the meeting will act upon no proposition except a Direct proposition to Lease upon that proposition Do you wish me to withdraw from the meeting or remain in the meeting no[t] voting

A&H—GP

Thomas J. Jarvis to F. M. Simmons
[Telegram]

Nov. 23ʳᵈ 1880

Read my letter to meeting. Then if the Private Stockholders are not willing to take action as to their wishes and interest in the Road leaving the Legislature to say what shall be done with the States interest withdraw.

A&H—SAA

Thomas J. Jarvis to S. A. Ashe

Executive Department.
Raleigh, Nov. 27 1880

Col. Kenan has just spoken to me about the proposed lease of the A&NC—R.R. and the withdrawal of the States proxy from the meeting.[225]

Last Saturday I wrote the States proxy a letter which was put upon my letter Book which sets out my position in full.

I would be glad for you to see this letter before you publish anything on the Subject. I will have it copied for you at any time you may desire it.

A&H—GP

Garland Sevier Ferguson[226] to Thomas J. Jarvis

Waynesville, N.C.
December 1st 1880

There is now pending in the Superior Court of Buncombe County, a bill of Indictment against Milton S. Littlefield & others for conspiracy &. for cheating and defrauding the State, in the Western Division of the Western N.C.R. Road.[227] Some days since I directed the Clerk of Buncombe Court to send me a copy

---

[225]At the New Bern meeting of the stockholders of the Atlantic and North Carolina Railroad, F. M. Simmons read Jarvis' letter of November 20 pertaining to leasing the railroad, and then he withdrew as instructed. With the withdrawal of the state's proxy, a quorum of the votes was not present. Thereupon the private stockholders resolved in favor of accepting the proposition to lease submitted by R. R. Bridgers (see Jarvis to Simmons, June 21, 1880, *n.* 166, in this volume). Nothing more was then done by the stockholders for several months. Brown, *State Movement,* 247–248; *News and Observer,* November 27 and 28, 1880; *Proceedings of the Occasional Meeting of the Stockholders of the Atlantic and North Carolina Rail Road Company, 1880, passim.*

[226]Lawyer of Waynesville; member of the General Assembly, 1876; Superior Court judge, 1903–1918. *North Carolina Biography,* V, 183–184.

[227]For a copy of this and other similar bills of indictments against Littlefield and his conspirators, see Governors' Papers. Not included in this volume.

of the bill for my inspection and examination When I have examined it I desire to have a copy of the record forwarded you to the end that you may make a requisition on the Gov. of Florida for the defendant Littlefield and I hope to have your cooperation in bringing the defendant to trial I am informed that a former Gov. of North Carolina (Caldwell) made a requisition on the then Gov. of Florida for the surrender of Littlefield and that the Gov. of Florida refused to have him arrested and surrendered to the authorities of North Carolina. I hope our State will now meet with better treatment at the hands of the Gov. of Florida—anyway I believe it Our duty to use all the means in our power to secure the trial of the defendant and if guilty his conviction and punishment

I will be pleased to have your views in regard to the matter.

A&H—GLB

Thomas J. Jarvis to G. S. Ferguson

Executive Department
Raleigh Dec 6th 1880

I am just in receipt of yours of the 1st and to show you how I concur with you I will mention briefly what I have already done.

In May 1879, I made a requisition upon the Gov of Florida for the rendition of Littlefield upon a Bill of Indictment now pending against him in Wake County. The Governor issued his warrant for the arrest of Littlefield but he was immediately released upon a writ of Habeas Corpus by a Radical Judge by the name of Archibald.

I then procured a copy of the Indictment against him in Haywood and Madison and Buncombe and made a requisition upon the Governor of Florida upon these indictments. The Governor refused to issue his warrant for his arrest and so I had to stop. I sent messengers to Florida both times and it cost the state considerable.

It is useless to send again to Florida. I hope we may have better luck in some other state. I will gladly second any effort you may make to bring Littlefield to trial.

A&H—GP

Henry J. Rogers to Thomas J. Jarvis

Dec. 7, 1880

The undersigned as Vice President of the Seaboard & Raleigh Rail Road Company, the President being deceased and his successor not yet elected, Respectfully begs leave to report.

1st The Stock of said company is by charter One Million of Dollars, with liberty to increase the same to Two Millions five Hundred thousand dollars.

2nd The debts of the Company amount to about Sixteen Thousand dollars, all being a lien debt on their purchase of the Williamston and Tarboro Rail Road

3rd The Cost of Construction of that portion of our line forming the Williamston and Tarboro Rail Road is as far as I am able to ascertain from the reports of the old Company about Two Hundred & fifty thousand dollars. Some Six thousand dollars addition have been expended by us in Surveys and obtaining rights of way.

4th The length of Road will be about one Hundred Miles exclusive of branches—

5th Of our line about Thirty three (33) miles are graded, but will need some dressing up to make it in proper shape for super–structure—

6th Seven and half (7½) miles 40# rail is now on the road. This however will have to be re–laid, as most of the crossties must be replaced.

7th Branch to Greenville will be about Sixteen (16) miles, the location not being yet decided on—Branch to Wilson, about nine (9) miles—

8th Length of Side track about one third (⅓) of a mile—All the Bridges are Tressle, and all in fair order except the one at Tarboro—

Negotiations are now in progress looking to an early completion of the road and I have every reason to believe that operations will begin early in January next—

A&H—GP

Edward Morse Nadal[228] *to Thomas J. Jarvis*

Wilson, N.C., Dec 9 1880

I write ask you to call the attention of the Legislature to the necessity of a law to regulate the sale of poisons in the State.

As you know, now, anybody can keep & sell poisons the same as calico to anybody who wishes to purchase.

The North Carolina Pharmaceutical Association at its last meeting adopted the draft of a bill to be presented to the Legislature at its next session, a copy of which I mail to you to–day, regulating the practice of Pharmacy in the state.[229]

I think, if you approve the main features of the bill, and will mention in your message to the Legislature the need and absolute necessity of confining the sale of poisons to qualified and licensed persons only, as the bill provides that it will aid us greatly in the accomplishment of our purpose.

Hoping and believing that you see the need of a law on the subject and will aid in the way you think best,

A&H—GLB

Proclamation, Dec. 11, 1880

Executive Department
Raleigh

Whereas the General Assembly did, at its session of 1879, propose Amendments to the Constitution as follows to wit.

Amend Section 6 Article 1. by adding to the end thereof the following.

"Nor shall the General Assembly assume or pay, or authorize the collection of any tax to pay, either directly or indirectly, expressed or implied any debt or bond incurred or issued by authority of the Convention of the year 1868, nor any debt or bond incurred or issued by the Legislature of the year 1868, either at

---

[228]Druggist and businessman of Wilson, and originator and first president of the North Carolina Pharmaceutical Association. J. G. Beard, "Edward Morse Nadal," *Carolina Journal of Pharmacy,* VIII (July, 1927), 263, hereinafter cited as Beard, "Edward Morse Nadal."

[229]Such a law was enacted on March 12, 1881. *Laws of North Carolina, 1881,* c. 355. For the formative years of the North Carolina Pharmaceutical Association, see Alice Noble, *The School of Pharmacy of the University of North Carolina, A History* (Chapel Hill: The University of North Carolina Press, 1961), 4–7, hereinafter cited as Noble, *The School of Pharmacy.*

special session of the year 1868, or at its regular session of the years 1868 and 1869, and 1869 and 1870, except the bonds issued to fund the interest on the old debts of the state, unless the proposing to pay the same shall have first been submitted to the people and by them ratified by the vote of a majority of all the qualified voters of the state at a regular election held for that purpose."[230]

Amend Section 10 Art XI by striking out all of said section and inserting in lieu thereof the following: "The General Assembly may provide that the indigent deaf mutes, blind and insane of the state shall be cared for at the charge of the state."[231]

And whereas said amendments were submitted to the qualified voters of the state at an election held at the several polling places on the 2[d] day of November 1880.

And whereas returns of the votes cast thereon at said election for and against said proposed amendments were duly made to the Chief Justice of the Supreme Court of the State[232] and were by him compared and counted in my presence on the 8th day of November 1880, in accordance with law:

And whereas it appears by said count certified to by the Chief Justice, whose certificate is now on file in this office, that there were cast for the first of said Amendments one hundred seventeen thousand three hundred and eighty eight (117.388) votes, and against it, five thousand four hundred and fifty eight (5458) the majority in favor of said amendment being one hundred and eleven thousand nine hundred and thirty (111.930) votes; and for the other of said amendments, there were cast eighty seven thousand one hundred and sixty three (87.163) votes, and against is, seventy thousand four hundred and fifty nine (70.459) votes, the majority in favor of said amendment being sixteen thousand seven hundred and four (16.704) votes:

Now therefore I, Thomas J. Jarvis Governor of North Carolina do, by authority of law, issue this my Proclamation and do proclaim that said proposed Amendments having been duly

---

[230]For the cause of this amendment, see Message to the General Assembly, March 15, 1880, n. 78, in this volume.

[231]The section had previously read "The General Assembly shall provide that all the deaf mutes. . . ." This amendment of 1880 was part of Jarvis' retrenchment program. See also Jarvis to Craven, February 22, 1879, n. 39, in this volume.

[232]William Nathan Harrell Smith, prominent political figure of Murfreesboro; member of the General Assembly, 1840, 1848, 1865; representative of the American party to Congress, 1859–1861; member of the Confederate Congress, 1861–1865; Chief Justice of the state Supreme Court, 1878–1889. Dictionary of American Biography, XVII, 366.

adopted by a majority of the qualified voters of the State have become apart of the constitution of the State of North Carolina.

Thomas J. Jarvis to G. W. McCrary

Executive Department
Raleigh Dec 22ᵈ 1880

Col John D. Whitford, President of the Atlantic and North Carolina Rail Road Company, will explain to you in person, that the Government has in possession at Fort Macon some thirty or more tons of Rail Road iron, belong[ing] to his Company.

As the Fort is practically abandoned, and these Rails are no further us[e] to the Government, I trust you will allow him to remove them, and place them along his Road, where they are much needed.

Thomas J. Jarvis to C. W. McLean

Executive Department,
Raleigh, Dec. 24ᵗʰ, 1880.

I am glad to hear of your efforts in the cause of immigration to this State.[233] It is a matter, in which I, as Governor of the State, take a deep interest, and will always be ready to encourage and promote. We want a steady, industrious people to come among us, and we will receive them cordially, and try to make their new homes among us, pleasant. The more capital they can bring with them, the better we will like it; but we prefer a sober, working man, without a penny, to an idler, with money.

There are vast resources here, that needs population and labor to develop. Among these, may be mentioned the fertile body of land, near Haverlock, on the A.&N.C.R.R., under your control, and of which you are endeavoring to make a Holland settlement. If the people, in the crowded cities in this and the old country, only could really appreciate our splendid climate, fertile soil, great resources of wealth and our generous, kind people, it would not be necessary to persuade them to come to

---

[233]For a partial explanation of this letter, see McLean to Jarvis, August 10, 1880, in this volume.

North Carolina;—they would come of their own accord. Take the splendid trucking country along the line of the A.&N.C.R.R. —with it, cheap and easy transportation facilities. If it and its advantages were only known to the truckers around Philadelphia, it would not be necessary to persuade them to come to it.— Can't you go out among them and induce some of them to come down and examine for themselves? Col. Pope will arrange cheap travel for them.

Hoping you may have success in an enterprise so valuable to the State, I am

UNC—UP

Thomas J. Jarvis to K. P. Battle

Executive Department
Raleigh, Dec 25 1880

In my message I want to say something about the University and the enclosed is a rough draft of what I have written. I am willing to add to or take from as you may desire. I can stand strong doctrine as I have taken a bold stand for education and burnt all the bridges behind me. Make such changes as you desire and return as soon as you can. Suppose you put in the number of boys that have attended the University free of charge for tuition since it was reopened. I will thank you for a strong paper of two or three pages on the University and I will report it. Give me freely any suggestions you may desire.

A&H—GP

Joseph B. Cherry[234] to Thomas J. Jarvis

Windsor, N.C.
27th Dec 1880

I send with this note, my report[235] of the State's Proxy in the A[lbemarle] & Chesapeake C[anal] Company. I have been sick, quite sick, & am now just up, or I would have remitted it sooner. You will see Governor, that I have touched upon some new

---

[234]Lawyer and planter of Windsor; member of the General Assembly, 1848–1858. Branson, *Directory for 1884*, 140; Connor, *Manual, 1913*, 503–504.

[235]"Deposit of the State Proxy in the Albemarle and Chesapeake Canal Company," *Public Documents, 1881*, No. 16.

thoughts (not to you) about our Inland navigation. I am a great advocate for this kind of Improvement in our navigation— Our friends of the Canal Company, would be pleased to see this report printed: It would perhaps be indelicate in me to ask you to aid us, so that the members of the Legislature might read it. You must attribute any thing that may look to be *too familiar* with you, to my strong friendship for you as a man, & as the Governor of our State, by my vote & all I could do for you— I hope to see you soon—

A&H—GP

J. A. Gray to Thomas J. Jarvis

Greensboro, N.C., Dec. 30th 1880

I hand you herewith a report[236] of the Condition of The C.F.& Y.V.Ry. Co. as required in Chapter 202 Laws of 1874-75. Our fiscal year closes March 1st. and all our accounts are made up to that date, consequently this report shows our condition at that time.

LETTERS FOR 1881

Thomas J. Jarvis to the General Assembly, January 5, 1881[1]

Gentlemen of the Senate and House of Representatives:

No general assembly has convened in the state for the last twenty years under such favorable auspices as those which greet your coming. As you journeyed from your homes to the capital, evidences of thrift and prosperity were seen in country and in town. During the year which has just closed abundant harvests and remunerative prices have blessed the labors of the husbandman; the mechanic and the laborer of every kind have worked with hope and energy, and have seen their anticipations of successful returns fully realized. Trade and business of every description have exhibited a healthy, steady increase. The despondency that for years has weighed upon our people like a pall, oppressing their energies, and retarding their progress, has

---

[236]Governors' Papers. Report not included in this volume.
[1]"Governor's Message," *Public Documents, 1881*, No. 1.

been lifted up, and all begin the new year with a will and a faith that must succeed.

Nowhere in the state has there been any disorder, riot or domestic violence, but everywhere the laws have been respected.

The two races are working together in peace and harmony, with increasing respect for each other. The colored population, I am glad to say, are becoming more industrious and thrifty. Many of them are property owners and tax payers. They seem to be learning the important lesson that they have nothing to rely upon but their own labor. I have tried, on every opportune occasion, to impress this lesson upon them, and to assure them of the sympathy and hearty co-operation of the white race in their efforts to make themselves good and useful citizens. They have held during the past two years, in the city of Raleigh, two industrial exhibitions that were exceedingly creditable to them. I attended both of these exhibitions, and made short addresses, and was glad to see the efforts of the colored race in this direction found so much favor and encouragement among the whites. I regard it as an imperative duty, from which the whites cannot escape, if they would, to see that in all things full and exact justice is done the blacks, and that they are not left alone to work out their own destiny. They are entitled, by many binding considerations, to receive aid and encouragement from the whites in their effort to be better men and women, and I have no doubt will receive it.

In compliance with the law and custom, I herewith transmit the reports of the heads of the several departments of the state government, the agricultural department, the board of internal improvements and the heads of the various charitable and penal institutions. From these reports you will learn, in detail, much of the operation of the state government and the different interests under its control for the past two years, and I beg that you will give to each of them your close attention and study. You will find the information they contain of much value to you in the discharge of your important duties.

By reference to the Auditor's[2] and Treasurer's reports, you

---

[2]Samuel Leonidas Love of Haywood County. Though a practicing physician, Love had wide experience in public service, serving in the General Assembly from 1856 to 1864, as member of the Constitutional Convention of 1875, and as state auditor from 1876 to 1881. Tomlinson, *Sketch–book,* 142.

will see that the total receipts for the fiscal year ending September 30th, 1880, were $546,996.04

Total disbursements........ 492,720.33

Balance in favor of receipts........$ 54,275.71

If all the expenses incurred in the quarter ending September 30th had been paid in that quarter, the balance in hand would not have been so great. It is likely, however, that as great an amount will not be paid in the quarter ending September 30th, 1881, so that this need not alter any estimate. The persistent effort of Dr. Worth, for ten years, to get our state debt adjusted has had its reward. Under the act to compromise and commute the state debt, passed at the session of 1879, he has taken up the old bonds of the state to January 1st, 1881, as follows:

Forty per cent. class $3,579,500

Twenty–five per cent. class 1,962,045

Fifteen per cent. class 1,928,700

Total $7,470,245

He has issued in lieu of these new four per cent. bonds of the state, to the amount of $2,211,616, upon which the interest was promptly paid on the 1st of January. The old bonds taken up were recorded as required by law, and burned in my presence.

A New Building for a Supreme Court Room

There is one matter in the excellent report of the able secretary of state to which I desire to direct your attention especially. On entering the office of the secretary of state, one can see at a glance its crowded condition, and how insufficient the room is for the uses to which it is necessarily put. It is apparent there must be more room provided in which to keep the records of the office, or injury and their loss are inevitable. Some of the most valuable and oldest records of the state have only recently been rescued from oblivion, in a heap of old papers in the arsenal, by the prolonged and continued search of Col. Saunders. Shall they again be cast away, or be put in a place where they will be perpetually preserved? So, too, with the state library. It is filled to overflowing with valuable books, which, for want of room, cannot be properly numbered, catalogued and placed upon shelves ready for inspection. The accummulation of records in the supreme court clerk's office has been so great that there is scarcely room for more. I beg that you will visit and inspect all three of these rooms. I urge, as a remedy for the crowded condition of these rooms, that you pass an act appointing five commissioners to select a site for a new building, to be called the "Supreme Court Building," with power to erect thereon one in every way suitable. The southeast corner of the capitol square would, in my opinion, be an excellent location; but if it is deemed best by your honorable body not to encumber Union square, then the commission should have the power to build on Nash square or some other suitable place. The lower floor of this building should be fitted up and used for the supreme court room and library, the clerk's and attorney general's offices, a consultation room for the judges, and other necessary rooms. The second floor should be fitted up in good style for a state library, and occupied for that purpose. The rooms now occupied by the supreme court and the clerk could then be given to the auditor, and the room now occupied by the auditor to the secretary of state. The room now used by the state library should be set apart as the repository of the old and valuable records of the state, and a law passed requiring them to be placed therein, and forbidding them, under heavy penalties, from ever being removed therefrom. Some of them are now so mutilated that it is absolutely necessary that they be printed while it is yet possible to decipher them. I suggest that the trustees of the library be allowed to do this and pay for the same out of the library fund. I call your attention to the librarian's[3] excellent report.

A New Governor's Mansion.

Burke square, northeast of the capitol, belongs to the state, and, in my opinion, is the most desirable location for a governor's mansion that can be procured upon any reasonable terms. I urge that this commission be authorized to erect on said square a new and suitable mansion for the governor. I do not know that I shall care to occupy it myself, but I think the state, by all means, ought to have such a building. I have a pride in seeing one erected, and am anxious to see it done during my administration, and ready for my successor.

Both of these buildings can be built at very little cost to the tax–payers of the state, if you will authorize the commissioners to sell the property known as the "Old Mansion," and Moore

---

[3]Sherwood Haywood of Raleigh. After studying law at Columbia Law School in New York, he returned to Raleigh and served as state librarian from 1875 to 1881, when he resigned his position and began the practice of law in Raleigh. Tomlinson, *Sketch–book*, 143.

The Yarborough House, opened in 1852, under the proprietorship of Edward Marshall Yarborough, served as the residence of Governors Zebulon B. Vance and Thomas Jordan Jarvis during their terms in office. It was the unofficial political and social center of the state in the period when there was no executive mansion and for many years afterward was considered as the "third house" of state government. It was destroyed by fire in 1928.
(Photograph from files of the State Department of Archives and History.)

square, now used by the city merchants as a cotton yard, and to draw from the treasurer the seventeen thousand dollars for which some out–lying lots belonging to the state were sold some three years ago to build a governor's mansion. The commissioners should have power to utilize the convict labor, and any material that can be made at the penitentiary, and to get stone from the quarry belonging to the state. With these resources, the commissioners can, without drawing much money from the treasury, erect these two buildings, so much needed, and which will be ornaments to the state and city.

Education

The report of the excellent superintendent of public instruction will give the condition of the schools and their work. The two normal schools established by the legislature of 1876–'77 have proven a decided success. The appropriation for each of these schools should be increased, if possible. They are doing a fine work in preparing and qualifying teachers for our common schools, in which I have been gratified to notice recently an increasing interest among the press and the people. Education I regard as the great interest of the state, an interest too great to be disposed of by a few paragraphs in a message. But while I may avail myself of another occasion to address you on this subject, I cannot now dismiss it without pleading with you for more money for the children. In the discussions I have seen in the papers, the system has been mainly the topic. Very little has been said about the money to carry on the system. While one system may be better than another, the most perfect is not worth the paper on which it is written without money to build school houses and pay teachers. Money is, and must be, the heart and life of every system. While I hope to see you make the system as perfect as possible, I beg that you will not forget to provide the money. This can only be done by taxation. Will you impose it? I think the people will approve it. The tax for schools is now only eight and a third cents on the one hundred dollars' worth of property, and twenty–five cents on the poll. Three times that on each would not be burdensome but wise legislation. The salary of the superintendent of public instruction should be largely increased, and I trust you will do this before the time comes for the gentleman elected to that position to qualify. Instead of degrading this very important office into a mere clerkship, as has been the case, it should be dignified and elevated to a rank so high that it will command at all times the best talent of the state.

It may not always be the case that a thoroughly capable and efficient officer can be found, like the present faithful incumbent, to make the sacrifices he does for the cause of education, in remaining here on such an inadequate salary. Nor can he, well qualified as he is, or any other man, without private fortune at his command, perform all the functions of the office, or the most important of them, under existing law.

The act of 1879 proposes to pay only fifteen hundred dollars a year to him who is charged with the great responsibility of superintending the education of four hundred and fifty thousand children. Then, as if to belittle and cripple the office still further, the same act declares "he shall not be allowed any sum for traveling expenses." Nothing is clearer to my mind than that the superintendent of public instruction ought to go out in the different sections of the state and address the people, inspect the schools, instruct the teachers and encourage the children. This, indeed, and much more, the law requires him to do, as will be seen by reference to Battle's Revisal, chapter 78. He cannot do it on his present salary and pay his own expenses.

The University

This noble institution is resuming her wonted place of usefulness and renown. But the trustees and faculty are endeavoring to educate so many young men, who are not able to pay any tuition fees, that the institution is laboring under financial embarrassments. There were in attendance at the session just closed one hundred and sixty-six students, of whom eighty-nine paid no tuition. Since the reopening, the university has given tuition free of charge, each year, to a like proportion of the students. A small annual appropriation of seven thousand five hundred dollars would relieve its embarrassments, and greatly enhance its usefulness. Upon the reorganization of the university in 1875, contributions were made by friends of the institution, out of their own private means, to the amount of about twenty thousand dollars, the greater part of which was used in repairs upon the buildings, all of which belong to the state.

The constitution of the state places the responsibility of the maintenance and management of the university on the general assembly. By article IX, section 7, "The general assembly shall provide that the benefits of the university, as far as practicable, be extended to the youth of the state free of charge for tuition." Little has been done in carrying into effect this mandate of the fundamental law. The state, it is true, pays to the university the interest on $125,000 of the land scrip fund received from the United States, which was invested chiefly in special tax bonds by a former board of trustees, and lost;[4] but the state was bound, by express contract, to make good this loss, or become liable to repay the whole amount to the United States. Moreover, in consideration of this, the university binds itself to receive from each county one student, who is recommended by the county commissioners, and certified to be unable to defray his own charges. This provision has seriously diminished the number of paying students. The university has been in the habit, in addition to this, of receiving all indigent young men of good character free of charge for tuition. I know that the institution is doing good work. Its faculty are able and zealous. They are educating large numbers of worthy young men, who, without this great benefaction, would grow up in ignorance. The number should not be curtailed but increased. I respectfully recommend that each county shall be allowed to send to the university two beneficiary students, instead of one, and that in consideration of this an additional seven thousand five hundred dollars be appropriated annually to the institution. With this amount the trustees could enlarge the faculty, and go forward in its liberal and beneficent course.

The normal school work of the university has been productive of great good. Thus far about eight hundred teachers of the state have attended the sessions and profited by the instructions of its skilled experts in their noble art. The president and professors of the university have, without compensation, co–operated with the normal school professors, and thus aided in uniting, to a greater extent than ever before, the university with the schools of the state.

Art. IX, sec. 14, provides that "as soon as practicable, after the adoption of this constitution, the general assembly shall establish and maintain, in connection with the university, a de-

---

[4]North Carolina had received 240,000 acres of land under the Land Grant Act of 1862, and the State Board of Education had sold this land at 50¢ an acre. All but $6,000 of the proceeds had been invested in special tax bonds. For the full story, see Battle, *History of the University*, II, 9–16.

partment of agriculture, of mechanics, of mining, and of normal instruction." By giving the aid I have mentioned, the general assembly will enable the trustees of the university to make greater progress in carrying out this mandate, which, it will be noticed, is imperative. They have done all they possibly could with the means placed in their hands. They have, as required by the land scrip act of 1862, used the $7,500 per annum paid them in "teaching such branches of learning as are related to agriculture and the mechanic arts, without excluding other scientific and classical studies." With the $2,000 per annum for normal school purposes, they have established a normal school, which has accomplished so much for the cause of education that our sister states of Virginia and South Carolina have copied their example. This was done without diverting a cent of the appropriations to the support of the other departments of the university. They have shown themselves worthy to be entrusted with greater means, in order to enable them to make a further advance towards realizing the idea of the sagacious framers of the constitution of 1776, viz: making the university an institution "where *all* useful learning shall be duly encouraged and promoted."

The State Board of Education

This board has in the hands of Treasurer Worth $91,500 in United States four per cent. bonds, derived from investments of fines, forfeitures and penalties, and the entries of vacant lands. The law required, and still requires, these investments to be made in United States bonds. These bonds are now worth one hundred and twelve cents in the dollars; so the $91,500 will bring $102,480. This fund, invested in the new four per cent. state bonds, which are worth, say, ninety cents in the dollar, will bring about $114,000, upon which the same rate of interest will be paid. I ask you to authorize the board to make this change in the investment, and I suggest that all laws requiring investments or deposits to be made in the new state four per cent. bonds.

Swamp Lands

There are large bodies of swamp lands belonging to the board of education, which, under the present laws, are not subject to entry and grant like other vacant lands, or to sale in any way. Some of these lands if cleared and well drained, would be valuable, while others are of less value. They are all liable to be pillaged by the public, and, so long as they remain as they are, can never yield anything to the state. I suggest that you fix a price upon these lands and make them subject to entry and grant like other vacant lands. The proceeds of the entry of all vacant lands, now liable to grant, goes by law to the educational fund, and so should the proceeds of swamp lands. I have never been able to appreciate the wisdom of making lands not swamp lands, subject to entry and grant, and swamp lands not so subject. It is true the title to one is in the state, and the other in the board of education, but it is but the state after all. The educational interest of the state will never stand in greater need of the help that the sale of these lands can give than now. These lands have lain idle in the hands of the board of education for half a century and more, yielding nothing to any one. It is better, in my opinion, that they pass into hands that will reclaim them, develop them, and make them pay taxes.

The Charitable and Penal Institutions

These institutions have been well managed by those in charge of them, as I believe; but you cannot examine into them too closely yourselves. They absorb one–half the taxes collected out of the people, and perform, within their respective spheres, important work for the state, for society and humanity. They occupy no inconsiderable place in the machinery of the state government, and the interests they have in charge are often the most difficult to deal with. Crime in all its degrees, insanity in all its forms, and the want of sight, speech and hearing in all its sorrowfulness, are the subjects they grapple with, to punish, to cure or to ameliorate. You are to make the laws and furnish the means by which this work is to be done. Too much thought and care cannot be given to the responsible part you have to take in their policy and management.

Penitentiary

There has been much more done on the walls and buildings of the penitentiary since the adjournment of the legislature in 1879, considering the scarcity of means at the command of the directors. I advise that you make as large an appropriation for the completion of the building as, in your wisdom, you deem proper. It is the design of the directors to make the institution self-sustaining by employing such of the convicts as have to be kept within its walls at some useful trade, but this cannot be done until suitable buildings for that purpose are erected. Impressed with the importance of expediting the work on the building as rapidly as possible, the treasurer, with my advice, permitted the directors to use the receipts from the hire of convicts on the Western North Carolina railroad for the support of the convicts and the furtherance of the work on the walls and buildings. This fund was not specifically appropriated to any purpose, but has been treated by the treasurer as a part of the receipts of the labor of the penitentiary, like the hire of any other convicts. By the report of the board you will see that the entire number of convicts on the 30th day of October, was nine hundred and ninety-three, which is considerably less than was in custody at the close of any one year for the last three. I do most earnestly hope that the number will continue to diminish. The most effective way to help on this diminution is to make punishment for crime swift and certain. Evil-doers must understand that while the law will not permit cruelty in officials, it will not tolerate idleness in convicts, but will require and enforce hard, constant work. They must be taught the lesson and driven by experience to learn it, that it is easier to live at home by honest labor than in the penitentiary by enforced laber.

The Insane Asylum

The asylum at Raleigh has lived for the past two years within the annual appropriation. The patients have been well cared for, but the buildings have not had all needful repairs. This institution has been and is now crowded to overflowing, with one hundred and ninety or more applications still on file for admission. There is scarcely a week that I do not have a painful appeal in person or by letter, begging for the admission of a friend or relative into the asylum. The obligation to provide for the safety, comfort and proper treatment of these unfortunate people is so weighty that nothing can excuse its longer neglect. I beg that you will make a sufficient appropriation to complete at once the wing and main building of the asylum at Morganton, so that it can be occupied by the insane not now provided for, who are the objects of the charity and care of the state. By reference to the report of the commissioners and the architect,[5] which is herewith sent, it will be seen that to prepare the wing and main building for the reception and custody of patients, will require for construction eighty thousand dollars, and for furniture twenty thousand. These reports, you will find, contain full information concerning the work done and to be done, and I beg that you will examine them closely. If you make this appropriation, then it will be necessary for you to make suitable laws for its opening and government.

The Colored Asylum

The colored asylum at Goldsboro is now open and has in it ninety-one patients. This building was erected probably with as little cost as any public building in the state, and by pushing the work rapidly on the main building and south wing, the commissioners were able to have it ready for use by the 1st of August last. The act passed for its creation provided for its opening, but when it was ready for use a question arose as to the fund applicable to that purpose. After consulting with the treasurer, we found that the tax levied by the legislature of 1879, for the support of the insane, would raise a fund in excess of the appropriation for the asylum at Raleigh, and as the act creating the Goldsboro asylum required all the colored patients to be removed from the Raleigh to the Goldsboro asylum, we determined to use this excess in the support of the colored insane, and consequently ordered the asylum to be opened on the 1st day of August. The expenditures have been economical, and vouchers are on file with the treasurer for the same. This institution needs some legislation for its management. I call your special attention to the report of the commissioners, and the necessity for an additional appropriation of twenty thousand dollars to complete the north wing. When the wing is completed, the building, it is thought will be sufficient to accommodate the colored insane of the state. It will be both humane and prudent to make the appropriation, and thus relieve the counties as speedily as possible of the ex-

[5]Samuel Sloan of Philadelphia, who also designed two of the buildings of the University of North Carolina. Archibald Henderson, *The Campus of the First State University* (Chapel Hill: The University of North Carolina Press, 1949), 198, 199, 249, hereinafter cited as Henderson, *Campus of the University*.

In March, 1875, the legislature appropriated $10,000 for the establishment at the Marine Hospital building, Wilmington, of a branch asylum for the Negro insane. The law stated no more Negro insane should be received at the Raleigh asylum and those already there should be removed to Wilmington. Later legislation indicated this plan was not followed. An 1877 appropriation of $20,000 and the unexpended appropriation of the previous legislature were designated for the establishment and support of an institution at some site in the state; provision was made for seven commissioners to procure a suitable building by purchase, donation, or "superintending erection thereof . . ." An appropriation of $20,000 was made in 1879 for additional construction at the Negro insane asylum near Goldsboro. The Eastern State Hospital was incorporated in 1881; in 1883 a $25,000 appropriation was made for completing and furnishing a new wing. The legislature of 1883 also suggested that the colored race should have some representation in the appointment of directors for the asylum.

The various divisions of the agriculture department were combined and located in one building in 1881. Governor Jarvis instigated purchase of the old National Hotel, which had formerly operated under the names of the Eagle and Guion hotels, to house the newly unified department. Photographs courtesy of the North Carolina State Department of Agriculture.

pense and care of these persons. Whatever legislation is perfected for the custody and care of the insane of the state must embrace the government of the asylum at Morganton, at Raleigh and at Goldsboro, and I would advise that it all be codified into one act. Whether these three institutions shall all be under one board of directors, chosen from different parts of the state, or whether each shall be under the exclusive control of a local board, is an important question for you to consider. My opinion is, after considerable thought and investigation, that it will be better for each institution to have its own local board, and I so advise.

In this connection I will call your attention to section 7 of article XI of the constitution, and to chapter 93 of Battle's Revisal, on "Public Charities," passed in pursuance thereto. The requirements of this provision, of both the constitution and the statute, are still in force, but are not complied with. An efficient board of public charities, composed chiefly of physicians, could be made of great service in visiting and inspecting the penal and charitable institutions of the state, and especially in looking into their sanitary condition, and medical treatment of the inmates.

The adoption of the amendment to the constitution concerning the insane, the deaf and dumb and the blind, renders necessary some legislation determining who shall and who shall not be considered indigent. After you have fixed the rule, I advise that you require all indigent applicants to be received first, and that no pay patient shall be admitted till all the indigent have been provided for.

The Institution for the Deaf and Dumb and the Blind

This well managed institution needs no legislation that I am aware of, except the appropriation for its support, which need not exceed, the directors say, thirty-four thousand dollars a year.

Department of Agriculture

This department, although in its incipiency, is doing a good work for the state, in the development of her resources, and in fostering her great agricultural interests. Much has been done to inaugurate and perfect a methodical system of immigration.

We are beginning to reap the fruits of these labors, and we hope for a large yield in the future. In the matter of immigration, the attention of the department has been turned chiefly to

England, with a view of inducing the small farmers of that over-crowded country to seek homes in North Carolina. A few have already done so, and are well pleased with the change. Many more are expected to come during this year. Col. A. Pope, the general passenger agent of the Wilmington and Weldon rail-road, the Raleigh and Gaston railroad, the Richmond and Dan-ville railroad, the North Carolina railroad, the Northwestern North Carolina railroad, and the Raleigh and Augusta Air-line railroad, with the approval of these companies, has recently en-tered into active co-operation with the board in its efforts to promote immigration. We can but hope for good results from the co–operation of so intelligent and energetic a man as Col. Pope, with such powerful aids as these lines of railway in this great work. The details of the labors of the board in this work and the plans and purposes of Col. Pope are elaborated more fully in the report of the board, to which I refer you.

If nothing else has been done, the protection given to the farmers against worthless fertilizers, has more than ten–fold over compensated for the labor and expenses of the department. Before this department was established, there were many tons of stuff sold in the state called fertilizers, which were not worth the cost of transportation. This imposition cannot be renewed so long as the department does its duty and the farmers rely upon the analyses made by the learned chemists employed by the board.

The new map of the state, which will be ready for exhibition and distribution before your adjournment, has cost the state geologist years of labor and research, but it is so far superior to any ever before published that its excellence will compensate for the delay, labor and expense, in its publication. He has at-tained a degree of accuracy and perfection that will render an-other survey and map of the state unnecessary for many years to come. His second volume of the geological report will also be ready for distribution before your adjournment, and will con-tain much valuable information about the state, her wealth and resources, never before published or known. The expense of the completion and publication of this map and report has been borne entirely, for the last two years, by the agricultural de-partment, and in estimating the benefits of this department, a just share of the benefits of these valuable works should be given to it.

As the whole expense of the geological work, under the laws

of 1879, chapter 50, has to be paid by the agricultural department, I beg to suggest that the second section of said chapter be repealed, and the board of agriculture authorized to select the geologist, as they do the commissioner and the chemist. I further advise that the board be authorized, out of the funds of the department, and with the use of convict labor, and material furnished by the penitentiary, to put up on Nash square, or such other place as you may direct, an agricultural building for the use of the department. The rents paid by this department amount to nine hundred dollars a year. The geological museum is probably one of the most extensive and valuable in any state of the union. This museum is much visited by persons in search of information concerning the wealth and resources of the state, and here they find specimens from nearly every county to interest and instruct them. This valuable collection ought to be permanently located in a building belonging to the state, known as the "Agricultural Building," where it can be safely preserved. And besides it is but meet and proper that there should be at the capitol a handsome building dedicated to the great agricultural interests of the state, so that when those engaged in this pursuit visit the capital they may know there is a place where they can learn something of the agriculture and resources of all sections of their state.

The Supreme Court

The supreme court judges are greatly over-worked. It is almost impossible for the present number to do the work that goes into that court. They certainly cannot give to the cases the thought and patient investigation they desire. For this there are two remedies—one, to increase the number of judges; and the other, to so regulate appeals as to diminish the work to be done. Since the abolition of the tax fee[6] the cost of taking a case to the supreme court has been so insignificant that the most trivial cases, as I am informed, are taken up; many, indeed, simply to delay execution. It would give considerable relief to the judges, I am advised, if they had the power to employ a man to attend upon them in their consultations to get the books they require, and to hunt up the references. This help can be given them with-

[6]In 1879 the General Assembly ordered that the "clerk of the supreme and superior courts of the State shall not include or charge in any bill of costs any attorneys' fee in any civil suit hereafter determined in any court of the State. . . ." *Laws of North Carolina, 1879,* c. 41.

out the cost of a penny to the state treasury, by imposing a tax fee of ten dollars on all appeals in all civil cases, and five dollars in all criminal cases for the benefit of the supreme court library. This person should be the supreme court librarian, and required to give bond for the custody and safety of the books. He should be required to make and keep a complete catalogue of all the books belonging to the library, open at all times to the inspection of the judges, and at all times subject to their control and orders. I advise that you give them this assistance, impose this tax fee for the use of the library, and restore the twenty-dollar attorney's tax fee. This, in my opinion, will greatly reduce the work of the court, without doing injustice to any one. The costs now in a case are about nine dollars. They are less than they frequently are in the court of a justice of the peace. Fifty dollars—twenty for the library, twenty for attorney's [*sic*] fee, and ten for other costs—would not be unreasonable, with the law still in force that allows the poor to sue in *forma pauperis*.

Even if you should determine to submit an amendment to the constitution to increase the number of judges, then some such help as I have suggested will be necessary, for it will be two years before the increase, if adopted, can go into effect.

The Superior Courts

The dockets of the superior courts in many of the large counties are so crowded that in some of them it is almost impossible to get a civil case trial without a special term. The time of the judges is so much taken up with their regular courts that it is not often that a judge can be had to hold a special term. I regard it as the imperative duty of the legislature, imposed upon them by the constitution, to provide courts for the people sufficient for the transaction of their business with promptness and dispatch. This necessity for more courts can be met in two ways: one, to increase the present number of superior court circuits and judges; the other, to establish two or more criminal circuits, each circuit, to be composed of several counties, which need not be contiguous. These circuits, if established, should include those counties where more courts are so greatly needed; and in such counties the superior court should be relieved of all criminal jurisdiction. After mature reflection, I greatly incline to the criminal circuits, and earnestly recommend their adoption. I believe this system will work well, and after it is tried will be popular. The judges and solicitors of these courts should be elected by the legislature, and the salary of the judges made sufficient to command the services of the best lawyers. The judges should be required to hold at least three courts in a year in each county, with power in some one to order other terms if necessary. No court requiring a jury of witnesses, either civil, criminal, inferior or superior, should be held in the month of June. Our people are eminently an agricultural people, and to take a large number of laborers out of the fields for a week, as is now done in many of the counties in the busy month of June, is a serious injury to the farmers of that county.

Codification of the Law

I desire to press upon you the importance of appointing a commission to codify the statute law of the state. The last codification was Battle's Revisal, which has been amended, and the laws amending that repealed and amended, till in many instances it is difficult, even for a skillful lawyer, to tell exactly what the statue law is. I know of nothing to come before you of more importance to the people than this, and I beg you not to adjourn without appointing such a commission. The people will bless the men that give them a code of plain, simple laws, so arranged that they and their county officers and justices of the peace can learn their duties and intelligently discharge them.

The Pardoning Power

I herewith transmit the list of reprieves, commutations and pardons granted since the last biennial message, with the information in each case required by the constitution. From this list it will be seen that I granted

in 1879

Reprieves	7
Commutations	2
Pardons	16
Total	25

in 1880

Reprieves		4
Commutations		3
Pardons		46
Total		53

The applications for executive clemency are numerous, and are often pressed with a zeal and a persistency that is hard to resist. I have given to each application a patient investigation, and have only exercised this fearful power when I believed mercy required, justice approved and the good of society did not forbid. Yet, after all, I think it probable I have granted mercy when it was not deserved, and refused it when it ought to have been granted. This duty gives me more care and anxiety than any other connected with the executive office. No one man ought to be required or permitted to discharge alone so delicate and often so painful a duty. If he be a good man, the responsibility is too great; if a bad man, the power is too great to trust in his hands. There ought to be a board of pardons, and I advise the creation of such a board, even if a change in the constitution be necessary. In some states the supreme court compose such a board; in others the state officers. In ours it might be either or both.

The Swepson Case

During the administration of Governor Caldwell, an indictment was found in Wake superior court against George W. Swepson and M. S. Littlefield for obtaining the bonds of the state under false pretenses. A farce of a trial was had before Judge Watts,[7] and, in the absence of the defendants, he ordered a verdict of "not guilty" to be entered, and the state appealed. The appeal, after being in the supreme court a long time, was finally decided against the defendants, during the administration of Governor Vance, who employed counsel to prosecute the case. This case has twice since been to the supreme court on collateral questions, and both times the decisions have been in favor of the

---

[7] Samuel W. Watts of Franklin County, who was appointed judge of the Superior Court in 1868. He resigned in 1877 when a committee of the General Assembly was appointed to bring impeachment proceedings against him on charges of bribery. Edward H. Davis, *Historical Sketches of Franklin County* (Raleigh: Edwards & Broughton Co., 1948), 155–157, hereinafter cited as Davis, *Franklin County*.

state. The counsel employed by my predecessor have been paid the sums agreed upon between him and them. Having given you this information as to the origin and progress of the case, I forbear to make any remarks upon it except to express the hope that it may soon be brought to a fair and impartial trial upon the merits of the case, without any further unnecessary delays.

The Littlefield Case

The defendant, Littlefield, has not been in the state since the indictment. In May, 1879, I heard he was in Florida, and having procured a certified copy of the indictment, I sent a messenger, with my requisition on the governor of that state, for his arrest and delivery to my agent. The governor issued his warrant promptly and Littlefield was arrested, but he was at once released upon a writ of *habeas corpus*, issued by a Judge Archibald, of that state. I then procured a copy of a bill of indictment, which had been found against him in Buncombe, and made a requisition upon that bill, but upon this the governor refused to issue his warrant, holding that it was substantially the same offence. I was then powerless to do more.

The Perry Case

In October last, the solicitor of the third judicial district sent me a certified copy of a bill of indictment, found against one Perry, in the county of Lenoir, for the forgery of a school order. He said he had information that Perry was in Washington city, and requested me to make my requisition upon the authorities of the District of Columbia for his arrest and delivery. This I did, and dispatched Dr. Bagby, of Kinston, as a messenger to bring the fugitive back to North Carolina for trial. After some delay the warrant was issued by the executive officer of the district, and the arrest was made; but Perry was at once taken in charge by the marshal, under a writ of *habeas corpus* issued by Judge Wylie. Dr. Bagby employed a good counsel to represent the State. The trial assumed the aspect of a political inquisition against the State of North Carolina. Instead of trying the case upon the papers before him, the judge proceeded to try the State upon the testimony of the defendant, his wife and mother, as to whether the man could get a fair trial if he should deliver him up to the State's agent. I doubt if any judge has ever done the like before. Perry, of course, was released, and the attorneys for the State appealed to the general term. The Hon. R. T. Merrick and R. S. Davis, Esq., are the attorneys that represent the State, and they have agreed to prosecute the appeal without further charge.

Railroads—Atlantic and North Carolina

The Atlantic and North Carolina railroad company is in a fairly prosperous condition. For the last two years it has met probably all its obligations, and paid promptly the accruing interest on its bonded and judgment debt. The bonded debt is $195,500, at eight per cent. interest, and the judgment debt $37,474 at six per cent. No part of this indebtedness was contracted in the last two years. During this time, I am informed, the company has paid cash for all its purchases, and has spent considerable sums in repairing roadway and rolling stock. Several offers have been made within the last year for the lease of this property, and on the 23d of November, a meeting of the stockholders was held to consider these propositions. As it was but a short time prior to your assembling, I took the responsibility of preventing any change in the status of this property till you could be heard. The private stockholders held a meeting, after the adjournment of the company meeting, and passed resolutions expressive of their opinions and wishes as to the proposed lease. I send you herewith a copy of the proceedings of their meeting. From this it will be seen that they are clearly in favor of a lease, and a majority of them to the Wilmington and Weldon railroad company. I have stated on more than one occasion, both publicly and privately, that this road was built chiefly for the benefit of the people east of Goldsboro, and that I desired to see it managed and operated in the way best calculated to develop and build up that section of the state, and that I had no policy or wishes in antogonism[sic] to the wish of the private stockholders along its line. It is now for you to give such directions concerning this property as you may think the interests of the state and the Atlantic section demand, and your action shall control. In the event you take no action, I shall not further interefere in the matter, one way or the other, but shall leave that question, as I do all others, to be settled by the company, without any interference on my part.

Albemarle and Chesapeake Canal Company

An act was passed on the 14th day of February, 1879, chapter 305, authorizing the public treasurer to exchange the stock of the state held in this company, for the bonds of the state, but there was a provision unwisely, as I think, inserted in the act, by which this authority expired on the 1st day of January, 1880. The company returned to the treasurer, before the act expired, one hundred thousand dollars in old bonds, and he surrendered to the company that much stock. The state still holds two hundred and fifty thousand dollars of stock in this company.

Cape Fear and Yadkin Valley Railroad

The work on this road has progressed more rapidly than was expected. The grading has been completed to Greensboro and fifteen miles beyond, and it is now ready for the iron. Negotiations for the sale of the first mortgage bonds of the company, authorized by the act of 1879, are going on, and it is believed enough money will be realized from the sale to iron and equip the road to Greensboro. Only thirty thousand dollars, of fifty thousand dollars appropriated, was paid out by the treasurer in adjusting the indebtedness of the company. The only aid the state is now giving this important work is the maintenance of the convicts, for which she is to receive the first mortgage bonds of the company. Upon those already received the interest has been promptly paid. The state, then, is taking the same kind of security for her convict labor that capitalists take for their money which pays for the iron and rolling stock. This the state can well afford to do for this or any other section, and I advise its continuance. By such a use of the convict labor the crime of the state can be made to contribute largely to the development of sections much in need of better transportation facilities. This road, I believe, will soon be running to Greensboro. It will then be only necessary to fill the gap of thirty miles between Fayetteville and Lumberton to open up another and shorter line of railway from Wilmington to Greensboro. With that or some such connection made and the road pushed as rapidly as possible into the northwestern counties, the benefits derived from a road running diagonally across the state, will be felt and appreciated by a large belt of the state, from Wilmington to the mountains. For the earnings of the convicts on this road I refer you to the report of the board of directors of the penitentiary.

Western North Carolina Railroad

The purchasers of the state's interest in this road have thus far complied with their contract with the state. They have paid promptly the hire of the convicts, and the interest on the first mortgage bonds of the company, as they contracted to do. They have paid off the floating debt of the company and have laid down about two miles of new iron. Their $30,000 deposit is still in the Citizens National bank of this city, as collateral security for the faithful performance of their contract.

Owing to hindrances and delays in effecting their organization, the work upon the road has not progressed as rapidly as was expected; but there are now five hundred convicts at work, and I am informed by the owners, as soon as the open weather of spring comes, the construction will be pushed rapidly forward on both lines.

Construction Bonds

The legislature, on the 14th day of March, 1879, ratified an act (chapter 138) to provide for an adjustment of that part of the state debt incurred in aid of the North Carolina railroad. By this act I was required to appoint three commissioners to make the settlement. This duty was performed by me by the appointment of the Hon. George Davis, of the city of Wilmington, Hon. Montford McGehee, of the county of Person, and Donald W. Bain, Esq., of the city of Raleigh. They entered at once upon the labors assigned them. The steady advance in bonds, in common with all classes of securities, the Swasey suit,[8] and a second lien upon the state's stock in favor of bonds issued to the Western North Carolina railroad, raised difficulties and caused delays in reaching anything like an agreement. Some time early in November the bondholders had a conference with one of the commissioners in person, and a plan of adjustment was agreed upon and signed by the bondholders, representing about two millions, and the commissioners. I herewith send you a copy of the agreement and the report of the commissioners,

---

[8]In 1871 Anthony H. Swasey and other holders of construction bonds, fearing that the consolidation of the Western North Carolina Railroad and the North Carolina Railroad would reduce the value of the state's stock in the North Carolina Railroad pledged against the construction bonds, asked the United States Circuit Court for the Eastern District of North Carolina to enjoin the consolidation. Court action had been postponed by mutual agreement for several years, and negotiation with these bondholders was part of the duty of the three commissioners. Brown, *State Movement*, 269–271.

Geroge Davis (1820-1896), born on his father's plantation at Porter's Neck, New Hanover
County, was of illustrious Colonial and Revolutionary ancestory. He studied law after graduating from the University of North Carolina and was licensed upon reaching the age of majority.
Davis was a Whig, an active Unionist, and a delegate to the peace conference of 1861. With
secession, he supported the Confederacy serving in the senate (1862-1864) and as attorney
general, 1864-1865. He joined President Jefferson Davis in his flight to Charlotte, was arrested
and later released on parole. Recognized as an able lawyer and scholar, Governor Vance
offered him the position of chief justice on the North Carolina Supreme Court but he
declined for financial reasons.

which I earnestly commend to your patient consideration.[9] By the terms of the act, the adjustment could not be consumated without the approval of the governor and treasurer. While we knew the commissioners had done the best they could, after taking a business view of the situation, we felt that to fix a new debt of $2,750,000 upon the people was a matter so serious that we ought to wait till you assembled, and learn what the people desired. We consequently determined to withhold our approval, and submit the whole matter to you.

In your investigation of this important question, those who are not familiar with the facts may find the following information serviceable. The state is the owner of $3,000,000 of stock in the North Carolina railroad company, and the private stockholders of $1,000,000. To pay for this stock, the state, in 1853–'54–'55, issued her bonds to run for thirty years, at six per cent. interest; and, to secure their payment, pledged the dividends accruing on her stock for the payment of the interest, and the stock itself for the payment of the bonds. In 1866, $205,000 of the bonds were taken up in exchange for stock held by the state in the Raleigh and Gaston railroad company, and by investments made by the literary board, leaving outstanding $2,795,000. The interest then due on bonds was funded in 1868, under the funding act of August of that year. The road was leased to the Richmond and Danville railroad company in 1871 for six and a half per cent, on the capital stock, and very soon thereafter a suit, known as the "Swasey" suit, was commenced in the federal court, to subject the lease money to the payment of the interest on these bonds. The court made the order and appointed Hon. S. F. Phillips[10] receiver to receive and pay out the dividends. This fund has been sufficient to pay the interest on such of the bonds as have been presented up to and including, I think, the January interest, 1877. There has been about $2,600,000 of these bonds presented to the receiver, upon which the interest has been paid. The reason the others have not been presented is, the holders do not know their value. This is known to be so, for quite a number recently presented to the receiver were first presented to the treasurer to be funded, and it was from him that the holders

---

[9]See "Report of the Commissioners to Adjust a Portion of the State Debt," *Public Documents, 1881*, No. 15.

[10]Samuel Field Phillips, lawyer of Chapel Hill and of Washington, D.C.; member of the General Assembly, 1852, 1864; professor of law in the University of North Carolina, 1854–1859; member of the Constitutional Convention of 1865; United States solicitor general, 1873–1885. Grant, *Alumni History of the University*, 493.

first learned their value. The interest on the other $195,000 is unpaid from January, 1869, and it is fair to presume that they will all be finally presented. These bonds fall due in 1883–'84–'85, and unless some adjustment is made before that time, the state's stock will be sold. If an adjustment is made on the basis suggested, the receipts from the lease of the North Carolina railroad will be sufficient to pay the interest on the new state bonds, and leave a surplus of some $12,000 annually, provided the present status of the road is continued. But if the lease should fail, or the road for any reason become non–paying, then the amount of tax to be raised out of the people for that purpose will be at least $170,000 each year. When this act was passed, both the treasurer and myself favored its passage, for at that time the bonds were worth from sixty to sixty–five cents, and it was thought they could be taken up with a new bond at seventy to seventy-five cents. Soon after the passage of the act, these bonds, like most other securities, began to advance, and have continued to do so, till now they are worth about ninety cents. The holders are not likely to accept a new bond for less than they can sell the old in cash.

In any consideration I have given to this matter, I have regarded the following as the settled fixed policy of the state: That however little regard there may have been paid to the old obligations of the state, all her new obligations must be held sacred and inviolable, and the interest promptly paid on any new bond she issues, no matter what may come. Hence new obligations ought not to be entered into without due consideration, and it was, in a great degree, this feeling to stand by the new obligations at all hazards, that induced me to refer this whole matter to the representatives of the people, whose debt it will be. Capitalists will be allowed to construct roads anywhere in the state they choose, with their own money, and no section shall be deprived of railroad facilities because it may hurt a road in which the state has or has not an interest. If you agree with me in this, the question whether any roads are likely to be built that will render the North Carolina railroad less valuable than now, becomes an important inquiry in your consideration of any adjustment. In fact, the whole question hinges very much upon the probable future of the North Carolina railroad.

In taking leave of this subject, I will only venture to make these suggestions: First, fix a price at which you are willing for the exchange to be made for new bonds; second, give the commissioners the authority to exchange stocks for bonds, giving the bond–holders the option, with the distinct understanding that if they decline both and sell the stock, no matter what it brings its proceeds will be all they will ever get. If anything is done, the second mortgage makes it necessary to retain the commissioners and the transcations to be had through them.

Centennials

The legislature, at its session in 1879, appropriated a sum not to exceed $1,500 to aid in the erection of a suitable monument on the battle-field of King's Mountain, and for other expenses connected with the centennial celebration. Of this sum I expended $1,060, leaving the balance $440, still in the treasury. Owing to a failure to get transportation over the railroads for the troops, I was unable to assemble the state guard upon the grounds, as I had desired to do, and only a few companies attended the celebration. It was, nevertheless, a great success, and will never be forgotten by the thousands who assembled there upon that sacred soil, dear to every true American liberty–loving patriot.

Cowpens

There is to be a centennial celebration on the battle-field of the Cowpens, with fit and imposing ceremonies. A granite column has been erected, to be surmounted by a bronze statue of Gen. Morgan, the hero of the battle. Each of the original thirteen states was asked to contribute $250 for a block in this column. Not wishing North Carolina to be behind her sister states in this patriotic work, and there being no authority to use the public funds for any such purpose, the state officers, out of their own means, forwarded this sum to the committee in behalf of the state.

Guilford Court House

The initiatory steps have been taken by the citizens of Guilford and surrounding counties to have a celebration on the battle–field of Guilford Court House on the 15th of March. While history does not record this battle as a victory for the patriots, every true and impartial reader of history must admit it had an important part in so crippling Cornwallis's army as to make his final overthrow seven months later, at Yorktown, possible. I trust you will take suitable action in reference to this proposed celebration.

Yorktown

In October, 1879, there was a call for the meeting of the governors of the thirteen colonial states, to take place in Old Independence Hall, in the city of Philadelphia. I attended that meeting, and then the initiatory steps were taken to have a grand centennial celebration at Yorktown, in October, 1881. In compliance with the plan of representation there agreed upon, I appointed R. B. Peebles,[11] Esq., of Northampton, as the commissioner to represent North Carolina, and he has, at his own expense, attended all the meetings of the commissioners. The United States government has made appropriations for the celebration, and will take charge of the ceremonies. I am anxious to see North Carolina bear a distinguished and honorable part in that memorable event. Her people, being the first to proclaim the great principles of liberty which triumphed at Yorktown, it will be eminently proper for them to participate in the ceremonies dedicated to their commemoration. I therefore urge you to take such action as will insure the state being properly represented on the occasion.

Druggists' Association

Within the last two years several persons have been poisoned in the state by mistakes made by druggists in filling prescriptions, or in the article sold. The communities were so shocked that it led to a convention of druggists, which was held in the city of Raleigh, at which an association was formed, and the draft of a bill prepared to protect the public against like mistakes in the future. This bill will be presented to you, and is worthy of your consideration.

Prohibitory Liquor Association

There is sold in the state another poison which numbers by the thousands its victims slain, debauched, degraded, impoverished, wrecked or made miserable and heart-broken. The results have so shocked the christian [sic] people of the state that

[11] Robert Bruce Peebles, lawyer of Jackson; member of the General Assembly, 1866, 1883, 1895; Superior Court judge, 1903-1915. Ashe, *Biographical History*, IV, 361-365.

they, too, have formed an association, and will present their petitions, praying for a law prohibiting the sale of this great destroyer of human happiness and human life. You are fresh from the people and are well informed as to public sentiment, and are the best judges as to whether it is better to undertake to prohibit or regulate the sale of intoxicating liquors. That legislation of some kind is needed cannot be successfully contradicted. What we now have on the subject is either evaded or openly disregarded. We have a statute against its being sold on Sunday, and yet I suppose there is not a city, town or village in the state, where it is sold at all, that it cannot be bought on Sunday. So too, we have one prohibiting its sale to minors, and yet they buy it openly, without stint, so long as they have the money with which to pay. In fact, there is but little regard paid to any law regulating its sale. If the traffic is to continue under the license of the state, some more stringent regulations are absolutely required. Upon this subject I offer these suggestions: Require the county commissioners to be very much more particular to whom they grant license. Increase the tax on license and permit none to be taken out unless the applicant makes his application in writing, and pledges himself to faithfully observe any restrictions placed upon the traffic and agrees to a forfeiture of his license for any violation. Confer upon the county commissioners the unquestionable right to refuse license in any county, and to revoke them at will, and require the board to make rigid investigation into the conduct of each person licensed. Require the attorney general to have published in convenient form a digest of all laws regulating the traffic for free circulation, and require each licensed liquor dealer to keep one posted up in a conspicuous place in his place of business. Make any violation of any restriction as a misdemeanor, punishable by fine and imprisonment and an absolute forfeiture of all license and allow no one to be licensed who has ever forfeited his license.

The State Guard

This military organization has received but little aid or encouragement from the state, but through the persistent efforts of the officers, and the sacrifice of the men, it has been kept up, and is to-day in every way creditable to both officers and men. I fear the importance of having such an organization scattered about over the state, ready for service at any moment, to aid the civil officers in the enforcement of the civil law, has not been properly appreciated. The fact that such an organization exists, ready to obey the orders of the civil officers, will contribute much to a continuance of the peace and quiet that now reign throughout the state. Adjutant–General Jones has given much of his time to the organization and discipline of the guard, and I renew the recommendation of my predecessor that his salary be increased to six hundred dollars.

Oxford Orphan Asylum

I cannot close this message without commending to your favor this noble charity, which is gathering up, feeding, clothing and educating the penniless and parentless children of the state. Under the protecting wings and fostering care of the masonic fraternity, that good, big-hearted man, Mr. Mills,[12] is preparing these little orphans to be useful men and women. Many dear little ones will be saved from the vices and dangers that beset children left without some one to watch over them, by this organized charity, that would otherwise fall and be lost. The aid now given by the state to this noble work is only three thousand dollars a year. I beg that you will make it five thousand. The grand lodge of masons, finding the capacities of the building not sufficient for the demands, ordered others to be erected. It will cost the fraternity no little to prepare these buildings, and they will be obliged to appeal to the charity of the people for help. In view of this increase of usefulness the state can well afford to increase her investment. I do not call it donations, for to have one hundred and thirty of her orphan children taken care of and educated, as is now the case, for three thousand dollars a year, is not giving, but receiving, not spending, but investing in good interest–bearing security, that will, in years to come, bring her large returns in mental and moral riches.

Conclusion

To these matters, lying within the appropriate sphere of your duty as legislators, I call your earnest attention, feeling assured

---

[12]John Haymes Mills. After graduating from Wake Forest College, he served one year as president of the Oxford Female Seminary. From 1863 to 1873 he was owner and editor of the *Biblical Recorder*. He was then superintendent of the Oxford Orphanage from 1873 to 1884, and of the Thomasville Orphanage from 1885 to 1895. Cox, *Encyclopedia of Southern Baptists*, II, 858.

that they will receive such consideration as their importance demands.

The citizens of North Carolina are to be congratulated that her interests are entrusted into the hands of men whose past records and personal characters warrant the assurance that such interests will be faithfully conserved. I shall heartily co–operate with you in all your endeavors to promote the general welfare. Wishing you a harmonious session and invoking, in behalf of your labors, the guidance of the great Law Giver,

A&H—GP

John Thomas Deweese[13] to Thomas J. Jarvis

Lewistown Pa. January 8/81

You doubtless remember my being with you at Raleigh some days ago, representing gentlemen of Philadelphia in reference to obtaining information from you about the Cape Fear & Yadkin Valley RR

You kindly gave me such information as you could at that time which I duly reported. In addition to the information then received the parties desire to know what the income and expenses were of that portion of the R.R. between Fayetteville and Gulf during the Year 1880.

Can you get such information for me? If you feel that you can give such information please let me know at your earliest convenience. I am unable to say what action the parties are disposed to take in the matter. I have stated to them the necessity of making a proposition while the Legislature is in Session if they desire to do any thing in the matter.

A&H—GP

Daniel Reaves Goodloe[14] to Thomas J. Jarvis

Washington, January 9th 1881

I have had so much pleasure in reading your message that I am prompted to express my gratification at its excellent tenor,

---

[13]After serving much of his early manhood in the United States Army, Deweese moved to North Carolina after the Civil War. From 1869 to 1871 he was Democratic representative to Congress. After being defeated for re–election, he left the state and began to practice law in Washington, D.C. *Congressional Directory*, 962.

[14]After practicing law in Louisburg with little success, Goodloe moved to Washington, D.C., and became a prominent author and editor. *Dictionary of American Biography*, VII, 390–391.

and at the very satisfactory presentation it makes of the condition and prospects of the State. What you say in behalf of the colored people is so wisely and well said that I cannot doubt it will be fruitful of the best influences upon both races. Such recognition of the rights of the emancipated blacks by the Governor of a Southern State cannot but produce happy consequences, socially and politically, at home and abroad. It tends to convince the colored people, and the northern people, that the dominant, ruling people of the South are coming up to their duty of contributing to the education and elevation of their former Slaves.

Your urgent recommendation of higher taxes in aid of education furnishes another cause for congratulation, and leaves room to hope that North Carolina is not always to remain behind all the states and territories in this essential element of civilization. The failure of the General Government to provide for the education of the colored race at the moment of giving it freedom and enfranchisement, furnishes a conclusive proof that the dominant party was chiefly, if not exclusively bent on securing votes; and that the elevation of the new voters was a secondary consideration. Humane people of the North have contributed liberally of their private means to this noble cause, but the Republican majorities in Congress have left it to the impovrished[sic] South to raise school funds by taxation, for the education of whites and blacks.

The senate, at the present session of Congress, has tardily come forward with a feeble and wholly inadequate measure in aid of education. It appropriates the proceeds of sales of the public lands to the cause of general education throughout the country, with the proviso that the distribution among the states be made in proportion to the number of illiterate persons in each.[15] Only the interest on the money derivable from this source is to be used, while the annual additions are to be saved and invested as a permanent fund. Its efficiency for a generation to come may be estimated in view of the annual proceeds of sales which now amount to only about one million of dollars. During the years 1877, 1878, and 1879, the proceeds of sales were respectively, $976.000, $1.080.000, and $924.000. Taking a million for the average, the interest at 4 per cent would be $40.000, to be divided among all the states and territories. The

---

[15]This bill had been introduced on December 17, 1880, by Senator Ambrose E. Burnside. *Congressional Record*, XI, 229.

interest for the second year, to be distributed, would be $80.000, and for the third year, $120.000, and so on. At the end of twenty years the annual interest to be distributed would be $800.000, between 80.000.000 of people, or one dollar for each one hundred inhabitants.

But if ante–bellum demagogism had not robbed the old states of their equal share in the public lands, which their valor had won and their money purchased; if Congress had not given the lands away by hundreds of millions of acres, before the war, during the war, and since the war, to the new States and Territories, to Railroad companies, and to "actual settlers," the fund to be distributed under the proposed law would make a valuable addition to the School systems of the southern states. The Annual Report of the Commissioner of the Land Office[16] for the year 1879 presents a statement of the aggregate proceeds of land sales to the close of that fiscal year, from the year 1796, when they were first put on the market. They amount to $204.547.812. 81. This sum or the annual interest which it would yield if invested ought to be distributed exclusively among the original Thirteen States, in order, approximately, to place them on a footing of equality with the new States, and territories, every one of which has been richly endowed by the generosity of Congress, at the expense of the old states.

As illustrations of the munificence of Congress at the expense of the country, in giving lands to "actual Settlers," the Commissioner's Report shows that from July 1st, 1868, to June 30, 1879, being eleven years, 47.143.410 acres were thus disposed of, at the cost of surveying and patenting. These lands, at the minimum value of $1.25 per acre would have brought $68.929.262.50. In 1878 the amount of land thus given away was 6.288.779 acres, and in 1879, 8.026.685 acres.

If the bill of Mr. Burnside, which has passed the Senate, shall lead to the funding of the $204,547.812.81, of aggregate proceeds of sales, for the cause of education in the old states, it will be a blessing indeed; but in its present shape it will amount to a homeopathic decoction, in the proportion of a drop of the medicine to a hogshead of water, well shaken.

---

[16]James A. Williamson of Iowa. *Register of Officers of the United States, 1877,* 273.

Inaugural Address, January 18, 1881[17]

"Inaugural Address of Gov. Thos. J. Jarvis Delivered, January 18, 1881[1] Before both the Houses of the General Assembly," Fellow–Citizens;—Every change in the progress of a state brings to the statesman new duties and responsibilities. Amid these changes, the public good must be ever in his mind and constant subject of his study and solicitude. To correct existing evils in the body politic; to remove impediments to the further progress of society; to aid established industries; and to develop new interests are obligations of the very highest nature resting upon those, who, under our form of government, have been elevated, by the suffrages of the people, to position and power. This power, under our system of government, rests upon no claim of right. It is a delegated trust for the benefit of the people, and a trust which our institutions were framed to enforce. These duties are always weighty, often burdensome; the responsibilities inseparably connected with power are frequently a source of embarrassment and trial. In such a position, the line of duty is not always clear; the judgment may often be misled by feeling the most honorable to our nature. What, then, must be the emotions of him, who, after a term of office more than ordinarily beset with difficulty and trial, finds himself, by the voice of a free people, again reinstated in his high position, again reinvested with the same high trusts? Such emotions it would be in vain to attempt to express. Let it suffice to say that, to a generous mind, such a tribute carries the highest reward that could be bestowed.

With a new administration comes new duties. To present these plainly, to appreciate them fully and to state the grounds upon which they rest, will be my object to–day. Were I called upon to formulate these duties into one sentence, it would be "North Carolina, the Development of Her Resources and the Education of Her Children."

The changes introduced by the war are many and various. Of one of these only is it my purpose to speak now. It is clear that the commonwealth moves with a quicker life now than formerly. The genius of the former state of things was repose; that of now is activity. The disasters sustained by our property–holders, while crushing and even fatal to a few, inspired the many with a determination to retrieve as far as possible their losses.

[17]*Public Documents, 1881*, No. 22.

The youth of our State entered life with the knowledge that their future lot depended upon their own exertions. That class of our population—about one–third in number—which were born, brought up and lived under the control of others, found themselves at the end of the war free agents, and possessed of the largest latitude of action. The scope of individual energy was thus expanded almost indefinitely. These newly developed and newly released energies flowed, some into the old, some into the new channels of business. Meantime, the drain upon our population which had so long gone on by emigration, particularly the emigration of our young men, nearly ceased. Meantime, also, an accession of population was gained by the incoming of many from the neighboring States. This accession was small in each instance, but in the aggregate very considerable. From these causes combined, our population has increased beyond any former ratio in the same period; business has been diversified and pushed on with exuberant energy, and a spirit of enterprise pervades all sections. The proofs of this meet us on every hand, in the expansion of our old staple crops and in the introduction of new industries; in the erection of cotton mills; in the multiplication of tobacco factories; in the amount of deposits in our banks; in the growth of our towns; in ways, indeed, without number.

But while individual prosperity is the rule, the progress of the State in its aggregate capacity leaves much to be desired. He who loves his State cannot reflect without a feeling of pain upon the fact that of the 32,500,000 acres or thereabouts embraced within the bounds of the State, a little less than one–half lies unimproved. And the fact even more painful, meets us in our survey of the State—the fact that so large a proportion of children of the State are growing up without the advantages of education. In these two facts lies the weakness of our commonwealth, and to these it behooves us to direct our attention.

What State can compare with ours in climate? Placed, as it were, on the border land between the North and the South, she knows the extremes of neither, while she possesses many of the advantages of both. No country better rewards the toils of the laborer. Her cereal crops are excelled by none, when they are cultivated with equal care. Her cotton ranks with the best. Her bright tobaccos have no rival in any market. While she produces materials for manufactures so abundant in quantity, so excellent in quality, her water power for propelling machinery is inexhaustible. The spindles of all the States may be driven by her streams. Her ores and minerals, if they alone were regarded, would, if developed, make her one of the richest of States. In her forests she has an almost boundless source of wealth; for here is found timber alike suited for the useful and the ornamental arts. We possess in very truth a goodly land. But of what avail is it to possess these unlimited resources of wealth, if they are to remain, as they have so long remained, practically dormant and undeveloped? If the rivers are forever to flow idly to the sea, the rich veins of ore to lie hidden in their earthen beds, the lands to sleep unvexed by the plow, it is folly for us to dream of a hopeful future. Who does not feel that it is an imperative duty to develop these resources and make them tributary to the comfort and wealth of our people and the world, according to the manifest design of Providence? How this development may be facilitated is a comprehensive question with which practical statesmanship must deal, and upon which I will risk a few observations.

They must be advertised. So little are they appreciated at home and so little are they known abroad, that it is necessary that their location, extent, value and all other facts connected with them, be published and circulated till they are sought after, as they will be when fully realized. Individuals advertise the superior advantages they offer to the public, and so must States. Many of our sister States, acting upon this business principle, spend large sums of money annually in publishing and distributing information about their resources; and for the sums thus expended they get large returns in capital and labor. We have done but little thus far in that direction. Until the Board of Agriculture was established, almost our total work in that regard consisted in the publication of a few geological reports, which, although valuable in themselves, found their way into the hands of but a few. So little have we felt its importance, that it has been seriously discussed for years that even this publication should be stopped; and but for the existence of the Board of Agriculture, it is likely it would have been done by the last Legislature. To show how little our resources are known and how important it is that we advertise them, I beg to mention a circumstance that occurred less than a year ago. Our State Geologist, with my approval, went to Pittsburgh, the great iron center of this continent, and delivered a lecture before the chamber of commerce on our iron ores. There he found the furnaces using each year hundreds of thousands of tons of ore, brought all the way from Africa to Baltimore by sea, and then inland four hundred and fifty miles by rail; while in many counties in North Carolina, not the distance of the length of the State away from these furnaces, inexhaustible quantities of better ores were to be found. When Prof. Kerr made known to them this fact and showed them samples of the ores and their analysis, they stood amazed. Just think of it for a moment. The iron men of Pittsburgh knowing more about the ores of Africa than of North Carolina! This is no reflection on their intelligence, but on our want of enterprise as a State. There is no lack of capital in the money centre seeking safe and profitable investments; for we have seen the rate of interest decrease from year to year until four per cent. bonds of the United States command a high premium, and the three per cent. British consols sold at par. Make known to capitalists our great resources, the advantages they offer for safe investments, and the work of their development is well advanced. This must be done by the State.

We need more people. If we would realize our want of population, let us compare our State with that of Massachusetts. These States were settled at no great distance of time from each other. At the census of 1870, Massachusetts, the only natural productions of which are ice and granite, had a population of one hundred and eighty–seven to the square mile. North Carolina, which, as shown by the same census, produced every crop then grown in the United States, had only twenty–one to the square mile. North Carolina, compared with her capacity to sustain population, may almost be regarded as uninhabited.

We need immigration on many accounts. The embarrassments created by the war have not been wholly cleared away from the landed interests; the sale of surplus lands would liquidate liabilities, and render the operations of the proprietor with the residue far more effective for his own and the general interests. Proprietors who are unembarrassed have a great excess of land. Immigration would enable them to dispose of this excess, so that lands now unimproved would at once become productive. At the same time, the capital they liberated could be turned to manufacturing pursuits. We have a large extent of land which has undergone partial exhaustion and now lies waste. For this state of things, immigration presents the speediest remedy. The methods of culture in the old world are much more thorough and pains–taking than with us. These exhausted lands would, under these methods, soon become fertile and fruitful. Immigration would bring among us new arts and new industries, and thus retain among us the money now paid out for the productions of other countries. Immigration brings wealth, and wealth stimulates all the elements of high civilization. We want immigration, in fine, because it is necessary to give to the State due weight in the councils of the country. If North Carolina possessed a population in proportion to her extent and resources, her wishes and wants, so far as the Federal government is concerned, would be at once met and supplied.

To the immigrant the State of North Carolina holds out unequalled inducements. Her laws are good, and nowhere are laws better administered. The two races which make up her population maintain each with the other relations of amity and even kindness. Labor complications, often formidable in the Northern States, generally a source of trouble and difficulty in the States to the South of us, have been almost unknown here, and have now wholly passed away.

While the investment of capital and the introduction of immigration into the State will greatly hasten the development of her resources, yet she must rely chiefly upon the labor and devotion of her own sons and daughters for the wealth and glory and power, which, of right, belong to her and will surely come. Labor is the creator of wealth and is honorable of all men. The man who, in the sweat of his brow, makes the hidden properties of the seed, the soil and the air, under nature's wondrous guidance, to grow into golden grain or fleecy cotton; or who, with fire and furnace, transmutes the rough ore into serviceable metal; or by forge and anvil, still further transforms the metal into tools for man's use, and with them builds houses and cities, creates the wealth of the State.

There is too great a tendency, I fear among our young men to leave the farms and work–shops of the country; some for employment in what they think the more honorable vocations in cities and towns; others, more ambitious, for the supposed ease and glory of professional life. Public opinion is not altogether blameless for this mistake, and should hasten to correct it; for it often leads these young men into failures and failures into vices. The successful farmer or mechanic is none the less honorable or useful than the successful lawyer or doctor; and how incomparably greater in both is he than the failure in the profession. I cannot forbear, in this connection, to refer to the example of a young friend of mine as worthy of imitation, and to ask young men to study it. Although a son of a distinguished ex–Supreme Court Judge and a nephew of one of the State's most useful Governors, he went into a work–shop as a boy, worked at his trade, and is now the master–machinist of a rail-road company.[18] The example of such men in any community is valuable, and will give to labor the dignity and respect it de-serves.

But while it is imperative to encourage every known method for the development of the resources of the State, it is just as important to guard against anything calculated to retard it. If this be so, then it becomes the duty of the law–making power of the State to see to it that the lines of transportation operating in the State do not, by their discriminating charges, transfer to other States the industries that properly belong to ours. I do not join in the wholesale abuse of the railroads that some heap upon them, but I do believe they ought to be required to do exact and equal justice to all sections. This I think to be their interest as well as their duty, and if they refuse, I have no doubt about the power of the State to compel it. But these lines of railway have been the great agency in the development of the State, and we ought to be just as careful to see that we do not treat them unjustly as we are to see that they treat us fairly. The most amicable as well as the most effective tribunal to adjust these matters, which has thus far been tried, is a first–class railroad commission. Such a commission, elected by the general assem-bly every two years, with proper powers, would, in my opinion, be of great service to the people.

The Education of Her Children

No scheme for the advancement of North Carolina and the de-velopment of her resources can be successful or permanent that does not encompass the education of her children. This I regard as of the very first importance; for without it, all our efforts will be in vain. Capital, proverbially timid, will not look for investments in a land of ignorance, nor will immigrants seek homes where there are no school–houses and churches.

Of the present state of education it is difficult to speak with moderation. It is difficult to refrain from trespassing beyond

---

[18] A reference to Basil Manly, master machinist of the Atlantic and North Carolina Railroad. His father was Matthias E. Manly and his uncle was Charles Manly. *News and Observer*, January 22, 1881.

the bounds of temperate language, when we think of the hundreds of thousands now growing up in our State in utter ignorance. It is an evil so tremendous in its nature and consequences, that all the energies of the State should be brought to bear to correct it.

It was a maxim with the founders of republican government, that such government could not live unless based upon the intelligence of the people. The education of the people was enjoined as a sacred duty by the framers of our constitution in 1776, and it is so enjoined in our present constitution. Unless we are to discard the opinions of those whose wisdom we have so long venerated—unless we are determined to set aside the positive mandates of our constitution we must make some adequate provision to carry out this injunction.

The duty of providing education for our people rests, however, not upon authority, venerable though it be. It is enjoined by other considerations of the very highest nature. The church, recognizing this obligation second only to the demands of religion, has worked for education with a zeal that has brought its reward in good to the church, to society, and to the State. It has provided the Sunday school, fostered the common school, built academies and supported colleges. The educated men and women it has sent out from these schools and colleges have helped to make the State what she is. Their lives and their works speak praises for the churches that established them that no tongue can utter. Dumb be the tongue and palsied the arm that is ever used to belittle or strike down one of these denominational colleges.

Individuals, too, moved by these high considerations, as well as the hope of reward, have done effective work in this great cause. By them high schools have been dotted about over the State like beacon–lights, whose value cannot be estimated or good influences told. The men who labor in these schools rarely grow rich or great, as the world estimates riches and greatness, but they lay the foundations upon which others do.

But as much as we admire the zeal of the church, and commend the enterprise of the individual in behalf of education, the State cannot afford to leave this, her greatest interest alone to their care. Among the heaviest burdens which she has to bear, are those which have their origin in crime. It presses upon the community with a deadly weight in the penitentiary, the jail and the criminal calendar of our courts. Much of that burden which we sustain in our asylums has its origin in crime. Every dollar expended in an effective system of education would be returned to us with ten-fold interest, in a higher moral tone and a healthier mental action of the community. It would be seen, too, in the decrease of those infirmities for which the institutions are intended to provide.

It is susceptible of proof that education is a source of wealth to a State. The difference is inconceivable between the efforts of an untutored mind and the efforts of the same mind quickened and trained by education. It is observable in the humblest sphere of labor, for labor is nothing but contrivance, and contrivance without intelligence is but the groping of the blind. In every other respect its effects are striking and everywhere visible. We have but to go into any State or country where universal education exists, to find in its improved agriculture, its ingenious mechanic arts, its prosperous commercial interests, its solid institutions of learning, the wider range of thought and discussion in its papers and magazines, (for these are made to suit their readers), its better modes of living, and its higher tone of manners and conversation, unmistakable evidences of its advantages. One other point: Among the recent experiences of our people, no lesson has been more favorably impressed than the vicissitudes of fortune. The war, in truth, only impressed upon a larger scale what the common experience of life makes so manifest. We have seen that the possessor of an ample estate to–day may to–morrow be struggling with straitened means, and be dependent upon the public institutions of learning for the education of his children. This is a consideration which appeals to the hearts of all men; for what is so powerful, so constant, so irradicable as paternal affection? That these institutions, then, should be at once put upon a footing which should prepare the children of every citizen for extended usefulness, becomes in this view an instinct of self–preservation.

The State, however, can only advance in this matter through her Legislature. It alone can establish this efficient system of common schools, which are peculiarly the people's schools. It is here that the children of the poor are to learn, or nowhere. Cut them off from these, and you doom them to grow up in ignorance, to grope in mental darkness, and it may be, die in disgrace. My fellow–citizens of the General Assembly, a grave responsibility rests upon you in this matter. How will you meet it? Will you send back the word to your constituents there is no hope, or will

[you] bid them say to their children the school–teacher is coming? Will you continue to crowd your penitentiary and jails with criminals rather than your school–houses with children? Decide, I pray you, in favor of intelligence and virtue, against ignorance and vice. That virtue is the companion of intelligence, and vice of ignorance, our own observation, as well as the statistics of our penal institutions demonstrate. If you doubt it, go to your penitentiary and search its records, so full of instructive lessons. Since it was first opened in January, 1870, up to Nov. 1st, 1880, three thousand eight hundred and twenty–two convicts have entered its gates. Of this number, there were three thousand three hundred and twenty–nine that could not read, three thousand two hundred and fifty–seven that could not write, while only fifteen had a good, one an ordinary, and two a collegiate education. Your jails and your criminal courts furnish the same overwhelming testimony. It is either taxation to support the schools or taxation to support the penitentiary and jails. It is either money for the child or money for the criminal. Which shall it be?

The time for a bold, onward movement in the great cause of education is propitious and the surroundings favorable. It is the beginning of an administration with no embarrassments. There are no works of internal improvements to be provided for. Our public debt, by its adjustment, is small and can no longer frighten us. Less than one hundred and fifty thousand dollars will pay its annual interest. Our rate of taxation is exceedingly low, as compared with other states. I have obtained officially the rate in twenty–seven states, and in them all it is higher than in ours, and in most of them greatly so. I do not know the rate in the others. Our assessments of property for the purposes of taxation, as everybody knows, is exceedingly low. If all the property was honestly listed and fairly valued at its cost value, the property of the state would be at least $300,000,000, instead of the $156,268,241, as now returned. Public sentiment is prepared for a large increase of taxation for schools and will sustain it. A friend of mine wrote me a few days ago, "I especially approve of your suggestion as to education, and am glad to find you are not afraid to advise necessary taxation. I had much rather pay taxes to educate people than pay taxes to support the penitentiary; for as long as our people are ignorant, the penitentiary will be full." This gentleman is one of the largest tax–payers in the state, and I think fairly represents public opinion on that subject.

But whether the people are ahead of us or not, they will go with us in this holy warfare for the redemption of the rising generation from the bonds of ignorance and vice, if we will but lead the way.

North Carolina has now reached a point when she must avail herself of every means of advancement and re-organize her institutions to the demands of the age, or else be content to occupy an humble place in the march of progress now going on among the States. I appeal to-day, as I have a right to do, to all her citizens, whatever may be their position, to come up to the full measure of their duty. My appeal is to all the people, without regard to party or to race, as all alike will be the objects of her care and bounty.

Now my democratic friends, a word with you before I close. While I appeal to all men of all faiths and creeds and parties to work for "North Carolina, the Development of Her Resources, and the Education of Her Children," I demand that you shall do it. You cannot, as a party, afford to stand still. The State must go forward, and if you will not seize this golden opportunity to guide and direct her progress, the people will look for leaders outside of your ranks. If you expect to receive popular support in the future, you must do so on works performed for the public good. If, under the administration which has to-day been inaugurated, peace and harmony shall continue, agriculture be fostered, immigration introduced, industries encouraged and schools established, the future of the party in the State will not be uncertain.

There is no cause for despondency, as a people or a party, because of your failure in the late canvass to elect your candidate for the Presidency. You failed, it is true, but barely so. Twenty-five thousand more votes in a city which could have given twice that number, had not its majority been thrown away in a selfish revolt against lawful authority for personal ends, and success would have been yours. For one, I do not take a gloomy view of the future. With a party having a majority in the Senate, a powerful minority in the House, and half of the voters of the country, to watch over the liberties of the people, the ruling party can do no harm, if they would. If our party leaders will look alone to the public welfare, and not to their own promotion or revenge, our standard shall again float in the sunlight of victory, and beneath its ample folds, all men of all sections shall dwell together in peace and unity. The party has stood defeat and it shall yet again endure success. It was born of the principles the fathers held, and as long as the principles live it cannot die. Some of its followers may be weak enough to desert it, others wicked enough to betray it, but none shall be strong enough to disband it.

A&H—GLB

Thomas J. Jarvis to C. M. Cooke[19]

Executive Department,
Raleigh, Jan. 20th, 1881

I am in receipt of a copy of a resolution passed by your honorable body, asking for "copies of the correspondence with the Governors of South Carolina and Tennessee on the free passage of fish up the Yadkin River and other streams."

Candor compels me to say that I did not know of the existence of any resolution requiring me to correspond with the Governors of South Carolina and Tennessee, until I received your communication; and consequently have had no correspondence with them.

The fish interests of the State have, by law, been made a part of the Board of Agriculture, and the fish Commissioner[20] under regulation of the Board has been in frequent and friendly intercourse with the fish Commissioner of South Carolina.

From our Commissioner, I learn that he has been informed by the Commissioner of South Carolina that the Yadkin and Catawba Rivers are open to the free passage of fish through the State of South Carolina.

A&H—GO

Resolution by Governor Thomas J. Jarvis before the Board of Public Buildings, January 23, 1881[21]

Whereas the walls and ceilings of the interior of the Capitol are in a dirty, dingy, smoky, unsightly condition, and the most, if not all the wood–work of the Halls of the Senate, House and

---

[19]Charles M. Cooke, speaker of the North Carolina House of Representatives. Connor, *Manual, 1913*, 611.

[20]A reference to S. G. Worth, superintendent of fish and fisheries.

[21]Taken from the Minutes of the Board of Public Officers, 1846–1893, Governors' Office, #104. This resolution passed and Jarvis also received permission to refurbish and repaint his offices.

various offices, is in the same condition; and whereas the roof
is leaky and damaging to the building; and whereas the curtains
of the windows of the Halls of the Senate and House of Representatives, and in most of the offices are but tattered and dirty
rags; and whereas the carpets on the floors of the Senate and
House of Representatives are but the ragged, dirty remnants of
worn out carpets; and whereas the Capitol, costing the people
over half a million of dollars, and being in itself a handsome
building, would be highly creditable to the State if put and kept
in good condition; and whereas the law not only authorizes but
requires this Board to keep it in proper condition; and whereas
it is believed by this Board that the people of the State desire
their Capitol to be kept in a condition creditable to the State; and
whereas it can be put in such condition at an expense not exceeding $15.000⁰⁰ or $20.000⁰⁰ and whereas the condition of the
treasury is such that the building may be easily put in such condition, without embarrassing the treasury or adding one penny
to the taxes of the people

Therefore, Resolved, That _____ and _____ be directed and
authorized to make all necesary contracts to have the roof and
the building thoroughly overhauled and put in first class condition; to have the walls and ceiling and wood work of the interior of the building cleaned and painted in decorative, first
class style; to have all necessary carpets put upon the floor and
suitable curtains to the windows; to have the furniture in the
Halls and the various offices repaired, and when necessary, replaced with new, and do all things else necessary to put the
building in first class condition

A&H—GP

E. K. Hyndman[22] *to Thomas J. Jarvis*
[Telegram]

Washington DC [January] 24 1881

"Personal"

Can the State sell its interest in Yadkin road without further
legislation?[23] Answer Carrollton Hotel Baltimore

---

[22]Unable to identify.

[23]Hyndman was interested in getting a charter from the General Assembly incorporating the South Atlantic and Ohio Rail Road Company, which
would run from Wise County, Virginia, to Smithfield, North Carolina.
Hyndman hoped to get control of the Carolina Central and the Cape Fear
and Yadkin Valley railroads and to construct about 120 miles of road to
connect these three lines. *News and Observer*, January 21, 1881.

A&H—GP

Thomas J. Jarvis to E. K. Hyndman
[*Telegram*]

Jan: 24th 1881

It will require an act of the Legislature to sell States interest.
No one has the authority to do so without such legislation

A&H—GP

E. K. Hyndman to Thomas J. Jarvis
[*Telegram*]

Balt Md Jany 24 1881

Personal

Have instructed Imboden[24] to write you our company should own
that Road for the mutual good of state & Road

A&H—GP

Thomas J. Jarvis to E. K. Hyndman
[*Telegram*]

Jan: 24 1881

Will await Gen Imbodens letter and will give it prompt attention

A&H—GP

J. D. Imboden to Thomas J. Jarvis

Bristol Tenn.
Jany 24. 1881

After parting from you on Saturday Mr. Hyndman and myself
were informed that it was probable the State of N. Carolina
would sell the 5500 shares of Stock she holds in the Yadkin
Valley R.R. Co, at something like the present market value of
the private shares held in the Company, say $8 to $10 per share,
to any responsible parties able and willing to complete the road.

---

[24]John Daniel Imboden, lawyer of Washington County, Virginia. He
pioneered in encouraging foreign and domestic capital to invest in Virginia,
and he was at this time president of the Bristol and North Carolina Narrow
Gauge Railroad Company. *Dictionary of American Biography*, IX, 460–461.

We discussed the matter very fully, and before we parted, about came to the conclusion, that it would be to the interest of both the State, and our proposed "South Atlantic and Ohio R.R. Co," that our Company should own and *complete* the line, at *both* ends, as a good outlet for our coals, both for local consumption in your mining regions, and for export from your coast—When we parted it was agreed that if some of our monied friends in the proposed new company concurred in these views Mr. Hyndman should telegraph me here authority to open negotiations for the purchase. I have just received such a telegram from him, and as our charter is not yet a law, and time is important in such matters, I make you the following proposition on behalf of Mr. Hyndman—to wit:

That he will give you $55,000 for the 5500 shares of the State, being at the rate of $10 per share. That if you or other competent State authority in the premises are willing to accept this offer, I will immediately return to Raleigh and deposit $5000. in your State Treasury as earnest money, to be forfeited to the State if default is made on the final payment of $50.000. That this final payment shall be made in gross on, say, the 1st day of May 1881 which will give ample time for the transfer, and for any legislation that may be needed, as well as for the full organization of our South Atlantic & Ohio R.R. Co. On receipt of this letter will you kindly telegraph me here, as early as possible *this* week whether the proposition is, or is likely to be, acceptable. If so I will immediately repair to Raleigh and make the deposit, and do whatever else is essential to conclude the purchase.

A&H—GP

Thomas J. Jarvis to J. D. Imboden [copy]

Executive Department,
Raleigh, Jan. 27th 1881

Yours of the 24th received, and I reply by first mail. The subject matter of your letter is too comprehensive to be treated about by telegraph; and even by letter my answer cannot be definite, because I have not the authority to make it so. I have no authority to either accept or decline your proposition. In this letter, I can only suggest the way of getting at an authoritative decision of the matter. The General Assembly is the only body that can authorize a sale of the stock of the State in the road. That body is now in session, and after it adjourns about the first of March, will not meet again in two years. If Mr. Hyndman desires to purchase the State's interest in the C.F.&Y.V.R.R., I suggest that he, or some one fully authorized to act for him and his Company, come to Raleigh at once, and make a proposition in detail for its purchase and completion. I think the completion of the road will be *the* consideration to which the State will chiefly look in any contract to sell her interest; and I suggest that you make your proposition explicit on that point. It ought to set out to what points you are willing to contract to build and by what time. My opinion is that the State would be willing to part with her interest in the road upon liberal terms, if satisfactory guarantees are given for its completion. Certainly I would advise such a course as best for the State, the sections to be benefited decidedly by the road, and, for your enterprise.

I shall be glad to receive further and fuller communications from you on the subject, and when the proposition is put in proper shape, to transmit the same to the General Assembly. There is but little time for delay, as it is not likely the Legislature will be in session longer than the first of March.

A&H—GP

James McLeod Turner[25] *to J. L. Robinson*

Office Keeper of Capitol
January 28th 1881

I have the honor to acknowledge the receipt of Senate Resolution passed January 27th 1881, directing me to place the two Rooms in the North end of the Senate Galleries in the Senate Chamber under the control of the Door Keeper of the Senate, to be used for the convenience of the Clerks and Committees of that body.

I beg leave to call your attention to the present use and condition of these Rooms.

The Room in the North East Gallery is occupied by the keeper of the Standard Weights and measures, and he has at this time

---

[25]Turner had served bravely in the Civil War and had attained the rank of lieutenant colonel. At the end of the war he was so disabled that he was unable to engage in business. In 1872 he became engrossing clerk to the Senate, and in 1877 Vance appointed him keeper of the Capitol. Tomlinson, *Sketch–book*, 144–145.

deposited therein many sets of Weights & measures for the Counties of the State when required by them in addition to the above the room contains the Standard Weights, Measures, Balances &c, furnished by the United States Government and on which depend the accuracy of the Weights & measures of the entire State depend. One set of these balances is secured to the floor and adjusted with great care and precision[.] the removal of this property will necessarily be attended with injury and loss to the State, and besides this there is no way by which the room can be heated, there being no fire place or stove flue. In relation to the Room in the North West Gallery I most respectfully call your attention to accompanying statement of Mr. Olds,[26] Clerk to Adjt General Jones.

To most of these facts I can bear testimony to their accuracy and to the importance value and condition of the property in the room, All of which is respectfully submitted

A&H—GLB

Thomas J. Jarvis to T. M. Holt

Executive Department,
Raleigh, Jan. 31st, 1881

I have the honor to forward for the consideration of your Board a copy of a resolution passed by the Board of Directors of the A.&N.C.R.R.[27]

The proposition to refer any claim the A.&N.C.R.R.Co. has against your Company to arbitration can but be fair.[28]

If they have a just claim, it ought to be paid; and if their claim is unjust, your Company will be in no danger from the arbitration.

The length of time that has elapsed ought not to be pleaded, but the claim ought to be settled upon its merits. These are two corporations in which the State has an interest, and I do not wish to see any advantage taken of one by the other, I will thank you to bring this matter before your Board.

[26]Frederick Augustus Olds of Raleigh. Besides his clerkship in the Adjutant General's Department, he was a life insurance agent and city editor of the News and Observer. Branson, Directory for 1884, 661.
[27]See Clark to Jarvis, June 10, 1881, in this volume.
[28]For the grievance of the Atlantic and North Carolina Railroad against the North Carolina Railroad, see Hughes to Jarvis, March 10, 1879, in this volume.

A&H—GP

Romeo Hicks[29] *to Thomas J. Jarvis*

Hicksville N.C.
Feb. 1. 1881

I live in Rutherford Co. NC adjoining Spartanburg Co. S.C.
There is considerable disturbance and misunderstanding in regard to the Fence Law of S.C. lately passed. S.C. so far as I
know is doing nothing towards building a line fence. Are we of
N C living along the border expected to build the line fence? Is
there any provision in our Law for the state or counties to build
said fence at public expense? If S C fails to build a fence on her
border we near the line will have to fence both our crops &
stock which would amount to an imposition, or build a fence on
the state line an expense we cannot afford, if you will give us
the information ask and any thing further in regard to the stock
law in S.C. You will greatly oblige a number of yr friends &
supporters.
P.S.
Another thing I would call to yr attention if there is a fence
built between S.&NC we ought to have a law protecting us from
being overseer from stock turned to our range from S.C. Hope
the Legislature will attend to this matter

A&H—GP

J. D. Imboden to Thomas J. Jarvis

Raleigh N. Carolina
Feby 7th 1881

On the 4th day of the present month an Act of the North Carolina Legislature was ratified, entitled "An Act to incorporate the
South Atlantic and Ohio Railway and Construction Company."
The objects of that corporation are fully set forth in the Pream-
ble and several sections of the Charter, and need not be repeated
here—
Acting as the general Agent and Attorney of those to whom
that Charter was granted, I have been instructed to organize and
place in the field immediately, a corps of Engineers to locate the
line of the proposed road from the Tennessee State line, on the

---

[29]Physician of Hicksville. Branson, *Directory for 1884*, 388.

border of Watauga or Mitchell County to some point East of the Blue Ridge Mountains, from which a convenient connection with the coast may be obtained for the shipment of coals and other tonnage.

I expect the Engineers to enter upon the surveys during the present week, and that within three months they will have obtained the necessary data to enable the Company to select the best route across the mountains, and commence the work of construction early in the coming summer—

The first route surveyed will be from Patterson in Caldwell County, crossing the Blue Ridge at Cooke's Gap, and thence down the water shed of the Watauga River to the Tennessee line, and to a connection with the company's works in Tenn. & V[a] Another route will then be surveyed from Cranberry in Mitchell County, across to the waters of Linville River, and thence to some point on the Western N.C.R.R. These surveys being completed, the company I represent, will select the one or the other route, as may appear most conducive to their interests—

Should the first mentioned route, with its eastern Terminus at or near Patterson be adopted, it may, and doubtless will, become a matter of great moment to the company that The Cape Fear & Yadkin Valley R.R. shall be speedily completed, and connected with their road across the mountains—My principals understanding that the State of North Carolina owns Five hundred & fifty thousand dollars of the stock of the Cape Fear & Yadkin Valley R.R. Co, the possession of which, by those I represent, would be desirable as an inducement for them to complete that road into Caldwell County, within the next two years I have been instructed to make the State the following proposition, to wit:

That the present Legislature shall pass an Act, authorizing a sale of the State stock in the Cape Fear & Yadkin Valley R.R. Co, Fifty five hundred shares of the par value of Five hundred and fifty thousand dollars, at the cash price of ten dollars per share, amounting to Fifty five thousand dollars, to be paid into the State Treasury, by or for, the South Atlantic & Ohio Railway Construction & Operating Company, at the time the stock is transferred—That said purchase shall be consummated, and the money paid on or before the 1st day of July 1881, otherwise the right to purchase by said South Atlantic & Ohio Company shall then cease and desist. That it shall be competent for, and shall be the duty of, the commission or agency created by the Act authorizing such sale, to exact from the purchasers of said stock, such reasonable & sufficient security as may be agreed upon, to insure the completion of said Cape Fear & Yadkin Valley Railroad to its Terminus in Caldwell County, within two years from the sale of the States interest in said road.

I need not discuss what, I think, would be valuable advantages to the State at large, and certainly to a large and exceedingly rich district, to result from such a combination of interests as this proposition suggests. It would pour into the great Iron & copper producing sections of your State the only lacking element for an unparalleled development of wealth—*cheap coke* of the highest excellence known in the United States—The coal for this fuel to the extent of over one thousand millions of tons lies within 100 miles of the border of your unequalled ore belt, and is controlled by those I have the honor to represent. For their own profit they seek a market in your State. And that line of principal transportation which they may finally adopt in N. Carolina, while it enriches them, will create great wealth and prosperity for your own people along its route, or prove to be an exception to the universal result of all similar works, that have *anywhere* united the great economic minerals of the world.

If compatible with your views of the public interests you represent, will you kindly give this proposition such direction as will secure for it, the early consideration of the Legislature of North Carolina.

A&H—GP

Donald MacRae to Thomas J. Jarvis

Wilmington, N. C. 8th Febry 1881

Having recently received a circular from the "Worlds Fair Exposition of 1883," addressed to me as one of the Comss^{rs}. from this state, requesting that an effort should be made to induce our Legislature to consider the propriety of making an appropriation for the purpose of having the various agricultural, mineral, and manufactured products of our state properly represented at the Exposition, and believing that such representation would depend upon the efforts and reccommendation of our Agricultural and Geological Departments I forward it to Montfort McGehee Esq. Comss^{r}. of Agriculture requesting him to take such action as he might deem proper in the premises.

Desiring to call your attention also to this important object I enclose for your perusal extracts from the New York Herald[30] giving assurance of the successful inauguration of the Exposition, and beg leave most respectfully to ask your official aid in presenting the subject to the Legislature at its present session for their consideration.

A&H—GP

O. E. Babcock to Thomas J. Jarvis

Baltimore, Md., February 17, 1881

I have the honor to enclose conveyances of the title to and cession of jurisdiction over the sites of Wade's Point and Roanoke River lighthouses, which I have to request you will execute and return to this office. Copies of the letters of the Lighthouse Board authorizing me to make this application are also enclosed.[31]

The following is a description of *Wade's Point* lighthouse site:

All that tract or parcel of submerged land situated on the north side of Albemarle Sound at the mouth of Pasquotank River, Camden County, North Carolina, containing 5 acres of land within a circle whose centre, marked A on the accompanying plan, is distant 3¾ nautical miles due E. from Wade's Point and 3¼ nautical miles W. by S. from North Point and which has, according to Coast Survey Chart No. 40 of Albemarle Sound, N.C., 1877, Lat. 36°09′(08″) N. & Longitude 75°58′(40″) W. and whose circumference or boundary line shall be 263.3 feet from the centre in every direction.

Roanoke River lighthouse site is described as follows:

All that tract or parcel of submerged land situated in Albemarle Sound, on the east side of the entrance to Roanoke River, Washington County, N. C. containing 5 acres within a circle whose centre, marked A on the accompanying plan, is distant 1⅝ nautical miles E. by N. from Terrapin Point and 3⅜ nautical miles S. ½ W. from Black Walnut Point, and which has, according to Coast Survey Chart No. 41 of Albemarle Sound, N.C., 1877, Lat. 35°56′(58″) N. and Lon. 76°41′(42″) W. and whose circumference or boundary line shall be 263.3 feet from the centre in every direction

---

[30]Governors' Papers, not included in this volume.
[31]Governors' Papers, not included in this volume.

A&H—GP

Thomas Branch and Company to Thomas J. Jarvis

Richmond, Va. 21st Feby 1881

We learn that the Committee of the Senate has reported adversely on the Contract made between the Construction Bondholder and the Commissioners.[32] We regret this but we think it will be agreeable to the holders of Bonds in the North. The people in the North have the most Extraordinary views of the future high value of Railroads, especially in the South, as the increase has already taken place in Western roads while ours have so far been somewhat neglected. Hence they think it will be best to wait until the maturity of the bond 1883 to 1885 and take the road, buying the State stock as cheap as they can and looking to the State for the balance. The sale of 3,000,000 of stock will of course break the price down so that the holders of the Construction Bonds will have a large claim against the State for the balance and whatever the present Legislature may do the State will pay this balance hereafter. If the Legislature will authorize you [and] the Commissioners to sell the State stock in the road to the private stockholders at such terms as will pay off and extinguish the Construction Bonds we think it probable the debt could be paid in that way. If you think favorably of such a scheme one of our firm will go to Raleigh to see you about it

A&H—GP

J. D. Imboden to Thomas J. Jarvis

Raleigh N.C.
Feby 22d 1881

On the 7th inst. I, as the Attorney of the South Atlantic & Ohio railway Construction and operating Company, incorporated by the Legislature of North Carolina, had the honor to submit to the State, through you, a proposition for the possible purchase,

---

[32]For a full explanation of the background of these negotiations, see Thomas J. Jarvis to the General Assembly, January 5, 1881, and "Report of Commissioners to Adjust a Portion of the State Debt," *Public Documents, 1881*, No. 15. When the General Assembly took no action on the contract referred to herein, the matter was left in the hands of the governor, the treasurer, and the commissioners. The contract finally agreed upon was very similar to the one rejected by the General Assembly. Ratchford, "The Adjustment of the North Carolina Public Debt," 164.

by the Company I represent, of the State's interest in the Cape Fear & Yadkin Valley railroad Company. Since the date of that proposition, which you kindly referred to the Legislature for its consideration, events have transpired, in the progress of perfecting the great enterprise in which my company is engaged, that enable me, in carrying out its purposes, and instructions to me,—to add to the proposition of Feby 7th. 1881, some points more specific, than I then felt authorized to submit, which may have a bearing upon the Legislative mind, in making a wise decision on the important questions involved. I therefore address you this supplemental note on the subject, and respectfully ask that you transmit it to the Legislature.

As I stated in my former note, I repeat here, that the disposition of the parties I represent to purchase at all, the State's interest in the Cape Fear & Yadkin Valley R.R.Co. will depend on the Surveys to be completed before July 1st 1881, of at least *two* routes from the N. Carolina & Tennessee State line in Watauga or Mitchell County, to a connection with the cis-montain railways in this state. If the Watauga, or more northerly route of the two, should prove the better of the two, then the speedy completion of the C.F.&Y.V.R.R. will become an important question to my Company. And it is in view of that possible contingency, that we hope this Legislature will take such action in the premises, as would avoid the postponement for two years to come of all operations on a work of so much importance to all parties concerned.

As suggestive of the Cardinal points to be provided for by the Legislature at this session, I propose specifically,

1st   That a bill shall be passed, authorizing a sale of the 5,500 shares held by the State, at $10. per share to the South Atlantic & Ohio railway Construction & operating Company, at any time between now and the 1st day of July 1881. The purchase money to be paid in cash at the time the stock is transferred—

2nd   That to represent the State, and with full power to act in the premises, a Commission of three or more officials, or other citizens of the State of North Carolina, shall be created, by the bill in question, to be called together whenever requested by the proposed purchasers, to execute the provisions of the bill—

3rd   That in consideration of the low price at which the State agrees to sell said stock, the purchasers shall enter into an obligation, that within two years they will complete the main line of said road as far Westward as Patterson in the County of Caldwell, and an extension thereof Eastward, to some point on the harbor at or below Wilmington: and that within three years they will complete a branch of said main line from some convenient point to, or as near as the ground may be found practicable to Mt Airy in Surry County. Time to be counted from the 1st day of July 1881. That as security for the fulfillment and performance of their obligation on the part of the purchasers in respect to the completion of the road & branch aforesaid, the 5,500 shares of state stock, when paid for at the above agreed price, shall be transferred in the books of the Company to the purchasers, but the certificates therefor shall remain in the hands of the Commissioners under the bill, as collateral security for the completion of the main line and branch aforesaid; and shall not be actually delivered to the purchasers, until trains of cars have been run over said main line & branch to their respective termini aforesaid. And if the purchasers are in default in the construction of said road & branch within the time stipulated, they shall forfeit all right and title to said stock, and to the purchase money paid therefore, and it shall be lawful for said Commissioners, or their successors or survivors to retransfer the said 5,500 shares to the State of North Carolina, and the purchase money to be retained by the State as liquidated damages for the non-fulfillment and performance of the Contract of the purchasers.

4th The question of gauge on said road shall be entirely subject to the decision of a vote of a majority of stockholders of the company, in the decision of which the purchasers as aforesaid of the States interest shall have the voice that their stock entitles them to under the present charter of the company at any meeting after they enter upon the work of construction and equipment under their said purchase and obligation: and so shall be decided all other questions affecting the relation of said Company to the purchaser's other railways, or other lines in the State that under their Charter they may connect with—

5th To afford the said purchasing Company all practicable facilities for the speedy completion of their work, the state shall consent & agree not to withdraw the convict force now in the employment of the C.F.&Y.V.R.R. Co, nor to diminish or abridge its rights to convict labour under existing laws; & shall further agree that as additional convicts, now in the employment of other companies in the State, are returned to the Penitentiary, the same shall be hired to the Cape Fear & Yadkin Valley railroad

Company, or to the South Atlantic & Ohio railway Construction and operating Company, until their works in this State are completed, on the terms usual in such cases, the hiring companies agreeing to pay the earnings of the convicts to the State, in money, monthly as the same falls due, under such contracts respecting the same as may be entered into.

In conclusion I may add, that in all its aspects, in whole or in part, this is a plain business proposition, pure & simple. The parties I represent are the owners of enormous coal mines within 100 miles of the borders of your State, in which they are engaged at this moment in rapidly developing so far as to reach this year a point of remunerative production. They seek, and must have an ocean outlet at some port or ports in North or South Carolina— I may add they *will* have this outlet because the way is already open to them, without additional legislation, to Georgetown & Charlestown South Carolina. Whilst that is *one* way now at their command, it may not be the *best* way—and they want the best way if it can be had on reasonable terms. Three or four months engineering can alone settle that question. If it shall be found that the *best* way both to reach the sea coast, and to develope on the route a demand for the coal and coke they have to sell and transport, lies entirely through North Carolina, they are prepared to open up that way—And as all the advantages will not accrue to them, they, as prudent business men, ask that co-öperation on the part of North Carolina which they think the mutuality of their interest and the State's entitles them to ask— If in the wisdom of the Legislature the terms I have indicated above, are inadmissible, I—as the organ of gentlemen of large means, and great enterprise, in whose service, I have been for nearly a year in South Western Virginia, where their large investments have been made through me,—can not but deeply regret the failure of my present mission here; at the same time however, I beg to assure you, that such failure if it occurs, must be ascribed to what I know will be an honest difference of opinion on questions viewed from different stand points—And it will then remain to be determined, whether other means of reaching a N. Carolina port, within the range of a reasonable expenditure of money, are attainable under the liberal charter your State has granted to the South Atlantic & Ohio railroad Company.

The whole question is one of dollars and cents on both sides. I have tried to present it briefly and fairly. If I have failed I will gladly supply the omission on any point left in doubt. I am not here, I have not been sent, to enter the lobby and buttonhole and annoy members of the Legislature in the personal solicitation of their support, but simply to explain what we want, and submit it to their unbiassed judgment. I lay the whole matter before them, through you in perfect good faith, as a business proposition, under instructions from those, about whom I know enough to say, unqualifiedly, that they are able to, and will execute to the letter any contract they may enter into—

A&H—SPI

Alexander Hicks[33] *to Thomas J. Jarvis*

Raleigh Feby 23ᵈ, 1881

I write you in the interest of the colored people, of the more extreme East, of which you were formerly a citizen. I hope, you will not consider this letter premature, as I am anxious about the matter.

In view of the fact, as recommended by the joint educational committee of the general assembly now in session, that there will be other Normal schools established in the State, than at Fayetteville,[34] I write to pray that the one to be established in the East, for the colored race, be located at Plymouth, for many good reasons,—some of which, I think I can make plain: Firstly, Plymouth is near the center of the 1ˢᵗ congressional district, and the central mail point of the East.

There all the mails connect regularly three times per week, from four points—East, West, North and South: We have the Black water steamer of Franklin [,] Va, touching all the points on the Chowan river and Albemarle Sound.

We have the steamer Oriole, running as far up the Roanoke river, as Hamilton and sometimes Palmyra, connecting there with the steamer Vesta of Halifax, and again making regular

---

[33]Negro teacher of Plymouth, who served as principal of the Plymouth Normal School from its beginning in 1881 to his death in 1883. He was a member of the General Assembly during the session of 1881. "Biennial Report of the Superintendent of Public Instruction, *Public Documents, 1883*, No. 6, 102; Connor, *Manual, 1913*, 843.

[34]On March 1, 1881, the General Assembly authorized the State Board of Education eight new normal schools—four for each race—for teacher education, and it appropriated $2,000 for the schools of each race. *Laws of North Carolina, 1881*, c. 141. As chairman of the Board of Education, Jarvis was to help decide where to locate the new schools.

connection with the cars from Washington [,] Beaufort County, which connects with all the mails from the counties of Pitt and Hyde.

We have also the steamer Bertie of Windsor [,] Bertie county, touching all the points on the Cashie river. We have in addition to all of these, a regular tri-weekly land route, from Columbia[,] Tyrell county, all meeting at Plymouth, three times per week; thus making Plymouth the only central mail point in the East, and the most accessable and convenient to the people of that section to reach. Furthermore, you are well aware, that the Albemarle section, has never received any aid from the state, outside the common school appropriation. While I feel thankful for the liberal consideration received at the hands of ex–governor Vance; and the colored people I warrant, feel grateful also, for the interest, which he exhibited in their educational, material and industrial welfare, yet, we of the more extreme East, have not been equally cared for, in all things; owing, I suppose, mainly to our remoteness. But, knowing you to be more identified with our section, needs and requirements, and while I would not ask or desire you to discriminate in favor of the East,—*and know you would* not, yet we do expect of you, that consideration, which we have heretofore, failed to receive. I read with pleasure both your message and Inaugural address, and took great delight, in forwarding copies to my constituents; and I am glad to say, as I have already said on many occasions, without the least hesitation, that while we recd much encouragement from governor Vance, and as much as could be expected under the circumstances, yet the encouragement which both of your addresses give to the colored people, especially as to their educational welfare, surpasses any heretofore extended to them in my time.

The liberality with which you express your self upon the Normal, and more particularly the common school system, and instruction, is all that could be said or requested. The encouragement of a higher rate of taxation and more Normal schools, have fully aroused the educational committee, and they are fully determined, so far as practicable, to comply with your request, and doubly improve our common school system. And I do hope, that the Eastern section may be considered in all of the proposed improvements. Consequently, the cause of this letter. Enclosed please find two recommendations, one from the citizens of my town as to my qualifications and character, and another from both chairmans of the house and senate branch of the educational committee, and the representatives and senators of the first congressional district.[35] I respectfully beg of you to examine closely the petition as to character, and give to each, your careful consideration; and I shall consider my–self highly favored at your hands. Besides, in a few days, I shall be pleased to call at your office, to converse with you upon the subject.

A&H—GLB

Thomas J. Jarvis to Thomas Branch and Company

Executive Department
Raleigh, Feb. 24th, 1881

Before the sale of the Western North Carolina Railroad, I was opposed to a sale of the State's interest in the North Carolina Railroad; but now the Western Road has been sold, I think the best thing the State can do with the North Carolina Road is to surrender the property for the debt.

I shall therefore favor such a proposition if it is proposed.

A&H—GLB

Thomas J. Jarvis to Donald MacRae

Executive Department,
Raleigh, Feb'y. 25th, 1881

Yours of 8th ins't. received.

I have communicated with the Legislature on the subject, but fear that body will take no action.

If they fail, I will then see what can be done by the Board of Agriculture.

A&H—GP

Thomas Branch and Company to Thomas J. Jarvis

Richmond, Va. 25th Feby 1881

We have yours of yesterday We represent somewhat over a million of the Construction Bond of the NCRR which are held in Va & N C and a small amount in Balt[r] We will accept for this million our proportionate share of the State stock in the road

---

[35]Not found.

surrendering to the State for Cancelation our Construction Bond. We do not know what the holder of the balance will do but we think a large part of them would join us in the Exchange on the terms proposed If the State determines to sell her stock on these terms we think it would be due to the private stockholder that they should have the refusal in proportion to their present interest that Each holder of one share should have the privilege of buying three more at the price agreed on and if he declined then the stock would be open to the public The large majority of the private stock being held in your State they would thus be able to continue its control. To accomplish this it would only be necessary to have a simple bill authorizing the governor &c &c to sell the State stock to the private stockholder or the public on best terms provided the price be not less than will pay off and Extinquish all the outstanding Construction Bond

We authorize you to say that the Bondholder will accept such a settlement and take the stock We speak by authority for a million and by an intimate knowledge of the views of the others for a second million The United States government (Interiour department) holds about $200.000 which would probably be subject to the action of Congress Then a half million would probably hold out against any Compromise no matter how just or fair as there are always stupid people who will oppose anything but we feel confident in offering you two million of the Construction Bonds for a proportionate share of the stock

A&H—SPI

W. A. Wilburn to Thomas J. Jarvis

Salisbury, N.C.
Feb. 28th, 1881

I have just learned that the Legislature has placed the sum of $4000 in the hands of the State Board of Education, for the purpose [of] establishing normals, where ever the Board may elect &c.

Now, Sir, I desire to put in a plea for the Rowan Teacher's Association, for a normal at Salisbury: because, as you well know, this [is] the most central as well as the most accessible point in this part of the State and as we so much need one, in this immediate section.

I have taught in Onslow, Chatham, Orange, Randolph and Rowan, and I am free to say that the common school teachers in
this section are at least fifty per cent behind those [of] any
other section of the State with which I am acquainted. Of about
sixty common school teachers in this county, not one has ever
attended a normal except my lady assistant and myself, who
were both employed from another county.

Of some twenty private teachers, only two have ever attended
any normal.

The result of this is, that teaching is at a very low ebb, and that
too, in *deep gutters*. This is very deplorable, but I am perfectly
satisfied it will not be any better for several years without the
normal and its benefits are brought nearer to their homes and
offered at less cost than at Chapel Hill.

We have a regular Teacher's Association in this county, probably the only one in the State that meets regularly. The Association, realizing the low status of teaching, have already determined to hold an Institute in this county during the summer.
But we, unanimously, prefer having a normal instead.

The Association proposes to employ English, Blair, Weatherly,[36]
or the best out side help possible,

We have canvassed the field and are satisfied we can secure
seventy five teachers for the normal here, who cannot attend
Chapel Hill, owing to cost, inconvenience &c. Our town will soon
have finished, the best public school building in the State. It will
be furnished with the most improved desk, maps, charts, stoves
objects, blackboards &c. They have authorized me to tend this
building for the use of the normal and to state they will do all
in their power to make it a success. Board can be obtained on
very reasonable terms.

Our Association would like to know the pleasure of the State
Board on this important subject, by our next monthly meeting,
March 12th, and if desirable we will have a committee to visit
Raleigh.

Will you do us the kindest to inform us, at your earliest convenience, the pleasure of the Board?

---

[36]Probably M. C. English of Greensboro, J. M. Weatherly of Jamestown,
and Franklin S. Blair, teachers at the University Normal School in Chapel
Hill. "Annual Report of the Superintendent of Public Instruction of North
Carolina for 1880," *Public Documents, 1881*, No. 6, 23–24.

A&H—GLB

Proclamation, March 1, 1881

Whereas, An Act was passed by the General Assembly of the state of North Carolina, on the 28th day of January, in the year one thousand, eight hundred and seventy–four, in these words:

"*An Act* to provide for the relinquishment to the United States, in certain cases, of the title to and jurisdiction over lands for sites of light-houses, beacons, or other aids to navigation in the waters of this state.

And whereas, application has been made by a duly authorized agent of the United States describing the site required for a light–house known as *Wade's Point Light–house*, situated on the north side of Albemarle Sound, at the mouth of Pasquotank River, Camden County, North Carolina; said site to contain five (5) acres of land within a circle, whose centre, marked A on the accompanying plan, is distant three and three–quarters (3¾) nautical miles due East from Wade's Point, and three and a quarter (3¼) nautical miles W. by S. from North Point; and which has, according to Coast Survey, Chart No. 40 of Albemarle Sound, N. C., 1877, Latitude 36°, 09′ (08″) and Longitude 75°, 58′ (40″) ; and whose circumference or boundary line shall be two hundred and sixty three and three–tenths (263.3) feet from the centre in every direction,—

Now, therefore, this deed witnesseth,

That Thomas J. Jarvis, Governor of the said state, in execution of the power and authority vested in him by the said Act of the General Assembly, does cede, convey, assign, transfer and make over to and for the use of the United States, the said tract or parcel of land situated and bounded as above described, containing not more than five (5) acres, together with all the jurisdiction which the said state possesses over the same. But this conveyance is to be operative and with the reservations in the said Act of the General Assembly set forth and not otherwise.

A&H—GLB

*George Henry White[37] and William W. Watson[38] to
Thomas J. Jarvis*

[n.d.]

In behalf of the colored members of the General Assembly, we communicate to you to ascertain what time it would be convenient for us to call on you for the purpose of presenting certain matters of deep interest to us as a race to your Excellency.

A&H—GLB

Thomas J. Jarvis to W. W. Watson

Executive Department
Raleigh, March 3rd, 1881

I have been compelled by a pressure of public matters to postpone till to–day receiving the visit of the colored members of the Legislature.

I will thank you to inform them that I will be glad to see them at the Executive office at 4:30 P.M. to–day.

A&H—GLB

William Stuart Primrose[39] to Thomas J. Jarvis

[March 3, 1881]

Last year the School Committee rented about 2 acres of the improved land connected with the mansion. This year we have also rented the same place to a colored man for 16⁰⁰ It seems

---

[37]New Bern lawyer and principal of the state Normal School at New Bern; member of the General Assembly, 1881, 1885; Republican representative to Congress, 1897–1901. *Biographical Directory of Congress,* 1690.

[38]Member of the General Assembly from Edgecombe County, 1881. Connor, *Manual, 1913,* 603.

[39]Businessman of Raleigh. After serving for several years as assistant cashier of the State National Bank, Primrose became an agent for the North Carolina Home Insurance Company. In 1885 he became its president. In 1881 he was chairman of the Raleigh school committee. Withers, *Davidson College,* 124.

that Mr. Tupper[40] has given him notice to stop work, as the Legislature has given an acre to his school.

I write to know your opinion as to whether Mr. Tupper goes into immediate possession, or whether, in your opinion, the tenant has a right to hold this year under our contract.

A&H—GLB

Thomas J. Jarvis to W. S. Primrose

Executive Department
Raleigh, March 3, 1881

In reply to yours of this date, I beg to say that as I leased to the Committee the Mansion property for this year, and as you sublet to the tenant in possession a part of it, the tenant cannot be disturbed during this year, unless Mr. Tupper makes satisfactory arrangements with you.

I answer this note, however, hastily, but will get the official opinion of the Attorney General if desired.

A&H—SPI

Braxton Craven to Thomas J. Jarvis

President's Office, March 9 1881

If it shall seem proper to the State Board, I should be glad for one of the four new normal schools to be at Trinity College. We have first rate accomodations and arrangements, and nothing would be charged for rooms, apparatus, black–boards, and the accommodations generally.

I am informed that if you and Mr. Scarborough should recommend it, that a donation would be given from the Peabody fund to the Normal School at Trinity established during the last Legislature. The Normal School thus established is under State control, as completely as is that at the University. I hope this may meet your views. We think [it] is of public utility, and in all

---

[40]Henry Martin Tupper, who had come to Raleigh from Massachusetts in 1865 as a missionary to the freedmen. In that year he founded Shaw University. *National Cyclopedia*, I, 270. The acre of land referred to had been granted to Shaw by the General Assembly in 1881 as a site for a medical school building, the money for the building having been raised by Tupper from northern philanthropists. *Laws of North Carolina, 1881*, c. 141.

senses fair, that a Normal School should be at Trinity, and a fair appropriation therefor

I make these suggestions, not knowing the plans contemplated by the State Board

A&H—GP

Johnson Hagood[41] to Thomas J. Jarvis

Executive Department
Columbia, S.C. 11 Mar 1881

May I enquire if your state has taken any action in view of co-operation in re–surveying the Boundary line between us. I ask because of the limited time allowed by the Act of the S.C. Legislature for having the work on the part of this State done.[42]

A&H—GP

W. L. Bragg et al. to Thomas J. Jarvis

Office of Railroad Commission of Ala
Montgomery Ala
Mch. 15th 1881

By act of the Legislature of the State of Alabama, approved Febry. 26th 1881, a Railroad Commission was provided for and the undersigned have been elected such Commissioners. The 31st Section of this act provides. "It shall be the duty of the Railroad Commission by correspondence, convention or otherwise, to confer with the Railroad Commissioners of other States of the Union, and with such persons from States having no Railroad Commissioners, as the Governor of such States may appoint, for the purpose of agreeing, if practical, upon a draft of Statutes to be submitted to the Legislature of each State, which shall secure such uniform control of Railroad transportation in the several States, and from one State, into or through another State, as will best subserve the interest of trade and

---

[41]Planter and lawyer of Barnwell, South Carolina. He served as governor from 1880 to 1882. *Dictionary of American Biography*, VIII, 85.

[42]In December, 1880, the South Carolina General Assembly authorized its governor to rerun and remark the boundary line between North and South Carolina. On March 12, 1881, the North Carolina General Assembly made a similar authorization. "Boundary Line Between North and South Carolina," *Public Documents, 1881*, No. 28, 3–4; *Laws of North Carolina, 1881*, c. 347.

commerce of the whole country; and said Commission shall include in their annual report to the Governor an abstract of the proceedings of any such conference or convention."

In obedience to this provision of the law, we respectfully invite your attention to what it contemplates, and beg leave to request an expression of your views respecting it, as early as may be convenient. It is believed by those who have given the movement some consideration, that such a convention held at some point that may be agreed upon, like for instance Louisville Ky., in the month of June or July next, might be productive of good in many respects.

Yours Respectfully
W L Bragg Prest
Jas Crook &   Associate Railroad
Chas P Ball   Commisssioners of Ala.

A&H—GLB

Thomas J. Jarvis to Johnson Hagood

Executive Department,
Raleigh, Mar. 16th. 1881.

I have delayed an answer to yours of the 11th ins't. till I could get a certified copy of the Act just passed by the General Assembly of this State, authorizing the re–marking of the line between our States. Owing to the pressure of business in the closing days of our Legislature, I have not been able to forward this Act earlier.

I will be ready to name the Commission on the part of this State at any time you may notify me of your appointment.

A&H—GLB

Thomas J. Jarvis to John F. Wooten[43]

Executive Department,
Raleigh, March 17, 1881

The Legislature, at its recent session, appropriated $500.00 for the erection of a monument at the grave of Gov. Caswell;

---

[43]Lawyer of Kinston, Branson, *Directory for 1884*, 415.

but, by a supplemental act, gave me the authority to have it erected in the town of Kinston.

It occurs to me that Kinston will be the more appropriate place, and, if it be the wish of the people of your town, I am inclined to designate that place. It also occurs to me that it will be proper to make the day of its unveiling something of a State occasion. Such is my purpose and such will be my effort if I can have the co–operation of the people of Kinston and Lenoir. If we were to fix the fourth day of July as the time and then work up the arrangements with energy, we could make it a day and an occasion long to be remembered by the people of the State. I cannot, however, succeed unless I can have the hearty co–operation of the good people of Kinston; and I do not care to undertake it without the assurance of such co–operation. Will you be kind enough to talk with some of your leading citizens about the matter and communicate with me on the subject? I expect to spend next week in Greenville and would be glad to meet some of your people there and talk the matter over with them. If there be any prospect of the people taking hold of it, I can come down any day after next week and confer with them and give them my idea of a programme, with some suggestions about a military parade and oration, a poem etc.

UNC—UP

Thomas J. Jarvis to K. P. Battle

Executive Department
Raleigh, March 18th, 1881

Mr. Supt. S. [carborough] is away and will not return till next week. I tried to see him yesterday after getting your letter[44] but found him gone. I expect to leave here Monday and will not return till 29th. So it will be some time before I can see him. I think you had better go on making your arrangements for the Normal as usual. The other normals will necessarily take away some whom you have been helping out of the Peabody Fund so that the aid you get from that will be sufficient. Of course I will help you and do not see why there should be any trouble.

---

[44]Not found.

A&H—GLB

Thomas J. Jarvis to W. L. Bragg

Executive Department
Raleigh, March 19th, 1881

There is no officer in this State authorized to act for the State in the matter referred to in your letter of the 15th ins't., nor have I the power to appoint one.

I agree with you that the question of transportation is getting to be of such vital importance to the people and their prosperity depends so much upon its proper adjustment, that it must be taken hold of and regulated by the law–making power.

I regret that, owing to the failure of our Legislature to act in the selection of a Railroad Commission,[45] North Carolina cannot be represented in a convention of the men charged with this important work.

A&H—GP

Circular [46]

Executive Department,
Raleigh, N. C., March 21st, 1881

The Legislature of the State, at its recent session, imposed upon the State Board of Education the duty of recommending a series of Text–Books to be used in the Public Schools of the State.

I deem this a matter about which our teachers throughout the State should be consulted, and their views as to the best series of Text–Books ascertained.

It is my desire that the Board shall adopt such books as will be satisfactory to the Teachers, and at the same time accomplish the best results for the children they instruct.

To enable the Board to choose wisely, as it is soon to meet, I respectfully ask that you will favor me with your opinion as to the comparative merits of the School Readers, Grammars, Geographies, Histories, Spellers, Arithmetics, Dictionaries and Copy Books with which you are acquainted.

---

[45]In 1879 the state Senate passed a bill establishing a railroad commission, but it was defeated in the House. *House Journal, 1879*, 805.

[46]This was a printed circular which Jarvis, as chairman of the Board of Education, sent to every educational institution in the state.

Please name the series, which in your judgment, are the most meritorious books on the subjects named.

An early answer will greatly oblige,

A&H—SPI

T. F. Klutzz to Thomas J. Jarvis

Salisbury N.C. Mar. 23/81

I take pleasure in heartily endorsing the application[47] for the establishment of a Normal School in Salisbury. The needs here are great, and the facilities excellent. We have a *live* Teacher's Association, which will guarantee the success of the Normal; and the new Graded School Building, to be shortly finished with all the modern accessories and appliances, will furnish a most desirable place for the Normal. Board is cheap here too, and this point convenient for the teachers of a large radius of country not penetrated by Rail–roads.

A&H—GP

John Duckett to Thomas J. Jarvis [48]

Apex N.C.
Mar. 24—1881

Yours of Mar. 21st relative to text books rec'd. I take pleasure in complying with your request.

Readers

I have used McGuffie's, Holmes', Sanders' and Appletons' readers. I have given all a fair test in the schoolroom. I am very decided in saying that my pupils have made far greater progress in reading since using Appletons' Readers than ever before. They teach more about the principles of reading than any other readers with which I am acquainted. McGuffie's revised readers are excellent and Holmes' are fair.

---

[47] See Wilburn to Jarvis, February 28, 1881.
[48] Jarvis received scores of replies to his circular letter of March 21 and they are all in the Governors' Papers. A few of those whose writers attempt to analyze the available texts are included here.

Grammars

It is hard to say which is the best series of grammars. None are perfect, and many are very imperfect. I have used Quackenbos' with success; but in some respects I think Reed & Kellogg's Graded Lessons superior. The latter makes analysis of sentences and punctuation important features, and gives concise rules that cover the whole ground on these subjects. I tried Holmes' Grammars one session and pronounce them failures. They are too difficult for the average pupil. No doubt Prof. Holmes is a master of the English Language, but he has been accustomed to teach young men in college whose minds, to an extent are already trained; consequently he does not know how to present rules and principles with sufficient simplicity, for the untutored minds such as we have in our common schools. No one can prepare text books for beginners who has never taught beginners.

Geographies

Maury's Manual and Physical Geographies are excellent books, but his Primary is not well adapted to beginners. The first named give more information about climate and the industries dependent upon it, and "The way the wind blows" than any other geographies with which I am acquainted.

History

Swinton's condensed history of the U. S. is a very good text book. If used by a skillful teacher, the pupil can be trained to arrange historical facts analytically and thereby have them at his command at any time.

Arithmetics

Prof. Sanford's arithmetics are undoubtedly the best mind–training books of the kind before the public.

Dictionaries

Worcester's dictionaries are superior in pronunciation, but Webster's are better in regard to definition.

Principal Apex Academy.

I recommend the following series.

1st   Appleton's Readers.
2nd   Quackenbos or Reed & Kellogg's Grammars.

3ʳᵈ   Maury's Geographies.
4ᵗʰ   Swinton's History of U. S.
5ᵗʰ   Sanford's Arithmetics
6ᵗʰ   Worcester's Dictionaries.
7ᵗʰ   American Spellers.
8ᵗʰ   Ivison, Blakeman & Taylor's Copy Books.

A&H—SPI

George Rockwell McNeill[49] *to Thomas J. Jarvis*

Wood Leaf, Rowan Co. 3/25—'81

At the request of my friend W. A. Wilburn, of Salisbury, I write to add my solicitations to his relative to your holding a State Normal School at this point (Salisbury).

You have already received the invitations extended to your Body by our County Board of Education, and by our Teachers' Association, to the latter of which my official signature as Secretary is appended. I can add but little to the arguments adduced in them.

I have been working in my humble sphere, for several years past to advance the interests of Education in Rowan—was myself the means of organizing a Teachers' Association in this County some five years ago—was one of the top teachers from Rowan who attended the first State Normal at Chapel Hill, and saw the great good to be derived therefrom, and, knowing these advantages, I am very anxious that out Western teachers may get the same opportunity. Salisbury is easily accessible to almost all the Western Counties, accomodations will be as cheap as in any neighboring town, and our Association, being already in good working order, will pledge itself to aid to the utmost in making the Normal a success.

Another argument that may be added, is, that, by another year, at least, the new School Law will require Institutes to be held in the different Counties,[50] by means of this Normal our

---

[49]After teaching for several years at Woodlief, McNeill in 1883 became president of Reidsville Academy. In 1889 he became president of La Fayette College in Arkansas. Withers, *Davidson College,* 58.

[50]A reference to a law of March 10, 1881, which allowed any county board of education to appropriate up to $100 out of the county school funds for the purpose of conducting teacher institutes. If this were done, all the public school teachers in that county must attend the institute. *Laws of North Carolina, 1881,* c. 200.

Teachers will be inducted into the *modus operandi* of such meetings and thereby be enabled to make these Institutes more profitable. Doubtless, however, all these and other more potential reasons for giving us a Normal are already in your possession, and I will not engress your valuable time further, hoping, however, that you will give our request an impartial and, if practicable, a favorable hearing.

A&H—GP

Sidney Michael Finger[51] to Thomas J. Jarvis

Newton, N.C. Mch 29 1881

Rev. J. C. Clapp[52] has informed me of the reception of your circular relative to text books. Allow me to suggest that, inasmuch as the books recommended two years ago[53] have been partially introduced throughout the state and are *good* books, if not the best, it might be unwise to make a change now. The law contemplates only a *recommendation* of books by State Board and does not make their use compulsory: therefore those counties that have introduced the series formerly recommended would not change now. Indeed I doubt whether, all things considered, there are any books extant better suited to our wants. My solicitudes about the school interests must be my excuse for thus troubling you.

A&H—GP

W. A. G. Brown[54] to Thomas J. Jarvis

[Hendersonville, N.C.
March 30, 1881]

In response to your circular asking the opinion of the teachers of the State in regard to Text–Books to be used in the Public

---

[51]After conducting an academy in Catawba for several years, Finger became a successful textile merchant and manufacturer. From 1874 to 1883 he was a member of the General Assembly, and from 1884 to 1892 he was superintendent of public instruction. *Cyclopedia of the Carolinas*, II, 421–422.

[52]Associate Reform minister of Newton. Branson, *Directory for 1884*, 196.

[53]For the list of school books recommended in 1879 by the superintendent of public instruction, see "Annual Report of the Superintendent of Public Instruction of North Carolina, for 1880," *Public Documents, 1881*, No. 6, 51–52.

[54]Teacher in Hendersonville and superintendent of public schools for Henderson County. Branson, *Directory for 1884*, 373–377.

Schools, I take pleasure in stating, as the sentiment of one teacher, that I am very much pleased with the Text-Books recommended by your Board something over a year ago. Personally, and as County Examiner, I interested myself in their introduction into the public schools of Henderson county. They have gone into almost exclusive use in the county—entirely so, except where old books already in hand have not been displaced, and these are all individual instances. The books recommended are in use to a greater or less extent in every school in the county—especially the Geographies, Readers and Arithmetics—no others are kept by the merchants. The few old books still in the hands of individuals are such as Webster's Speller, Smith's Grammar and Davies Arithmetic. A change now, so soon, would be a calamity to the schools, when parents are congratulating themselves that the book question is settled and there is to be no more change. To speak of the merits of the books lately recommend: I am acquainted with a very wide range of school books, and do not think a selection better adapted to the present wants of our Public Schools could have been or can now be made. Some of the books, especially the Geographies, Readers, and Common School Arithmetic, have special merits. So I would not recommend any change, but on the contrary advise the readoption of the books alread[y] in use as recommended by your Board. I know this to be the sentiment, likewise, of a very large portion of the people of this county.

A&H—GP

James F. Terry[55] *to Thomas J. Jarvis*

Roxboro, N.C., March 30th, 1881—

I have rec'd the enclosed circulars with request that I give such information as I may have. Our County Board of Education adopted the books recommended by the State Board, and I have no doubt the same will be the case again, upon the ground that the State Board are better prepared to make a wise selection. The books recommended by the State Board have given, in every instance, so far as I am informed, entire satisfaction.

The trouble in getting teachers to use them entirely, is owning

---

[55]Lawyer of Roxboro, and county school examiner for Person County. Withers, *Davidson College*, 132.

to the fact that we, after zealous effort, failed to get any one to keep these books for the Publishers at *introduction and exchange* rates for the commissions allowed by the Publishers. I am persuaded, from what information I can get, that in our Public Schools there are almost as many different kinds of books as there are pupils.

The late School Law meets with general favor with our citizens, and it is to be hoped that it will fully accomplish the end aimed at, and that our Public Schools may become to be *really beneficial* instead *the drags they now are*, owing in the main to the teachers who conduct them, and the little interest taken by the School Committee in them. There are exceptions of course, but they are comparatively few. The *County* Superintendent or Supervisor, if a good selection is made, in performing his prescribed duties, *can* and *will* do much to correct this.

A&H—GP

John Warfield Johnston[56] *to Thomas J. Jarvis*

Washington, March 30th 1881

The Yorktown Centennial Commission extends to you a cordial invitation to attend the ceremonies to be held at Yorktown—commencing on the 19th of October 1881—in commemoration of the surrender of Lord Cornwallis and his Army, to the Allied forces of the United States and France.

You will please extend this invitation to such of your Staff as you my desire to accompany you.

The Commission hopes for as large a military representation from your State as possible on that occasion and would be glad to know at your earliest convenience, what number of troops will probably attend—whether they will come by water or by rail—and whether they will furnish their own quarters on boats or cars—or desire to be assigned locations for encampment. This information is needed for the use and guidance of the officer detailed by the Government to lay off the grounds for an encampment, and to assign their positions to the various corps expected to be in attendance.

The Commission would also like to be informed of any action taken by your State Legislature, in this matter, and to receive copies of all official acts in connection therewith.

---

[56]Johnston represented Virginia in the United States Senate from 1870 to 1883. *Biographical Directory of Congress*, 1,158.

A&H—GP

S. S. Elam to Thomas J. Jarvis

Richmond, Va., Mch. 31 1881

The object of this note is to ascertain if the Board of Public works of NC will entertain an offer from "myself" and associates" to purchase the States interest (12.666 shares) in the Atlantic and North Carolina R R Co, at the present market value of the Stock which is $5 per share. The object of the association is to extend the Road from New Bern to Salisbury; which will give western NC a deep water outlet—

A&H—GP

Frederick Becton Loftin,[57] *George K. Bagby, and*
Lemuel Harvey[58] *to Thomas J. Jarvis*

Kinston, N.C. March 31st 1881

We have been appointed by the Caswell Memorial Association to confer with you,[59] and to obtain your consent to have the money appropriated by the General Assembly for the purpose of erecting a monument to the memory of Gov Caswell, used in conjunction with other moneys which said Association proposes to raise in erecting said monument on the Court House Square in the town of Kinston. It has been suggested that it would suit your convenience to come down any time next week, if so. we would respectfully suggest that you meet us in Kinston next Tuesday the 5th day of April, and advise with us in regard to the matter,

A&H—GLB

Thomas J. Jarvis to S. S. Elam

Executive Department,
Raleigh, April 2nd, 1881

In reply to yours of the 31st ult., I have to say that the General Assembly is the only body in this State having the authority to sell the State's interest in the A.&N.C.R.R.Co.

---

[57]Lawyer of Kinston; member of the General Assembly, 1870, 1883. Branson, *Directory for 1884,* 415; Connor, *Manual, 1913,* 681.

[58]Prominent businessman and truck farmer of Kinston. Talmage C. Johnson and Charles R. Holloman, *The Story of Kinston and Lenoir County* (Raleigh: Edwards & Broughton Company, 1954), 125–126, hereinafter cited as Johnson and Holloman, *Kinston and Lenoir County.*

[59]See Jarvis to Wooten, March 17, 1881, in this volume.

As the Board of Internal Improvements has no authority to sell at any price, the proposition of yourself and associates to buy at $5. per share, of course, cannot be entertained at any price.

The construction of a road from Goldsboro to Salisbury on something like a direct line would, however, develop such a fine portion of North Carolina, that, in my opinion, the General Assembly would be most liberal with the State's interest in the A.&N.C. to any association that would construct such a road, with a view of making Newberne and Morehead City the outlet for the traffic of their line. If such an enterprise is in serious contemplation, I shall be glad to advance it in every way in my power.

A&H—GLB

Thomas J. Jarvis to F. B. Loftin, G. K. Bagby, and Lemuel Harvey

Executive Department,
Raleigh, April 2nd, 1881

It will be my pleasure to use the $500. appropriated by the Legislature for a monument to Gov. Caswell, as indicated in your letter of March 31st, which did not reach me till to–day.

It is exceedingly gratifying to me to know that the people of Kinston and Lenoir, the home of North Carolina's first great Governor under a constitutional form of government, have taken hold of this matter in earnest. I hope to see their effort successful and to be present and witness an occasion worthy of the great Carolinian, who now sleeps in an unmarked grave.

Unless prevented by some unforeseen cause, I will come down on Tuesday and have a conference with your committee and such others as may be with you.

A&H—GLB

Thomas J. Jarvis to T. S. Kenan

Executive Department,
Raleigh, Apr. 12th, 1881

I desire to take the State Guard to Yorktown[60] a thousand strong, if it can be done in a manner that will reflect honor upon

---

[60]See Johnston to Jarvis, March 30, 1881.

the State. I am not willing to see them go at all, unless their soldiery appearance will be equal to that of the troops of any State in the Union.

To put the Guard in condition that all Carolinians who visit the Centennial will be proud of them, I shall be obliged to have the services of the Adjutant General in perfecting their organization and in making all necessary arrangements.

He cannot give this service upon his present salary of $300.⁰⁰, and no expenses allowed.

Have I the authority, under existing laws, to order him on active duty for such time as may actually be necessary, and to pay him for his services?[61]

A&H—GLB

Thomas J. Jarvis to John Goode[62]

Executive Department,
Raleigh, April 12, 1881

This will introduce to you Gen. Johnston Jones, Adjt. Gen'l. of North Carolina. He visits New York as my personal representative to attend your meeting on the 30th ins't., to get the details of the part the States are to take in the Yorktown Celebration. I feel it important for me to know exactly what part the States are expected to take in the Celebration, and what each will have to do for the comfort and encampment of its own troops, so that I can know what I shall have to do for the troops I hope to send from this State.

I beg to suggest that you settle everything as definitely as possible, and I request that you inform Gen. Jones.

[61]Kenan replied in the affirmative. See Kenan to Jarvis, April 12, 1881, Governors' Papers, not included.

[62]Lawyer and statesman of Virginia, whose public career spanned half a century. At this time he was Democratic representative to Congress, and president of the Yorktown Centennial Celebration. *Dictionary of American Biography*, VII, 382–383.

Thomas J. Jarvis to Jacob W. Bowman[63]

Executive Department,
Raleigh, April 13th, 1881

The petition of certain citizens of your County for the appointment of Mr. C. D. Stuard[64] Supervisor of Convicts on the M. [arion] & A[sheville] Turnpike, and your letter to Col. Fuller seeking his services to secure a compliance with the act of the General Assembly donating convicts to said Turnpike, has been sent to me.[65]

I beg to assure you that it is entirely unnecessary to employ any one to compel the Board of Directors of the Pen., or any officer of the State Government to comply with the law. Any money spent in that direction will be uselessly spent.

It will give the Board pleasure to comply with the provisions of the act when it is in their power to do so, and, until it is in their power, all the lawyers in the State cannot compel it.

There was an act passed about the same time as your act was, appropriating fifty convicts to the Scotland Neck R.R., in Halifax County. These convicts are to be paid for by the Company, and the State to have no expense. The Warden of the Penitentiary informed Mr. R. H. Smith,[66] of Scotland Neck, in my presence on Monday last, that it would be impossible to furnish the convicts, because they were not in the Penitentiary.

The State has a contract with the purchasers of the W.N.C. R.R., to furnish five hundred able–bodied convicts to that work for $125. a year each. I am sure you would not have the State violate that contract. It takes every able–bodied convict in the Pen. to fill this contract, and at this time the number is about twenty short. Then there is an act of four years standing, giving two hundred to the Cape Fear and Yadkin Valley R.R. The number on this work is only one hundred and thirty, and most of them such as will not be received on the W.N.C.R.R. The number of convicts which can be sent out of the Pen. has greatly decreased in the last year or so. It is a source of great gratification to me that the colored people of the East are beginning to

---

[63]Lawyer of Bakersville; member of the General Assembly, 1868, 1872; member of the Convention of 1875; Superior Court judge, 1899–1900. Branson, *Directory for 1884*, 478; Connor, *Manual, 1913*, 451, 704, 889.
[64]Unable to identify.
[65]Neither the petition nor the letter referred to herein has been found.
[66]Lawyer of Scotland Neck. Branson, *Directory for 1884*, 357.

quit stealing and are going to work. I would that I could say there was not one in the Penitentiary.

Now these are the facts in the case, and from them you will see the convicts can only be sent you in one of three ways. First, have crime to increase. I know you would not have that. Second, have the State violate her contract with purchasers of W.N.C. R.R., or have the Board violate the law giving two hundred convicts to C.F.&Y.V.R.R. Are you prepared to accept them in either of these three ways? If not, can you suggest any other? Had the convicts continued to come in as they did some years ago, there would have been no trouble about your getting them.

I shall be glad to help in the matter when it can be done.

A&H—GLB

Thomas J. Jarvis to W. B. Hazen

Executive Department,
Raleigh, Apr. 16th, 1881

In reply to yours in reference to the Signal Service, I beg to say that Prof. W. C. Kerr, the Geologist of this State, has been for years having weather observations taken at some twenty or more points in the State. I had a talk with him yesterday, and he thinks he can have all the work done which may be necessary to give you a fair report from all sections of the State.

I turned over to him your letter and the accompanying papers. I beg to suggest that you correspond with him.

UNC—KPB

A. S. Buford to Thomas J. Jarvis

Richmond, Va., April 27 1881

I have yours of yesterday[67] and reply at once. I exceedingly regret having had no previous information as to the circumstances which you seem to think so urgently require the immediate completion of the University Railroad.[68] We have been

---

[67]Not found.

[68]In 1873 the General Assembly granted a charter for the construction of a railroad from Chapel Hill to University Station, located a few miles west of Durham on the North Carolina Railroad. Since the Richmond & Danville controlled the North Carolina Railroad the management of the former agreed to help build the University Railroad. Battle, *History of the University*, II, 246.

waiting for the readiness of General Hoke[69] and his associates, to go with placing the track on the terms indicated by him, which would make it quite practicable to both them and us. I suppose he had his own, and satisfactory reason for not making progress more rapidly. I have heard nothing from him or Colonel Andrews very recently on the subject, and while, as you know, I would do anything in my power to accommodate your wishes in such matters, I do not see now how it is possible to effect what you wish in time. The understanding about it was that Gen. Hoke's Company were to contract with certain rail makers for a given amount of rails to be delivered in exchange for ones from their mine, which rails we are to use in replacing old rails on the N.C. Road, which latter will be taken up and used in making track for the University Road; and without some such arrangement as this, we have no rails to apply in that way, or at any rate, nothing like a sufficient quantity to track the road. As I learn from Colonel Andrews, the better portion of the old rails taken from his road are necessarily used about as fast as they are obtained for repairs of other portions of his old track, leaving none of the old rails so taken up on his road to dispose of, except the short and worst worn portion, which are only fit for sale to manufacturers, and are certainly unfit to track a new road like that for the University branch.

If I am correct in this, therefore, the thing cannot be done within the time you indicate, for want of material, and it is utterly impossible to get new rails from the mills faster than they have contracted to deliver during the summer and fall.

If we had the rails now on the ground it would be as much as could be done to get them placed and the road surfaced up so as to make it passable for trains within the thirty days to elapse between this and the first of June. As it is, our material is scattered over the line, would have to be gathered together, and when so collected would be utterly unfit to make a track out of.

This is the way the case looks to me, and while I very much regret the disappointment either to yourself or your friends, yet you will perceive that we are in no sense responsible for it. In fact while I have had through Col. Andrews the understand-

---

[69]Robert Frederick Hoke of Lincolnton, who possessed wide holdings in North Carolina cotton mills and iron works. *Dictionary of American Biography*, IX, 126–127. Hoke owned Iron Mountain, one mile north of Chapel Hill, and at this time the price of iron was so high that he invested heavily in the University Railroad to give his ore an outlet to the furnaces of Pennsylvania. Battle, *History of the University*, II, 246.

ing about it which I have stated above, yet we have never had anything like a definite contract with the owners or managers of the University Road upon which alone I could undertake to carry out the work as desired.

I suppose it will take about one thousand, or twelve hundred tons of rails to complete the track. I have no idea Col. Andrews has on his line one–fourth of that amount of old rails at all fit to put upon that road to remain there for use. To put down a track of such inferior material as might possibly be scraped up would neither be safe nor creditable. In fact if useful at all it would have to be taken up very soon at the expense of a double track-laying, not to add other possible inconveniences or damage.

Suppose you talk with General Hoke and Col. Andrews about it. If their arrangements with the rail makers are such as to enable them to go on at once we will be gratified to do anything we can to expedite the opening of the road.

Speech, April 28, 1881, Before The
Raleigh Prohibition Convention[70]

The Governor was gracefully introduced by Major McRae,[71] and said that he knew that a body of men was here assembled which had the good of the State at heart. It gave him pleasure to witness the proceedings, and to give his countenance and whatever influence he possessed to the cause. This call was, no doubt, as much to find out his views as anything else. "The public think, no doubt, that I belong to that class of politicians that regard this question as a ticklish one. But I have an opinion. Candor obliges me to say that at first I doubted the benefit of absolute prohibition, thinking a rigid system of licenses sufficient; but the Legislature has passed the law, and I must take one side or the other. I should be false to the 1,400,000 people of North Carolina if I remained silent, and I must take my position. In taking it I propose to do just as I have done in all public questions since I first took office. I have always, God knows, taken a stand for the best interests of North Carolina, and I propose to meet this question in the same way. I never walk these streets

---

[70]Taken from the *News and Observer*, April 29, 1881.

[71]James Cameron McRae, lawyer of Fayetteville; member of the General Assembly. 1874: Superior Court judge, 1882–1890; state Supreme Court justice, 1893–1895. In 1899 he became dean of the Law School of the University of North Carolina. Oates, *Story of Fayetteville*, 548. McRae was president of the Prohibition Convention of 1881.

or ride over the State but I see melancholy victims of intemperance. Knowing what is best for North Carolina and North Carolinians, I declare for the prohibition movement, and for prohibition I intend to go. [Great applause, continued for many minutes.] Whatever may be in the bill that ought to be out, or out that ought to be in, can be put there by subsequent legislation or law. I think I know something about the sentiments of the people and how to win their good wishes, opinions or co–operation. This cannot be done by coercion, but by kindness and proper argument. The way to succeed in the matter is by going out and making friends of the people, of all classes, religions and opinions. Party has nothing to do with this question. If this movement means to organize a political party, I do not go with it, but if it means to do the good work of eradicating vice, I go with it heart and soul.

Another question to which I intend to address and devote myself is a similarly grand one, and that is the education of our people, both races alike. If this is done, even if prohibition does not receive the public majority in this election it will have to come, and that soon. There is not a day that I do not have some painful appeal for clemency, growing out of intemperance. There is now on my table a petition asking that a man, once a prominent physician, who, in a fit of drunkenness, made a most brutal attack upon his wife, be pardoned out of jail where he now lies a prisoner. Yet this case is but one of hundreds. My observation leads me to know and assert that for every dollar received as taxes from the sale of liquor, ten dollars go out of the public purse." Thanking the audience for their kindness, he closed.

A. B. Andrews to Thomas J. Jarvis, Z. B. Vance, and J. M. Worth, April 30, 1881[72]

To the Honorable Thos. J. Jarvis, Zebulon B. Vance and J. M. Worth, Commissioners:[73]

This petition of A. B. Andrews, president of the Western

---

[72]Taken from the *News and Observer*, September 1, 1881.

[73]The act of the General Assembly selling the Western North Carolina Railroad to Best and his associates also appointed Jarvis, Vance, and Worth as commissioners to see that the new owners fulfilled their parts of the contract. The main interest of the commissioners was to see that the road reached Paint Rock and Murphy at the designated time. *Laws of North Carolina, 1880*, c. 26.

Alexander Boyd Andrews (1841-1915), Raleigh resident, was born in Franklin County. Before the Civil War Andrews was employed by his uncle, General P. B. Hawkins, in construction work on the Blue Ridge Railway in South Carolina. Following secession he returned to North Carolina and joined the Ninth North Carolina (First Cavalry) Regiment. Andrews was again engaged in railroad work after the war, holding executive positions with the Raleigh and Gaston, the Richmond and Danville, and the Atlantic and North Carolina railroads. As president of the Richmond and Danville, he was primarily responsible for completion of the Western North Carolina Railroad to Tennessee. When the Richmond and Danville became a part of the Southern Railway Company, he became vice-president of the company. Andrews was actively interested in several insurance companies and banks in Raleigh and was a trustee of the North Carolina Soldiers' Home in Raleigh and of the University of North Carolina.

North Carolina Railroad[74] Company, respectfully represents that in pursuance of the act of the General Assembly, ratified March 29th, 1880, entitled "An act to provide for the sale of the State's interest in the Western North Carolina Railroad Company and for other purposes," the Western North Carolina Railroad has been reorganized, and the work of completion of said road has been begun and the same will be prosecuted with the utmost diligence and energy, and as an indication of its earnestness the company has already advertised for one hundred hired laborers, who are being daily employed and placed upon the work, and advertisements are to be posted immediately for five hundred additional hired laborers, making six hundred in the aggregate, which, joined to its force of five hundred convicts furnished by the State, will soon give the company a total working force of eleven hundred hands, and it is its purpose and intention to keep all of this force, or as many as it can place on the road, employed during the whole working season just now opening. But it is respectfully submitted to your honorable board that, notwithstanding the employment of this large force, and the costly expenditures which will thereby be necessarily incurred, the company has serious apprehensions that they will not be able to reach the points indicated in the short time left them under the provisions of the act of the 29th of March, 1880. The petitioner respectfully shows to your honorable board what is well known through the public documents of the Senate of North Carolina, that the original grantees lost four months of the most valuable and suitable time given them by the Legislature, to–wit: from the 29th of March to the 31st day of July, 1880, and which was the basis of estimate when the Legislature prescribed the 1st of July, 1881, as the time when the road should be completed to Paint Rock and Pigeon River, and it was at this gloomy period in the history of this contract on which North Carolina had based so many bright hopes that the asignees were urged to assume the burden of the contract and complete the road; and that they did at that late day, after four months had been lost

---

[74]After agreeing to buy the Western North Carolina Railroad, Best found that he could not raise the necessary money from his colleagues. On July 31, 1880, he assigned his rights to the railroad to W. P. Clyde, A. S. Buford, and T. M. Logan for 7,500 shares of stock in the railroad. *News and Observer*, September 1, 1881. This negotiation delayed the beginning of construction for four months. See also, Best to Jarvis, May 21, 1880, in this volume. At a meeting early in April, 1881, the stockholders of the Western North Carolina Railroad declared terminated the offices of President Best and his board of directors, and then elected a new board of directors with A. B. Andrews as president. *News and Observer*, April 13, 1881.

without any fault of theirs, assume the responsibilities of the contract under the assurance that a liberal policy would be pursued towards them by your honorable board in the exercise of the large discretionary powers granted in said act.

And your petitioner further shows that the work on the road which was begun in the early autumn was obstructed and at times almost forced to cease by a winter season unparalleled in its coldness in the history of this State; the snow and frosts were so severe and continuous that it would have been cruel and inhuman at times to compel the convicts furnished by the State to be exposed in them. And your petitioner further shows, as a further reason for asking an extension, that it has not been practicable, or perhaps possible, for the State to take her convicts from the penitentiary, or remove them from other public improvements and furnish them to the company according to the provisions of the act, and that the assignees have submitted to this curtailment of its labor with the expectation that a like spirit of accommodation and liberality would be extended to them, if they should be compelled to ask for an extension of time.

For the reasons set forth above, the undersigned respectfully asks your honorable board to grant him, in writing, over your own signatures as commissioners, an "extension of time" for the completion of said road to Paint Rock and Pigeon River, to wit: an extension of four months, which is less than the time lost by the failures and delays of the original grantees, and for which the present assignees ought not to be held legally responsible.

In conclusion, your petitioner is advised that your honorable board are empowered, by virtue of the 23d section of the said act, under the circumstances above mentioned, and for the cause set forth, "to allow a reasonable extension of time for the completion of said lines." He, therefore, asks that the prayer of their petition be granted.

The additional laborers referred to in this communication will be employed and put upon the work as soon as the labor can be employed at reasonable compensation, either in hired labor or by contract, and of this six hundred additional laborers or their value in contracts we will employ at least one-half on the Ducktown line, and will keep a sufficient force on said line to complete it to Pigeon River by the time required by the con-

tract as extended by this application. But it is distinctly understood that this extension, if granted, shall not affect any other
provision of the contract.[75]

A&H—GP

A. Pope to Thomas J. Jarvis

New York, May 4th 1881

Yours April 21[st][76]—has been read attentively I appreciate the
kind sentiment and well wishes you express—I have been communicating regularly with the Commissioner of Agriculture
touching my actions[77]—

I have sent into North Carolina within the last week over 150
people of whom 100 or more are of the very best class of German
laborers—I have located an "Immigrants Home" at Salisbury
and assigned an agent to service in assisting these people in
obtaining Employment.

It Depends upon the people of North Carolina by the manner
in which they treat these people whether or not accessions may
be expected and whether it will be Desirable to continue these
efforts—

I recognize the importance of sending people who have the
means to buy property and I will very shortly present abstracts
of lands and all information of interest in connection—therewith
—that will attract such people—this publication will be made
jointly for our interests in each of the four States and also *separately*—

I am in constant communication with **Mr. Fall**[78] Emigrant
Agent in England and hope to advise of having perfected a satisfactory plan of cöoperation with him

[75]This last paragraph was an amendment added by Jarvis. *News and
Observer*, September 1, 1881.
[76]Not found.
[77]At this time Pope was general passenger agent for the Associated Railways of Virginia and the Carolinas, representing the Piedmont Airline,
the Central Short Line, the Atlantic Coastline and the Seaboard Airline.
These roads had offered their co–operation in distributing information on
North Carolina and its resources and in furnishing cheap transportation
to immigrants. "Report of the Board of Agriculture," *Public Documents,
1881*, No. 9, 21.
[78]Samuel J. Fall, commissioner of immigration for the state of North
Carolina in Great Britain. See Stone to Jarvis, June 23, 1881, in this
volume.

A&H—GP

Johnson Hagood to Thomas J. Jarvis

Executive Chamber
Columbia May 7th 1881

I have the honor to inform you that I have made a contract
with E. L. Spencer, Civil Engineer, to re–run and re–mark a portion of the Boundary Line between this State and North Carolina in accordance with the act of December last of which a copy
has been heretofore sent you.

Mr Spencer has contracted to do the work for the gross sum
of nine hundred and ninety four ($994.) dollars.

His Post Office is Bishopville, Sumter Co. So.Ca.; and I would
suggest that your Commissioner, upon his appointment, immediately communicate with him in view of arranging prelimi-
naries.

A&H—GLB

Thomas J. Jarvis to Robert Todd Lincoln[79]

Executive Department,
Raleigh, May 9th, 1881

I propose to attend the National Celebration at Yorktown in
October next with about one thousand of our State troops. We
have no tents and no funds with which to purchase any. I have,
therefore, the honor to request that you loan us for our use on
that occasion, seventy–five hospital tents, with the necessary
poles and pins. We would want them for the space of one week
in October—say from the 17th to the 22nd. I would be glad to
have the use of them for a short time in the month of July or
August, for the purposes of a preparatory encampment. I can
furnish you any bond that may be required for the preservation of the property and its safe return to the government authorities, and will hold myself in readiness to perform such conditions as may be imposed.

Should you be unable from any cause to comply with this
request, I would ask that you establish a camp at Yorktown for
the use and accommodation of the troops from this State for

---

[79]Lincoln devoted most of his life to his law practice, but he was secretary
of war under Garfield and minister to England under Harrison. *Dictionary
of American Biography*, XI, 266–267.

the space of time indicated;—the same to remain under Federal supervision and control, and the State to be answerable to you for any injury or damage which may be inflicted upon the tents by our troops during such occupation by them.

Whatever arrangements you may make for encamping the troops from this State, either by a loan of tents or otherwise, will be highly appreciated.

A&H—GLB

Z. B. Vance to Thomas J. Jarvis

Washington, May 12, 1881

Circumstances coming to my knowledge since our meeting in Raleigh induce me to withdraw my consent to the extension of time asked for by A. B. Andrews, president.[80] No legal application by the assignees has yet been presented as Andrews promised,[81] and I have reason to believe that none will be soon. I will explain fully when I see you. Meanwhile, please notify Andrews that I do not hold myself bound any longer to accept his proposition when made. He ought to know at once. I will be at home early next week and can go over the work with you.

---

[80]The syndicate which had acquired Best's rights in the Western North Carolina Railroad had recently petitioned Jarvis, Vance, and Worth—commissioners appointed to supervise the completion of the railroad—for a four months' extension of Best's contract. The commissioners met in Raleigh on April 30 to consider this petition. Andrews to Jarvis, Vance, and Worth, April 30, 1881, in this volume. They agreed to the extension if the lessees would put 600 more convicts to work on the road. "Proceedings of the Commissioners of the Western North Carolina Rail Road, 1881-1884," Governor's Office Correspondence, hereinafter cited as "Proceedings of the Commissioners on the Western North Carolina Rail Road." About this time, however, Best told Vance in Washington, D.C., that he had formed a new syndicate and had money in hand to redeem his mortgaged interest in the Western North Carolina Railroad. News and Observer, October 2, 1881. To some extent the "circumstances" referred to above were personal. During early May, Vance received what he considered reliable information that the new management of the railroad were practicing shoddy construction methods. News and Observer, August 28, 1881. Vance felt that under Best the Western North Carolina Railroad would be well constructed. In addition he was convinced that the new syndicate intended to use the railroad to build up Richmond, Virginia, at the expense of the North Carolina cities; whereas Best's plans were primarily for a North Carolina system. News and Observer, September 8, 1881. These factors partially explain this letter to Jarvis.

[81]See Jarvis to Vance, May 13, 1881, in this volume.

Thomas J. Jarvis to A. B. Andrews[82]

Raleigh, May 13th, 1881

I am just in receipt of a letter from Hon. Z. B. Vance, in which he asks me to notify you that he withdraws the assent given by him to an extension of time for the completion of the Western North Carolina Railroad to Paint Rock and Pigeon River. Please accept this as such a notice.

The Application presented to me by you last Monday,[83] signed by W. P. Clyde,[84] T. M. Logan and A. S. Buford, assignees, was in form as agreed upon, and I shall, when the commissioners meet, vote to give the conditional extension as indicated in the memorandum made at our meeting in Raleigh some weeks ago.

Thomas J. Jarvis to Z. B. Vance[85]

Executive Department,
Raleigh, May 13, 1881

I am just in receipt of yours of the 12th inst., and have informed Col. Andrews of its contents, and given him the notice requested.

On Monday, the 9th inst., Col. Andrews presented me with the paper prepared strictly as agreed upon, with all the suggested amendments, made and signed by Messrs. W. P. Clyde, A. S. Buford and T. M. Logan, assignees. He wished to have it presented to each of the commissioners at once, but I told him to hold it till we met to examine the work, as that was our understanding. He will so present the paper when we can be got together.

I have recently been very much encouraged with the belief that the present owners are about to begin work in earnest on both lines of the road; and I shall regret to learn that you have in your possession any facts to prove that they do not so intend to act.

If it shall turn out that I am right as to their purposes, I trust

---

[82]Taken from the *News and Observer*, September 1, 1881.
[83]This is the petition of Andrews to Jarvis, Vance, and Worth, April 30, 1881, in this volume.
[84]William Pancoast Clyde of New York City, steamship owner and railroad promoter. For a time he controlled the Richmond and Danville Railroad. *National Cyclopedia*, XX, 57–58.
[85]Taken from the *News and Observer*, September 8, 1881.

that no question of reasonable time shall prevent their going on with the work.

If, on the other hand, it shall turn out that I am deceived and that they do not intend to work on the Ducktown line, you will find me ready to do my full duty in the matter.

I am determined, as far as in me lies, to have this road completed without cost or trouble to the State, and I believe by proper management it can be done. To declare the contract forfeited throws the road back upon the State—a thing I should be slow to do as long as there is a reasonable prospect of the work being done in any reasonable time.

Thomas J. Jarvis to J. M. Worth[86]

Raleigh, N.C., May 14, 1881

You will remember that at the meeting of the commissioners of the Western North Carolina Railroad it was agreed by yourself, Gov. Vance and myself that we would extend the time for the completion of the road to Paint Rock and Pigeon River, upon the application being made to us, signed by Clyde, Buford and Logan, with the amendment suggested by us. Upon this promise of ours, they have advertised to let the road to contract from Asheville to Pigeon River on the 18th. They presented to me last Monday the application for the extension in the form and signed by the parties as agreed upon by us, as you will see by an examination of the paper itself. They have done all on their part that they agreed to do or were required to do; and for one, I propose to do what I agreed to do.

Governor Vance wrote me yesterday that circumstances had come to his knowledge since he was here which induce him to withdraw his assent to the extension and asked me to so inform Colonel Andrews. This I at once did, and I fear it is about to seriously retard the work. Of course they cannot let the road to contract or go on with the work in a satisfactory way unless they have an assurance that they will be allowed to go on.

The situation then seems to be that we have to take the responsibility to extend the time or the responsibility to stop the work. I choose to take the responsibility to extend the time. If you agree with me, you can, in your own way, say so to Andrews in writing. I have already done it for myself.

[86]Taken from the *News and Observer*, September 1, 1881.

A&H—GP

James Clarence Harper[87] *to Thomas J. Jarvis*
[with endorsements]

Patterson N.C. 10th June 1881

The Caldwell and Watauga Turnpike Company was chartered by the Legislature of 1846–7 under the name of Caldwell and Ashe Turnpike Company and soon afterwards constructed the road from this place to the Tenn State line. The State owns one half of the Stock $1,250, and individuals the remainder $1,250. The rates of toll have been very low and the whole amount collected has been spent in keeping the road in repair, much of the road being located on the rocky Southern side of the Blue Ridge where there is no ordinary road labor to be obtained. Although no dividends have ever been paid the State has long since been repaid in the increased value of taxable property as well as in the sale and settlement of large tracts of land made accessible by the road which would have remained vacant without it.

In compliance with amendments made by the Legislature from time to time the road at present extends by its Charter only from this place to Shulls[88] on the west side of the Blue Ridge. About 9 miles of distance from Shulls to the Yadkin Spring is not much used by market wagons, and we asked for and obtained from the last Legislature an act amending the Charter so as to allow the Company to surrender that portion of the road to the County of Watauga and thereupon to extend the Southern terminus of the road to Lenoir (7 miles) This section crosses the Brushy Mountain range and is very hard to keep in repair. In fact much of it becomes impassable during the market season from Nov to March. The proposed change meets with general approval but to make it effective we must accept it at a meeting of stockholders which has been called to meet at this place on Wednesday the 22nd inst. After a lapse of more than 30 years much of the stock has been lost to sight and we find it impossible to secure a majority of stock in a meeting unless the State is represented. I therefore respectfully ask that you appoint a State proxy as has

[87]Merchant, textile manufacturer, and planter of Patterson; Conservative representative in Congress, 1871–1873. In 1881 he was president of the Caldwell and Watauga Turnpike Company. *Biographical Directory of Congress*, 1,062-1,063.
[88]Shull's Mill, seven miles southwest of Boone.

been done heretofore to enable us to organize a meeting and accept or reject the proposed amendment.

I very respectfully recommend Samuel L. Patterson[89] or Edmund Jones[90] for the position either of whom will serve the State with ability and satisfaction. I will promptly forward the necessary fees to the Executive Clerk on the rept of the paper. Please excuse the unseemly length of this paper. I could not well make it shorter.

[*endorsement*]

Hon: Tho⁸ S. Kenan
       Atty Gen.

Dear Sir

Have I the power to make the appointment asked for in the above letter of Mr. Harper.

I am Resp Yours
Tho⁸ J. Jarvis Gov

[*endorsement*]

Atty. Genl's Office
14 June 1881

To The Governor:

Chapter 61 of the Rev. Code, as brought forward in Chapter 62 of Bat. Rev. was re–enacted by Chapter 83 of the acts of 1874–75.

It is therefore the law, and provides that when the State makes an appropriation to any work of internal improvement, it shall be considered a stockholder therein &c sec. 8. The charter granted this company in 1846–47, shows that the state was authorized to make an appropriation in the manner therein set out, and, I take it, did so. In such case the Internal Improvement board has au-

---

[89]Samuel Legerwood Patterson, large land owner of Patterson; member of the General Assembly, 1891, 1893; commissioner of agriculture, 1895–1908. Ashe, *Biographical History*, II, 344–351.
[90]Lawyer of Patterson; member of the General Assembly, 1868–1872, 1879. *North Carolina Biography*, IV, 108–109.

thority to appoint an agent to represent the stock of the state. sec. 38.

The amendment alluded to by **Mr.** Harper may be found in the acts of 1881, ch. 131.

Very respectfully &c
Tho S Kenan
Atty. Genl.

A&H—GP

C. C. Clark to Thomas J. Jarvis

Newbern, N.C., June 10th 1881

I have, on behalf of the A.&N.C.R.R.Co, brought suit against the N.C.R.R. Co, to recover the value of the iron which was taken from the former in 1865.

The Defendant wanted 60 days to answer, in order that its Directors might decide whether to plead the statute of limitations. The time was granted.

I thought it proper as you represent the State in both Companies to inform you what had been done—[91]

A&H—GLB

Thomas J. Jarvis to T. M. Holt

Executive Department,
Raleigh, June 11th, 1881.

I am informed that suit has been brought by the A.&N.C.R.R. Co., against the N.C.R.R.Co., to recover the value of some iron.

It seems to me that it is not a proper case in which to plead the Statute of Limitations, and I trust it will not be done. The case ought to be settled upon its merits.

A&H—GLB

A. B. Andrews to Thomas J. Jarvis

Raleigh, N.C., June 13 1881

I have received a letter from Maj J. W. Wilson Chief Engineer Western North Carolina Railroad in which he says. "Both

---

[91]For the explanation of this letter, see Hughes to Jarvis, March 10, 1879, and Jarvis to Holt, January 31, 1881, in this volume.

bridges are finished and we will on Monday begin to push the track down the river. The work is not progressing as rapidly as I wish, so many convicts being in the hospital from scurvy. At Sandy Mush Quarters, the day I spent there forty–two were in, over one fourth of the working force,—Last winter we lost a great deal of time from frost bite caused by improper clothing and this summer from improper diet—This is unfair to the Railroad authorities and humanity to the prisoners demands a different treatment. I mention this matter so that steps can be taken in time to remedy it in the future."

I refer this matter to you directly and without delay in order that you may be officially acquainted with the condition of and the causes thereof that a speedy remedy be instituted from which latter the Railroad may derive relief and benefit

A&H—GLB

Thomas J. Jarvis to E. R. Stamps

Executive Department,
Raleigh, June 13, 1881

I herewith send you a copy of the letter received from Col. A. B. Andrews, Pres't. of the W.N.C.R.R.Co.

I desire you, and I know it will be your pleasure, to take immediate steps to see whether there has been any suffering or sickness among the convicts, as suggested in his letter, on account of a want of proper clothing or food.

As I suggested to you some days ago, I expect to go with the other Commissioners over the Western Road on Wednesday of next week; and would be glad to have you go along with us, if it suits your convenience.

I know it is your purpose to see that the convicts are properly cared for, and I know of no better way to secure it than for you to make frequent and rigid inspections of their treatment.

A&H—GP

T. M. Holt to Thomas J. Jarvis

Haw River, N.C. June 14th 1881

Your favour of 11th recd. last evening. In reply have to say, that the matter refered to, has been considered by my Board, since Maj. Smith[92] took charge of the road, & committees have been appointed to investigate it, & so far all have denied that the Atlantic road has any claim, or has been injured. Col Whitford attended the meeting of our Board at it last meeting, when the subject was fully discussed pro & con, & the vote stood 3 for paying, the balc 8 against it, the Pres. not voteing. It has two sides to it & I think if you were to hear both sides, you might think it is not a very plain case. The Board were under the impression that suit would not be commenced for the present, but Col Whitford did bring suit, & served notice on Mr. Kornegay,[93] who paid but little attention, or rather no attention, to it, until Thursday of the 2nd week of the court, when he Telegraphed Mr. Ruffin[94] at the Shops,[95] to know if I had employed council, that the case was in court, & would come up. Mr. R. sent me the Telegram [sic], which was the first intimation I had of it, & for fear a judgmt might be taken by default I went to the Shops & Telegraphed Mr. Kornegay, to go to New Berne at once, & employ council, & resist it in any way possible, & plead the Satute [of Limitations]. I did this knowing that it was the sentiment of the Board, on which were two Lawyers, Craig[96] & Burwell.[97] I learn from Mr. Kornegay, that 60 days, has been allowed in which, to file pleas, in the meantime, we will have a meeting of the Board, when I will bring the matter before them again, & will act as they direct. I am not Lawyer enough to say, what the law would decide, but the discussion, which was full & free, led me to believe, that it was doubtful, if there was any equity in it. It is by no means a plain case, but one that admits of argument on both sides. The Board will meet in Goldsboro, on Wednesday July 13th, & I presume Col. Whitford will be present. I will then bring it before them, & ask for positive orders in regard to it.

[92]William Alexander Smith, prominent merchant and planter of Ansonville. In 1881 he was president of the North Carolina Railroad. *National Cyclopedia*, XXVII, 217–218.

[93]William F. Kornegay, merchant, manufacturer, and planter of Goldsboro. In 1881 he was the director of the North Carolina Railroad on the part of the state. *Cyclopedia of the Carolinas*, II, 586–587.

[94]Peter Brown Ruffin of Hillsboro. He served for more than thirty years as treasurer of the North Carolina Railroad. Grant, *Alumni History of the University*, 540.

[95]Company Shops, in Alamance County, principal office of the North Carolina Railroad.

[96]Kerr Craige, lawyer and banker of Salisbury; member of the General Assembly, 1872; 3rd assistant postmaster general during Cleveland's second administration. In 1881 he was a director of the North Carolina Railroad. *National Cyclopedia*, XXVIII, 92–93.

[97]Armistead Burwell, lawyer of Charlotte; member of the General Assembly, 1881; state Supreme Court justice, 1893–1895. *North Carolina Biography*, V, 361–366.

ADDRESS[98]

Mr. President and Fellow–Members of the Society of Alumni,

Ladies and Gentlemen:

To–day there comes back to me with a vivid distinctness, almost akin to pain, a scene that transpired just twenty–one years ago, when, with a proudly beating heart, I received the diploma awarded to me by the authorities of Randolph Macon College. The hand that gave it to me is still, and the voice that uttered the words, "Accipe hoc diploma," is hushed in death; but I can see the venerable form of her President, look upon his strongly marked face and listen to his words, just as if it were all now taking place. With his prayer following me and his tender benediction resting upon me (for no graduate ever left there without them), I went forth from her quiet shades and friendly sympathies into the struggles of life, to confront, as best I could, its labor and responsibilities.

Then it was, brethren of the Alumni, that I gave the parting clasp of the hand to those of you with whom I stood to receive the rewards of our years of study, as they are now about to be bestowed upon the new generation henceforth to be enrolled in our ranks, and each of us went forth in the proud flush of early manhood in pursuit of the objects of our ambition.

The paths through which my journey up the rugged hill has lain, have led me away from these annual reunions, which serve so happily to bind with the sympathetic chords of brotherhood of the old graduates to the new; so that not until to–day have I been permitted to return to the hallowed associations of the olden time, and to renew my vows of allegiance to our charished mother.

There was, however, a small reunion to which my memory will always recur with a melancholy pleasure. In the summer of 1864, just four years after the close of our college life, I lay wounded and ill in one of the hospitals at Richmond. Four years! and yet almost an ordinary lifetime had been crowded within that eventful epoch. The careless boys had become grave men upon whom their country's future for weal or woe in part depended. The precise place was the Baptist Female College, which

---

[98]"Address Delivered By Hon. Thos. J. Jarvis, Governor of North Carolina, Before The Society of Alumni of *Randolph Macon College*, June 15th, 1881." (Richmond, Virginia: Jones and Goolsby, 1881).

was then used as the officers' hospital. Oh! how gratifying the thought that the innocent, tender girls that bound through that building with happy and joyous hearts, know nothing of the tales of suffering and pain its walls could tell had they tongues to speak!

Borne from the field of carnage and death dangerously wounded, I lay helpless in this house of suffering heroes, tenderly watched over by Virginia's noble women. Their gentle ministration, their unflagging patience and never-failing liberality to the sick and wounded through those long years of agony, are the brightest of all the bright jewels that sparkle in the diadem of the City by the James. While there, I was visited by four members of our Society—three of them of my own class; and in that crowded ward, surrounded by suffering and dying men, and uncertain whether the morrow's sun would greet me a living man, we forgot the war and its scenes of horror over which we had but lately walked, and unmindful of the roar of Grant's artillery, and the frowning future that menaced us, we talked of the happy days of our college life, with its lasting, tender associations.

Tears and blood hallowed that gathering, for as each questioned the other of old associates, it was found that many a bright young life, so full of eager anticipations of future fame or usefulness, when we had clasped hands and bidden each other Godspeed on the threshold of manhood, had been laid, a willing sacrifice, upon their country's altar. And we had not escaped; for between the five there brought together on that Sunday afternoon, there was a strange, sad bond of sympathetic union: two were permanently disabled in their right arms, and from the shoulders of the other three, their [sic] dangled three empty sleeves.

But in the presence of bright youth, with its buoyant hopes, across whose horoscope no shadows have yet fallen and in the face of brilliant beauty, whose eyes have never been bedewed with more scalding tears than the tender cries of sympathy, it is an ungracious task to touch upon great woes that have wrung agony from human hearts and have crushed out brave and noble lives by the hecatomb. Begging pardon for this brief but painful retrospection, I come, my brethren, after this long separation, to greet you with a heart brimful of love for each of you and with undiminished devotion to our grand old mother, Randolph Macon College.

It is your misfortune at this reunion that your choice should have fallen upon one who has not been in a position to have kept up a sufficiently intimate acquaintance with the personal history of the different members of the Society to tell of the hopes and aspirations, the successes and honors, of those who have been faithful to the lessons of wisdom learned here.

My lot has been so cast and my time necessarily so occupied in the midst of the conflicts which for me were but fairly begun at Appomattox Courthouse—for is not an active civil life but another series of campaigns, requiring all the energy and vigilance of a soldier in battle?—that in the midst of different scenes and pursuits, I have lost sight of those with whom I once walked, so familiarly side by side, on the campus of old Randolph Macon. Here and there, amid the records of an outside world which scarcely seemed any longer my own, as I struggled on in my limited orbit, some dear name would gladden my eye and bring joy to my heart as I would hear or read of brave deeds done, victories won, honors achieved by beloved comrades. Yet I know there are many more, far worthier than he who now addresses you, whose lives, with the incidents that ennobled them, and whose very places of residence are unknown to me. So that instead of coming here, as is the custom on such occasions, to tell you of our brethren, I have had to inquire of them and about them, and have thus, in the last twenty hours, gleaned about as much as I had previously known in almost as many years.

Brief epitomes of life or death, with only glimpses of the great aggregate of failure or success, are necessarily the limit of my information upon these subjects. My position is quite anomalous to day. I feel that I am at home, and yet how changed the scene! So few of the old familiar faces greet me as I look over the vast assemblage! I look out upon the campus, and it is not the one upon which I walked and talked, studied and played. Not a familiar object meets my searching look. The place, too, is different. Presidents and Professors have come and gone. Good, gifted Dr. Smith, whose interest in his boys never flagged, has long since gone to meet his reward. Other Presidents have served with pre-eminent distinction, and have passed away, with tears for their memory and immortality for their fame. Of the Professors and their assistants, none remain but my dear friend Shepard. Place and people, President and Professors, all changed, and strangers, and yet I feel at home! I feel, as I stand here today, as I would feel at no other institution of learning on the earth. I have no words—there are no words—to express these emotions. People and places, Presidents and Professors, may all change, but this to me is old Randolph Macon College! The location is an hundred miles and more away from my college reminiscences, but the name and associations are here; and while these last, recreant indeed would I be did not my heart fill with pride and devotion at the mention of that honored name! I scarcely realized till I reached here how little there was left for me save memory; but as that comes pouring in upon me its flood–tide of rich treasures of the olden days, I am loath to break away from her spell to greet the new and living scenes of to–day by which I find myself surrounded.

The thought would be an inexpressibly sad one but for the comfort that no mere wanton iconoclasm has been here. Randolph Macon of the olden time is no more, but on its changed location, the new Randolph Macon has arisen, strongly and more nobly equipped for the great work before here. May heaven prosper and great success attend her!

Thus spanning the chasm which divides the old from the new, the remainder of my time will be taken up with some practical remarks intended more particularly for those who are about to be enrolled among the Alumni. They are about to exchange the quiet harbor, where they have been carefully guarded and skillfully fitted out, for the waves of the wide sea where their safety depends much upon their own pilotage. Those of us who have been tossed and buffeted for years upon these waters know how furiously they do sometimes lash our little barks, and how necessary it is when these storms come that wisdom shall be our pilot and courage our helmsman. Out on this sea, my young friends, it is sometimes storm, sometimes calm, sometimes rain and sometimes sunshine; sometimes the winds are prosperous and sometimes adverse. I would not have you believe that there are no havens of rest and beauty along the voyage. There are many, thank God! dotted along life's coast, planted there by the hand of an all-wise and beneficent Creator. It will not do, however, to linger too long within these pleasant retreats. Ulysses could not forever remain in the enchanted island with Calypso. The ship that lies in port is of but little value to her owners. To bring revenue to them, she must sail out upon the ocean and brave perils. So too must man. Many that go out are stranded upon the shoals and never return. So too many make shipwrecks of themselves. Beacon–lights have been erected to warn the mariners of the dangers upon which others were destroyed. The lives of those who have gone before us will serve, if we will but utilize the experience, to warn us o[f] our dangers or to give courage to our efforts and good cheer to our labors. It is possible that I may say something which will cause some one of them, when the storm approaches, to look to these beacons; and, taking the lessons of truth and wisdom they have learned here as their chart, steer straight forward with their eyes fixed on right, as their polar star. If so, I shall be more than repaid.

Neither the jostling world nor the practical age in which they are to live tolerates a dreamy sentiment or Utopian follies. Practical ideas and practical wisdom are their chief characteristics; and he will succeed best who best utilizes the lessons he has learned and the means placed at his command.

It was the custom, in the days of knight–errantry, for the chieftains to have a sentiment or motto engraved or painted upon their banners. These sentiments, expressed in epigrammatic words, were intended to give some idea of the character or the motives of the person whose armorial bearings they were. The custom has been followed even to our day, and not without reason and good results. Who has ever seen the motto of the Mother of States, that did not take in at the sound of the words, "*Sic Semper Tyrannis,*" the hatred of liberty–loving Virginia to the rule of tyrants? The liberty societies of this institution have their mottoes, and the members long remember them and the lessons they teach. So I would have these young gentlemen have their motto and then live up to it.

We will not permit the hypercritical historian to draw in question the truth of the familiar tradition of Crecy. The blind old king of Bohemia, when the hosts of France on that fatal day were wavering in confusion, making fast his bridle rein to those of his trusty attendants and asking to be led so far in the fight that he might strike one blow with his sword, rode fearlessly on to his death. But the triple–feathered crest of the fallen Bohemian king and his royal motto, "*Ich dien,*" adopted by the Black Prince, have since graced the escutcheon of Britain's eldest son. It is upon these simple words "*Ich dien*" (I serve), that I propose to make a few practical observations to–day. I would have each of these young gentlemen adopt them as his motto, and, like the king of Bohemia, having borne them in honor in life's conflicts, die with them boldly displayed in its last great battle.

Service has been the natural condition of man since the divine decree went forth, "In the sweat of thy face shalt thou eat bread, till thou return unto the ground." It is universal in its application, and its obligation ends only with the grave. No man is exempt from it, and he who refuses to obey it is a failure. It is *the* condition of success. He who succeeds must work. The idler may be harmless, but he is a drone in his household, a burden to society, and a curse to any community. All honest labor is honorable, and should have the favor of all good people. He who is not fitted for the professions, will find it in the eyes of proper–thinking people just as honorable to serve on the farms, in the workshops, or at the trades. The successful farmer, merchant or mechanic is the equal of the successful lawyer, doctor or politician; and incomparably greater than the professional failure! I desire to emphasize this because too many of our young men are disposed to linger around the portals of the many storied temple of the professions who have but little hope of mounting even to the first floors. This inclination is strengthened by the false notion that manual labor is not honorable. The ladies, generally our leaders in the paths of duty and the ways that are good, are not altogether blameless for this false idea about labor. The more fashionable and less thoughtful of them sometimes frown upon the man who works with his hands for an honest living, while they smile upon the dainty darling of fashion. Let me at least hope they do not know the evil they do. Such sentiments drive young men to idleness, idleness to want, want to crime and crime to disgrace. If you encounter this sentiment anywhere, young gentlemen, let it have no influence upon you. It comes of thoughtlessness, and is not worthy of respect. Never be idle. Be always at work—never out of service. Neither turn your back upon manual labor or those who are engaged in it, for it is the man who, in the sweat of his brow, makes the hidden properties of the seed, the soil and the air, under nature's wondrous guidance, to grow into golden grain or fleecy cotton; or who, with fire and furnace, transmutes the rough ore into serviceable metal; or by forge and anvil, still further transforms the metal into tools for man's use, and with them builds houses and cities, that creates the true wealth of a State.

A word of advice to the young ladies present. It is this: Whomsoever else you wed, do not marry a lazy man. He is not worth marrying. His sluggish hands will not make bread nor his idle brain buy dresses, and it is not altogether fashionable or very convenient to do without either. Rather trust the man who is never idle, even if his hands be brawny and his service humble.

There is a moral in the mythological union of Venus and Vulcan—the goddess of beauty and the tawny king of the anvil. There is grandeur, as well as fidelity to nature, in the picture drawn by the great Scotch novelist in the marriage of the Fair Maid of Perth to lion–hearted and iron–handed Smith, rather than to the silken–gloved Rothsay, or any of his lute–playing courtiers.

The great incentive to all service is the hope of reward. It spurs on man's flagging energies and often keeps him at the post of duty. But for the hope of gathering the fruit of our toils, labor would become an intolerable bondage. It is well that an all–wise Creator has so adjusted the affairs of this life that wise and well-directed service is sure of its reward; while nothing but failure may be expected from that which is ill–advised or badly performed. A few suggestions as to *how* this service should be performed may not prove amiss.

First, it must be performed with energy and determination. Feeble, faltering, hesitating service does not deserve and will not achieve success. "Whatsoever thy hand findeth to do, do it with thy might," is not only the scriptural, but a wise rule.

Secondly, it must be done bravely. In the battle of life cowards seldom win. Courage is not more necessary in the sharp encounter of hostile armies than in the every day conflict of life. Difficulties will arise, but they will be overcome if met with a bold unconquerable will; and the greater the difficulty and the stronger the courage, the greater the victory.

Thirdly, let the performance of the service be straightforward and direct. Never resort the methods of indirection. They seldom succeed and are never commendable. An open, manly course is not only the surest road to success, but it will always command, even in the untoward accident of failure, the respect of your fellow–men.

Fourthly, the service must be right no matter how tempting the offer or how great the promised reward, no service should be undertaken that is not strictly legitimate in the sight of the law of God and of man. Unless it has the unqualified approval of your conscience, let it alone. If its propriety be debatable, touch it not.

Fifthly, it must be continued till the work is done. There is to be no forfeiture of contracts or failure of obligations; nor is there to be any end of service. "Till thou return unto the ground" was the decree. But all along you will receive your rewards, and they will be just in proportion to the efficiency of the service. While the service ends with the grave, the rewards, thank heaven! do not. The good deeds done in service will live after you, and generations to come will bless your name and keep your memory green.

Sixthly, it must be performed solely in the interest of the party for whom the service is rendered. It will not do, while you are pretending to be in the service of one man or cause, to be secretly in the service of another. Fidelity to whatever cause you undertake to serve, must be a rule as unalterable as the laws of the Medes and Persians. If, for any cause, you cannot give that fidelity to the man or cause you serve, the proper thing to do is to quit the service.

There is nothing new in these six suggestions thus formulated, nor are they all that might be made. But they are none the less valuable on account of their age. They are the simple rules that should govern in the every–day transactions in life, and that will govern if our lives are regulated by the rules of right and justice. There is no service to which they do not apply—from the boot–black to the statesman—and the higher and more noble the service, the more binding they become. I fear, however, they are oftener violated by the statesman than by the boot–black, or at least the last one. The service must be solely in the interest of the party for whom it is performed. Can any rule be laid down more absolutely demanded in the administration of government than this? What right has a man, while in the service of his country, to think of any other interest but that of his country? What right has he to use the public service to promote his own or another's ends? None. And the man who trades and traffics in a public trust commits a crime against the public. And yet men, in these days of debauched politics, are daily violating this principle. They do not ask, as did the fathers, how can I best use this public trust for the public good, but how can I best use it for my own promotion or for my enemies' downfall? Such men may flourish for a season, but they have violated a rule of ethics that no man can violate with impunity, and their end shall speedily come. Gaining position through unpatriotic influences, they may maintain their position by exaggerating these influences and keeping them before the people. By appealing to sectional prejudice and animosities, or local questions of state or local interests, they may, for the time being, be able to divert the attention of the people from the manner in which they are performing their service; and while the attention of the people is thus diverted, they may peculate and trade in their public trust to the public harm. The unusual and unnatural issues that give them power cannot last. The people, always honest and always right in their second sober judgment, will see that their confidence has been abused, and their trust betrayed. They will turn upon their betrayers and sweep them from position and power with the besom [*sic*] of destruction. The fate and the memory of Arnold shall be no worse than theirs.

While I cannot advise you, my young friends, to become politicians in the restricted and popular sense of the word, yet I must tell you that you cannot disregard the obligations you owe your country. There is no service in which you can engage, save that of your Creator, more sacred than that of your country. No man who does his duty can withdraw himself entirely from such service. Particularly is this true of men who have received their mental training and moral teaching within the classical and hallowed walls of Randolph Macon. Let me entreat you, young gentlemen, when you do engage in the service of your country, no matter in what capacity—whether it be as a maker or minister of the law, or whether it be as that highest type of an American citizen—a voter—to discard every other consideration from that service but the best interest of your country. Ask only the question, how can I best use this great trust for the benefit of my country? Study only that question. Seek information only upon that, and when you have determined it, let no self–interest keep you from doing it like men.

It was such a spirit as this that animated that liberty–loving band of North Carolina heroes when, on the 20th of May, 1775, in the county of old Mecklenburg in that state, they startled the creatures of King George, as well as their own timid compatriots, with these bold words:

"*Resolved.* That we do hereby declare ourselves a free and independent people, are, and of right ought to be, a sovereign and self-governing association, under the control of no power than that of our God and the general government of the congress; to the maintenance of which independence we solemnly pledge to each other our mutual co–operation, our lives, our fortunes and our most sacred honor."

It was this same spirit that fired the brain and nerved the arm of Thomas Jefferson, when he wrote the great Magna Charta of human liberty the Declaration of Independence. It was this spirit that stirred the souls of the Continental Congress and gave them courage, on the 4th day of July, 1776, to publish this declaration to the world. It was this spirit that drew our fathers from their quiet homes to give their treasure, their blood and their lives to make good that declaration. It was this spirit, and this only that sustained our fathers through all those long years of hardship, privation and war, in defeat and in victory, till finally they gathered on the plains of Yorktown to strike the last blow for freedom. As they stood on those memorable shores on that ever–to–be–remembered night, with the starry canopy of heaven for their only shelter, how many of them do you suppose thought of anything but their country? Not one asked how can I best use this trust to promote my own ends, but how can I best perform this service for my country's good: and if, in response to this inquiry, the God of battles said "Die," each was ready to be offered up upon his country's altar.

> "Pass not on
> Till thou hast blest their memories, and paid those thanks,
> Which God appointed the reward
> Of manly virtue. And if chance thy house
> Salute thee with a father's honored name,
> Go, call thy sons, instruct them what a debt
> They owe their ancestor, and make them swear
> To pay it, by transmitting down entire
> Those sacred rights to which themselves were born."

And, finally, it was by the inspiration of this spirit that our fathers met in council and framed that greatest of instruments ever penned by mortal men—the Constitution of the United States.

Such an impetus as this given to truth and to liberty could not soon lose its force, and for half a century the government was administered in this spirit, and the people were happy and the country prosperous. Had all the public servants always possessed this spirit—had they always made their country's good their first care—had the peace and happiness of the people always been the goal of their ambition—had love of country and not love of self always been the inspiring motive—the bloody pages of our country's history would never have been written. But alas! too many allowed other and improper motives to influence their action, and ere long we found ourselves in a cruel, devastating war, from which the country emerged with its most beautiful and fertile section laid waste. For many long, weary years of patient endurance, this devastated section of our country has felt the bitter pangs of prostituted public service. Had those upon whom the responsibility of shaping the course of events after the surrender of Lee and Johnston, devoted themselves patriotically and alone to the best methods of binding up the wounds of their war–scarred country, of rebuilding her waste places and reconciling her estranged children, we would have had the blessings of Reconciliation and not the curses of Reconstruction. But they acted otherwise and strife has been kept alive, reconciliation postponed and the prosperity of the country retarded. But, thank heaven! the clouds are disappearing, the sun of fraternal harmony once more begins to shine upon us, and the men who have so long delayed his blessed coming are one by one passing away. Not many years hence the last one of them shall be forgotten. Let the history of the past fix this determination in your minds, my countrymen : to allow no thought of self to enter into any service you render the public : to support no man for any public position who can be moved by any other consideration than a faithful performance of his high trust solely in the public interest.

I pray God that this great Centennial year will be the end of all strife in this land of ours. As this year one hundred years ago was the end of the struggle for freedom, may this year be the end of our struggle for reconciliation; and, as from the bloody plains of Yorktown in 1781, the sun of liberty rose to shed his beneficent rays for all time to come upon free America, so, in 1881, from these fields, may the sun of an absolute and everlastlingly reconciled brotherhood rise, never again to be dimmed while time shall last. Yes, my friends, as the people gather from the North and from the South, from the East and from the West, and meet upon that sacred soil, may the spirit of an hundred years ago fall upon them, and bind them together in bonds of love and confidence that can never be rent asunder. And when they leave that hallowed ground, may that spirit go with them, and abide with them, and all the people, forevermore.

That such will be the case I verily believe. I have an abiding faith in the people and in their determination to preserve the institutions of their fathers. I have never seen the hour, even in the darkest days of our country's history, that I had any fear of these institutions being overturned. The talk of empire and of change in our form of government, of which we have heard so much of late years, has given me no concern. That men did contemplate such a revolution, I had no doubt; but that they would be able to accomplish it, I had no fears. The people stood in the way, and in them I had the utmost confidence. So the people will ever stand, upholding the right and trampling upon the wrong. If you would have their favor, you must study their interests and make right and justice the rule of your lives. Do not let the fact that the people themselves are sometimes misled by designing men, ever encourage you to do wrong. They will surely find out their trust has been betrayed, and they will speedily remit their betrayers to private life and to oblivion. No Centennial pageant shall ever gather upon the field of their exploits to shed tears over their graves, or to inscribe their names upon the tablets of memory.

Any speech on the duties of man which fails to impress its hearers with the fact that man's Creator demands his first and best service is incomplete. So any life, however brilliant or useful, that does not render this service, is, after all, but a sad failure. If I may, in the presence of so many commissioned ambassadors of Christ, venture to speak of the spiritual life, I invoke you, young gentlemen, to enter at once openly and forever into the service of the great Creator and Sovereign of the Universe. Do not, I pray you, listen for a moment to any system of philosophy that does not teach that God is the Creator of all things and the Ruler of all things, and as such is entitled to the service of all men. Let nothing shake your faith in the Christian religion, or keep you from obeying its teachings and walking in its ways. It is hard to have no friend to cherish; it is worse to have no country to serve; but it is death eternal to have no God to love or religion to comfort. Man without a friend is a misanthrope, and knows nothing of the sweets of life. Without a country he is an exile and a wanderer—an aimless Arab in the desert. Without a religion, he is in a wilderness of uncertainty without a guide— in the dark without a light—in the world without a hope. Life in these conditions is like a ship at sea without a chart or star, driven hither and thither by the changing winds till chance finds her at the bottom of the sea or wrecked upon the shore. Take no part or lot in such a life, but rather choose the certainty, the light, the hope, the joy and the reward the Christian religion is sure to give. With uncovered head and an humble spirit, I pray God from the great deep of my heart that your lives' service may be such as to merit a rich reward in this life and a crown of glory in the life to come.

Once again, brethren of the Alumni, I greet you all. I have performed the service assigned me by your kind partiality as best I could. Whatever may be its merits, it has at least been cheerfully rendered. This reunion has been to me a pleasure which for years I have earnestly desired and which I shall long remember. Tomorrow we separate again, and with many of us for years—it may be forever. Whenever we go, let us remember our dear old *Alma Mater's* eyes are upon us, watching over us with tender care and affectionate solicitude. And in return it is our high and loyal duty to render glad service, worthy of such a mother, to keep her fair name untarnished, her bright record unstained.

A&H—GLB

Thomas J. Jarvis to T. M. Holt

Executive Department,
Raleigh, June 18, 1881

Yours of the 14th to hand; and in reply, I beg to say that I did not, nor do I now mean to intimate that the A.&N.C.R.R.Co. had a valid claim against your Company for one cent. I did not, nor do I now advise to pay them one cent. All I did suggest, and I think it only a fair suggestion, is, that if you do owe them anything, you ought to pay it and not plead it out of date.

I know of no better tribunal than the Court to say whether one Company owes the other, and think the case ought to be tried on its merits. If you do not owe anything, then you are in no danger. This is all.

A&H—GLB

Thomas J. Jarvis to Johnson Hagood

Executive Department,
Raleigh, June 21st, 1881

I beg to inform Your Excellency that I have appointed Prof. W. C. Kerr, the State Geologist of North Carolina to represent this State in re-running and re-marking the line between this State and South Carolina. This appointment is made in pursuance of an act of the General Assembly of this State, ratified 12th day of March, 1881, a certified copy of which I sent you some time ago, and which is Chapter 347, Laws of 1881.

This act is more comprehensive than the act of your State, and I trust will enable the Commission to do the work to the entire satisfaction of both States.

A&H—GP

S. M. Stone[99] to Thomas J. Jarvis

Franklin Co—N.C. June 23rd 1881
Wake Forest P.O.

I was pained on yesterday 22nd June, to see in News & Observer the obituary notice of that good man—Saml. J. Fall— "Agt of Immigration for N.C." "at Wellingborough Eng—." How is the law in regard to filling the vacancy? But as a matter of course, his Excellency has the appointing power to fill all state vacancies; if not implied, so understood. When that vacancy be filled–have notice of same put in News & Observer. Agriculturilist [sic] were taking more interest in Immigration than, perhaps, you were aware of. The farmers eye was rapidly being turned in that direction: Mr. Fall's agency being in our own language — farmers were in direct communication with him — in making offers and arrangements with the Immigrants themselves, without middle men, a plan that was bound to succeed well, but for the untimely death of the Agt—Mr. Fall. Can we get his place supplied? Will give you an Idea about the harmonious working of Mr Fall's agency. I was in communication with Mr. Fall, relative to manage arrangements direct with Immigrants Fall and through him the Immigrants would accept our terms. for myself and neighbors for another year, they to land next Dec^m at our Depot a certain day, and we to be there with our teams to take them all home. We have this year to arrange houses and plans for their reception and first year's subsistance. I wrote our terms of hire and terms of our share system to Mr— Fall and through him the Immigrants would accept our terms. My last letter of arrangement to Mr Fall is unanswered—by his death, then I had another arrangement to offer for some neighbors, stating their offer and accommodations, and if Mr Fall had lived, next Dec. (in time for next year's cropping) we would have had eighteen families land on board the cars of R & G.R R, at Wake Forest. That is the farmer and laborers and house ser-

---

[99] Farmer of Wake Forest. Branson, *Directory for 1884,* 665.

vants all doing their own business in their own satisfactory way (without the interposition of any middle–men.)

Then after our landing of laborers and servants a plenty for those who–sent–the rest of our farming communities would do likewise. Am sorry our plans are brought to an end by the death of Mr—Fall, but hope you can help me out with the plans. I know it is not legitimately your work, but then if we get these Immigrants through Mr. Mcgehee or Col— Pope— we get them promiscuously— not like from Mr. Fall—he would fill out my bill of requirement and that of my neighbors and after careful selection of picking them, book their names to each one of us, so many by name to me and so of the rest— obviating any confusion of division and homes on their arrival—. Can't you see beauty and convenience in such an organized plan? We need a change— since the present laborers and labor system in our section is a failure, and we can not succeed as agriculturist[s] any longer with such, but merely drag our slow years out, without any progression. The labor question is a serious one just now with our people and country.

.   .   .   .

A&H—GP

A. B. Andrews to Thomas J. Jarvis, Z. B. Vance, and
J. M. Worth [with enclosures]

Raleigh, N.C., July 4th 1881

I herewith have the honor of enclosing to you copies of letters recently sent to the Chairman of the Board of Directors of the State Penitentiary, which explain themselves.

The recent outbreak of scurvey among the Convicts, has been a cause of great regret to us, not only on account of sympathy with the unfortunates, but also because it seriously hampers, and delays our work upon the Railroad.

It is to be hoped that prompt measures will be taken to eradicate the disease

[enclosure—copy]
A. B. *Andrews to E. R. Stamps*

Raleigh, N.C., June 28th 1881

Allow me to call your attention to the fact (which I am satisfied you are aware of.) that we have about 450 Convicts on the W N.C. Road.

The law gives us 500 *able bodied* Convicts, on account of scurvey and other diseases caused by improper diet, and clothing, we have less than 250 at work, making these men cost us double what the law contemplated.

I had trouble to get the Commissioners to extend my time

Had the State furnished 500 able bodied Convicts, as they promised under the Act. March 29th 1880 the road would have been finished today. So you see the State Authorities and not the R R. Authorities are responsible for these delays.

Will you please have the quota of able bodied Convicts provided for in the Act furnished at once.

[enclosure—copy]
A. B. *Andrews to E. R. Stamps*

Raleigh, N.C., July 2nd 1881

I greatly regret to be obliged again, to call your attention to the condition of the Convicts upon the W.N.C.R.R. Advices recently received from Maj J W Wilson, Chief Engineer, and Supt of Construction state "On June 28th Convicts more than ever are down: on June 29th 78 sick at Sandy Marsh today, an increase," and on same day." the number of the sick are increasing instead of diminishing," and the same complaint on July 1st

While I am sure that the prevalence of disease, especially one like scurvey, is a source of keen regret to your Board, and that you desire to use all means in your power to check it.

It must be remembered that the State contracted to furnish Five hundred able bodied Convicts, and to maintain that number: and that by the present painfull state of affairs, difficulties are thrown in the way of our completion of the work upon the

Western N.CRR. in accordance with the terms of our contract, by causes *entirely* beyond our control, but not *entirely* beyond the control of your subordinate officers, who are in fact employees of the State of North Carolina

If you decide to send up your Physicians, as you have suggested in conversation, I will gladly furnish a pass, and will aid your Board in any way in my power to alleviate the condition of the Convicts, as well as to secure better and more effective laborers.

A&H—GP

M. F. Morris to Thomas J. Jarvis

Washington, D.C., July 6th 1881

My partner, Mr. Merrick, was called to Chicago this morning; but requested me, before his departure, to attend the session of the General Term of the Supreme Court of the District of Columbia to–day, and promptly announce to you its decision in regard to the Extradition Case of Samuel L. Perry, the "exodus" man.[100]

I regret to have to inform you that the decision is adverse to the claim of the State, and that the previous judgment of Judge Wylie, discharging the fugitive from custody, has been affirmed. The ground of the decision is, that the indictment is defective, inasmuch as it does not set forth a crime upon which a conviction could be sustained. The opinion has been taken down in short hand, and will be written out, and sent to you. Mr. Merrick will be absent in the West about a week or ten days. I presume he will write to you upon the subject on his return.

A&H—GP

Charles Foster[101] to Thomas J. Jarvis
[Telegram]

Columbus O Jul, 10 1881

Present indicates strongly encourage the hope that the President [Garfield] will recover from the effects of the horrible attempt upon his life—It may occur to all that it would be most fitting

---

[100]See Merrick to Jarvis, November 11, 1880, in this volume.

[101]Governor of Ohio and close personal friend to President Garfield. *Dictionary of American Biography*, VI, 544–545.

for the Governors of the several states and Territories to issue proclamation setting apart a day to be generally agreed upon for thanksgiving & praise to Almighty God for the blessed deliverance of our President and for this great evidence of his goodness to this nation If this suggestion meets your approbation permit me to name the Governors of N York Pennsylvania Kentucky Maryland & Ohio[102] as a Committee to fix upon a day to be so observed please reply.

A&H—GP

Edward Thomas Boykin[103] to Thomas J. Jarvis

Clinton, N.C., July 29., 1881

We are very anxious to secure the 100 convicts granted to us in our charter by the Gen. Assembly of '81 to aid in building the Clinton & Faison R.R. It is very important that we should get them by Jan 1. '82 if possible. By their aid, we can certainly build the Road. Without it, there is much doubt.

Have you any idea when the W.N.CRR. & the C.F.&Y.V.RR. will be completed? Do you know any reason why we can't get the convicts for our Road after the grant of convicts to the above roads, expires? I wish you would be kind enough to give me information as to the above unless they are matters of state that it is not proper to divulge at present.

I am asking purely for business reasons.

Thomas J. Jarvis, Z. B. Vance, and J. M. Worth to W. P. Clyde, A. S. Buford, and T. M. Logan[104]

Morehead City, N.C., Aug. 1, 1881

We have the honor to herewith inclose you a copy of an agreement entered into on the 25th day of May, 1881, between W. J. Best and his associates and ourselves as individuals and com-

---

[102]Respectively these governors were Alonzo B. Cornell, Andrew G. Curtin, Luke P. Blackburn, William T. Hamilton, and Charles Foster.

[103]Lawyer of Clinton; member of the General Assembly, 1881–1885; Superior Court judge, 1885–1896. In 1881 he was chairman of the Sampson County Democratic Committee. Oates, *Story of Fayetteville*, 681.

[104]Taken from the *News and Observer*, September 13, 1881.

missioners of the Western North Carolina Railroad.[105] Mr. Best and his associates have placed in our hands the sum of $250,000, which we hereby tender you, to reimburse you for your expenditures upon the Western North Carolina Railroad, legitimately and properly made under what is known as the Best contract, and we are authorized to say if this is not sufficient such further sum as may be due will be paid to you. Mr. Best and his associates having in pursuance of said agreement obtained a lease of the Atlantic and North Carolina Railroad, and having deposited the sum of $85,000 as required by said agreement, and being now actively engaged in making the necessary preliminary surveys of the line of the railway between Goldsboro and Salisbury, we have to inform you that if they shall continue to prosecute vigorously the work of constructing and building said road, we shall in good faith and literally comply with our part of the agreement above referred to, both as commissioners and individuals.

A&H—GLB

Thomas J. Jarvis to Johnson Hagood

Executive Department,
Raleigh, Aug. 11th, 1881

I enclose you a copy of a letter[106] received by Prof. Kerr, in reference to running the line between our States. Prof. Kerr, as you know, is the surveyor and Commissioner for this State, and is a scientific man. He wants to do the work well, and I write to inquire if you will approve the plan suggested in this communication to Prof. Kerr.

---

[105]A year previously, Best and his associates, who had been incorporated as the Midland North Carolina Railroad Company, had assigned away their interests in the Western North Carolina Railroad to Buford, Clyde, and Logan, representing the Richmond Terminal Company. See Andrews to Jarvis, Vance, and Worth, April 30, 1881, *n.* 74, in this volume. Best and his associates now wanted to regain their interests. See Vance to Jarvis, May 12, 1881, *n.* 80, in this volume. Feeling that the state's interests would fare better with the railroad under Best's management, the commissioners on May 25 entered an agreement with Best. They would help Best procure the retransfer of the railroad if Best and his associates fulfilled four conditions: 1) lease the Atlantic and North Carolina Railroad as part of a proposed through-line, 2) deposit $85,000 as security for its rental, 3) build a direct line from Goldsboro to Salisbury, and 4) deposit $250,000 for reimbursing the Richmond Terminal Company for its work the last year on the Western North Carolina Railroad. *News and Observer*, October 2, 1881. For further details of the agreement of May 25, see Carruth to Jarvis, November 7, 1881, in this volume.
[106]Not found.

A&H—GP

A. H. Canedo[107] to Thomas J. Jarvis

Raleigh N.C.
Aug 17th 1881

I beg leave to submit herewith, as the authorized representative of a body of capitalists, of New York;—A Proposition to purchase the interests of the State of North Carolina in the Cape Fear and Yadkin Valley Railroad, with the view of making it the neucleus[sic] for a general main line from Wilmington N.C. to Cincinnatti Ohio, via Fayetteville, Greensboro, and Mt Airy, branching near the head waters of the Guyandotte in West Virginia and down that river to Huntington on the Ohio River

I propose to give satisfactory guarantees for the fulfillment of the project in so far as that we will complete the construction of the line projected within the limits of the State of North Carolina.

I beg leave to ask your Excellency to respond to this, with your views on the matter, and the requisites to enable us to enter upon the contract in accordance with the law as it exists upon the subject.

A&H—GLB

Thomas J. Jarvis to A. H. Canedo

Executive Department
Raleigh, Aug 17th 1881

I am just in receipt of yours of this date, and as requested reply at once.

The continuation of a line of Railway diagonally across the State from Wilmington in the South–Eastern border, to a point on the North Western border has, for years, had my warm support. Its completion would be hailed with delight by all our people. Now add to such a line its extension to the Ohio thus uniting Wilmington with the great North West by a direct line, such as you propose, and no one can tell the advantage to accrue to the State generally but more particularly to Wilmington our

---

[107]New York physician who had gone into railroad development. At this time he was vice–president of the New York and Southern Railroad and Telegraph Construction Company, a New York corporation which so far had had no dealings in North Carolina. *News and Observer*, November 24, 1881.

chief seaport. Our people will welcome to the State the capitalist who engage in this great scheme. Nor do I believe all the advantages in this project are on the side of the State. I have no doubt it will be a paying road yielding large profits to its owners.

This I think can be clearly demonstrated by a review of the country through which it will pass, and the great amount of business it must bring from the great west to this near and easy point of water transportation—the City of Wilmington. But these are questions I have no doubt you have well considered.

The Legislature of this State passed an Act which Prest Gray has furnished you authorizing certain Commissioners with approval of the Governor and his Council; and the stockholders of the C.F. and Y.V.R.R. Company to sell the State interest in said road upon the terms and conditions set out in said act.[108] I think I can say with very great confidence your syndicate will have no trouble in completing the purchase of the State's interest when you satisfy the Commissioners of your purpose and ability to complete the road as required by said act.

I beg to suggest as a practical way of getting at the matter that you forward to me at as early day as suits your convenience a formulated proposition signed by the persons who propose to go into the project. Let the proposition set out in detail your plans as fully as you may deem it to the advantage of your enterprise to develop them. The only point about which I apprehend there is likely to be much difference of opinion is the question of guarantees that you will complete the road. On this point I beg to suggest that the proposition be explicit and the guarantees as strong as the interest of your scheme will allow. Of course the character of men who propose to engage in this enterprise will have much to do with this question and for this reason I desire that you give us their names as early as possible. As soon as I am put in possession of the proposition proposed as indicated and have the desired information I will assemble the Commissioners and lay all the papers before them.

---

[108]On March 14, 1881, the General Assembly had established a commission of thirteen members with authority to sell the state's stock in the Cape Fear and Yadkin Valley Railroad subject to the approval of the governor and his council and of the vote of a majority of the stockholders in the railroad. The minimum acceptable price for the stock would be $55,000. *Laws of North Carolina,* 1881, c. 374.

A&H—GLB

Thomas J. Jarvis to T. S. Kenan

Executive Department,
Raleigh, Aug. 20, 1881

I think it a matter of great importance to the people of the State that the railroads of the State be subject to such laws as the General Assembly shall choose, in its wisdom, to pass for their control.

I believe it is conceded that such roads as have been chartered since the adoption of the Constitution of 1868, are subject to such control; or, at least, it is in the power of the Legislature to enforce upon them obedience to its will. As to roads chartered before 1868, there is a strong opinion, in which I do not concur, that they are, in many particulars, beyond the reach of the Legislature. I say I do not concur in this opinion because I do not believe there is any vested right, as between the State and the corporation that is the creature of the State, which the General Assembly cannot alter or repeal. But, be this as it may, if they are compelled to take out new charters, then it will no longer be a matter of doubt.

I therefore beg to request that you will investigate the charters of the roads chartered before 1868, and see if any of them, for any cause, have forfeited their charters; and, if you find that any road has, that you will take such action in the matter as, in your opinion, the case requires and the law justifies.

A&H—GLB

Thomas J. Jarvis to T. S. Kenan

Executive Department,
Raleigh, Aug. 20, 1881

The State is burdened with a debt of over $3,000,000. for the construction of the North Carolina R.R. and with a debt of considerable magnitude for the construction of the Atlantic and North Carolina Railroad. The State still owns a large interest in both of these roads, yet we see the North Carolina Railroad now so operated as to not only cripple the Atlantic and North Carolina Railroad, but to cut off the people of the whole eastern section of the State from the freight privileges of the North

Carolina Railroad. This I get from a circular issued by Sol [omon] Haas, General Freight Agent of the Associated Lines of Railways, (No. 88), in which he prohibits any freight rates beyond Goldsboro to points along the A.&N.C.R.R.[109] One of the results of this outrageous proceeding on the part of the lessees of the North Carolina Railroad is, that the middle sections of the State, in which the corn crop has almost been destroyed by the excessive drought, will not be able to procure a supply from the east, where the crops have been more favored with rains, except at greatly increased rates and by circuitous routes.

This action of the managers of the North Carolina Railroad I consider an outrage upon the people of the State, taken to vent a little personal spleen, regardless of the rights and benefits of the people.

I have no doubt that other instances might be found in their management, if not so glaring, yet pernicious to the best interest of the people.

In view of these facts, I beg that you will examine into the lease of the North Carolina Railroad and the advisability of instituting a suit to vacate the lease and recover back the road, so that it shall not be operated against the best interests of the people of he State.

A&H—GP

Johnson Hagood to Thomas J. Jarvis

Executive Chamber
Columbia 21 Aug 1881

Yr favor of 11th covering communication from Prof Kerr relative to survey Boundary line rec'd.

The terms of the act of the Legislature of this State of which I have heretofore forwarded a copy will not admit of my going into such elaborate work as suggested.

Mr. Spencer the contractor to re run & remark a portion of the line on behalf of S.C. has therefore been directed to procede as originally contemplated—& I would be glad of your cooperation.

---

[109]For an explanation of the nature and purposes of Circular No. 88, see Buford to Jarvis, September 1, 1881, enclosures.

A&H—GP

Z. B. Vance and J. M. Worth to Thomas J. Jarvis[110]

Raleigh, Aug. 25, 1881

We, the undersigned, Commissioners appointed by the "Act to provide for the sale of the State's interest in the W.N.C. Railroad and for other purposes," ratified 29th March, 1880, do hereby report to you in accordance with the provisions of section 15 of said Act, that, from time to time, we have examined the work on said road, and find that the Assignees of the grantees in said Act mentioned have failed to prosecute the same with diligence and energy; that they have failed to keep a force of work on the Ducktown line, after the road had reached Asheville, sufficient to insure its completion to Pigeon River by the 1st of July, 1881; and that they have failed to complete said road to that point and to Paint Rock by the 1st of July, 1881.

In addition to the foregoing, we also find, upon examination, that the company of the Assignees are daily discriminating most injuriously in freights and charges against North Carolina towns and cities and railroads, contrary to the provisions of section 20 of said Act, and their contract made in pursuance thereof.

A&H—GP

W. P. Clyde, T. M. Logan, and A. S. Buford to Thomas J. Jarvis, Z. B. Vance, and J. M. Worth

Richmond, Va. Aug. 25th 1881

Your letter of August 1, 1881, has been received, together with a copy of the agreement therein referred to, of date, May 25, 1881, between yourselves and W. J. Best.

These papers have received from us the careful and respectful attention and consideration, which their importance demands, and as emanating from gentlemen entrusted with the important duties conferred on you by the State of North Carolina in this regard, and occupying towards us a business relation scarcely less peculiar than important in its character.

---

[110]Vance, Worth, and Jarvis met in the latter's office on this date and agreed to send the following commissioners' report to the governor. "Proceedings of the Commissioners on the Western North Carolina Rail Road."

Eng by E. G. Williams & Bro NY

John Milton Worth (1811-1900), a Guilford County native, studied at the Medical College of Lexington, Kentucky, but returned to Montgomery County, North Carolina, to farm. He moved to Randolph County, opened a general store in Asheboro, and also became interested in mining. A Whig, Worth was a member of the state Senate (1842-1848); he was appointed state treasurer by Governor Curtis Brogden in 1870, elected in 1876, and re-elected in 1880.

We beg to assure you, that the delay which has occurred in making reply has resulted only from the fact that, owing to the absence of one of us, it was impossible to obtain an immediate conference.

Candor compels us to say, that we did not at first escape the impression naturally to be derived from the apparent import and tenor of your letter and the accompanying contract, to the effect, that it was intended to indicate that in your character as Commissioners of the State of North Carolina, acting under the powers and limitations conferred and imposed by the Act of Assembly referred to, you had entered into an engagement with Mr. Best and his associates, to compel us as the assignees of Mr. Best, by such means as might be at your command, upon certain contingent events over which we have no control, to surrender the just and lawful rights acquired and held by us under the said act, and the assignment thereof from Mr. Best; and that your letter was intended to imply a demand upon us to surrender these rights under penalty of all the powerful adverse influence, both official and personal which you could exert.

Upon more careful consideration, however, we do not think that this could be your intention, and for several reasons. Among others, for the reason that the Commissioners, especially Governor Jarvis and Senator Vance, are fully aware of the peculiar circumstances under which we assumed the execution of this contract with the State of North Carolina, and all the circumstances attending the assignment made to us by Mr. Best; and were fully cognizant of Mr. Best's utter and acknowledged inability at the time of making his assignment to us, to take the first step towards the fulfillment of his undertaking. That at the time of such assignment we were made sensible by numerous representations directly and indirectly from the Commissioners and other prominent and influential citizens of the State, that consequences most disastrous to the interests of the State and its people, would ensue, if it then became apparent that the Best Act was a failure; and that with the full knowledge of these things you not only consented to it, but were largely instrumental in inducing us to accept the assignment of the said contract.

More particularly is it worthy of note in this connection that Senator Vance was present at several of the interviews had in New York with Mr. Best, and was active in promoting the negotiation then thought by yourselves in common with others of the State, to be important and even essential to the interests of the

State and of those citizens of the State who had been actively instrumental in procuring the original law and the contract thereunder, to be enacted and made.

It is moreover proper to say, that the commissioners are and were at the time, aware that this assignment *was not sought by us,* but only taken at the *urgent solicitation* of those who were most deeply interested in its successful consummation, yourselves most conspicuously and influentially among the number; and that under these circumstances we stepped into the breach when every other resource had failed, and assumed an onerous burden which all others had declined, and thereby averted the disastrous consequences apprehended by yourselves and others from a failure.

It seems to us also, that you cannot mean to demand a surrender of our just and fully recognized rights under this contract, because there can be no possible ground for such a demand.[111]

We feel assured that you are fully aware that ever since we assumed the responsibility of this assignment, we have proceeded to push forward the work in accordance therewith, with a diligence and vigor which, considering the unexpected, unexampled and almost insuperable obstacles presented, have shown upon our part, not merely good faith, but a sincere and earnest desire and purpose to comply with and carry out our contract in its true intent and spirit.

At the same time, we know that you are fully informed of the fact that for reasons in no wise attributable to us, the contract on the part of the State has not been performed in essential particulars, that have not only seriously retarded the progress of the work, but greatly increased its cost.

The State has not furnished, and as we are informed cannot now furnish, the five hundred convict laborers to which we are now and have always been entitled under the Act.

For these reasons, as well as others that might be assigned, we cannot construe your communication to be a demand for the surrender of our rights and interests; much less that such de-

---

[111]The commissioners were not in the legal position to make such a demand. In answer to a Senate resolution asking, among other things, information "in respect to the present ownership and control" of the Western North Carolina Railroad, Jarvis had replied that Best and his associates could sell their interest "without our consent, and even against it." The commissioners could only insist that "the grantees, or some one for them," continue the work as agreed upon in the contract. "Message of the governor in relation to the ownership of the Western North Carolina Railroad," *Public Documents, 1881,* No. 33, 3-4.

mand should be made under a menace of whatever injuries your high official position and your personal influence might enable you to inflict.

We can therefore, only understand your communication as intended to place before us a proposition which we may consider from the standpoint of the interests we represent, and which without any risk of injustice, may be accepted or declined.

If, as we assume, this interpretation be correct, it will be presented to all the parties interested, and respectfully and duly considered, in connection with all the rights, interests and obligations that are involved in the whole transaction.

We await your reply to learn whether or not we place the proper interpretation upon your communication.

We can offer you no better assurance of the good faith with which this contract is being carried out, than the fact that notwithstanding all the difficulties which have surrounded the work, arising from Mr. Best's original default and the extreme rigors of the Winter following the assignment to us, it has been pushed forward so rapidly as to insure its completion both to Pigeon River and to Paint Rock by November 1st 1881, at which latter point the Tennessee system of roads is under contract to meet and connect with it, and thus open to the State the shortest and most direct route to the great markets of the West.

We beg to assure you that you will always find us, as you found us when approached on this contract, ready to coöperate heartily in protecting and promoting the real interests of the State, in which we represent as you know, a very large and constantly increasing permanent investment of capital; and we in turn respectfully and confidently ask your cordial sympathy and continued cooperation in our work. Inspired by your appeals for our aid at an alleged crisis, and to prevent the indefinite suspension of a great work of long cherished value to the people of N. Ca. we assumed this undertaking, and, if not interrupted, propose to stand by it until executed.

A&H—GLB

Proclamation

I, Thomas J. Jarvis, Governor of North Carolina, do issue this my Proclamation, declaring the result of the election held on the 4th~day of August, 1881, to take the sense of the people on the question of Prohibition, to be, according to the returns made to the Board of State Canvassers, as follows:

There were cast at said election two hundred and twelve thousand, one hundred and ninety-four (212,194) votes; of which forty-eight thousand and sixty-one (48,061) votes were cast "For Prohibition," and one hundred and sixty-four thousand, one hundred and thirty-three (164,133) votes were cast "Against Prohibition": the majority "Against Prohibtion" being one hundred and sixteen thousand and seventy two (116,072) votes.

A&H—GLB

Thomas J. Jarvis to A. S. Buford

Executive Department,
Raleigh, Aug. 26, 1881

Twenty-six days ago, I, with the other Commissioners of the W.N.C.R.R., addressed a communication to you and your associate assignees. Up to this time, none of us have received any reply to that communication.

I now have the honor to forward to you a copy of a letter received by me from the Commissioners on yesterday, relative to the conduct of the work on said road and the management thereof in the matter of freight.

I also send you a copy of a letter I have addressed to the Attorney General of the State, relative to the lease of the North Carolina Railroad, and also a letter addressed to him on railroads generally.[112]

Unless the allegations set out in these papers prove to be untrue or the cause of the complaint is speedily removed, I shall feel it to be my duty to use whatever power the State administration possesses, to oust the Richmond and Danville Railroad people from the control of any railroad in this State in which the State has a direct or contingent interest.

A&H—GP

A. B. Andrews to Thomas J. Jarvis

Raleigh, N.C., Aug 29th 1881

I have the honor to request that you furnish me copies of the records which the commissioners appointed under the act to

---

[112]See Jarvis' two letters of August 20, 1881, to T. S. Kenan.

provide for the sale of the Western North Carolina Railroad, have ordered to be made, or that you permit me to have copies transcribed myself—Your early answer will much oblige

A&H—GP

A. S. Buford to Thomas J. Jarvis [with enclosures]

Richmond, Va.,
September 1st 1881

Your letter of the 26th August, with the copies therein enclosed of the letter of Commissioners Vance and Worth to you, and your two letters of the 20th August to Attorney General Kenan, have been received and have had my attention, and I now take the earliest opportunity to reply to the several matters referred to by you, and in the order in which you mention them.—

First:—I regret that circumstances over which I had no control, necessarily delayed the reply of Messrs Clyde and Logan and myself to the communication of the Commissioners appointed by the Act of the General Assembly of North Carolina relating to the sale of the State's interest in the Western North Carolina Railroad, bearing date the 1st August 1881, to which you refer. This reply was forwarded yesterday to your address, and I now have the honor to enclose you a copy of it, and beg to call your attention to the statements therein contained as pertinent to the matters of which you write.

Second:—I observe that Messrs Vance and Worth, two of the three Commissioners, officially report to your Excellency, "that the assignees of the grantees in the Act mentioned have failed to prosecute the work with diligence and energy, that they have failed to keep a force at work on the Ducktown line after the Road had reached Asheville, sufficient to insure it's completion to Pigeon River by the 1st July 1881, and that they have failed to complete said Road to that point and to Paint Rock by the 1st July 1881."—

The fact that the lines were not completed to Paint Rock and Pigeon River on the 1st July 1881 has been known to the Commissioners ever since that day; and they also knew that the assignees did not expect to be able to complete them by that time, long before the 1st July.

It is well known that the President of the Western North Carolina Railroad Company presented a petition to the Commissioners on the 30th day of April 1881, asking for an extension of four months' time from the 1st July for the completion of the work to the points named, and the record of the proceedings of the Commissioners shows that this petition was duly considered, and that the Commissioners agreed to grant the prayer of the petitioner upon certain conditions, all of which were faithfully complied with. And after this petition had been amended as required by the Commissioners, and signed by the assignees as was also required, your Excellency, acting in the capacity of a Commissioner, finding that the assignees had fully complied with the requirements of the Commissioners, promptly gave,— as all the Commissioners had agreed to do,—your consent in writing to the extension as prayed for. Hon. J. M. Worth on the next day signed a writing of similar import. When these papers were obtained, the assignees proceeded to prosecute the work with vigor, diligence and energy. If the consent had not been given, they would have been forced to abandon it.

It is unnecessary to refer to the reasons for the application for an extension of time, or to the reasons which induced the Commissioners to grant it. It is enough to say, that they were then deemed altogether sufficient.

These being the facts of the case, all of which were well known to Commissioners Vance and Worth, I am at a loss to know why it is that they report the assignees as delinquent in failing to finish the work to the points named by the 1st July.

The Act of Assembly makes it the duty of the Commissioners under certain circumstances, to grant certain extensions of time. These circumstances existed. And it will not be denied that the State itself has been delinquent, and is to this day delinquent, in failing at any time during the progress of the work, to furnish the number of convicts which she agreed to furnish.

I have seen in the public prints that Commissioner Vance has stated, that the grants of the extension of time signed by your Excellency and Commissioner Worth were invalid, because the signature of Commissioner Worth to the paper had been fraudulently obtained. And he states, as the ground upon which he makes this serious charge, that the signature was obtained before Commissioner Worth had been informed that *he—Commissioner Vance*—had determined, for reasons satisfactory to himself, to decline to comply with his agreement to grant the extension, and had withdrawn his consent.[113]—

Without stopping to enquire whether Commissioner Worth would have felt himself justified in refusing to fulfill his own solemn promise, because Commissioner Vance had declined to comply with his, I will only say, that you yourself know that you communicated to Dr Worth, in your letter of the 14th May 1881, the fact that Commissioner Vance had withdrawn his consent, and that Commissioner Worth received and read this letter before he signed the paper.

Relying most implicity upon the good faith of the Commissioners in their action of the 30th of April 1881, and upon the consent to the extension given in writing by Commissioner Worth and your Excellency, the assignees pressed forward the work most vigorously, and employed labor as soon as they could. In a short time they placed three hundred (300) additional hands upon the Pigeon River line, and have had during the month of August an average of over seven hundred (700) men on that line, and about six hundred (600) on the other—, notwithstanding the fact that the State is still delinquent, in failing to furnish the five hundred (500) convicts, as she contracted to do.—

I am unwilling to believe that any one of the Commissioners will in view of these facts, undertake to have the contract forfeited, because the lines to Paint Rock and Pigeon River were not completed by the 1st July. However this may be I think it proper to inform you, that the assignees will rely upon all their legal rights in the premises, of which I can not assume it is the desire or purpose of the Commissioners to endeavor to deprive them.

I beg to state further, that the circumstances and inducements under which the Best contract was assigned to Messrs Clyde and Logan and myself, and under which the obligations thereof

---

[113]Vance agreed that early in May he had agreed to an extension. But he claimed that soon after returning to Washington, D.C. he learned that the new assignees were procrastinating to gain time. So in his letter of May 12 to Jarvis, Vance withdrew his consent to any extension and begged Jarvis and Worth not to act without him. Jarvis received the request the next day; but Worth's letter had to be readdressed to Asheboro and thereby took several days to reach him. Jarvis signed his agreement of an extension of time despite Vance's advice, and Andrews hurried to Asheboro and obtained Worth's signature to an extension before the latter received Vance's letter. Vance, therefore, argued that a majority of the commissioners' votes were obtained by fraud. *News and Observer*, August 28, 1881. Andrews denied all this. *News and Observer*, September 1, 1881.

were assumed, are stated with some detail in their letter in reply to that of the Commissioners of the 1st August, a copy which of is sent you herewith, as before stated: and you may well imagine that the assignees were surprised to learn that, notwithstanding these facts, the Commissioners had, as far back as the 25th May 1881, actually entered into a formal agreement with Mr Best, looking to the recession or re-assignment of said contract, of which agreement the assignees were kept in total ignorance for more than two months, notwithstanding they were re-doubling their energies and sparing no effort or expense to carry out and complete the contract, relying upon the extension of time which had not only been granted, but granted without controversy as to their right to claim it.

Third—Commissioners Vance and Worth also say in their letter, that they find upon examination that the Company of the assignees are daily discriminating in freights and charges against North Carolina towns and cities and Railroads, contrary to the provisions of Section 20. of the Act relating to the sale of the Western North Carolina Road. In behalf of the assignees, we say, we know that no such discrimination has been authorized or intended, and we believe none such exists. In confirmation of this, I beg to say, that since the receipt of your letter communicating this charge, I have talked freely with Col. Andrews, President, and Mr. Macmurdo,[114] General Freight Agent of the Western North Carolina Railroad Company, who emphatically declare that no such discrimination has been intended, and, as far as they know or believe, none exists. I have personally examined their tariff rates, and can find no evidence of any such.

There may be isolated cases in which freight bills are improperly made out, but these errors are promptly corrected upon application, or when attention is called to them. In a large business clerical errors will sometimes unavoidably occur. I am informed that the General Freight Agent's attention was called to the Section of the Act referred to, and he was instructed not to violate it, and he assures me that he has not done so, which he is prepared to verify by his tariff sheets, that I beg to say are always subject to the inspection of the Commissioners.

Fourth—In regard to what your Excellency has to say in your letter to the Attorney General, as to the present operation of the North Carolina Railroad affecting injuriously the interests of the

---

[114]John R. McMurdo of Salisbury.

people of Eastern North Carolina, based upon a certain circular issued by Sol. Haas, General Freight Agent, allow me to say, that, as you will see from what follows, you have wholly misapprehended the actual facts of the situation.

Mr Yates,[115] Manager of the Atlantic & North Carolina Railroad, complains by letter of the 16th August 1881 to Mr Haas, General Freight Agent of the Associated Railways, of certain alleged inequalities of rates. To this Mr Haas replies next day, explaining that the rates complained of were so made to enable *Newbern* to *compete* with Wilmington, Richmond and Norfolk for the same trade, the Atlantic & North Carolina Railroad having the same relative rates as the lines from the last named cities. But, that in view of his, Mr. Yates', objections to the rates, he issued the notice in question, and requested Mr Yates to "furnish him at the earliest moment with such rates to competitive points as he was willing to prorate, and what proportions he was willing to accept to Goldsboro on all classes of freight to W & W and N. C. stations." Please see copies of these letters herewith submitted, from which it is clear that the temporary withdrawal of through rates was intended only to enable the Manager of the Atlantic & North Carolina Railroad to arrange rates satisfactory to himself, which action on his part was requested to be taken at once. Meanwhile the actual interchange of traffic was practically undisturbed, and the rates paid by shippers not at all increased.

In the absence of the General Freight Agent, I have requested the attention of our General Manager, Col. Talcott,[116] to this matter, and herewith submit copy of his letter of this date in reply. I also submit herewith for your information copies of letter of Mr Yates to Mr Haas, of date August 20th 1881, and of Mr Haas' reply thereto, and his order revoking the former one.

Upon reading these papers you will hardly need a word of comment to satisfy you, that, if any disturbance of freight arrangements between the North Carolina and the Atlantic & North Carolina Roads has occurred, it has resulted from the action of the Atlantic & North Carolina Railroad, and can be continued only by it's failure to meet the General Freight Agent of the North Carolina Railroad in his urgent proposal to have the rates settled and agreed.

[115]John B. Yates of Salem, who succeeded John D. Whitford as manager of the Atlantic and North Carolina Railroad. *News and Observer*, August 13, 1881.

[116]T. M. R. Talcott of Richmond, Virginia. Poor, *Railroad Manual*, 314.

I can, therefore, assure your Excellency of my conviction, that, in the order referred to, Mr Haas had no intention whatever to encroach upon the rights or interests of the Atlantic & North Carolina Railroad. What transpired was, of course, without my knowledge at the time. The General Freight Agent necessarily regulates these traffic arrangements, subject to control and supervision. He has no authority to treat unfairly any traffic passing between the North Carolina Railroad and the Eastern portions of the State, and knows that he would not be allowed so to do, were he so disposed, which I do not believe.

You are yourself witness of the endeavors that have been made by the lessees of the North Carolina Railroad, to aid those sections in their transportation interests. We shall continue to do so if allowed, as far as practicable consistently with our duties and obligations to the North Carolina Railroad Company, and the people and interests along it's whole line. We utterly disclaim any objects or interests in the management of the North Carolina Railroad, except in accordance with our acknowledged lawful rights, and our declared purpose to do impartial justice to every section of the State into which it's business relations extend. Beyond this, it will not be expected that we shall willingly allow it to be injuriously used for the purposes of rival corporations or of unfriendly individuals. We seek to discharge faithfully our obligations, legal and moral, to the public and to individuals, asking only to be accorded the peaceful use of the properties we lawfully hold and lawfully use, in like manner as is accorded to all who so act.

If we have inadvertently departed in anything from this course of action, when shown we will promptly correct whatever error we have made. Can we do more? Can we ask less? Will less or more be expected and demanded of us by the authorities or the public sentiment of a law- and justice–loving people?

[enclosure]
J. B. Yates to Solomon Haas

Newbern, N.C, Aug't 16 1881

I wish to call your attention to what appears to me to be a grave inequality in freight rates against this Road.

I cite at present two instances:—First.—the rate on corn from Newbern to Greensboro is 26¢ pr C. We get 5¢ which includes

1¢ for transfer here. In other words you get 21¢ for 130 miles, and we get 5¢ for 59 miles.

Again the rate on corn to Wilson on the W & W from this point is 14¢.—Our proportion of this is 5¢. That is you get 9¢ for 25 miles and we get 5¢ for 59 miles. The above are but samples of cases which I have under consideration.

I respectfully ask some explanation for this (to me) unjust discrimination against this Road.

[enclosure]
Solomon Haas to J. B. Yates

Richmond, Va. Aug. 17th 1881

The rates from Newbern which you are pleased to term unjust discrimination against your Road, were made to enable Newbern to compete with Wilmington, Richmond & Norfolk, your Road having the same relative rates from Goldsboro as were charged from the other points mentioned. This business is competitive to your Road & is not competitive to the Roads on which stations you mention are situated.

If you will inspect the rates to competitive points, you will find your Road very liberally provided for.

In view of your apparent dissatisfaction with these rates, I have issued a notice withdrawing all rates between your Road & the Roads I represent. I will be glad if you will at the earliest moment furnish me with such total rates to competitive points as you are willing to pro–rate & what proportion you are willing to accept to Goldsboro on business to W&W&NC stations on all classes of freight.

[enclosure—copy]

Richmond, Va., August 17 1881

Circular No. 89.—

Upon receipt of this notice you will withdraw all rates to & from A&NC.R.R. stations Newbern & Morehead & name rate for these points to Goldsboro only until further advised.

New rates will be issued & furnished you as soon as practicable.

(Signed.) Sol. Haas

[*enclosure*]
J. B. Yates to Solomon Haas

Newbern, N.C. Aug. 20, 1881

In reply to your letter of Aug. 17, I am sorry you considered it necessary to take "snap judgment" and annul your rates. However, as the rates were of your own making, I am respecting them and shall continue to do so, until we come to a decided understanding or misunderstanding. I positively state I do not wish to break up any system or cut rates. I send you herewith, for your consideration what I consider our just proportion on grain, without disturbing the rates,—for instance, take Greensboro, the point mentioned in my letter of 16 inst. You receive 39¢ for 130 miles, and we 13 for 95 miles, this is on the new rate,—good pay for you and assists us in paying considerable extra expense in an incurring in employing agents and solicitors —We are trying to build up and foster the grain trade by rail. We guarantee to increase the shipments, so that the increase in the business will allow you to be somewhat more generous with us on this line hereafter, than even the proportions we ask for now.

The Coal rates you will see we have not disturbed.

The local rates to and from points on this road are satisfactory to us, in other words, we accept the tariff made and promulgated by you.

We also send you rates for Cotton from Raleigh and stations along W. and W.R.R. would like your opinion on this. We also desire you to propose rates on cotton and mchdze between Goldsboro & Northern and eastern cities. We consider we are entitled to some of this business from Goldsboro, and hope we can pleasantly and to our mutual interest so to say *pool* the freight, so that our little road may have something to show on the credit side from this important station.

Ad interim, I pledge ourselves to adhere to present rates until as above we agree to disagree.

We call your attention to the fact that we charge no transfer on grain—the proportion we ask for covers this.

[*enclosure*]
Solomon Haas to J. B. Yates

Richmond, Va., Aug. 20 1881

Absence prevented a sooner reply to your valued favor.

Had the divisions complained of not been made by myself, I could perhaps not have taken what you term "snap judgment."

As you express a willingness to continue former divisions, I issue an order to–day restoring all rates & divisions in force previous to "order 88."

The tariff—local tariff—of N.C. Road has been revised, making material reductions, which, if you will continue your former propositions, will reduce the rates from your section; thus giving to the public the benefit of the reduced local tariff for those stations.—If you insist upon increasing your propositions, please advise me & I will make up a set of rates, based upon whatever figures you want for your Road to Goldsboro.

The W. & W. Tariff is undergoing revision now & will be ready in a few days.—I can then better answer as to rates for stations on that road.

To the stations in South Carolina contained in your list, these roads demand & receive locals from all Lines.—no matter where the business originates.—We can not, under the circumstances, do otherwise then pay these locals, & prorate remainder to junction points.

To competitive points,—which road & south of Charlotte & Wilmington, have heretofore prorated—we can not allow you an arbitrary, but will prorate rates to such points.

[*enclosure*]
No. 128

Piedmont Air Line
Office Genl. Freight Agent, Richmond, Va. Aug. 29th 1881
To Agents

The Genl Manager of the Midland N.C. Rwy.[117] having temporarily withdrawn his objection to rates from Newbern More-

---

[117]The Midland North Carolina Railway Company, which had been chartered in 1873, had been organized to build and operate a line from Beaufort to the Tennessee line. By 1880, W. J. Best had secured control of the Midland Company, and on July 1, 1881, the Midland leased the Atlantic and North Carolina Railroad for thirty years. Brown, *State Movement*, 242–249.

head and A.&N.C. Stations in effect prior to issue of order No 126 from this office that order is now revoked and former rates are restored.

Through rates based on New reduced local tariff of R.&D.R.R. Sept. 1st 1881 will be issued as soon as possible.

Sol. Haas.

[enclosure—copy]
T. M. R. Talcott to A. S. Buford

Richmond, Va., Sept. 1st 1881

In reply to the charge that Mr Haas, G. F. A. of the Associated Lines, by his General Order No. 88. *"prohibited any freight rates beyond Goldsboro to points along the Atlantic and North Carolina Railroad."*

I would call attention to this order referred to as in itself refuting this charge. That no *prohibition* of rates was either made or intended is evident, for this order states, that *"new rates will be issued as soon as praticable."*

Mr Haas might have stated in the order the reason why the old rates were withdrawn so peremptorily, but his correspondence with Mr Yates, Gen'l Manager of the A & NC. Railroad, shows that it was because Mr Yates not only objected to the existing rates, but, in view of the fact that they were made by Mr. Haas, as the General Freight Agent of the A & N.C. Railroad, Mr Yates' language (in his letter of Aug. 16) could be construed only as a direct charge against Mr Haas, personally, of malfeasance while representing the A & N.C. Railroad.

Moreover the fact stands, that the temporary withdrawal of the through rates, which the Governor of No. Carolina characterizes as an *"outrageous proceeding on the part of the lessees of the No. Carolina Railroad"* merely left the freight to be forwarded to local points on the No. Carolina Railroad at local rates, which were precisely the same as the No. Carolina Railroad's proportion of the through rates which were withdrawn.

So far as the through rates to competitive points were concerned General Order No. 88 merely suspended them temporarily on account of the objections made by Mr Yates in behalf of his Company. These rates were divided *pro rata per mile* because the business was competitive and no more liberal division was possible.

If any other evidence is needed to show that the "outrageous proceeding" on the part of Mr Haas was the result of the objections raised by Mr Yates, and not an attempt on his part to *"prohibit* rates beyond Goldsboro to points along the A&NC Railroad" it is furnished by the correspondence between Messrs Haas and Yates, wherein it is made apparent that Mr Yates' efforts were all directed towards the securing of larger proportions of the rates and consequently increased revenue for his Road, even by "pooling" the business if Mr Haas would assent. There is positively nothing in this correspondence to indicate that either Mr Haas desired or intended to *prohibit* through rates or that Mr Yates for a moment even suspected him of such a desire or intention.

Thomas J. Jarvis to A. S. Buford[118]

Executive Department,
Raleigh, September 2, 1881

Yours of the 25th of August, in reply to the letter of the commissioners of the Western North Carolina Railroad of 1st of August, was received by me on yesterday. The commissioners will meet on the line of the road on the 12th instant, at which time I will lay your letter before them. In the meantime, I wish to say for myself that I do not regard your letter in any way responsive to ours. Nor do I admit that there is any trouble in construing our letter. If you found it difficult to get at our meaning or purposes, it was so easy to ask us what we meant, without consuming pages of paper in recounting a long history of the troubles of the past.

An east and west line, running from Morehead City to the western borders of the State and beyond, with its outlet at Morehead City, and operated solely in the interest of North Carolina ports, cities and towns, would be of such immense advantage to the State that I would feel bound to do everything in my power that was honorable, whether as an individual, a commissioner or as Governor, to secure such a boon for her people. Will you not frankly say it would be my duty to do so? This is what I meant by the letter of the 1st of August, and this is said without any threat, expressed or implied, to injure any one.

I do not know that any such line will be built, or that it is

---

[118]Taken from the *News and Observer*, September 13, 1881.

likely to be; but if it is, I trust you will exhibit the same willingness to serve the State that you claim in your letter to have done
when you took up the work on the Western North Carolina Railroad. I think you could do so without any injury to the substantial, permanent interest of your lines, and I am sure such a
noble act would make all North Carolinians your friends.

Now, a word about the manner and the circumstances set out
in your letter under which you undertook this work. I have always found you a frank, candid, straight–forward man, and, I
have always said and believed, a gentleman. In this spirit I ask,
did you have no desire for the Western road at the time you
took up the Best contract? Did you do it solely to help the State
and her people, and for no other purpose? Is it true or not true
that, at the time Best was negotiating for the purchase of the
road, some of those interested in your lines met and discussed the
question of becoming yourselves bidders against Best? Would
you not have become a bidder had you not have become satisfied that Best was not in the interest of a line hostile to yours?
I ask these questions because your persistent pushing upon us
the suggestion that you took up the contract to avert a great
calamity make them pertinent.

But from whatever motive you act, you certainly cannot say
you entered into the contract at my solicitation. I did not ask,
nor did I even know you and your friends had done so till after
it was done. It is true that I knew there was trouble between
Mr. Best and his associates, and they were likely not to be able
to organize. Col. Andrews had been for years my warm personal friend, and was then, as now, a member of my staff. I
asked him to go to New York and see what the trouble was, and,
if possible, remedy it. I also telegraphed to Senator Vance to go
to New York and aid in the adjustment.[119] I felt that it was a
crisis in the history of the road, and that if the contract broke
down and the work failed, then it would be a long time before
the people of the west would see the road and hear the whistle
of the engine. I also knew that you were in New York, and that
you did not want the work on the road to stop or the contract
to fail, and I supposed the fact that you knew the road would be
an important feeder to your line had something to do with your
anxiety and feelings in the matter. But, as before stated, I did
not know who assumed the responsibilities of the contract till
after it was done. There is not connected with this whole matter,

---

[119]See Jarvis to Andrews, May 22, 1880, in this volume.

from the day Mr. Best first came to Raleigh to the present time, one single act, word or line of mine that I would have concealed or kept from the public. I therefore beg that you will cease to write in such vague general terms, and say what it was that I did to induce you or your friends to take up the Best contract. What promise did I make or what inducement did I offer? Now, let us have it all out in plain, unmistakable words, giving time, place and circumstances. I do not wish to evade any obligation or responsibility I am under, but I do want to know what it is. I write to you thus individually, because I know you well, while I barely know Gen. Logan and do not know Mr. Clyde at all.

Col. Andrews was an ardent friend of mine for the nomination by the Democratic party and election by the people for Governor. I have no doubt that he thought that a failure of the enterprise at that time would seriously affect me in both ways, and that, on this account, he worked all the harder to get the matter adjusted; and, I expect, urged it as a reason for his efforts, and, if the truth was known, even used his own money to save the contract.

I shall not soon forget the services of Col. Andrews, and will never fail to reward them when I can properly do so, and I am sure he would not have me do so improperly.

I think you and your friends rendered the State and myself a service in taking up the contract at the time you did, no matter from what motive you act, and I think you are entitled to be treated at least with fairness and justice if not with liberality. I so propose to treat you, and I believe my associate commissioners will co–operate with me.

But, because of these things, you must not expect us to turn our back upon or be indifferent to a great enterprise for the development of the State, like the one proposed by the Midland scheme, if its projectors shall show their good faith by their works, especially when it is proposed to compensate you for all your expenditures and all your troubles.

If the commissioners helped to get you and your friends into a bad bargain, as you say, they have offered to help to get you out without loss. If it has turned out to be a good bargain, so much the better for you, so that you have not been injured by them. If the time shall ever come when the commissioners are required, either as commissioners or individuals, by the memorandum of the 25th of May, to do anything, I do not understand that they are required by said memorandum to do anything dishonorable or improper, and I have no idea that either of them will.

A&H—GP

Ethan A. Allen to Thomas J. Jarvis

Thomasville
Davidson Co. N.C.
Sept 3. 1881

If you still wish to capture that swindler Genl. M. S. Littlefield I can bring such result about through an acquaintance of mine who will decoy him to within four miles of the N.C. & Virginia line, if you will agree to pay this acquaintance of mine a satisfactory reward.

Please let me hear from you as soon as possible & oblige

PS. As I have not the pleasure of your personal acquaintance I beg leave to refer you to my old friend Col. Wm. H H Tucker[120] of Raleigh.

I have been down here for the last three years from New York engaged in the Gold Mining business
I was formerly engaged in N.Y. in the wholesale Dry Goods business.

A&H—GLB

Proclamation

[September 4, 1881]
Executive Department.

I, Thomas J. Jarvis, Governor of North Carolina, do issue this my Proclamation, inviting the people of the State to assemble at their respective places of worship on Tuesday, Sept. 6th, A.D., 1881, between the hours of ten and noon, to unite with the people of the other States in prayer to Almighty God for the recovery of the President.

---

[120]William Henry Haywood Tucker, drygoods merchant of Raleigh since 1846. *News and Observer*, May 27, 1882.

A&H—GLB

Thomas J. Jarvis to E. A. Allen

Executive Department,
Raleigh, Sept. 5, 1881

In reply to yours of the 3rd ins't., I beg to say that I am anxious to capture the person referred to in your letter, and if you will put your friend in communication with me, it is possible that we may agree upon the plan to be adopted and the terms of the capture.

A&H—GP

W. C. Murphy to Thomas J. Jarvis

South Washington N.C.
5th Sept 1881

Can not the convicts for the Angola Bay public Road be sent forward at once? Our citizens have with commendable energy & public spirit cleared away the Timber & undergrowth, & only the ditching remains to be done. I appeal to you personally to lend your influence & aid in the completion of this, to us, & also the school fund, important work

Please write me if we can expect any aid from the authorities at the Penitentiary.

A&H—GLB

Thomas J. Jarvis to W. C. Murphy

Executive Department,
Raleigh, Sept. 8, 1881

In reply to yours of the 5th ins't., I regret that I cannot give you any encouragement in your application for convicts on the Angola canal. You have no doubt seen it often stated in the public prints that the State is unable to furnish the 500 convicts to the Western N.C.R.R. Until that contract is filled, it will be impossible for the Penitentiary authorities, under existing laws, to send convicts elsewhere.

A&H—GP

E. A. Allen to Thomas J. Jarvis
Confidential

Thomasville
Davidson Co. N.C.
Septr 9. 1881

Refering you to my communication of 3rd Inst. to which your reply of 5th came duly to hand, I beg leave to say the name of the party whome I propose to put you in communication with is Mr. Eugene A. Albee[121] who has been residing in this place for the past 15 or 16 months and is *well* acquainted with the person desired by you.

It occurs to me, that it might be best for you to inclose to Mr. Albee tickets to visit Raleigh, & pay his Hotel bill in Raleigh while waiting on you, he is willing to visit Raleigh at any time that you may wish an interview.

A&H—GLB

Thomas J. Jarvis to A. S. Buford

Executive Department,
Raleigh, Sept. 10, 1881

Yours dated Sept. 1st was not received at this office till the 7th ins't.

I have read the letter carefully and the exhibits and copies it covers; and have tried to do so in a spirit of fairness. I shall not undertake to reply to the matters it contains in the order in which they occur. I may have been a little hasty and harsh in my strictures on Gen. Order, No. 88, in my letter to the Attorney General. All I knew at the time was, that it had been issued, and I knew what would be its bad effects upon the people of the State. What the motive was that prompted it or how long it was to continue, I did not know and could not know, because they were secrets locked up in the bosom of Mr. Haas, and he did not choose to give them to the public. I will most respectfully submit, though, that the respectful letter of Mr. Yates of Aug. 16th, was not of itself a sufficient cause for the order; and I am obliged to dissent from Col. Talcott's view that the letter was a

---

[121]Unable to identify.

reflection upon Mr. Haas, or that imputed to him any malfeasance in office. But I have no inclination to take any part in any controversy between Mr. Yates and Mr. Haas. The correspondence shows this fact: that harsh language I used in my letter to the Attorney General was unjust as to any one else but him; and if unjust as to him, I regret that such language was used. Col. Talcott's own letter in his defence undertakes to excuse Mr. Haas on the ground that he felt personally aggrieved. In other words, he issued the order in a moment of personal pique. I hold that, because one railroad official is offended with another, he has no right to put the public to inconvenience to avenge himself. But the order has been revoked, and I do not care to pursue these reflections any further. If I have, without cause, used harsh language, I regret it and retract it.

Now, as to the discriminations on the Western North Carolina Railroad. It is insisted, on the one hand, that there are discriminations, while, on the other hand, it is denied. I propose, as one of the Commissioners, to investigate this matter next week as best I can. I hope it will turn out the charge is a mistake, and that the alleged discrimination does not exist. But I will suggest, Colonel, that, in my view of the case, there are other ways to discriminate besides in the mere matter of freight charges.

In your letter, you are pleased to say: "We utterly disclaim any objects or interests in the management of the North Carolina Railroad, except in accordance with our acknowledged lawful rights, and our declared purpose to do impartial justice to every section of the State into which its business relations extend." This declaration of yours opens the way, I trust, to a better understanding between us on the question of railroad management in this State. If I understand the demands of the people, it is that North Carolina interests, North Carolina enterprise and North Carolina industries shall have an equal chance in the race for public favor with her sister and adjoining States, Virginia, South Carolina, and Georgia. We ask for nothing more and we will have nothing less. We do not ask that any favors shall be shown us, but we do demand that no hinderances shall be put upon us. In this, we are terribly in earnest. I say it in all kindness, but with a solemn pledge made to myself to stand by it and to accept nothing less. I think this much you ought to concede without a struggle and without reservation or stint; and I indulge the hope that I am not asking too much of you to ask you to give the matter your personal attention, and to have your tariffs reconstructed on this basis. Now, it is not fair to make Winston, Reidsville, and Durham pay a greater freight on manufactured tobacco to cities and towns in the South than Richmond pays. To do it throttles one of the great industries of this State, and, of necessity, creates complaint. Take another case: A. is coming South to invest in cotton factories. We claim that North Carolina possesses peculiar advantages as a manufacturing State, and we urge Mr. A. to locate here. He investigates, as a business man will do, the question of freight; and he finds he can take his machinery right by Greensboro, High Point and Haw River several hundred miles further south to Columbia or Augusta by your line, and pay much less freight, and that the same discrimination exists as to other things. I am told that it takes a hundred and fifty thousand dollars in North Carolina to overcome one hundred thousand dollars invested at Columbia or Augusta, on account of the difference in freight. This is unjust to the State, and as long as this discrimination exists, the development of this industry is crippled. In our efforts to build up this great industry, is it surprising that we should get mad when we find a property that we created made to play this part against us?

Then take the subject of merchandise and commerce generally. Any legislation that undertakes to force men to trade with certain cities and towns, is wrong; and so is any railroad management that forces them away from one place and to another, wrong. That is to say, if Richmond, Norfolk, Baltimore or New York offers better inducements to trade than Wilmington, Charlotte or Raleigh, purchasers ought to be allowed to go there; but; on the other hand, if Wilmington, Charlotte or Raleigh offers better inducements, purchasers ought not to be kept away by freight discriminations.

You are now in control of more than half of the miles of railway in this State, and you can do much to hasten or retard her prosperity. Which shall it be? If you help us, you are obliged to receive benefits from our increased prosperity, and all strife and bickering will cease. If we are to be weighed down by these discriminations, your lines are obliged to suffer in loss of business, and If I have been misinformed as to the allegations of discrimination suggested in this letter, I shall be glad to be set right. If any cause exists for these complaints, I trust to your sense of justice and spirit of fairness to have such cause removed.

A&H—GP

W. J. Best to Thomas J. Jarvis
[Telegram]

Boston Mass Sept 13 1881

Coleman[122] and other friends here have seen your letters to Buford and Attorney Gen and greatly encouraged thereby are today buying Iron for new road please tell other Commissioners

Thomas J. Jarvis, Z. B. Vance, and J. M. Worth to W. P. Clyde,
T. M. Logan, and A. S. Buford[123]

Asheville, N.C., Sept. 14, 1881

Your letter dated August 23d, in reply to ours of August 1st, was received by Commissioner Jarvis on September 1st and delivered to the commissioners yesterday, this being the first meeting held since it was received by Commissioner Jarvis.

Candor compels us to say that your letter is not an answer to ours, but is an evasion thereof. One-half of it is consumed by disingenuous accusations of possible improper motives and intentions on the part of the commissioners, and the remainder consists in a denial of these same accusations, for reasons found in a statement of facts, many of which do not exist in truth, and the enumeration of which aggravates the offensive character of the first suggestion.

Conscious as we are of no intention on our part to do any act, or put ourselves in any position inconsistent with the rights, duties and proprieties imposed upon us by the law which called us into existence, or that may be in any way unbecoming the position we occupy as citizens, we respectfully decline to answer the question you see proper to put as preliminary to a response to our letter.

We beg to repeat our question which you so completely evaded, to–wit: If the Midland Company shall complete their road from Goldsboro to Salisbury, or so far prosecute the work

---

[122]Lewis Coleman, businessman of Boston. Coleman was a director of the Shawmut Insurance Company from 1875 until its demise in 1882. In 1881 he joined the Board of the Pacific National Bank and in 1882 became its president. After this bank closed in 1883, he confined his activities to a hosiery and glove store which he had started much earlier. Information furnished by Mrs. Sarah W. Flannery of the Boston Public Library.
[123]Taken from the *News and Observer*, September 24, 1881.

thereon as to insure its completion, and shall demonstrate to the satisfaction of the commissioners their ability to complete and fulfill the Best contract, and we, both as commissioners and as individuals, request you, for the good of the State, to reassign to Best and his associates the interests in the Western North Carolina Railroad, which you acquired from him, will you do it upon being paid in cash in full for all your expenditures—principal, interest and reasonable compensation for time and trouble? We will thank you for an early reply.

A&H—GLB

Thomas J. Jarvis to E. R. Stamps

Executive Department,
Raleigh, Sept. 17, 1881

You were kind enough some week or more ago to inform me that your Board [of Directors of the Penitentiary] had made an order to withdraw a part of the convict force from the C.F.& Y.V.R. Road to make up the five hundred on the W.N.C.R.R., and to ask me if there were any reasons why the order should not be at once executed.

There are some negotiations going on about this road and some trouble about the iron for it.[124] Besides, I consider the road of great importance in the development of the State. To withdraw a part of the convicts at this time would, I fear, have a bad effect upon the present prospects of the road. I therefore beg that you will suspend the execution of the order for the present. I will be glad to advise with you in person about the matter.

A&H—GLB

Proclamation

Executive Department,
[September 23, 1881]

Whereas, The final funeral ceremonies of James A. Garfield, late President of the United States, will be had on Monday, the 26th day of September, 1881, between the hours of two o'clock

---

[124]For the cause of the dispute between the two railroads, see Hughes to Jarvis, March 10, 1879.

and four o'clock, P.M.; And whereas, Chester A. Arthur, President of the United States, has appointed that day as a day of humiliation and mourning, and has recommended all the people to assemble on that day in their respective places of divine worship, there to render alike their tribute of sorrowful submission to the will of Almighty God and of reverence and love for the memory and character of the late Chief Magistrate; And whereas, It is eminently fit and proper for the people of North Carolina to join in these solemn observances, and thereby give expression to their deep sympathy with the occasion and their abhorrence of the work of the assassin that has brought the whole country to mourning;—

Now, therefore, I, Thomas J. Jarvis, Governor of North Carolina, do issue this my Proclamation, earnestly urging all the people of the State to close their places of business and to abstain from work of every kind, as far as practicable, between the hours of two o'clock and four o'clock, P. M., on Monday next, the 26th of September, 1881, and that all who can, will repair to their respective places of worship, and there engage in fitting religious exercises in memory of the deceased.

A&H—GP

Thomas J. Jarvis to J. A. Gray [*copy*]

Raleigh, Sept. 23rd 1881

I leave to morrow for Cleveland to attend President Garfield's Funeral. The South will give Arthurs Administration a loyal support. The Western [N.C.] Rail Road fight cannot effect your enterprise.[125] The people and the administration will stand by the men who invest their money in the State. We will soon overcome the short crop. Urge the men to come and see for themselves.

---

[125] A New York syndicate was interested in buying the state's stock in the Cape Fear and Yadkin Valley Railroad. See Canedo to Jarvis, August 17, 1881, in this volume. Jarvis approved of the proposed sale and Gray, as president of the railroad, was in New York promoting the completion of the transaction. *News and Observer*, November 24, 1881.

A&H—GP

W. P. Clyde, T. M. Logan, and A. S. Buford to Thomas J. Jarvis, Z. B. Vance and J. M. Worth

New York Sept 27. 1881

In reply to yours of the 14th, we beg to express our regret that our letter of the 24th[25th] of August to the Commissioners should have been so materially misconceived by them as to its import, tenor and spirit. We endeavored to be explicit, direct and respectful, We think any impartial judge would say we had succeeded reasonably in the effort.

Your communication[of August 1], bear in mind, was not merely your brief letter, but also the agreement of the Commissioners with Mr Best of the 25th of May, of which a copy was sent and intended to be taken as a part of that communication. That agreement revealed a new, an unknown and an unexpected attitude of the Commissioners towards us. Was it not most natural that we should be startled by such a revelation, and to feel the uprising inquiry. What does this mean? Do these Commissioners mean to put their official and personal pressure upon us, to make it necessary for us to abandon this contract and return it again to Mr Best? The communication looked that way. The letter and agreement taken together, *very much* that way. But, recurring to what we understood of the history of the whole matter, we did not see any conceivable reason for such a reversal of position by the Commissioners towards us, and thought it was due alike to the Commissioners and to ourselves, that we should not mistake the true purport of their communication. Hence the reply we made. Nothing in it was intended, nor as far as we can now perceive, can anything be found in it desrespectful, either in expression or implication. We attempted to make a plain statement of facts, as we understood them, without color or exaggeration, and for the reason assigned by us in our reply. We are not conscious of any inaccuracy in that statement, or of having done the slightest injustice to any party referred to therein. We did not, in anything we said to the Commissioners, make any reference to their motives. We referred to facts only and for the purpose assigned; that our transactions with the Commissioners should be in no sense ambiguous, or the results inconclusive. While we were thus without motive, disposition, or apparent effort, to be in any sense discourteous in our reply, we are at a loss to conceive why it should be charged. We respectfully and absolutely disclaim it, and refer to a careful and dispassionate judgment of the document for our vindication.

In reply to your proposition to surrender to Mr Best, and his associates, our rights and interests acquired by assignment from him, we beg to assure you that it would give us great pleasure at any time to gratify your personal desires; but in this matter our situation compels us respectfully to decline your proposed request. When by the final assignment from Mr Best, we became the absolute proproprietors [*sic*] of the Western North Carolina Rail Road, the requirements and restrictions, in the act of March 29th 1880 compelled the creation of very large obligations in the necessary organization of the Capital, adequate to the undertaking; and the better to secure the success of the enterprise, we have deemed it expedient at a large outlay, to acquire other interests, connected with and dependent upon the Western North Carolina Railroad.

In the accomplishment of these arrangements, our interests as derived from the assignment have become so blended with those of others, that we no longer have the sole personal control of this property, and therefore cannot properly agree to surrender it without the consent of others, who decline to release their interests.

We are performing all our obligations as we understand them under the contract, and desire and intend to continue to do so if permitted. We therefore recognize no just or reasonable ground on which its surrender can be claimed, or expected from us. In declining the request proposed to be made to us, we desire further to say, that we do not wish to hinder Mr. Best and his associates in any purpose entertained by them to construct another road to Salisbury. If they do so, it will be alike our interest and policy to accord to such road impartial access to the Western North Carolina Railroad, and upon terms just and equitable to every portion of the state to be benefitted thereby.

We take this occasion to express the strong interest we have felt in the successful prosecution of this enterprise, from the date of our present connection with it; and by some of us long anterior to that date; and to signify our cordial sympathy with the citizens of North Carolina in their desire to see this important work fully completed, and even extended according to its original design, until connected with the Railroad systems leading to the Mississippi Valley; some of our strongest and most influential associates urging with earnestness, the direct extension of the line from Murphy to Chattanooga.

We assure the Commissioners that it is our intention and purpose to have the work prosecuted on both lines of the road with diligence and energy until they are completed to Murphy and Paint Rock; and in every thing to cause the contract we have entered into to be faithfully and literally complied with.

We hope to receive from you encouragement and cooperation, that nothing which may hasten the work or help its utility shall be left undone, nor anything done which may retard or impair it

Speech Delivered October 2, 1881, at The Raleigh State Fair[126]

Gov. Jarvis spoke substantially as follows:

It has been the custom for years for the Governor to open the State fair, and in obedience to that custom I am here to–day to perform that service. I regret that the fair opens under unfavorable auspicies. The long–continued drought and the early biting frost have cast a gloom over a large part of our citizens engaged in agricultural pursuits. Notwithstanding these untoward circumstances, through the untiring energy of the executive committee and the officers of the State Agricultural Society, the exhibits and arrangements of this fair will compare favorably with those which have preceded it. Every person, no matter in what pursuit engaged, must sympathize with the despondency that has overshadowed the agricultural interests of the middle section of the State, because all pursuits and interests are more or less affected by whatever affects the great agricultural interests of the State. Our farmers must not yield to this despondency, but must enter upon their great work with renewed energy and determination. This year's experience, in my opinion, teaches two important lessons—first it will not do for the farmers to rely too much and go in debt too heartily for manufactured, purchased fertilizers. They must rely more and be more careful in the preparation of home manures.

Second, no matter whether it be wet or dry, the man who ploughs and hoes his corn and cotton best will gather the best crops. There is nothing that can be substituted for earnest, hard work. I take a deep interest, as every Carolinian must do, in the progress and success of the State Agricultural Society. Whatever

---

[126]Taken from the *News and Observer*, October 3, 1881.

tends to the development of the State, and adds to her wealth and prosperity, has my earnest sympathy and hearty co–operation. I believe the bringing together annually of the Agriculturists of the State, the talks they have with each other, the information they impart and receive, the tending to encourage and stimulate each other, is one of the potent means of developing the general agricultural interests of the State, and hence it has my warnest sympathy and most earnest co–operation. Its officers and members are doing a great work in this particular, and should be encouraged.

There is no cause for gloom, but every reason why we should take fresh courage and look forward to a bright and hopeful future for our State. I predict, then, in the next year there will be more miles of railroad completed in the State than in any year in her past history. I predict that before the Agricultural Society meets again, more capital from without her borders will be invested permanently within her borders than in any year since the war. I predict that within the next year more immigrants will be settled among us than any one year has ever witnessed within the memory of the oldest of us. I make these predictions, not as mere speculation, but I speak advisedly. It will be my great purpose to contribute all I can to these ends, and I expect to have the co–operation of every true North Carolinian. And from no agency can I hope for more aid and support than from this society.

In declaring the 21st annual fair open for exhibition, and in welcoming you to its grounds and inviting you to view its exhibitions, I beg that as you wander around viewing the stock, articles, implements and other things on exhibition, that you will not do so for the purpose of criticism, but for the purpose of information and emulation. No man ought to say he has better stock at home. If he has, and has not brought it here for exhibition, he has not done his duty to himself or his State. No lady dare say she has better poultry at home than she finds here, without convicting herself of a failure of duty. But rather examine the stock, farm products, etc., with a view to see how you can improve upon them, and vow to yourselves that during the coming year you will work more honestly, energetically and industriously for your State, this society and yourselves, and that in the coming years you will put something on exhibition superior to anything you find here. The man who raises one additional pound of pork, and the woman who raises one additional chicken adds something to the aggregate wealth of the State.

Then let us all, in leaving these grounds, determine to do all that within us lies to add to the wealth and glory of North Carolina.

A&H—GP

Thomas A. Love[127] to Thomas J. Jarvis

Bakersville N.C.
Oct. 4. 1881

My Dear Governor I am requested by Mr. Irby[128] to call your attention to pledges that the people of this county say that you made them during last campaign in regard to their public roads and the working of them out by convict labor. They say that it pertains to Democratic faith that they be allowed the convicts on their roads and that you as a Democratic Governor pledged them your influence in securing the convict labor for the purpose above mentioned Now as a democrat and one who wishes you great success as our Executive leader I would with your approbation suggest that if there is any aid that you could give us in the way of convicts on our roads that it would add greatly to your popularity in the counties of McDowell Mitchell Yancey and Watauga as Governor as the people of those counties are expecting that they will get them through your influence and would undoubtedly remember you kindly in the future with their support in political matters if you should hereafter desire to become a candidate

A&H—GLB

Thomas J. Jarvis to T. S. Kenan

Raleigh, Oct. 7th, 1881
Executive Department,

I will thank you to examine all laws appropriating convicts to public works, whether to canals, turnpikes, dirtroads or to railroads, and give me your opinion as to the powers and duties of the Board of Directors of the Penitentiary under these laws in sending out convicts to these several works.

---

[127]Lawyer of Bakersville. In 1886 he turned to farming because of ill health and became a large and prosperous land owner. *North Carolina Biography*, VI, 298–299.

[128]Joseph K. Irby, merchant and mica mine proprietor of Bakersville. In 1881 he was chairman of the Mitchell County Board of Commissioners. Branson, *Directory for 1884*, 458–459.

The number of convicts is wholly insufficient to fill the appropriations made by the Legislature, or to supply the demands made upon the Penitentiary authorities under these appropriations. The authorities of the Penitentiary have no other purpose to serve than to simply obey the law, and to send the convicts where the law directs. The Board has been criticised by persons who have a local interest to be served, without a proper regard for the obligations of the Board to obey the law; and there is much discussion among those locally interested as to what the law is.

To settle all these questions in the way pointed out by the law and to the satisfaction of all law-abiding citizens, I beg that you will indicate in your opinion to what works the convicts must be sent.

A&H—GP

T. S. Kenan to Thomas J. Jarvis

Attorney General's Office
Oct. 10. 1881

In compliance with the request contained in your letter of the 7th inst., I have examined the acts of Assembly appropriating convict labor to railroads, canals, turnpikes and other public roads, and for the purpose of draining swamp lands. There are a great number of these acts—passed at the sessions of 1879 — 1880 — 1881 — giving to the different works of internal improvement in various parts of the state, from twenty to five hundred convicts. The great majority of them provide that the state shall pay the expense of guarding, feeding, clothing, &c. out of the fund appropriated for the support of the penitentiary; and in a few instances the counties or companies employing the labor are required to pay such expenses.

The number of convicts, as stated in your letter, is insufficient to meet the requisitions upon the directors of the penitentiary. Under these circumstances, I think it is the duty of the directors, first, to supply the number granted to the Western road, then, the Cape Fear and Yadkin Valley road, and then, such other works as may be entitled under the law. The reason for this is threefold.

1. Upon examination of the acts referred to, it will be seen that nearly all of them contain a proviso that the number of

convicts assigned to the Western N.C. Road or any road in which the state has an interest, shall not be reduced, thereby giving a preference to those works.

2.   Because the Governor and directors are specially required to apportion among the various works to which convicts have been, or shall hereafter be assigned, all the convicts of the state in such manner as they may deem just and right—having regard to the respective numbers assigned to the several works—*Provided,* that the number employed on the Western Road and the Cape Fear & Yadkin Valley road, shall not be reduced—Acts 1879, ch. 278.

3.   Because the contract of the state to supply the number of convicts agreed upon in pursuance of the act of 1880 for the completion of the Western Road, creates an additional obligation on the penitentiary authorities.

While these expressions of the legislature would seem to be sufficiently explicit in directing how the apportionment is to be made, yet I think every one will recognize the controlling effect of the contract. And in view of the fact, that by the terms of said contract the state is to receive for the 500 convicts assigned to that road the sum of $125.00 per annum for each convict, the legislature no doubt reduced the appropriation for the support of the penitentiary, for without it, the appropriation might have been inadquate.

I am therefore of the opinion that the Western road should first be supplied then the Cape Fear and Yadkin Valley—then to apportion the convicts (if any remain) in the manner provided for in Chapter 278 acts 1879, if the appropriation for the support of the penitentiary be sufficient, otherwise to assign them to works of internal improvements which are carried on without charge to the state, as indicated in chapter 333 Acts 1879.

A&H—GLB

Thomas J. Jarvis to the Editor of the Kinston Journal [129]

Executive Department,
Raleigh, Oct. 12, 1881

In your issue of last week, you did the Directors of the Penitentiary a very great injustice. You charged them with giving

---

[129]The editor was H. S. Nunn. *News and Observer,* December 4, 1881.

false reasons for their official conduct and of using a public trust for political purposes. These are very grave charges and should not be made, except upon the most ample proof. I trust the opinion of the Attorney General, of which I enclose you a copy,[130] with a copy of my letter, will convince you that you made the charge without due consideration and without cause; and being thus convinced, you will withdraw these unjust charges as publicly as you made them. I know the gentlemen who compose the Board of Directors are incapable of discharging a public duty in the way you have charged, and I did not seek the opinion of the Attorney General to convince me of that fact. The Attorney General is an Eastern man with a pride and an interest in the East, and I take it you will not dispute the correctness of his opinions. I beg further to remind you that there is an important enterprise in his own native and adjoining County applying for convicts; and yet, notwithstanding all these facts, the law is such that he is obliged to give an opinion which, for the present, is adverse to the claims of his own section.

Speech Delivered October 27, 1881, Before The Atlanta Exposition[131]

Governor Jarvis, of North Carolina, was introduced, and made a splendid speech.

He said:

My heart is too full for utterance. I have seen the evidence here to–day that for years I have been struggling to help bring about, that I have been hoping to see—the material prosperity and advancement of the South. Atlanta, distinguished as she has been in years that are past and gone, as a scene of struggling armies, however much that may have gained her a name in the history of our country, these memories must, in the presence of the grand achievements of the arts and sciences and peace, be buried and forgotten forever.[Applause.] My friends, I so much rejoice that the scars that were made by the tramp of these armies have been healed. I rejoice that everything of bitterness, of strife, is gone. It was my good fortune to meet upon the historic ground of Yorktown the people of all this

---

[130]See Kenan to Jarvis, October 10, 1881.

[131]Taken from the Atlanta *Constitution* and printed in the *News and Observer* of October 30, 1881.

country of ours. They were from New York and Maine and
Rhode Island—from the north, the east, the west and the south.
We met upon that sacred soil as the people of a common country,
and as we met there the spirit of our ancestors, the spirit of a
hundred years ago, came over us and we shook hands with the
common flag floating over us and determined that forever
hereafter we should vie with each other in our devotion to
our country and in developing the material things of the land,
[Applause.] I mentioned a moment ago, my friends, that Atlanta was to be memorable in the history of this country,
for having inaugurated this great enterprise for exhibiting
the arts and sciences, the commercial wealth, the mineral
wealth, the agricultural resources, and the energy and prosperity of our people. This occasion and this presence, my
friends, knows not the muskets, the bayonets, the swords nor
the cannon, but instead I see the implements of husbandry, and
the insignia of peace and prosperity. My friends, the prosperity
of the north has taught us lessons that we of the South may do
well to heed, and will do well to practice. It may be out of taste,
and out of place to say anything that looks like a lecture, and yet
at the risk of your censure I will say this—there is, as Governor
Hoyt[132] said, a glorious future, a grand and glorious destiny for
the people of the South. [Applause.] There is a great future for
all the States of the South. We have here beneath our soil un-
told millions of wealth. Our soil is susceptible of the highest
cultivation, and products of our soils find a market in the markets of the world. We have the climate, the soil, the wealth, and
everything of it lies idle here, and it but waits the touch of—
what? It but waits the labor of the young men of the South.
Now, we hope for immigration. We invite it and capital. God
knows the people of North Carolina and the people of Georgia
welcome the capital that crowds the Northern States. But
while we do that, the great problem must be worked out by
our own people. Young men, the future of your country depends
upon you. There is one thing that I love, and one thing that I
turn my back upon. Whereever I see a young man of the South
that is not afraid or ashamed to work, I want to take him by
the hand. [Applause.] And whenever I see one that is a loafer,
and idle, I have no kind word for him, but good-bye to him. I
accept the kind hospitality and the good works of my brother

---

[132]Henry Martyn Hoyt, governor of Pennsylvania from 1878 to 1882. He
was a guest at the Atlanta Exposition. *National Cyclopedia*, II, 292-293.

Governor. It was not necessary, except as a matter of form, that he should have tendered the hospitality. We know it as we shook hands, as we saw the kindly welcome, and we were well assured of that before we came."

Thomas J. Jarvis to Z. B. Vance
[Telegram]

Raleigh, Oct. 31, 1881

When can you go over the Western Road and when do you wish us at Charlotte?[133]

Speech Delivered November 3, Before the
Colored Fair at Raleigh[134]

After making their tour of inspection the party repaired to the large hall devoted to oratorical displays, which was neatly arranged for the occasion. The formal exercises of opening the exhibition then began. Governor Jarvis was introduced in a pleasant manner, and said: Two years ago this exposition of the colored people of North Carolina was inaugurated, and it was my privilege as Governor to formally open it. A year ago I had the pleasure of being with you again, at your second fair. Now I am here for the third time, to witness and participate in the interesting exercises. I told you from the first that I felt as deep an interest in this movement, and would do as much as any person in our State to make it a success. I have watched your progress and watched it with deep interest. I am exceedingly glad to know and see that the colored people during the twelve months past have not been idle, but have been at work. This association and its aims are valuable, not only to the colored people but to the whole State. Whatever affects the colored race, which is one—third of our population, intellectually, morally or financially, in all respects affects similarly the growth and happiness of North Carolina and North Carolinians. If you become industrious, en-

---

[133]The commissioners to supervise the completion of the Western North Carolina Railroad had agreed to meet in Charlotte and complete their investigation of the freight rate discrimination allegedly being practiced by the management of the railroad. "Proceedings of the Commissioners on the Western North Carolina Railroad," November 7, 1881.

[134]Taken from the *News and Observer*, November 4, 1881.

terprising and intelligent, all the white people share in your honor and glory as much as you yourselves. These exhibitions and things of this kind give the colored people something to hope for, something to look forward to; an ambition, as they toil in heat and cold—an ambition to bring something of their own manufacture or product of their tillage, and show what a success their race is carving out for itself. I am glad to see that those who have brought articles have brought such as do credit to themselves. The white farmers of North Carolina, with all their advantages, did not show at the State fair such hogs as are on exhibition here, nor did they send such fine poultry to that exhibition. I am exceedingly gratified at what you have done. It teaches the lesson that the colored people of the Old North State are finding the roads to happiness and prosperity, in honesty, industry and hard work. I am glad to see the handiwork of your women well displayed. Upon them much depends. If they beautify their homes their husbands and children will be taught habits of refinement and virtue. A grave responsibility rests upon me as your Governor to see that the colored people have the full benefit of the public schools. I have before said that I am pledged to aid in securing the education of the colored children. That pledge I have kept and am keeping. It is a duty that the older colored people owe to see that their children and their neighbors are properly instructed. I heartily condemn idleness, drunkeness and spend thrifts. Save the results of your labor and buy homes. Then you will be linked to the soil by those ties which make men good citizens. Show me a colored man who has a home of his own, well cared for, and I will show you a man whom I can trust. It is my desire to aid in the advancement of your people, and it always gives me pleasure to respond to your demands."

A&H—GP

W. J. Best to Thomas J. Jarvis
[Telegram]

New York Nov 6 1881

Judge Carruth[135] has addressed a letter to the Commissioners on behalf of the Boston gentlemen engaged in the Midland which I beg may receive attention before the next meeting of the commission   please wire me when this meeting will take place.

---

[135] William W. Carruth, originally of Newton, Massachusetts. After

A&H—GP

W. W. Carruth and D. J. Sprague[136] *to Thomas J. Jarvis*

New York Nov. 7th 1881

Soon after the adjournment of the General Assembly of North Carolina, last Spring, several gentlemen of Boston & New York were invited by Mr. Wm. J. Best to an interview in regard to the railroad interests of your state. At that time some of these person's had a large pecuniary interest in Mr. B.'s scheme to secure the Atlantic & North Carolina Railroad & extend it to Salisbury. He now made known his purpose to consolidate it with the Western N.C.R.R. & thus complete a Grand Trunk line to develope[sic] the resources of the State.

To accomplish this he said he would require financial assistance from other persons than those present & solicited their advice & co–operation in carrying out his plans. The enterprise seemed to offer a prospect of a fair remuneration & a company was immediately organized & its stock promptly taken by a number of men of large personal wealth & influence, who thus placed at Mr. Best's disposal sufficient means to complete his scheme of railroads.

As representives of this company, Messrs. Lewis Coleman, Wm. S. Denny,[137] and the undersigned, as representing the interests of both the New York & Boston gentlemen, accompanied Mr. Best, in May last, to Raleigh, where, by your invitation, we waited upon you at the Executive Chamber. It was there our pleasure also to meet Senator Vance & State Treasurer Worth, who, together with yourself, constituted the Commissioners on the part of the State to deal with the Western North Carolina Railroad.

Understanding that there was likely to be a contest over Mr.

---

finishing Harvard Law School in 1869, Carruth began practicing in Boston. In 1883 he shifted his practice to New York City, but in 1887 he return to Boston and was a prominent lawyer there until 1902. He was called "Judge" Carruth because for a few years he served as judge of the Police Court of Newton. Information furnished by Mrs. Sarah W. Flannery of the Boston Public Library.

[136]Daniel J. Sprague, businessman of New York City. Nothing has been learned of his interests. Information furnished by the New York Public Library.

[137]William Sprague Denny was president of the Shawmut Insurance Company from 1877 to 1882. When this company closed in bankruptcy, he became involved in a number of other projects, one of which was the position of treasurer of the Midland North Carolina Railroad during 1883 and 1884. In 1885 he settled down in the insurance business. Information furnished by Mrs. Sarah W. Flannery of the Boston Public Library.

Best's full possession & physical control of the Western N.C. R.R., and being determined on our part not to proceed in the enterprise without being first satisfied that that road would soon come into Mr. Best's hands, we discussed that matter with you at great length. This discussion involved not only Mr. Best's relations to that road but the power of the Commissioners in the premises.

At the close of this discussion, you personally asked each of us, privately, if we would take a lease of the Atlantic & N.C.R.R. & go forward with the building of the road from Goldsboro to Salisbury, without having first obtained possession of the Western North C. Railroad.

Each of us, (not knowing that such a question had been put to any other member of our committee) ; replied that we would neither lease the Atlantic & N.C.R.R. nor build any portion of the new line unless we could have the W.N.C.R.R. or be forthwith put in possession by the Commissioners. The scheme, we said, was good as a whole, but we did not, & would not entertain it in parts.

Subsequently, & before we left Raleigh, the memorandum of Agreement dated May 25 '81, was drawn up & signed by the Commissioners & sent to us through the counsel of our company in North Carolina.

That agreement required us to do three things. Viz:

1st. To place in the hands of the Commissioners, "The sum of two hundred and fifty thousand dollars ($250.000) to reimburse A. S. Buford, W. P. Clyde & T. M. Logan, x x x for their expenses upon the Western North Carolina Railroad, legitimately & properly made under what is known as the 'Best Contract' for the purchase of the state's interest in that road."

2nd. To "deposit at a place, and in a manner satisfactory to the Board of Directors of the Atlantic & North Carolina Railroad Co., the sum of thirty five thousand dollars ($35.000) as rental for the lease of the Atlantic & N.C. Railroad, when the same shall have been obtained, and the further sum of fifty thousand dollars ($50.000) as collateral for the rolling stock of said last mentioned company."

3rd. "So soon as the lease of the said Atlantic & North Carolina road shall have been obtained, [to] proceed at once to prosecute vigorously the work on the Midland North Carolina Railroad between Goldsboro & Salisbury."

For and in consideration of the foregoing to be performed

on our part, "the said Commissioners agree & promise that they will use all the means in their power, as Commissioners, and as individuals, to procure the surrender & re–assignment of the interest heretofore conveyed by the state of North Carolina to W. J. Best and others in the Western North Carolina Railroad Co., to be made to W. J. Best, W. W. Carruth, D. J. Sprague, Wm. S. Denny, Lewis Coleman & such others of their associates as they may designate."

Relying upon this contract and upon the verbal assurances of the Commissioners of their hearty co–operation in our plans to even a greater extent than they cared to express in writing, we returned & reported to our associates that you & the other Commissioners would act with & for us, & that so soon as our company had complied with the conditions of the Agreement set set forth above you would at once take such measures as would speedily place us in possession of the W.N.C.R.R.

We most respectfully call your attention to the fact that the three conditions required of us in the agreement hereinbefore set forth above you would at once take such measures as would

1st. On the Eleventh of June last we placed in the hands of the Commissioners the sum of two hundred & fifty thousand dollars to re–emburse Messrs. Buford, Clyde & Logan.

2nd. On the second of July last we leased the Atlantic & N.C. R.R. & deposited the sum of eighty five thousand dollars as security for the payment of the rent & rolling stock.

3rd. Early in July the preliminary survey of the new line was begun and on the twenty sixth of September we placed in the field as large a force as could be obtained, which force has been constantly on the increase until, at present, it numbers about six hundred men. We believe you must concede that the work has been *"vigerously"* [*sic*] prosecuted & we expect to complete & put the line in operation as far as Smithfield by the close of this year.

In addition to the work required of us under the agreement, we have also expended large sums in restoring & improving the Atlantic & N.C.R.R. in its road bed & buildings and in the purchase of new rolling stock. We have also purchased at the present time steel rails for sixty miles of the new road.

From the time of our leaving Raleigh, in May last, rumors reached New York & Boston that we were not likely to get the W.N.C.R.R. "because the Governor was friendly to the Rich & Danville people & not to us." We treated these rumors with contempt & the matter being spoken of at a meeting of our Board of Directors, held in Boston, in June last, Mr. Best read the following from a letter received about that time from Mr. Caddigan:

"Gov. Jarvis told Mr. Gatling[138] before leaving yesterday, (June 21) "That as soon as Best gets his friends to put up the $85.000 for the lease of the A.&N.C.R.R. if the R.&D. dont give up the W.N.C.R.R. to the M^d Co. quietly, he (Jarvis) would turn the militia of the State on them & drive them out at once.' "

These rumors continuing, & some of our friends manifesting uneasiness as to the action of the Commissioners, more particularly as to the position which you occupied towards the Midland & the R & D., Mr. Best privately & under the pledge of secrecy submitted to Mr. Coleman & a few others your letter of August 5 last to Mr. John Gatling.[139]

From this letter I quote as follows:

"The memorandum signed on the 26th [25th] of May by Z. B. Vance, J. M. Worth & myself was signed by us as Commissioners and as individuals. It contains an obligation on the part of Mr. Best & his friends to do three things before we are required to take any action on our part. They have performed the first, the deposit of the two hundred and fifty thousand dollars ($250.000) and the second, the lease of the A.&N.C.R.R. but the third & most important remains to be done. The vigorous prosecution of the work in constructing a road from Goldsboro to Salisbury is the consideration of that agreement; and when that obligation is complied with by Mr. B. & his friends I have no doubt the Commissioners will faithfully do their part. x x x Till the work is vigorously prosecuted I do not feel that we are called upon to do more than we have done. Yet for one I am willing to give still further assurance of the active & hearty support of the State Administration, & I will add my position & influence as Governor to the agreement of the memorandum of the 26th [25th] of May. x x x x I shall give to Mr. B. & his friends all the support I can command as Governor of the state if they proceed vigerously with the work on the road from Goldsboro to Salisbury. The Western road being a necessary part of this scheme I shall stand ready to do all I can to make it a part of the [Midland] system.

If the Buford—Clyde—Logan syndicate will not of their own

---

[138]John Thomas Gatling, Raleigh lawyer of the firm of Gilliam and Gatling. He was a member of the General Assembly in the session of 1885. Grant, *Alumni History of the University*, 215.

[139]For additional information of Jarvis' letter of August 5 to John Gatling, see Jarvis to Carruth and Sprague, November 14, 1881.

accord accept the money refunded, with interest & fair compensation, I shall feel justified in using positive measures and if they still persist in standing in the way of this great interest of the state then I shall feel called upon to use harsh measures even to attacking the lease of the North Carolina R.R. & the charter of the Piedmont road. But my action in these matters must be dependent upon the work on the road from Goldsbo[ro] to Salisbury & what I mean by work is the actual construction of the road."

These assurances satisfied the minds of our Directors as is shown by the money they have expended on the strength thereof.

Your letters of August on the same subject addressed to Attorney Gen. Kenan, & which were printed in New York and Boston, still further encouraged our associate to look for prompt action against the R.&D. people, and the early surrender of the W.N.C.R.R. to the Midland Co. Since these publications, we have been in constant expectation of some decisive & final action on your part.

We most respectfully ask that such action may be taken

A&H—GP

Joseph B. Cherry[140] to Thomas J. Jarvis

Windsor, Bertie Co N.C.
12th Nov. 1881

In compliance, with my commission received from your Excellency two years past, appointing me, Proxy for the State of North–Carolina, in the Corporation of the Albemarle & Chesapeake Canal Company, I was notified to attend a meeting of the stockholders of said corporation which I did attend in person in the city of Norfolk Va on the 27th day of October past the time of the annual meetings of the stockholders in said company, and participated in the deliberation of the meeting. I deem it due to your Excellency, for your kind consideration in bestowing this appointment upon me, to make a brief report of the proceedings of the corporation.

It being the time, at which the regular annual election of the

---

[140]Planter and lawyer of Windsor; member of the General Assembly, 1836, 1848–1852, 1856–1860. Grant, *Alumni History of the University*, 109.

officers [of] the company takes place, I found, upon a full and satisfactory examination into the affairs of the company, that all the officers, who at this time control its management, were entirely acceptable to the individual stockholders, and with them, I united without a dissenting vote, in re–electing these officers to the position they have so long filled. For Marshall Parks,[141] who for the 27th annual election in succession to the position as President of the Canal Company, I took much pleasure in casting the vote of the state of North–Carolina, the confident belief, that my conduct in so doing would meet the approbation of your Excellency.

The conduct of all the other officers is equally meritorious— As your Excellency is well aware, an act was passed by the last General Assembly of our State to exchance the Bonds of the A&C.C. Co— for Bonds of the State. I am fearful, that in consequence of the great advance in the price of State–Bonds, the Company may not be able to effect the exchange. Nothing has been done in that connection as yet. An act of the General Assembly was passed two years [ago] to incorporate a Company, to effect a better canal navigation, between Beaufort Harbor & the Neuse River, by improving what is known as club–foot & Harlow Creek Canal. Under that charter, the A&C.C. Co. authorized the subscription of an amount of stock ($50.000) to secure the charter of what is now known as the New bern & Beaufort Canal Company. Fully impressed with the importance & usefulness of this work, to the company which I represent, and to the entire shipping & commerce of Eastern North Carolina as well, and believing, that I fully reflected the wishes & sentiments of your Excellency, I cast the vote of the State of North Carolina for the proposed enterprise. In my last report to your Excellency two years ago,[142] I somewhat elaborated the importance of this Inland connection of our eastern waters. I trust my action will meet your aprobation.

The Annual Report of the President of the Company, shows a gratifying increase in our business—It will soon be remitted to

---

[141]The Albemarle and Chesapeake Canal Company was organized in 1855 under the name of Great Bridge Lumber and Canal Company, and Marshall Parks of Norfolk served as its president from 1855 to 1885. In the 1880's he and his associates built a narrow gauge railroad from Norfolk to Virginia Beach, and in 1883 they erected the Princess Anne Hotel at the latter place. Information furnished by Mrs. Frank C. Pinkerton of the Norfolk Public Library System.

[142]"Report of the State Proxy in the Albemarle and Chesapeake Canal Company." *Public Documents, 1881*, No. 16.

you,[143] & will give your Excellency a more accurate insight into the operation of the Company, than anything I may say. Before I conclude this very brief report, allow me again to return to your Excellency, my high appreciation of the Honor confer[r]ed upon me, as the representative man of your administration in the company; & which, I hope may add something to your already unequalled & renowned administration.

A&H—GP

L. A. Potter and R. W. Chadwick[144] to Thomas J. Jarvis

Beaufort, N. C. Nov 14 1881

The Legislature of 1868–69 passed an act— ratifying the same Mch 11. 1869—making an appropriation of $5000. for the "North River Turnpike Road," leading from North River, this Carteret County, to Adam's Creek, Craven County, a distance of 9 or 10 miles.

Only a part of this appropriation, we understand, has been expended, while the road remains in an unfinished state. Under the act of July 18, 1875, this unexpended balance is in charge of the Board of Internal improvements.

It is very desirable that this road be completed, and that the balance in the Treasury (some $2500.) be used for that purpose.

We beg leave, respectfully, to inquire whether, in the judgment of your Board, the appropriation in question, is still available for the completion of this work, notwithstanding the resolution of Dec 13. 1871—[145]

We beg leave to state further, that we have the opinion of eminent lawyers, to the effect, that said resolution does not virtually repeal the act of appropriation as some have supposed.

On behalf of the citizens interested in this important public work the desired information is respectfully asked.

---

[143]Governors' Papers, not included in this volume.

[144]Editors and publishers of a weekly Beaufort newspaper, the *Telephone*. Branson, *Directory for 1884*, 710.

[145]This resolution prohibited the state treasurer from disbursing any more money for work "purported to have been done" pursuant to an act authorizing a turnpike road in Cartaret County. *Laws of North Carolina, 1871–1872*, 391–392.

A&H—GLB

Thomas J. Jarvis to W. W. Carruth and D. J. Sprague

Executive Department,
Raleigh, Novr. 14, 1881

Yours of the 7th ins't. came while I was away with the other Commissioners on a tour of inspection on the Western Road. This accounts in part for the delay in my answer. Then, there was a part, at least, of this answer which I felt but fair to **Mr.** Gatling that he should see. He has just returned from one of his Courts, so his absence added to the delay.

At the interview referred to in your letter as having taken place in the Executive office in May, Mr. Sprague was the chief speaker for Mr. Best and his friends. He explained the scheme to be to obtain a lease of the Atlantic and North Carolina Railroad, to get the Western North Carolina Railroad and to build a road from Goldsboro to Salisbury to connect the two; to complete the Western Road to the western extremities of both lines and beyond and then operate the whole line as an east and west line from and to Morehead City. His presentation of the scheme contemplated the possession of the Western Road, or if not its actual possession, the reasonable certainty of it in the near future, as a condition precedent to the investment of any money in the scheme by the syndicate. I have a very distinct recollection that I replied that the Western Road did not belong to the State; that it had been sold and that the Commissioners had no power to put **Mr.** Best and his friends in possession of the road. It was after this declaration that I put the question to the gentlemen—I will not say whether separately or altogether—whether or not they were willing to lease the Atlantic Road and build the road from Goldsboro to Salisbury, taking their chances of getting the Western Road. I was asked what I thought of the chances of Mr. Best and his friends getting the Western Road. My reply was that I believed if they leased the Atlantic Road and built the Midland to Salisbury, that they would get the Western Road. I also distinctly remember that I said to the gentlemen present that while I was anxious to see the Midland Road built, I did not wish to do or say anything to mislead them, and that this was only my opinion, in which I might be mistaken. I was appealed to direct to know if I would as Governor, give the scheme my support. I replied, "When you give me safe ground to stand upon;" that Mr. Best had failed once in his contract with the State and, no matter from what cause, it was a failure which seriously threatened the interest of the State, and that I could not afford to have any more failures. I was then asked what I meant by "safe ground to stand upon." I replied, work and labor done so that I could feel secure and the public feel confident that there would be no failure. "When this is done," said I, "I will write the assignees a letter as Governor, as Commissioner and as a citizen, begging them to turn over the Western Road to you." Senator Vance spoke up at once and said, "Yes, and I will carry it." This interview lasted for several hours. There were some dozen persons present and I think all had more or less to say; and, of course, I do not undertake to repeat all that was said or the order in which it was said, but I do say that the above is a fair synopsis of the substance of what was said to me and of what I said in reference to my action about the Western Road. That night at the Yarboro House there was much discussion, chiefly through your attorneys, as to the terms upon which the Atlantic road could be leased. These were finally agreed upon and there the memorandum of the 25th of May was drawn up by Major Dowd,[146] as embodying the result of the suggestions agreed upon at the afternoon and evening conferences. This memorandum, as you correctly state, requires Mr. Best and his friends to do three things, to—wit, to make the deposit of $250,000., to secure the lease of the Atlantic Road and to vigorously prosecute the work in constructing a road from Goldsboro to Salisbury, before my promise to do anything became binding. The deposit was made in due time; the lease of the Atlantic Road was obtained at the earliest possible moment; but it is doubtful if it can be said that the third and, by far, the most important thing, has yet been done. It can hardly be said that the grading of eight miles of a road one hundred and fifty miles long, is vigorously prosecuting the work. I do not wish to be understood as complaining, for I think about all has been done that could well be in the length of time; but the point I wish to make is that *you* have yet no grounds of complaint. I did not, however, wait, as I might have done, till your part of the memorandum was fulfilled to the letter. I have used all the means I

---

[146]Clement Dowd, banker and lawyer of Charlotte; Democratic representative to Congress, 1881–1885. He had been Z. B. Vance's law partner before Vance made politics his profession. *Biographical Directory of Congress,* 918.

deem lawful and proper to substitute the Boston syndicate for the Richmond and Danville in the ownership of the W.N.C.R.R., because I felt if it could be done, a great service would be rendered the State. I say it would be a great service to the State to substitute the Boston syndicate for the Richmond and Danville, because the Boston syndicate proposes to build one hundred and fifty miles more of road than the other and to operate the whole line as an east and west line. As much as I desire to see this result accomplished, I shall not use any means I deem improper or unlawful to bring it about; and of these I propose to judge for my self.

I do not wish to criticize or complain of your syndicate, but your letter puts me in a position where I feel, in justice to myself, I am called upon to say something that may look that way. It seems to me a business–like view of the situation, suggested after the meeting of the 25th of May, that two things be definitely fixed. First, that it be distinctly settled that you would not take the lease of the Atlantic Road nor do any work on the Midland till you got the Western Road; or, secondly, that you would take a lease of the Atlantic Road and go to work with a fixed determination to build the Midland, taking your chances in getting the Western Road. After you took the Atlantic Road, the question of building the Midland ought never to have been discussed, but ought to have been acted upon by the syndicate as a fixed thing. Had this course been pursued in a quiet, determined, business–like way, your syndicate would to–day have a strong hold upon the sympathies and confidence of the people of the State; and as you pushed your way along with your Midland Road through the very heart of the State, you would have gained a position and an influence in the State that would, in my opinion, have made the acquisition of the Western Road easy. This view I tried to impress upon some of your people and upon your attorneys. Had it been adopted, your friends, who were ready and willing to give you their support and influence, could have done so with effect.

A very different (and I say it with due deference to the opinions of others)—a very suicidal policy has been pursued. There seems to have been no fixed determination about anything. No one seems to have been authorized to push forward in the accomplishment of a fixed purpose. This hesitation and uncertainty did not have the effect to make friends for the Midland scheme. Meeting after meeting and conference after conference was asked for and often held and, of course, it all ended in talk. It could not end in anything else. One result of this policy of much talk, many meetings and little work has been a vexatious warfare of words in the news-papers of the State, which has engendered bitter feelings and, I think, contributed but little towards securing a transfer of the Western Road to the Boston syndicate. It has given the enemies of Mr. Best and his schemes an opportunity and an excuse to rehearse and rehash his promises and failures of 1880 in connection with the Western Road, to excite the fears of those who have so long hoped to see the road built and to consolidate the whole western part of the State in their support of the Richmond and Danville syndicate, which has been for months pushing the work on the road with such remarkable diligence and energy. Work, and not words, wins the confidence of a people who for thirty years have been anxiously watching for the coming of the railroad. It was during one of these periodical, almost endless talks, while at Morehead City, that I was pressed to take some decided action outside of the premises in the memorandum of the 25th of May and in advance of the performance of the agreements by the syndicate. I absolutely refused, but afterwards I penciled off a draft of a letter addressed to John Gatling, Esq., I first handed it to Senator Vance, who was at that time at Morehead, to read to get his opinion about it. I then handed it to Mr. Gatling and asked him to read it. It was written in pencil and not signed. He kept it for some time, It may be a night or day or both—I do not now remember—and handed it back to me. I held the letter up for more mature reflection and finally decided not to write it at all. Mr. Gatling never mentioned the matter to me again, nor I to him. I did not know he had made any use of it, and I was greatly surprised when I read in your letter to me a substantial copy of it.[147] The draft of the letter which I handed Mr. Gatling is now in my possession and has been all the time since he examined it. Having given this statement of facts about the matter, it is but due to Mr. Gatling to say that he did not understand the matter as I did. He is incapable of being untrue to a friend or a client, and had he understood the matter as I did, he never would have permitted a copy of the letter to have been made; for in doing so he might do a friend injustice and mislead a client—neither of which he would do knowingly. I have had a talk with him

[147]For the relevancy of the letter in question, see Carruth and Sprague to Jarvis, November 7, 1881, in this volume.

about the matter since I received your letter, and we have together gone over, as well as we can remember it, what took
place at the time; and while we do not differ materially as to
what took place, we do entirely concur in the inferences upon
which he acted. But we do both concur in the declaration that
it was an honest misunderstanding of each other's purpose.

There is one other matter in your letter which demands a reply. I quote it in full: "Gov. Jarvis told Mr. Gatling before leaving yesterday (June 21st) that as soon as Best gets his friends
to put up the $85,000. for the lease of the A. & N.C.R.R. if the
R. & D. don't give up the W.N.C.R.R. to the M'd. Co., he (Jarvis)
would turn the militia of the State on them and drive them out
at once." How such a thing as this ever came to be written I do
not know and will not undertake to say; but I will say I never
said anything of the kind and I am sure Mr. Gatling will confirm
this. Had I said such a thing as this, I could not have expected
any prudent man, who believed I would do it, to invest his money
in building railroads in this State. Neither the rights of persons
nor the rights of property have ever been determined in this
State by military power. Our people would not tolerate anything
that had the semblance of it. So fixed are they in this that no
man will dare attempt it. Money invested in this State in any
species of property—railroads not excepted—will always be exempt and secure from the rude touch of the mailed hand of military power.

Now, in conclusion, I will state two things upon which I wish
to be distinctly understood. I thought I had been till your letter
cast a doubt upon it. The first is that I will do nothing to throw
the Western North Carolina Railroad back upon the hands of the
State so long as the work on it is continued with diligence and
energy. The second is that I will do what I can that is proper for
me to do to substitute the Boston for the Richmond and Danville
syndicate, because I believe it would be greatly to the advantage
of the people of the State to have an east and west line from
Beaufort Harbor, running through the middle of the State, to the
Tennessee and Georgia lines and beyond.

If my position on any question shall still be in doubt, it will
be my pleasure, as well as my duty, to speak out so plainly that I
cannot be misunderstood.

Thanksgiving Proclamation, November 16, 1881

Executive Department

Custom, law and gratitude alike requiring that at least one day before the close of each year should be devoted to giving thanks to Almighty God for His manifold mercies and blessings, I, Thomas J. Jarvis, Governor of North Carolina, do issue this my Proclamation, setting apart Thursday, November 24th ins't. as a day of thanksgiving and prayer, and do earnestly request all the people of North Carolina properly to observe the same. Let the churches and other places of public worship be opened and the places of business closed. Let the people, resting from their labors, spend the day devoutly, as becomes a thankful Christian people. On that day, let not the poor, the widow and the orphan anywhere be forgotten, remembering that to give to these is to lend to Him from whom all blessings come. Especially let not the Oxford Orphan Asylum be forgotten, the necessities of whose unfortunate inmates, never greater than now, I especially commend to the generous consideration of a grateful people.

A. H. Canedo to Thomas J. Jarvis

Raleigh, N.C., Nov. 21st, 1881

I beg leave to refer to the brief letter I had the honor to address you on 17th August last past, looking to subsequent negotiations for the purchase of the stock of the State in the *Cape Fear and Yadkin Valley R.R. Co.*

Since that time, a Company has been organized in the City of New York under a charter obtained in the State of New Jersey, entitled the *New York and Southern Railroad and Telegraph Construction Co.*, with full power to purchase such interests and with ample financial ability to carry any contract it may make for the completion of said road.

I now have the honor to make a direct proposition to purchase said stock upon the terms set forth in a memorandum of a contract herewith annexed and made a part of this letter.[148] This proposition is made for and in behalf of said N.Y.& Southern

---

[148]Governors Papers, not included in this volume.

R.R. & Tel. Co. and by virtue of a resolution of said Company under its seal and signature of its President and Secretary, and hereto attached.

The object of the Company, as briefly alluded to in my letter of Aug. 17th, is to construct a grand trunk line from Wilmington, N. C., via Fayetteville, Greensboro, M't. Airy, through Va. and Kentucky to Covington, opposite Cincinnati, Ohio; with branches down the Guyandotte River, W. Va. and down the Tug Fork of Big Sandy from Prestonsburg, Ky. to Ashland on the Ohio River, and by connection at M't. Sterling, Ky. with Louisville. Also, a branch from Lloyd's, near Germanton, up the Yadkin valley to Patterson, Caldwell Co., N.C., and a subsidiary branch to Ore Knob; and also to construct a line from Florence, S.C. through Fayetteville to Goldsboro, N.C. I would further say that although it is not specifically referred to or mentioned in the memorandum of the contract submitted herewith, it is the intention of the contracting parties whom I represent that, in addition to the $55,000. paid for the State stock to pay off the entire floating debt of the C.F.&Y.V.R.R. Co., amounting to about $100,000. (as reported to me) before the final consummation of the sale and delivery of the road.

And I would beg leave to call your attention and that of the Commissioners to the necessity for such legislation, at as early a day as practicable, as may be necessary to enable us to make a new issue of bonds and fulfill our obligations and push the work to an early completion of the main line between its initial and objective points.

Now, therefore, I would ask you to assemble the Commissioners appointed by the Legislature at its session of 1881 to sell the above mentioned interest of the C.F.&Y.V.R.R. held by the State at as early a day as to you may seem proper, to consider this proposition.

A&H—GLB

Thomas J. Jarvis to A. H. Canedo

Executive Department,
Raleigh, Novr. 23, 1881

I am in receipt of yours of the 21st ins't., enclosing a copy of certain resolutions of your Company, authorizing you to negotiate for the purchase of the State's stock in the C.F.&Y.V.R.R. Co.

and a draft of a contract setting out the terms upon which you propose to make this purchase. This memorandum of a contract and your letter, both together forming a proposition, I will submit to the Commissioners appointed by the General Assembly to consider any proposition for the purchase of this interest. They are the persons authorized by law, as you know, who are first to pass upon the proposition; and as a convenient way of getting them together, I shall issue a call for them to meet in the Senate Chamber in the City of Raleigh at four o'clock, P.M. on Monday, the 19th day of December, A. D., 1881. As this memorandum and letter is only submitted as a proposition open to discussion and amendment by the Commission when it meets, I suggest that you and the President of your Company and such others as you may desire attend the meeting of the Commissioners prepared to give any information that may be desired and to accept or reject any other conditions that may be suggested.[149]

Your scheme is of such magnitude and importance to the State and promises such benefits to many of her sections and particularly to Wilmington, her chief city, that you need give yourself no concern about its receiving the warm, cordial support of our people as soon as they have reasonable assurance of its being carried out.

As suggested to you in my letter of August 17th, the only possible trouble you need apprehend is to be able to satisfy the Commissioners of your ability to carry out that part of the scheme lying in North Carolina and to offer them satisfactory guarantees that you will do so. To this end I beg to urge that you come before the Commissioners as strongly backed as possible. In the meantime you may expect many questions to be asked and a strict inquiry to be made about the ability of your Company.

Proclamation, November 23, 1881[150]

Executive Department

Whereas the General Assembly, at its session of 1881 (chapter 374) appointed A. J. DeRosset, of Wilmington; Levi M.

---

[149]Representatives of Canedo's company were at the meeting of the commissioners as Jarvis suggested herein. After two days' discussion, the sale was made on the terms outlined in Canedo's letter to Jarvis of November 21, 1881. *News and Observer*, December 20, 22, 23, 1881. For a complete copy of the contract, see the *News and Observer*, December 31, 1881.
[150]Taken from the *Union Republican*, December 1, 1881.

Scott[151] and Julius A. Gray, of Greensboro; E. L. Vaughan, of
Alleghany; George M. Rose, A. A. McKethan, Jr.,[152] and A. B.
Williams,[153] of Fayetteville; Orrin A. Hanner,[154] of Chatham;
Jesse F. Graves, of Mt. Airy; Tyre York, of Wilkes; A. J.
Boyd,[155] of Rockingham; Hugh, [sic] Parks,[156] of Randolph; and
W. A. Lash,[157] of Stokes, commissioners to receive any proposi-
tion that may be made to the Governor or otherwise concerning
the purchase of the stock of the State in theCape [sic] Fear and
Yadkin Valley Railway Company; and whereas, a proposition
has been formally made to me for the purchase of said stock
by the New York and Southern Railroad and Telegraph Construction Company: Now, therefore I, Thos. J. Jarvis, Governor,
do request said commissioners and each of them to meet in the
Senate Chamber in the capitol, in the city of Raleigh at 4 o'clock
P. M., on Monday, the 19th day of December, A. D., 1881, to
receive said proposition and any other that may be made for the
purchase of said interests.

If any of said commissioners decline to serve or cannot attend, they will please notify me in time so that their places can
be filled according to law.

A&H—GLB

Thomas J. Jarvis to James Sanders Amis[158]

Executive Department
Raleigh N.C. Nov. 23rd 1881

I am in receipt of yours of the 25th. inst. I trust for the sake
of the good name of the people of Oxford and for the sake of the
law abiding people of the whole State, that no effort will be
made to resort to violence towards the murderer of Mr. Lynch.
I have tried since I assumed the responsible duties of the Gov-

---

[151]Lawyer of Greensboro; member of the General Assembly, 1856. Ashe,
Biographical History, II, 386–393.
[152]Junior partner in the many business enterprises of A. A. McKethan &
Sons of Fayetteville. Oates, *Story of Fayetteville*, 846–847.
[153]Arthur Butler Williams, merchant of Fayetteville. Branson, *Directory
for 1884*, 251.
[154]Unable to identify.
[155]Andrew Jackson Boyd, lawyer of Rockingham County; member of the
General Assembly, 1864. Ashe, *Biographical History*, VII, 48–51.
[156]Textile manufacturer. Ashe, *Biographical History*, IV, 355–360.
[157]Merchant and manufacturer of Walnut Cove. Branson, *Directory for
1884*, 602.
[158]Lawyer of Oxford; member of the General Assembly, 1850–1854, 1862,
1864. Grant, *Alumni History of the University*, 19.

ernor's office to do my part in the faithful and prompt execution of the law. I have exercised the pardoning power very sparingly, and I fear have with–held it in some cases where I ought to have exercised it. More men have been hanged during my three years than in many years before. I have been called by some bloody Tommy. It will be a poor return for my efforts to suppress crime by a certain exaction of the sentence of the law for the people themselves, whom I am trying to protect, to turn criminals and violators of the law. I have no patience with crime of any kind, and particularly that kind which is generally the result of idleness. Men will eat. Those that work earn their bread honestly. Those that idle away their time become drones or criminals living either by the toleration of the community or by crime. Society must see that the loafer, the idler and the drone have no countenance or room in its midst. The law must see to it that the criminal meets with swift and certain punishment. Then crime will rapidly decrease. The place for the people to begin is upon the idler and the loafer. *There* they may and can do much in the suppression of crime. It will not do for them to undertake to deal with the criminal. The law must do that. With all my abhorrence of crime, I cannot tolerate any spirit of violence towards a criminal; and I trust this spirit will not show itself among the good people of Granville.

If it is deemed advisable for any cause to have a Court in your county before the regular term, I will, of course, order it upon having the proper certificates filed with me. In this communication I beg to call your attention to the Special Court provided for in Ch: 17th Sec. 11a. and to the court of Oyer and terminer provided for in section 11b. in same Chapter. It seems to me that the Special Court is much the better of the two. But this is only a suggestion.

With an earnest hope that your people will set an example of absolute obedience to Law,

A&H—GLB

Thomas J. Jarvis to A. J. de Rossett

Executive Department,
Raleigh, Nov. 24, 1881

A Dr. A. H. Canedo, of the City of New York, has just submitted to me, as you will see by the morning papers, a proposition for the purchase of the stock of the State in the Cape Fear and Yadkin Valley Railroad Company, with a view, as he says, of constructing a road from Wilmington direct to the Ohio River. If he has the ability to carry out this scheme and does carry it out, I know of nothing that has taken place in the State in many years so full of promise to Wilmington. Of this ability I cannot speak, because I am not myself informed. It is a question that ought to be well looked into before the meeting of the Commissioners on the 19th of December. It was to give ample time to do this that I put off the meeting to so late a day.

I trust, in view of the great interest involved, I am not asking too much when I beg you to see that this investigation is made in a spirit of fairness, but thorough and complete. I have never thought the people of Wilmington manifested a proper interest in the Cape Fear and Yadkin Valley Road. Your leading paper, with its usual patent— right claim to wisdom and sagacity, ever opposed the passage of an act to appoint this very Commission. But it is not my purpose to complain or speak of the past. It is the present that demands our attention. It seems to me that there is enough in this proposition of Dr. Canedo to induce your people to look into it; and to this end, I beg to suggest that some of your citizens be sent to New York to talk with the gentlemen proposing to undertake this great scheme, and learn all about them that may be necessary to be known. I hope you will find it convenient to visit New York yourself in this interest. Dr. Canedo will be in Wilmington in a few days, I am informed by him, and will call to see you.[159]

Trusting that I have not offended the proprieties of the occasion in making these suggestions, I beg to subscribe myself.

A&H—GLB

A. J. de Rossett to Thomas J. Jarvis

Wilmington N.C. Nov 26. 1881

I beg to acknowledge the rect today of your kind favor of 24th inst. & to thank you for the suggestions given in regard to the important proposition for the purchase of the C.F.&Y.V. Rail Road, which is to be submitted on the 19th prox. to the Commissioners appointed by the last Legislature—

[159]De Rossett was one of the commissioners named in the act of March 14, 1881, authorized to sell the state's stock in the Cape Fear and Yadkin Valley Railroad. *Laws of North Carolina, 1881*, c. 374.

I received several days ago, a pamphlet endorsed by A. H. Canedo setting forth in detail a scheme for constructing the "Ohio & Carolina Railway" from this place to the Ohio River—but having never heard of Dr. C. or his Company before, I did not fully understand the object until yesterday, when I saw in the News & Observer, the correspondence on the subject & the call for the meeting of the Commissioners on the 19th prox.

I have already written to New York, & know of others who have done, or will do so, to make enquiry as to the parties proposing the scheme, & hope our information will be received in time to prepare us for Dr. Canedo's visit—

Many of us here appreciate, with intense interest, the importance of the proposition in question, & feel indignant at the apathetic—not to say hostile course of the "leading paper" to which you refer—

There will doubtless be a call soon for either a public meeting of Citizens—or of the Chamber of Commerce, to give expression to our views as to a matter of such supreme importance to our City & to take measures in ascertaining the standing of the parties proposing the scheme—

A&H—GLB

Thomas J. Jarvis to J. A. Gray

Raleigh, Nov'r. 29, 1881
Executive Department,

I have the honor herewith to send you printed copies of a letter from Dr. A. H. Canedo addressed to me, covering a proposition for the purchase of the States stock in said Company. I also send you a printed copy of the proposed contract of purchase.

I have called the Commissioners together to meet on the 19th day of December to consider this proposition. When they meet, they will, of course, desire all the information possible to be had to enable them to act intelligently and to the best interest of the State and the Company.

I know you feel a deep interest in this matter and that you have already spent much time and labor—to say nothing of money—in looking into and in aiding in working up an interest in it; yet I feel obliged to tax your time and labor still further.

As President of the Company, the Commissioners will properly look to you for such information as they may desire. I therefore beg that you will visit the City of New York in the interest of this enterprise and make a close investigation into it before the meeting of the Commissioners. I suggested that you take with you Maj. J. C. MacRae, the attorney of the Company and any other persons you may think proper. If the proposition is bona fide and the parties making it have the ability to carry it out, I feel that we ought to give them all proper encouragement. If either element is wanting, we had better know it before any contract is made. It is therefore iminently proper that you see the parties and that you talk with them frankly face to face and let them understand exactly how the people of the State feel about their scheme.

A&H—GLB

Thomas J. Jarvis to J. B. Cherry

Executive Department,
Raleigh, Nov. 29, 1881

Your report of the condition of the State's interest in the A.&C. Canal Company was received in due time.[160] I am obliged to you for your faithful attention to this trust and am glad to hear such good reports from the Company. I am especially glad to hear of the prospect of work beginning on the A. &C. Canal at an early day. This will be an important work for the State and I desire to see the interest of the State in the A. &C. Canal used to construct this new work.

Parks is a man of wonderful powers, full of energy and enterprise. He will accomplish what most men would not begin. It was his energy that built the A. & C. Canal, and but for that I do not see what would have been the fate of Eastern North Carolina during the sixteen years since the war.

A&H—GLB

Thomas J. Jarvis to J. A. Bonitz

Executive Department,
Raleigh, Nov. 30, 1881

In reply to yours of the 29th,[161] I beg to say that I have no special suggestions to make to the Board [of Directors of The

---

[160]See Cherry to Jarvis, November 12, 1881, in this volume.
[161]Not found.

Colored Insane Asylum]. Of course, I share with them their anxiety to administer the institution in the best interests of the State and the poor, unfortunate inmates that fill its wards. The advance in all kinds of provisions will make it all the more necessary for the Board to see that the utmost economy is practiced in the administration of the institution consistent with a proper care for the patients.

There is one matter to which I will call the attention of the Board and will avail myself of the occasion offered by your kind letter to do so. Complaint has been made to me by the authorities of the Penitentiary of a want of courtesy and a failure to comply with the law by the Supt. of the Goldsboro Asylum.[162] It seems that some time ago some insane persons were sent to the Asylum from the Pentitentiary. The Superintendent not only refused to admit them, but it is reported to me that he even refused to allow them to be lodged for one night in the Asylum: so that the State was not only forced to incur the expense of taking them back to the Penitentiary, but was forced to the expense of taking them to jail and keeping them there the over night. Sec. 47, Ch. 85 (page 679), of Battle's Revisal, is relied upon by the Pen. authorities for their action, and under this they have never had any trouble with the Asylum at Raleigh. I suppose the Supt. had not long been in harness and was not familiar with the courtesies usually existing between the officers of the different institutions. I certainly do not suppose that he intended any disrespect to the authorities of the Penitentiary.

Please call his attention to the matter and suggest to him to adopt a different rule.

A&H—GLB

Thomas J. Jarvis to J. D. Imboden

Executive Department,
Raleigh, Dec. 1, 1881

I send you by to–day's mail a printed copy of a proposition which has been submitted for the purchase of the State's stock in the Cape Fear and Yadkin Valley Railroad Company. The Commissioners have been called together to consider this proposition, and they will meet in the City of Raleigh for this pur-

---

[162]Dr. William Harding Moore of Goldsboro. "Report of the Chairman of the Board of Directors of the Asylum for the Colored Insane," *Public Documents, 1881,* No. 12, 2.

pose on the 19th (Monday) ins'th. We will be glad to see you with us on that day and to have a bid from your Company.[163]

A&H—GLB

Thomas J. Jarvis to L. A. Potter and R. W. Chadwick

Executive Department,
Raleigh, Dec. 1st, 1881

Yours of the 14th of Nov. was received in due time and now has my attention.

The whole matter referred to in your letter was brought to my attention last winter by the Representative of Carteret[164] and its importance was strongly urged by him. I submitted the question to the Attorney General for his opinion. Your Representative had an attorney to appear before me and, I think, also before the Attorney General. The opinion of the Attorney General was filed on the 16th of Feb., and was adverse to the wishes of your Representative.[165] I send you enclosed a copy of that opinion. Whether your Representative sought to procure the additional legislation, which the Attorney General says is necessary, or not, I cannot say, for I do not know. He was, however, I know, very earnest in his efforts before the Board of Int. Imp. It may be that, knowing the difficulties that were before him in the Legislature, he did not attempt it. How that was I cannot say.

It may be that the eminent lawyers to whom you refer are correct in their opinions, but the opinion of the Attorney General is the one that I am bound by and that the law requires me to observe. I am sure the Attorney General gave the matter a very thorough investigation and I think his conclusions will be accepted as the law. With this construction of the law before us, the Board of Int. Imp. can do nothing till the suggested additional legislation is obtained.

---

[163]Earlier in the year Imboden had expressed an interest in buying the state's stock in this railroad. See Imboden to Jarvis, January 24, 1881. He had not submitted a formal bid, however, since the General Assembly set up a commission to sell this stock. See Jarvis to Canedo, August 17, 1881, n. 108, in this volume.

[164]George W. Smith of Beaufort. *House Journal, 1881,* 5.

[165]Governors' Papers, not included in this volume.

Open Letter to the News and Observer[166]

Executive Department,
Raleigh, December 3, 1881

The following paper was prepared to spread upon the records of the commissioners at their meeting the 10th of November. It was read by Commissioner Vance, and for reasons deemed sufficient it was not put on the record, I now beg that you will publish it with this note. Truly yours,

Thos. J. Jarvis.

My conduct as a commissioner of the Western North Carolina Railroad having been misrepresented and unjustly criticised by one of my associate commissioners and by the assignees and their supporters, I deem it a duty I owe to myself and to the trust I have had in charge to place upon record the facts in the case, as I understand them, and the misrepresentations that have formed the basis of these criticisms.

Although Commissioner Vance and myself have not been in entire accord in every particular in our action as commissioners of the Western North Carolina Railroad, yet I have never questioned his motives or criticised his course or permitted any one else to do so in my presence. I know he has discharged this duty, as he does every other public trust, as he believed in the best interest of the State. But while I concede to him this perfect integrity, I claim for myself the same honesty of purpose, and I deeply regret that I have not enjoyed the same measure of exemption from criticism by him.

The strictures by Commissioner Vance of which I complain are contained in the three extracts which I shall make from his recent address[167] to the people. The statements made by him in these extracts, so far as they refer to me, are, to say the least, inaccurate, as I think I will be able to conclusively show. Not supposing the commissioner intended to misstate the facts, I would have paid no attention to them had not inferences and conclusions been drawn from these misstatements prejudicial

[166]Taken from the *News and Observer*, December 7, 1881.
[167]This address, which was first published in the Charlotte *Observer*, may be found in the *News and Observer* of October 2, 1881.

and unjust to me. In fact, the commissioner himself, assuming these misstatements to be true, expresses his astonishment at my course.

The first extract I wish to make refers to my action on the question of extension, and is the following, to–wit:

"Although I invited a suspension of action on the part of the other commissioners, and promised to explain to them in full the reasons for my course, this was not accorded me."

To show the inaccuracy of this statement of the commissioner, I quote his own letter:[168]

.   .   .   .

This is the only letter or message of any kind I received from him on this subject, and there is not the slightest request or invitation in it for "a suspension of action on my part." On the contrary, the letter left me completely in the dark and entirely at liberty to take the course I should deem best under the circumstances.

The same quotation I make is upon the same subject, and has in it a similar inaccuracy. The commissioner says: "I quote the following letter to Gov. Jarvis in answer to his of the 13th of May, in which he implied that he would wait and hear my explanation." My letter referred to is as follows:[169]

.   .   .   .

This is the only communication of any kind the commissioner had from me, and in this I submit there is not the slightest intimation that I would wait and hear his explanation. The fact is, I did not know he wanted me to wait, and, therefore, could not have intimated a purpose to do so. I think if there is any intimation of my purpose in my letter, it is that I felt my own responsibility in the matter and that I intended to meet it in my own way. I told him it was either to declare the contract forfeited, and throw the road back upon the State, or to extend the time. On these alternate propositions I think I gave no uncertain sound. Said I to him, I am determined, as far as in me lies, to have this road completed without further costs or trouble to the State; and I believe by proper management it can be done. To declare the contract forfeited throws the road back upon the State, a thing I shall be slow to do as long as there is any reasonable prospect of the work being done in any reasonable

---

[168]See Vance to Jarvis, May 12, 1881, in this volume.
[169]See Jarvis to Vance, May 13, 1881, in this volume.

time." Now, might I not well say, judge of *my astonishment* when I saw that the commissioner had stated that he invited me to suspend action till I could hear him, and that I had intimated I would do so? But, to enable one fully to understand my action upon the question of extending the time in which the assignees were to complete the road to Paint Rock and Pigeon River and to completely acquit myself of the unjust reflections made by the commissioner upon this action, I will give the facts in the case.

At the meeting of the commissioners, held in Raleigh on the 30th of April, an agreement was entered into between the commissioners on the one side and Col. Andrews, representing the assignees, on the other.[170] The agreement was to the effect that if the assignees would reform their application for an extension of time by inserting certain promises in it, which have been heretofore published, and the assignees themselves sign it, the commissioners would give the assignees a four months' extension. The suggested amendments were handed Col. Andrews, and then, at his request, the exact form in which the extension was to be drawn upon was discussed and agreed upon. It was then written out by me, read over and agreed to by all the commissioners. This paper, not signed, was delivered to him in the presence of all the commissioners and with their approval. It was then agreed that the commissioners would go over the road on the 16th of May. I had to go to Spartanburg on the 11th, and could not go before, and Commissioner Vance had to return to Washington, but felt certain he could get away by that time. On the 9th of May, Col. Andrews, as before stated, handed me the new application, reformed strictly as agreed upon. I told him to hold it till we met on the 16th, and we would then sign the extension as agreed upon. This was entirely satisfactory to him. He did not question that the commissioners would keep their promise, but remarked to me that he would go on with his preparations to let the work to contract on the 18th, as advertised, and that he hoped to be able to do so while the commissioners were up there. On the 13th, I received Commissioner Vance's letter, requesting me to notify Col. Andrews of his withdrawal. This I at once did by a written notice, and in that very notice I pledged myself to stand by my promise; and it was to this written pledge I referred in my letter to Commissioner Worth, and it was to this,

---

[170]See Andrews to Jarvis, Vance, and Worth, April 30, 1881, in this volume.

I presume, Mr. Badger referred when he told Comissioner
Worth that I had already signed the extension. As soon as Col.
Andrews got the notice of Commissioner Vance's withdrawal,
he came to see me and asked me what it meant. I told him I did
not know, that the letter of the commissioner left me completely
in the dark. He then asked me what he had better do. I told him
to go on with the work, that I had no doubt it would all be made
right when the commissioners met. He replied that he could not
afford to enter into new contracts which required the expenditure of large sums of money upon such uncertainty; that he must
know absolutely before the 18th that the extension would be
signed or he would be compelled to abandon letting the work to
contract. I still urged him to go on and that it would all be right.
He replied that until the action of Commissioner Vance the verbal promise of the commissioners was sufficient, but now the extension must be in writing before he could afford to spend money
on the faith of it. I replied that he already had my agreement to
the extension in writing. "That is only one," said he; "I must
have two before I can know that I am safe." He then asked me
to telegraph Commissioner Worth to come to Raleigh at once.
This I declined to do. He urged me to do so on the ground that
the commissioner would come on my telegram, but not on his,
and offered to pay all the expenses of the telegram and of the
messenger from High Point. I still declined. He then said there
was nothing left for him to do but to go or send a messenger to
Commissioner Worth at his home in Randolph. I replied promptly that was exactly what I would do, were I in his place. His final
determination to send a messenger to Commissioner Worth was
not reached till about night on Saturday, long after the passenger train had left. After he concluded to send a messenger, he
asked me to write a letter to Commissioner Worth. This I readily
did and wrote the letter which Commissioner Vance denominated
"urgent" and which has already been published.[171] In that letter
I told Commissioner Worth of Commissioner Vance's withdrawal and of my idea of the situation, to—wit, that he and I had to
take the responsibility to extend the time or to stop the work. On
the return of the messenger on Monday, the 16th, at Colonel Andrews' request, I drew out my consent to the extension more
formally than I had done in my note to him on the 13th. In thus
detailing what took place between Colonel Andrews and my-

---

[171]See Jarvis to Worth, May 14, 1881.

self, I have only attempted to give the substance. We were together on Friday and several times on Saturday and talked much about the matter. The situation gave us both much concern. He was anxious about the extension and I about the work on the road, which I feared was about to be stopped. I could not conjecture what the circumstances were that had come to Commissioner Vance's knowledge. I remembered that in our April meeting the commissioner had expressed the belief that the assignees did not in good faith intend to work on the Ducktown line, while I expressed the belief that they did. I wondered if it were possible that any facts had recently come to his knowledge to strengthen him in that belief. Such thoughts as these were running through my mind, as any one can see, when I wrote my letter to him. On the other hand, Col. Andrews gave me the most positive assurances that he did intend to push the work on the Ducktown line as soon as the extension was a fixed fact. I believed him. It was important to him to have this question settled at once, and when he proposed to send a messenger to Commissioner Worth I encouraged him in it. I not only felt bound by my agreement of the 30th of April, but I felt to break up that agreement was likely to lead to a stoppage of the work on the road. Entertaining these views and feeling this necessity of a prompt decision, I could not have suspended action on my part even if Commissioner Vance's letter had contained an invitation to me to do so. When the Best contract was made I had high hopes of seeing both lines of the western road completed, and notwithstanding one of the leading journals of the State denounced any man as an idiot who believed that a spadeful of dirt would ever be thrown on the Ducktown line, yet I have believed that the contract was such as to insure the completion of both lines. It is true that work under this contract had been too long delayed, but it was then, in my opinion, about to be begun in good earnest. Impressed with these beliefs and inspired by these hopes I could not let the wishes of any man, however much I esteemed him, influence me to do anything that tended to longer hinder or delay this work. Hence I did not hesitate to sign the extension.

When I came in office as Governor, no ray of light had pierced the great tunnel, no train of cars had crossed the mountains. Before I go out, I hope to be borne on a train through the tunnel, over the mountains, along the valleys and into Cherokee. This result, however little I may have contributed to it, will richly repay me for all the misrepresentation and abuse to which I have been subjected, and for all the anxiety and trouble I have endured.

Much has been said and written about the agreement entered into on the 25th day of May between the commissioners and the Boston syndicate. It was of this agreement that Commissioner Vance was speaking when he said: "The paper, when signed, was left with Governor Jarvis (a copy perhaps) with the understanding, as soon as the money was deposited, a tender of it, with a copy of the agreement, would be at once made and delivered. That this was not sooner done was certainly not my fault, nor the fault of Mr. Best, for he deposited the money within ten days." This is the third and last extract I shall make from his address. The inaccuracies in this statement of the commissioner are, first, that the paper was left with me; secondly, that a copy of it was; thirdly, that there was an understanding that a copy of it was to be sent to the assignees; and, fourthly, that the money was deposited within ten days. The corrections I make in these statements are, first, the paper was not left with me; secondly, a copy of it was not left with me; thirdly, there was no understanding that a copy of it should be made and sent to the assignees; and fourth, the money was not deposited within ten days. In support of these corrections I make the following statements: The paper, when signed, was delivered to Mr. Best, and, so far as I know and believe, has all the time been in his possession. Before I signed, I had my clerk to make a copy of the paper for myself, which I kept for my own use; but this, I think, was unknown to Commissioner Vance till the first of August, and I think unknown to the others present except to Maj. Dowd. Anyhow, it was not left with me in the sense used by the commissioner, but was made by my clerk without any understanding of any kind, and without any purpose whatever, except for my own use. It has been an invariable rule with me to preserve a copy of any letter, telegram or paper of any kind I have ever signed, sent or received, in any way connected with the Western road, and these copies are all in their proper places. In taking a copy of this paper, I was simply observing that rule. There never was a word said about sending a copy of this paper to the assignees till the first day of August, and then it was first suggested by myself. At the conference at Morehead City, on the first of

August, it was agreed to make a formal tender to the assignees
of the $250,000 deposited with the commissioners. The question
then arose as to the particular manner in which it should be
done. I suggested that the proper way to do it was to send the
assignees a copy of the agreement of the 25th of May, and to say
to them that if Best and associates complied with their agreement we would, in good faith, comply with ours, and this I allege
was the first time that any suggestion was ever made to send
the assignees a copy of this paper. I then told him I had a copy at
my office, which I took at the time it was signed, but that I supposed we could get the original from Mr. Best, as he was then in
the hotel. We got the paper from Mr. Best and a copy was made
and sent. The deposit was made on the 11th of June, seventeen
days after the signing of the paper, instead of less than ten.
This is, however, unimportant, except to show the inaccuracy of
the commissioner's memory on these questions.

As before stated, there has been much discussion of this 25th
of May agreement. The assignees and their active friends have
labored to make some capital out of it. While I avow my full
share of the responsibility of that paper and have been ready at
all times, and am ready now to perform all that it requires of
me, I protest against the construction and direction attempted
to be given to this paper by the assailants of the commissioners.
The words used in this paper, like those used in most other paper
writings, may be distorted and made to give the agreement a
meaning that was never intended and which does great injustice
to the parties to it. There has been a studied effort in this case
by totally perverting the meaning of the paper to bring odium
upon the commissioners. I do not think the thought ever occurred to the commissioners at the time they signed the paper
that they were doing an act in the slightest degree improper or
censurable, and I now declare they have been unjustly criticized.
The purpose of the commissioners was to serve the State, but to
do nothing inconsistent with her honor and good faith. This will
more fully appear by a recital of what took place at the meeting of the 25th of May, at which this paper was signed. This
meeting was held in the afternoon at the Executive office in the
city of Raleigh, the three commissioners, Mr. Best and his attorneys, Messrs. Gatling, Dowd and Henderson,[172] and Mr. Sprague, of New York, and Messrs. Coleman, Denny and Carruth of

---

[172]Unable to identify.

Boston, of his associates, being present. They declared the purpose of this newly formed syndicate to be to lease the Atlantic and North Carolina Railroad, to build a road from Goldsboro to Salisbury, and to secure and complete the Western North Carolina Railroad, and thus open an important line of railway, running east and west from the sea to the western boundary of the State and beyond. They declared their ability to carry out this project in its entirety, and their willingness to put up collaterals as a pledge of their good faith. The question was then asked me direct if I would favor such a scheme. I answered without a moment's hesitation, yes. I was then told that there were two obstacles to be over come: one, to obtain a lease of the Atlantic and North Carolina Railroad, and the other to obtain the possession of the Western North Carolina Railroad, and I was asked if I would help overcome these difficulties. My reply was, "When you give me safe ground to stand upon." I was then asked what I meant by "safe ground to stand upon." I replied that for the lease of the Atlantic and North Carolina Railroad they must put up collaterals to such an amount that in no event could there be any loss to the company or the State, and that they must then show by work and labor done their purpose and ability to build the road from Goldsboro to Salisbury, and then fully satisfy me of their ability to complete the Western road. "When you have done these things," said I to them, "I will write a letter as Governor, as commissioner and as a citizen, to the assignees, begging them to turn over the Western road to you." Commissioner Vance instantly said, "Yes, and I will go and carry it." Soon after this, we all went to the Yarborough, and there the discussion turned upon what terms I would impose for the lease of the Atlantic and North Carolina Railroad. After some deliberation, I announced my *ultimatum*. The terms I imposed were considered hard and were not at first accepted, and the whole thing looked as if it would break up. I was appealed to by the North Carolina friends of the enterprise to modify the terms. Commissioner Vance suggested to me that I was driving a hard bargain and that I might safely let up a little. But I told them all that for the lease of the Atlantic and North Carolina Railroad I alone would be held responsible, and that I intended to see that a safe bargain was made, or it would not be leased. After some delay the terms were accepted, and the memorandum of the 25th of May was then prepared by Major Dowd in accordance with these suggestions, and was signed by the commissioners. The most casual reading of the paper was given when presented for signature, for it was at once apparent that it embodied the general features agreed upon in the afternoon and evening conferences, no special attention being paid to the language used. However, upon a critical examination of the words used by the draftsman, it seems to me that any man seeking to get at the true intent and meaning of the commissioners could not, in common fairness and impartiality, reach any other conclusion than that suggested by the facts as herein set out, to–wit, a promise on the part of the commissioners to aid in a voluntary "surrender and reconveyance" of the road to the Boston syndicate. Can they be justly censured for making such a promise? I think not. The Boston syndicate promised to do all for the Western road that the assignees did, and, in addition to that, to build some hundred and fifty miles of new road through the heart of the State, along her best water powers, from Goldsboro to Salisbury, and to operate this whole line in the interest of our own cities and towns. No one can say that the completion of such a line of road will not greatly add to the prosperity of the State and the good of her people. As the Western road was a necessary part of this line, I had no hesitation in promising to do all in my power to "procure a surrender and reconveyance" of this road to the Boston syndicate as soon as I became satisfied by tangible evidence that there were to be no more failures. I believed, and so often expressed myself, that if the Boston syndicate pushed the work on the Midland road with vigor, so as to command by their works the confidence of the people of the State and the confidence of the assignees, it would not be long before the assignees would agree to reconvey the road to the Boston syndicate, upon being repaid in full. But it was never any purpose of mine, however, to undertake to hasten this result by violating or withdrawing my agreement I had made with the assignees for an extension of time or by dealing unjustly with them in any way. I had no idea, as is well known to my associates and to the attorneys of the Boston syndicate, with whom I had repeated conferences, to declare the contract of the Western road void or to stop the work thereon; but I did intend to do what I could, as soon as I become entirely satisfied as to the good faith and ability of the Boston syndicate, to substitute it in the ownership of the Western road for the Richmond and Danville syndicate upon terms just and fair to both. This I felt I could do with service to the State and without dishonor to myself. This, I think is in harmony with a fair construction of the agreement of the commissioners as set forth in their agreement of the 25th of May.

I know of no reason why the paper was not made public. There certainly was no desire on the part of the commissioners for it to be kept secret nor understanding that it should be done. Mr. Best could have published it if he desired at any day. There was no reason why the commissioners should either keep it secret or publish it. They had done nothing improper and therefore had no reason for it to be kept secret. Nor did they have any reason to publish it, because their promise was contingent upon the syndicate doing three things, and as they might never be done they might therefore never be called upon to act. The three things to be done by the syndicate were, first, a deposit of a sufficient sum of money to reimburse the assignees; secondly, to procure the lease of the Atlantic road; and thirdly, to prosecute the work with vigor on the Midland road from Goldsboro to Salisbury. The first of these was done on the 11th day of June, and the second on the first day of July. In fact, there was no secret about it, for much of the substance of it was published in The News and Observer on the 31st of May. Just here I will state a fact which I am sure Col. Buford will confirm. I had a long conversation with him on the 24th of June while on this tour of inspection about the road. I expressed to him my desire to see it a part of the Midland scheme, and asked him then to agree to reconvey it to the Boston syndicate if they pushed on to Salisbury, upon being paid for all their expenditures with interest and reasonable compensation. After some hesitation he declined to recommend such an agreement to his friends. In this conversation he asked me if I thought Mr. Best's new syndicate had any money. I told him that they had deposited with the commissioners $250,000, and told him substantially the purposes and conditions upon which the deposit was made, but did not go into details nor tell him of any written agreement, so that he knew as early as the 24th of June of this deposit of money, although not formally tendered to him.

In this paper so far, I have been speaking chiefly of my conduct as a commissioner and of my purposes as such. I wish, in conclusion, to say a word as to my more important and extensive duties as Governor, touching railroads and investments in them in North Carolina. I do not believe there is any cause to apprehend danger from them to the people. I believe they, like other property and persons, are subject to law and that they can be made to obey the law. I declared this belief in strong terms in my inaugural address, and I have had no reason to modify this opinion, but on the contrary, much to strengthen me in it. I at the same time urged the creation of a railroad commission, composed of three of our best citizens, as the best known method of enforcing the legislative will. For causes which need not now be given, the measure did not become a law, although both Houses by very large majorities favored it As some are now favoring the proposition who were then opposed to it, I hope to see such a law passed when the Legislature convenes again. I have no doubt if it is done, that the railroads will conform to the law and abide by the decisions of the commissioners; and if any of them refuse, I have no doubt about the power of the State to compel them. So that unjust discriminations and exorbitant and improper charges exist, in my opinion, because the legislative branch of the government has failed to provide the proper legislation; for there is in the Legislature ample power to protect the people. Believing that the roads are thus subject to such laws as may be passed for their government, I at the same time believe they are entitled to the protection of the law, and by no act of mine shall they ever be unlawfully deprived of it. Their property and their rights of property, are entitled to the same protection and to the same methods of adjudication that other property and other persons enjoy. I wish to emphasize this, because I have and do invite capital to come into the State and build new roads for us. In many sections they are greatly needed and the people are anxious for them. They must be built, if at all, largely by foreign capital, and I desire to give to this capital the most positive assurance of security and protection.

A&H—GP

J. D. Imboden to Thomas J. Jarvis

Bristol, Tenn, Dec 5th 1881

Your letter of the 1st inst: reached me here this morning— The copy of printed proposition has not yet come to hand. I thank you for your attention—

It is not probable that our company will be competing bidders for the C.F.&Y.V. road—Last winter they would have bought the State's interest at the price named in the proposition I had the honor to submit to you. But before the necessary legislation could be had such manifest opposition existed on the part of the road officials, and the private stockholders, that I greatly doubted the wisdom of a purchase of the State's interest, with the certainty of discord in the future management, and so advised our company. To still further embarrass the purchase, if we should attempt it, the C.F.&Y.V. Compy loaded itself by purchase, as we learned through the newspapers, with another road in even worse financial condition than itself, and which never could have become of value of to us—[173] Under these circumstances our company has not considered the question of purchase for many months, but kept steadily at work to ascertain the best *possible* attainable route from this place to the Eastern foot of the Blue Ridge, knowing very well that thence to the sea a very direct and easy route could be had—The practicability of our mountain line was demonstrated some months ago, but our able & cautious Engineer Capt. Dwight suggested an exhaustive examination of other possible routes over the worst part of the line—The company approved his recommendations, & he has been thus engaged since August, and is drawing his work to a conclusion— We shall have a line across the mountains that must become the *trunk* for several of your roads in the Eastern part of the State to reach the West. I have no doubt the proposed purchasers of the C. F. & Y.V. road will find it to their advantage to connect with us somewhere on the upper

---

[173]General opinion in Wilmington was that Imboden represented the Richmond and Danville Railroad, and that if he and his associates controlled the Cape Fear and Yadkin Valley Railroad they would direct traffic away from Wilmington and into Virginia. Largely because of pressure from Wilmington, the directors of the latter railroad temporarily decided in April, 1881, against selling or leasing their line. Instead they sought to reinvigorate it by purchasing and adding to it the Fayetteville and Florence Railroad. *News and Observer*, March 7 and April 9, 1881.

Yadkin in Wilkes or Caldwell—So with the Chester & Lenoir road—So with the Fayetteville & Winston road, & even Mr. Best and his friends may find their easiest way out of the toils of the Clyde Syndicate, by a junction with us.

Thanking you again, I close by saying that I shall probably be in Raleigh shortly, but not likely on the 19th

A&H—GP

T. S. Kenan to Thomas J. Jarvis

Attorney General's Office
Raleigh Dec. 9th 1881.

Your letters of a recent date[174] addressed to me upon the management of railroads operating in this state presents a subject of importance, and I have given it such consideration as I could, in view of the other pressing duties of this department. My reply is now respectfully submitted:

I will first call attention to acts of assembly incorporating railroad companies, but will cite only extracts of such parts of their provisions as undertake to prescribe rates of charges for fare and freight. I have confined myself to this particular branch of the subject, because I apprehend from the general tenor of your communication that it constitutes the main ground of complaint. The amendments to these various acts have not generally been brought within the limit of my research, as it is believed they have made no substantial change and do not materially bear upon the question.

The acts prescribing rates for railroads now in operation are as follows:

Raleigh & Gaston—Act of 1850—51 ch. 123 § 9, (and act of 1852-53) prescribes a charge for transportation, not exceeding 6 cents a mile for passenger and 8 cents per ton per mile for freight.

Wilmington & Weldon—Act of 1833, sec. 26, page 344 of second volume of Revised Statutes: Not exceeding 6 cents a mile for passenger, and 9 cents a mile per ton of 2000 pounds of freight

Atlantic, Tennessee & Ohio—(Charlotte & Statesville) Act of

---

[174]See Jarvis' two letters to Kenan of August 20, 1881, in this volume.

1854-55 Ch. 227 sec. 16—Not exceeding 5 cents a mile for passenger; and 35 cents per 100 pounds on heavy articles and 10 cents per cubic foot on articles of measurement for every 100 miles.

Piedmont (Greensboro & Danville) Ordinance of the Convention of Feby 8, 1862, pages 91, 92, sec. 13, 14. At such charges as may be fixed by majority of board of directors, provided they shall have no power to discriminate on either freight or travel against the North Carolina railroad or roads in North Carolina connected with it.

Wil. Col. & Augusta (Wilmington & Manchester) Act of 1846-47, ch. 82 sec. 29, Not exceeding 6 cents a mile for passenger; and 50 cents per 100 pounds for each 100 miles on heavy articles and 15 cents per cubic foot on articles of measurement.

Char. Col. & Augusta (Charlotte & South Carolina) Act of 1846-47, ch. 84 sec. 15—Regulated by directors; but subsequently the act of 1848-49 ch. 89 sec. 10 prescribed not to exceed 6 cents a mile for passenger, and 50 cents per 100 pounds and 15 cents per cubic foot for every 100 miles. And the same applies by act of special session of 1868, ch. 8, to the *Atlantic & Charlotte Air Line.*

Seaboard & Roanoke—Act of 1832, 2 Rev. Stat. page 318, prescribes 6 cents a mile for passenger and 8 cents per ton a mile on freight; but by the subsequent act of 1836–37, several material changes were made, among them the rate per ton a mile on freight was reduced to 4 cents.

Spartanburg & Asheville—(Greenville & French Broad, consolidated) Act of 1854–55, ch. 229 sec. 13. Regulated by company. But by subsequent act of 1873–74, ch. 83 sec. 3, no greater discrimination than 25 per cent between rates for local and through freights.

Petersburg & Weldon—Act 1830 of the Virginia legislature, adopted by our act (2 Rev. Stat. page 285) with certain modifications and additions. Rates prescribed during time of construction, afterwards to be fixed by "board of public works." Sec. 18. Va act. And it was further provided by section 8 of our act that the provisions should be subject to be altered, amended or modified, except so much thereof as prescribed rates of freight.

North Carolina railroad—Act 1848–49 ch 82 sec. 18. Charges for fare and freight regulated by majority of board of directors. And the same provision is made for the following companies, to wit, Carolina Central (W.C.&R) act 1854–55 ch. 225 sec. 17; Western North Carolina, act 1854–55 ch. 228 sec. 25; Raleigh & Augusta (Chatham) Act 1854–55 ch. 230 sec. 18; North Western (Salem) Ordinance of Convention 1868 ch. 17 sec 11; Oxford & Henderson, act 1870–71 ch. 150 sec 1; Norfolk & Eliz. City, act 1869–70 ch. 18 sec 8; University Road, act 1868–69 ch. 22 and act 1879 ch. 100; Atlantic & N.C. act 1852–53 ch. 136 sec. 17; Midland, act 1872–73. ch 54 sec. 17; Chester & Lenoir, act 1872–73 ch. 35, and act 1871–72 ch. 130.

It is stated in your excellency's letter, "that it is of importance to the people that the railroads in the state be subject to such laws as the general assembly shall choose in its wisdom to pass for their control"; and in this connection it may not be inappropriate to refer to statutes now in force bearing upon this subject:

The act of 1874–75 ch. 140, to prevent discrimination in freight tariffs provides in substance as follows:

1. That it shall be unlawful to charge for transportation of freight over a railroad, a greater amount of toll than shall be charged for an equal quantity of the same class of freight, transported in the same direction, over any portion of same road of equal distance; and any company violating this section shall forfeit two hundred dollars for each offence *to any person su[e]-ing for the same.*

2. Or to allow freight to remain unshipped for more than five days after receipt of same, unless otherwise agreed upon, and the company violating this section shall forfeit twenty five dollars for each of the freight remains unshipped as aforesaid, *to any person su[e]ing for the same.*

3. As amended by the act of 1879 ch. 237. That nothing in this act shall prevent a company from making special contracts with shippers of large quantities of freight, to be of not less in quantity of bulk than one car load.

And section 2 of said chapter 237, prohibits the pooling of freights or allowing rebates on same, and any person violating this section shall be guilty of a misdemeanor, and on conviction be fined not less than $1000, or imprisoned not less than twelve months.

The act of 1879 ch. 182, prescribes a penalty of $50 for refusing to receive freight, and makes it the duty of every transportation company to keep posted at depots a list of its charges for freight, such charges not to be increased without giving 15 days notice, under a penalty for violation of not less than $50, nor more than $100.

The act of 1874–75, ch. 202, amended by act of 1879 ch. 281, provides that the chief officer of railroads or other works of in-internal improvements in which the state owns an interest, shall make an annual report to the board of internal improvement to be submitted to the legislature—person failing to report guilty of misdemeanor—suit to be brought against persons so failing, on application of board of internal improvements, to whom authority is also given to have the affairs of any such road investigated by a member of the board, who shall have power to send for persons and papers, administer oaths &c—sheriffs to execute summons as in other cases—refusal to obey summons a misdemeanor.

From these statutes it appears that the remedy for a violation of their provisions is given to the party aggrieved, and also by indictment in the superior court. A case arose under section 2 chapter 240 of the acts of 1874-75 where a railroad company was sued for the penalty incurred in allowing freight to remain unshipped more than five days after receiving it, and the court held the act to be constitutional and the plaintiff entitled to recover. *Branch* v. *Wil & Wel. R R Co,* 77 N.C. 347.

The act of 1866–67 ch. 105 empowers directors of railroads in the state to enter into agreements with each other to secure through freight and travel, without expense of transfer of freight, or breaking bulk, and in section 2, authorizes the directors of the Western N.C. Railroad to connect with the roads from Tennessee and Georgia, but in making such connections, no discrimination shall be made against railroads or sea ports of this State, and that the terms upon which said connections are made shall be approved by the legislature.

And under a resolution, ratified on the 14th of December 1865 (Acts 1865–66, page 11) it is provided that in the event of any contract having been entered into by any railroad company in this state with any person or company, whereby preferences or exclusive rights of transportation, either in priority or arrangements, are given to such person or company, suit may be brought against the company for a forfeiture of its charter.

In the contract of lease of the North Carolina railroad entered into on the 11th day of September 1871, to be found in the legislative documents of 1871–72—cod. no. 27—, the lessees covenant to pay $260,000 annual rent, to deposit bonds to secure the same, in the first national bank of Charlotte or in such other banks as may be approved by the directors of the North Carolina road, and on failure to comply with the above, possession of the road may be resumed by the lessors on notice required by the contract; also to keep the road in good repair with bond for faithful performances of same; and not to establish local fare or freight at higher average price from station to station, than the average rate for same as established by the North Carolina road on September 1st 1869.

General Order No. 88 referred to in your letter, I am informed by your excellency was revoked, and did not go into practical operation.

It is provided by the general statutes that a suit may be brought against a corporation to vacate the charter and annul its existence, whenever it shall exercise a franchise or privilege not conferred by law. Bat. Rev. ch. 17 sec. 362 *et seq*; ch. 26, sec. 39; Rev. Code ch. 26 sec. 5 and 25. And upon a judgment of dissolution the corporate body is continued only to enable the company to settle its affairs, and not to carry on the business for which it may have been established. After collecting debts owing to it, selling its property, and paying its creditors, it is provided that the surplus be distributed among the stockholders or persons entitled thereto. Where the franchise and property of a corporation are sold under an execution at the instance of creditors, the corporation in the hands of the purchaser retains the same powers &c, as before such sale. Rev. Code ch. 26 sec. 9–13; *Gooch* v. *McGee,* 83 N. C. 59. By the act of 1874-75 ch. 198, the legislature directed suit to be brought to dissolve the Roanoke Navigation Company. After providing for the appointment of a receiver, a sale, &c, it makes the purchaser a new corporation under any name mentioned in the deed of conveyance, and specially provides that the corporation thus created shall succeed to the rights of the old. By direction of this act a suit was brought and a judgment of dissolution obtained. Sec *Attorney General* v. *Roanoke Nav. Co,* 84 N. C. 705. There is also a provision in section 14 of the act incorporating the Raleigh & Gaston road, to the effect, that whenever the legislature may be of opinion that the charter shall have been forfeited, it may by joint resolution direct a writ to issue returnable before the Supreme Court calling upon the company to show cause why the charter shall not be forfeited. (I suppose however that now the remedy would be the same as in like cases under the general law.)

I have collated these statues from time to time, as other duties permitted, to show what the legislature has done in respect to this subject and the result of these different modes of procedure against corporations.

To constitute the basis of a suit to dissolve a corporation, vacate its charter, and annul its existence, for exercising a franchise or privilege not conferred by law, it is necessary that the allegations of cause of forfeiture should be specific as to time, place and overt acts, as was said by the late Chief Justice Ruffin in the case of *Attorney General* v. *Petersburg RRCo*, 6 Ired 456. This was a suit to vacate and annul the charter of the defendant company, and it is declared by the Chief Justice in delivering the opinion of the court, "that when the legislature required the grounds to be set forth, on which the forfeiture is alleged, nothing less was meant, than that the information, like an indictment, should state with certainty to a common intent the facts and circumstances which constitute the offence." And it is also essential to a successful prosecution of the same that the allegations must be established by proof. I take it that this particularity is required perhaps on account of the consequences which result from a judgment dissolving a corporation, as referred to above. When the facts necessary to meet these requirements of the law shall have been furnished, I shall deem it my duty to give the same a fair consideration and to institute suit in cases affecting the public interest. To extend the investigation to obtain the facts of any particular case and proof to sustain them, would impose me a labor so great, as to seriously interfere with the proper discharge of the duties of this department. It will be observed by reference to the act of 1875, above cited, that the board of internal improvements are clothed with certain powers in investigating the affairs of any road in which the state owns an interest. Whether these powers should be extended so as to include all railroads in the state, or whether authority should be given to any other person or commission to send for persons and papers to make a preliminary examination into their management upon complaint made, are questions for legislative consideration.

While I think the beneficial character of railroads is universally recognized, and that investments in these and other enterprises ought to be encouraged, yet at the same time it is important that such regulations for their management should be matured as will prevent their being operated to the injury of the people of the state; and that the same should be reasonable in themselves, and subservient to the public good. Additional legislation if any should be thought necessary framed upon this basis, might conduce to the welfare of the public, and work an injury to no class of business, whether conducted by individuals or corporations; but its particular character I cannot anticipate, nor is it a proper subject for me to enter upon. Of that, the legislature after receiving the recommendations and suggestions of your excellency, will be the judge.

Thomas J. Jarvis to the News and Observer[175]

Raleigh, N. C., December 12, '81

I see in your paper of a recent date a report of the proceedings of a meeting of the citizens of Chatham county at which certain resolutions were passed condemning my action as one of the commissioners of the Western North Carolina Railroad.

I recognize the right of the citizen to criticise and, if he chooses, to condemn the conduct of his servant. This right is a part of the foundation upon which our system of government rests, and its exercise must never be denied or abridged. It is also essential that the time shall never come when it will be considered indelicate or improper in a public officer to respectfully show the people, if he can, that they have been misled by the information upon which they acted. The truth is what the people want, and this they will, sooner or later, have. The sooner they get it, the better. Give them this, and they never err in their judgment. Sometimes they go astray because they act upon information and statements which they believe to be true, but which are in fact false. In this way the people are often misled, but as sure as day follows night, truth will light up their pathway and they will ultimately reach correct conclusions and form infallible judgements. All this I verily believe, and believing it, I have never been afraid to submit any question, in which I felt that truth was on my side, to the people. Nor am I afraid of the verdict of the people of Chatham on my conduct when they get all the facts—the truth, the whole truth, and nothing

---

[175]Taken from the *News and Observer*, December 14, 1881.

but the truth in the case. It is to furnish these facts upon which they may form their more matured judgment that I address you this communication.

It will, no doubt, be remembered that in the early winter of 1880 Mr. Best came to Raleigh to negotiate a purchase of the Western North Carolina Railroad. He came with the most pronounced assurance of his ability. He was antagonized by a very strong and a very respectable sentiment in the State.

The Mud Cut circular, conceived in a spirit of spite and issued in secresy, [sic] full of misrepresentations and mischief, created in the State a condition of things which made the future of the Western North Carolina Railroad very uncertain, to say the least of it. The proposition of Mr. Best to buy and complete the road without further cost to the State, coming right upon the heels of the Mud Cut boom, precipitated upon me a condition of things which required me to trust him. I was cautioned in many ways not to do it. I felt that the best interest of the State required me to do it. I did it. The road was sold to him. He then made a speech, and, like his Pittsboro speech, it was taken down by his own shorthand reporter. He told us that in less than sixty days he would be at work, and I felt that I had done well and that all was safe. Time wore on and nothing was done by this "railroad builder," as he styles himself. On the 21st of May, only eight days before the expiration of his [contract he said that] his associates refused to organize [and that this][176] meant no good to the State or himself and that he wished to separate from them; that he could find several gentlemen in all respects more desirable, and that, free to act, he was satisfied a few days would suffice to put him in position to pay the State its disbursements and vigorously to begin work. This letter was sent all the way from New York by special messenger, and contained a request that myself and co–commissioners give our consent to his associates assigning their interests. We replied that we did not have the authority either to consent or object and that we refused to do either. They did, however, assign their interests, and it turned out afterwards that his new and more desirable associates were Messrs, Buford, Clyde and Logan. They became his new associates and furnished the money that saved the contract from failure and whatever consequence that might have attended such failure. Mr. Best and his new associates soon

---

[176]Manuscript mutilated.

quarreled. Whose fault it was I do not know. Their quarrel still progresses. After Mr. Best and his new associates quarreled and separated, he came to me with his complaints, statements and explanations. I positively declined to take any part in his quarrel, on the one side or the other. The fight was transferred to the Legislature and still I kept silent, although assailed and maligned day after day. So much for his first scheme; now to the second.

In 1872 73 a very liberal charter was granted by the Legislature of North Carolina to the Midland North Carolina Railway Company. Sometime last fall (I think it was) Mr. Best got control of this charter. During the winter he repeatedly told me it was his plan to lease the Atlantic and North Carolina Railroad and to extend it to Salisbury. He said he was advised by the best of counsel that he could compel, through the courts, a reconveyance of the Western road, and that he would soon begin a suit for that purpose. The subject about which he wished to talk with me was the lease of the Atlantic road. I listened to him patiently, attentively and respectfully. I did not say to him, as I might have done, "Mr. Best, 'a burnt child dreads the fire.' You came to me less than a year ago to buy the Western road, with the strongest assurance one man could give another of your ability to do anything you promised. I trusted you, although warned not to do so. I even took the responsibility to call the Legislature together. You left me after the Legislature acted, telling me you would soon be back in full force; that soon I would see car load after car load of picks, spades, shovels, wheelbarrows, powder, dynamite, drills, etc., etc., passing by Raleigh soon to be followed by tons of steel rails, all on their way to the Western road, for you intended to bring them in at Morehead and take them up the North Carolina Railroad that the people of the State might see them. I looked for their coming; I listened for the news of their coming, and I looked and listened in vain. Instead of that the air was full of rumors, and day after day I was asked, 'When is he coming?' My friends grew timid; my enemies grew bold. I inquired, 'What is the matter?' and you replied, 'All will be right.' Meanwhile the contract was executed and then we all took fresh courage. You returned at once to New York, leaving behind you the most positive assurances of your speedy return, ready to commence work in good earnest. You did not come, but painful rumors of your failure did. Each day added to the embarrassments as day after day passed and no Best, no implements, no rails, no money came. I asked some of my friends and telegraphed to others to go to New York to see what was the trouble and to aid in removing it, if possible. They went and they found you, as they told me, utterly broken down. You appealed to them for help and they responded, some in one way and some in another. Several thousand dollars in cash had to be raised at once to save the contract, and the floating debt, amounting to $30,000 more, had to be paid off. Right there in the great city, the money centre of this continent, the city in which you 'have been able to command hundreds of dollars by a few hours' labor,' you appealed to those friends of mine to help you raise that sum. Even in this crisis you would not risk one dollar of your own money to fulfill your contract to the State and to redeem your promises to me. I was in great danger, the Western road in a critical condition and the best interest of the State in peril, and all because you failed to keep your promises. No, Mr. Best, I cannot trust you again: 'a burnt child dreads the fire.'" I say I might well have talked this way to him, and, had I "consulted my own interest," I would have done so. I did not do it because I did not think of my own interests. It was alone the interest of the State to which I looked. I thought I saw in Mr. Best a man full of energy, of fine intelligence and an unconquerable will—just such a man as would undertake great enterprises and do much for them if he did not accomplish them. I was willing to trust him a second time because his scheme looked to the development of the State, and I felt it my duty to encourage it no matter what the risk to myself. Effort after effort was made to repeal his Midland charter, but I stood by him and his charter, determined to give him another chance.

The Legislature adjourned about the middle of March. Mr. Best left the city about that time. It may have been a short while before. I heard nothing more of his Midland scheme till the middle of May. On the 30th of April, when the extension was granted on certain conditions to be subsequently performed by the assignees of Mr. Best, it was not known to me that Mr. Best would ever be heard of again in this connection. Nor had I heard of his Boston syndicate when, on the 14th of May, I reaffirmed my action as one of the commissioners of the 30th of April. I was first told of its successful organization by one of Mr. Best's attorneys of the 15th of May, and I then told him I had signed the extension. On the 25th day of May, Mr. Best and some of his Boston friends came to Raleigh and had a conference with the commissioners, and devolped fully their Midland scheme. This was the first time that Mr. Best exhibited any ability to go forward with it. I was very favorably impressed with the gentlemen he had with him. I was asked if I would give their scheme my endorsement. After alluding to Mr. Best's former failure so delicately that it touched the sympathies of heart and mind I told them I would. When asked if we would help them to get the Western road we told them the commissioners had no power to put them in possession of the road. They replied they knew that, and that it was our moral influence they were after. I told them they could have that as soon as I felt confident of their ability. There was much talk about what would satisfy me.

The result of this talk was the memorandum of the 25th of May. The Midland project had my full sympathy then and it has it now. I would be false to myself, false to my record, false to my State, false to her people and to her best interest, did I withhold from such a scheme anything in my power to push it forward. No misrepresentations of Mr. Best or any of his new–born supporters could sting me into withholding from it any support that I can give it. I have done all for it in that I could, and I utterly deny that I have done anything or failed to do anything inconsistent with my promise of support made in the paper of the 25th of May. In that paper I promised "to use all the means in my power to procure the surrender and reassignment of the interest heretofore conveyed by the State of North Carolina to W. J. Best and others in the Western North Carolina Railroad Company to be made to W. J. Best, W. W. Carruth, D. J. Sprague, W. S. Denny and Lewis Coleman." Before I was required to do anything, the Boston syndicate was required to do three things, to–wit: First, to make a deposit of $250,000; secondly, to obtain a lease of the Atlantic and North Carolina Railroad; and, thirdly, to prosecute the work "vigorously on the Midland road from Goldsboro to Salisbury." The first was done promptly and the second as soon as it could be. Who is prepared to say that the third and by far the most important of the three things has yet been done? It is some hundred and fifty miles from Goldsboro to Salisbury, and up to the Clinton meeting about ten miles, I think, had been graded. It will cost some two millions of dollars to complete the road from Goldsboro to Salisbury. The grading of the ten miles, I suppose, cost ten thousand dollars. Can it be safely said that with this small amount done, in comparison with what remains to be done, the time had come when the commissioners were called upon to act? I think not. In our letter of the 1st of August to the assigners we said: "If they" (the Boston syndicate) "shall continue to vigorously prosecute the work of construction and building said road" (meaning the Midland) "we shall in good faith literally comply with our part of the agreement" (referring to the 25th of May agreement). Have they yet constructed or built a mile of road?

Here I might rest my case. But I concede that they have done as much as they well could do in the time they have had, and that they have complied with the spirit of their agreement. So have I. I did not wait, as I might have done, till they had built and constructed several miles of road, but having faith in those whom I had met, I commenced as early as June my efforts to bring about the reassignment referred to in the agreement. I have steadily pursued that course, using all means that I considered legitimate and proper, because I felt that the success of the Midland scheme in its entirety was of such value and importance to the State as to require me to do it. There is a difference of opinion among many good people as to the propriety of my having made this promise of the 25th of May, as well as a difference of opinion as to whether I have kept it. This difference of opinion, however, like most others, results, I opine, from the difference of meaning given to certain words. In this case, I take it that the words, "all means in our power," furnish the grounds of difference. It may be that it was unfortunate that more definite words were not used. Be that as it may, I have always proposed, and do now propose, to be my own judge of the means I shall use. I am always glad to have the approval of my fellow-men, but I must first of all have the approval of my own conscience. Without that, their approval would be worth but little. In this case I have it most unqualifiedly. I have gone over with myself carefully and in detail all that I have had to do with Mr. Best and his schemes, and I can say of a truth I have not done or said one thing that I did not believe honorable and for the best interest of the State. My conscience does not reprove me, let the tongues and pens of others lash me as they may. But back to the words, "all means in our power" No reasonable man will say they required me to do anything unlawful or immoral. Now the particular "means" which I am censured for not using is my failure to vote for Commissioner Vance's resolution at the

Clinton meeting, declaring the contract of the assignees forfeited and throwing the Western road back upon the State. I
could not do that because I believe it would have been both illegal
and immoral, and, if so, I was not required by my promise to do
it. Why do I say it would have been both illegal and immoral in
me? It would have been illegal, because, on the 30th day of April,
the commissioners gave the assignees four months' extension of
time, conditional upon the assignees doing certain things. These
certain things were done by the assignees as speedily as possible. Had none of the commissioners signed the extension, I
have not the slightest doubt, and never had, that, after the assignees performed their part, a court of equity would have compelled the commissioners to do theirs. But I did sign the extension on the 13th of May, but more formally on the 16th, and
Commissioner Worth on the 15th. The granting of the extension
was on the 13th of April, and not when Commissioner Worth
and myself signed it, nor on the 17th day of November at the
Clinton meeting, as some have supposed. Had I voted with Commissioner Vance at the Clinton meeting I would have been voting, as I believe, to force the State into a lawsuit on the Western
road, in which, after long and expensive litigation, she was, in
my opinion, bound to be beaten. I had no legal right to put the
State in such a position. It would have been immoral in me to
have so voted, because I had time and again specifically promised
that I would give a reasonable extension. I promised Mr. Best,
while he was interested on that side of the question, I would do
it for him, if he needed the time. I promised his assignees that
I would give it to them. I voted for it at the April meeting and
signed it in my own handwriting on the 13th and 16th of May.
It would have been immoral in me to have violated that oft-re-
peated promise. I have never deceived any one in this matter, or
concealed from any one my purpose in reference to it. I have all
the while declared it to be my purpose to stand by the extension, if the assignees continued to perform their part of the
agreement.

I have said the actual granting of the extension was at the
meeting of the commissioners in the city of Raleigh on the 30th
of April, and not when Commissioners Worth and myself signed
the extension, or at the Clinton meeting, when we voted to uphold it. The following paper, unanimously agreed upon by the
commissioners at said meeting of the 30th of April, is, I think,

conclusive on the question. The paper is as follows, the italics being my own:

"The commissioners having considered the application of Buford, Clyde and Logan, assignees of W. J. Best and associates, for an extension of four months' time under the contract in which to complete the Western North Carolina Railroad to Paint Rock and Pigeon River, *and being of opinion the causes set out in said application are sufficient to entitle them to the extension asked for,* it is agreed by us, the said commissioners, that the time be and is hereby extended four months in which to complete said road to Paint Rock and Pigeon River under the said contract; provided, the said applicants shall comply with all the conditions and requirements set out in their said application."

This paper was, as I have said, unanimously agreed to, and was delivered to Colonel Andrews, not signed, but with an agreement that it would be signed by us at our meeting, which was expected to take place two weeks hence, upon the application being reformed in the particulars there agreed upon.

This paper is valuable for another purpose. It shows what the commissioners thought of the merits of the grounds upon which the extension was asked. It shows that, notwithstanding there had been delays on the part of the assignees in pushing the work, still the commissioners unanimously declared "the causes set out in said application are sufficient to entitle them" (the assignees) "to the extension asked for."

Having said this much in explanation of my course as a commissioner, I submit the question at issue to the verdict of that tribunal which I have never yet been afraid to appeal—the people. If they shall say I have erred, I regret it. I did what I thought was right.

One more word and I am done. The Midland road is for North Carolina, and being so, I am for it. It would do much for the development of the State if built. I trust the Boston syndicate will see their way clear to continue the work. If they do, I shall do all in my power, consistent with my ideas of right and the best interest of the State, to make the Western road a part of the Midland system, and no amount of cajoling or abuse can change my purpose.

A&H—GP

Charles Wendell[177] to Jarvis[copy]

New York, Dec 12 1881

I regret exceedingly that I did not see you when you were in this City and now regret all the more that I am unable to visit your State as I intended to do by reason of sickness in my family and the multifarious interests that demand my constant supervision here.

I beg to add that I fully appreciate the great interests at stake in the matter of the proposed Trunk Line and its importance to North Carolina, and to assure you, that when the action of the Commissioners results in a favorable consideration of our proposition, very prominent Capitalists will come forward as connected with the enterprise, able to carry it through.—

They are fully alive to the scheme if certain assurances can be had from your State as also from the other State through which the road is to pass.—

Personally, I have no anxiety upon the Subject, believing your people will aid in every way possible

A&H—GP

H. D. Roberson to Thomas J. Jarvis

Robersonville N. Car.
December 16th 1881

We have commenced work on the Raleigh & Seaboard R. R. that is known as the Williamston & Tarboro R. R. — I have taken the contract from Williamston to Tarboro, to clear off the tract to its former width, and have about one hundred hands at work on said Road bed—I write to know if you can furnish the company of said Road any convict labor when we get to regrading the Road—The parties have not said anything to me about the convicts, but there was a Bill passed the Legislature in its session of 1879–1880—making provisions for some convicts to be turned over to this Road when needed—Should the company need them,

[177]President of the Columbia Fire Insurance Company of New York City, and one of the investors in the New York and Southern Railroad and Telegraph Construction Company, the syndicate interested in buying the state's stock in the Cape Fear and Yadkin Valley Railroad. See Canedo to Jarvis, November 21, 1881.

can you have them or part of them furnished—I want to have the R. R. tract cleared off by the 1st day of January–1882—Please accept thanks for the invitation extended, to visit the Atlanta Exposition—It would have afforded me much pleasure to have gone but my present state of health would not permit me—

A&H—GP

James E. Broome[178] to Thomas J. Jarvis

New York Dec[r]. 23rd 1881

I have a European party who desires to invest for business in some large tracts of low priced Southern land well timbered in part with Cypress or Juniper. A friend has informed me that your state holds such lands in or around the Dismal Swamp. If you have such and will name a *very low price* and give an option on one or two hundred thousand acres to extend four months to give the party an oportunity to Examine the land, I think I can furnish you a cash buyer, and one who will be an acquisition to your state. Excuse me for saying my Father was a North Carolinian. My second wife was the widow of Arthur Macon, and daughter of Col Joseph Hawkins and grand daughter of Nat Macon distinguished in the politics of your state and all names long and favorably known in your state. I am a native of South Carolina and from October 1853 to October 1857 was Governor of Florida. I make these allusions only to introduce my self as a Southern man and a Gentleman. I have been here 15 years and have handled much Southern land but none in your state. If you have lands for sale, I would be pleased to register them on my books aside from the present demand for the Cypress & Juniper.

I am now organizing a department to handle state & Rail Road Bonds and would be obliged to you for a list of your Bonds, that are recognized as valid by your state Government with any suggestions in regard to your impression of their future value.

---

[178]Merchant and planter of Florida, and governor of the state from 1853 to 1857. In 1865 he moved to New York City, where he resided until his death in 1883. *National Cyclopedia*, XI, 378.

A&H—GP

Tyre York[179] *to Thomas J. Jarvis*

Trap Hill NC
Dec 26 1881

Since my arrival home I have taken a good–deal of pains to learn the feelings of the people in regard to the sale of the [C.F&Y.V. RR.] road and I find every body well pleased. It is the universal cry by every one well done so far

And as I heard it spoken of before leaving Ral[e]igh that you might require a *bonus* of Dr Canedo before signing the contract[180] and as it might possible[*sic*] get you into some little trouble I thought as a friend I would make a few suggestions to you. If you should require the bonus and he should refuse to give it he might say and show through friends that he was ready and willing to pay over the $155000. and comply with the contract as agreed upon by the commission and the exaction of a bonus was not thought of and in the event of a failure throw all the responsibility and blame on you

Under the circumstances if I were you I would not require a bonus I would give him a showing and in the event of a failure the blame will rest with him. The people are so extremely anxious about the matter I do hope he will succeed. The people return you their heart felt thanks for the interest you have shown for our end of the road, do the best you can. Keep your eyes wide open every body will look to the results with much anxiety. If any new developments should occur I would be glad to hear from you. Excuse my suggestions I do it as a warm *friend*

A&H—GLB

Thomas J. Jarvis to J. E. Broome

Executive Department,
Raleigh, Dec. 27, 1881

Your favor of the 23rd to hand. The State is the owner of some large bodies of land in the eastern part of the State. These lands,

---

[179]Planter and physician of Trap Hill; member of the General Assembly, 1865, 1870, 1879, 1881, 1887; Democratic representative to Congress, 1883–1885. *Biographical Directory of Congress,* 1,736.

[108]For an explanation, see Vaughan to Jarvis, December 29, 1881, in this volume.

as a general thing, are accessible to water transportation and much of them set with juniper and cypress timber. A great deal of this land, when cleared and well–drained, will be very productive, as the soil is very rich: while other parts of it are worth but little except for the timber. You can therefore see it will not be practicable to fix any price upon it unless we know exactly what it is the party wants to buy. The State Board of Education holds the legal title to these lands and have the power to negotiate for their sale.[181] If there be any probability of a purchase by your party, we will be glad to have some one to examine these lands, and to this end I suggest that you send out an agent.

There is one body, said to contain 300,000 acres, lying in the Counties of Hyde, Beaufort, and Washington and Tyrrell, to which the State still holds the title, which can be bought without any negotiation with the State. The State contracted to sell this body to a party in 1870 for the sum of $50,000.—the State to retain the title till the purchase money was paid.[182] The party paid a part of the purchase money, but has been unable to pay the balance. I am sure the party would be glad to substitute your party in their stead, and the State would not object. I think there are cypress and juniper both on this land.

If you will at any time make your inquiry about the bonds referred to in your letter sufficiently definite to indicate the information you desire, either myself or the State Treasurer will give the desired information with pleasure. If you refer to State bonds alone, I can say now that the only bonds the State will pay are her new bonds, issued since July, 1879, to compromise her debt. These are four per cent bonds, and are marked "Consolidated Debt of the State."

It will give us pleasure to give you any further information in our power on either of the matters referred to in your letter.

---

[181]Article IX, section 4 of the North Carolina Constitution specified that the income from the sale of all swamp land belonging to the state "shall be securely invested and soundly preserved as an irreducible literary fund," the income from which should be used "for establishing and perfecting in this State a system of free public schools, and for no other purposes or uses whatsoever."

[182]By the authorization of an act of the General Assembly of March 26, 1870, the Board of Education sold this land to Samuel T. Carrow and Daniel P. Bible. After paying $5,000, the purchasers defaulted, and the swamp land reverted to the state. "Annual Report of Superintendent of Public Instructions, 1870," *Public Documents, 1870-1871*, No. 6, 318. See also Jarvis to Broome, January 12, 1882, in this volume.

Augustus Summerfield Merrimon (1830-1892) was born in Transylvania County. He studied law, passing the bar in 1853, and practiced in Asheville. An active Whig, he was elected to the House of Commons in 1860. Merrimon joined the Buncombe County "Rough and Ready Guards" on the outbreak of the Civil War. He continued his interest in politics following the war. Though an unsuccessful candidate for governor as a member of the Conservative Party, he succeeded, by a coalition of Republicans and Conservatives, in winning the senatorship from a vote of the two houses of the legislature and served in Congress, 1873-1879.

A&H—GLB

Thomas J. Jarvis to A. S. Merrimon

Executive Department,
Raleigh, Dec. 27, 1881

I feel I would not be doing my duty to the State or her taxpayers did I not request you to protest against the interference
of the Federal Court in the levying and collection of taxes by
the State under her Constitution and upon property in her own
borders. I beg that you will move to have the Logan, Clyde, Buford–Western North Carolina Railroad case,[183] now before Judge
Dick,[184] transferred to the State Courts; and if he refuses, that
a plea be made to the jurisdiction. The more I think of the slap
in the face that Buford, Clyde and Logan have given the State
Judges, the more indignant I get. But there is more involved in
my objection than mere sentiment. Nearly all the railroad property in the State is owned by non-residents. If this action of
Clyde, Logan and Buford is to go unrebuked and to be taken as a
precedent, then, when the State passes any law to regulate these
roads, some non-resident stockholder brings his suit in the Federal Court to render these laws nugatory. I regret to say it, but
it seems to me that the tendencies and disposition of the Federal
Courts look to a constantly increasing jurisdiction over State
matters; and, in many cases, seem to regard their mission to be
to set at naught State laws. I say I regret this, because it is not
subserving the interests of the State or the country at large.

This suit was not brought, I presume, in the name of the W.N.
C.R.R. Co., because, both plaintiff and defendant being residents,
that would have given the case to the State Courts. Buford,

---

[183]The Associated Railways of Virginia and the Carolinas had recently
filed a bill of equity in the United States District Court in Charlotte
against the counties of Burke, McDowell, and Buncombe, and against the
trustees of the Western North Carolina Railroad. Notice was also served
that a motion would be made for an injunction against the collection of
state and county taxes from the Western North Carolina Railroad. The
Associated Railways Company maintained that the title to the Western
North Carolina Railroad, not having passed to them by their fulfillment of
the conditions of their contract with the state, was still in the possession
of the state. *News and Observer*, December 13, 1881. In the Governors'
Papers, dated January, 1882, there are three printed documents relating to
this case. One document consists of the case of the plaintiffs, and the other
two documents relate to the defense. Governors' Papers, not included in
this volume. Eventually the railroad authorities agreed to pay taxes for the
years 1881-1884, on a valuation of $2,250 a mile. *News and Observer*, Febru-
ary 17, 1882.

[184]Robert Paine Dick, federal district judge of North Carolina since 1872.
Dictionary of American Biography, V, 287–288.

Logan and Clyde being non-residents, their names were used to get the case into the Federal Courts.

Do the plaintiffs allege that they are *now* the owners of the interest sold by the State? I read the bill hurriedly, and do not remember how that is. In a letter to the Commissioners, dated Sept. 27th, Messrs. Clyde, Buford and Logan use this language: "In the accomplishment of these arrangements, our interests as derived from the assignment have become so blended with those of others that we no longer have the sole personal control of this property, and therefore cannot properly agree to surrender it without the consent of others, who decline to release their interests."

These are only intended as suggestions. I leave the management of the suit with you with this single request. I desire the defence as complete and vigorous as possible. The plaintiffs, I think, have shown their contempt for our State Courts, and are entitled to no consideration at her hands.

A&H—GP

A. S. Merrimon to Thomas J. Jarvis

Raleigh, Dec. 28th 1881

I am in receipt of your letter of suggestion and instruction in respect to the suit of Clyde, Logan and Buford vs. yourself and others, in Equity in the U. S. Cu Ct. at Charlotte.—I long to assure you that I will constantly endeavor to carry out your wishes as far as possible in the respect you mention. I will submit for your consideration the rough of your answer as soon as I can have a conference with Maj. Graham[185] on the subject.—I fear the Court has *jurisdiction*, as the case is presented, but I think we will be able to make it manifest that Messrs. Clyde, Logan & Buford have no interests in the property of the West N.C.R.R.Co. that entitles them to sue as they seek to do, in the U. S. Cu Ct. or elsewhere.

---

[185]Probably James Washington Graham, lawyer of Hillsboro; member of the Convention of 1868; member of the General Assembly, 1870, 1876, 1907, 1911. Grant, *Alumni History of the University*, 228.

Asa Owen Gaylord[186] to Thomas J. Jarvis
[Telegram]

Plymouth N C 28 Dec, 1881

There is an unprecidented[sic] riot in this town & I am unable
to suppress it by the Civil authority of the County, and Earnestly
request you to order several Military Companies to be here at
the Earliest time possible to suppress it. There are three hundred
Negroes here defying the Law. All are armed with guns. please
do this at once answer.

Ellis Leftridge Vaughan[187] to Thomas J. Jarvis

Sparta N. C—
Dec 29th 81

Before leaving Raleigh you asked my opinion in regards to your
requiring a deposit from Canedo & Co before acting upon the
contract made by the Commissioners You will remember that in
reply to the question I advised that if there would be a special session of the Legislature and the time we gave would not elaps[e]
before the adjournment of the Legislature I thought it would
be well to require the deposit otherwise not On my way home and
since my arrival I find that Public sentiment so universally demands that the parties with whom we contracted should be given
the opportunity to comply with the terms of the contract that I
deem it but a duty that I owe you to give you the information that
gentlemen can to say that I think it would be hard for any one to
justify his act before the public if by demanding the deposit the
parties were to be prevented from moving the time set out in
the Contract in which to pay the ($155.000) I write this merely
as your friend not desiring that it should influence your action
in any way but that you may have all the information I have on
the subject

---

[186]Merchant of Plymouth, and mayor at this time. Branson, *Directory for
1884*, 671; Gaylord to Jarvis, December 31, 1881, in this volume.
[187]Lawyer and farmer of Sparta; member of the Convention of 1875;
member of the General Assembly, 1876–1881. Tomlinson, *Sketch-book*,
50–51. At this time he was a member of the commission authorized to sell
the state's stock in the Cape Fear and Yadkin Valley Railroad. See Jarvis
to Canedo, August 17, 1881, *n.* 108, in this volume.

A&H—GP

Thomas J. Jarvis to David N. Bogart[188]
[Telegram]

317 PM
Greenville N C Dec. 29 1881

Take Your company to Plymouth at once and report to Mayor or Sheriff.[189] Use such force in restoring peace and Law in aid of the civil authorities as may be necessary

A&H—GP

Thomas J. Jarvis to John Whitaker Cotten[190]
[Telegram]

4 PM
Greenville N C Dec 29th 1881

I am just informed that Plymouth is in the hands of an armed mob of Negroes. I have ordered the Washington and Edenton Co's there You are hereby commanded to proceed on land by horse tonight to Plymouth and take command of the troops. Use the military to support the civil authorities in restoring order. Report to me at this place via Washington by courier and telegraph the condition of affairs as soon as you arrive and if anything further is required.

A&H—GP

D. M. Bogart to Thomas J. Jarvis
[Telegram]

Washington N C 29 Dec 1881

Plymouth thirty five miles no way to go except to walk. one third of the members out of town my men are now uniformed have made effort from evry stable to obtain wagons without success

---

[188]Druggist of Washington and captain of the Washington Light Infantry. *Cyclopedia of the Carolinas*, II, 223.

[189]Dempsey Spruill. Branson, *Directory for 1884*, 670.

[190]Constable of Tarboro and lieutenant colonel in the state militia. Branson, *Directory, 1878*, 108; "Adjutant General's Report," *Public Documents, 1881*, No. 20, 13.

A&H—GP

Thomas J. Jarvis to J. W. Cotten
[Telegram]

Greenville N C Dec 29ᵗʰ 1881

Order the Tarboro Company to follow you at once. Provide them with wagons for Baggage and have them to take Boat at Williamston if you can procure one.

A&H—GP

Thomas J. Jarvis to Cyrus Wiley Grandy[191]
[Telegram]

Greenville N C Dec 29 1881

I desire you to go to Plymouth tomorrow to take charge of the Riot investigation. I go over from here. Do not fail to go

A&H—GP

Thomas J. Jarvis to Harry Skinner[192]

[Telegram]

Washington N C 30, Dec. 1881

We get the news that things are quiet We will return as soon as all things are safe.

A&H—GP

Thomas J. Jarvis to G. L. Dudley
[Telegram]

Plymouth N C 30 1881

I arrived here at four P.M. and find that Four men were wounded in Saturdays riot one died today. The Sheriffs posse had made arrests of principal rioters before arrival of troops. Everything now orderly and quiet. Troops will return at once

---

[191]Lawyer of Elizabeth City; member of the General Assembly, 1872. *Cyclopedia of the Carolinas*, II, 141–142. At this time he was solicitor for the first district. Jarvis to Grandy, January 14, 1882.

[192]Lawyer of Greenville; member of the General Assembly, 1891; Populist representative to Congress, 1895–1899. *Biographical Directory of Congress*, 1,529.

A&H—GP

A. O. Gaylord to Thomas J. Jarvis

Plymouth, Dec. 31st 1881

In compliance with your request and as the mayor of the town of Plymouth I have the honor to herewith submit a statement of the events and occurrences commencing on Saturday the 24th day of December 1881, and culminating in an open and armed opposition to the enforcement of the civil law.

In the forenoon of the 24th a fight occurred between one Wise, a white man and a negro named Everett, which was soon quieted. Shortly thereafter a difficulty occurred between two negroes, which was also soon quieted with but little difficulty. Up to this time there was not in my mind, or so far as I have reason to believe in the minds of others, the slightest apprehension of any more serious or grave trouble than those spasmodic disturbances of the peace usually happening about the holidays, when large crowds are gathered together and drinking a little freely. But late in the evening of the same day, and at or about sunset a fight occurred between two negro men in the public streets of the town and in view of the police officer on duty, who promptly arrested one of them and started to carry him before the mayer. The party thus arrested — named Williams — after proceeding a short distance with the officer of police — named Blount — stopped, declared his intention of proceeding no further, seized the stick of the officer and violently and with great force[illegible] it from him. A struggle instantly commenced between the prisoner and the officer. Immediately, as if by a preconcerted movement they were surrounded by a large body of infuriated negroes, who boldly declared that the prisoner should be released and that the law should not be executed. In this perilous situation the officer called for assistance from the few bystanders who were present, other than those seeking to rescue the prisoner. Three or four persons went to the relief of the officer, when a general melée ensued, which I found myself utterly unable by any means in my power to suppress. The result can easily be anticipated, when we remember that on one side was the officer of the law, assisted by not more than half a dozen whites, and on the other a hundred or more negroes, excited by anger, by evil advice and by an over indulgence in drinking. In this conflict, a Mr. Wolfe had the temporal artery

severed; the police officer received a painful wound through the
arm from a pistol shot; a Mr. Arnold was felled to the ground
by a blow upon the head, and a Mr. Butler had his skull broken
in two places. These were all whites. No negro was injured in
the slightest. The prisoner was released, violent threats were
made, and I found myself powerless to preserve the peace, or
enforce the law. The wounds inflicted upon Wolfe, Arnold and
Blount, though painful are not serious. But I regret to say, that
Mr. Butler after lingering unconscious for five days, died on
Friday evening. Anticipating the death of Mr. Butler, I have
made careful inquiry into the circumstance surrounding his
death, and am satisfied that the mortal blow was stricken by one
John Hoskins, a negro; and that he was aided, abetted & assisted
by another negro named Gus Williams. Immediately after the
conflict, John Hoskins fled and has not up to this time been
taken. On the following day, Sunday, a large crowd of negroes,
notably among whom were Gus Williams, Matthew Wilson and
Elias Jennett, well known for their turbulant characters, prome-
naded the principal street of the town, openly, loudly and boldly
expressing their defiance of the officers, both municipal and
county, and declaring that under no circumstances should the
said Gus Williams be arrested. On Monday, Gus Williams applied to me for a warrant against one Henry Wolfe, on a charge
of assault and Battery, which warrant I immediately issued and
caused to be executed. Williams thereupon submitted to arrest
upon the original charge against him. The case was continued
till the 5th of January 1882 for hearing, and both defendants
recognized for their appearance. I did not at that time have the
information regarding his—Williams—complicity in the murder of Mr. Butler. On Monday and Tuesday there were larger
bodies of negroes congregated in the principal streets of the
town, gathered together in knots at the street corners, keeping
aloof from the whites, and plainly showing by their demeanor
their determination to resist the execution of the law to the
end, and by whatever means might be necessary, Under these
circumstances having no force at my command, the sheriff being
absent, and being unwilling to precipitate a difficulty, the result of which could not be foreseen, I did not undertake to make
any arrest, and the negroes made no active demonstration, except such declarations as that they would resist arrest, and if
necessary would tear down the jail building. On Wednesday I
concluded that the time for action had arrived. I therefore is-

sued a warrant for the apprehension of Gus Williams upon the charge of assaulting the officers and for complicity in the wounding of Mr. Butler. The officer succeeded in making the arrest and bringing the prisoner before me. Upon the investigation I ordered the prisoner to be committed to jail to await the result of the wounds inflicted upon Butler, it appearing by the testimony that they were mortal and would cause death. While the investigation was being held a large crowd of negroes gathered in the court room and in front of it, and when the order of committal was entered, declared with loud and angry cries, the order should be changed and that Williams should not be sent to prison. I directed the officer to carry the prisoner to jail. Immediately the mob of negroes, numbering certainly more than fifty led on and encouraged by the afore mentioned Matthew Wilson, Cain Jennett and Elias Jennett, rushed upon the officer, tore the prisoner from his grasp, and protected him until he escaped. Great excitement immediately ensued. The quiet and peaceable portion of the community became greatly alarmed, and a number of influencial gentlemen waited upon me, and declared that if nothing was done for their protection they would be compelled to remove their wives and children to a place of safety. Having no means at my hand to execute the law, to resist mob violence or to protect the lives and property of our citizens, I caused to be sent, on Wednesday night a telegram, asking your Excellency to furnish military assistance for the restoration of peace and order. On the following day sheriff Spruill arrived with a posse hastily summoned from the body of the county. I at once issued warrants against Matthew Wilson, Cain Jennett, Elias Jennett, John Johnson and Albert Nixon. The sheriff with his posse arrested them, and fearing an attack upon the jail here, I caused them to be confined in the prison of Chowan County. The Negro named Gus Williams has absconded and thus far has evaded arrest. I should have notified your Excellency of the facts supervening the sending of my telegram but for the fact that I could not do so before Friday, when it was too late, nor is it to be regretted since the presence of the troops has had, and I trust will continue to have a very salutary effect.

LETTERS FOR 1882

A&H—GP

Thomas J. Jarvis to G. L. Dudley
[Telegram]

Greeneville NC Jan 2 1882

Just returned from Plymouth Left everything quiet I am tired and will rest here until Wednesday unless there is something to call me at once to Raleigh

A&H—GP

A. H. Canedo to Thomas J. Jarvis

New York, Jan 3ᵈ 1882

Meeting Col Fuller at the 5th Ave Hotel on Sunday night (while on his way to Boston) I was surprised to learn that the Assembly was to meet on Monday last. I had been under the impression it was not to meet untill 8th Jan.

It was contemplated by those interested with us in regard to the C F & Y.V. to go down the last of this week, it being impossible to get anyone to move untill after the holidays, though I desired to go earlier. I have prepared a rough draft of a bill which I proposed to submit for action.

I will send it by next mail so that Prest Gray may embody it with his, or so much thereof as may be consistent with his views, and in accordance with the suggestions of such R R men and Capitalists as I have consulted, and particularly with the wishes of the Syndicate of London who have engaged to take the Bonds where issued

I would suggest that the Resolution of the Stockholders of the Western Railroad, of   18
               see page 31 of Charter, be adopted and acted upon in the matter of preparing the way for issuing new bond.

It has been suggested that a new Charter be granted with all the provisions necessary and covering from Wilmington to Fayetteville and all under the new name of the "Atlantic and Cincinnatti" One of the hitches we meet in our negotiations is that our contract calls for the building of a line from Wilmington to Fayetteville for which there is no provision in the Charter, and which of itself makes the contract nil. In regard to the change of name, this had better be done in any event, for if, for instance, we do not enter into any arrangement for the purchase of the Road.

I have accomplished a great work in negotiating for the sale of the bonds under the new name

which piece of work could not be done again by any one else, under a year and not so favorable rates, for, if this arrangement fails, the moneyed Syndicates of Europe (who are, after a fashion, interchangeable) would not reconsider, and besides, the markets of Europe are flooded with R R Schemes going a begging.

but as I fortunately happened to strike a favorable opportunity I followed it up, and presented the matter in such a favorable shape supported by such voluminous testimony, that it interested them exceedingly. And I have been privately informed that, an expert has been or is now on the ground to verify my Statements in detail. He is incog.

Now to sum up, there is, as the results of my years work, a number of parties ready to put up the money whenever the legislation and a suitable contract is had.

I take it for granted that the Assembly will not get down to actual work untill say 10th. and would suggest that no action be taken on R R matters earlier than 15th or 20th.

A&H—GP

J. E. Broome to Thomas J. Jarvis

New York Janny 4 1882

Your favr of 27th December was duly received, and you have my thanks for the attention. There is a tract of land of about 110000 acres said to have been sold at about ten (10) cents per acre which has been returned to the State. My party enquired of me in regard to this tract particularly, and it was this that I had a prospect of placing. Can it be purchased at or about that price?

If you will give me the address of the party with whom negotiations may be opened for the 300,000 acres, I will write him. It may be that I can place that tract with a European Syndicate to whom I am disposing of some large tracts in West Virginia. Should you be able to furnish me maps or descriptions of any tracts owned by the State I shall take pleasure in using efforts for their disposition.

Has your State disposed of all her mineral lands?

A&H—GP

Richard Jordan Gatling[1] to Thomas J. Jarvis

Hartford, Conn. U. S. A.
January 5th 1882

We have the honor to call your attention to the Gatling gun, which fires one thousand shots per minute and is undoubtedly the most effective arm in the world for suppressing mobs &c.

We have sold these guns to nearly all of the principal governments of the world and have supplied them to many of the states, to be placed in the hands of militia, so that in time of peace their use may be thoroughly learned.

For the purpose of quelling or preventing riots the Gatling gun is especially adapted. Some years since a mob was suppressed in Indiana by the mere presence of these guns, and on another occasion a formidable mob, gotten up by Dennis Kearney[2] in San Francisco, was quelled by their presence without bloodshed. Such has been the moral effect of this truly death dealing weapon.

The writer—the inventor of the gun—is a native of North Carolina, and as a matter of pride wishes that the "Old North State" should have some of his guns, and respectfully requests that you order some of them.

The U. S. War Dept. will furnish these guns on your requisition, to apply on the quota due *or to become due* your state out of the annual appropriation made for arming and equipping the militia

We enclose herewith our price list, and trusting you will make your requisition for some of these guns,

---

[1]Originally of Hertford, North Carolina, Gatling had lived in the North since 1844. In 1862 he obtained a patent for the "Gatling gun," and was now president of the Gatling Gun Company of Hartford, Connecticut. *Dictionary of American Biography*, VII, 191–192.

[2]President of the Workingmen's Party of California, a protest movement against various economic and political conditions operating against the well–being of the laboring interests. Kearney and his party are best remembered for their opposition to Chinese immigration. *Dictionary of American Biography*, X, 268–269.

A&H—GP

A. H. Canedo to Thomas J. Jarvis

New York, Jan 9th 1882

I beg leave to inform you that we have this day submitted to you by Adams Express the contract for the purchase of CF&YV RR Stock, duly signed and certified.

A&H—GLB

Thomas J. Jarvis to R. J. Gatling

Executive Department,
Raleigh, Jan. 10, 1882

Yours of the 5th instant was received by me in due time.

I have taken a commendable pride, as a North Carolinian, in your success as the inventor of the "Gatling Gun." It would be a matter of pride with us to have in this State a small battery of these guns; and, at some future time, when our quota of arms due from the Government will justify, we may take the necessary steps to procure one. I believe, however, that we will never have in this State a condition of things that will require them to be used.

A&H—GLB

Thomas J. Jarvis to J. E. Broome

Executive Department,
Raleigh, Jan. 12, 1882

I rather expect that the 110,000 acre tract of land, referred to in your letter of the 4th instant, is the same as the 300,000 acre tract, referred to in my letter and likewise alluded to in yours.

In 1869–70, the Legislature of this State passed an act authorizing the State Board of Education to enter into a contract of sale for all the State lands in the Counties of Hyde, Beaufort, Washington, Tyrrell and Dare for the sum of $50,000. The Board did enter into a contract of sale with a man by the name

of Bible,[3] of the City of New York, and S. T. Carrow,[4] of the
town of Washington, of this State. Under this contract, the title
was not to be made until the lands were paid for. I think about
$14,000. was paid. This is the only tract of land sold by the State
which has not been paid for; and it is of this tract that I expect
you have heard. Mr. S. T. Carrow, I have understood, acquired
whatever interest his partner had; and, I have reason to believe, he would be glad to sell his interest upon easy terms. The
State would be glad to see it taken up by parties able to complete the contract—not so much for the money as for the development of her lands. I have referred to this body of land as
containing three hundred thousand acres. It has never been
surveyed, and it may contain a great deal more: I hardly think
it can be any less.

There are other bodies of State land in this State, the title to
which is in the State Board of Education. Any negot[i]ations for
the purchase of these lands will have to be made with this
Board. The Board has fixed no price upon these lands because
there there has not yet been any very great demand for it.

I shall be glad to give you any further and more definite information that I may have.

A&H—GLB

Thomas J. Jarvis to C. W. Grandy

Executive Department
Raleigh, Jan. 14, 1882

I regretted that you were not able to meet me at Plymouth. I
hope you are now entirely recovered, and that you will be able
to give the riot cases your attention. My desire is that the offen-
ders shall be brought to a speedy trial and, if found guilty, to
merited punishment. An example ought to be made of this case
that will deter others from like conduct.

All of those who were engaged in the riot of Saturday — the
day and time Butler received his wounds — are in law guilty of
murder, and the leaders at least ought to be so indicted. There

---

[3]Daniel P. Bible. Unable to identify.
[4]Samuel Topping Carrow, large landowner and gristmill operator of
Washington. Branson, *Directory for 1884*, 136–138.

ought to be a second indictment against them all for resisting an officer, and a third against all for a riot. There were, as I understand the case, quite a number actively engaged in the disturbance on Saturday.

The trouble on Wednesday I regard as much more serious than the affair on Saturday, although three men were wounded and one other mortally in Saturday's riot. On Saturday, there was likely much drinking, and men may have become involved in the riot upon the spur of the moment who had no *purpose* to violate or resist the law. But not so Wednesday. Their conduct then, in undertaking to brow-beat the Magistrate and in rushing upon the Deputy Sheriff and rescuing the prisoners, is without any mitigation of which I have heard, and showed a spirit of defiance of the law which ought to be rebuked by the law's swift and severe punishment. Their conduct on that day showed a *purpose* to violate the law. I understand there were fifty or more present on Wednesday. Every one there who in any way aided, abetted or encouraged that action of the mob, ought to be indicted, tried and, if guilty, punished.

If I am correct in my view of the whole affair, then there is more work for the Solicitor and the Court growing out of these cases than can possibly be done in one week, and as the regular term of Washington Superior Court only lasts one week, I have thought it advisable for you to have a Special Court for the investigation and trial of these cases. If you concur with me after you have made such investigation of the case as you may desire and will make the application provided for in section 11ᶜ, chapter 17, Battle's Revisal, I will order a Court of Oyer and Terminer to meet some time about the middle of February, so as to get through in time for your circuit to begin. I can send Judge McKoy,[5] who rides the circuit. We can hold the Court and go from there to Currituck. If this course is pursued and the indictments all found and such of the trials had as can be, with justice to the State and defendants, the whole matter can be closed up at the regular term. But if nothing is done till the regular term and then either the State or the defendants are not ready, or a case is removed to another County, it will throw the trials over till the fall, and all the beneficial effects of a prompt action lost.

You will find, when you begin to investigate the affair, that

---

[5] Allmand Alexander McKoy, lawyer of Clinton; member of the General Assembly, 1868; member of the Convention of 1865; Superior Court judge, 1874–1885. Oates, *Story of Fayetteville*, 679.

the testimony is voluminous and conflicting. To sift this mass of testimony, to get just what you want, to prepare the bills, prepare the cases and try them properly, is a work of no small moment. I do not well see how one man can do it alone and do it well. If, therefore, you desire help you shall have it. You can select any one to assist you that you prefer. Maj. [L. C.] Latham was with me at Plymouth and I consulted with him about the matter, but he may not be able to attend the Court. If he is, he will appear with you. If you desire help, however, you had better not depend upon him. In making these suggestions as to help, I beg that you will not think I mistrust your purpose or ability. I do it solely because I know the magnitude of the *work* before you. Nor do I wish you to feel under any obligations to apply for the Court because I have suggested it. After the investigation I made of the case while in Plymouth, I would order the court of my own motion if I had the authority to do so.

I deeply regret the whole affair; but now that it is upon us, it had better be dealt with in a way that it will be the last of the kind. I am glad that it was not so serious as at first reported and that the troops had nothing to do after they arrived but to return home.

The supremacy of the civil law must be maintained and all men made obey her ministers, however humble they may be. Without this, neither life, liberty nor property is secure. It has been my purpose, as the Chief Magistrate of the State, to make every citizen feel that the law will be enforced rigidly and impartially. I want the humblest to feel that the law is always about him to guard and protect him, while he is obedient to the law. I want the strongest to feel that the law is always about him to arrest him and to punish him if he commits crime. In these feelings I am sure you share to their fullest extent, both as a citizen and as an officer.

Nothing will do more to *fix* this in the public mind as the purpose and settled determination of those in authority than speedy trials and certainly punishment. When our laws are so made and their administration is such that the people accept this as the policy of the State and the practice of the Courts, we will be exempt from those two terrible curses — mob law and lynch law.

Pardon the length of this letter and the fact that I indulged so much in these general suggestions. I have strong feelings and convictions of duty to do all I can to have order and law in the State, and when I get to talking or writing about it I hardly know when to stop.

A&H—GP

W. S. Denny to Thomas J. Jarvis

Boston Jany. 19. 1882

Since writing you on the second ultimo[6] concerning our deposit of $250.000 with the Commissioners, your letter of Nov 14th to Mess. W. W. Carruth and D. J. Sprague, receipt of which was delayed a month by lack of delivery in N.Y., has come to hand.

Its contents caused us to carefully consider the whole situation and as the result of such consideration we deem it proper to call for a return of the Certificate of Deposit as provided in the receipt given us by the Commissioners.

Had we more fully realized the situation as we now do, it would in our opinion have been proper long ago to have called for its return — and, we might add, had we preseen the present consideration of things we would have regarded it folly to deposit the check, as the funds could have been converted into interest bearing Securities and thus save a loss to us of some six to eight thousand dollars in interest to the present time, and at the same time afford equal satisfaction and Security to the Commissioners.

It seems from your letter that we misapprehended the situation, or at least that we did not understand it as you did.

When these funds were pledged by us, we believed, as we had been led to, that the Western North Carolina Railroad would be turned over to us in a very short time — a few weeks at most.

It was to ascertain the correctness of our impressions that we availed ourselves of the opportunity to meet the Commissioners on the 25th of May last, for without the Western N. C. Railroad, as you are well aware, we would not for a moment think of investing a dollar in the proposed enterprise. We, of course took the chances of delay when we finally launched into the undertaking, but it was, with the distinct understanding and agreement that the Commissioners would *use all the means in their power* to have the road conveyed to us in time to be used in connection with the Atlantic road so soon as we should get possession of the latter, and we did not count upon any luke–warmness or indifference on the part of our Syndicate, or the Commissioners. Upon these points we felt sure and secure — and

---

[6]Not found.

with these influences committed in our favor, we were willing to take all the chances of delay which would be likely to arise from unwillingness on the part of the Richmond & Danville syndicate to surrender at once. The first of July had been fixed upon as the time, previous to which we should be in possession of the Western N.C Road. We do not feel sure that our interview with the Commissioners, taken by itself, would authorize such a belief, but having such impressions at the outset, we felt that the interview served to strengthen and warrant them.

Subsequently, on the same day, we received from the Commissioners a memorandum of agreement, which, though lacking in precision of dates or means *to be employed*, distinctly stated that the Commissioners "will use all the means in their power" as commissioners and as individuals to procure the surrender &c.

We did not then understand, nor do we now comprehend why, if the road is to be turned over to us, it should not be transferred at once. If money is to be expended in completing the road, why should it be dispensed by those who have no interest in an economical expenditure rather than by those who furnish the money.

Taking such a view of the case is it not reasonable that we should feel assured by the conference with the Commissioners and their written agreement that the representations previously made to us had been fully confirmed. At all events we did feel so, and without further hesitation we proceeded at once to fulfill the requirements of the Commissioners.

The $250.000 was placed at their disposal. The $85.000. in North Carolina Bonds were pledged as required and a lease of the Atlantic & No Carolina road obtained even at a cost of $5.000 per annum in advance of the price named by the Commissioners.

We proceeded "at once to prosecute vigorously the work on the Midland No. Carolina Railway between Goldsboro and Salisbury" thereby literally fulfilling *all* the requirements of the Commissioners.

We did all this in good faith as evinced by a continuation of the vigorous prosecution of the work until we now have over 20 miles of the road ready for the rails — enough of which are now on the way from England to lay 60 miles of road As we write this a telegram announces the arrival at Morehead of one of the vessels.

There seems to be some question whether or not we were entirely justified in assuming that, there was a full understanding that the Western N C Railroad was to be turned over to us at once. It was however so plainly promised us that from our standpoint the question admits of no doubt.

That the Commissioners so understood it at the time is evidenced by the written agreement over their individual signatures — embodied in the receipt for the $250.000 — providing for a return of the funds if the road should not be turned over to us by July 1st — the exact language being "if the object of this deposit shall not be accomplished by July 1, 1881"

It is not our present purpose to utter any complaint at what to us seems an unaccountable delay — trusting still that, tho there may be a difference of opinion as to the proper means to be employed, all are acting in good faith, according to their own individual views, and "using all the means in their power" to procure a surrender to us of the Western North Carolina Railroad at the earliest practicable moment.

In our withdrawal of these funds we desire that it shall be distinctly understood that it shall in no way prejudice our position or delay the delivery to us of the Western North Carolina Railroad — and that we still stand ready, as heretofore, to furnish or call the amount of money expended upon said road under what is known as the Best contract — our only object in recalling the certificate being to save some forty dollars per day in interest. With much esteem I am

A&H—GLB

Thomas J. Jarvis to A. S. Buford

Executive Department,
Raleigh, Jan. 19, 1882

I do not like to play the role of complainer, and I often endure great personal inconvenience rather than complain. But when the inconvenience is one that affects an interest of any portion of the people of the State, whose every interest I am anxious to serve, I cannot shrink from playing this role. The complaint to which I now call your attention I do not think unreasonable, and I therefore confidently expect the cause to be removed as soon as it is made known to you. Col. Andrews is not here, or I would see him about it before writing to you.

There was great trouble in this State last year in getting fertilizers brought into the State to meet the demand. All the lines of transportation were taxed to their utmost capacity and were then unable to do the work required of them. If there is any one interest to which the roads can well afford to make concessions, it is the interest directly affecting the crops. This, I take it you will readily admit. What I shall ask of you is not a concession to that interest, but a simple act of justice.

The way some things should be done is so clearly marked out by nature and the commonsense view that any effort to do them differently entails a loss and often ruinous results upon the man that tries it. Nothing is clearer than that the way for the dealers and the farmers between this point and Goldsboro to get their fertilizers is via Newbern or Morehead City and the Atlantic Road. Any railroad management that shuts up this way is wrong in principle and does a great injustice to the people; and no personal quarrel between the managers of the different roads can justify it. To bring these goods all around by West Point and the R.&D. is impracticable for two reasons. First, the haul is so great that it makes it expensive, and then your business at that point is so great that it will be almost impossible to get them at any price, as I am informed. If they are brought by Norfolk and the R.&G. Road to this place, then, the gauge being different, bulk has to be broken; and besides, there is but little courtesy, as I am told, between the two roads at this place. The same may be said as to Wilmington and coming over the W.&W. Road to Goldsboro.

In view of these facts and the interest of the farmers involved in them, I ask you, notwithstanding your antagonism with Mr. Best, to see that proper facilities and rates of freight are given to the people who wish to get their fertilizers over the Atlantic Road. Whatever may be your opinion of Mr. Best or your feelings towards him, I trust you will rise above personal considerations when the interest of the people along the line of your road is involved.

This letter is written by request of interested parties, and I hope it may not be in vain.

A&H—GLB

C. W. Grandy to Thomas J. Jarvis

Elizabeth City, N. C.
Jany 19th 1882

Enclosed please find letters[7] from Bro Charles Latham Legal Adviser of the Board of Commissioners of Washington County, & from John W. Latham[8] Chairman of the Board — from which we learned that they believe it entirely unnecessary to ask your Excellency to order a court of Oyer and Terminer for said County to try the rioters, as indicated in your letter —

I am satisfied that these gentlemen who are citizens of the County & witnessed the late trouble are better enabled to Judge what is necessary to be done in the premises than myself, is my reason for writing to them

A&H—GP

J. E. Broome to Thomas J. Jarvis [with enclosure]

New York Jany 20th 1882

I have received your favor of 12th Inst, and beg leave to hand the enclosed communication of Col William B. Sipes,[9] who desires to purchase the 300 000 acres of Land of which you spoke. If his terms of payment are satisfactory, you will identify with your State, a Gentleman of much intelligence and fine social position a man who would be an acquisition to any Community, and one whose business capacity would guarantee Success in his enterprise.

I note your remark in regard to your State board of Education and will ask you to turn this communication over to that Board, I shall be pleased to serve the board in regard to this or any other land that the State may have to dispose of.

I make no charge for registering lands, but a commission of 5 per cent on consumation of sale

---

[7] Governors' Papers. Letters not included in this volume.

[8] Proprietor of the Latham House in Plymouth, and agent of the Southern Express Company and of the Roanoke Steamship Company. Branson, *Directory for 1884*, 671–672.

[9] The New York City Directory listed Sipes as a broker of that city. Information furnished by the New York Public Library.

[*enclosure*]
William B. Sipes to J. E. Broome

New York, Jan. 19, 1882

I wish to make a proposition for the Lands you have so kindly brought to my attention belonging to North Carolina and located in the Eastern portion of that State, on or near the navigable waters of the Atlantic. As I understand, these lands are in area not less than 300,000 acres and are to be sold as of that extent — (the excess, if any, to belong to the purchaser —) are partly timber and portions are susceptible of agricultural development. For these lands, being in fact all the State owns in that locality, I will pay the sum of $50.000 on the conditions following:

I to have an opportunity to examine the lands, which are to be designated by some person accredited by the State so to do, and if they are as above stated, I to pay $5000 in cash on the execution to me of a warranty deed, clear of all liens and encumbrances, and to execute upon the entire property a mortgage for $45,000 payable in annual payments of $5000 each bearing interest at the rate of 5% per annum — the purchaser to have the right to extinguish the mortgage at any time by the payment of the balance due with the accrued interest.

My object in offering to purchase this property is to utilize it in two ways: first — to secure its settlement which I think may be accomplished during the existing influx of immigration by properly presenting its advantages (if it has any) in certain portions of Europe; and, second, to manufacture the timber for a market. To accomplish these results will require the expenditure of money, independent of the payments to the State, therefore I have proposed the terms herein stated. If I succeed in the enterprise, the State will, in all probability, receive the entire purchase money long before the expiration of nine years.

Should my offer be entertained, I will endeavor to examine the lands as early as the weather will permit; but, taking into consideration the swampy character of the country where they lie, I hope to be accorded sufficient time to make this examination satisfactorily.

A&H—GLB

A. S. Buford to Thomas J. Jarvis

Richmond, Va., January 21st 1882

I have received yours of the 19th, and have given the matter therein referred to a careful personal investigation. I am aware there was great trouble last year, in getting fertilizers distributed, not only in North Carolina, however, but throughout the Southern States. Most of this was due to circumstances not likely soon to recur, on our lines at least.

In the first place our equipment then quite as full as the average of Southern railways, has since been very largely increased; and in the Second place, the block of last year was materially aggravated by the protracted inclement and severe weather which restrained the distribution of fertilizers after arrival at their Stations, and in that way quite a large proportion of the cars so employed were held for the convenience of consignees, who were unable promptly to unload the cars after arrival. The unusual character of the season also had precipitated much of this traffic into a limited period, requiring an amount of accommodation for that purpose theretofore unprecedented.

However, as I have said, to provide against any possible recurrence of this trouble, this Company at an expense of nearly a million dollars, has made an addition to its equipment of last year of nearly one thousand freight cars, and about twenty-five locomotives. We hope therefore, that for all legitimate demands for transportation, we shall be able to accomodate the public with that promptness which we desire to provide.

In reference to the special accommodations for the transmission of business passing from the N. C. Midland Road at Goldsboro, I beg to say, that it is not within our purpose to do less than furnish all usual and practicable facilities on our part to handle any such traffic. I was not aware that there was any cessation of interchanging cars at Goldsboro, between the North Carolina Road and the North Carolina Midland.

Without present provision of equipment I do not see that there should be any difficulty in making a proper interchange of cars when required by the regular course of trade between the two lines.

Simultaneously with the receipt of your letter, our General Manager received a similar communication forwarded through Col. Andrews, Superintendent, from the General Manager of the North Carolina Midland, making the request for more satisfactory arrangements in regard to the interchange of cars; and instructions accordingly have been forwarded to the Superintendent of the North Carolina Railroad to extend proper facilities in this respect; and I imagine that no proper ground of complaint on this score will continue, if it has heretofore existed. At any rate, if brought to our attention, we will see that whatever is reasonable will be done on the part of the management of the North Carolina Road, to do full justice to the trade relations between the Eastern portion of the State, and the Central and Western portions accommodated by the North Carolina R. R.

It is a question of business in which we recognized the interests of the public as well as of the railways; and we desire and intend, that the North Carolina Road shall continue, (as we have endeavored always heretofore to secure) to provide all practicable and reasonable facilities for the conduct of such transportations as the citizens of the State require, as well on its own line as on those connections that reciprocate this spirit of fair and regular business intercourse.

In conclusion I beg to assure you, that I do not receive these representations in the light of mere complaints, but will be at all times gratified to have your suggestions as to what may appear from the sources of information within your reach, to be just and necessary in the regulation of our business operations in that State. In this way matters may be brought to our attention, which require correction and control. When practicable, it will always be done as efficiently and promptly as possible. If beyond our reach we will then be able to have you so advised, and thus assured of our dispositions to do no injustice to the interests of any, but simply to conduct our operations in such manner only as a prudent regard for the welfare of the citizens and railways concerned shall require.

A&H—GLB

Thomas J. Jarvis to W. S. Denny

Executive Department,
Raleigh, Jan. 23, 1882

Yours of the 19th was received by me on Saturday.

I think the request to have the certificate of deposit of $250,000., which was deposited with T. J. Jarvis, J. M. Worth and Z. B. Vance to you, is not unreasonable. As the certificate is made payable to the order of all three of the Commissioners, it will be necessary, I presume for all three to endorse it. Commissioner Vance, as you know, as in Washington, and Commissioner Worth is at his home in Randolph. We expect to have a meeting in the near future, at which time I will lay your letter before them and suggest that we endorse the certificate and return it.

I regret that you and your friends should ever have understood the Commissioners as promising what they could not perform. I have a clear and distinct recollection that in my office on the afternoon of the 25th day of May, I distinctly stated that we had no power to deliver you the Western Road. I also remember that I stated that I was anxious to have the Midland Road from Goldsboro to Salisbury built, but that I was not willing for you to commence the work under any false impressions that we had the power to deliver the Western Road to you. I did believe at the time and so stated that I thought it was likely that Messrs. Buford, Logan and Clyde could be induced to *reconvey* the Western Road, and I believe it could have been done but for bitter controversy over the matter. I promised to do all in my power to bring about the *reconveyance,* but nowhere did I ever promise or think of promising to declare the contract forfeited and throw the property back upon the State. By declaring the contract forfeited, we could put Buford, Clyde and Logan out (it might take us a day, a month or year), but we have no power to put you in. The State would be compelled to hold the property till the meeting of the Legislature and then go through another squabble over the sale. While I was willing to do all I could to induce a *reconveyance* of the property so that you could take their place and go on with the work, I was not willing to throw the road back upon the State and to take upon myself the responsibilities and to impose upon the State the bad results. My duties to the State would not allow it, and, as a reasonable man, I do not believe you would ask it if you understood the whole situation. I do not think that our promise of the 25th of May, fairly construed, looks to anything but a *reconveyance* and a promise on our part to do all we could to procure it. I can truly say that I have complied with this reasonable view of the promise. I usually try to be so definite in what I do and say that there can be no misunderstanding about it; and I deeply regret that I ever signed the paper of the 25th of May as long as it contained words which might be misunderstood. I was and am now in sympathy with the spirit of the paper and would sign it again to–day if more carefully drawn.

I submit that a proper construction of the *fact* that you required the certificate of deposit to be returned on ten days' notice at any time after the first day of July was plainly a *recognition* of the doubt as to your getting the Western Road at all. Now I will tell you how the "first of July" came to be fixed as the time in the receipt which we gave for the return of the certificate. The receipt as originally drawn by Mr. Best and Maj. Dowd did not have the first of July in it, but required us to return the certificate upon ten days notice: thus still more strongly recognizing the doubt as to getting the Western Road. When it was presented to me to sign, I suggested that some time ought to be fixed before which the certificate could not be called for: otherwise I would not feel willing to undertake to assist in procuring a *reconveyance* of the road, as I would have no certainty of the funds to pay the parties in case they agreed to *reconvey.* Mr. Best replied with some spirit that he did not intend to have $250,000. of his money locked up doing nothing upon the uncertainty of his getting the road. I told him he could do as he pleased; but after some considerable talk over the matter, he himself fixed the first of July as the time. I deem this explanation due to myself and the facts in the case, as you seem to put some stress upon the fact. The certificate has been subject to your order since the first of July, and I submit we are in no way responsible for any loss upon the money by way of interest or otherwise since that time.

I trust a way may yet be opened up to you to go on with your enterprise in this State with both profit and pleasure to you and your friends. The enterprise you have undertaken, if carried out, will add greatly to the development and prosperity of the State, and I do most earnestly hope you will not feel obliged to abandon it. I know with you it is a matter of business, and I hope you will see your way clear as a matter of business to go on with the work on the Midland Road.

A&H—GP

James Powell to Thomas J. Jarvis

Chicago, Jan 24 1882

I am to present a paper this spring before the Congregational Churches of the States of Mich Ohio Ills & Iowa. My subject is

The Freedmen. Are they *rising* or *falling*? Are they advancing or going back?

What say those who live among them and are able to testify from observation? I wish to present the opinions of a few leading Southern men with such facts as they may feel inclined to furnish.

Pardon me for asking you to give me your opinion — I know you are busy — very busy — I would rather not refer the request — but the subject is of such importance that I must turn to those who can give authoritative opinions and sterling facts. How much property do the negroes own in your State? Are they interested in Schools? How are they in respect to morals?

May I hope to hear from you — any facts or opinions you may give will be gratefully received

Have you knowledge of amount of property owned by negroes in your State?

J. P.

A&H—GP

W. S. Denny to Thomas J. Jarvis

Boston, Jany. 26. 1882

Your esteemed favor of the 23ᵈ inst is just recd.

I would not burden you with an extended reply except to correct some evident misapprehensions. First, the certificate of Deposit if returned to us does not need the indorsement of the Commissioners and further delay therefore need not be made for that purpose. Second — The impression you seem to have obtained, that we expected a forfeiture declared, or something else done that could not be performed must have been gained through some other channel than my letter, for the writer never received or entertained the impression that you promised a forfeiture and from a copy of Mess Sprague & Carruths letter to you, which is indirectly connected with mine, I do not find that they intimated such a view. Such a construction has been talked about as we knew, and having yourself been aware of that fact, doubtless it was from inference that you received the suggested impressions

I may not in my letter have fully reflected the views of every one interested with us — possibly not of a majority — but the general sentiment, as I understand it, including my own.

I doubt if we ever had any agreed or positive individual expectations as to the precise manner in which the Commissioners were to bring about the desired result, but I do think that each and every one of us felt determined to do our part and fulfill to the letter all your requirements, leaving to you, the responsibility of deciding what means were in your power or what should be adopted.

Your explanation concerning the insertion of "July 15" in the memorandum, causes us to better understand why your impressions were not necessarily the same as ours upon the significance of the record, and it illustrates how easily a misunderstanding can be formed. From our stand point we thought there was every reason to suppose that we should be in possession of the road at once — not later than July 1st

Now my dear Governor, allow me to suggest that could you spend even a day or two with us here in Boston, aloof from all your official cares and responsibilities, where we could sit and freely discuss all the features of our enterprise we could arrive at a much better understanding of each others views, intentions and expectations — and enable us to more fully co–operate in the development of our enterprise and in the internal improvement of your States interests.

We still understand from your recent documents, rather than from your letter to me, that you yet desire to do all in your power to procure for us possession of the Western N. C. Railroad.

It is very likely that you may have had misgivings, from Statements for which we are in no way responsible, as to our perfect good faith in wishing to co–operate with you in all practicable means for the good of all; and we know that some of our people, for similar reasons, have at times doubted the sincerity of some of those interested — but in our opinion, if we could base our impressions only upon existing facts, we could accomplish immeasurably more good.

Thomas J. Jarvis to W. S. Denny

Executive Department,
Raleigh, Jan. 31, 1882

I send you to–day per express the certificate of deposit for $250,000., as requested in your letters of the 19th and 26th. I send it per express because I think it safer to do so.

It would give me very great pleasure to visit Boston if it were possible for me to leave the State so far and my official duties so long. I have never been that far North although I have long desired to do so. I see no hope of being able to do so in the near future.

I should greatly regret to see your Company withdraw from the State. I had hoped to see it extend the Atlantic (or, as you call it, the Midland) Road up into Chatham and Randolph, where you will strike a water–power that is not excelled by any on this Continent. As soon as your road was completed to this point, I had hoped to see some of your wealthy enterprising manufacturers locate there and, with the surplus capital of which your section has such an abundance, open up and develop this magnificent power. I still mean to be understood as ready to cooperate with you in any way that I can to push forward your enterprise. And I need not be misunderstood, for I will answer any question in a plain, direct way. It is a matter of deep regret with me that any question or answer should have been left so indefinite that any misunderstanding could arise.

Please present my kind regards to the gentlemen whom I have met.

Thomas J. Jarvis to James Powell

Executive Department,
Raleigh, Feb. 1st, 1882

Yours of the 24th ult., making inquiries into the condition of the negroes of the South and propounding certain questions in reference to that race, has been received.

My answer will be confined to the negroes of this State, as I do not profess to be familiar with their condition in the other States.

Your first questions are: "Are they *rising* or *falling*? Are they advancing or going back?" To these questions I unhesitatingly answer, "They are *rising, not falling; advancing, not going back.*" You ask, "What say those who live among them and are able to testify from observation?" I think I have given the opinion of all well–informed men. "How much property do the negroes own in your State?" you ask. I have no means of answering this question definitely, but I am delighted to be able to say that many of them are becoming to be property–owners and tax–payers. "Are they interested in schools?" is another question asked by you. My answer it, "Greatly so." "How are they in respect to morals?" This question I am also glad to be able to answer favorably, but I cannot do it as briefly as I have done the others. "They are improving" is probably the best brief reply I can make.

I have thus given a categorical answer to your inquiries, and with this I might be excused by one less interested in the colored people of my State. I shall, however, avail myself of your patience to hear me still further on this important subject. Both as a citizen and as an official, I have taken the deepest interest in the colored people of my State. I have done for them exactly what I thought was best for them and I have made them and their advancement the subject of many hours of deep concern.

All things considered, I think their career since the close of the war has been a most remarkable one. Cast, as they were, out upon the world, homeless and penniless, their accumulation of property has been all that could be expected. Having lived in a state of ignorance, their thirst for learning and the rapidity with which they acquired it, have been wonderful. Subjected, as they were, to bad influences immediately after the war and during the days of reconstruction, their esteem and love for their former masters are a living monument to their generous, confiding, submissive nature. During these years to which I have referred there were race antagonisms, but happily these conflicts have passed away, and now the two races are living upon the most amicable relations, each helping the other in their march of improvement and advancement. The State is doing what it well can in providing schools for both races, and, in addition to what the State is doing in this particular for the colored people, there are quite a number of high schools in the State of excellent quality for the education of the colored children which have been established by donations from the good people of the North. These schools are doing a good work and the colored people, anxious to learn, are being greatly improved by them. Through these different agencies the advance of the colored people has been very marked in the last few years.

In 1879, the colored people of this State organized a State Industrial Agricultural Society, which was largely attended by the better class of their race and by a goodly number of the white people. The exhibition did the race great credit and stimulated them to better efforts of labor and economy. It was my privilege to formally open the exhibition with an address. In 1880 the exhibition was better and in 1881 it was a great success. County fairs have been organized by them in quite a number of our counties. These exhibitions are having a good effect upon the colored people, and I think encouraging them to get homes and accumulate property. It is certain there is a marked improvement in the general condition of these people in this particular.

This improvement in the moral habits of these people, though not so marked, is still perceptible. Crime has considerably decreased among them in the last few years. Good agencies and good influences are at work among these people and I look forward with bright hopes to good results. One third of the population of this State is made up of these people, and I can but feel a deep interest in them and take an active part in whatever tends to their improvement.

A&H—GLB

Thomas J. Jarvis to Charles Wendell

Executive Department,
Raleigh, Feb. 4, 1882

The contract entered into about the last of December between your Company and certain Commissioners on the part of the State for the purchase of the State's stock in the Cape Fear and Yadkin Valley Railroad Company,[10] was duly returned to me from New York upon its execution by your Company. On the

---

[10]See Canedo to Jarvis, November 21, 1881.

18th of January 1882, the contract was submitted to the Governor and the Council of State and by them approved. On the 2nd day of February ins't., it was submitted to the stockholders of the C.F.&Y.V.R.R. Co. and was by them also approved. The contract is now deposited with me, it having received all the sanction and approval required by the law authorizing the sale.

It only now remains for you to pay the money, take possession of the property and begin the work. I trust there will be no unnecessary delay in doing either of these things. It is a great work and I hope to see the enterprise start off in a way to win the confidence of our people and the public generally in the beginning.

In my opinion, this system, when completed, will be one of the most important lines for trade and traffic yet projected. It will be greatly to be regretted if so important a work is crippled in its progress and usefulness by delays and mishaps before it attains a position of assured confidence and strength.

I hope to soon have the pleasure of welcoming you and your friends to North Carolina, whose people, as well as myself, will give you a hearty welcome.

A&H—GLB

Thomas J. Jarvis to J. E. Broome

Executive Department,
Raleigh, Feb. 7, 1882

Yours of the 20th ult. was received in due time, but it has remained till now unanswered for the reason that I felt it necessary for me to see the attorney — Col. T. C. Fuller, of this city — of the party who holds the contract of purchase of the 300,000 acres of which you wrote. Col. Fuller has been sick and to-day was the first time I was able to see him. I explained to you that one S. T. Carrow held a contract of sale which he had long ago forfeited, but there has been no decrees of foreclosure. My plan was to have him join in the conveyance, and it was to this end that I desired to see his lawyer.

Col. Fuller informs me that he will co–operate with my view and for this purpose will write to his client, Col. Carrow, to–day.

I beg to suggest the propriety of Col. Sipes taking a run down to the State to look at these lands and fully inform himself as to their location, value etc.

Col. Carrow lives in Washington, Beaufort County, of this State, in which County part of the lands are situated, and he will take Mr. Sipes or any one he may send down to see them at any time. It is but a day's ride in a buggy from Washington. It may be after he sees them he may not want them or it may be that he will like them very much. If he likes them, I think there will be no trouble about his making a trade.

A&H—GP

Charles Wendell to Thomas J. Jarvis

New York, Feby. 7th 1882

I have the honor to own receipt of your letter of the 4th inst. stating that the contract for the purchase of the States interest in the Cape Fear & Yadkin Valley R.R.Co. by this Co. had been approved by yourself and Council and that it had likewise, been ratified by the stockholders in that Company, on the 2d inst. and returned to you to be deposited in the archives of the State.—

It now remains for us to comply with the terms of said contract all of which we propose to do in good faith and carry out our project with the help of the Legislature and the people of North Carolina.

A&H—GP

S. S. Elam to Thomas J. Jarvis

Richmond Va., Feby 18 1882

Please do me the favor to inform me what amount of stock the State of NC owns in Atlantic & NoCR.R.Co.
Also let me know if your Board of Public Works would entertain a bid for their interest in the stock of the Co.

Thomas J. Jarvis to Dennis Simmons[11]

Executive Department,
Raleigh, Feb. 24, 1882

The State is the owner of a body of swamp land in the Counties of Jones and Onslow, known as the "White Oak Swamp," and said to contain about 85,000 acres. There are two or three propositions pending before the State Board of Education for the purchase of this body of land. The Board feel that they are not sufficiently informed as to its value to act intelligently upon these propositions. The Board to-day wisely determined to get some one qualified as a judge of such things to examine the lands and report to the Board upon their value; and I have been instructed to employ you for that purpose. We want you to go immediately to Jones and Onslow Counties and make an examination of these lands; and we suggest that you make the examination without mentioning for what purpose you are making it. To reach the lands you will go to Kinston and from Kinston to Trenton, which is 22 miles from Kinston. From Trenton it is five or six miles, I think, out to a place called Quaker Bridge, where these lands begin. From Quaker Bridge there is a good road leading seven miles into the swamp, which was built a year or so ago with convict labor. At Trenton inquire for Mr. Furney Simmons,[12] who will give you all the necessary information as to where the lands lay in Jones. In Onslow, you can get the information from Mr. Franks.[13] What we want to know is what would be a fair value per acre for this land in its present condition, including good, bad and indifferent. You can make the examination as if you were investigating it for yourself and you can do it in a few days. Of course we expect to pay you a liberal compensation for your services. I beg that you will do this work for us at once, for I know of no one so well qualified as yourself. You can come here before you go to arrange about the matter, if you prefer it.

---

[11]Farmer and lumberman of Williamston. Branson, *Directory for 1884,* 437–439.

[12]Farmer of Pollocksville, Branson, *Directory for 1884,* 412.

[13]Probably E. E. Franks or E. L. Franks, both of whom were farmers of Richlands. Branson, *Directory for 1884,* 503.

Thomas Kenan (1838-1941) of Kenansville attended Wake Forest College one year, graduated from the University of North Carolina, and studied law under Judge Richmond Pearson. He was a captain of the Duplin Rifles and a colonel of the Forty-third North Carolina Regiment; he was wounded and captured at Gettysburg. Kenan was a member of the legislature, 1865-1867, mayor of Wilson, 1869, state attorney general, 1876-1885, and clerk of the Supreme Court. He was a civic leader and strong supporter of the Oxford Orphanage and Soldiers' Home in Raleigh.

A&H—GLB

Thomas J. Jarvis to S. S. Elam

Executive Department,
Raleigh, Feb. 27, 1882

The State owns about two thirds of the capital stock of the Atlantic and North Carolina Railroad Company. Her interest is $1,266,000.

There is no authority vested in any board or person to sell this stock. It can only be done by the Legislature or some one authorized by it to do so.

Our Legislature will, I think, meet in extra session some time in April. If you will make a proposition for the purchase of their stock, I will submit it to the General Assembly when it convenes.

A&H—GO

Thomas J. Jarvis to T. S. Kenan [copy]

Executive Department,
Raleigh, Feb. 27, 1882

As you are aware, a new apportionment act has recently passed Congress giving North Carolina nine members of the House of Representatives. It is provided in the act that where a State gains a member of members, such State may elect such gain by the State at large. By this act North Carolina gains one member. Have we any election machinery in this State by which an election can be held, returns made, and canvassed for a member of Congress to be chosen by the votes of the State at large? It is desirable that our State have that representation in Congress to which she is entitled by law; and if we have no machinery by which a member of Congress can be elected by the State at large, then I shall feel it to be my duty to submit to the Council of State the question of calling the Legislature in extra session to provide for such election or to divide the State into nine districts. I will thank you to examine the question fully and to give me your official opinion at as early a day as convenient.

A&H—GP

Henry Otis Hyatt[14] to Thomas J. Jarvis

Kinston N.C.

Feb 28th 1882

As soon as I got home I had the remainder of the Public lands in Onsalow [*sic*] entered for my associates and myself and without duly thinking over the matter wrote a letter to Mr Scarborough saying that I would give the Board 18cts per acre for the White Oak and locate immigrants or I would give 25 and not bind myself to do so. I now want evry acre that we have enterd in Jones and Onsalow [*sic*] Some of the land is absolutely valueless but we will take it all if we can agree upon a price. It is to the interest of the State to get clear of it It will keep out the taxes of Jones and Onsalow and we think we can make something out of it and give that section a boom unheard of. Send a man down and we will show him over the entire field Let me hear from you

A&H—GLB

A. C. Avery to Thomas J. Jarvis

Morganton, March 2, 1882

You are aware that an action is pending in the Superior Court of Rowan County, in which W. J. Best is plaintiff and W. P. Clyde and others are defendants, and that the action involves the title to the Western North Carolina Railroad.[15] It is of course important to the parties and to the public that the matter should be decided. I can not try the case or even hear a motion in it. I am a director of the company in possession; but if there were no other objection to my acting than grows out of that fact, I should remove the difficulty by resigning. I am also a stockholder and, moreover, nearly connected by marriage with Major J. W. Wilson, one of the defendants. With a view to removing the trouble, I had a conference with Judge Eure,[16] now riding the

---

[14]Prominent surgeon of Kinston. *Cyclopedia of the Carolinas*, II, 264–265.

[15]Best was now resorting to the state courts in an effort to regain the Western North Carolina Railroad from his assignees. He was defeated in the Rowan County Superior Court, and the state Supreme Court refused to hear his appeal. *Best v. Clyde*, 86 N.C. 24 (1882).

[16]Mills E. Eure of Gates County, Superior Court judge, 1874–1883. Connor, *Manual, 1913*, 450.

8th Judicial District, on yesterday. He concurs with me in requesting you, if the reason offered shall be deemed sufficient, to authorize and order an exchange between us to apply to certain counties and to take effect on Monday, April 24th, 1882. We propose that he shall hold the courts in Surry, Stokes, Forsyth and Rowan counties in the 7th District, and I shall hold, instead of those courts, the spring terms of Mitchell, Watauga, Ashe, Caldwell and Alexander. We propose to make the exchange on April 24th because the court in Alleghany ends at the same time that Judge Eure finishes Yancey; and the transfer on the part of both can be more certainly and easily effected then than at any subsequent time before the commencement of Rowan court. You will find that the General Assembly, in the act of 1879, which provides for the rotation of Judges (I have no copy before me) clearly recognizes your power to make the order, as does the act of 1876–'7, regulating the ridings of the twelve Judges. I think, too, that both acts are constitutional. The section of the constitution in reference to rotation, I think, does not prohibit the exchange except as to the courts of districts collectively.

I shall be at Lexington for two weeks from Mar. 6th.   Judge Eure will be at Newton till the 2nd Monday in March and then for two weeks following at Morganton. I should be pleased to hear from you on the subject.

A&H—GLB

Thomas J. Jarvis to H. O. Hyatt

Executive Department,
Raleigh, March 2, 1882

The Board at its last meeting ordered some further information to be collected as to the value of the White Oak Swamp lands. As soon as we get that information, we will be prepared to make a direct response to your offer.

I think your last offer — twenty–five–cents per acre for the whole swamp except Judge McKoy's entry — will strike the Board more favorably.[17] For myself, I think the best obligation you can give that you will have the lands settled up is to pay

---

[17]For action on the bids by Hyatt and McKoy, see "Biennial Report of the Superintendent of Public Instruction," *Public Documents, 1883*, No. 6, 52-54.

a good price for them. I send you by this mail a copy of my last Message, and from this you can see what my opinions are about the propriety of the State's parting with these lands.

A&H—GP

T. S. Kenan to Thomas J. Jarvis

Attorney General Department.
Raleigh, March 6th 1882

To The Governor — My reply is respectfully submitted:

Our election law (Acts 1876–77, chap. 275) makes no provision for holding an election "for a member of congress to be chosen by the votes of the State at large." For the purpose of selecting representatives in the Congress of the United States, section 48 of the act prescribing the manner says, that the State shall be divided into eight districts — designating the counties embraced in each. Under the Constitution of the United States (Art. I sec. 4), "the times, places, and manner of holding elections for senators and representatives, shall be prescribed in each state by the legislature thereof; but the Congress may at any time by law make or alter such regulations, except as to the place of choosing senators" — which is fixed by section three. So that, among the powers delegated by the states to the Federal government, is the one permitting the Congress "to make or alter such regulations." That power has not been exercised in the Apportionment Act; it only says that if the state be entitled to an additional representative, he may be elected at large, and if the number be decreased, the whole delegation shall be elected at large, unless the legislature has provided or shall otherwise provide before the time fixed by law for the next election of representatives; it has not undertaken to designate the "places" or prescribe the "manner" or "make" any "regulations" for holding such election. And our statute fails to meet either contingency — an increase or decrease in the number of representatives. A change in the number, necessitates a corresponding change in our election law. And the necessity for such change is as manifest in the case of a "gain of one member," as it would have been if the number of representatives had been decreased.

In other words, there must be an express warrant of authority to hold a legal election. The machinery, the details, must be provided by the law itself, and not supplied by inference or implication. The very fact that our law authorizes the election of officers *therein named* by general vote, furnishes the best reason that it does not apply to officers *not therein named*. And it is certain the legislature did not contemplate that its provisions would be extended so as to authorize the election of a congressman at large.

I do not think any one will seriously contend, as a matter of law, that the Governor has a right to order an election to fill a vacancy, as provided in section 50 of our election law, until a vacancy occurs in one of the eight districts established by that law. That section must be construed in connection with the other sections of the same statute. And the apportionment act giving this state an additional member, starts out by saying; "That after the 3rd of March, 1883, the House of Representatives shall be composed of 325 members," of whom North Carolina will be entitled to nine. So that there can be no possible ground to suppose that a vacancy can exist, owing to the increase in our representation, before that date; for the state will not be entitled to be represented by nine members, until then. If therefore it is desirable that no such vacancy may occur, it will be necessary to take action in advance, and that action would in my opinion be illegal unless authorized by some positive statute.

I take it that the electoral privilege of the citizen depend upon the written law, and that by it the extent of those privileges and the manner in which they may be exercised must be defined.—by the constitution and the laws passed in pursuance thereof — and acting upon this rule, the legislature at its last session made specific provision in detail, for holding a general election on Thursday after the first Monday in November, 1882, for an associate justice of the Supreme Court, a judge of the Superior court for the first to the sixth districts, inclusive, and for solicitors. See Acts 1881 chap. 327.

I propose now to refer to the various acts germane to this subject, as it may be a matter of interest at this time. And to enable me to do so without unreasonable delay, I requested Secretary of State Saunders to search the records and documents on file in his office, and supply me with necessary the data. By the courtesy of that officer they were furnished, and constitute the basis of the following collation:

Federal Apportionments — The first apportionment was made in the federal constitution itself, (and was intended to last only until a census could be taken) and specified the number of representatives to which each state was entitled. Art. I, 2.

In 1792, and every ten years thereafter, apportionments were made directly by act of Congress, until 1852, when congress (having fixed the number of members of the House) directed the Secretary of the Interior to make the apportionment and certify the same to the Governors of the states. In 1862, the former mode was again adopted and Congress itself made the apportionment by act of March 4th of that year. There was no provision in any of these acts affecting the election laws of a state. The act of 1842 approved June 25 required each representative to be elected from his own district, section 2 thereof providing, "that in every case where a state is entitled to more than one representative, the number to which each state shall be entitled under this apportionment, shall be elected by districts composed of contiguous territory, equal in number to the number of representatives to which each state may be entitled, no one district electing more than one representative." And in 1862, by act of July 14th, the provisions of this section were enacted into a separate general statute by congress. So according to this general law, the states were prevented from electing their representatives "at large," except where the State was entitled to only one representative) until 1872 when the act of February 2nd permitted it to be done in case of an increase in the number of representatives, but was silent as to the case of a decrease. And by section 3 of the last mentioned act, the tuesday next after the first monday in November, 1876, and in every second year thereafter, was established as the day in each of the States for the election of representatives — thus exercising the power given by the Constitution, so far as fixing the *time* is concerned.

Congressional Districts—North Carolina was first laid off into five congressional "divisions", as they were then called, by act of assembly of December 18th 1789. On the 1st Thursday and Friday of February, 1790, an election was held for five members, the number allowed by the Constitution, to represent the State in the "United States Legislature," as the Act of Assembly called it. The fifth or western "division" embraced the State of Tennessee, and was composed of two districts — the district of "Washington," the returning officers meeting at Jonesborough, and the district of "Mero," the returning officers meeting at Nashville. This territory was ceded to the Federal government in 1790, and it then became necessary to re–district the state, which was done by the act of December 15th of that year. On December 31st 1792 — the census having been taken and the apportionment made — the state was divided into ten districts, and elections directed to be held on the 1st Thursday and Friday in February, 1793, and every two years thereafter. A gain of two members in 1802 necessitated a division into twelve districts, and in 1812, having gained still another, thirteen districts were created, and the time of holding the election changed from February to August of the odd years. And so the districts stood until 1842, when the state having lost four members was divided into nine districts. In 1852, it lost another, and divided into eight districts. By the census of 1860, it lost still another, and after reconstruction in 1868, seven members were elected to Congress from districts created by what was called the Constitutional Convention of that year. The apportionment under the census of 1870, gave the state a gain of one member, and it was redistricted the last time — into eight districts — by chapter 171 of the Acts of 1871–72, which was brought forward and incorporated into our election law of 1877, above referred to.

It will be observed that before the war, owing to the fact that congressional elections were held in the odd years, and because of annual sessions of the legislature at the time of the apportionment in 1872, there was no necessity of special sessions to arrange the districts to meet the requirements of apportionment acts. But the present difficulty, I apprehend, will occur every ten years hereafter, (in case the census involves a change in the number of representatives) unless Congress exercises the power delegated in the clause of the Constitution above cited or shall change the time of holding the election, or shall be more prompt in passing acts of apportionment; or, unless the legislature shall provide in advance for such a contingency, or the time of holding its sessions be changed.

Presidential Electors — The case has been different in the matter of providing for choosing presidential electors. The state voted for President for the first time in 1792, and has been obliged to resort to extraordinary legislation three times, to provide in time for the election of electors — in 1792, 1812, 1852 — and would have been forced to do so in 1832, but for the fact that the apportionment of that year made no change in the number of representatives; and also in 1872, had it not been for the annual sessions of the legislature at that time.

The act of apportionment under the census of 1790, giving the state ten members of the House of Representatives, was not ratified until April 13th, 1792, and the legislature was not in session that year, after that date, until the 15th of November, when it met in Newbern. The electoral college was to meet on the 5th of December ensuing, and to provide for the election of electors in time to take their seats, an act was passed on the 23d of November, 1792 dividing the state into four electoral districts, and requiring the members of the legislature from each district to meet on the 26th of the month and choose three persons resident in their district, as electors, which made up the number (12) to which the state was entitled in the electoral college. But at the same session the state was divided into districts, and the election of electors given to the people. They have continued to be so chosen until the present time, with a single exception, to wit: in December, 1811, the legislature, anticipating an increase in the number of members of our electoral college under the census of 1810, passed an act directing the whole number of electors to be chosen on joint ballot by the legislature of 1812, which was done on Saturday the 29th of November of that year — the number being fifteen — and the only instance it is believed in which they were so elected in North Carolina. This legislation however met with serious opposition, and the records of both Houses show protests against the passage of the act. And in 1812 when it was proposed to have a ballot in acordance with its provisions, Judge Gaston in the Senate, and Judge Cameron in the House of Commons, both strongly opposed it — Gaston desiring that the expedient resorted to in 1792 should be adopted (rather than an election directly by the legislature on joint ballot.) as it was then the nearest approach to popular suffrage. In 1852, Gov. Reid called a special session of the legislature which met on the 4th of October of that year, and on the 19th of the month passed an act providing for choosing electors. He stated in his message that the necessity arose in consequence of the apportionment made under the census of 1850, by which the state was entitled to only ten electoral votes, while the then act of assembly provided for the election of eleven electors. See House Journal, Session, 1852.

A&H—GO

Thomas J. Jarvis to the Council of State

Executive Department.
Raleigh, March 6th 1882

The question which I submit to you to day is, "Shall the Legislature be convened in Extra Session." Upon this question I ask your advice; and if your advice be in favor of the call, what time will you suggest as likely to work the least inconvenience to the members?

The extraordinary occasion which, in my opinion, makes an extra session necessary is the new apportionment act giving North Carolina nine members of the House of Representatives of the Congress of the United States. Since and before the passage of this act I have given the matter a thorough and close investigation, and I can find no authority or machinery for the election of a member of Congress by the State at large. But desiring to get authoritative information on this subject, I asked the Attorney General for his official opinion, intending to let his decision of the question be my guide. My letter to him and his reply are herewith submitted.

My constitutional legal adviser having decided that there is no machinery by which a member of Congress for the State at large can be elected, there is nothing else left for me to do but to ask your consent and advice to call the Legislature together to provide the necessary legislation. However others may feel and act I am not willing that North Carolina by any act or omission of mine shall be deprived of any part of her representation and influence in the National Legislature. Nor am I willing to take part in holding an election which I am advised by the Law Office of the State is without authority of Law.

A&H—GP

J. A. Gray to Thomas J. Jarvis

Greensboro N.C., Mch. 6th 1882

I got home Saturday night.[18] Did not write you because I kept hopeing something would be brought to the point every day during my stay in New York which would look solid and encourag-

---

[18]See Jarvis to Gray, November 29, 1881, in this volume.

ing, but I waited and hoped in vain and came home no wiser than I went. Canedo and Wendell say the money will be forthcoming in due time and that all will work out right. They even said they expected to forward to the treasurer in a few days a certified check for the $55.000. and would place $20.000 in my hands to buy x ties with. But I did not see any body except the same *old set* and listened to the same line of talk as on former visits. They are raking fore and aft to get somebody to take hold who has money but I think there is scarcely a shadow of chance for success. There is a very panicky state of feeling in many circles in N.Y. and I think it will be harder to raise money now than for a year past.

I hope you will call the Legislature at an early day and will be prepared to submit a proposition for the purchase of the States Stock — Not upon such terms as offered by Canedo but such as prudent business men who expect to put their money in it are willing to make and such as will, if accepted, assure the building of the road.

A&H—GP

J. D. Whitford to Thomas J. Jarvis [with enclosure]

New Bern
March 7th 1882

We had our Directors meeting this morning — All present except Morehead[19] Faison[20] & Grainger — Enclosed find Resolutions offered by C. C. Clark who stated he would not press a vote & on Motion Judge Thomas[21] they went over to next meeting I think they will want your views, all was done in good temper, Mr. Clark offered a resolution which was unanimously adopted, that the President notify the experts that they had no business in the valuation of the Midland Rolling Stock or other property of that Co. their duty being to see the A&NCRR prop-

---

[19]Eugene Lindsay Morehead, banker and tobacco manufacturer of Durham. Ashe, *Biographical History*, II, 265–271.

[20]Paul F. Faison, cotton broker of Raleigh. Branson, *Directory for 1884*, 646.

[21]Charles Randolph Thomas, lawyer of New Bern; member of the Convention of 1861; Superior Court judge, 1868–1870; Republican representative to Congress, 1871-1875. *Biographical Directory of Congress*, 1,607.

erty was kept in as good condition as when turned over to the Midland Railway Co[22]

This will prevent misunderstanding & trouble hereafter — Judge Thomas offered a resolution protesting all the time he is not an Atty of the Midland Railway Co (Sometimes he that drops the work leaves a greater sign that his feet would make you know, to appoint an agent to act with the agent of the Midland R. Way Co in taking down bonds in Bank &c — Name left blank, Mr Clark in a very fine but temperate speech opposed it as the Midland had not complied with Contract of Lease, there upon Thomas (again & again Stating he was not Atty &c.) informed us that but two hundred tons of the iron had been taken out of Bond by Best & Co. that they had been in trouble [illigible] of the owners of the iron, Barring & Co had been down to Beaufort & if we did not release them it was this last feather breaking the camels back. He did not know that the last Ship load had been paid for thought it had not & duties due on all except 200 tons sent forward no doubt, to fit Directors Meeting as dispatches used to fit the meetings of you worth & Vance, Best friends looked serious, Clark[,] Caho[23] Wooten[24] voted against it, I did not vote as I expected my name to be one offered for the   . After Resolution was adopted, Judge Thomas moved to put in Mr Geo Allens[25] name where upon mine mine was Substituted. Thomas & W. C. Wooten voting against the change. Thomas apologizing and giving as a reason he wanted to go out of the Board as the duties might conflict with that of Director as Mr J. C Wooten had been suggested to him for the place & he opposed it for similar reasons Mr Clark then informed Thomas it could not possibly conflict as the decision of the Agent was final unless it went to the Courts — I dont intend to be factious but we will know before Any bonds are taken down what those luxurious cars & who they belong to Cost I assure you the Best men & State affair were silent & for

---

[22]According to the lease, the physical condition of the Atlantic and North Carolina Railroad must be maintained until all the terms of the lease had been fulfilled. "Proceedings of the Twenty-eighth Annual Meeting of the Stockholders of the Atlantic & North Carolina Railroad Co.," 3.

[23]William T. Caho, lawyer of Pamlico County; member of the General Assembly, 1876, 1883. Branson, *Directory for 1884*, 512; Connor, *Manual, 1913*, 744, 824.

[24]John C. Wooten, merchant and farmer of Kinston; member of the General Assembly, 1862. Branson, *Directory for 1884*, 417–418; Connor, *Manual, 1913*, 681.

[25]Banker, merchant, and manufacturer of New Bern. Branson, *Directory for 1884*, 240–242.

one Mr Clark stated again & again he was for Best if Best was for & could carry out the contract The meeting was pleasant, I stated to the Board to keep down expense, I had concluded not to visit Washington again about our claims without consultation; It was expressed I had better go & see what could be done — Your recollect our Claim is $200,000 When I go may stop & see you at backing up *if no other consideration* — However, there is no Sweetheart love in it if you do think it is time, Mr James A Bryan[26] was at my house last night & said to me the Midland people wanted him to meet you to explain certain things He is not as sanguine as he once was though is still somewhat in the Best faith. Governor, I am satisfied Best has had no money or backing lately & all is done out of the earnings of our Road. Yet if he can do let him do in any way that will benefit us, You will see in the papers about the Onslow R R Meeting, Would you believe it Some of our Trent River Steam Boat men went to encourage it, Of course the Rail Road Connection out there would kill the Trent River works, But such is life, I am for it I write in a hurry to get this mail to day —

[*enclosure*]

March 7th 1882

Whereas the provisions of the lease to the N C Midland Railway Co have not been complied with:

And whereas it has been authoritatively stated that the work on the stipulated extension to Salisbury will be stopped at Smithfield And whereas, according to the terms of the Said lease, it is competent, for the causes stated, for this Company, to declare a forfeiture thereof:

And whereas it is the duty of the Board of Directors to see that said contract of lease is, in all respects, faithfully executed:

And Whereas, no effective or decisive action can be taken in the premises without the sanction & cooperation of the Governor of the States, Therefore,

Resolved. That a Committee of ten be appointed to confer with the Governor & call to his attention the matters herein stated,

---

[26]Farmer and lumberman of New Bern. Branson, *Directory for 1884*, 243–244.

and ascertain if some immediate steps cannot be taken, either to compel a performance of the conditions of the lease, or to declare the same forfeited —
Action postponed till next meeting

A&H—GP

A. H. Canedo to Thomas J. Jarvis

New York, March 14th 1882

I beg leave to call your attention to a matter brought to me by some Capitalists who are arranging to *come in with us.*

They say it is the law in this State that when an extra session is called the matter to be legislated upon should be mentioned in the call and no other business can be brought up for legislation.

A&H—GLB

Thomas J. Jarvis to A. H. Canedo

Executive Department,
Raleigh, March 16, 1882

In this State the Governor is required, in calling an extra session of the Legislature, to specify in his proclamation the object for which it is called. This does not, however, exclude the Legislature from considering and acting upon other questions. The only limitation put upon the Legislature in an extra session, not applicable to a general session, is the number of days for which the members shall draw pay.

The time in which your Company is to put up the $155,000.00 is rapidly drawing to a close. I am often asked about you and whether the money has yet been put up. I trust there will be no trouble about the matter and that your Company will be able to comply with their contract. I shall be glad to have your assurance to this effect.

A&H—GLB

Thomas J. Jarvis to R. T. Lincoln

Executive Department,
Raleigh, March 16, 1882

When the city of Raleigh was laid out in 1792 upon land purchased by the State from Joel Lane, the State reserved the title to certain lots or squares within the city boundaries and certain lots without the boundaries. At the sale of these outside lots in 1819, lot No. 35 was retained by the State and the unquestioned title has always remained in the State. In 1863 the State authorities, without any legislative action, as a measure of humanity, verbally granted to the Confederate authorities the right to erect hospital buildings upon the lot and it was used as a hospital for State, Confederate and Federal soldiers up to the occupation of Raleigh by the United States army in April, 1865. There was never any conveyance or lease of the lot to the Confederate authorities and the sole action taken was a verbal permission to occupy the lot for hospital purposes.

From 1865 up to 1877 the lot was used by the various detachments of the United States army stationed at Raleigh as barracks. In 1877 (I think it was) the post was abandoned, and since that time the lot (known as Camp Russell) has been under the control of the Sergeant who has charge of the Federal cemetery and not used by the Government for any purpose. Permission has been granted to use it for the annual exhibitions of the N. C. Industrial Association.

My predecessor made application in 1877 for the restoration of the property to the State, but for reasons deemed sufficient by the Secretary of War [G. W. McCrary], the request was not granted. In 1879 an officer of the U. S. army, representing himself as the agent of the Department, came to Raleigh to investigate the facts concerning this property, and I believed that upon his return an order would be issued restoring it to the State. But as this has not yet been done and as the buildings are growing greatly dilapidated and are now of small value, I deem it my duty to call your attention to the matter and to repeat the request that the same may be delivered to the State.

The Government occupied this property about twelve years as a barracks when it was useful to the Government to do so, and for five years more it has with-held the property from the

State without its being a penny's benefit to the Government.

It seems to me that a proper regard for right and justice requires that this property be *at once* restored to the State and that a reasonable allowance be made to the State for its use during the seventeen years it was occupied by the Government. I trust that the time has come when this property will be restored to the State without further delay, and I respectfully ask that you will have an order issued to this effect by the proper officer; and if for any cause you may not deem it proper to issue such an order, that you will give the State your aid and influence in the recovery of the possession of the property.

A&H—GLB

Thomas J. Jarvis to M. W. Ransom and Z. B. Vance

Executive Department,
Raleigh, March 16, 1882

In 1879 an officer of the U. S. Army came here to investigate the occupancy of Camp Russell by the U. S. Government. Not being familiar with the facts myself, I employed Mr. F. H. Busbee to look up the matter and place them before the officer properly. In this way Mr. Busbee is familar with all the facts, and while in Washington on other matters, I have asked him to interest himself in behalf of the State in our effort to recover the property.

I will thank you both, as well as our Representatives, to take hold of this matter and to do whatever may be necessary to secure the return of the property to the State and the payment of reasonable rent for its use.

A&H—GP

G. L. Dudley to Thomas J. Jarvis [*with enclosure*]

Chamber of the Council of State,
Raleigh, March 18, 1882

By instructions from the Council of State, I have the honor to transmit herewith to your Excellency a copy of the resolution adopted by them at their meeting of the 17th, in reply to your communication of the 6th instant.

[enclosure]

Copy of Resolution

Whereas, there exists a difference of opinion among the members of the Bar as to the authority of law and machinery in this State for the election of a Representative in the United States Congress for the State at large:

Therefore, resolved, That this Council, having considered the question according to the information to be had, upon examination of the law and precedents of former times, and in other States, is of the opinion that the present law regulating elections is sufficient for the election of such Representative at large, and advises the Governor that the necessity does not exist for convening the General Assembly in extra session.

A&H—GP

A. H. Canedo to Thomas J. Jarvis [with enclosure]

New York, March 18th 1882

Enclosed please find letter from one of the Syndicate of Capitalists who have been arranging to come in to our Company with the money requisite to carry out our matter. I see by the papers that the session will not be called, I send you the letter that you may Judge from their stand–point the necessity of the Extension

During the last few weeks a depression in R R financial operations existed. To day, things are entirely changed, and confidence is becoming stronger, and the financial outlook for American Securities are extremely good. And large orders come from abroad for the purchase of, and investment in, such securities.

The probabilities are that we will be on time. Yet we must anticipate, therefore we ask for the Extension thirty days We urge this the more strongly from the fact that when the purchase was made, we were assured that we should have this legislation at an early day, and but for that assurance re-iterated to our friends, we could not have made this purchase.

We have arranged our details for Rolling Stock, Iron, and perfecting our organization on other portions of the line beyond the State.

I leave for Richmond tomorrow to carry measures for the Charter across Virginia. Our agents ar[e] arranging matters in Kentucky, and I am corresponding with Genl M. P. Taylor[27] and others in perfecting the route between Fayetteville and Wilmington.

[enclosure]

Edward D. McCookey[28] *to A. H. Canedo*

New York Mah 18 1882

After a full investigation of the status of the New York & Southern R R. & Telegraph Construction Co and its connection with the purchase of the Cape Fear & Yadkin Valley R.R., and examining into the charter and amendments to the charter of the latter, we have come to the conclusion that it would not be politic or safe to risk investment in the same until an assurance that the legislature be called, and such enabling acts be passed as would ensure beyond peradventure, the stability of the road on a sound footing, and facilities to carry it beyond the limits of the State or at least within the State.

This is all the work necessary at this juncture while the temper of the people and the present Members and Executive [sic] are I am informed are in harmony on this subject.

Should this opportunity pass by there is no knowing what antagonisms political changes—New rulers and antagonistic legislators there may develope.

Hence as it appears the legislative body may convene about the last of April as you say. (and one month later than we had been led to expect) it appears we cannot bring about a unanimity of action on the part of our Capitalists in time for the 2nd of April and therefore would ask that your Governor extend the time for the payment.

If a call was made so that it would be known that the legislature *would meet* would be an assurance quite enough, as evidenced by the Governor and other letters from different members of the house. And in the event the legislature doesn't meet it is all the more necessary for the extension to afford time to

---

[27]Matthew P. Taylor, insurance agent of Wilmington, and a brigadier general in the state militia. Branson, *Directory for 1884*, 490–493.
[28]Unable to identify.

arrange with you upon a different footing, that the financial matters may be carried upon the present Mortgages of $4000 per mile which though inadequate may be made to carry out the contract for the present year

You should urge this upon the Executive the more strongly from the fact that when the purchase was made you were assured you should have such legislation —

A&H—GLB

Thomas J. Jarvis to J. E. Broome

Executive Department,
Raleigh, March 20, 1882

I have seen Col. Carrow and he is anxious to join in a sale of the swamp lands about which we have been corresponding.

I beg to suggest that Col. Sipes come out at once and make an inspection of the lands and learn for himself all about them.

I think I can confidently say the body can be bought for $50,000.—the only difference being in the payments, and I think this can be managed if your friend likes the lands after seeing them. If he buys at all, I prefer that he shall buy upon his own inspection and not upon any representation of mine.

A&H—GP

F. H. Busbee to Thomas J. Jarvis

March 21, 1882

I have been delayed by the temporary indisposition of Senator Vance and the absence of Senator Ransom, together with the absence of the Secretary of War from his office where I called twice on yesterday.[29]

Today both the Senators called on the Secretary, accompanied by myself. I presented your letter which he read carefully and seemed favorably impressed with. In fact if the matter had not already been submitted to his predecessors the order would have

---

[29]For an explanation of this letter, see Jarvis to Lincoln, March 16, 1882, and Jarvis to Ransom and Vance, March 16, 1882, in this volume.

issued forthwith. But he referred the communication to the Judge Advocate General, with instructions to inquire into the matter and report at once.

The Senators pursued the hunt and called on Judge Advocate General Swain.[30]

He received us courteously, said he had investigated the Charleston Citadel case, and agreed that the property did not of right belong to the United States, if our case was similar.

I have just telegraphed you asking if I shall remain a day or so until the matter is definitely acted upon. I think the order will be issued this week — or if no order is issued that no objection will be made to the States' taking possession of the property.

The question of rent will necessarily be referred to Congress for such action as they shall see fit to take.

The delegation is improving in health, though nearly all have been indisposed lately. Gen. Scale is confined to his room.

A&H—GLB

Thomas J. Jarvis to A. H. Canedo

Greenville, Pitt Co., N. C.,
March 23rd, 1882

This is my home and I am here for a few days of rest and pleasure with friends. Your letter of the 18th ins't., with the letter of Mr. Edward D. McCookey addressed to you, was forwarded to me here from Raleigh, and I answer from here at once.

It is true the Legislature will not be convened till the regular session, 1st of Jan., 1883, but it is also true that no certain promise could have been held out that it would meet sooner. There was considerable talk about an extra session, but nothing could have been said of a definite character.

There was a general opinion expressed at the time you and the State Commissioners were arranging the contract of purchase in Raleigh, that whatever legislation was necessary to enable you to carry out your contract you could get without any trouble. I still have no doubt you will be able to get such legis-

---

[30]David G. Swain of Ohio. *Register of Officers of the United States, 1877,* 224.

lation if, when the Legislature meets, you have complied with your contract up to that time. Although you may not be able to get the legislation as soon as you may desire it, I think I can say with great confidence you will be able to get such as you want if you shall then be able to go on with the work.

The present State officers will continue in office till the first of January, 1885, and you may give your friends and associates strong assurances that you and they can rely upon our warm support if your works shall merit it. I think I can give you also the most positive assurance of the warm support of the people from Wilmington to Ashe and Surry if you give them a reasonable hope of your purpose and ability to build the road. I can go even further and say you will have the warm support of the people of the whole State.

I know of no other lines of railway that are likely to antagonize your enterprise. If any antagonism should manifest itself, it can amount to nothing.

Now as to the proposed extension. The stock–holders meet in regular annual meeting on the 5th of April. Both myself and the stock–holders will go to the full extent of our authority in giving you any reasonable extension or help, if that extension or help will enable you to fulfill your contract. I beg, however, to urge you to make the payment, if possible, before the expiration of the time. This compliance will help your position very much. I also suggest that you attend the stock–holders' meeting and that you be prepared to give them the actual condition of affairs.

A&H—GLB

Thomas J. Jarvis to J. A. Gray

Executive Department,
Raleigh, March 31, 1882

I regret that I was not at home when you were here. I would have been glad to have seen you and had a talk with you about the C.F.&Y.V.R.R.

I send you enclosed a copy of a letter from Dr. Canedo and a copy of a letter to him which he enclosed to me and a copy of my answer.[31] I do not only send them for what they are worth.

---

[31]See Canedo to Jarvis, March 18, 1882, and enclosure; and Jarvis to Canedo, March 23, 1882.

If Canedo should by any possibility come up during the month of April and pay the money, I would be in favor of letting him do so and take charge. There need be no formal extension given to allow him to do this, as I suppose it is not likely that anything better can be done during that time. I do not, however, think this ought to prevent your looking out for something else in other quarters, as I have but little hope from the Canedo Company.

The only suggestion that I can make is that the stock–holders pass a resolution giving the Board of Directors full authority, and then we will do the best we can. The road *must* be built and I am almost inclined to say it *shall* be built.

I have to go up on the Western Road on Monday and will be gone all the week or I would go down to your meeting.

A&H—GP

A. H. Canedo to Thomas J. Jarvis [with enclosures]

New York, Mch 31st 1882

Your response to my letter of 18th duly received, and enclosed please find copy of letter of this date to Mr. Gray, which explains itself.

I send two slips from reputable financial papers here. It is such paragraphs as these that make capital cautious about venturing in operations in North Carolina, and it is only upon our personal assurances, and the character of your encouraging letters that give them confidence to go on with the work after the extension is granted. The probabilities are that the payment may be made and work begun, before the Month is out (April)

[enclosure]
Charles Wendell to J. A. Gray

New York, Mch 31st 1882

In view of the approaching annual meeting of Stockholders of your Company to be held on the 5th inst. I beg to submit the following suggestions and statements to be presented at the meeting referred to and to ask that you kindly give the matter your personal attention.

The time limited by the Contract with this Co in which the $155.000 — is to be paid will expire on the 2ᵈ of April and as the amount cannot be paid I deem it my duty to communicate the fact to you and to give the reason for the failure on the part of this Co to carry out the provisions of the contract.

At the time the Contract was entered into and subsequently, assurances were given by prominent parties, that you would have an extra session of the Legislature at which session the needed legislation could be had to enable us thoroughly and efficiently carry out the enterprise.

Upon such assurances Capital Stock of the Co has been subscribed for and no small amount of work and planning has been done, and money expended. — The failure to have (what we find Capitalists seem to regard as quite important) the desired legislation at this time, has disturbed our plans for the time being, and a *"new departure"* is necessitated — Dr. Canedo our Vice President addressed a letter to his Excellency Gov Jarvis upon this subject in which he requested that 60 days extension be granted this Co in order to enable it to arrange work upon a basis of $4.000 a mile by hypothicating the bonds until such time as legislation can be had.

Negotiations pending for a continuation of the line and contracts for construction Rolling stock Rails &c will necessarily be modified to conform to the changed circumstances.

[*enclosures*]

[*newspaper clippings*]

North Carolina Bonds.

The Wilmington, N. C., *Star* says: "We wonder what Northern papers will say when they read that North Carolina paid $8,819.745 of debt with $2,598,850 of bonds? It seems that all those holding the old bonds are not anxious to swap them for new bonds on the terms proposed by the Legislature. There are still outstanding nearly $4,000,000. Will the papers hint at repudiation? Does Mahone & Company propose any more sweeping repudiation than the above fact indicates?"
North Carolina Special Tax bonds are said to be a good "gamble," in view of a movement being started to encourage outsiders to buy. That is it. They are a "gamble," nothing more,

with the cards stacked in favor of insiders. The chance of a dollar ever being paid by the State of North Carolina for the redemption of these bonds is even more remote, if possible, than the payment of Confederate bonds by the United States Government.

A&H—GP

W. G. Curtis to Thomas J. Jarvis

Smithfield April 1st 1882

I regret to inform you that the Quarantine Hospital near this place was burned to the ground yesterday — On investigation I found that the fire caught in the roof, and that a violent wind was blowing at the time. So that nothing could be done to arrest the flames —

The keeper who was alone with his family in the building, managed to save most of the furniture and bedding, which was all he could do

This hospital was built in 1869 at a cost of about $2000 upon a tract of two acres of ground at Pine Creek, purchased for the purpose by the State — Although not often used, it is of absolute necessity as part of a Quarantine Establishment, and has served to isolate many cases of yellow fever and small pox, to the great advantage of the community —

I suppose nothing can be done towards rebuilding, until an appropriation can be obtained from the Legislature, although the law provides that there shall be a hospital for the better care and nursing of the Sick with contagious diseases — I should be pleased to receive instruction from your Excellency as to what had better be done under the circumstances, and I would suggest that it is probable the old light house at Pine Creek might be obtained from the U S government for temporary use, if a hospital should be required the coming Summer — This building can, I think, be made to answer without cost to the State and if so instructed by you. I will make application to the proper department for the loan of the building to the State until such time as provision can be made for the erection of another hospital

A&H—GLB

Thomas J. Jarvis to A. A. McKethan

Executive Department,
Raleigh, April 4, 1882

I am for building the C.F.&Y.V.R.R. and am ready to co-operate with any movement that promises success.

In the present condition of things, it seems to me about the best thing that can be done by the stockholders is to elect the same Board of Directors and officers and then give them all the power possible.

If Canedo finally fails, I have faith that the Board, with what little help I can give them, will be able to evolve some plan to go on with the work. The road must be built. It is a road of vast importance to the State and it has and will continue to have my best labors for its completion.

If Canedo should, in the next thirty or sixty days, come up with the money and show his ability to go on with the work, I presume there will be no objection to receiving his money and turning the road over to him, even without any formal action extending the time. There certainly will be no objection on my part.

I had intended to be at your meeting, but I leave to-day for an examination of the Western North Carolina Railroad, so I will not be able to be with you.

A&H—GLB

Thomas J. Jarvis to W. G. Curtis

Executive Department,
Raleigh, April 4, 1882

Yours of the 1st, informing me of the burning of the hospital building, has been received.

I think your suggestion as to the old lighthouse a good one, and Senator Vance, who is here at this time, thinks the Government will give you the use of it. He promises to aid us.

I therefore suggest that you make a formal application to the Chief of the Lighthouse Bureau for this building, stating all the facts, and have it recommended by any Federal officer and the

Collector of the Port, who will give it a favorable recommendation.

After the papers are completed, send them to me and I will endorse them and forward them to Washington and get our Senators and Representatives to look after the matter.

A&H—GP

James A. Bryan to Thomas J. Jarvis

Goldsboro, N.C, April 20th 1881 [1882]

Upon my arrival here this afternoon, I made a comparison of the mortgage being registered here today by Best,[32] with that which I submitted to you & find it in all essentials identical. — I write to ask you since it covers the A&N.C.RR'd itself & every right & species of property belonging or appertaining thereto, placing a lien of $15,000 per mile on the Road if non–action upon the part of the A&N.C. Directors before the meeting of the stockholders, would not be, in law, construed into tacit consent. — I do not wish to take any precipitate action, or to do anything in the premises contrary to yr views, wishing, on the contrary, to conform the action of Craven County strictly to that of the State; but the course of Best, which I hardly thought he would take just now, seems to me to demand a prompt protest upon the part of the A&N.C.Co. followed up by such action as you & the Directors, acting in consonance with your views, may deem best —

I go to Newbern in the morning.

A&H—GP

S. G. Worth to Thomas J. Jarvis

Avoca, April 4th 1882

I received your kind inquiry about the steam launch in a letter of recent date from Mr Robinson. I have not yet succeeded

---

[32]Best, as president of the Midland North Carolina Railroad Company, had just mortgaged the recently leased Atlantic and North Carolina Railroad to the American Loan and Trust Company of Boston for $10,000,000 at 6 per cent interest. Under the deed of trust signed by Best and the railroad stockholders, Best could mortgage the railroad for as much as $15,000 for each mile of road in operation. *News and Observer*, April 21 and 30, 1882.

in obtaining a launch but am hopeful. I enclose a slip from the Washington Post (2 insertions) & a letter which is my first reply. I do not know but the "Endeavor" is a bargain to one with money to purchase. I will send other replies to the advertisement should any come worthy of notice. Meanwhile there is a small tug boat at Edenton the "Lizzie May" in the employ of the E. C & Norfolk Rail Road whose duties are confined to forenoon service except an *occasional* tow of fishing boats becalmed or disabled which keeps her busy as late as 2 p.m. Dr. Capehart[33] thinks that we *may* get *her* if we do not succeed in another direction. I shall probably purchase a 26 foot sail boat this week at Edenton to transfer fish fry to the steamer wharf. She will cost me about Sixty-dollars She is a fast sailer & I will attend Roanoke fisheries in her till a launch is secured. She will be safer than a launch & as quick when there is any wind.

Dr. Capehart "Sends his love to you & hopes your shadow may never grow less nor your nose paler" he is catching 200 shad & 2 to 3 thousand herrings. I send three of my force to the sein hauls this p.m. & procured from three hauls 165000 eggs. They look well & one in the cones. My new pump & boiler are working in the best manner. The telephones are working & worth their weight in gold. The Dr says he wouldnt take anything in the world for them that he had no idea of the convenience. They have indeed made a new phase here in all our work. Everything bids fair to be successful my force being excellent — I have only ten men here. We have not idled a half day. I cannot put the bottles up before next week my piping being behind. I am in exuberant spirits — tho' I have not had but one drink today — & hope that nothing will prevent your coming

A&H—GLB

Thomas J. Jarvis to J. A. Bryan

Executive Department,
Raleigh, April 22, 1882

Yours of the 20th, written from Goldsboro, was received in due time. The only reply I can make is to express the desire for the Board to look into the matter referred to in your letter as

---

[33]William Rhodes Capehart, who had forsaken medicine and now was a successful fish dealer in Avoca. Branson, *Directory for 1884*, 141.

well as all other matters affecting the interest of the A.& N.C.R R. I cannot see how any mortgage placed or attempted to be placed upon the property of the A.& N.C.R.R. Co. by the Midland Company, can, in any view of the case, bind the property of the Atlantic Company or in any way become a lien upon it. There are, however, several good lawyers on the Board of Directors of the Atlantic Company and I suggest that a copy of the Midland mortgage be submitted to them and their opinion obtained as to whether it in any way jeopardizes the interest or property of the A.& N.C.R.R. Company. I cannot suggest to the Board any action beyond this. I am fully satisfied that the Board is both competent and prepared to act wisely.

As I told you when here, I desire the property and interests of the A.& N.C.R.R. Co. protected. At the same time, I am just as anxious that no advantage shall be taken of Mr. Best or his Midland scheme. I desire that every reasonable chance shall be given him to go on with his Midland scheme and that, instead of any obstacles being thrown in his way, he be supported and encouraged as long as there is any reasonable hope of his success.

I think the Board is in a position in which the interest of the Atlantic Company can be protected without detriment to the Midland scheme. I feel that I can trust the Board to do both.[34]

A&H—GP

D. C. Salisbury[35] to Thomas J. Jarvis

Old Fort.
McDowell Co
April 24./82

I wish very respectfully to call your attention to the manner in which the W. N. C. Rail Road are working "mud cut" by sluicing with water. It [is] making the water in Catawba River unfit for cattle or horses, killing the fish, and destroying the "spawn,"

---

[34]The Board of Directors of the Atlantic and North Carolina Railroad met on May 9 and resolved that, according to the terms of the lease, the lessees could not sub-let, mortgage, or in any way assign the lease. The resolutions also stated that the contract was liable to forfeiture, because the lessees were not prosecuting the construction of the line from Goldsboro to Salisbury with the vigor stipulated by the contract. The board, however, postponed action against the lessees to give the latter opportunity to explain their action. *News and Observer,* May 11, 1882.

[35]Gristmill operator of McDowell County. Branson, *Directory for 1884,* 442.

and doing great damage to mill dams by filling them with mud. Knowing you had the welfare of WNCRR in view, as well as the legal, and natural rights of the citizens of the state in your keeping — I thought it best make my complaint to you & I have no doubt a word from you to the President of the Road will induce him to work out that cut with care, which I think can be done cheaper and better than any other way

A&H—GLB

Thomas J. Jarvis to R. T. Lincoln

Executive Department,
Raleigh, April 26, 1882

I am in receipt of yours of the 21ˢᵗ instant,[36] asking for information as to any changes in the Congressional Districts of this State under the apportionment act of February 25, 1882.

No changes have yet been made. The Districts — eight in number — will remain as they are until after the meeting of the General Assembly in January, 1883. The ninth member to which this State is entitled under the new apportionment, will be elected by the State at large at the election next fall. I will gladly notify you of the changes in the Districts after they are made, if you shall then so desire it.

A&H—GLB

Thomas J. Jarvis to D. C. Salisbury

Executive Department,
Raleigh, April 27, 1882

Yours of the 24ᵗʰ instant to hand and its contents noted.

The Commissioners of the Western Road are not charged with any supervision of that part of the Road east of the point to which the trains were running when the Road was sold.

However much I may regret any damage done by the washings from Mud–Cut to the people along the upper Catawba, it is a question of private rights with which I can have nothing to do, either as Commissioner or Governor.

---

[36]Governors' Papers, not included in this volume. For explanation, see Jarvis to Kenan, February 27, 1882, in this volume.

A&H—GP

George Dewey[37] to Z. B. Vance

Office of the Light–House Board,
Washington, April 29th, 1882

Dear Sir:

Referring to your endorsement of April 18th, in the letter of the quarantine physician, Wilmington, N. C., making, by direction of the Governor of North Carolina, application to the Light House Board for the temporary use of the abandoned light house at Price's Creek, N.C., for hospital purposes,[38] I beg to inform you that the Board, at its session on April 27th, ordered that the application be granted on the condition that the property be left in as good order as when received, and that it be restored to the custody of the Light House Establishment on due notice.

Major A. C. Hains, U. S. Engineer, Engineer of the 6th Light House District, has been directed by the Board to turn the property over to the quarantine physician, on these conditions.

A&H—GP

C. S. Hewitt[39] to Thomas J. Jarvis

Maysville Jones Cty NC. May 20/82

During the session of the Legislature 1881 an act was passed authorizing the employment of a number of Convicts (20 I think) to work upon certain roads in Onslow County, as by reference to the act. You will see the provisions of the bill This road crosses as fine a body of State lands as any in the State numbering thousands of acres, a large portion of which has been taken up by entry, awaiting the completion of the road, which when done, the State will begin to realize a great source of revenue as applications for patents will be continually forthcoming at the office of Sec. of State This Road is now ready for the reception of the Convicts, the road bed having been cleaned of all rubbish, consequently the next thing wanted is the spade & shovel.

---

[37]At this time Dewey was naval secretary of the Light-house Board. *Dictionary of American Biography*, V, 269.

[38]See Curtis to Jarvis, April 1, 1882, in this volume.

[39]Unable to identify.

It is the hope of the Commissioners appointed under the provisions of this bill, one of whom is your humble servant, that your Excellency will give this matter its proper attention as a very large number of the citizens of Onslow are deeply interested in the completion of this work, and are already beginning to despair of any State aid I trust it will be the pleasure of your excellency to confer with me, and give me all the information I may need as to the time when the convicts provided for in the bill can be had, and to whom is the proper authority to apply to for them. Please write me upon reception of this and please to be as explicit as you can

A&H—GP

John T. Patrick[40] *to Thomas J. Jarvis*

Wadesboro, N. C., May 23rd 1882

Please let me know by return mail what you will do in the immigration matter. I am receiving from two to ten letters per day from parties in the Northern States. Received seven to–day. One of them writes "Our organization is about compleate. Rev W. B. Evers, Pres. H. V. Mohn, Sec. These are men of some means and energy. There are now 20 families belonging to it. They want 20000 acres. The land will be divided into 100 & 125 acre lots They will bring in good moral citizens Religious people preferred but must be moral and industrious. Please see those parties owning large tracts and secure them for us. Find out first cash price, 2nd time price, 3rd cash amt in four annual payments without interest &c. They are planning for two hundred families. Let me hear from you as soon as you can so as they can arrange to come down." — RAW.

Another letter reads, "I desire to change my location for one father South. I ask you to show me some of the inducements of N. C. I am a farmer and know nothing else. What is horses worth cows & land. Could not take over five or six thousand dollars with me"

---

[40]Patrick was editor and publisher of the *Pee Dee Herald,* but at this time he was becoming increasingly interested in town promotion and developing. In 1884 he stopped newspaper work and devoted himself entirely to promotional work. *North Carolina Biography,* VI, 174–176.

Without some aid I can not attend to all the applications that I am receiving, and besides we have not the places in our county to place them. If I had the state to work in there is no doubt, but I could place during the next twelve months five thousand *good* famelies.

A&H—GP

A. H. Canedo to Thomas J. Jarvis

New York, May 27ᵗʰ 1882

In developing our scheme to the most eminent Bankers and Capitalists, English, German and Americans, we find there is not a dissenting voice as to the brillancy of the scheme, its practicability and outlook for profitable business as well as the great advantage to the State of North Carolina and its chief sea port Wilmington.

But no inducement thus far presented however brilliant, can be of any avail in bringing in capital to the enterprise while the contract, as it now exists, contains such unbusiness like and illiberable conditions.

I refer especially to the clause where the stock [of the C.F. & Y.V.R.R.] is retained by the State as a lien.

It is obvious that when we pay in $155.000 and go on with the work, the State has the benefit of it if ye did nothing more.

We cannot sell or carry off the road, we cannot sell bonds for more than every five miles as built.

Capitalists who put in their money are not going to stop short and sacrifice it all; and, admitting we sold the stock, which at present is valueless in this market, would we not lose control of the road?

If we built a portion of the road and abandoned it we would be the only losers, the State having been paid for the stock, and all the work done inures for the benefit of the road and the State and other stockholders; therefore it is unjust to ask us to put money into an enterprise and have no control of it, forfeit all we have done and more too.

The stock should be transferred, as in all other stock transactions, upon payment of the purchase money.

Again, it is conditioned that the State retain control of the bonds & c.

In no case has ever a railroad bond been invested in except in the country or state when the money is paid or advanced upon it; hence there should be a trustee in behalf of both parties, in the City of New York or in London or wherever the arrangement is made for the hypothecation at 50¢ on the dollar, to be paid out only, upon completion of portions of road as agreed on, say five miles at a time, cross ties and rails. These bonds will be hypothecated only, not sold, so that we can take them up, cancel and make a new issue after legislation.

The modifications sought for then — are, an absolute transfer of the State stock to the purchasers, to be held by the State as provided, as a lien or forfeit until the first year's contract is completed, and no further forfeit required.

An entire surrender of the bonds &c. to a trustee jointly designated at or in a place indicated by the capitalists, the proceeds of such bonds to be placed to the credit of the Construction Company upon every five miles of road, cross ties and ironed (steel rails) certified upon engineer's sworn certificate.

The contract in other respects to remain the same and be carried out.

The enclosed letter[41] embodies the provisions called for, the writers references are Winslow, Lanier & Co., Vermilyea & Co. Bankers.

Rails and rolling stock will be ordered at once upon conditions asked for being granted as stipulated. We can complete the first year's contract from Rae Mont to Greensboro in five or six months, and go on with the rest of the work as provided.

Now I respectfully suggest to your excellency that you, as the executive power in the absence of the legislature, might modify the contract as desired, and be sustained by the endorsement of the legislature at its next session; all the more readily that the contract will be carried out in building the road to Greensboro within the time specified, and the wisdom of your action could not but meet the approbation of all concerned.

---

[41]Not found.

A&H—GP

A. H. Canedo to Thomas J. Jarvis

New York, May 29th 1882

With this I send you some of our correspondence, which please return,

I would appreciate any publicity of the accompanying letter, particularly to the press, as they will be so apt to garble or make unreasonable comments, and besides we do not want our operation known to other corporations and individuals who may be inimical to our scheme

If the modification is made we will begin work in a short time and complete the work to Greensboro by the time the contract calls for. Thus after all nothing will be lost.

The contract was accepted as it is, in the hope the extra session would give us the modifications and relief now sought for.

PS
I have been assured by Messr Jones,
York, Vaughan, and others, that they
will support any measure that facilitates the scheme.

A&H—GP

A. B. Andrews to Thomas J. Jarvis

Raleigh, N. C., June 5 1882

The completion of the Western North Carolina Rail Road to Paint Rock and its business connections with the Tennessee system of roads render it necessary to make some changes in the freight tarriffs of the W.N.C.R.R. in order to protect and foster the trade and business of the towns along its lines — It is my desire to give the towns along the line of the W.N.C.R.R. such tariffs as will enable them to command all the trade that properly belongs to them without any detriment to the other cities and towns of North Carolina — By doing this I am not only helping to build up towns along the line of road, but am also enabled to make business for the road itself — At the same time I wish to conform strictly and in good faith to the provisions of the act and contract forbidding any discrimination against cities and towns in North Carolina —

As it is not my purpose to violate this provision of the act I do not wish to make any tariffs of which the commissioners may complain — And as it will not be pleaesant to be arraigned upon charges of discrimination when I am in good faith trying to comply with the act and build up the towns of North Carolina. I beg that you will indicate in advance your construction of the contract and inform me upon what principles a tariff can be made which will not be considered a violation by the commissioners

You will remember when the commissioners were in session early in April in Asheville the matter was discussed so far as Asheville interests were concerned by a committee of the Board of Trade and yourselves and myself though separately and apart — While no definite conclusion was then reached I hope the matter was sufficiently discussed to open the way for some plan now to be adopted by which a tariff can be made that will serve the best interests of the people along the line of the road and at the same time be in harmony with the spirit of the law and will not give rise to any further trouble between the commissioners and the authorities of the Western North Carolina Rail Road

A&H—GLB

Thomas J. Jarvis to A. H. Canedo

Executive Department,
Raleigh, June 6, 1882

I have carefully read over your letter of the 27th of May and its enclosures. As I have heretofore written, I am anxious to do any and everything in my power to push forward and encourage your project of connecting Wilmington with Cincinnati by rail. While that is so, I am obliged to say that whatever provisions are to be found in the contract made by the New York and Southern Railroad and Telegraph Construction Company with the State for the purchase of the State's stock in the Cape Fear and Yadkin Valley Railway Company and for the completion of the said road, that may be called illiberal and unbusinesslike, were put there with the consent of your Company. The time to have raised these objections and made these complaints was before the contract was signed by your Company. But notwithstanding that, what we want is the road built, and if you will

Nerus Mendenhall of Guilford County, Dr. Eugene Grissom of Wake, Honorable William A. Graham of Orange, Thomas G. Walton of Burke, and Dr. M. Whitehead of Rowan were appointed commissioners by the legislature of 1874-1875 to superintend construction, within three miles of Morganton, of the Western Insane Asylum. They were instructed to employ convict labor and an appropriation of $50,000 was made for the first year and $25,000 for the second year. A joint committee was appointed in 1876 to visit the institution and report on the appropriations necessary for construction and on progress and management there. In January, 1877, the legislature provided for three superintendents to supervise completion and construction of the main building and one wing. The Western Insane Asylum was incorporated by the 1881 legislature; upon completion, all inmates in the Raleigh institution from counties most convenient to Morganton and insane inmates of jails were to be transferred there. The 1883 legislature declared the Western Insane Asylum was exclusively for white patients, designated any remaining funds for furnishing and maintenance, and appropriated $40,000 for the next biennium.

come here with the $155,000. and show us your ability to go on with the work, you can get from Commissioners, Governor, Legislators and people the most liberal terms and a hearty support.

A&H—GLB

Thomas J. Jarvis to T. S. Kenan

Executive Department,
Raleigh, June 6, 1882

I will thank you to examine the laws of the State and inform me if there is any law authorizing the opening of the Western Insane Asylum and any law making an appropriation for the *support* of the patients that may be admitted. I am informed that the building will be ready for use in the fall and what I want to know is whether it can then be opened for the reception of patients or will it be necessary to wait till an appropriation is made by the General Assembly for the support of the patients?

A&H—GP

T. S. Kenan to Thomas J. Jarvis

Attorney General Department.
Raleigh, June 7th 1882

After an examination of the acts relating to the subject matter of your letter of the 6th inst., I have the honor, in reply, to say, that the act of 1881 ch. 297 §14, provides that when, in the judgment of the directors of the Asylum at Morganton, the same shall be opened for the admission of patients, they shall receive from the Asylum at Raleigh the patients whose homes are most convenient to the Western Asylum — not to exceed one hundred in number. And *such additional* patients as the Western Asylum may be prepared to accommodate shall be received under the provisions of said Chapter 297, and upon the warrant of the Governor "draw such sums as may be actually necessary for their support and maintenance."

If the one hundred are removed to the Western Asylum, after its directors declare it ready to receive them, I know of no statute appropriating money for their support. But, if the removal be deemed practicable before a specific sum is appropriated for the Western Asylum, no reasonable objection could be raised if the directors of the Asylum at Raleigh should continue to support them out of the general appropriation made for that institution by the Act of 1881, ch. 182; provided their funds be adequate. Although the law *authorizes* them to use the appropriation for the Raleigh Asylum, yet under the circumstances and in the interest of humanity it would not *forbid* them from continuing to support those patients in the event of their removal to the Western Asylum.

But under the latter clause of said section, the Governor is expressly authorized to issue his warrant upon the Treasurer for such sums as may be necessary for the support of such *additional* patients (over and above the one hundred) as may be properly received into the Western Asylum.

I believe this to be the proper construction of the act, though practical difficulties may result from it, and the opening of the Western Asylum for the accommodation of patients temporarily delayed; for I do not think the legislature intended to increase the appropriation for the insane, except in the manner above indicated.

A&H—GLB

Thomas J. Jarvis to John A. Dickson[42]

Executive Department,
Raleigh, June 13, 1882

I have this day drawn a warrant in your favor as Treasurer Western Insane Asylum for five thousands dollars. This makes $70,000. that has been drawn under the appropriation of 1881. There is $10,000 now due you.

I write especially to ask you to see Capt. Walker[43] and ascertain from him if it be *certain* that the $10,000. be sufficient to put the wing and centre building in readiness for the furniture

---

[42]Insurance agent of Morganton, and secretary and treasurer of the Western Insane Asylum. Branson, *Directory for 1884*, 161; "Report of the Committee of the Western Insane Asylum; also a report of the Architect," *Public Documents, 1881*, No. 11, 5.

[43]James Walker, master builder of Wilmington. *Public Documents, 1879*, No. 12, "Report of the Commissioners of the Western Insane Asylum," 2.

and for occupancy by patients? I will thank you to answer this question definitely, as it is important for me to know.

If your answer be that it will be sufficient, then I wish to know the earliest day the institution will be ready to be opened for patients. I suppose the work is now so far advanced that you can safely fix upon a day when it will be ready. It is also important for me to know this and I beg that you will be as accurate as possible in your estimate.

A&H—GP

George Davis et al. to Thomas J. Jarvis [with enclosure]

Raleigh, N.C., June 14th, 1882

Sir: The undersigned appointed Commissioners "to adjust and renew a portion of the State debt," under the act of 1879, chapter 138, beg leave to submit for your consideration and that of the Treasurer of the State, the accompanying agreement entered into between them and those of the holders of the construction bonds of the North Carolina Rail Road, whose names are signed thereto.

In its essential principles this agreement does not differ from that formerly submitted to you and by you to the last General Assembly.[44] The principle of settlement indeed is prescribed by the act and was, of course, adhered to in both. There is a difference, however, in some of the details, by which, while it has been made more acceptable to both parties, it is at the same time, rendered more explicit in its terms, and easier to carry into execution.

The former agreement was not, it is true, approved by the last General Assembly, but inasmuch as the act was not repealed but left in full force, it is plainly a sanction of the principle of the Settlement as established by the act of 1879. Nor can the continuance of the commission be otherwise regarded than as an expression of the Legislative will that some equitable adjustment should still be sought.

There is little doubt that the failure to secure the approval of the General Assembly arose out of an opinion that more favorable concessions might be obtained from the bondholders. Eighteen months have elapsed since the first agreement was

---

[44] See Branch to Jarvis, February 21, 1881, *n.* 32, in this volume.

made, during which time the bondholders have made no over-
ture of any kind to the commissioners, and taken no action looking to an adjustment. It seemed evident from this circumstance
that the former offer to compromise was made in good faith on
the part of the bondholders; that they, in their judgment, had
conceded all that a just regard for their own rights would
admit; and that they had come to the conclusion that further
concession involved such a sacrifice that justice to themselves
demanded that they should abide the result of the foreclosure of
the mortgage under which their bonds were secured, whatever
that result might be.

In this state of facts it seemed to the commissioners that the
only prospect for bringing the matter entrusted to their charge
to a successful issue was for them to reopen negotiations. In the
progress of these negotiations, it abundantly appeared how
unfounded were the opinions of those who supposed that better
terms of settlement could be obtained. It was not, indeed, without much reluctance, that the same terms were now conceded
that had been voluntarily proffered before.

The undersigned submit this agreement as presenting solid
claims to your approval and to the approval of the Treasurer.
They are confident that it embraces the best terms upon which
an adjustment can be made. They are confident, also, that this
adjustment will be in the highest degree beneficial in every
aspect in which it can be viewed. It disposes finally of all those
financial questions which have so long disturbed the minds of
our people and retarded the prosperity of our State. A great
property now all but lost — a property acquired by the self-
sacrificing efforts of many of her most patriotic sons, and identified with the memories of men held in honor by all our people
— is at once revested securely in the State.

These results are accomplished without imposing one dollar
of taxation either for the recovery of the property, or for the
payment of the interest which will accrue upon the bonds issued
for effecting the settlement. Nay, by the terms of this compromise a fund is provided for the final extinction of these bonds.

While it thus takes care of the interest of our whole people,
it in an especial manner preserves the interest of those of her
citizens who subscribed for the construction of this great work,
or which is held by their descendants. It lifts from the State a
burden of debt of more than three quarters of a million. This
involves on the part of the holders of these bonds a surrender

of two hundred and forty dollars on each bond. And when it is considered that this concession is made by creditors whose debts are secured by mortgage upon which foreclosure and sale must follow in a few months, it cannot be regarded as other than a liberal one.

The present value of this great property, which, since the completion of the Western North Carolina Rail Road, forms a most important link in the line of communication between our seaports and the great valley of the West in one direction, and an equally important link in one of the great highways between the North and the South in another, cannot in the most sober judgment be estimated at less than double the amount of the bonds exchanged for its redemption. Its value, when these bonds shall reach maturity, no one conversant with interests of this kind, with the present rate of increase of wealth and population; both of which must be greatly accelerated when the tide of immigration shall be turned to the Southern States, could estimate at less than treble the price fixed by this adjustment. Moreover, by this agreement, this great line of travel and transportation, destined to a factor of incalculable power in the future progress of the State, is held under her own control, and she thus retains the means of adjusting, through conditions inserted in future leases, all those complications to which inequitable discriminations have so often given rise.

For a further exposition of the considerations which have influenced the undersigned in entering into this agreement, they beg leave to refer to their former report.[45] Upon one point only they desire to add a remark. In speaking then of the source from which the dividends for the payment of the interest on the bonds are to be derived, they expressed the opinion that the lease of the road could be continued without difficulty.

What was then expressed as matter of opinion they are now

---

[45] Report of the Commissioners to Adjust a Portion of the State Debt," *Public Documents, 1881*, No. 15.

able to affirm as a matter of fact. It is now known that a lease of the road can be effected for the whole time during which these bonds have to run.

We have the honor to be
Very respectfully,
Your obedient Servants,
Geo. Davis
M. McGehee
D. W. Bain.
Commissioners

[*enclosure*]

The Agreement

Whereas, under an act of the General Assembly of the State of North Carolina, ratified on the 14th day of March, A.D., 1879, entitled, "An act to adjust and renew a portion of the State debt," the Governor of said State was authorized to appoint three commissioners to carry said act into execution by the exchange of the bonds therein mentioned for new bonds to be issued by the said State under the provisions of the said act; and

Whereas, George Davis, Montford McGehee and Donald W. Bain have been appointed by the Governor of the said State commissioners for the purpose mentioned in said act:

Now, therefore, We, the undersigned, holders of bonds of the said State in said act mentioned and described, do hereby severally, and not jointly, propose and agree to and with the said George Davis, Montford McGehee and Donald W. Bain to exchange with them, as Commissioners as aforesaid, all of the said bonds owned, held and controlled by us respectively, on the following terms, viz:

We are to deliver said bonds to said commissioners, with coupons attached thereto falling due on the first day of July, 1878, or the first day of October, 1878, as the case may be, and all coupons falling due subsequent to that date. In case any of said coupons have been detached from said bonds and are not delivered therewith, the amount of such detached coupons shall be noted on the certificate of the commissioners; and in the issuing of the new bonds, the Treasurer shall cut off from them and retain the first maturing coupons for thirty dollars to the amount of the missing coupons and shall deliver the coupons so cut off to the holders of the said old missing coupons, in exchange therefor, whenever the same shall be presented. The balance due on coupons of said bonds due anterior to the first day of July, 1878, is to be paid without interest out of the balance of dividends on the stock owned by the State in the North Carolina Railroad Company, not heretofore distributed in the suit known as the Swazey suit (hereafter mentioned); and if that is not sufficient for that purpose, then out of the surplus of the dividends on the stock owned by the State in the said railroad company, which shall not be applied to the payment of the interest on the new State bonds to be issued under the said act.

In exchange for the bonds thus delivered to us, we are to receive new bonds equal in amount to the principal of the bonds delivered by us to said commissioners, which shall be issued by the said State in all respects in accordance with the provisions of the act above referred to, with semi-annual coupons attached thereto for interest of thirty dollars each, the first of which shall become due and payable on the first day of October, 1882, except that the first coupon of the new bonds issued in renewal of the old January and July bonds shall be for forty–five dollars, instead of thirty dollars: so that the interest on each class of bonds may be equalized — it being the intention of this contract that the bondholders shall rebate to the State two hundred and forty dollars of interest on each bond delivered for renewal. The surplus of the dividends received under said act on the stock owned by the State in the North Carolina Railroad Company and applicable to the said old bonds, after paying the interest on said new bonds, shall remain as and constitute a sinking fund for the payment of the interest due before the first day of July, 1878, on such of the said old bonds as have not been presented and proved in the suit known as the Swazey suit, now pending in the United States Circuit Court for the Eastern District of North Carolina, and after such interest is paid, then for the payment of interest and principal of the said new bonds issued under said act, and shall be sacredly held and applied to this purpose and none other: and such surplus shall be invested in the purchase of the new four per cent. bonds of the said State and all of the bonds thus purchased shall be stamped and marked as the sinking fund for that purpose.

The certificate for the stock owned by the State in the North Carolina Railroad Company shall be held by the Public Treasurer, after the same shall have been returned to the State by order of the Court in the said Swazey suit, until the said new bonds are paid in full; and no lien, mortgage or other incumbrance shall be placed or made on the said stock or by the said railroad company, which shall have a priority over the lien of said bonds on said stock.

And it is understood and is hereby expressly declared to be the true interest and meaning of this agreement that the new bonds to be issued hereunder are given, not in payment, but in renewal and extension only, of the old bonds, and without prejudice to the lien of said old bonds on the State's stock in the North Carolina Railroad Company; which lien is preserved unimpaired for the security of the new bonds as fully as the old bonds are now secured thereby.

John P. Branch,	$500,000.	Bonds.
F. Davenport, Jr.,	34,000.	da.
F. Davenport, Jr., Prest.,	51,000.	da.
James H. Dooley,	75,000.	
A. S. Buford,	35,000.	
Jos. Bryan,	26,000.	
John Stewart,	228,000.	
Chas. S. Stringfellow,	5,000.	
Thomas Potts,	5,000.	
Marshall M. Gilliam,	15,000.	
Andrew Kevan,	17,000.	
D. B. Tennant,	23,000.	
A. Y. Stokes,	23,000.	
W. M. & C. Watkins,	45,000.	Bonds
Tho. Branch,	35,000.	
Bradley T. Johnson,	18,000.	
Clara C. Colston, per F.M.C.,	3,000.	
Wm. C. Seddon,	7,000.	
Freeman Clarke,	225,000.	
William H. Fogg, $1000. each,	40, Bonds.	
Jos. H. Wilson,	3,000.	
J. H. McAden, 67 Bonds,	67,000.	

The undersigned, Commissioners for the State of North Carolina, appointed under and by virtue of the act of 14th March, 1879, entitled, "An act to adjust and renew a portion of the

State debt," do hereby, in behalf of the said State, approve, ratify and adopt the annexed and foregoing agreement and contract.

Geo. Davis,
M. McGehee,
D. W. Bain,
Commissioners.

Executive & Treasurer's Offices,
Raleigh, June 14, 1882

We, the undersigned, Governor and Treasurer of North Carolina, having examined the plan of adjustment of that part of the State debt contracted for the construction of the North Carolina Railroad, as set forth in the foregoing contract, do hereby approve the same and do fully authorize, so far as we are empowered to do, the Commissioners to proceed with the settlement as set forth in said contract.

Thos. J. Jarvis,
Governor
J. M. Worth,
Public Treasurer

A&H—GLB

Thomas J. Jarvis to A. S. Buford [with enclosure]

Executive Department,
Raleigh, June 16, 1882

Things have been going so smoothly in the State of late in railroad matters that I had hoped the managers of the roads in this State, seeing that in serving the best interest of the State and people, they were serving the best interest of their roads, had determined to pursue that policy. I had also hoped that the roads had determined to pursue such a liberal policy in the State as to give no reasonable grounds for complaint. I had still further hoped, after the exceedingly kind and liberal letter written by you to me on the 21st day of Jan. 1882, in reference to the transfer of fertilizers at Goldsboro coming over the A.& N.C.R.R. and the rates of freight thereon, I would not be again called upon to complain about any disregard of the interest of that section of the State. Nor do I now for one moment suppose that the matter which I now beg to call to your attention, was before known to you, because it is so much in conflict with the sentiments expressed in your letter. I know something of men being censured, and often abused, for the acts of others; for there is hardly a week that I do not have to endure it; and hence I do not propose to use any harsh words for what your freight agents have done, but only to ask you to have it corrected. The matter of which I speak is the recent increase of rates on corn from Newbern to this place. I send you enclosed a copy of a letter from J. V. Williams[46] & Co., of Newbern, who are simply one of the many complainants at Newbern and at this place. Corn is very scarce in this section and money with which to buy is, if possible, still scarcer; and to nearly double the freight from Newbern here just at this time is a very great hardship. Besides, Newbern is the natural place, the cheapest place and the most convenient place for this section to buy corn, if not hindered by unjust railroad discriminations. I have tried and shall continue to try to do the railroads full justice. I do not join in the hue and cry against them, but, at the same time, I will not sustain one of them in any wrong attempted to be perpetrated by any of them on any section of the State. And until we have a railroad commission, who shall have this matter specially in charge, I feel it to be my duty to look specially after it and to champion these complaints when they are well founded. I consider this complaint which I now prefer reasonable and I rely upon your sense of right to have the cause removed.

This letter would have been written several days ago but for the absence of Col. Andrews, with whom I wished to talk about the matter before writing to you. He tells me he knew nothing about the change and suggested I write to you.

[enclosure]

J. V. Williams to Thomas J. Jarvis
New Bern, N. C. June 8th, 1882

The Richmond & Danville road yesterday advanced freight rates on grain from this place to Raleigh from 9 to 16 ¢ pr. 100 lbs. and I think it will have the effect of giving the entire market (Raleigh) to Richmond

---

[46]Broker and wholesale dealer in grain. Branson, *Directory for 1884*, 242.

You can see how unjust this is when the fr'ts from Richmond to Raleigh are 16¢ they want to make it 16 from Newberne & compel Raleigh to quite their market (near by & own production) to buy Chicago corn from Richmond. I suppose that this place shipped to Raleigh last month (May) 75 cars corn, we shipped 32 cars. I simply call your attention to these things that you may help our people and the state if you have the opertunities — This is geting to be quite a corn market and large quantities are coming here from North Counties — It is supposed by some here that your sympathies are not with the Midland road and eastern N.C. but this of course I do not believe as you are an eastern man and will look out for the good of the state. If you can I hope you will use your influence to have these rates reduced —

A&H—GLB

Thomas J. Jarvis to T. S. Kenan

Executive Department,
Raleigh, June 16, 1882

One of the guano companies, which has paid the $500. tax for the privilege of selling in this State the fertilizer manufactured by said company, submits to the Board of Agriculture the following question:

Have the town authorities of any town the authority to levy a tax on all fertilizer companies, selling through their agents, on such sale?

I desire to refer this question to you as it involves a construction of both our revenue laws and the laws taxing sale of fertilizers in this State.

I will thank you to examine the various statutes referring to this matter and for your official opinion in answer to the above inquiry.

A&H—GP

J. A. Gray to Thomas J. Jarvis

Fayetteville, N. C., June 16th 1882

I have today forwarded to Treasurer Worth the "return" of this [C.F.&Y.V.R.R.] company for assessment of Franchise upon which your Board will act next Monday, and beg to say a word for your consideration.

Every dollar of the earnings of this road goes into operating expenses, repairs, betterments &c. and it does seem to me that we ought not to be taxed until our earnings amount to more than is absolutely needed to keep it up. Indeed as the State owns so large an interest would it not be proper to relieve us of all taxation so long as the earnings are all used in keeping up the present line and carrying on the work of construction. When the road is completed and begins to earn something it will be no hardship to pay the tax but as it now stands every dollar so paid cripples and retards our progress to that extent.

In addition to the Tax upon franchise, we now pay upon real and personal property at a valuation of $35.000. to the County of Cumberland and the same to the Town of Fayetteville. We also pay upon all our real and personal property in Harnett, Moore and Chatham. The amount assesed against us in each of these counties I have been unable to get though Mr. Rose[47] has written for it several times. But altogether our Taxes amount to no inconsiderable sum and when you fix the assessment upon our Franchise I beg you to favor us all you can. —

A&H—GP

J. A. Dickson to Thomas J. Jarvis

Morganton, June 17th 1882

I find I can not answer the questions in your favor of the 13th, as definitely as you desire. As soon as I can positively I will do so, the coms meets the 21st to consider this subject, will inform you of the result. I think now we will complete by some time during the fall, possibly not until Xmas, & that the cost will

---

[47]George McNeill Rose, lawyer of Fayetteville; member of the General Assembly, 1876, 1881, 1883. Rose was the attorney for the Cape Fear and Yadkin Valley Railroad. Dowd, *Sketches of North Carolinians*, 65.

exceed the appropriation by about $5000. The excess is due to the advance in prices, especially of labor & freights, the uncertainty about the date of completion is owing to the delay of a few parties in filling contracts for material, our chief trouble at present is flooring & finishing lumber, out of a contract for 218,000 feet made in New Bern which was to be delivered in Jany last, only about one half has yet arrived. I will lay your letter before the coms & ask them to direct a reply.

T. S. Kenan to Thomas J. Jarvis

Attorney General Department
Raleigh, June 19 1882

In reply to your letter of the 16th inst. I have the honor to say that I do not think town authorities have the right to levy the tax.

The constitution requires the legislature to establish a department of agriculture, (and then of course to support it). Act. 9 sec. 14. Accordingly, the same was done by the act of 1876-77, ch. 274. That act provides:

Sec. 8. That the manufacturer or importer of the fertilizers, named therein, shall pay to the State treasurer a license tax of $500 to obtain the privilege of selling such fertilizers in this state.

Sec. 22. *All moneys arising from the tax and licenses &c.* shall be paid into the State treasury, and kept on a separate account for the exclusive use and benefit of the agricultural department.

This is the only fund appropriated for its support; and it was also intended that the department should be organized to protect the public from imposition, to keep the traffic in fertilizers in the hands of responsible persons, and to make the means to that end self-sustaining by a license tax. *State* v. *Norris,* 78 N. C. 443.

It would seem therefore upon general principles and the ground of public policy, as well as upon analogy to adjudicated cases, the legislature did not intend that the companies, after paying the privilege tax, should also be subjected to a municipal tax. A tax levied by all the towns and counties in the state, might have the effect of causing a withdrawal of "fertilizer companies" from business in the state — thereby diverting the tax

from the purposes intended, — decreasing the amount necessary
to the support of the agricultural department — and seriously
impairing its efficiency. And it cannot be supposed that the
power was given to municipal corporations thus to indirectly
weaken and obstruct the measures adopted by the legislature
for an institution established under the requirements of the
constitution itself. It will be noticed upon reference to the acts
of assembly, that objection was made to the "50¢ ton tax" provided for in section 8 of the original act establishing the department, for very soon thereafter, and by chapter 291 of the laws
of the same session (1876–77) it was repealed; and then, a
similar tax in section 19 and 20, was repealed by the act of
1879 ch. 175. It is true that the last act repeals *sections* 19 and
20 of the original act, but taking the whole legislation together,
it may be, that the repealing act might have been directed
towards the obnoxious "ton tax," and also to relieve parties who
had paid it, and not to the proviso "that no municipal corporation should tax any of the privileges or subjects taxed by the
State." But be that as it may, I do not think it a material question, for by eliminating, entirely, sections 19 and 20 of the
original act, the result is as above stated.

A&H—GP

A. S. Buford to Thomas J. Jarvis

Richmond, Va., June 20th 1882

I have yours of the 16th enclosing a letter of Mr. J. V. Williams, Newberne, of date June 8th, representing his complaint
in regard to corn rates from Newberne to Raleigh. I have made
full enquiry into this matter and beg to state the facts as they
exist, in reply and explanation.

The former rate from Newberne was an old one adopted, perhaps temporarily, for special reasons which do not now exist.

When rates from Newberne, were recently advanced to 16¢,
they were also advanced from Portsmouth to Richmond, to 18¢,
so that Mr. Williams apparent justification, that the advance
was made in order to force purchases to be made at Richmond
of Western corn instead of at Newberne, for North Carolina
corn, is entirely unfounded.

The fact is, I am assured and believe, that in the recent adjustment of rates from the several North Carolina & Virginia ports, the endeavor was to give each port that consideration to which it was fairly entitled, taking pains so far as we could control the question, that there should be no inequitable discrimination against the North Carolina ports.

Please bear in mind that the line from Portsmouth to Raleigh is not run by this Company & only one of the two lines from Richmond to Raleigh is run by this Company; the other line from Richmond being the shorter, and claiming the right to regulate the rate.

I understand the rule for many years has been to give Wilmington, Portsmouth and Richmond the same rates to Raleigh, — that in the recent revision it was thought that Newberne should have the advantage of a somewhat lower rate than either of the other ports mentioned; but as this in some instances would have been possibly somewhat unfair to Wilmington, it was concluded that inasmuch as they were both North Carolina ports, that both Wilmington and Newberne should be allowed to share in the advantage, and therefore, a *lower* and equal rate was given to each.

Please also bear in mind, that a large portion of the corn producing districts of eastern North Carolina, is directly interested in having equitable rates from Portsmouth, as against any other port, whether in Virginia or North Carolina. This claim had to be respected in the consideration of rates. As Portsmouth has always done & claims to do a portion of the North Carolina grain trade, & the people of that section find it to their interest to use that shipping point.

So far as discrimination, therefore, is concerned against the North Carolina ports in favor of Richmond, or even Portsmouth, you see there is no foundation for it whatever. The only question is, have the rates been advanced from *all* the ports unreasonably? If they be reduced from Newberne, the other ports will claim a like reduction, and it is not seen where the Newberne shipper can derive any advantage as between that point and others; and as this Company can only adjust rates from all the points named upon agreement with other lines, for the reasons above stated, you will see that it is impossible for us to do more than to ascertain what will be done by these other lines; for example; the Richmond and Petersburg line from Richmond, & the Raleigh and Gaston line from Portsmouth.

Fountain at Round Knob, N. C.   "On Line of Southern Railroad."

    In 1870 railway transportation development was more or less abandoned by the state and taken over by private enterprise. The first step was the leasing of the North Carolina Railroad to Virginia and northern capitalists. They also acquired the Richmond and Danville Railroad as well as several other companies. When Governor Jarvis concluded the state was steadily losing money in the Western North Carolina Railroad and was unable to complete proposed construction, he gained support for its sale to W. J. Best and a New York syndicate. Best assumed an $850,000 mortgage and paid the state $600,000 in cash for its outlay on the railroad since 1875. He also agreed to complete the road to the Tennessee border. The Richmond and Danville Railroad subsequently acquired the Western North Carolina Railroad and in 1894 it was, in turn, reorganized into the Southern Railroad Company. Andrew's Geyser, a familiar landmark on the Western North Carolina Railroad, was given in tribute to Alexander Boyd Andrews by George Fisher Baker, president of the First National Bank of New York.

Our General Freight Agent is now endeavoring to ascertain from the other lines how and to what extent they will consent to some suitable reduction, based upon either an equality of rates from the different ports named, or such proximate equality as will protect the trade in eastern North Carolina from any apprehended discrimination.

You will observe that the question with the Newberne shipper is not so much what the rate is as *how it is* in comparison with other neighboring ports in North Carolina and ports in North Carolina and Virginia. At present, rates are absolutely in favor of both Newberne and Wilmington by a difference sufficient ordinarily to control business.

If the other lines consent, a reduction on the rates from all the ports may be made, and if made, we will endeavor to see that no unfair discriminations are made against any of the markets which have occasion to use our lines.

I return herewith the letter of Mr. Williams which you enclosed me, & beg you to accept my thanks for the unprejudiced opportunity now or hereafter, to explain or correct any irregularities supposed or real in connection with our Railroad interests in your State.

A&H—GLB

Thomas J. Jarvis to George Davis, Montford McGehee, &
D. W. Bain

Executive Department,
Raleigh, June 21, 1882

I have received the contract which you have entered into with the holders of what are known as the "construction bonds" for the adjustment of that part of the State debt created for the construction of the North Carolina Railroad. This contract, as you state in your letter conveying it to me, I find to be, on examination, substantially the same as the one submitted to me in the latter part of the year 1880. I did not approve that contract for the reasons stated in my message to the Legislature. In that message, I stated that the wisdom of the plan of adjustment "hinged upon the probable future of the North Carolina Railroad."

I have approved this contract because I think the situation is very different now to what it was when submitted to me before. Then the completion of the Western North Carolina Railroad was by no means as certain as now. It was not then certainly known that this burden would not be again thrown back upon us and the State become again burdened with her obligations concerning it. It may now be fairly assumed that the State is not likely to be again burdened with this road. The completion of this road to Paint Rock and its extension on the Ducktown line makes the Western North Carolina Railroad an important feeder to the North Carolina Railroad and, I think, goes far to fix its future value. In fact, I think the question upon which I suggested to the Legislature the wisdom of the proposed adjustment depended, has been answered. I now regard the problem as to the future of the North Carolina Railroad settled. Situated as it is; with the present prosperity of the State and her bright outlook for the future, the road, it seems to me, can but be regarded as a very valuable piece of property. The plan of adjustment of the debt agreed upon and submitted to me, will, I believe, save this valuable property to the State without imposing upon the people one dollar of taxation. With the change in the condition of things since the fall of 1880, when this question was submitted to me before, the doubt that I then had as to the wisdom of the proposed settlement, have been removed. While I think it a good settlement for the bondholders, I also think it a good settlement for the State and I have therefore approved it. As a part of the bonds fall due January the first, 1883 — before the meeting of the Legislature — it is necessary that there shall be no unnecessary delays in the settlement: so I have approved the contract at once and herewith return it to you, with the approval of the State Treasurer, to be filed in the vaults of the Treasury. Unless this settlement be effected, the State's stock may be sold; and being sold for cash in large blocks, it is not likely to bring par or anything like it. Thus the State may lose the property and still have a considerable debt hanging over her. I therefore beg to suggest that you have the new bonds printed as early as convenient and that you proceed with the exchange.

J. D. Whitford to Thomas J. Jarvis

Newbern, N. C., July 4th, 1882

Up to this time (night) we have heard nothing from the Midland N.C.R way Co. respecting the $20,000 now due for the rental of this Road. To–morrow, I will see our Attorney, Mr [C. C.] Clark, & if necessary we will take such steps as may prevent embarrassment hereafter — I will inform you of our consultation, We will act upon prudent advice —

Some of the coupons from our bonds are already in Bank here for collection & will be posted for payment — When we had money it bothered us to get in the debt & when we havent it bothers us to push it off — I suppose when you receive this you will have the "wisdom" of the State at hand. Well he that runneth, whoever *he* may be will find his mamas boy well abused ere he is elected or defeated. —

.   .   .   .

Speech before the State Democratic Convention in Raleigh, July 5, 1882[48]

Long and loud were the calls for Gov. Jarvis, who in response took the stand amid continued cheering and applause, and made a speech which was a model. He said he would not make a campaign speech but only say a few words of caution and encouragement to this grand assemblage of the representatives of the good old Democratic party. Ever since the Republican party in 1867 dragged its corrupting body into North Carolina he had as a member of the Democratic party participated in every political campaign. He did not propose to make this campaign an exception and remain quiet during its progress, but proposed to enter the canvass and stay in it. He believed as honestly and as earnestly as he did in any fact ever proved, that the best interest of North Carolina and the Democratic party were one and the same. [Cheers] Empanel a jury of any twelve honest colored Republicans and he believed that in their hearts they would find it to declare that it was to the interest of North Carolina that the Democratic party should control the State. Two State conventions, both calling themselves political conventions,

---

[48]Taken from the *News and Observer*, July 6, 1882.

have recently assembled in this city. One took to itself the name of the "Anti-Prohibition, Liberal Convention."[49] He did not know what others might think, but it was his idea that this name was well chosen. People who were in Raleigh in 1868–69, and familiar with the actors in the Republican arena at the capitol then, saw on the 7th of June last many familiar faces, for as a matter of fact the men who controlled that convention were the same old set who congregated around the capitol in other days. There were such men as William A. Moore,[50] J. J. Mott,[51] James H. Harris,[52] J. E. O'Hara,[53] I. J. Young[54] and others, who were leading spirits on both occasions, and many others might be enumerated. As to the appropriateness of the term "Liberal," the Governor read some figures taken from the Auditor's books, which showed that during the period from September, 1868, to September, 1870, when the Republican party had absolute control of the State, the ordinary expenses of the State government were $1,893,637.08. Now, wasn't that truly "liberal?" [Great laughter and cheers.] Hence, when the convention of June 7th called itself liberal it called itself rightly. The Republicans were the most liberal people in the world so far as collecting taxes from the people and then squandering the money. Then, their name of "Anti-Prohibitionists" was an apt one, for it was their desire to get in power and thus put a stop

---

[49]In the spring of 1882, a faction of the North Carolina Republican party sought to take advantage of the increasing sentiment against prohibitionism and Bourbon Democracy. On June 7 they held a convention in Raleigh and organized the Liberal Anti-Prohibition party. They drew up a "liberal" platform and chose a slate of candidates for the approaching November elections. A week later the Republican convention endorsed the candidates and platform of the new party. Daniel J. Whitener, *Prohibition in North Carolina, 1715–1945* (Chapel Hill: University of North Carolina Press [Volume 27 of *The James Sprunt Studies in History and Political Science*], 1946), 73–77, hereinafter cited as Whitener, *Prohibition in North Carolina.*

[50]Lawyer of Edenton; member of the General Assembly, 1868. Branson, *Directory for 1884,* 218; Connor, *Manual, 1913,* 560.

[51]John James Mott, physician of Iredell County, and member of the General Assembly, 1868. Mott had been one of the leading Republicans in the state for the past fifteen years, and from 1876 to 1886 was chairman of the state Republican Committee. Since 1872 he had been collector of internal revenue for the sixth district. Ashe, *Biographical History,* IV, 331–339.

[52]James H. Harris of Raleigh; member of the Constitutional Convention of 1868; member of the General Assembly, 1869, 1872, 1883. For the past several years he had been deputy collector of internal revenue. Dowd, *Sketches of North Carolinians,* 70–71.

[53]James Edward O'Hara, lawyer of Halifax County; member of the General Assembly, 1868; member of the Convention of 1875; Republican representative to Congress, 1883–1887. *Biographical Directory of Congress,* 1,369.

[54]Unable to identify.

to Democratic economy and honesty which now prohibited Radical stealing. Here the Governor read extracts from the Auditor's reports showing that, in the past two fiscal years, from September, 1879, to September, 1881, the expenses of the State government, under Democratic rule, were only $925,000. Look at this, on the one hand, and the $1,800,000 spent by the Republicans on the other, and we see at a glance that Radical government costs the people just twice as much as the Democratic rule. The Democratic party has stood, stands, and will stand like a stone wall against this "liberality" of the Republicans. The Republican party has sought to reinforce its ranks by an "assistant party," for so the Liberal party has been aptly termed. Hungry Democrats had joined hungry Republicans. If he had to turn either loose in the Treasury, he would say turn the Republican in. [Laughter.] Now who cast the bulk of the Republican votes in the State? Why the 105,000 negro voters. The Republicans in Congress have an idea that all the negroes vote the Republican ticket, so they only ask if the voters are black or white, believing that if the former they are sure to vote the Republican ticket. They calculate, and pretty safely calculate, that these votes shall be wielded a solid mass. In addition to this colored vote are the revenue officers, a power and a plague in the land. How many thousands there are of these, nobody knows. The system has an army of employees, who swarm everywhere. When an election comes off it appears from investigations now in progress at Washington, their number is greatly reinforced. The revenue collectors, it is charged, go about with blank commissions buying votes, and they have thus purchased for a consideration some Democrats. His definition of a "liberal" was a "purchasable Democrat." Not long since a prominent Republican had declared that the Liberals made the Radicals appear good by comparison. So the revenue people go about and find some person who loves $4 a day better than he does his State. So we have the run of the Republican party, the darkey, its backbone, the revenue officers and the liberals or hungry Democrats.

Governor Jarvis went on to say that so long as that crowd of people banded together as one, so long as the colored voters stand together, controlled by revenue officers, just so long will the white people stand together. As a matter of fact he thought it would be best if parties were only divided on great questions of public interest. But this, it seemed, was not to be the state of facts, for though we wish these things so, we cannot have them so. He had tried earnestly, steadily and conscientiously to do his duty to the colored people, both as an officer and as a citizen. They had in all respects had full and equal justice. He had advocated and would advocate taxing the whole people to give the whole people free schools. Their muscle and their labor are to–day aiding in building up North Carolina. It is our duty to see that they are improved, educated, made good citizens. The white people will see that full and fair justice is done them. But so long as they stand together with the men who so nearly ruined the State in 1868 and 1869, just so long will the white people stand for themselves. The administration of affairs under Democratic rule was such as to command public confidence. He defied any man to show that under that administration one dollar of the people's money had been expended save in accordance with law; and he defied any one to find one cent not properly accounted for. [Applause.] He forcibly contrasted this with the Republican rule of plunder and lavish extravagance. He went on to speak again of the revenue system, aptly termed "infernal," saying that it was doomed. Then he took up another very important matter, vigor of action on the part of Democrats. They must all vote, all be earnest, be vigilant, be steadfast, have a speaker everywhere to meet and match each Republican speaker, and contrast the pure record of the Democratic party with the black and odious one of the Republican party. He pledged his personal efforts on the stump in the campaign. Now the State is prosperous and happy. Will the people go back to the dark days? [Cries of no.]

A&H—GP

J. D. Whitford to Thomas J. Jarvis

Newbern, N. C., July 5th 1882

Rec'd 16th Section of the lease — We cannot give notice before 30 days expire from the 1st July therefore, will keep quiet until then, unless when we have to explain when demands are or as for money due. Agreeably to the contract of lease we notified the Bank here not to allow any more of the Coupons for interest on the bonds they hold as security &c cut off of bonds until rental is paid — They had been taken off on May 1st as they are payable May & November. We now have no money — Not a dollar, in our Treasury — Neither the Treasur nor myself draw our Salary for June. I mention this as I have heard we take care of each other, if some small bills were left unpaid by us — I did not think Mr. Best would have paid the interest on the 1st July as if he designed to pay about that, he would have had it done before our Stockholders Meeting, We can do nothing but wait for the expiration of the 30 days or for the interest in the meantime.

A&H—GP

A. H. Canedo to Thomas J. Jarvis

New York, July 17th 1882

I am requested by the Capitalists who propose to enter upon our matter, to ask you if it would be agreable to meet their representative, Mr. A. N. Martin of firm Post & Martin of this City at either Morehead City or Montgomery White Sulpher Springs, Va. — preferable the latter — within the next ten days — notice of the exact day to be telegraphed you after the reception of your answer to this — or, setting your time, to suit your convenience and that of Mr. Gray, who will be written to under this date on this subject. — It is proposed that Mr. Gray, Mr. De Rosette, Mr. Merrimon or Mr. Fuller, of Counsel and myself, with Mr. Martin meet you as above to discuss measures whereby we may facilitate immediate action on the Rail Road matter.

While we are aware that the time for the payment of the money &c. has lapsed, we beg to assure you that we have been diligent in working up the matter, and have expended much time and money to bring the enterprise to a successful issue.

We consider ourselves in the field, and in any discussion of the subject that may come up, by that you will recognize the fact that we are, *defacto*, the Contractors, until the field is otherwise occupied. —

Mr. Martin will be provided with a certified check for $155.000. — to be transferred upon an understanding to be had at our meeting. —

Will you be good enough to cause a half dozen copies of each, the Proposition and Agreement to be sent me by next mail and oblige

[Postscript:]

Kindly advise Mr. Gray of this and of your action in the matter. —

A&H—GLB

Thomas J. Jarvis to A. H. Canedo
[Telegram]

Raleigh, N. C. July 27, 1882

You can see me at Morehead on the 1st of August or at Greensboro on the 9th.

A&H—GP

R. T. Lincoln to Thomas J. Jarvis

Washington City.
July 27th, 1882

Referring to your letter of the 16th of March, last, requesting that Lot 35, in the city of Raleigh, the property of the State of North Carolina, and known as "Camp Russell," and which is under control of the Superintendent of the National Cemetery at Raleigh [G. A. Dichte], may be restored to the custody of the State, I have the honor to inform you that the Quartermaster General[55] has been instructed to direct the Superintendent in charge of Russell Barracks[56] to withdraw himself from the custody and protection of the ground and buildings thereon.

This Department will interpose no obstacle to possession of the property in question being taken by the State.

A&H—GP

Thomas D. Hogg[57] to Thomas J. Jarvis

Raleigh N.C. July 29th 1882

I have carefully examined the A.& N.C.R.R., & I deem it proper to say to you that the Road is in far better order than I

---

[55]Brigadier General Samuel B. Holabird of Connecticut. *Register of Officers of the United States, 1883*, I, 261.
[56]Unable to identify.
[57]Independently wealthy resident of Raleigh. Daniels, *Tar Heel Editor*, 260.

expected.[58] My predecessors had put the value of the iron at Twenty one Dollars ($21.) a ton, & that no doubt influenced my opinion.

The track is a better one than the track of the N.C.R.R. from Greensboro to Goldsboro. I do not say that in depreciation of the N.C.R.R., for that has been getting better every year for four years, but I give it as a standard by which you may judge. Also to estimate what public opinion is worth.

The road-bed needs ditching, and more section–masters of which we have taken notice in our report. Our report may be ready in a week or two.

The cars were not properly marked. I shall go over the Road again to see that that is properly done.

There is one valuation on which we have differed. We will *probably* make Col. Devine[59] of the W.&W.R.R. our umpire on the value of one car.

Thinking you would like to have this information before my report goes in, I have taken the liberty of writing you.
P. S.

I have reported the condition of the Eastern and of the N.C.R.R several times as fully up to the terms of the Lease.

A&H—GP

John Gatling to Thomas J. Jarvis
[Telegram]

Morehead City 5 Aug [1882]

Can you meet Denny myself & others in Raleigh or Morehead next Wednesday. Answer.[60]

---

[58]For reasons stated above (see Jarvis to Bryan, April 22, 1882, *n.* 34, in this volume), stockholders of the Atlantic and North Carolina Railroad were considering terminating the lease of their railroad by the Midland North Carolina Rail Road Company. The stockholders wanted to make sure that the physical condition of the road had been maintained (see Whitford to Jarvis, March 7, 1882, *n.* 22, in this volume), and Hogg's job was to ascertain the road's condition.

[59]John Francis Divine of Wilmington; general superintendent of the Wilmington and Weldon and the Wilmington, Columbia and Augusta railroads. Ashe, *Biographical History*, VI, 197–201.

[60]When the stockholders of the Atlantic and North Carolina Railroad finally sought to regain their railroad from the Midland Company, John Gatling was appointed receiver of the Atlantic and North Carolina Railroad Company. Brown, *State Movement*, 249.

A&H—GP

J. D. Whitford to Thomas J. Jarvis

Newbern, N. C., Augst. 8th 1882

It will be recollected the Board of Directors of this Co. in consequence of the trust Mortgage executed by the Midland NC Rway Co. to the American Loan & Trust Co, of the City of Boston, rescinded the order, at a meeting in Raleigh, on the 9th of May last,[61] appointing an Agent to act with one from the Midland N.C.R. Way Co. to assess new rolling Stock to take down bonds in bank & s — While we have heard nothing official on the subject of rolling Stock or Mortgage since the appointment of our agt, on the 7th day of last March, from the Midland NC Rway Co, yet, as it is stated, by some of the officers of that Company, the rental will not be paid, though now due over a month, I write to ask you whether you think it necessary that I should call, at once, a Meeting of our Board to have the Agent referred to appointed that we may be ready for any plea or contingency — If the rental were not paid I designed calling a meeting of our Board again to towards the end of this Month — Enclosed, I send you a paragraph from the *Goldsboro Messenger*[62] which first appeared in the *Daily Journal* of this place, It will explain itself —

. . . .

UNC—MG

Thomas J. Jarvis to John Gatling
[Telegram]

Received at Morehead City N. C.   Aug 11 1882.
Dated, Raleigh N. C.

All right I will be down Sunday night.

---

[61]See Bryan to Jarvis, April 20, 1882, *n.* 32; and Jarvis to Bryan, April 22, 1882, *n.* 34, in this volume.
[62]Governors' papers, not included in this volume.

A&H—GP

W. S. Denny to Thomas J. Jarvis [with enclosure]

August 16. 1882

I have the honor to inclose to you herewith a copy of Resolution passed by our Stockholders at a meeting held on the 15th ultmo concerning the Construction of our railroad from Goldsboro to Salisbury.

[*enclosure*]

Aug 16 1882

At a meeting of the Stockholders of this Company held on the 15th ultimo the following Resolution was unanimously passed viz:

"Resolved That The Midland Improvement and Construction Company will go forward with the Construction of the link between Goldsboro and Salisbury as soon as the ownership of the States' Stock in the Atlantic and North Carolina Railroad is acquired or the Legislature of North Carolina shall guarantee to The Midland Improvement and Construction Company or The Midland North Carolina Railway Co. the ownership of said States' Stock upon completion of the road to Salisbury" [63]

A&H—GP

W. C. Kerr to Thomas J. Jarvis

Washington D.C.
Aug. 19. 1882

When I was invited some time ago by the Director of the U. S. Geological Survey[64] to go on that survey & proceed at once to the Rocky Mts. to take part in the work there, in exploring & mapping the territories, I declined to accept, before the end of the year, on the ground that my second volume must be finished, before I could quit the survey of N.C.[65]

---

[63]For an explanation of this resolution, see Sprague to Jarvis, September 4, 1882, in this volume.

[64]John W. Powell of Illinois. *Register of Officers of the United States, 1883,* I, 592.

[65]For the completion of the *Geological Survey,* see Jarvis to the Senate, March 11, 1879, *n.* 54, in this volume.

Now, the U.S. Survey having been extended over the States, by a recent action of Congress, I am invited to take charge of the southern division of that survey, which will cover the territory of the South Atlantic states.

My objection in this case, on the ground of my unfinished report, is met by the following suggestions: —

First, I will be allowed to select my own central point of operations: & I had suggested the mountain region of N.C. from which seven states could be readily reached by working out radially from that point: in this way N.C. will receive the earliest advantage & the U. S. Survey will be firmly and permanently planted there, & all my work hitherto, used as a basis for the work in the adjoining states:

Secondly; The Director of the U. S. Geological Survey offers to publish all the results of any previous work, embodied in my reports to that Department, which will secure the dissemination of these results much more widely than is possible to N.C.; in folio, illustrated editions, of hundreds of thousands of copies, instead of our plain editions of 3000. These seem to me to be advantages not to be lightly refused, And further, I will have the opportunity in the winter, after the field work is ended for the season, to finish my report to the Board of Agriculture, if they still wish to continue the publication of it. I can at the same time put the Geological Museum in order & arrange the specimens in the new cases.

It seems to me plain, therefore that the interest of N. C. requires that I accept the position offered me, as United States Geologist; & with your approval & that of the Executive Committee, I will enter at once upon the work indicated, retaining my official relations to the Board until my report is published, or such terms as may approve themselves to your judgment & that of the Board.

I congratulate myself, that just as my long term of service in the State Geological Survey was drawing to a close, I am thus enabled not only to continue but to enlarge it, & to renew the prospect, which had faded out of my hope, of seeing a work, to which I had given the best years of my life, & which is intact only fairly begun, taken up again & pushed forward with ampler means toward the certain & speedy accomplishment of plans & achievement of results of the greatest importance to the prosperity of the state.

I suggest that during my absence Mr. W. B. Phillips be placed in charge of the Geological Museum, keep up the correspondence of the office, attend to the routine work, forwarding to me any letters that may require my attention; & that if agreeable to [the] Board, as soon as he can be spared from the Laboratory, he be appointed Assistant Geologist, with a salary of $1200. Mr. Phillips is better qualified for this position than any one in the state, whom I could name to you. He is capable & assiduous, fond of the work & enthusiastic in the pursuit of information, & I am satisfied will prove efficient.

In referring these important matters to your decision, I rely with entire confidence upon your clear judgment & devotion to the true interests of North Carolina.

A&H—GP

A. H. Canedo to Thomas J. Jarvis

New York, Aug 21st 1882

We wrote to our counsel Messr Merrimon & Fuller, full details of our affairs and prospects with reference to the CF&YV. RR. — that they might be the better prepared to advise us, and act in our behalf where occasion required.

We instructed them to advise with you relative to the necessity of your visit to New York to confer with some gentlemen who have the matter of the CF&YR. seriously in hand:
Mr Gray said last fall that if the emergency arose he would come on to N Y and bring you with him.

Now, the matter is urgent from the fact that there are two setts of Capitalists, who would like to see you; and it would not be convenient, or polite for so many to go down simultaneously to N.C.

The points to be discussed are; Some arrangement by which the Certificate of Stock and outstanding bond ($54.600) can be placed in a mutual Trust Co here, pending an immediate cancellation of the existing mortgage. — the making of a new mortgage, and the issuing of new bonds or Certificate for the same. And there upon, (the cash being in hand) the full amount placed to the Credit of the State by the Trust Co, all by our simultaneous action. And we then enter upon our work. And also to consult with you as to such modifications as you may feel justified in acting upon through or by virtue of your prerogative.

You will not be pressed to commit yourself to any action inconsistent with your executive powers, but, rather to give your views as to what course to be pursued to obtain legislative action covering our requirements; and, lastly, as these gentlemen have been impressed by us with the conviction that you are deeply interested in the success of the enterprise, not only for the interests of the State, but

as a measure calculative greatly to enhance your prestige, which it will certainly do. The gentlemen spoken of will all be here in the City this week and from that time on, and I would be glad to know at your earliest convenience when it would suit you to come.

You will be met and conveyed to suitable quarters.

A&H—GP

Aristides Monteiro[66] *to Thomas J. Jarvis*

New York Aug 28th 1882

There is now a lively interest in Southern lands manifested by the Capitalists of New York. I have seen several parties that are disposed to buy such lands as the State of North Carolina offers for sale; Will you be kind enough My dear sir to, inform me, or instruct me how to procure the information as to a description and the number of acres & price asked by the State for the mountain lands; Mr Scarborough has kindly informed me of the character number of acres &c, of eastern North Carolina, and I have found parties here who have concluded to make an offer for the same. These lands I have been told are under the control of the Board of public Education. While the Capitalists here are disposed to invest in Southern lands, I feel assured the State can sell all her mountain lands at the price mentioned to me by Mr Scarborough when I met him at Wilson last June. Please let me know what State office can enable me to place this question before the monied men looking toward Southern investments. Knowing the deep interest, you have always manifested in the welfare & prosperity of your grand old Commonwealth & her noble people, I have presumed to intrude this letter upon you. . . .

[66]Physician of Columbia. Branson, *Directory for 1884*, 620.

Thomas A. Jarvis to A. H. Canedo

Executive Department,
Raleigh, Aug. 29, 1882

I hardly think it will be convenient for me to visit New York to have an interview with those who wish to join you in the purchase of the State's interest in the Cape Fear and Yadkin Valley Railroad. I shall be glad, however, to see any of the capitalists to whom you refer in Raleigh at any time that suits their convenience and talk the matter over with them. Or, if they prefer, I shall be glad to have a communication from them.

I beg to call your attention to the fact that our Legislature meets the first of January next and, as that is only four months off, it will be better to wait until then for any amendments that your friends may desire in the contract or in the charter of the company, as that body alone has the authority to make such as you are likely to desire. I also desire to impress upon you the importance of perfecting your plans by the meeting of the General Assembly (if you desire to pursue the matter further), as there are likely to be other bidders for this property next winter.

Thomas J. Jarvis to Aristides Monteiro

Executive Department,
Raleigh, Aug. 29, 1882

There are two classes of vacant lands in this State—one is the swamp land and the other land not swamp land. The swamp lands lie in the eastern part of the State in large bodies. The State Board of Education holds the title to these lands and is authorized to sell them at prices to be agreed upon by the Board and the purchaser. The State holds the title to the vacant lands not swamp lands. They are subject to entry and grant at 12½ and 15 cents per acre, according to quantity; but the State does not gurantee the title. The State does not own any large bodies of these lands of which I am aware. Whenever a man thinks a piece of land is vacant and applies for a grant, we issue it to him upon his paying the price and he takes the chances as to whether he gets any title or not. There are large tracts of land for sale in the western part of the State, but they are owned by individuals. It may be that in the mountains some vacant lands can be found, but we have no record as to where they lie or anything as to their value.

If you desire at any time any definite information as to the swamp lands, Mr. Scarborough will gladly give it to you.

A&H—GP

J. D. Whitford to Thomas J. Jarvis

Newbern, N. C., Augt 29th 1882

Yesterday Cashier Guion[67] gave out in the morning that Col Caddagan told him the $20,000 rental would be in Bank North for him if he would pay it here, which he promised to do on rect of telegram from Northern Bank to that effect. Last night the post Master[68] here informed me that Guion had received the telegram as above — thus, I suppose the contest about the Road is ended for the present. Hereafter unless Best & Co. are made to pay interest they will take the advantage of the two months & make our rental payable every 8 months instead of every six months — What think you? — I have called our Directors to—gether to-morrow Gatling goes up to day & I learn will come back to the meeting, talk with him & Faison, if opportunity offers about our future action.

Dr. Hogg's report is in & you will no doubt be gratified to know we have one of the *very* best Roads in the State — Only 400 tons of new rails will be required in years, the Road bed is in splendid condition So is the Superstructure & bridges & so also is the Rolling Stock. It will be a Capital report to send to the Legislature & will prove to that body heretofore we have had the least abused Road in the State.

---

[67] John A. Guion, cashier of the National Bank of New Bern. Branson, *Directory for 1884*, 242.

[68] John S. Manix. Branson, *Directory for 1884*, 238.

A&H——GP

Thomas J. Jarvis to M. W. Ransom

[*Telegram*]

Raleigh Aug. 29 1882

Whites one hundred & thirty eight blacks eight hundred & fifty six[69]

A&H——GLB

Thomas J. Jarvis to W. C. Kerr

Executive Department,
Raleigh, Aug. 30, 1882

I am in receipt of your communication of the 19th instant, concerning your work as State Geologist and your desire to enter the work proposed by the United States in extending its geological survey of the States and Territories to the Atlantic States.

I believe that North Carolina possesses mineral wealth and geological importance equal, if not superior to any of the Atlantic States. Neither capital nor science has ever been properly attracted to these resources, because they have never, until recently, been properly advertised and made known. I consider this opportunity to get these things published in the geological reports of the Government of the United States, of great value, if we but properly avail ourselves of it. If you take charge of the survey for the South Atlantic States, I shall feel confident that North Carolina will receive the position she merits in these reports. I have talked the matter over with Dr. Battle, one of the Executive Committee of the Board of Agriculture, and we have agreed to give our consent to the proposed arrangement, relying upon the Board and the Legislature to give whatever sanction to our action that may be necessary.

You will put Mr. W. B. Phillips in charge of the museum and your office as your assistant and give him such directions as to the business of the office as may be necessary.

---

[69]Apparently Senator Ransom had recently asked Jarvis for information on the convict situation in North Carolina. On August 29 Jarvis requested a quick and brief report from the warden of the penitentiary (not found), and on the same day the warden submitted such a report to him. Hicks to Jarvis, August 29, 1882, Governors' Papers, not included in this volume.

I am aware that this arrangement will delay the publication of the second volume of your report for some months, but I think the advantages of the arrangement will greatly more than compensate for the delay. It is, however, my desire that you push its publication as rapidly as possible and that, as soon as the inclement weather of winter comes on, when field work is suspended, you devote yourself assiduously to this work.

A&H—GP

William Simpson[70] to Thomas J. Jarvis

Raleigh, N. C., Sept. 1st, 1882

In accordance with the provisions of the "Pharmacy Act 1881," I have the honor to submit to your Excellency the following report of the proceedings of the Board of Pharmacy for the year ending Sept. 1st, 1882:

On May 17th 1881, the members of the Board, consisting of Messrs. Wm. H. Green, Wilmington E. H. Meadows, New Bern, E. M. Nadal, Wilson, A. G. Lee and Wm Simpson, Raleigh,[71] holding commissions from your Excellency, met in the town of Goldsboro; the Board was duly organized and the following officers elected viz. Wm. H. Green President and Wm. Simpson Secretary and Treasurer. The term of service of the several members expiring in one, two, three, four and five years, the term of each was determined by lot, with the following result, Mr. Lee for one year, Mr. Meadows for two years, Mr. Green three years, Mr. Nadal four years, the Secretary's being fixed by law at five years.

A circular letter, reciting the provisions of the Pharmacy Act, and calling the attention of all Druggists and Pharmacists of the State to whom the Act applied, to the requirements thereof, was prepared and mailed to every Druggist whose address the Secretary could procure, ninety days previous to the time when the Act would go into effect. A notice of the same nature was also inserted in several of the leading newspapers of the State.

---

[70]Druggist of Raleigh, and secretary of the North Carolina Board of Pharmacy. Branson, *Directory for 1884*, 649.

[71]These men were druggists in their respective towns as described. Branson, *Directory for 1884, passim.*

The second meeting of the Board was held in the city of Raleigh on August 30th, 1881. All the members present. In response to the circular letter before mentioned, two hundred and seventy applications for registration were received and passed upon by the Board. One applicant for license to practice Pharmacy appeared for examination, and, after due examination he was adjudged properly qualified and a license was granted him.

The third meeting of the Board was held in the town of Goldsboro on May 23rd, 1882 for the purpose of examining such applicants for license to practice Pharmacy as might appear before it. Five applicants presented themselves, three of whom passed a satisfactory examination and were granted licenses, the others failed to pass upon such examination.

The fourth meeting was held in the town of Winston, Aug. 9th 1882. All the members present, and at which three applicants for license appeared for examination, one of whom, failing on a former examination passed satisfactorily at this one. The others failed to pass.

The following statement will show in detail the receipts and disbursements of the Board to date.

.   .   .   .

A&H—GP

D. J. Sprague to Thomas J. Jarvis

New York 4 Sep 1882

I was not aware till about ten days ago that I had been appointed on a Committee with Messrs Denny, Carruth and Gatling to confer with you relative to our interests in the Midland North Carolina Railway and Atlantic and North Carolina Railroad Co. It is impossible for me at this time to leave important business in New York or I would gladly go to North Carolina and meet you.

It is necessary for me to recall to your mind the fact that the gentlemen composing the Boston Syndicate exercised much caution, before entering upon any railroad enterprise in your State, and that cash was not advanced or invested until we had received the strongest assurance of your earnest cooperation and your official support.

We had informed you that we would not take a lease of the

A.&N.C.R.R. and build the link between Goldsboro and Salisbury unless we could have more than that. Having received assurance that we should soon become the owners of the States' Stock in that road, we went forward vigorously with the work of construction and have now twenty two miles of new road in good working order.

We now find that it is vitally important that the State's interest in that road be so placed that there shall be no possible contingency in regard to its ownership and that no political or other organization can leave us owners of a line of Railroad between a leased road on the one side and a, perhaps, hostile road on the other. As our line is pushed forward toward Salisbury, from Goldsboro, we feel that we must control and own permanently with our new road the whole line to the sea board.

It is now absolutely necessary to the further carrying on of our work that some plan be devised by which we are made sure of the Atlantic and North Carolina stock upon the completion of the road to Salisbury. — unless this can be arranged, it is certain that our people will not make a further investment of capital. If it can be arranged, it is also certain that they will complete the railroad to Salisbury and carry out the original scheme. You were assured of this by the unanimous vote of the Stockholders taken at their meeting in Boston on July last.

Last year the Boston gentlemen felt that the Directors of the Atlantic and North Carolina Rail road, nominated by you, should have been men who were pronounced in favor of the Midland. This year they had the greater occasion for surprise at their nomination in view of the friendly speech you made and also in view of the fact that during the past year these same directors have shown no friendship for our scheme, if they have not acted positively in hostility to it.

One proof of your hearty cooperation with us would have been given had they not been appointed. We are often asked for some positive and irrevocable evidence that you will assist our enterprise.

I beg leave to suggest two methods of securing the States interest in this stock, either of which would be acceptable to us.

First: let the State sell us the stock outright taking in payment therefor the note of the Midland Improvement and Construction with satisfactory security, said not to be void or to be regarded as fully paid by the completion of the road to Salisbury; but to be paid in full at maturity, if the road should not be completed and running within the time agreed upon.

Second let the State's interest be placed in escrow in the hands of the American Loan and Trust Company of Boston to be delivered to us on the completion of the road to Salisbury.

It may be that some other plan will suggest itself to you which will bring about the same result. Permit me to urge in behalf of all the gentlemen connected with the enterprise that you confer at once with Mr Gatling and Judge Carruth, my associates appointed on this committee, and devise some method whereby we may immediately control and own this stock, thus assuring the completion of a work of great importance to your State and the development of interests long cherished by yourself.

P. S.

Judge Carruth will be in N.C. within a few days

A&H—GLB

Thomas J. Jarvis to D. J. Sprague

Executive Department,
Raleigh, Sept. 12, 1882

Yours of the 4th inst. was received some days ago. As your letter notified me of Judge Carruth's early visit, I withheld my reply till he came. He, in company with Mr. Gatling, called upon me Saturday and had a long talk with me about the Midland enterprise. The point in the interview was the same as is emphasized in your letter, to wit, the desire of the Boston syndicate to have something definite about the State's stock in the Atlantic Company. I told him, as I now am obliged to tell you, that I have no authority to do anything with the stock and I cannot assume powers that do not belong to me. There are two certificates of stock, belonging to the State, for stock in this Company, locked up in the vaults of the Treasury. One is for 10,666 shares and the other for 10,000 shares. I have no power to remove or pledge these certificates in any way till authorized so to do by the General Assembly.

As I said at Morehead, I think the State can well afford to give your syndicate the stock if you will complete the road from Goldsboro to Salisbury and I will urge the Legislature so to do when it meets in January if the syndicate is prepared in good faith to go on with the work upon the passage of a bill to that effect.

The practical question now to be met is the meeting of the stockholders on the 28th of this month. I had hoped at the June meeting that a new impetus would be given to the Midland enterprise. It was, I think, manifest that the people along the line of the Atlantic road were disposed to warm up to the Midland and give it a hearty support. The syndicate, I think, had an opportunity of strengthening itself and winning the confidence of the people, but I regret to say the opportunity has been thrown away. The thing has been left almost to itself to drag along as best it could. If the President of the Company has been in the State or given the enterprise any attention since the June meeting, I do not know it. The rent was not paid till the very last moment. I know that some of the stockholders begin to feel that the enterprise is practically abandoned and that it stands them in hand to begin to look after their property. I trust you will be able, at the meeting of the 28th to lay something definite before the stockholders. I am still prepared to help the enterprise if its managers will give us any reasonable assurance of their purpose and ability to go on with the work.

A&H—GLB

Thomas J. Jarvis to T. M. Holt

Executive Department,
Raleigh, Sept. 20, 1882

Referring to our conversation of some days ago in reference to the prompt payment of interest on the new bonds of the State, given in exchange for the bonds issued to build the North Carolina Railroad, you fully understand the importance of the interest being promptly paid and my anxiety that it shall be so paid. You also understand why it is that the dividends are not this time sufficient to pay the Oct. interest. It grows, as you know, out of the fact that in order to make all the interest fall due in April and Oct., it was necessary to make the first coupon on some of the bonds forty-five dollars, as some of the old bonds fell due in Jan. and July. This will not occur again and the excess of the dividends over what is required to pay the interest hereafter will soon redeem this present deficiency. The present difficulty can easily be bridged over by the help of your Board. I trust the Board, appreciating the importance of a prompt payment of the *whole* interest, will aid the Treasurer. I am not willing for him to do anything in the matter not fully authorized by law. The deficiency, as I get from Mr. Bain, will be some ten or fifteen thousand dollars; the exact amount cannot be given as we cannot tell now exactly how many bonds will be in by the 1st of Oct. What I desire the Board to do is to authorize your Treasurer to invest enough in the coupons of the new bonds due on the 1st of Oct. as are not paid by the dividends turned over by the receiver. If the Treasurer does not have the funds on hand, then a second resolution will be necessary, authorizing the President to borrow such an amount as may be needed for that purpose. The details of the loan and carrying out of the resolutions can of course be left with you. All the Board need do, as I understand the case, is to pass the two resolutions I have indicated.

I only throw out these suggestions as to the method of accomplishing the purpose; of course, leaving the better judgment of the Board to devise a better plan.

Mr. R. H. Battle, the attorney of the Company, went to Washington City, at my request to see Mr. Phillips, the receiver, and took with him Mr. Bain. I will thank you to see that Mr. Battle's bill is paid and, in doing so, please allow $21³⁰, actual expenses of Mr. Bain. As all of this is a part of his employment as attorney of the Company, I prefer it being paid out of the funds of the Company to paying it out of the funds of the State.

A&H—GP

Rufus Sylvester Tucker[72] to Thomas J. Jarvis

New York, Sept 21 1882

You may be a little surprised to get a letter from at this place, but I cannot permit the opportunity to pass without dropping a word into *your* ear (no body else.) in regard to the A & NCRR. I have seen parties here who are interested with their money in the enterprise & who know nothing of the mangment, but have their money in it. I have also talked with Judge Caruth & he says & they say they must have an extension of time on their contract, or — every thing will be busted up — that it is their intention to build the line, have built 21 miles & will in time

---

[72]Merchant and planter of Raleigh, and at this time president of the Board of Trustees of the North Carolina Institute for the Deaf, Dumb, and the Blind. Dowd, *Sketches of North Carolinians*, 255–257.

complete the remainder, that the Stock holders nor the State can have any thing by delay, that the Pacific Boston Bank failure has interfered with their project but that they have money men at their back & as soon as they see their way a little clear they will push it on; They put their money in it, but can't go out there to attend to it they trust to Best &C[oleman] to do the managing — &c Caruth speaks very kindly of you & says he hopes you will lend your influence to extending the time till next year.

We go out next Tuesday He did not ask me, nor does he know or may care that I am or would write to you I have done so as a citizen and as your friend — if for any cause, their failure or otherwise, they are driven out of N.C. it will hurt us a long time to come. The citizens along the Road are pleased with the management so far & it does seem to me, that if no harm is done by letting them hold on, it will be the best for the present. I have other reasons regarding yourself personally which I can tell you better when I see you we are in the midst of a close election. And a few hundred votes might be of importance to our party. You must excuse me for writing you as I have & I assure you I have no axe to grind. have sold my stock in the Road some time since — & am under no obligation to any one on the Road but I write what I written & from the best motives to you & the State

Please consider this letter entirely *confidential, No one to know* & tear up when read

Keifer proprietor of this Hotel has 20,000 in the Enterprise —

A&H—GP

John De Jarnette Pemberton[73] *to Thomas J. Jarvis*

Wadesboro N.C
Sept 21 1882

Under sec. 11 of the Machinery Act of 1881[74] the value of the franchise of Rail Roads shall be given in by President or chief officer of said roads and shall be assessed by Treas. Auditor & Gov. of the State. The Cheraw & Salisbury R Road, running from Cheraw to Wadesboro, has not been assessed by the officers named.

The Road runs for (14) fourteen miles in N. C. They claim

---

[73]Lawyer of Wadesboro. Branson, *Directory for 1884*, 121.
[74]*Laws of North Carolina, 1881*, c. 117.

the road bed & c are exempt from taxation, but Judge Shipp[75] held in an action testing the matter such is not the case. They do not so far as I know claim that the franchise is also exempted — As Attorney for Anson Co. — Com[rs] I respectfully call your attention to this matter, and ask you to at once assess the value of the franchise of this Road —

In the case tried of Judge Shipp. I should have stated that the R R Co appealed to Supreme Court, where the case is now depending —

A&H—GP

W. C. Kerr to Thomas J. Jarvis

Bristol, Tenn. Sept. 22 1882

Yours of the 30th Aug. reaches me here on my return for a few days from Roan Mountain & Mitchell Co. where I have just started three parties on the topographical survey in connection with the U. S. Geological survey. I have one party working between this point & Cumberland Gap, & shall begin work my self, with a fifth party, in Burke Wilkes & McDowell next week. So that you see the U. S. Geol. Survey is fairly inaugurated in N C & the adjacent states; & I am sure your anticipations & mine in regard to the benefits likely to insue to N. C. from this movement are much more certain to be realized than if we had held aloof from it.

I am gratified that your views of this matter, as expressed in the letter above referred to accord so entirely with my own. And as to the desire you express, in closing, that the report, thus temporarily suspended, shall be resumed in the winter & pushed to completion, be assured that my wish & purpose are in full accord therewith.

---

[75]William Marcus Shipp, lawyer of Charlotte; member of the Convention of 1861; member of the General Assembly, 1862; attorney general, 1871–1873; judge of the Superior Court, 1881–1890. Grant, *Alumni History of the University*, 561.

A&H—GP

W. S. Denny to Thomas J. Jarvis

Boston, Sept 23 1882

I learn to day that Mr Best is sick in New York. A letter from him to Mr Coleman however expresses his intention of being at Newbern next week and he urges us to go also.

I have seen all of our Directors and have but little confidence that many, if any, will be able to go next week. I am requested to write to you however and say that we shall stand by the resolution of our Stockholders at meeting of July 15th last a copy of which I had the honor of transmitting to you on the 16th ultimo and which reads as follows viz —

"Resolved That The Midland Improvement and Construction Company will go forward with the construction of the link between Goldsboro and Salisbury as soon as the ownership of the State's stock in the Atlantic and North Carolina Railroad is acquired or the Legislature of North Carolina shall guarantee to the Midland Improvement and Construction Co. or the Midland North Carolina Railway Co. the ownership of said State's Stock upon completion of the road to Salisbury."

The above resolution was prompted not through any misgiving that you had not or would not do anything in your power in aiding us to carry out our project in its whole breadth and scope, but at the outset we had been led to believe that there would be no difficulty in obtaining possession at once of the Western No. Carolina Railroad and, in a short time, the Atlantic & No. Carolina Railroad which as you know, we regarded of vital importance to our scheme. We went to work at once, having no doubt as to the early consummation of our expectations, and expended several hundred thousand dollars in carrying out our part of the agreement before we realized that our hopes might result in disappointment. When doubts upon this point began to arise, our people, or some of them at least, felt that we ought to have some tangible evidence that our money was not being expended in the very way we had assured the Commissioners we should *not* expend it viz: in building a local road without through connections. In view of these doubts it was natural and as we think, reasonable for our Stockholders before expending more money to require some pledge or positive guarantee from the State that our expectations concerning the ownership of a through line should be realized providing we should fulfill our part of the undertaking.

We did not feel sure that such a pledge could be given until the Legislature should be in Session, and if not, we saw no way but to wait its coming to–gether.

This seems to be our present situation and if we, or any of us find it possible to be present at the adjourned A&N.C. meeting, we could not give any assurances further than is expressed in the above resolution.

. . . .

C. C. Clark to Thomas J. Jarvis

Newbern, Oct 19. 1882

It is currently humored here that upon the lessees of the Atlantic Road putting on two locomotives, and replacing old with a mile or two of new iron, that indulgence will be granted them to give them an opportunity to apply to the Legislature for the State's stock.

It is natural, Governor, that I should feel a deep interest in the future of this Road, on the management of which depends, to a large extent, the material interests of this section, and I thought you would pardon me, a Director by your appointment, for enquiring whether there is a foundation for the rumors.

I do not, after the interview I had with you in Morehead, scarcely think there can be; yet these rumors have a tendency to create a feverish anxiety which it is pleasant to have allayed, and I hope you will do me the honor to inform me whether anything has occurred, or is likely to occur, which can change the purpose you expressed at the time referred to.

. . . .

Thomas J. Jarvis to C. C. Clark

Executive Department,
Raleigh, Oct. 20, 1882

In reply to yours of the 19th, I beg to say that I appreciate your interest in the Atlantic Road and the section largely dependent upon it for its prosperity.

I have had no communication, either directly or indirectly, with any of the lessees of the Atlantic Road since the adjournment of the stockholders' meeting last of September. Any statement which any of them or their employees may give out or rumor handed around as to any opinion or purpose of mine, is without even the semblance of authority. The condition in the lease to build a new road from Goldsboro to Salisbury was *the condition* with me upon which I supported the lease. I have never had any other purpose than to see that that *condition* of the lease was complied with or the Atlantic Road given up. I have of late lost all hope of *this condition* being complied with and it will take a great deal to restore confidence. I shall be glad, however, if they are able to do it. I shall try to keep myself in a position to pass impartially upon any proposition they may make. The only change, I regret to say, that has taken place in my views since the stockholders' meeting, is that the evidences of the failure of the enterprise have greatly increased. I think these are about the views I expressed to you then and they are the same now.

I shall be glad at all times to give you my views upon this or any other public question when you deem them of any consequence.

A&H—GP

W. C. Kerr to Thomas J. Jarvis

Blowing Rock
Oct. 20, 1882

After trying the Red Sulphur Springs four weeks I find myself but little improved. I expect to go in a few days to Lenoir, & visit a new spring between that place & Taylorsville. As soon as I am located, I will write further & decide whether I am able to push thru' the publication of the report.

I hope to get down to Raleigh before long & to see you in person about it, after the dust & confusion of the Exposition are over, & the canvass.

A&H—GP

L. D. Starke[76] to Thomas J. Jarvis

Norfolk, Va., Oct. 20, 1882

I take the liberty of calling your Excellency's attention to what I regard as a matter of public concern as affecting certain interests in your State — I refer to the habit lately sprung up, of building islands or making land in Currituck and Albemarle Sounds, (and possibly in other waters of the State,) and then making entries of such lands and applying for grants from the State for the same.

Apart from the public injury thereby done in obstructing navigation, an unseemly scramble is likely to be engendered between persons who wish to obtain the benefit of these artificial islands, unless checked by the prompt action of the authorities of the State.

Legislation may become necessary; but at all events, I think it would be wise in the Executive Department of the State Government to lay down a line of policy which should govern its administration in this particular, absolutely refusing to issue grants for such lands, and discountenancing all attempts in that direction.

I feel that you will appreciate my motives in writing this letter, from your knowledge of my interest in every thing that affects the welfare of North Carolina; but I will add, that I have a special interest in this matter, viz: that some clients of mine, prior to their becoming such, were disposed to enter into the project of making lands and obtaining grants therefor. I have set my face against the proceeding as unwise and impolitic both in the State and in individuals; and I shall persist in this course unless the State shall recognize a contrary policy.

I should be very glad to have your views, at your early convenience, upon this subject, not to be used except for my own guidance and with your permission.

---

[76]Lucien Douglas Starke. Before the Civil War, Starke had been a newspaper editor in Richmond, Virginia, and in Elizabeth City, North Carolina. After the war, he practiced law in Norfolk, Virginia. Information furnished by Mrs. Frank C. Pinkerton of the Norfolk Public Library System.

A&H—GP

A. B. Andrews to Thomas J. Jarvis

Newbern, N. C., October 25 1882

Mr. Caddagan informs me that you were told in Raleigh that I had given passes in blank to individuals to go over the road to get up meetings and expressions from the people addressed to you, with a view to influenceing your action on the 10th of Nov. I beg most respectfully to say this is not the case.

In my conversation with you, I told you the people of Smithfield intended calling a meeting to memorialize you, but that I had not in any way interested myself — nor would I do so.

Speaking with a gentleman from Chatham Co: next day, he wished me to give him some facts as to the standing of this Company, and their intentions for the future, with a vew to writing an article and to calling a meeting in Pittsboro. And asked me to come there and state them to the people; I did think of doing so at that time, but on second thought I decided that if any memorial or resolutions however respectful they might be should emenate [sic] from our officers it would have an observe effect, rather than the one desired I therefore determined not to say one word to the public. but if they chose to ask you to postpone action until after the meeting of your Legislature, I would not interfere; but that I would neither by word, letter, or action interest this company in the movement and turned my attention to addressing our president and the Syndicate, urging them to personally interview you before the 10th and settle upon a basis for the future, assuring them that I believed that you would be governed by a desire only to serve your state and protect their money and interests

I am aware that we are surrounded by enemies, and every thing having a tendency to injure us is reported to you. Our critical situation forbids our exciting a feeling by even refuting the slanders against us

In this instance I feel personally called on to sit myself right before you.

To prove my sincerity in what I have said about the memorials to you, I hold a letter from the leading Smithfield people addressed to you in early September — previous to the adjourned meeting at Morehead, on this same subject, which I did not deem prudent to give you, but withheld it, together with the resolutions of a meeting of the same character, fearing it might be considered as emanating from this company or its officers.

While I think you hear all our enemies have to say, and we have been silent in our own defence — nor heard what our patrons and friends could urge in our behalf. Yet I do not think our cause would be benefitted by calling from the public an expression at this time of their preferences or wishes regarding the control and management of the A&NCRR hence I do not propose saying one word to influence them in their actions. It is a matter more properly between our Syndicate and yourself and your State

A&H—GP

Edmund Jones to Thomas J. Jarvis

13ᵗʰ Nov 1882
Patterson N. C.

I desire earnestly to call to your attention the importance of your calling the notice of the Legislature to the condition of the C.F.&Y.V.R.R. especeally[*sic*] of the Yadkin Valley branch. An idea has been prevalent in this section for some time that the Democratic party influenced by companies that are supposed to be hostile to this branch has virtually abandoned it: This impression has done more to bring about our disaster in this section than all other causes combined. If this notion is not counteracted in some way before the next election, we shall certainly lose every county from Greensboro to Yancey in the next election, even to Caldwell. We all earnestly hope that in your message you will recommend favorable legislation to this enterprise. We are the more encouraged to ask this from the fact of your having been constantly the friend of this line. We do not propose to ask any increased taxation for our benefit, but only to make the road build itself, which can be done if the General Assembly will act liberally and fairly by us.

A&H—GLB

Thomas J. Jarvis to J. D. Whitford

Executive Department,
Raleigh, Oct. 31, 1882

In asking you to get the expert of the A.&N.C. Road, Dr. Hogg, to get certain information for the stockholders' meeting on the 10th of Nov., I did not mean to be understood as objecting to the board of directors getting any other information from any source they desired, for the meeting. On the contrary, I think it to be the duty of the board — and I shall be glad to see them do so — to get *all* the information for the meeting of the stockholders, important for them to know, as to the condition of the property and to lay it before the meeting. If, therefore, the board desires Gen. Lewis[77] or any other person to make any examination of any kind, I beg that you will not understand me as objecting, but as approving. I did want Dr. Hogg to get certain information which I pointed out to you; and that is all I want to say and all I think I did say. This request of mine does not in any way interfere with the proposed action of the board. Had it done so, I would not have made it; for I propose to hold the board of directors responsible for the property in proper limits.

A&H—GP

J. D. Whitford to Thomas J. Jarvis [with enclosure]

Newbern, N. C., Nov 14th 1882

Herewith you will find an agreement with Midland N.C.R. way Co. There seems to have been given some authority to the President of the A&N.C.RW Co., by the Stockholders of the Co. I shall do nothing without your advice & cooperation, — I want to be in Raleigh a few days & will wait upon you for instructions

---

[77]William Gaston Lewis, civil engineer of Edgecombe County. J. Kelly Turner and John L. Bridgers, *History of Edgecombe County, North Carolina* (Raleigh: Edwards & Broughton Printing Company, 1920), 202, hereinafter cited as Turner and Bridgers, *History of Edgecombe County.*

[*enclosure*]

North Carolina
Wayne County

Whereas the Atlantic & North Carolina Railroad Company by a vote of its stockholders, in General Meeting assembled, declared the Lease heretofore made by it to the Midland North Carolina Railway Company void & forfeited and now desires repossession of its road, property, and franchises, and the said, the Midland N C Rwy Company desires sufficient time to enable its stockholders and managers to consult together, in order to determine what shall be done in the future as to their surrendering the said, the Atlantic & N C R Road and the property thereof without litigation —

It is this day agreed between the said, the Atlantic & NC RR Company of the first part, and W S Denny W W Caruth, & Jno P. Caddagan, representing the said, the Midland NC RW Company and the Midland Improvement & Construction Company, so far as they can bind the said Companies, of the second part, as follows: The party of the first part will not, for a period of thirty (30) days from the date hereof, take any legal steps, or otherwise attempt to gain such repossession of its said road and property: Provided that the said Midland NC Railway Company shall immediately so repair Trent river bridge, as to make it safe for the transportation of trains, and shall, during said thirty days, put said Atlantic & NC Railroad in safe condition —

The party of the second party will, at the expiration of said thirty days, quit & deliver up possession of said road and property & unless before said expiration, the party of the second part shall determine to carry out the provisions of said lease by the immediate expenditure of money on the road of the party of the first part, sufficient to put the same and its equipment in as good order as it was at the date of said lease, in case it is not now in such order, and immediately take such other steps as shall restore the party of the second part to the confidence of the party of the first part, as to financial ability and intention to carry out such provisions —

In case the party of the second part shall quit & deliver up possession of said road and property as aforesaid, and any dispute shall arise between the said, the Atlantic & NCRR Company and the said, the Midland NCRW Company as to any moneys due by either to the other, or as to the ownership of any property or right over the same, or as to any matter of account between the two, all such matters of dispute shall be referred for decision to two referees, one to be selected by each party: Should the referees disagree, an umpire shall be by them selected, and the decision of the referees, or that of the umpire, shall be final — The party of the second part shall earnestly endeavour to determine its course as aforesaid, and notify the party of the first (1ˢᵗ) part of such determination on or before the first day of December 1882, unles the full period of thirty (30) days, heretofore limited, shall be found to be necessary to that end —

And it is hereby expressly agreed that a demand for the possession of the said Atlantic & NC Railroad & other devised property has been made upon the party of the second part, and that it has refused to surrender said possession —

Nothing herein contained shall be so construed, as to in anywise impair the effect of the declaration of forfeiture aforesaid, or waive the right of the party of the first part to repossess itself of its said road and property, after the expiration of the time hereinbefore limited —

Witness the signatures of John D Whitford President of the said, the Atlantic & North Carolina Railroad Company, representing the party of the first part, and the signature of W S Denny, W W Caruth, & Jno P. Caddagan party of the second part, hereto affixed this 11th day of November 1882 —

A&H—GP

James G. Hall[78] to Thomas J. Jarvis

Hickory, N. C. Nov 14ᵗʰ 1882

Our work at the Asylum has reached that point at which we so much need the advice and cooperation of the Board of Directors of that Institution.

---

[78]Resident of Hickory and manufacturer of wagons and of plug and twist tobacco. *Branson, Directory for 1884*, 194. Hall, J. C. Harper, and W. S. Pearson were commissioners appointed to supervise the construction of the Western North Carolina Insane Asylum. "Report of the Board of Directors of the W.N.C. Insane Asylum," *Public Documents, 1883*, No. 13, 7.

When it may be your pleasure to constitute that Board, will you please so arrange that a meeting with our Board may at once take place.[79] This past week has been to me one of great suspense in respect to our political success.

A&H—GP

Washington Bryan[80] *to Thomas J. Jarvis*

New Berne, N. C.,
Nov. 15th; 1882

It is with considerable reluctance that I trespass upon your valuable time, and, if I did not believe that you were always ready to listen to any of your friends, and, if I did not think that somewhat of interest might perhaps be found within these pages, I would hold my peace

Since my arrival here, I have found a feeling of exasperation — it is best to speak the unvarnished truth — among our citizens in regard to the Midland Ry., and a conviction that the Boston Syndicate is by hook or by crook to keep the road, and no argument can convince them to the contrary. They say that it is a notorious fact that the road is horribly unsafe, and yet that these strangers are allowed to stay from adjourned meeting to adjourned meeting and still further run it down, and that at each meeting under some pretext the road is kept for a longer time in their hands, and that even after public opinion has forced a declaration of forfeiture matters have been so arranged that the legislature shall be in session before it can be gotten out of their possession. They also say that the thirty days allowed the Boston folks by the Board of Directors will bring the time to the 10th of December, and then that the additional twenty days required by by-law for notification of Stockholders will fool the time up to the 1st of January, and that at this stage of the proceedings the whole matter will be turned over to the general assembly in order to give Best & Co. an opportunity to buy up the representatives and to get the State's Stock for a song. It is further

---

[79]For the Board of Directors which Jarvis immediately appointed, see "Report of the Board of Directors of the W.N.C. Insane Asylum," *Public Documents, 1883*, No. 13, 1.

[80]Lawyer of New Bern, president of the North Carolina Railroad under Governor Scales. Josephus Daniels, *Editor in Politics* (Chapel Hill: University of North Carolina Press, 1941), 447, hereinafter cited as Daniels, *Editor in Politics.*

stated that the Board was influenced to grant the time by an assertion of one of its members that such was your desire.

To give color to all these rumors and suspicions, I understand that the Midlanders still claim that it never was part of your original intention that they should leave the State, but that it was a question which you did not care to deal with, and that you were and are quite willing that they should have another trial at the road after they reorganize, and that they will be allowed to present their claims to the legislature.

The Midland Co. is inducing the people to think that they (the people) have no help in you; that you are in some unaccountable way leagued with them, and that it is useless to suppose that they intend to leave, and many of the people do believe it, I am sorry to say. They feel that they have been deserted, and that the administration of their own party has left them to their fate: that they can look no where for a redress of their grievances: that they have got to bend their necks to the domination of this Boston Radical Ring; that their property and the value of their Stock is being destroyed and depreciated before their eyes; that when they could have freed themselves from this intolerable yoke that the Governor of their State interfered and saved these people time and again — people whom the public know to be a set of adventurers here to wreck and pilfer. To add more fuel to this flame these Boston men have professed to know what you were going to do, and what would be the result of each meeting, and thus far correctly; and as your friends told you long ago they would do, by bold assertion and subtle innuendo they have begun to sap the confidence of the people in you, and are slowly but surely teaching them to hate you and to regard you as a public enemy; and if they remain here, a popular cry will soon sound from Morehead to Goldsboro, and they will make it echo and re–echo through this Eastern Country, and the disaffected throughout the state will take it up, and it will be "Down with Jarvis." And Governor Jarvis, you will have to thank the Midland Syndicate for it.

I see the trouble brewing here in New Berne. It is beginning. the people are exasperated. Harper[81] is a ready tool to work your political destruction. The Midland is doing all it can in an underhand way. Your friends are being led astray and estranged, and

[81]James Warren Harper of Lenoir County. Graduating from the University of North Carolina, he studied law under Judge Richmond M. Pearson; later he edited the Kinston *Journal*, and, in 1882, the New Bern *Journal*. He died in 1883. *News and Observer*, January 30, 1883.

let these Boston people spend a little money in the legislature — it matters not if it be Democratic — and they are established in North Carolina, and then will come their open enmity. I know perhaps that you will smile at what I have told you, but one needs only to stand at the street corners and to go into the offices to hear it, and even more. Harper has just published a most outrageous editorial — "Too Much Jarvis in Politics," ascribing the Democratic losses to you, and to your interference in R.R. matters &c &c. I will send you the paper if I can get it. So you see he is already bolder and is trying to accomplish your ruin.

Now, Governor, I have told you some unpleasant things, but you can come to this part of the country and verify them, for they are facts. I and mine have been your friends since we knew you, and we have been honest friends. We do not ask anything from you. We can take care of ourselves and therefore what I have written, I have written because I thought you ought to know it; because I thought that the Governor of this State ought to be kept informed by his supporters of what was going on, and of what was uppermost in the popular mind. I have told you the truth and I have told it because it was the truth, even at the risk of your displeasure. I have made this venture of my own accord, but it will not be repeated save at your own request — never again otherwise —

I told Mr. [C.C.] Clark of your conversation with me in regard to Col. Whitford. He fully admitted the justice of what you said, but I have no idea that he will tell him—

Yesterday there came to our Bank a draft from the Rhode Island Locomotive Works upon the A.&N.C.R.R.Co. for $23000 — for two locomotives. The bill of sale by which it was accompanied was made out to the Midland Improvement & Construction Co. So you see that it was never contemplated that the *Midland Ry. Co.* should have any title to them, but that the *Midland Improvement & Construction Co.* which is not known in the lease should be the owners, and so it is with whatever else they have — It all belongs to the Improvement & Construction Co., and in case of trouble we would hardly be able to touch anything, and if the road ever rests in the possession of the Stockholders again, even for ever so short a time, I expect we shall find out that they have utilized the time that has been so constantly granted them to cover up everything. Their credit does not seem to have been very good at the North — not as good as that of the old A.&N.C.R.R. upon which they instructed, I suppose, the manufacturer to draw. It has created quite a sensation. Caddagan refused to pay the draft when presented to him by our Cashier who remarked that it was probably meant for him. Payment was of course refused by the A.&N.C. Co. and the draft went back protested. The discovery that the property is owned by the Improvement Co., and the Road run by the Ry. Co. creates much comment. I was looking over some of our papers to day, and I find that they overdrew their account in Dec., Jan., Feb., March, April, May, June, July, Aug., Sept., October, and $1700 — thus far this month, on all of which we charged them one and one half (1½) percent. per month, and we have just gotten our money — So you see again to what straits they are driven — 1½ per cent per month is ruin to anybody. There has just been a man named Griffith, from Baltimore, here looking after ten tons of guano lost between New Berne and La Grange. He was very bitter. The trains are still behind time in spite of the new engine, the Bragg, just out of the shops, so it must be the condition of the road. I have not told you the half of the complaints, but shall end by saying that everything is ripe here for their expulsion. The people want them out. They want the Governor of their own State openly on their side — They are the natives. They have borne the heat and burden of the day — They want protection. They want his power for once exerted to effect in their behalf. They say you cannot realize how matters stand. The men want their pay — Some of them have not had it for a month and a half. They say the Syndicate promised at Morehead to get out at Goldsboro if they did not go on; that the track &c should be in better order. They have done neither and unless some steps be taken they have an extension of time to Jan. 1st 1883 — They say no natives would be treated in so lenient a manner, that you would be disposed to exact the letter of the contract from them, and that it is now time for charity to begin at home. Hope deferred has made their hearts sick, and your friends, not those whose axes have been ground, but your disinterested friends, say if ever there was a time for the Governor of North Carolina to stand up in his power for the protection of his people against outside speculators, that it is now, and they expect you to do it, and those who know you do not expect that you will disappoint them. We all want the road leased to parties who have no object in swindling the people, it does not make much matter who they are, but let me beseech you not to let this dangerous force be player in our midst any longer. Pardon me, please if I have spoken too freely, for I am at least sincere.

A&H—GLB

Thomas J. Jarvis to A. J. Galloway

Executive Department,
Raleigh, Nov. 16, 1882

In reply to your question if I will offer any opposition to a lease of the Atlantic and North Carolina Railroad to the Wilmington and Weldon Railroad Company, I answer as follows:

In 1880, I stated that I desired to see the Atlantic road operated in the interest of that section of the State east of Goldsboro and that if the people in that section desired the road leased to the Wilmington and Weldon Company, I would offer no objection. In a stockholders' meeting of the Atlantic and North Carolina Railroad Company subsequently held, when the road was about to be leased to the Wilmington and Weldon Company, I withdrew the State's proxy for reasons that I then deemed sufficient. The Midland project was then under discussion and it being just before the meeting of the Legislature, I deemed it wise to wait till the Legislature meet and to submit the question to that body. The Legislature took no further action than to direct that no lease be made without the consent of the Board of Directors. In 1881, a lease was made to the Midland Company, which has recently been declared forfeited. I favored that lease because of the hope it held out of getting one hundred and fifty miles of new road built right through the very heart of the State. But to my great regret, the project has failed and I now recognize the fact that something must be done with the Atlantic road. I still repeat what I said in 1880 that I desire to see the road operated in the interest of that section of the State east of Goldsboro. The most of the Directors live in that section and they and the stockholders are supposed to know what is best for that section and for the Company. If, therefore, the Directors and the stockholders shall agree to lease the road to the Wilmington and Weldon Railroad Company, I shall offer no objections to such lease. In fact, I will say the same of a lease to any other party.

A&H—GLB

Thanksgiving Proclamation, November 17, 1882

State of North Carolina,
Executive Department

Gratitude for the many blessings the people of North Carolina have enjoyed during the year now drawing to its close, as well as respect for custom and law, require that at least one day shall be specially devoted to giving thanks to our Heavenly Father, from whom cometh every good and perfect gift.

The crops have been more abundant than ever before harvested in the State. Peace has everywhere prevailed within our borders. The health of the people has been extraordinarily good; while their progress in educational and material interests and in the cultivation of a high moral and religious sentiment, has been equally satisfactory.

For these and all His other manifold services and blessings, I, Thomas J. Jarvis, Governor of North Carolina, do issue this, my Proclamation, setting apart Thursday, November 30th inst., as a day of thanksgiving and prayer, and do earnestly request all the people of North Carolina properly to observe the same. Let the churches and other places of public worship be opened and the places of business closed. Let the people, resting from their labors, spend the day devoutly, as becomes a thankful Christian people.

On that day let not the poor, the widow and the orphan anywhere be forgotten, remembering that to give to these is to lend to Him from whom all blessings come. Especially let not the Oxford Orphan Asylum be forgotten, the necessities of whose unfortunate inmates I especially commend to the generous consideration of a grateful people.

.   .   .   .

A&H—GLB

Thomas J. Jarvis to Washington Bryan

Executive Department,
Raleigh, Nov. 17, 1882

Yours of the 16th inst. was received to–day and carefully read. I beg to assure you I appreciate the kind motives which prompted you to write so freely and frankly. None but a *true* friend would so have written.

I sympathize with the people in their anxiety as to what is to be done with the Atlantic road and I can see how easy it will be for a man like Harper, who cares nothing for the wrongs he inflicts upon others, to add to that anxiety and to injure any man he assails with a newspaper, for the time being. But I am a great believer in the correctness of the final judgment of the people and I shall patiently await that judgment. Conscious as I am that I have no other motive or desire than to serve the best interest of the people, I have no fears as to what that final judgment will be. I am now as indifferent to Mr. Harper's criticisms as I will then be to his praise.

I am under no sort of obligations to any of the Boston syndicate nor am I in any way in league with them. I do, however, desire to see them treated justly and shall not take any part in any effort to take advantage of them. After the stockholders had declared the lease forfeited, two of the syndicate, Messrs. Denny and Carruth, had an interview with me in the presence of John L. Morehead,[82] Eugene Morehead, Julius A. Gray, John Gatling and others. In this interview, they made a request that two weeks be given them in which to have a meeting of their associates to consider the situation in which the action of the stockholders had placed them and to see what could be done to help them out of their losses. I replied to them, if they would agree to surrender, without litigation, if they could do nothing which would meet the demands of the board of directors, that I thought the board would act wisely in giving them the two weeks. There was then nothing said about thirty days, nor did I hear anything said about thirty days until I heard the board had given them thirty. I will not, however, say that the board acted unwisely in making the time thirty days, for I think it the surest, and possibly the speediest way to a repossession of the property by the Atlantic company.

To show you how little foundation there is for the wild rumors and conjectures referred to in your letter, to the effect that there will be other delays and that all sorts of unreasonable things will happen, I enclose you a copy of a letter that I yesterday had occasion to address to A. J. Galloway, Esq., I supposed, un-

---

[82]John Lindsay Morehead, banker and manufacturer of Charlotte. He was a large stockholder in the Atlantic and North Carolina Railroad. Grant, *Alumni History of the University*, 441.

til I received your letter, that everybody was expecting and preparing for a new lease of the road. The only discussion I expected to hear was as to whom it shall be leased. That question I proposed to leave, as indicated in my letter to Galloway, with the directors and stockholders. If the people will but be patient three weeks longer, they will see how unfounded have been their fears and how unreasonable their suspicions. If I know myself, I am incapable of failing in my duty to the people. They have always confided in me and stood by me and they may rely upon me now and at all times to stand by them.

UNC—SMT

Thomas J. Jarvis to S. M. Tate

Executive Department.
Raleigh, Nov 17ᵗʰ 1882

Yours of the 14ᵗʰ [83] has been received and I heartily congratulate you upon your splendid victory.[84] Burke did nobly. I doubt if any other county in the State was the scene of such a fight. You have cause to be proud of Burke and of your victory.

I shall appoint the Directors [of the Western Insane Asylum] in a few days and will be certain to appoint Perkins,[85] and Davidson if I do not feel called upon to scatter the Board. As this Board elects officers it may be best not to put too many of them in one county. After the organization is made then it will be best to have them as near the Institution as possible.

---

[83]Not found.

[84]Tate had been re-elected to the North Carolina House of Representatives. Connor, *Manual, 1913,* 523.

[85]Elisha A. Perkins, farmer of Morganton. Branson, *Directory for 1884,* 163.

A&H—GLB

Thomas J. Jarvis to B. J. Burgess

Executive Department,
Raleigh, Nov. 23, 1882

Maj. B. J. Burgess,
    Principal Savannah Military Academy,
        Savannah, Ga.,

Dear Sir:
    Yours of the 21st. instant[86] has been received. I do not thinkit will be possible to induce the Legislature to make an appropriation for the establishment of a State military school. Whatever appropriations the Legislature may make to any school, outside of the appropriation for the common schools, will likely be made to the State University or to State normal schools. I think our Legislature will be more likely to make appropriations to train persons in the art of teaching rather than in the art of war. Our people have never taken very warmly to military schools. It is true there are several private schools in the State at which military tactics are taught, and many of these schools are well patronized; but it is the mental training the boys get, and not the military feature, that attracts the patrons. I could not, with my ideas of public sentiment in North Carolina and of the needs of the educational interest of the State, approve or recommend an appropriation for the establishment of a State military school. You must remember, however, that in this State the Governor has no veto power and my opinions need not necessarily prevent your making the effort.

A&H—GP

Edmund Jones to Thomas J. Jarvis

23rd Nov 1882

My project for the building of the C.F.&Y.V.R.R. embraced the idea of a sale to parties that would build at least a large portion of the road. If any party or parties will take the road and build the whole line, that is a solution of the question. But I have been

---

[86]Governors' Papers, not included in this volume.

of the opinion that the prospective purchasers would wish to leave off the Y.V. branch and in case nothing better can be obtained, I think the Y.V. branch can be built if the Legislature will give to that branch as a separate division or new corporation all the assets to be made out of the old company by a transfer of the same. The state excepting from the sale its interest in the Y.V. portion of the road, and the same to remain under the control of the state. This is of course not desirable if we can get responsible purchasers to build the whole line. It is only an alternative—and the only chance I see for us of the NW without heavy appropriations which are I suspect not readily obtainable. I shall see you before the meeting of the Legislature when matters shall have cleared themselves of some of their obscurities, and we can talk the matter over fully. You must not understand from my last that the opinion if it was an opinion that the Dem party were weakened on the C.F.&Y.V. was entitled to any credence. I only mentioned the matter because I have heard that that report was used in particular in the campaign in Wilkes, and was thought to have damaged us sadly, and as an indication of how the people up hear [sic] feel on the matter.

A&H—GP

William A. Hearne[87] *to Thomas J. Jarvis*

Newbern, N. C., Decr. 5. 1882

Of my own volition and unknown to any one, I beg to tender a suggestion for your consideration, and I do it in good faith, and all that that implies.

You have from the very necessities of the situation been compelled to take a hand in the affairs of the A&NC RRCo. and you are not only the guardian of the State's interest in that property as Governor, but you are *ex officio* President of the Board of Internal Improvements, and in that capacity charged with the State's interest in all Public Works.

---

[87]Possibly Wiliam A. Hearne, formerly of Arkansas, who had served as an assistant paymaster in the Confederate Navy. *Journal of the Congress of the Confederate States of America, 1861–1865* (Washington, D.C.: United States Government Printing Office, Fifty-Eighth Congress, Second Session, *House Document No. 234*, 7 vols., 1904), IV, 176, 203, hereinafter cited as *Journal of the Confederate Congress.*

A great deal is said pro and con about the present condition of the A&NCRR property and the improvements made under the lease, and you naturally desire to know the exact truth.

Now as President of the Board of Internal Improvements, I suggest, and with great deference and respect, that your Board make a close personal inspection of the Road from one end to the other, and upon the finding of your Board, base whatever action you may be called upon to take.

Mr. Cooke is an honorable and intelligent man, and fully capable of passing an intelligent opinion upon the condition of any Railroad property he might take the pain to inquire into and examine. Col. [William] Johnston, the other member is a Railroad Expert, and in my opinion equal to the best.

In my opinion the proper thing to do, and the best, is to have an official examination and report from this authorized body of State officials, of a property in which the State is principal owner, and with the administration or disposal of which the Governor of the State is charged; and in regard to which the Legislature may be called upon to act in some manner during the approaching session.

The Company has had reports from its expert Dr Hogg who examined the Road in company with the Midland Expert, openly and in a dignified and business like manner — Not satisfied with Dr Hogg's statement, they sent Gen. Lewis, secretly and in the disguise of a prospector for rice lands, in which character he masqueraded from one end of the Road to the other — Of course a report thus made cannot have weight with the public, nor with you. Any report that the Midland Company may make through its officers and employees, you and the public will take with some grain of allowance; while at large Dr Hogg may not be recognized as a RR expert, though he is as good as the best. But anything coming officially and by authority of the State from the State Board of Internal Improvements will be accepted by everybody.

This Company will, I think, cheerfully submit its books to an examination by your Board.

A&H—GP

R. H. Battle to Thomas J. Jarvis

Tarboro, N. C.
Dec. 4th 1882

I am requested by Col Peter Dorsch, our Superintendent, to ask you if the State requires him to make a report of the condition of the "Seaboard and Raleigh Railroad," as is required by his native state, N.Y. of the Railroad of that State: if so, please send him blank forms. Never having given this question any consideration I am unable to enlighten him on this point.

Our infant Road is gradually assuming manly propo[r]tions and I trust the time is not distant when the whistle of our engines will be heard by the citizens of our Capitol City —

The radical elect county officers of this county have so far failed to give Bond and we are hoping to have Democratic officers throughout.

A&H—GP

Thomas J. Jarvis to Z. B. Vance

Copy.

Executive Dept
Raleigh Dec 7/82

I desire to be able to give the General Assembly definite information as to the condition of the Western Road and the progress of the work thereon. It will therefore be necessary for us to make a trip over it before the meeting of the General Assembly — The time that will best suit me is to leave here on Sunday afternoon, the 17th inst. Can't you get a leave of absence and join us at Greensboro Sunday night, the 17th — It will take us 3 or 4 days — I trust you will be able to go. If any other time between now and the first of Jany. will suit you better, write me; and if you will not be able to go at all, write me also. I shall have to go up there a few days anyhow, whether you can go or not.[88]

---

[88]Vance declined because of the press of business in Congress. He asked that Jarvis and Worth make the examination without him. Vance to Jarvis, December 11, 1882, Governors' Papers, not included in this volume.

A&H—GP

F. Warburton to Thomas J. Jarvis

Richmond Va
9th December 1882

On my travels through your State I met Doctor Gentry,[89] at one time a member of your Legislature, who informed me that it was proposed to sell the narrow gauge R R from Greensboro for $55,000 to any Company who should guarantee to extend it through Western N. C.

Dr Gentry informed me that I could obtain any particulars from you.

I am about to proceed to England in view of interesting Capitalists in enterprises in your state and should be glad to have some reliable information on the above and any other kindred Subject, specifying such important conditions and particulars as will enable them. to take a comprehensive view of any matter laid before them.

I have recently retired from the English army.

I enclose my card[90]. . . .

A&H—GLB

Thomas J. Jarvis to F. Warburton

Executive Department,
Raleigh, Dec. 14, 1882

In reply to yours of the 9th instant, I beg to say that at the session of the Legislature in 1881, an act was passed appointing a commission to sell the State's interest in the Cape Fear and Yadkin Valley Railroad Company upon the conditions named in said act. The act itself can be seen in the Laws of 1881, chapter 374. A contract of sale was made with some parties in New York, but they failed to comply with their agreements: so they acquired no right under the contract. The property is still for sale and I would be glad to have you examine it and make a bid for it. Our Legislature meets on the 3rd of January next and I have reason to believe that there are other parties who will

---

[89]Probably Dr. L. C. Gentry of Ashe County, member of the General Assembly, 1881. Connor, *Manual, 1913*, 493.

[90]This card identified Warburton as a lieutenant colonel, retired, of the British Royal Engineers.

submit a proposition to purchase the State's interest in the road. I give you this information because it may be too late if you delay the matter till after your proposed visit to Europe.

Mr. Julius A. Gray, the President of the Company, lives at Greensboro, and will give you any information about the property you may desire.

A&H—GP

J. F. Graves to Thomas J. Jarvis

Mt Airy N C
Decm 15ᵗʰ 1882

I hope you will pardon me for calling your attention to some matters in which I am feeling a very considerable interest. First, you will remember that you suggested to me the propriety of my going on to New York with President Gray and others to investigate the standing of Canedo and his US Security, and that I did accordingly go and use my best endeavors to find out the real financial condition of the parties. With what success I did my part was shown by the result of the Canedo negotiations for the purchase of the C.F.&Y.V.R.R. Canedo and his associates as I reported were men of ventures without means.

In the next place I desire to call your attention to the terms of the Act authorizing the Sale of the CF&YV.RR. As I have probably heretofore explained to you the terms of the act authorizing the sale contains provisions and limitations which render a sale under that act utterly impracticable. If you should concur with the opinion that a sale of the road is desirable if you deem it for the public benefit I should be glad to have you recommend some legislation on the Subject such as you deem wise. I have information which I deem reliable that induces me to believe that a sale of the road can now be effected to Responsible parties most of them North Carolinians, men of interprize[*sic*] and of means. I suppose however you have much more definite information in regard to the sale of the road than I have. Of one thing I do feel assured and that is that the only way to have the road complete is to sell it. Of course the terms of sale will have to be nullity of contract and the state ought to get the best terms possible but I should favor a sale upon almost any terms which will require the completion of the road or even of any considerable portion of it. Indeed rather than see the project fail I would be calling for the State to surrender even the claims for current labor already over. So that the purchasers might take the road unencumbered.

I have ventured to make these suggestions because they refer to matters in which I have dearest interest. I trust I have not too greatly trespassed on your patience.

A&H—GLB

Thomas J. Jarvis to L. D. Starke

Raleigh, Dec. 15, 1882
Executive Department,

In reply to your letter [of October 20] concerning the issuing of grants for lumps of made land in Currituck Sound, I beg to say:

That several months ago the Kitty Hawk Club filed with the Secretary of State an entry of certain parcels of land in Currituck County, upon which they asked that grants might issue to them. Soon after application was made for these grants, a protest was filed by Mrs. Nye[91] against their being issued, on the ground that the land (so called) had been made by the parties applying for the grants to the detriment of the public and, especially, the land–owners. The Secretary of State referred the matter to the Attorney General for his opinion as to whether it was his duty to issue the grants, or not. Before the Attorney General gave his opinion, the Kitty Hawk Club bought out Mrs. Nye. The protest was withdrawn and the application for the grants abandoned. So the Attorney General gave no opinion and no grants have ever been issued. Under our law, the Secretary of State issues the grants—it being his duty to examine all the papers and to determine whether they fulfill the requirements of the law, or not. The Governor authenticates them with his signature and the Great Seal of the State. So the Secretary of State is the officer who has the practical control of the matter and he would not know whether the land for which the applicant applies for a grant, is made land or not, unless, as in the case of Mrs. Nye, some protest could lay down any line of policy about it. He might issue a number of grants for such lumps of

---

[91]Unable to identify.

land and not know anything about it. A sure remedy for the alleged evil that presents itself to me, is some legislation forbidding the entry–taker to survey any such land. The propriety of such legislation will be a question for the representatives of Currituck particularly, as it is more or less a local question.

A&H—GLB

Thomas J. Jarvis to R. H. Battle

Executive Department,
Raleigh, Dec. 15, 1882

There is no law in this State requiring reports from railroads like the Seaboard and Raleigh road.

The only report required is for the purpose of taxation and a blank will be sent out next spring for that.

. . . .

A&H—GP

Adolphus Williamson Mangum[92] to Thomas J. Jarvis

Chapel Hill, N. C.,
Dec. 15, 1882

While I am greatly interested in the general business of the University I am naturally *most interested* in that one of my several professorships which may be called "The Chair of Moral Science and Christian Evidences." To this I prefer to devote the remainder of my life. Of course I would expect to add to the work that it requires whatever other branches of instruction the exigencies of the University might demand.

I now proceed to suggest a few reasons why I think you ought to recommend the State endorsement of this Chair, — I mean, in your message to the Legislature.

1. The skeptical tendencies of the day warn the guardians of the University to make all practicable provision against those tendencies. Science is most popular, and, unless care be taken, it is

---

[92]After holding pastorates in several important North Carolina Methodist churches, Mangum in 1875 became professor of moral philosophy, history, and English literature at the University of North Carolina. Battle, *History of the University*, II, 81.

sadly apt to shake the faith of the young. So of the Reviews of the day, &c. Our sons should be trained under the aegis of the faith of their fathers.

2.   The conservative sentiment of North Carolinians of both parties and all churches (Except the Catholics & the Hardshells) will heartily approve any action looking to this vital interest. Perhaps I should not except the Hardshells.

3.   The means at command of the Trustees do not enable them to provide adequately for this Chair.

The proposed chair would embrace the whole department of metaphysics.

4.   The denominational colleges could not safely oppose such an appropriation.

5.   The appropriation would enable the Trustees to make more satisfactory arrangements for thorough and extensive instruction in the English Language.

6.   The annual Endowment of $2000. would enable the professor to live and to obtain now and then some facilities to render his department more efficient.

7.   The proposed Endowment will strengthen the University, *at once,* at the very point at which the people have least confidence in the institution. Think of this. Whatever you give or refuse to give, you must not fail in this. I'll add no more reasons now. I hope Col. Saunders will concur. Take this down & read it to Mrs. Jarvis — & see if she doesn't approve it.

What would be a higher honor to the Jarvis Administration? Pres. Battle favors this & promises to use his influence in favor of it. I am willing to take any responsibility needful in the case. Of course the Endowment of one chair, helps every other chair.

A&H—GP

A. H. Canedo to Thomas J. Jarvis

New York, Dec 19th 1882

After several months negotiations with a Syndicate in London, by letter and by cable, we have arranged for the sale of the Bonds of the A.W&CRR on the whole line and its branches,[93]

---

[93]For an explanation, see Canedo to Jarvis, January 3, 1882, in this volume. However, the English firm which had agreed to take over the Cape Fear and Yadkin Valley Railroad bonds refused to do so. Canedo's company was therefore unable to pay the purchase price of the state's stock within the specified time and the contract became void. Eutsler, "The Cape Fear and Yadkin Valley Railway," 432-433.

upon satisfactory terms to both sides.

The *terms* have been settled and now it remains for them to verify my statement as to the actual condition of the road, viz: the Charter, surveys & profile, right of way, number of miles completed number of miles graded, extent and character of equipment &c, &c, which being done and the bonds prepared they will be cashed as every thirty miles is completed.

They understand that the road is to be cleared by us of all recorded liens, the name changed, the right of merging or consolidating and other legislative acts as will put the matter in good shape.

We are now in receipt of intelligence, that the matter is practically settled, so far as the Bonds are concerned, and it is by the strongest financial Syndicate on the face of the Earth.

I have also negotiated for a Charter, Survey, Profile and Right of Way of over five hundred miles in Virginia, Kentucky & Tennessee upon equitable terms, all of which will be tributary to the C.F&Y.V. concentrating its traffic at Wilmington N.C. and have also made preliminary contracts for the steel rails for the whole line to go into effect as soon as we have acquired the road.

Now these are not theories or hypotheses, but facts, which I have for the last year developed with all my power and strength.

In view of these facts, there are parties who will put up the money to clear off encumbrances when they are assured that the obnoxious features of the contract are removed.

From information recently received, I find there are parties who, under pretence of entering in with us have so acquired information and offered the matter to R & D and other corporations and are now on the ground utilizing our work for their own ends, looking only to the acquirement of the CF&Y.V. for local and speculative purposes.

These persons have recently returned from Greensboro, where they have been quietly looking over the ground. There are others in behalf of the Denny Syndicate who control the Virginia, Tennessee & Georgia and seek to make the CF&Y.V. tributary to Norfolk.

Now, our systems as now developed, connects with Huntington, Cincinnati Louisville and St Louis, Nashville and via Hickman Ky. New Madrid Md. with the Iron Mountain and Southwest Systems, all of which our people will prosecute at once, as my arrangements with the foreign Syndicate engage to purchase bonds upon any prolongation or branches of the System which communicates with the Seaboard and agreed harbor.

I expect to be with you in a few days.

A&H—GP

Lewis Coleman to Thomas J. Jarvis

Boston December 20 1882

When I was down Raleigh last May I had a talk with you about the Rail Road Matter and then and there I told you we would not continue to build beyond Smithfield until we had a guaranteed[*sic*] from the State of N. C. that we could have the Atlantic & N. C. on the conditions which you talked about and you agreed with with [*sic*] me you know very well it would be very foolish thing for us to build the Road from Goldsboro to Salisbury unless we knew just the terms we was to have the Atlantic and N. C R. Road now I have not one particle of doubt but we can carry out build the road if we had the time granted us you said you would give us three or five years to do it in you know very well when Mr Best made the contract *with* the State about, the Western N. C. you asked us if we would build the road to Salisbury if we could not have the Western N. C. *Road.* We all answed *No* and by our given you the cheque on Pacific Bank for 250 M dollars which we supposed by what was said and agreed upon and approved by [illegible] J.T. Gatling and [Z.B.] Vance we did not consider any doubts but we should have the W.N.C. Road in a very few weeks therefore you see by by [*sic*]keeping the money in Pacific Bank waiting for you we made a loss by the Bank by so doing and now I have the largest amount of Stock and I have paid bills of the company to the amount of 50 M dollars more to help the roads a long now I thing [*sic*] in justice we should have a chance to go on with the road I know Mr Best has neglected the road by given his time elsewhere but now he is willing to retire from the road and put in some good rail road man to manager and Mr *Gatling* has expressed his willingness to take an interest and to get some N. C. people interested with *us* and I believe we can make success of it if we can have what I have told you what we wanted I hope and trust when your Directors come together of the At-

lantic and N. C Rail road you will consider the matter in our favor and grant us to Dec 31 I have not any doubt we can make arrangement *Satisfacty* and one quarter *is out there*
Mr. Carruth left Saturday for the South

A&H—GP

Johnstone Jones to Thomas J. Jarvis

December 21st 1882
Asheville

Today at 2.30 P.M. Incl. a telegram from Genl M P Taylor, Wilmington, requesting me to send authority to Captain Hoke[94] (Commandant of the "Southern Stars") Lincolnton to report to the Sheriff of the County[95] to supress a riot which is threatened, & also to send amunition. I immediately notified you by telegram of this request.[96]

I therefore telegraphed Taylor that I could only order out the troops upon application from the civil authorities, & wired Hoke to the effect that if the Sheriff would telegraph me to send him military aid, & would state that he apprehended a riot & *required* the assistance of the troops I would order a company or two to his assistance.

The law Chap 272 S2 says that "in time of riot or reasonable apprehension thereof" the Commander-in-Chief may order out the troops.

I instructed Hoke, in the meantime to act with the Sheriff as a *posse Comitatus.*

I have heard nothing further today.

A&H—GP

Johnstone Jones to Thomas J. Jarvis

Dec. 27 1882
Asheville

Ther[e] is an organized movement going on among the companies throughout the State to petition the legislation for aid in the

---

[94]Michael Hoke, merchant of Lincolnton. Branson, *Directory for 1884,* 421.
[95]A. S. Haynes, Branson, *Directory for 1884,* 419.
[96]Governors' Papers, not included in this volume.

organization, mainly in shape of appropriation for assistance to individual companies for annual encampment &c, and among other things for an increase in the salary of the Adjt Genl. to $1500 to $2000 — what it is on the average in other States.

If you say in your message anything about the militia I would be glad if you would reiterate your former recommendation that this salary be increased; but $600 is altogether too little. I, incidentally, am of course not to be considered in the matter; it is to the public interest I think that the office at the head of the military be enabled to give more time to the duties.

The Adjt Genl of N. C. [illegible] a salary of $1500, & a clerk at $1200. $1800 is about the average salary, in the States.

I have a full report of the trouble in Lincolnton which I will submit with my annual report in Jany. The report is from Capt. Hoke, Comdt of the "Southern Stars." The Co. was on duty twice, & helped the Sheriff to arrest & lodge in jail 31 negroes.

The State Guard proposes to meet in convention at Raleigh Jany 22 or 23d to prepare & present to the Legislature a memorial. When you transmit this memorial to the Genl Assembly the time would be opportune for an elaborate presentation of yr views on the importance of a good militia & the means for maintaining such a force.

INDEX

A

E

East Carolina University, established, lviii.

East Tennessee, Virginia & Georgia Railroad, xxxi.

Eastern Hospital for the Insane, see Goldsboro Asylum.

Eastern North Carolina Railroad, xlvii.

Ecumenical conference, lii.

Education, Board of, in Jarvis' administration, xxiv-xlix, *passim*, 76, 116n, 153-154, 193n, 266-267, 305, 311-312, 314, 337, 344-348, 363-365, 366-367, 370-371, 374-375, 375-377, 378, 643, 650-651; mentioned, 76, 188-189, 314, 363n, 366-367, 374-375, 527-528, 548.

Edwards, Theophilus, identified, 48n.

Egypt, 43.

Eighth North Carolina Regiment, assigned to Roanoke Island, xvi; further activities of, xvii.

Elam, S. S., letters from, 381, 547; letters to, 381-382, 550.

Election laws, explanation of, 553-557.

Election of 1868, xviii; of 1870, xix; of 1872, xix-xx, 15-17, 37-38; of 1874, xx, 18-19; of 1876, xxi-xxiii, 20-21, 26, 282, 286; of 1878, xii, 25-28, 33-38; of 1880, xxxiv-xxxvi, 235-236, 258, 275-276, 295-297; of 1882, 603-606, 642, 646; of 1892, lv; of 1894, lv; of 1896, lv; of 1898, lvi.

Elections, discussed, xxi, 15-16, 19, 26-28; proclamation concerning, 429-430.

Electors, presidential, 295-297.

Elizabeth City, xvii.

Elizabeth City & Norfolk Railroad, 575.

Emigres, from Romania, 277-278.

Engelhard, James, nominated, xxi.

Engelhard, Josephus Adolphus, identified, 51n.

England, 68, 320.

English, M. C., identified, 367n.

Ervin, Samuel James, identified, 167n; letter from, 167-168.

Erwin, Alfred Martin, identified, 173n; letter from, 173-174.

Erwin, George Phifer, identified, 163n; letter from, 248-249.

Estes, Llewellen G., identified, 6n.

Eure, Miles E., identified, 551n.

Evarts, William Maxwell, identified, 241n.

Evers, W. B., 579.

Examiner (Fayetteville), 239.

Executive mansion, see Governor's Mansion.

F

Fagan, N. B., identified, 28n.

Fain, Mercer, identified, 109n; mentioned, 113-114, 136-137.

Fairs, see Colored Industrial Fair.

Faison, Paul F. identified, 559n.

Fall, Samuel J., death of, 415-416; identified, 392n.

Farmer's Alliance, liii.

Farrow, Tillman, identified 12n.

Fayetteville, xxviii, 43, 79n, 80-81, 327, 336, 524, 566.

Fayetteville & Centre Plank Road, 189.

Fayetteville & Warsaw Plank Road, 189.

Fayetteville & Western Plank Road Company, 189.

Fayetteville & Winston Railroad, 497.

Federal occupation of Raleigh, 563-564.

Fence laws, 355.

Ferguson, Garland Sevier, identified, 299n; letter to, 300.

Fertilizers, 215-216, 230, 320, 534, 537-538, 593, 595, 597-598.

Fiedler Steamship Company, makes claim against Brazil, li.

Finger Sidney Michael, identified, 378n; letter from, 378.

Fish, James D., identified, 166; letter from, 180; mentioned, 181, 184, 186, 187, 188, 202, 254-255.

Fish commissioner, 349.

Fish industry, 349.

Fitch, G. A., letter from, 225; letter to, 224-225; mentioned 217, 220.

Flint, M., 254.

Florida, 67-68, 86, 95-96, 103, 240.

Florida Central Railroad, 68n, 96.

Florida conspirators, 77-78, 240-241.

Florida railroads, 68n, 77-78, 95-96, 99-100, 103, 240-241.

Forsyth County, 16.

Fort Bartow, xvii.

Fort Macon, Ga., 93.

Fort Macon, railroad iron at, 304.

Foster, Charles, identified, 418-419; telegram from, 418-419.

Fowle, Daniel Gould, identified, 167n; mentioned, 235-236; seeks Democratic gubernatorial nomination, xxxiv, lii.

Murphy Walter Calton, identified, 271n; letter to, 446; letters from, 271, 445.
Myers, Charles D., identified, 113n.

N

Nadal, Edward Morse, identified, 302n; letter from, 302; mentioned, 618.
National Hotel, Board of Agriculture purchases, xli, xlii-xliv.
National Military Cemetery, Raleigh, 256, 608.
Navigation companies, 94, 104, 189-192.
Negroes, education for, 363-365, 544-545; hold industrial fair, xxix, 119-121, 461-462, 545; organize State Industrial Agricultural Society, 545; references to, xxix, 119-121, 327, 337, 363-365, 369, 461-462, 518, 519, 520, 521-523, 524-525, 540, 541, 543-545, 605-606; riot in Plymouth, 518, 519, 520, 521-523, 524-525, 528-530, 535.
Neuse River, 268, 468.
New Bern, xvii, 49n, 381-382, 435-437, 439, 534, 594-595, 598-599, 601, 636.
New Orleans Exhibition of 1884, North Carolina exhibit at, xlvi-xlvii.
New River Navigation Company, 191.
New York, 67-68, 463, 480-481, 504, 506, 559.
New York & Southern Railroad and Telegraph Construction Company, organization of, 475, 478, 583; references to 475, 478, 511, 566-567.
New York Central Railroad, 244.
New York World's Fair, 241-242, 357-358.
"New South" address, xlvi.
Newbern and Beaufort Canal Company, xlv, 468.
Newberry, S. H., identified, 218n; signs petition, 283.
Newport, 270, 274, 285.
Newport News, Va., 1.
News (Kernersville), 236n.
News (Raleigh), 116, 250.
News and Courier (Charleston), 248.
News and Observer (Raleigh), letter to, 503-510; references to, 116n, 180, 481, 494; speeches from, 387-388, 454-455, 603-606.

Nixon, Albert, 523.
Norfolk, Va., xvi-xviii, xxxi, 49n, 134, 156, 435, 437, 534, 652.
Norfolk & Elizabeth City Railroad, 499.
Normal schools, establishment of, xxviii, xxxvi-xxxvii, xxxix, 76n, 77, 82, 105, 363-365, 366-367, 370-371, 373, 375, 377-378; references to, 40, 66, 76n, 77, 82, 105, 311, 313, 363-365, 366-367, 373, 375, 377-378.
North Carolina, boundary surveys, xxviii-xlix, *passim*, 110, 123, 125, 371-372, 393, 414-415, 420, 424; colonial records of, xxxviii, xlv-xlvi; commerce, xxxi-xxxiii, 44-45, 49n, 50, 117, 175; congressional representation of, 550, 553-558, 565, 577, 624; crime in, 277; economic conditions in, xxiii, xxxvi, 18, 42-43, 340-342, 454-455; mentioned, 16, 38, 114, 118, 278, 325, 333, 337, 434, 441, 447, 570, 580, 612, 617; militia of, xix, 518-520; salary scale, xlix; treasury, 12, 209, 212.
North Carolina Agricultural Society, 454-455.
North Carolina bonds, funding of, xxvi, xxix-xxx, xxxvi, 54-55, 59, 115, 227-229, 514, 571; references to, xxv-xxvi 54, 114-116, 129-131, 227-229, 246-247, 291, 328, 330-332, 359, 365-366, 587-593, 601-602, 622-623.
North Carolina Code, xxxvi, xxxviii, xliii, xlvi, 323, 398.
North Carolina Constitution, xviii, xx-xxi, xliv, 2-11, 23, 202, 205n, 250-251, 260, 302-304, 312-314, 423.
North Carolina Department of Agriculture, experiment station of 213-215, 231-232, 274-275; references to, xxiv-xlix, *passim*, 40, 51n, 61-62, 101, 214-215, 231-232, 274-275.
North Carolina Insane Asylum, lii, *see also* Raleigh asylum.
North Carolina Pharmaceutical Association, incorporated, xxxviii; requests prohibition on sale of poisons, 302, 333.
North Carolina Railroad, bonds for, xxvi; indebtedness of, xxvi, 191-192; lease of, xxvii, xxxiii, 50, 156n, 430, 467; rates on, 498-499; references to, xxx-xxxi, 28, 50n, 59-60, 61, 62, 80, 95-96, 98-100, 103, 114-115, 116, 129, 131,

DATE DUE
